PCs
ALL-IN-ONE

FOR
DUMMIES®
A Wiley Brand

6TH EDITION

by Mark L. Chambers

PCs All-in-One For Dummies®, 6th Edition

Published by
John Wiley & Sons, Inc.
111 River Street
Hoboken, NJ 07030-5774
www.wiley.com

About the Author

Mark L. Chambers has been an author, computer consultant, BBS sysop, programmer, and hardware technician for almost 30 years — pushing computers and their uses far beyond "normal" performance limits for decades now. His first love affair with a computer peripheral blossomed in 1984 when he bought his lightning-fast 300 BPS modem for his Atari 400. Now he spends entirely too much time on the Internet and drinks far too much caffeine-laden soda.

With a degree in journalism and creative writing from Louisiana State University, Mark took the logical career choice: programming computers. However, after five years as a COBOL programmer for a hospital system, he decided there must be a better way to earn a living, and he became the Documentation Manager for Datastorm Technologies, a top communications software developer. Somewhere in between writing software manuals, Mark began writing computer how-to books. His first book, *Running a Perfect BBS*, was published in 1994 — and after a short 15 years or so of fun (disguised as hard work), Mark is one of the most productive and best-selling technology authors on the planet.

His favorite pastimes include collecting gargoyles, watching St. Louis Cardinals baseball, playing his three pinball machines and the latest computer games, supercharging computers, and rendering 3D flights of fancy — and during all that, he listens to just about every type of music imaginable. Mark's worldwide Internet radio station, *MLC Radio* (at www.mlcbooks.com), plays only CD-quality classics from 1970 to 1979, including everything from Rush to Billy Joel to the *Rocky Horror Picture Show*.

Mark's rapidly expanding list of books includes *MacBook For Dummies,* 4th Edition; *iMac For Dummies,* 7th Edition; *MacBook All-in-One For Dummies,* 2nd Edition; *Mac OS X Mountain Lion All-in-One For Dummies; Macs For Seniors For Dummies,* 2nd Edition; *Build Your Own PC Do-It-Yourself For Dummies*; *Building a PC For Dummies,* 5th Edition; *Scanners For Dummies,* 2nd Edition; *CD & DVD Recording For Dummies,* 2nd Edition; *Mac OS X Tiger: Top 100 Simplified Tips & Tricks; Microsoft Office v. X Power User's Guide; BURN IT! Creating Your Own Great DVDs and CDs; The Hewlett-Packard Official Printer Handbook; The Hewlett-Packard Official Recordable CD Handbook; The Hewlett-Packard Official Digital Photography Handbook; Computer Gamer's Bible; Recordable CD Bible; Teach Yourself VISUALLY iMac; Running a Perfect BBS; Official Netscape Guide to Web Animation;* and *Windows 98 Troubleshooting and Optimizing Little Black Book*.

His books have been translated into 15 different languages so far — his favorites are German, Polish, Dutch, and French. Although he can't read them, he enjoys the pictures a great deal.

Mark welcomes all comments about his books. You can reach him at mark@mlcbooks.com, or visit MLC Books Online, his website, at www.mlcbooks.com.

Dedication

This book is dedicated to my daughter in-between, Chelsea Chambers — movie fanatic, *Gilmore Girls* expert, and musical diva — with all my love.

Author's Acknowledgments

Books don't produce themselves — and no book that I've written is complete without a round of sincere thanks (and applause) that's due to everyone involved!

First, my appreciation to my technical editor, Brian Underdahl, who spent weeks checking every fact and verifying every Start screen item (and Ribbon button, and pop-up selection . . .) in this book. I do a lot of technical editing myself, and I can tell you that it's no simple task to wade through this many chapters — it takes a combination of long nights and lots of soda.

Again, the Wiley Composition Services team has outdone itself in designing and preparing the material. All the beautiful formatting in this book (including every single figure and screen shot, all the step-by-step procedures, and the regular appearances of Mark's Maxims) is a testament to this team's hard work.

As with all my books, I'd like to thank my wife, Anne, and my children, Erin, Chelsea, and Rose, for their support and love — and for letting me follow my dream!

And I won't forget the patience and the guidance of Kyle Looper, my acquisitions editor, and Linda Morris, my project editor. Kyle, I hope I kept any headaches to a minimum, even with a tome this size — and Linda, your direction has improved every chapter in this edition, and I appreciate all your hard work! My heartfelt thanks to you both.

Publisher's Acknowledgments

We're proud of this book; please send us your comments at http://dummies.custhelp.com. For other comments, please contact our Customer Care Department within the U.S. at 877-762-2974, outside the U.S. at 317-572-3993, or fax 317-572-4002.

Some of the people who helped bring this book to market include the following:

Acquisitions and Editorial

Project Editor: Linda Morris

Acquisitions Editor: Kyle Looper

Copy Editor: Linda Morris

Technical Editor: Brian Underdahl

Editorial Manager: Jodi Jensen

Editorial Assistant: Annie Sullivan

Sr. Editorial Assistant: Cherie Case

Cover Photo: © SAKIStyle/iStockphoto

Composition Services

Project Coordinator: Patrick Redmond

Layout and Graphics: Carrie A. Cesavice, Melanee Habig, Joyce Haughey

Proofreaders: Jessica Kramer, Dwight Ramsey

Indexer: BIM Indexing & Proofreading Services

Publishing and Editorial for Technology Dummies

    Richard Swadley, Vice President and Executive Group Publisher

    Andy Cummings, Vice President and Publisher

    Mary Bednarek, Executive Acquisitions Director

    Mary C. Corder, Editorial Director

Publishing for Consumer Dummies

    Kathleen Nebenhaus, Vice President and Executive Publisher

Composition Services

    Debbie Stailey, Director of Composition Services

Contents at a Glance

Table of Contents

Book IV: PC Troubleshooting and Maintenance 251

Book VI: Fun with Movies, Music, and Photos 445

Introduction

What's the definition of a reference book? Well, I like to think of this book as a snapshot. Sure, it's an extremely heavy photograph, weighing in at more than 700 pages. But nevertheless, it captures the current state of PCs, including hardware, the most popular applications, and of course, the latest and greatest incarnation of the Windows operating system that we all cherish (in this case, Windows 8).

That covers a lot of ground, especially when you consider how the PC has branched out into all sorts of new directions in the past 20 years or so. What used to be primarily a simple word processing platform in the early days of DOS has now become a hub for digital video and audio, an optical recording center, an Internet communications system, a digital darkroom, a 3D gaming console, an office productivity center — the list goes on and on. Therefore, fitting the features and functionality of today's PCs into a single volume was a challenge for me — *and* it proved singularly rewarding because PCs are both my career and my favorite hobby!

With that comprehensive approach in mind, this book still holds true to the *For Dummies* format: step-by-step instructions on major features within Windows 8, Microsoft Office 2013, and other popular PC applications, with a little personal opinion, my recommendations, and my attempts at humor mixed in to add spice. I take the time to explain each topic for those who have just entered the PC universe, but you'll uncover plenty of advanced information as well. With this book in hand, you can set up a wireless network, navigate an Excel spreadsheet, diagnose hardware problems, benchmark your graphics card, and even work magic with your digital camera.

I sincerely hope that you enjoy this book and that it will help open up the countless possibilities offered by your PC. Thanks to the efforts of all those software developers, engineers, and hardware manufacturers, you and I get to play!

What's Really Required

Here's a short section for you — for this book, I assume that you have a PC, laptop/netbook, or tablet PC, preferably running Windows 8.

(I told you it was short.)

What's Not Required

If you've read any of my earlier books, you already know the score. But just in case you haven't (hint, hint), here's the list of what you don't need:

✦ **A degree in computer science:** Computers are supposed to be *easy.* I like 'em that way, and I get *very* testy when faced with anyone who tries to make a PC artificially complex. 'Nuff said.

✦ **All sorts of expensive software:** Because Microsoft Office 2013 is so doggone popular, I cover it here, but virtually everything else is either included in Windows 8 or is inexpensive.

✦ **An Internet connection:** Some folks should be reminded that PCs are quite productive by themselves. Naturally, you need an Internet connection to use Internet Explorer and Windows Live Mail or Outlook, but you **don't have to be online** to enjoy your computer.

About This Book

Each of the nine minibooks in this desk reference squarely addresses a specific topic, and there's no need to read this whole book in a front-to-back fashion. You certainly can, if you like, but it's not necessary. Instead, each minibook (and on a lower level, each individual chapter) is self-contained. That is, you can jump from chapter to chapter to pursue information about what you're working on right now — happy in the knowledge that when you decide to invest in an external hard drive (or a scanner or a memory upgrade) and you need help with installation, it's covered!

Occasionally, we have updates to our technology books. If this book does have technical updates, they will be posted at `www.dummies.com/go/pcsaio6efdupdates`.

Conventions Used in This Book

Like other *For Dummies* books, this volume uses a helpful set of conventions to indicate what needs to be done or what you'll see onscreen.

Stuff that you type

When I ask you to type something, like a command or an entry in a text box, the text appears like this, in bold:

Type me

Press the Enter key to process the entry.

Menu commands

When I give you a specific set of menu commands to use, they appear in this format:

Edit⇨Copy

In this example, you should click the Edit menu and then choose the Copy menu item. (This format applies to programs with old-fashioned menus.)

I describe selecting items from the Ribbon in Office programs similarly. For example, when I ask you to "choose Insert⇨Picture," this is shorthand for "click the Insert tab of the Ribbon and then click the Picture command button."

Display messages

If I mention a specific message that you see on your screen, it looks like this on the page:

```
This is a message displayed by an application.
```

How This Book Is Organized

Here's a quick summary of what's included in those nine minibooks (with cross-references where appropriate, included at *great* expense).

Book 1: Getting Started with PCs

It's not a PC without the hardware. In this minibook, I discuss the standard equipment (like your monitor, keyboard, and mouse) as well as optional items that you can attach (like a scanner or printer). I also cover the different ports on your PC and the proper methods of maintaining your PC hardware.

Book 11: Windows 8

A minibook for the Big 8 generation — with everything you need to know about today's most popular PC operating system, including the new Start screen and Metro apps, as well as the basics, advanced customizing topics, maintenance, the included applications — and (insert ominous chord here) troubleshooting. Wherever possible, I also try to include tips for both mouse wranglers and touch-screen types.

Book 111: The Internet

The obligatory Internet information fills this minibook. Discover how to navigate the web, read all that incoming e-mail, and — most important — keep your computer secure while you're online.

Book IV: PC Troubleshooting and Maintenance

Every PC owner should be familiar with basic hardware and software troubleshooting, and this minibook walks you through the process. I also cover the maintenance steps you should follow to keep your PC running smoothly. (Someday, PCs will be smart enough to clean themselves.)

Book V: Office 2013

Okay, so I decided to cover the behemoth. The major components of Microsoft Office 2013 are Word, Excel, PowerPoint, Access, and Outlook — and the gang's all here, with each application covered in a separate chapter, along with Microsoft's online SkyDrive storage system. If you use Office 2013, you'll treasure this minibook. And if you don't use Office, you'll still enjoy it as a spellbinding work of nonfiction. (Sure, Mark.)

Book VI: Fun with Movies, Music, and Photos

Your PC is now a digital, multimedia production center — and an excellent combination for watching video and listening to music, to boot. In this minibook, I show you the latest cutting-edge fun you can have with your MP3 player and your digital camera. Wait until your PC does the DJ work at your next party . . . automatically!

Book VII: Upgrading and Supercharging

The gloves come off in this minibook: If you're hankering to turn the corner and become a PC power user, use these chapters to help you upgrade your PC's hardware, including your system RAM, your graphics card, and even external connections like eSATA, USB 3.0, and Thunderbolt. "To the BatCave!"

Book VIII: Home Networking

If you've decided to install a home (or small-office) network, you've come to the right place. In these chapters, I demonstrate how to install your own wired network as well as how to expand with the latest wireless technology. Then I turn your attention to security so that you can use your network without fear of intrusion.

Book IX: Gaming

This final minibook is new to this edition, and it's devoted to one of the fastest-growing segments of the PC population: heavy-duty gamers! You'll discover what hardware should be the focus of every gamer, how to benchmark your system, software and peripherals that make gaming easier and more enjoyable, and even learn how to select the best PC games for your taste. (Those things are expensive, let me tell you!)

Icons Used in This Book

In a book stuffed to the gills with icons, my editors have decided to use — you guessed it — more icons. Luckily, however, the book's set of icons acts as visual signposts for specific information that you don't want to miss.

Mark's Maxims represent way-important stuff, so I call your attention to these nuggets, like this:

> These are My Favorite Recommendations — in fact, I'll bet just about any PC power user would tell you the same. Follow my maxims, and you'll avoid the quicksand and pitfalls that I've encountered with all sorts of PCs!™

A Tip icon points to a sentence or two that might save you time, trouble, or, quite possibly, cash.

Consider these tidbits completely optional, but if you're captivated by all things technical — as I am — you'll find trivia of interest here. (The information in these paragraphs is intended for those who enjoy cutaway drawings of the *Titanic* and those who know what JPEG means.)

Speaking of the *Titanic, always* read the information next to this icon first! Your PC is usually quite a safe harbor, but icebergs can appear from time to time, if you're not careful.

As you might expect from its name, this icon highlights information that you might want to, well, remember.

Book I
Getting Started with PCs

Visit www.dummies.com for great Dummies content online.

Contents at a Glance

Chapter 1: Starting with the Basics

In This Chapter

- ✏ Defining hardware, software, and peripherals
- ✏ Identifying the common components of all PCs
- ✏ Comparing desktop and laptop PCs
- ✏ Understanding RAM and your PC's CPU
- ✏ Defining the operating system

If your name is Hemingway or Faulkner or King, the first chapter is always the toughest to write. For me, however, this chapter was fun to write because it tackles the basic questions, such as which components make up your PC and why you need an operating system. You'll discover more about the specific parts of your PC that determine how fast it is, and I also discuss the pros and cons of choosing a laptop (or netbook or notebook) over a desktop PC.

If you're a hardware technician or a PC power user, you might decide to eschew these basic concepts and move on — and that's okay. But if you're new to the world of personal computers running Windows 8 or you're going to buy your first PC running Microsoft's latest and greatest version of Windows, this chapter is a great place to start. In fact, you would be amazed by how many folks I talk to who have owned their PCs for a year or two and still don't know some of the terms that you'll read here!

Here's the first Mark's Maxim for this book:

> It takes a solid foundation to build a power user.™

So read on!

Basic Terms

My high school English teacher, a wonderful lady whom I have always admired (even then), always told us, "Never jump into anything before defining your terms." (I owe her a lot.) No small coincidence that my favorite editors at Wiley say the same thing!

Before you venture further, commit these terms to memory to take a giant first step toward becoming a PC power user.

There's no reason to walk around with these definitions tattooed on your arm; you certainly don't need to know these technicalities just to check your e-mail or use Microsoft Word. However, when you grow more knowledgeable about Windows and your PC, you find that these terms will crop up in your computer conversations more and more often.

Hardware

In the PC world, *hardware* is any piece of circuitry or any component of your computer that has a physical structure. For example, your computer monitor is a piece of hardware, as is your keyboard. Even those components that you normally can't see or touch — the ones buried inside your case — are considered hardware, too, like your PC's motherboard and power supply. (And yes, your computer's case is technically a piece of hardware even though it's not electrical.)

Figure 1-1 illustrates a common piece of hardware — in this case, a video card with a PCI connector.

Software

The other side of the PC coin is the software you use. *Software* refers to any program you run, whether it resides on your hard drive, a floppy disk, a CD or DVD, a USB flash drive, or somewhere on a network.

When you hear folks discussing a software *upgrade, patch,* or *update,* they're talking about (you guessed it) *another* piece of software! However, the upgrade/patch/update program isn't designed to be run more than once; rather, its job is to apply the latest features, bug fixes, and data files to a piece of software that's already installed and running on your PC, to update it to a new *version.* (Virtually all software developers refer to successive versions of their software, such as Version 1.5 or Version 3; the later the version, the more features the software includes.)

Figure 1-1:
Hardware,
like this PCI
video card,
is, well,
hard.

Typically, think of software as an application that you buy or download, such as Microsoft Office 2013 or Nullsoft's Winamp (see Figure 1-2). However, the term *software* applies to any program, including Windows itself and the driver programs that accompany the hardware you buy. Unfortunately, computer viruses are software as well.

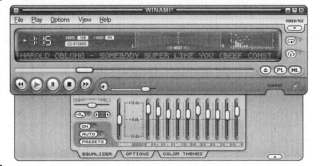

Figure 1-2:
Use
software
to perform
tasks,
such as
listening to
your digital
music
collection.

And software might be cheap!

You'll probably encounter two other types of "ware": freeware and shareware. A *freeware* program has been released into the public domain — in which case the author generally releases the programming code needed to modify it or maintains the rights to it — but you can still use it for free. *Shareware,* on the other hand, is not free. You get to try it before you buy it; if you like it, you send your payment directly to the author. Because there's no middleperson (you won't catch me using a sexist term) and you're not paying for an expensive box or advertising, shareware is usually far cheaper than a similar commercial program.

Before using freeware or shareware, check to make sure that the author offers regular updates. When you work for peanuts, you usually can't afford a Quality Assurance department or comprehensive beta testing!

From time to time, you might see the word *firmware* in a magazine or on a hardware manufacturer's website. This sounds like a strange beast, but I can explain: *Firmware* consists of the software instructions you find stored in the internal memory or the internal brain of a piece of hardware, so it's not quite software, and it's not quite hardware. For example, your DVD recorder has a firmware chip inside that controls the mundane tasks required to burn a disc; likewise, your video card's firmware contains instructions for all sorts of 3D magic that can be turned on and off by those games you play. Generally, you don't have to fool with firmware, but a manufacturer might release a firmware upgrade to add support for a new version of Windows or fix bugs that have cropped up with a piece of hardware (or even add new features). To upgrade firmware, you run a software utility program supplied by the manufacturer.

Peripherals

Peripherals are items that reside outside your PC's case, which can include all sorts of optional hardware. Examples include

+ Printers
+ External DVD recorders (such as the model shown in Figure 1-3) and hard drives
+ Webcams
+ Graphics tablets
+ Portable music players

✦ Joysticks and other game controllers

✦ Network hardware, such as Internet-sharing devices

✦ Scanners and digital cameras

Figure 1-3:
This external
DVD
recorder
peripheral
enjoys
sunshine
and
clean air.

Three pieces of external hardware that are found on every PC — your monitor, keyboard, and mouse (or trackball or touchpad) — are generally *not* considered peripherals because they're required in order to operate your PC. Call 'em "hardware" instead.

Peripherals connect to your computer via the ports built into the back (and often the front) of your PC. I go into more detail on ports in Chapter 3 of this minibook; any PC power user worthy of the name can identify, on sight, any common port on a computer. (If you're a hardware technician, you can identify the ports in the dark, the way a soldier knows his weapon. Just don't ask me why — I'm not at liberty to discuss it.)

The Common Components of a Desktop PC

Although a PC is hardly a living thing, your system can grow like one — and it can become quite unwieldy and tough to move. Turn your attention to the components that you find equipped on just about any desktop PC you buy (or assemble) these days.

The computer

The computer itself is housed in a case, which protects all the internal parts from damage. (Unfortunately, dust still finds its way inside, which is why I recommend that you remove the case at least once a year and blow out all that dust by using a can of compressed air.)

Lingo alert: You'll hear techs refer to your PC as *box, CPU, chassis,* or possibly even *$*Q(#*$*!%* (reserved for special occasions). You meet your PC's *CPU* — central processing unit; a single integrated chip — later in this chapter.

Not all PCs are created equal; several different *form factors* are available. (Jeez, another two-dollar term for a 50-cent concept.) A *form factor* determines the height and "footprint" of your computer, depending on the size of its case. (In the original days of the IBM PC, all computer cases were designed to straddle your desk, parallel to the floor; however, folks soon realized that a PC takes up far less room when standing vertically.)

Your desktop PC's case can look like any of the following:

✦ **The standard tower machine:** Because a tower case (see Figure 1-4) gives you the largest number of expansion bays and room for multiple fans, it's the case favored by PC power users and network administrators. A tower case is often placed on the floor because it's sometimes too tall for your computer desk.

✦ **The minitower machine:** The standard case offered with most PCs, the minitower is simply a shorter version of a tower case. The minitower is suitable for home and standard office workstation use — however, don't expect it to have as many expansion (or *card*) slots or as many empty drive bays waiting for you to fill with additional hard drives and another DVD recorder.

✦ **The lunchbox, all-in-one and pizza box machines:** These are the smallest PC cases, built for those areas where space is at a premium (or you know ahead of time that expansion won't be required later). These machines are often used in larger corporate offices, hospitals, banks, and the like. All-in-one PCs often offer touch-screen input (in addition to a standard keyboard and mouse). Figure 1-4 shows a pizza box case, which sits flat on your desktop rather than standing upright.

You might be interested in buying a PC with a special color scheme. Typically, these machines are black or brushed aluminum, but I've seen them in every color of the rainbow as well. (I particularly fancy the neon green and Florida orange.) Many high-performance gaming machines use wild color schemes that will knock you back a few feet. Use caution, though: Finding a neon green Blu-Ray drive in any store — online or otherwise — is more difficult than getting a teenager to stop texting.

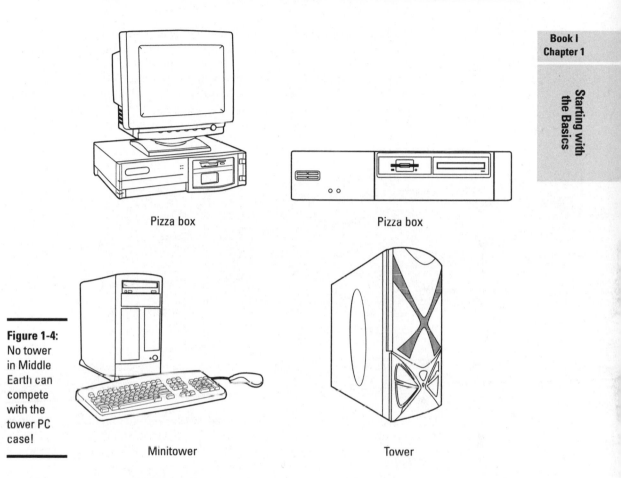

Pizza box   Pizza box

Figure 1-4:
No tower
in Middle
Earth can
compete
with the
tower PC
case!

Minitower   Tower

The monitor

Monitors come in two varieties:

✦ **The traditional CRT monitor:** A cathode ray tube (CRT) monitor is big
   and brassy and offers better color quality than a liquid crystal display
   (LCD) monitor in all lighting conditions, but CRTs use more electricity, get hot while you use them, and emit all sorts of radiation (nothing
   harmful, mind you, but it's there all the same). Because CRT monitors
   use older technology that's similar to a TV set, they're bulky, especially
   at larger screen sizes, such as 19" and 21". Most CRT monitors are flat-
   screen models; older designs with curved screens tended to distort the
   image you see.

✦ **The LCD monitor:** LCD monitors — also called *flat-panel* monitors — share the same technology as laptop computer screens, so they're very thin and use much, much less electricity than CRT monitors. (Many are even designed to hang on the wall.) LCD screens don't emit heat or radiation. LCD monitors have generally replaced dinosaur CRT monitors globally, and most LCD monitors are available in widescreen displays (good for watching DVD movies or working in a graphics program). See Figure 1-5.

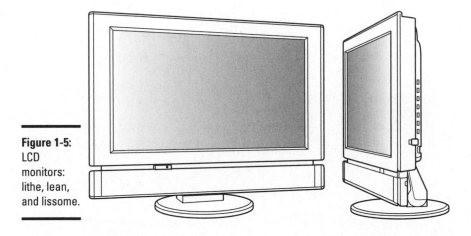

Figure 1-5: LCD monitors: lithe, lean, and lissome.

Either type of monitor is fine for a home or office environment, but I recommend (naturally) using an LCD monitor. The larger the monitor size, the easier it's likely to be on your eyes, and the more windows and documents you can stuff on your desktop at one time.

The keyboard and mouse

Keyboards are rather mundane. All models now have the Windows-specific keys, which will help any PC power user — but I still have a suggestion or two:

✦ **Consider using an ergonomic keyboard.** The cool, curved appearance that makes ergonomic keyboards, such as the keyboard that's part of the Microsoft Natural Ergonomic Desktop 7000, stand out in a crowd isn't just for looks. You can type longer and faster and with less strain on your wrists if you use an ergonomic keyboard like the one shown in Figure 1-6.

✦ **Keyboard tasks are easier with one-touch buttons.** Many keyboards now on the market — and most that ship with new systems — feature one-touch keys that you press to automatically display your e-mail program or web browser, print a document, or mute your computer's audio. Even if you don't use the standard functions for these keys, they can generally be reprogrammed to work with other applications. For example, I reprogrammed the Print key on my server's keyboard (which has no access to a printer) to run my network management application instead.

Figure 1-6:
Ergonomic
keyboards
are friendly
to your
wrists;
trackballs
are friendly
to your
fingers.

On the other side of the coin, most PC power users eventually look for a different mouse or pointing device; the standard-equipment mouse rarely gets the job done unless you're buying a more expensive system that comes with a premium mouse. Mouse-y features to consider include

✦ **Cordless:** This mouse type is sans tail: Instead, it uses a built-in infrared (IR) emitter or Bluetooth wireless connection to communicate with a separate base station, which in turn connects to your PC. The base station often acts as a battery charger for the mouse when you're not using your PC. Many folks find this type of mouse liberating because it has no tail to drag around and you can place the mouse farther away from the computer.

✦ **Optical operation:** Optical mice advantages include no mouse ball to clean, far fewer moving parts, and better control — it's no wonder that optical pointing devices are so popular! If you're still using an old mouse with a ball, jettison it and pick up an optical mouse.

✦ **Multiple buttons:** Most new offerings have a programmable third button and a scroll wheel, which you use to scroll the contents of a page just by turning the wheel with your fingertip. (For example, I have the middle button programmed as a double-click.) Some mice meant for gamers have additional buttons that can be programmed to "type" several keys automatically when clicked.

✦ **Trackballs and touchpads:** Many tech types swear by these alternatives to the traditional mouse. To use a *trackball,* which is kind of like a giant stationary mouse turned on its back, you move the ball with your thumb or the tips of your fingers. (Refer to Figure 1-6.) With a touchpad (like what's found on many laptops), you move the tip of your finger across a pressure-sensitive pad.

Speakers

Today's multimedia PCs are just as attractive to an audiophile as traditional stereo systems. If you think that you're limited to two desktop speakers and a chintzy volume knob, I invite you to contemplate the latest in PC speaker technology:

✦ **Flat-panel speakers:** As LCD screens are to CRT monitors, flat-panel speakers are to older PC speakers. Most flat-panel speakers are less than a half-inch thick yet provide the same power and punch as their older brethren.

✦ **Dolby Surround sound:** I get into more detail about high-fidelity PC audio in Book VII, Chapter 5. For now, suffice it to say that with the right sound card and multiple speakers, your PC can equal the clarity and realism of a home theater system. Your ears become just as important as your eyes when you play the latest 3D games!

✦ **Universal Serial Bus (USB) digital connections:** For the ultimate in sound quality, the best digital speakers now connect to your system through the USB port — you can say goodbye to old-fashioned analog forever.

Desktop PCs versus Mobile PCs

Should you buy a desktop PC, a laptop PC, or a netbook/tablet PC? Naturally, if the portability of a laptop PC is a requirement for you — say, your job or your lifestyle demands plenty of travel every year — you really have no other choice than a mobile computer.

Today's laptops are as powerful as desktop PCs, with features such as high-resolution graphics, large hard drives, and DVD recording, which used to be very expensive options in the laptop world. Oh, and don't forget the all-important wireless networking that all laptops include these days — no longer just for students, either, because these days everyone craves wireless networking!

Then there are those who take portability even more seriously — many PC owners choose either a *tablet* like Microsoft's Surface (which looks and operates much like the Apple iPad) or a *netbook,* which looks more like a conventional laptop (but on a significantly smaller scale). Both the tablet and the netbook offer light weight and long battery life, although neither design offers the power and peripheral connectivity of a laptop.

However, if you're sitting on the fence and portability is a lesser requirement, I generally recommend a desktop system, for the following three reasons:

✦ **Laptops aren't as expandable as desktops.** Although you can hang plenty of peripherals off a modern laptop (using USB, eSATA, Thunderbolt, and FireWire ports), desktops are just plain easier to expand and upgrade (especially the processor and your graphics card, which are practically impossible to swap on a laptop).

✦ **Laptops are more expensive than desktops.** My friend, you pay dearly for the portability of a laptop or tablet. (The cost exception is today's netbooks, which are very inexpensive, but they have fewer features and less power than a typical laptop or tablet and lag far behind any desktop.) So if you don't need it, jump to the desktop side of the fence. It's as simple as that.

✦ **Laptops cost much more to repair.** If the sound card fails in your desktop, you can replace it yourself with a new, relatively inexpensive adapter card. However, if the sound hardware fails in your laptop, it's time to pull out your wallet because you can't fix it yourself and the entire motherboard inside the unit probably needs to be replaced. (Remember: Part of that portability stems from the fact that laptop manufacturers put all the graphics and video hardware on the motherboard to save space.)

Luckily, most of this book is still valuable to laptop owners. Just ignore the parts about upgrading the components you can't reach.

RAM and Processors: The Keys to Performance

When you hear PC owners talk about the speed and performance of their computers, they're typically talking about one of three different components (or all these components as a group):

✦ **System memory, or random access memory (RAM):** The more memory your PC has and the faster that memory is, the better your PC performs — especially Windows, which enjoys memory like the proverbial hog. I tell you more about slops — sorry, I mean *memory* — in Book VII, Chapter 2.

✦ **Central processing unit (CPU):** Most PCs now use either an Intel Core i3, Core i5, or Core i7, or Intel's less-expensive and slower cousin, the Celeron. The other popular processors are the Athlon II series or the Phenom II series from AMD, along with AMD's less-expensive and slower cousin, the Sempron. The speed of your processor is measured in giga-hertz (GHz), with 1 GHz equaling 1000 MHz. The faster the speed of your processor, the faster your PC performs. (I go into this topic big-time in Book VII, Chapter 1.)

✦ **Graphics processing unit (GPU):** This item is the chipset used on your video card. The better the chipset, the faster and the more realistic 3D graphics your PC can produce. For the skinny on graphics cards, visit Book VII, Chapter 5.

You can always display which type of processor your PC uses, its speed, and how much RAM your PC has. From within Windows 8, move your mouse to the upper-right corner of the Start screen to display the Charms bar, and then click the Search icon. Click the Settings button under the Search box, and then type **System** in the Search box. Click the Show Which Operating System Your Computer Is Running button in the Search results pane, and you should see a window like the one in Figure 1-7, with these interesting facts.

Processor type

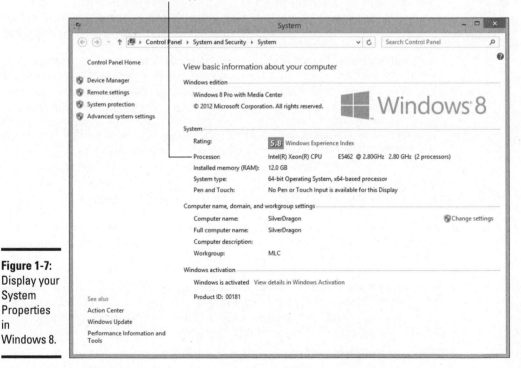

Figure 1-7: Display your System Properties in Windows 8.

Your Friend, Your Operating System

Windows, which is your PC's *operating system,* is the program that you run to

✦ Navigate through the files on your hard drive

✦ Run other programs

✦ Listen to music, view pictures, or watch movies

✦ Copy, move, and delete things, and much more

Windows is composed of hundreds of smaller programs, but you rarely notice anything else running. Instead, Windows presents a cohesive and relatively easy-to-use interface to the world. (The tech word *interface* simply refers to the design of the screen and the controls you see when you're using software.)

In this book, when I refer to Windows, I'm talking about Windows 8. If your PC meets the minimum requirements, I recommend that you upgrade to it (especially if you're using a tablet PC with a touch-sensitive screen). (Book II is completely dedicated to Windows 8 — there's another reason to upgrade!)

I should mention, however, that Windows 8 isn't the only operating system that runs on a PC. For example, you can run UNIX, Linux, Windows 7, Windows Vista, or Windows XP. To be honest, your PC's hardware couldn't care less — but it's a good bet that the programs you want to run are designed for Windows, and much of your PC's hardware either won't work or will be harder to configure if you use another operating system. Therefore, I heartily suggest that you stick with Windows Vista or Windows 7 (for a machine more than three or four years old) or Windows 8 (for a PC designed or rated as compatible with the Big 8).

Chapter 2: Additional Toys Your PC Will Enjoy

In This Chapter

✔ Comparing printers

✔ Adding a scanner to your system

✔ Upgrading your input devices

✔ Adding a game controller

✔ Introducing digital cameras and digital video (DV) camcorders

✔ Adding new storage to your system

✔ Guarding your PC with surge protection

You bought a PC — congratulations! — or you decided to finally turn on that totem pole of a desktop computer that you've been looking at for the past six months. Here's a friendly warning for you in the form of a Mark's Maxim:

> Serious computing requires serious peripherals.™

In other words, PC owners who are hoping to get the maximum return and explore the maximum power of their computers need additional stuff (*peripherals,* as you can read in Chapter 1 of this minibook) that connects to your PC to take care of specific jobs. Printers are a good example; a PC certainly doesn't produce hard copy without one.

In Chapter 1 of this minibook, I discuss hardware and software. This chapter is designed as both a showcase and an introduction to PC peripherals that will familiarize you with the most popular additional toys for your computer. Some of these devices are covered in great detail later on (for example, scanners have Book VI, Chapter 1 to themselves), and others are covered primarily right here.

This chapter can be hazardous to your wallet or purse.

Printers

The first stop in the world of peripherals is the most common (and most folks would say the most useful) device: the system *printer,* which allows your PC to produce hard copies of documents, artwork, and photographs.

Inkjet versus laser printers

In the digital days of yore (in other words, more than 20 years ago), making a choice between an inkjet and a laser printer was ridiculously easy. After all, laser printers were prohibitively expensive, and they couldn't print in color. Therefore, every home PC owner picked up an inkjet printer (or got an inkjet printer as a bundled peripheral with a new PC) and got on with his or her life. These days, however, the line between inkjet and laser printers has blurred; this section lists the advantages of each one so that you can shop with the right type of printer in mind.

Laser printer advantages

Monochrome laser printers now start at around $80 (all dollar amounts in this chapter are in U.S. greenbacks), which is still mind-bendingly weird for an old hardware hacker like me who still remembers the days when the *absolute* cheapest (and likely refurbished) laser printer you could find set you back $1,500 to $2,000. Advantages of the laser printer include

✦ **Speed:** Most laser printers can turn out pages more quickly than the average inkjet printer can.

✦ **Low cost:** Over time, toner costs for a laser printer total far less per page than refilling and replacing inkjet printer cartridges.

✦ **Quiet operation:** A laser printer is generally quieter than a low-cost inkjet printer — which is a big deal in a quiet office, where the printer usually occupies a central location.

✦ **Best-quality text:** No inkjet printer — no matter how much you pay for it — will ever turn out black text and line graphics as crisply as a laser printer does.

Also, if you can afford to pony up $300 or so for a color laser printer, you'll find that it offers better-quality color output than most low-cost inkjet printers. With these advantages in mind, pick a monochrome laser printer if most of the pages you print are text and if color isn't a requirement. You'll be glad that you chose the laser model after you go three months without changing a single toner cartridge!

The monochrome laser printer shown in Figure 2-1 can produce 12 pages per minute without blinking an eye (if it had one).

Figure 2-1:
Invest in a low-cost monochrome laser printer for document printing.

Inkjet printer advantages

Inkjet printers are still somewhat cheaper than laser printers. You can find an acceptable color inkjet printer for well less than $100 anywhere on the planet, and it's still the color printing solution for the home PC owner. Other advantages include

- **Versatility:** A color inkjet can print on many types of media, including craft paper, T-shirt transfers, and even printable CDs/DVDs.

- **Smaller size:** Save some space on your desktop.

- **Larger paper sizes:** If you spend more, you can add to your system a large-format inkjet printer that can print 11-x-17-inch or larger items.

The inkjet printer shown in Figure 2-2 costs less than $100 yet includes both Ethernet and Universal Serial Bus (USB) connections. It can print near-laser-quality black text and photo-quality color images. You can even set this model to print on both sides of the paper.

Photo printers

Photo printers are specifically designed to create photographs that rival any 35mm film print. They either use the best-quality inkjet technology or rely on dye-sublimation (dye-sub) technology (also called *thermal wax* printing). A *dye-sub* printer transfers heated solid dye from a ribbon to specially coated paper, producing the same continuous tones that you see in a photograph produced from a negative. Photo printers can often accept memory cards from digital cameras directly (or by using a USB cable connection to the camera), so you don't need a PC to print your digital photographs.

Most photo printers on the market are smaller than typical inkjet printers. (They can't use standard 8.5-x11-inch paper, and they're lousy at printing black text, which makes an inkjet printer far more versatile.) Both photo and inkjet printers can produce borderless images (just like a film print), but a true dye-sublimation photo printer is far slower than an inkjet, and the special paper and dye ribbon it requires make it much more expensive over the long haul.

If you're a serious amateur or professional digital photographer, a photo printer is worth the expense. For a typical home PC owner, however, a standard color inkjet printer is the better path to take.

Label printers

Before I move on, I want to discuss the popular personal *label printer,* like the DYMO LabelWriter I use. The LabelWriter 450 Turbo uses a USB connection and sells online (www.dymo.com) for about $130.

This printer might look a little like a toy — it's not much bigger than the label tape it uses — but I've found that a label printer is worth twice its weight in gold (see Figure 2-3). For example, the LabelWriter 450 Turbo can produce all these materials with aplomb:

✦ **Address and shipping labels**, complete with your logo

✦ **Bar codes and U.S. mail codes**

✦ **CD and DVD labels**

✦ **File folder labels**

✦ **Floppy disk labels** (for those who still use floppy disks, anyway)

✦ **ID badges**

Figure 2-3:
A personal label printer is a convenient tool for printing all types of labels.

When you design your labels, the software that ships with the LabelWriter gives you control over fonts, time and date stamping, line drawings, and even thumbnail photographs. You can rotate and mirror text or set up bar coding with ease. Plus, you get the capability to print labels directly from applications such as Outlook, Word, and QuickBooks.

Just as valuable as the output, however, is the sheer convenience you get from one of these printers! A label printer frees you from the hassle of designing and preparing labels on your inkjet or laser printer, and you don't have to hunt for your label sheets every time you need to print a new batch. (Anyone who has fought tooth and nail to align and print a bar code or address labels on a standard laser printer knows just what I mean.)

Scanners

Scanners are interesting beasts — and man, you get a lot of bang for your buck! In fact, a perfectly serviceable USB scanner (as shown in Figure 2-4) is waiting for you at your local Maze O' Wires store for less than $100, and it can do all this:

✦ **Produce digital images from magazine and book pages, photographs, and just about any other printed material.** These images can later be edited to your heart's content, sent as an e-mail attachment, or recorded to CD or DVD.

✦ **Read text from a printed document into your word processor.** This trick — optical character recognition (OCR) — can save you hours of typing and prevent introduction of typos and finger fumbles.

✦ **Produce images that you can fax with your PC's fax/modem.**

✦ **Produce images from transparencies or slides (with the right attachment).**

✦ **Create copies of a document (in concert with your printer).**

The scanner shown in Figure 2-4 features seven one-touch buttons on its front. You can e-mail, copy, or even create PDFs from the original — or even run your OCR software with a single punch of a button. *Sassy!*

Figure 2-4:
Use a
scanner
to bring
all sorts
of printed
material to
your PC.

Specialized scanners are designed especially for things such as bar codes — perfect for those who collect audio and video — and business cards. I go into more detail on scanners in Book VI, Chapter 1. For now, just remember that they're the very definition of the cat's pajamas. (In fact, many printer manufacturers include scanning and faxing features with specific printer models, calling them *multifunction printers* or *all-in-one units.* Talk about a Swiss Army knife!)

Keyboards, Tablets, and Pointing Things

Gotta have 'em. Using a desktop PC without an input device is . . . well, I guess it's like playing Ping-Pong without paddles. (Naturally, a tablet PC also needs an input device — in fact, the tablet's screen is actually the input device, acting just like an oversized laptop trackpad.)

In this section, I discuss the upgrades you can make to your PC's existing keyboard and mouse. (Although they're technically not peripherals, as I mention in Chapter 1 of this minibook, some of these hardware devices are too cool not to cover.)

Tickling keys wirelessly

As I discuss in the previous chapter of this minibook (and as you can read in Book II, Chapter 1, when I start talking Windows 8), the folks at Microsoft have remodeled the hoary PC keyboard in their own fashion by adding extra keys that make it easier to control Windows. If you're using a PC built in the past five years, you already have these keys handy. I mention a few keyboard features to look for in Chapter 1 of this minibook, such as ergonomic keyboards that can help reduce the strain of typing on your wrists. But what if you want to relax in a better chair several feet away from that big-screen monitor?

Enter the wireless keyboard, which is the perfect complement to a wireless mouse or trackball. The wireless keyboard shown in Figure 2-5 also comes with a wireless mouse and uses the Bluetooth short-range wireless network technology (covered in Book VIII, Chapter 3). This keyboard is festooned with no less than 11 one-button hotkeys and even includes a set of audio CD player controls for listening to your music.

Figure 2-5:
This wireless keyboard/ mouse combo is the nomad's dream.

Putting a graphics tablet to work

If you're a graphic artist, a professional photographer, or someone who wants to paint or draw freehand, consider getting a *graphics tablet* (shown in Figure 2-6) on which you draw or make notes with a stylus in the familiar old-fashioned method. Like an ergonomic keyboard, a tablet can also help ease the strain on your wrist.

Figure 2-6: A graphics tablet makes drawing within many applications a breeze.

"But what about the fine control I get with paper or canvas?" No problem! Today's tablets can recognize thousands of different levels of pressure. Some can even detect the angle of the stylus, allowing you to tilt your virtual brush in graphics applications like Photoshop and Corel's Painter 12 (`www. corel.com`) for special effects with watercolor, chalk, and pencil filters.

A typical tablet, like the Intuos4 from Wacom (`www.wacom.com`), has no batteries or cords on its stylus, and it even comes with its own mouse. The tablet uses a USB connection to your PC, and it sells online for about $350 — that's the 5.5-x-8.8-inch model. (The 8-x-12.8-inch model is about $120 more.)

Repeat after me: Buy a trackball!

I can't work with a traditional mouse any longer — I'm now firmly set in the trackball camp. A trackball offers a number of benefits:

✦ **Compact:** Trackballs require far less space on your desktop because just the trackball moves (rather than the entire device).

✦ **Control:** Many folks find that using a trackball provides a finer level of cursor control.

✦ **Clean:** A trackball stays cleaner than a mouse. (Even optical mice get dirtier than trackballs.)

Figure 2-7 illustrates a trackball mouse that you control with your thumb; on other trackballs, you use your index finger to control the ball. This particular model uses either a USB or PS/2 connection to your PC and sells for about $35 U.S. online. (For more detail on PS/2 and USB connectors, visit Chapter 3 of this minibook.)

Figure 2-7:
A trackball
is much
more
efficient
than the
traditional
mouse.

Big-Time Game Controllers

Ah, do you remember the old Atari joysticks that ushered in the age of the video game (and the Atari personal computer after that)? A plastic tube, a base with a single red button, and a cord — what more could you possibly want, right?

Because modern game players want a lot more than one button, witness the arrival of the game controller (which I think has a much grander sound than just *a joystick*). For example, check out the controller shown in Figure 2-8 — does that look like an old-fashioned joystick to you? In fact, this model is more like a combination of a mini-keyboard and a gamepad (reflecting the current complexity of PC games, which rely as much on the keyboard as on the pointing device you're using). Your entire hand fits on top of the controller, much like with a trackball, and your fingers press the keys while your thumb operates the gamepad directional control. (You can also use this controller along with your regular mouse or trackball.) This model, which sells for about $30 U.S. online, can even be programmed to fit your preferences for each individual game you play. *Sweet!*

Another popular feature of today's game controllers is *force feedback,* where the controller rumbles or provides resistance to your hand that matches the action onscreen, such as a steering wheel that gets tougher to turn in curves or a joystick that shakes each time your WWII fighter is hit by enemy fire.

Figure 2-8:
It's a bird, it's a plane — no, it's a modern PC game controller!

Consider the Logitech Driving Force GT steering wheel, which has the same 900-degree rotation as an actual car. It even has its own onboard processor, which keeps track of what's happening within the game and activates the wheel's internal motors to provide the matching feedback. (Naturally, it also has a sequential shifter.) Anyway, you get the steering wheel and a set of pedals to boot for about $150, making you the hit of your NASCAR crowd!

Video and Digital Cameras

Images and full-motion video have traditionally been based on film (which retains an image when exposed to light) or magnetic tape. That whole approach, however, is now strictly '90s — and very early '90s to boot. Digital cameras and digital video camcorders now have heavy-duty advantages over film cameras and tape camcorders:

+ **No processing at your local MegaMart is required.** Your digital images can be downloaded directly to your PC (or printer).

+ **Editing is easy,** using programs like Adobe Photoshop (static images) or Adobe Premiere (for video). You can also download free programs from Windows that will get you started with digital video and film editing.

✦ **No film to buy.** Instead, you simply delete images from your digital camera's memory card after they're downloaded.

✦ **Images and videos can be saved to a CD or DVD for permanent storage.**

✦ **Images can be sent by e-mail or displayed on your web page.**

✦ **You can create your own DVD movies from your video clips.**

A specialized model of DV camcorder (about the size of a golf ball) is designed especially to sit atop your desktop PC: a *webcam*. Folks use them to send digital video over the Internet, to add a video signal to their web pages, or to record simple movies from their chairs. Webcams have been in use as Internet videoconferencing tools for years, most cost less than $50, and they use either a wireless or USB cable connection to your PC. Many laptops are equipped with built-in webcams as well.

Figure 2-9 illustrates a typical digital camera, which looks and operates much like its film counterpart; it also shows a camcorder, ready to record straight to digital video, which you can transfer over a USB or wireless connection to your PC.

Figure 2-9: The image and video makers of the new millennium: the digital camera and the camcorder.

For the skinny on digital cameras, see Book VI, Chapter 5. And, for a look at how the video clips you take with your DV camcorder can be turned into movies, see Book VI, Chapter 3.

External Drives

Now consider how simple it is to add fast storage — or the ability to record your own CDs, DVDs, and Blu-Ray discs — to today's PCs. If you're the least bit nervous about digging inside your PC's innards to add more hard drive space, you'll be pleased to know that you can easily connect a fast external hard drive to your system — as long as you have the FireWire, USB, Thunderbolt, or external SATA ports available on your desktop or laptop PC. (If you're not familiar with these types of high-speed connections, fear not: I launch into a complete discussion of all four in Book VII, Chapter 4.)

In fact, not every form of external storage even needs a cable. Read on to see what I mean.

Portable hard drives and DVD/Blu-Ray recorders

Forget the huge external hard drives of just five years ago. Those doorstops have been replaced by slim, trim models (see Figure 2-10) that run faster and are more reliable yet are no bigger than a pack of playing cards. At their current prices, you can pick up an external 500GB hard drive for less than $50 that's a mere 1-inch thick and shock resistant yet can connect effortlessly to PCs with either FireWire or USB ports. These drives are usually bundled with backup software that can automatically safeguard your PC's data — more on this in the next section.

Figure 2-10:
This external drive means mobile storage.

On the DVD and Blu-Ray recording scene, you find six major types of drives:

✦ **CD-R/CD-RW drives:** Can store around 700MB on a CD

✦ **DVD-R/DVD-RW drives:** Can store 4.7GB on a DVD

✦ **DVD-RAM drives:** Can store 9.4GB on a double-sided DVD

✦ **DVD+R/DVD+RW drives:** Can store 4.7GB on a DVD

✦ **Dual Layer (DL) DVD+R drives:** Can store 8.5GB on a DVD

✦ **Blu-Ray BD-R/RE drives:** Can store 25GB on a Blu-Ray disc

The *RW/RE* in the drive moniker stands for *rewriteable,* which means that you can reuse a CD-RW, DVD-RW, DVD+RW, or Blu-Ray BD-RE over and over. All these recorders can produce audio CDs and standard data CDs and DVDs, but only the drives that can record the DVD-R and DVD+R formats are likely to create DVD movies that can be played in your stand-alone DVD player. Unfortunately, the rewriteable DVD-RW and DVD+RW standards aren't compatible with older, standalone DVD players; you have to watch your discs on your PC. (Insert sound of palm slapping forehead here.)

Backup drives

Backup drives used to mean inexpensive, slow-running tape drives — however, typical 2 terabyte (TB) and 3TB drives are now simply too humongous for such tapes to be worth much anymore. Heck, I remember when everyone backed up to floppy disks, and now even the highest-priced digital audiotape (DAT) drives are losing ground fast in the backup-storage world.

Instead, you now have three choices to pick from when backing up your system:

✦ **Blu-Ray recorder:** As I mentioned earlier, 25GB per disc makes optical backup reasonable.

✦ **Online backup:** Use a commercial Internet backup service. *Note:* This solution is viable only if you're using a broadband connection to the Internet; backing up a big hard drive takes too long over a pokey 56KB modem.

✦ **External FireWire, USB, eSATA, and Thunderbolt backup hard drive:** An example is the 3TB Western Digital My Book (www.westerndigital.com), which provides full, automated backups of your system on a regular schedule.

The My Book drive isn't cheap at $150, but how much are your documents and files worth? No matter which backup method you use, I strongly urge you to do your duty as your PC's guardian and *back up your system!*

USB flash drives

One storage toy is something different: a *USB flash drive,* which is a keychain-size unit that needs no batteries and has no moving parts! Instead, it uses the same method that digital cameras use to store images. Your files are stored on memory cards (either removable cards or built-in memory inside the unit). Most USB drives now range anywhere from 2GB to 256GB of storage. Just plug one into your PC's USB port and copy data there. Then, just unplug and go: the ultimate in portable data storage. These drives don't need any extra software — Windows recognizes them instantly — so they make a great "digital wallet." These drives are now so common and downright handy that you can find novelty drives in different shapes and colors (for the style-conscious individual)!

Figure 2-11 illustrates a 16GB flash drive that sells for about $20 online. It even has a write-protect switch so that you can safeguard your data from being accidentally erased.

Figure 2-11: Carry 16GB in your pocket with a USB flash drive.

Surge Protectors and UPS Units

You know, one clear sign of a PC power user is at the end of the PC's power cord. True power users use either surge protectors or UPSs to safeguard their systems. However, I always make sure that I stress the following fact when I'm talking about surge protectors and UPS units: Neither can protect your PC from a direct lightning hit on your home or office wiring! (That's just too much current for any commercial surge device to handle.)

Otherwise, using either a surge protector or a UPS helps guard against less serious power surges, and both provide additional AC sockets for your rapidly growing system. If you can afford to spend $75 to $200, a UPS is the better choice because of the following reasons:

✦ **Safety nets:** A UPS provides a number of extra minutes of AC power if your home or office experiences a power failure — generally enough so that you can close any documents you're working on (like that Great American Novel you've been slaving over for 20 years) and then shut down your PC normally.

✦ **Auto shutdowns:** More expensive UPS models can automatically shut down your PC in case of a power failure.

✦ **Current cleaners:** Most UPS units filter the AC current to smooth out brownouts and noise interference from other electronic devices.

✦ **Audible alerts:** Some UPS units sound an alarm whenever a power failure or significant brownout occurs.

How long (in minutes) your UPS will last during a power failure depends on the power rating of the battery and the power drawn by your PC.

If you're using a dialup or any broadband modem connection, make sure that you get a surge protector or UPS that also protects your modem from electrical surges. That juice can travel just as easily across a phone line as across your power line. (For this reason, some electric utility companies are now offering insurance safety plans that cover your home against surge damage.)

Chapter 3: Connectors, Ports, and Sundry Openings

In This Chapter

✔ Connecting all sorts of devices

✔ Putting the antique serial and parallel ports to rest

✔ Connecting your monitors

✔ Locating the jacks and ports on your sound card

✔ Connecting your mouse and keyboard

*I*n the beginning (okay, last century), there were the serial port and the parallel port — who would have needed anything else? If you could afford a printer back then, it was connected to the parallel port, and your modem (or perhaps your mouse) was hooked to your serial port. End of story.

The typical PC of today might not have either of those original two ports, though. The serial port is all but extinct, and although some current motherboards still provide a parallel port, it's on the way out as well. Modern PCs rely on a number of relatively new connectors that greatly expand the range of peripherals you can add to your system. In this chapter, I help you make sense of the various ports and sundry openings that you find on the back and front of your PC.

Using USB Stuff

The first port on the tour is the most important standard PC connector on the planet these days. A *Universal Serial Bus* (USB) port (see the following figure) allows you to connect all sorts of peripherals, and it's just as popular for connecting keyboards and mice. Intel is responsible for this most versatile of ports.

USB

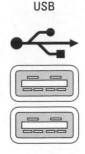

A USB connection is the cat's pajamas because

✦ **It's plug and play.** You don't even need to reboot your PC after you connect a USB device because Windows 8 automatically recognizes the connection, and you can start using your USB peripheral immediately.

✦ **One port supports dozens of devices.** A single USB port can support as many as 127 different devices, either connected in a daisy-chain configuration or by using a USB hub. I doubt that you have that many connections to handle. (If you do, please take a photo of your system with your digital camera and send the picture to mark@mlcbooks.com because I can hardly wait to see it.)

✦ **It's relatively fast.** USB devices come in three flavors. The oldest is USB 1.1, which is nearly extinct now and has all but disappeared. USB 2.0 is the current standard, and it's fast enough for most external devices. However, the latest USB 3.0 port offers much faster performance than a USB 2.0 port (and, as you might imagine, a USB 3.0 connection is much better for external hard drives, USB flash drives, and the like). USB 3.0 is backward compatible, so you can still use that USB 2.0 external DVD recorder that Aunt Harriet gave you two years ago.

Note that many USB cables have a different type of connector on each end, as shown in Figure 3-1. One end will connect only to your PC, while the other connects only to the device (like a cellphone, scanner, or digital camera). As long as you use the cable supplied with the external device, all is good!

I discuss USB connections in greater detail in Book VII, Chapter 4; for now, just remember that any device with a USB port connection is a better choice over the same device with a serial port or parallel port connection.

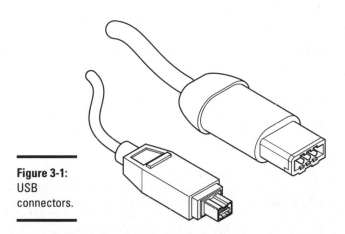

Figure 3-1:
USB
connectors.

Making the FireWire Connection

Until 2001 and the arrival of the USB 2.0 port, the FireWire port (sometimes referred to by its more official name, *IEEE 1394*) was the fastest port on any personal computer. For a time, it was the standard for digital video (DV) camcorders and high-resolution scanners — both of which produce honking big files that need to be transferred to your computer as quickly as possible. Apple Computer is the proud parent of FireWire.

IEEE 1394
FireWire

Unlike USB ports — which are now included with every new PC — FireWire ports are generally available as optional equipment. (Of course, you can always buy an adapter card to add FireWire ports to your computer.) Like USB, FireWire is a plug-and-play connection; a FireWire port can support 63 devices (using a daisy-chaining technique).

Find more information about FireWire in Book VII, Chapter 4, where I introduce the FireWire 800 standard, which ups the ante in the port speed race by churning an 800 Mbps (megabits per second) — or twice as fast as original FireWire!

Riding in the Fast Lane with eSATA and Thunderbolt

Now we arrive at the two speed demons of the PC peripheral racecourse: eSATA (or external SATA) and Thunderbolt are the two fastest external connections you can make between your PC and a peripheral.

✦ **eSATA** (short for external Serial Advanced Technology Attachment, of all things) is essentially an internal hard drive . . . outside your PC's case! Don't worry, the explanation is forthcoming: If you're familiar with the internal SATA (serial ATA) hard drives that are commonplace in the PC world today, an eSATA drive is an extension of that same technology. An eSATA drive delivers approximately the same performance as an internal SATA drive, just like it was mounted inside your PC's case. eSATA connections are very popular for adding superfast external hard drives (and hard drive arrays, which include more than one physical drive) to your system.

✦ **Thunderbolt** was developed by Intel and made its debut on Apple Macintosh computers, but this fast external port is gaining slow acceptance in the Windows world, as more high-end PCs and laptops ship with Thunderbolt ports, and more Thunderbolt devices appear on the market. Thunderbolt is literally more than 12 times faster than FireWire 800 — heck, Thunderbolt is twice as fast as a USB 3.0 connection. Unfortunately, however, Thunderbolt hardware is still very expensive at the time of this writing, so you'll pay top dollar for that performance.

I discuss both eSATA and Thunderbolt in Book VII, Chapter 4, including speed comparisons between all of the common peripheral ports in use today.

Your Fossilized Serial Port

Okay, perhaps the serial port isn't *fossilized*, but it is one-half of the original dynamic duo that first appeared with the premiere of the IBM PC.

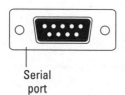

Serial
port

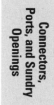

Most new peripherals nowadays are USB. However, you can still find the following serial devices from time to time (usually used, and probably on eBay):

✦ Modems

✦ Game controllers (especially the more complex joysticks)

✦ Scanners and older Zip drives

✦ Digital cameras

✦ Personal digital assistant (PDA) docks for Palm and Pocket PC units

Serial devices aren't plug and play, so you have to reboot your PC before Windows recognizes them, and most serial peripherals need drivers for Windows that have to be installed for things to work. Also, serial devices — especially modems — might require additional manual configuration inside Windows, such as editing files with Notepad and turning off certain port features. Oh, and did I mention that serial ports are slow as molasses compared to USB?

All in all, go USB. Everyone else has, and it's A Good Thing.

The Once-Renowned Parallel Port

Ah, I remember those days: the early 1980s, when the parallel port was truly the Queen of the PC Connections. Printers were hideously expensive peripherals that only a doctor, lawyer, or Supreme Court justice could afford. And, if you did have a printer, it was connected to your PC's parallel port (see Figure 3-2) with all the pomp, grace, and grandeur of the *RMS Queen Elizabeth II*. (Perhaps I need more Diet Coke.)

Figure 3-2:
The antique
25-pin
parallel port.

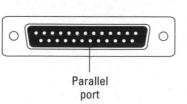

Parallel
port

Laptop Connectivity 101

Like their desktop brethren, today's laptops lean heavily on USB ports to provide all the connections to printers and other external devices. However, there are two types of ports that are generally considered specific to laptops that you may encounter from time to time:

✔ **Infrared:** Many laptops once featured an infrared port (commonly called an IrDA port, short for Infrared Data Association) that can be used to communicate with devices such as PDAs and other laptops. Windows provides full support for an infrared connection. However, these ports don't do diddly squat if the external peripheral you're trying to communicate with doesn't have its own IrDA port — and not many do, so you can't use this whiz-bang technology with many devices.

✔ **PC Cards:** Speaking of laptops, PC Cards are used with laptop computers to provide all sorts of external connections: wireless network adapters, FireWire and eSATA ports, external hard drives, and even cellular phone service. Most laptop models can accommodate either two or three of these credit-card-sized adapter cards — note, however, that most netbooks and ultrabooks don't have PC Card slots. When you pack up your laptop, your PC Cards can be ejected to streamline your computer for the road — when you get to your destination, it takes only a second to pop them back in.

Again, I'm sorry to report that the parallel port's days are numbered. The popularity of the USB port as a printer connection has doomed the parallel port to obsolescence, and we can wave goodbye to her with a wistful smile. As with the serial port, this Mark's Maxim prevails:

Buy USB. You'll be happier.™

Meet Your Video Port

At last, a port that has been around for many years and still (occasionally) rocks! Yes, friends and neighbors, most video cards still offer the same 15-pin, D-SUB video port that originally appeared with the IBM Video Graphics Array (VGA) specification. However, the 29-pin DVI-I port has gained ground fast. A *DVI-I port* is used to connect digital flat-panel (also called *liquid crystal display,* or LCD) monitors to your PC, as well as to many flat-panel televisions. Figure 3-3 shows the business end of a typical video card that offers both ports onboard.

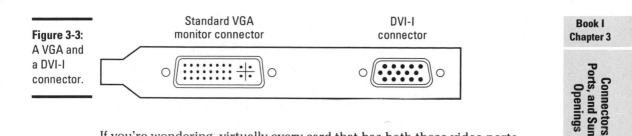

Figure 3-3:
A VGA and
a DVI-I
connector.

Standard VGA
monitor connector

DVI-I
connector

If you're wondering, virtually every card that has both these video ports
can use two monitors at a time (either showing an *expanded* desktop, where
your mouse moves seamlessly from one monitor to the other, or two separate and discrete desktops). Figure 3-4 illustrates this kind of rig.

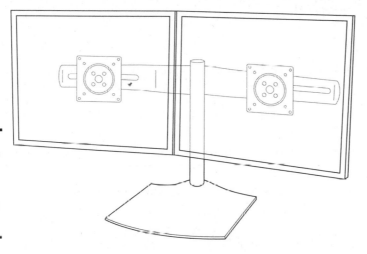

Figure 3-4:
Two side-
by-side
monitors
offer a huge
Desktop.

Some video cards now sport an HDMI port as well as DVI-I and VGA — and
yes, that's the same HDMI port that connects to today's high-definition TVs
and computer monitors. Imagine viewing your computer games and movies
on a 60" flat screen (or projector), and you can understand why an HDMI
port is rapidly becoming standard equipment on a Windows PC.

Audio Connectors You Likely Need

Today's speakers connect to your PC's sound card in one of four ways:

✦ **Standard analog Line Out/Speaker jacks on the card:** You find these familiar audio jacks on the card itself, just like the headphone jacks on an MP3
player. Most PC speakers use these jacks, shown in Figure 3-5.

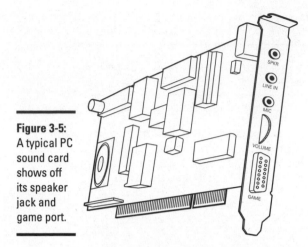

Figure 3-5:
A typical PC
sound card
shows off
its speaker
jack and
game port.

✦ **Standard analog RCA jacks on the card:** Some cards also have the RCA jacks that most folks associate with a stereo system or VCR. These jacks are more convenient than the Line Out/Speaker jacks because you don't need a miniplug-to-RCA adapter to use your stereo system with your PC's audio output.

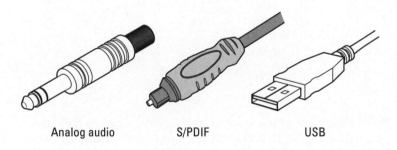

Analog audio   S/PDIF   USB

✦ **Standard optical (TOSLINK) and coaxial digital (SPIDF) connectors:** Audiophiles who truly want the best sound reproduction are willing to spend the extra dollars on an all-digital connection betwixt card and speakers (or card and high-end stereo system). These connectors are also standard equipment on most Dolby Surround sound systems.

✦ **The USB port:** Surprise! Our new/old friend makes another appearance. This time, your speakers can use any USB port on your system for a digital audio connection — analog gets tossed out the door, and audiophiles can wax enthusiastic about their pristine digital sound.

You might also find a PC game port on older audio cards, allowing you to connect a joystick or another game controller. The game port is going the way of the dodo (thanks once again, as you might guess, to USB game controllers).

Keyboard and Mouse Ports on Parade

The final stop on the port tour is the ubiquitous PS/2 keyboard-and-mouse port. Figure 3-6 illustrates the plug that fits in these ports. Each port is typically color coded and marked with an icon to indicate which piece of hardware gets connected where.

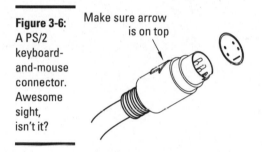

Figure 3-6: A PS/2 keyboard-and-mouse connector. Awesome sight, isn't it?

Make sure arrow is on top

I hate to bring it up, but at the risk of sounding like a broken record, virtually all PC hardware manufacturers are turning to USB keyboards and USB mice. (See why I stress just how important USB is to the modern PC?) In this case, however, I see no real advantage to using a USB keyboard or mouse over a PS/2 keyboard or mouse because the latter really doesn't require any configuration, and it's not continually being unplugged and reconnected. Plus, most of today's PCs still include PS/2 ports for keyboards and mice, so we're not quite to the point of an "orphan" PS/2 connection yet.

Book II
Windows 8

Visit www.dummies.com/extras/pcsaio for more on customizing the Start screen.

Contents at a Glance

Chapter 1: Shake Hands with Windows 8

In This Chapter

✔ Celebrating the advantages of Windows 8

✔ Starting and shutting down Windows 8

✔ Introducing Windows controls

✔ Using the keyboard

✔ Searching for help

✔ Contacting Microsoft for support

The Windows 8 operating system offers the most current appearance, performance, and functionality available for your PC — that is, as long as you're using an Intel or Advanced Micro Devices (AMD) processor with sufficient muscle. If you're using an older, slower Pentium or Athlon single-processor machine, consider sticking with Windows XP because your PC doesn't have the necessary horsepower to provide real performance in Windows 8.

In this chapter, I present you with the beginning of your Windows 8 manual — the invaluable, indispensable paper volume that you *didn't* get when you bought Windows 8 or your PC. (Can you tell that I used to write software user manuals?) This book assumes no experience with Windows, so I start with shutting down your PC and the most important controls and keys that you use in the following chapters.

A Windows 8 Primer

Start off by seeing what's new in Windows 8. And for those readers on the fence trying to decide whether to upgrade — and whether your current machine has the juice to support Windows 8 — I've got you covered.

Why Windows 8, anyway?

If you're wondering why Windows 8 is the pick of the Microsoft litter — and why it's time to upgrade from an older Windows version, such as XP, Vista, or 7 — allow me to point out the advantages of Windows 8:

✦ **Support for tablet and touch-screen PCs:** Microsoft has done a lot of work to add tablet and touch-screen PC support to Windows 8, including the company's own Surface line of tablet PCs. Although Windows 8 can still be controlled with a mouse or trackball, for the first time Windows can truly recognize your finger as a PC pointing device. (Sorry, I had to add that, I couldn't resist.)

✦ **Speed:** Run on a PC built within the past year or so, Windows 8 performs better than older versions of Windows — and that includes Windows 7, which was used as the foundation for Windows 8. For example, startup and shutdown times have been dramatically improved over Windows 7.

✦ **Customizability:** You can tweak, remove, and reengineer such elements as the Start screen, toolbars, menus, and your desktop within Windows 8. (In this chapter, however, I stick with the default settings, to avoid confusing you with my crazy preferences!)

✦ **Ease of use:** No downside here! Older versions of Windows made it harder to take care of common tasks, such as creating an Internet connection and adding a printer to your system. The folks in Redmond have been working overtime to help automate these processes.

✦ **Support for the latest standards:** Again, this is nothing but the very definition of Good. Windows 8 can handle all the acronyms you want (but might not yet know): MP3, MPEG, JPEG, USB, Wi-Fi, DSL, and many more. (All those cryptic escapees from a bowl of alphabet soup are explained in this book.) Unlike some earlier versions of Windows — which either don't even support the latest technology or require additional software to use it— Windows 8 has built-in support for today's neatest toys.

✦ **More secure:** Windows 8 includes better protection against all sorts of malware and viruses (without being as intrusive as Vista or Windows 7 when it comes to protecting your system). With better defenses, you can get up from your PC for lunch without worrying whether it will still be running when you return.

Flavors à la Windows

Windows 8 comes in four editions: the basic edition (simply titled Windows 8) is by far the best seller. Windows 8 Pro is the Cadillac, including all the features Microsoft can pack into Windows. Windows RT is especially designed for tablet PC users and runs only on the ARM CPU — in other words, a desktop PC owner can't install Windows RT. Finally, Windows Enterprise is sold to companies and organizations for network-wide distribution (so you won't be able to buy it in a retail store).

The Windows 8 edition is probably the best low-cost choice. (At the time of this writing, the basic edition is selling for around $70 at most online retailers, with an upgrade from Windows 7 going for about the same amount.) For a typical home PC owner or small-office PC user, the Windows 8 and Windows 8 Pro editions are just about identical in look, taste, and smell. (Pro Edition includes a number of advanced features, like remote desktop capabilities and support for system-wide encryption.) Everything you find in this chapter applies to both the basic and Pro versions of Windows 8. (When disparities occur later in this minibook, I send up a flare.)

Microsoft allows you to upgrade from Windows 8 to Windows 8 Pro with the Windows 8 Pro Pack (about $100 at the time of this writing). If you're running Windows 8 Pro, you can bump up yet again — this time to Windows 8 Pro with Media Center for $10, which includes the ability to watch DVD movies and record live TV broadcasts (with the correct hardware, of course).

Upgrade or clean install

To upgrade, or to perform a clean install? A question worthy of the Bard himself (if he were using Windows 7, that is). If you've never heard the term, a *clean install* involves backing up your existing personal data from your Windows 7 system — the files and information that you created — and then formatting your hard drive and installing Windows 8, fresh as a daisy. You have to reinstall all of your data and programs, of course, but your system should perform at its best with a clean install.

Upgrading from Windows 7 to Windows 8 is certainly possible, but you're more likely to encounter minor problems and bugs, and you'll likely have to reinstall at least some of your applications. Also, your PC may not perform as well as it would if you had done a clean install.

Personally, I recommend a clean install, which results in the best possible performance for Windows 8 and also allows me to "clean house" by determining what programs I *really* need to reinstall.

System requirements for the Big 8

If you're upgrading to Windows 8, it's time for that moment that you've feared all along: coming to grips with the demands that the Big 8 will make on your PC. Is it ready for the upgrade? Do you need to add RAM, or will you run out of hard drive space?

I cover the basics in this section, but don't forget that Microsoft offers the Windows 8 Upgrade Assistant, which scans your PC's current configuration and provides you with a listing of possible issues that you might have while upgrading. You can download the Assistant at

```
http://windows.microsoft.com/en-US/windows-8/upgrade-to-
    windows-8
```

Processor and RAM

For a typical installation of Windows 8, you need at least a 1 GHz processor (preferably with multiple cores) and at least 1GB of random access memory (RAM).

These are the minimum requirements as recommended by Microsoft. I wouldn't run Windows 8 on any PC with less than a dual-core processor and at least 2GB of RAM.

Hard drive space

Installing Windows 8 Home Premium costs you at least 16GB in hard drive space, and that's the very definition of A Bare Minimum.

Those figures don't include the extra hard drive territory that Windows 8 demands for features such as temporary files and virtual memory, so you should add another 10GB (or even 20GB) to those totals if you want better performance from Windows 8. With today's hard drives, a spare gigabyte of space is easy to come by, so there's no reason to feel claustrophobic. My call? I'd opt for a minimum of 30GB for Windows 8.

Mr. Potato Head on parade

Over the years, Windows has inflated like a Macy's parade balloon on Thanksgiving Day. On my desk is an original copy of Microsoft Windows/286 — version 2.1 of Windows, which dates back to the late 1980s and was designed for 80286-powered PCs. I keep it as a conversation piece. The entire installation took a whopping seven low-density floppy disks, and only one holds the operating system! (The other six disks store applications, fonts, printer drivers, and such. And you can forget the floppies — Windows is available only on DVD-ROM or as a download now.)

Graphics card

You need a graphics card of recent manufacture — one that supports at least DirectX 9 — to enjoy the visual perks of Windows 8 without slowing down your PC.

And now for the rest of the story

To enjoy some features of Windows 8 to the fullest, I would also recommend the following "luxuries" (luckily, most of them are either included with a PC of recent vintage, or they're easily obtained at your local Maze O' Wires electronics store):

+ To use the full power of Windows 8 and the programs I describe in this tome, you'll need an Internet connection.

+ For those interested in watching or recording TV directly, a TV tuner is a must.

+ Sharing files and printers using HomeGroup requires a network and PCs running Windows 7 or 8.

+ DVD/CD recording (with a third-party application) requires a compatible optical drive.

**Book II
Chapter 1**

**Shake Hands
with Windows 8**

Starting and Shutting Down Windows 8

Starting (or, as technotypes continue to call it, *booting*) your Windows 8 PC is as easy as pressing the power switch. Some diagnostic and troubleshooting options are available during the startup process, but I cover those in detail in Chapter 5 of this minibook. For now, just remember the power switch.

There's more to consider, however, when you're ready to shut down Windows 8. In this section, I discuss the five methods you can use to shut down completely or partially.

Shutting down completely

The first option is the full deal: turning off your PC completely. Move your cursor to the upper right corner of the screen to display the Charms bar — it's a strip of icons that appears at the right side of the screen. (If you're using a touch-sensitive screen, you can swipe to the left from the right side of the screen to display the Charms bar.) Click the Settings icon (which looks like a gear) to display the Settings pane (shown in Figure 1-1), and then click the Power button. Click Shut Down from the pop-up menu. Your PC turns itself off automatically.

If you're using the Windows 8 Desktop (which I discuss in more detail in the next chapter), you can also press Alt+F4 to display the Shutdown window, where you can choose all of the options I cover in this section.

Windows tries to be a friend by automatically closing any applications you're running before it shuts down. However, if a program has an open document or file that hasn't been saved, the application is *supposed to* prompt you to save your changes first. Note that I said *supposed to*: Some misbehaving or badly written programs *don't* prompt you before they zap themselves out of existence, so don't use the Shut Down or Restart options (see the next section) unless you manually saved all open documents (or you trust any application that's open, such as Microsoft Word).

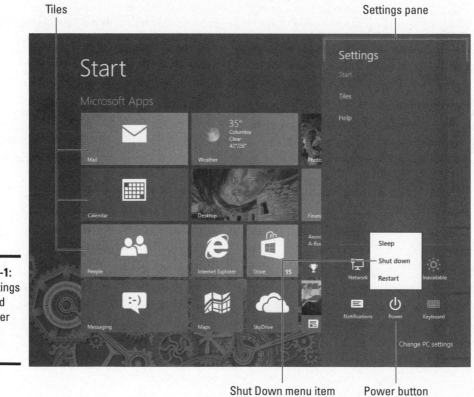

Figure 1-1:
The Settings pane and the Power pop-up menu.

Tiles

Settings pane

Shut Down menu item

Power button

Restarting your PC

Restarting your PC consists of shutting down Windows and then immediately turning it back on. (Restarting is also called *rebooting*.) To restart your computer, close all open programs and documents, display the Charms bar by moving your cursor to the upper right corner of the screen, click the Settings icon, and then click the Power button and choose Restart from the pop-up menu. You don't need to press the power button to turn your PC back on again. Dame Windows, she can do it all.

You might need to restart when you install new software or upgrade existing software. (You typically see a dialog box that displays a Restart button.) I also recommend rebooting if your PC starts acting flaky — like when error messages keep appearing, programs refuse to close, or strange graphics appear on your desktop.

Using sleep mode

Sleep mode immediately puts your PC in a low-power mode: The monitor goes black, and Windows appears to shut down. However, you can return to your work just as you left it by pressing one of the arrow keys on the keyboard or moving the mouse. It's rather like your monitor waking up from a screen saver snooze: It saves time and electricity and makes it easier to return to your work "already in progress." To go into sleep mode, display the Charms bar, click Settings, click Power, and then choose Sleep from the pop-up menu.

Not all PCs support sleep mode. Check your PC or motherboard manual to see whether you can use this feature. If you can use Windows's sleep mode, you may also be able to set your PC's power switch to activate sleep mode rather than turn off the computer. Or, your PC can go into sleep mode automatically after a certain amount of inactivity.

Manually save your documents before putting your PC in sleep mode because putting your machine into sleep mode does *not* save to your hard drive the files you're working with — instead, they're saved to your PC's memory. You lose everything if your PC is hit with a power failure and you haven't saved your documents.

Multiuser options

Three system choices in Windows 8 are useful in a *multiuser* environment: in other words, when multiple people are sharing the same PC at different times and using a different user account for each person:

✦ **Switch User:** If another user simply needs the PC for a short time, you can use the Switch User feature, which allows another person to log on and take care of business. Unlike signing out, however, your applications continue running in a *hidden* state. When that other person has finished using her account, she can sign out, allowing you to return to your far more important tasks! (In other words, Windows 8 is allowing *two* accounts to run at the same time but allowing only one person to use the PC.) To switch users from anywhere within Windows 8, press the now-infamous "Three Finger Salute" combination (Ctrl+Alt+Delete). Click Switch User on the screen that appears and then click the desired user icon. After the usurping user has finished and signed out, click your user icon to return to your world.

If you've been using PCs for many years, you may hesitate to press Ctrl+Alt+Delete because it used to immediately reboot your PC! This is not the case, however, for Windows XP through Windows 8. I use this shortcut all the time.

✦ **Sign Out:** Leave your PC running but allow others to log on to the PC if they enter a valid username and password. Like a true shutdown, signing off in Windows 8 automatically closes most applications and any open documents. To pass the computing torch to someone else, press Ctrl+Alt+Delete, and then choose Sign Out. Windows 8 displays the date/time screen you see whenever you start your PC — click anywhere to sign in. (From the Start screen, you can also click your account name at the upper-right corner of the screen to sign out.)

✦ **Lock:** Press Ctrl+Alt+Delete and click Lock, and Windows 8 immediately displays a password-protected screen that prevents anyone from logging in or using the machine until the proper password is provided. (If you're thinking security while you visit the restroom, you're a winner.) In effect, a Locked system operates just like it would with a password-protected screen saver. (You can also click your account name at the upper-right corner of the Start screen to lock.)

Windows 8 keeps track of each different user's account data and documents, so you can be assured that everything you don't want seen by others remains private. I go over multiuser operation in Chapter 4 of this minibook, so don't worry — all will become clear there.

Your Windows 8 Controls

After you become an expert in starting and shutting down your PC, survey the landscape of Windows 8. I show you the various graphical WUDs (short for *Wondrous User Devices*) represented on your Start screen and Desktop and how you can use them to exercise your will within.

Icons

The first stop on your journey is the lowly icon — often jeered at and often the target of a string of impassioned and unprintable words. Yet, icons are still the building blocks of today's graphical user interfaces (GUIs; that's a 10-cent synonym for operating systems such as Windows, Apple's OS X, and Linux, which all use a mouse). Believe me, icons will be around long after you and I are no longer worried about PCs.

Icons look like a picture, and that's no accident because they're simple representations of different locations and items on your computer. For example, Windows 8 displays different types of icons on your Desktop to represent items such as these:

✦ **Files and folders**

✦ **Programs you can run**

✦ **Hardware, such as hard drives, DVD drives, and printers**

✦ **Internet connections**

✦ **Other computers on your home or office network**

Let's talk right-click

You can also click your right mouse button *(right-click)* when the mouse cursor is resting atop something to display a pop-up menu that includes commands that are specific to the item you're hovering over. (To technonerds, the term for this pop-up is a *contextual menu.* Geez.) For example, if you right-click a digital photograph that you saved to your hard drive, you can choose to preview it, edit it, or print it. Personally, I'm a big fan of contextual menus because they usually contain everything that applies to a particular file. Some programs, such as Photoshop, even add their own commands to the contextual menu.

If you're using a touch-screen PC or tablet PC, however, the method you use to right-click varies by manufacturer — generally, you right-click by tapping on the item with two fingers instead of one, but I've also used PCs that required you to tap and hold to activate the contextual menu or hold down a key while tapping with one finger. Check your device's user manual for the proper method of right-clicking.

Figure 1-2 shows a gaggle of different types of Desktop icons in their natural environment. I go into much more detail about what you can do with icons in the next two chapters of this minibook. For now, just remember their versatility and that they represent something else on your system besides a thumbnail-size picture.

Tiles

Tiles are simply another form of icons, acting as buttons to activate or open programs and files, as well as display "live" information that's constantly updated — the big difference is where those tiles hang out, which is the Start screen that debuted with Windows 8. (More on the Start screen in a page or two.) As you might also have guessed, tiles are far easier to control with your finger if you're using a touch-screen or tablet PC.

That constantly changing cursor

Within Windows 8, your cursor is more than just a focus for your clicking finger — although that is its main use. Your cursor can be moved by a pointing device (like a mouse or trackball) or with your finger (on a touch-screen or tablet PC). When your cursor isn't pointing the way (depending on the action you're performing or the application you're running), it can also show

+ **Status:** PC activity, such as loading a file or applying a command

+ **Selection:** Selected text or graphics (to do something nefarious, I'm sure)

+ **Location:** Your position in a document

+ **File movement:** Progress while you're copying or moving files

The Start screen

If you've used earlier versions of Windows, it's time to brace yourself for a shock: The familiar face of the Start menu is gone from Windows 8! The Start menu has been replaced by the Start screen, shown in Figure 1-3 — from here, you can begin most of the activities and tasks that your PC can perform. (And again, the Start screen is easier for a touch-screen PC or tablet PC owner to activate and use.)

Figure 1-2:
I have always depended upon the kindness of icons.

Figure 1-3:
Tiles are the center of your Windows 8 Start screen.

Here's where tiles take center stage: each tile on your Start screen represents a different program, activity, folder, or even information source. I show you in later chapters how to *pin* (add) and remove tiles from your Start screen. Some tiles are automatically updated with new information, like the Weather, Sports, and News tiles.

Your Start screen might look different from mine. You can customize your Start screen to fit how you work, like how I did.

To display the Start screen from your Windows 8 Desktop, move your cursor to the top-right corner of the screen to display the Charms bar, and then click or tap on the Start icon (which looks like a windowpane). With the Start screen displayed, move your cursor to a tile or icon, and then click or tap.

You can press the Windows logo key (which looks like a waving windowpane) on your keyboard to switch between the Start screen and your Desktop.

Your user account name and picture appear at the top of the Start screen, identifying who's using the PC and allowing you to lock your PC and switch users (as I described earlier in this chapter).

I discuss many of the tiles and features of the Start screen in later chapters of this minibook.

The Desktop and taskbar

"Wait, Mark, does that mean that my Windows Desktop is gone for good as well?" Fear not, good reader, Microsoft hasn't made *that* dramatic of a change! Your Windows Desktop is now available from the Desktop tile on the Start screen, and (as you can see in Figure 1-4) the familiar *taskbar* — that little strip of buttons and miniature icons that runs along the bottom of the Desktop — is still alive and well.

The taskbar is another useful control that you can use to accomplish all sorts of tasks, and it remains out of sight until you need it. (Depending on the settings you choose for your taskbar, it might remain hidden until you move your cursor to the bottom of the screen.) I talk more about configuring the taskbar in Chapter 3 of this minibook.

Don't worry if your taskbar doesn't look like mine in the figure here. The appearance of the taskbar varies according to the programs you're running and the custom controls you added to it. You can use the taskbar to

✦ Switch quickly between open applications (and even multiple documents or windows open in the same program, as shown in Figure 1-4).

✦ Run the programs that you specify with a single mouse click.

✦ Control background programs that normally run hidden, such as your antivirus software.

✦ Control hardware, such as your printer and modem.

✦ Connect and disconnect Universal Serial Bus (USB) and FireWire peripherals, such as digital cameras and external DVD recorders.

✦ View the time and date.

✦ Access File Explorer.

You can find the full scoop on the taskbar in Chapter 3 of this minibook.

Figure 1-4:
Use the
taskbar
to switch
between
multiple
documents
in one
program.

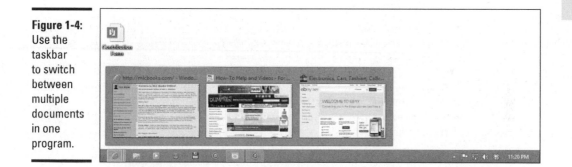

Menus and the Ribbon

Here's one more set of Windows 8 common controls, which are found in just about any program you run because they're part of Microsoft's grand user interface design standard. (It makes all Windows programs easier to understand and use, often without the need to refer to that ridiculous web-based user manual you got with your latest application.)

Remember the toolbar?

Still somewhat confused by the idea of a Ribbon? If you're familiar with the *toolbar*, which appeared in older versions of Windows (and is still used widely in the world of PC software), you're halfway there. Think of the Ribbon as a stationary toolbar that changes each time you click a tab.

Many applications — Adobe Photoshop, for example — have either "floating" toolbars or toolbars that can be resized and relocated. A Ribbon, however, remains firmly fixed at the top of the program's window.

The miracle of menus

Menus are the drop-down secret to life itself. Each menu contains either a group of similar commands or a group of commands that fall under the same category. To use a menu, you can either

✦ **Go mousing.** Click the menu name and then click the command from the list that appears.

✦ **Go digital.** Hold down the Alt key, press the underlined letter (the *hot key*) in the menu name, use your cursor keys to choose a command, and then press Enter to use the command.

For example, to open a file in a Windows application that uses menus, click the File menu at the top of the window and then choose Open from the drop-down list that appears. Alternatively, while holding down the Alt key, press F (the hot key for the File menu) and then press O (the hot key for the Open menu).

That tremendous Ribbon

What could be even easier and more efficient to use than the time-honored menu? How about Microsoft's popular Ribbon? (Someone should get a steak dinner for this one.) A *Ribbon* is a strip of tabs at the top of a program window (including the File Explorer, as well as virtually all Microsoft software). Each tab displays a different strip of buttons that allows you to use the most common commands in a program with a single click. The Ribbon appears within Photo Gallery at the top of the screen, as shown in Figure 1-5.

Figure 1-5:
The Ribbon
abounds
in the
Windows
world.

To illustrate how easy it is to use a Ribbon, consider opening a file. If the application you're using has an Open button on the Ribbon, click it — end of story. (The moral is, Ribbons rule!)

Using Bill's Funky Keys

Not all Windows-specific controls are meant for your mouse. Thanks to the Power of Bill, PC keyboards now come complete with additional keys that are tied directly to Windows, so you can use your keyboard, rather than your mouse, for navigation. As any PC power user will tell you, the mouse that can move faster and more efficiently than your fingertips hasn't been (and likely never will be) invented.

Most of the keys on your computer keyboard work like they do on standard typewriters. For instance, pressing Shift in combination with another alphabetic key still creates a capital letter. PC keyboards, however, also sport nifty special keys for navigation, functions, and (sometimes) Windows-specific commands. For your reference, Figure 1-6 illustrates a typical modern 104-key PC keyboard.

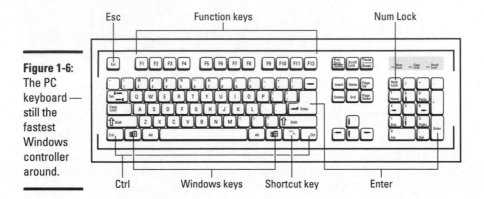

Figure 1-6: The PC keyboard — still the fastest Windows controller around.

The Windows keys

 Ah, the Windows keys — they rest snugly between the Alt and Ctrl keys on both sides of the spacebar on your keyboard. You can press either of these keys at any time to display the Start screen. Additionally, a number of other keys can be used in combination with a Windows key. Just hold down a Windows (Win) key and try one of the keys listed in Table 1-1.

Table 1-1	Windows Key Combinations
Key Combination	*What It Does*
Win+D	Displays the Windows Desktop (even when displaying the Start screen, or with other programs running)
Win+E	Opens the Computer window on your Desktop, where you can manage your files
Win+F	Opens the Files box on the Start screen Search pane, from which you can locate a file or folder
Win+L	Locks your computer
Win+R	Opens the Run dialog box, from which you can run a program by typing its name

In fact, just press the Windows key by itself, and Windows displays (or hides) the Start screen. What will they think of next?

The Shortcut key

Remember how enamored I am of contextual menus? A quick poke at the Shortcut key — located on the right side of the keyboard between the Windows and Ctrl keys — acts as a right-click (displays a contextual menu) when you select an icon anywhere in Windows. After the pop-up menu appears, you can use your cursor keys and the Enter key to choose a command.

Other important keys

These old friends have been around since the days of Genghis Khan — or at least the beginnings of the IBM PC, whichever came first. (Scary thing is, I remember the latter vividly.) Anyway, these keys still come in quite handy in the Windows world:

**Book II
Chapter 1**

Shake Hands
with Windows 8

◆ **Enter:** PC keyboards have two of these beauties: one above the Shift key on the right side of the alphabetic keys and the other in the lower-right corner of the numeric keypad. Within your word processor, of course, pressing Enter creates a new paragraph. But elsewhere within Windows, pressing Enter almost always starts a command or selects an item. (A friend of mine still calls it the *Submit key,* from the days of mainframe computing. He's great fun at parties.)

◆ **Arrow (navigation) keys:** This tightly knit group of four keys performs a number of different functions, depending on what you're doing at the moment, but it's always something to do with movement. For example, you can scroll through a document in a word processor or spreadsheet or move through the items in a list. Heck, many games you play will even use the arrow keys to select a direction or move your character forward or backward.

◆ **Escape (Esc):** Press Esc (in the far-upper-left area of your keyboard), and you're jetted off to your favorite vacation spot with a ton of cash to spend and your favorite movie star. (No, not really — although the Redmond engineers are rumored to be working on the new enhanced Escape key for the next version of Windows.) Actually, you use Esc to back out of things. Pressing Esc can cancel many commands, close some windows, and close dialog boxes.

◆ **Num Lock:** Press this key (in the upper-left corner of the numeric keypad) to toggle those keys between the numbers — useful for spreadsheets and data entry — and navigational keys. (Note the cursor arrow symbols on the 2, 4, 6, and 8 keys.)

◆ **Ctrl (Control):** These two keys (on either side of the spacebar) are used in conjunction with other keys for editing and keyboard commands within many applications. For example, pressing the combination Ctrl+B within Microsoft Word makes selected text bold.

✦ **Alt (Alternate):** Like the Ctrl keys, your Alt keys are used in league with other keys, typically for invoking menus and special features within your applications.

✦ **F (Function) keys:** These 12 sentinels across the top of your keyboard are used for different purposes throughout Windows — and in many cases, even within specific applications (hence the generic name). They're usually abbreviated as *F1* through *F12*.

Other keys on your keyboard — for example, Home, End, Page Up, and Page Down — also have specific uses within every application. To become a power user of a certain application, consult that program's Help system for the special keystrokes it uses. You'll zip through documents while others plod along!

Using the Windows 8 Help System

Speaking of help, I'm happy to say that Windows 8 comes with the best Help system that has ever shipped with any version of Windows. It even has online components that you can refer to for the latest information on features (and the *occasional* bug). With the Help system, you can

✦ **Locate specific help.** Find help for nearly any topic.

✦ **Follow task tutorials.** They guide you step by step through all sorts of procedures (such as printing, troubleshooting, and updating Windows with the latest patches).

✦ **Search the Microsoft Windows 8 communities.** All you need is an Internet connection.

✦ **Scan tips and tricks.** Get help from Windows experts (if you have an Internet connection).

✦ **View the latest headlines.** Read all about new Windows 8 features (if you have an Internet connection).

Displaying Help

To display the Help system within Windows itself, click any empty spot on your Desktop and then press the F1 key to load the top-level Windows Help system window, which you see in Figure 1-7. (When you're using a program, pressing F1 displays the Help system for that program.)

To display application-specific help from the Start screen, press Win+I and click Help.

The Windows Help system requires an Internet connection.

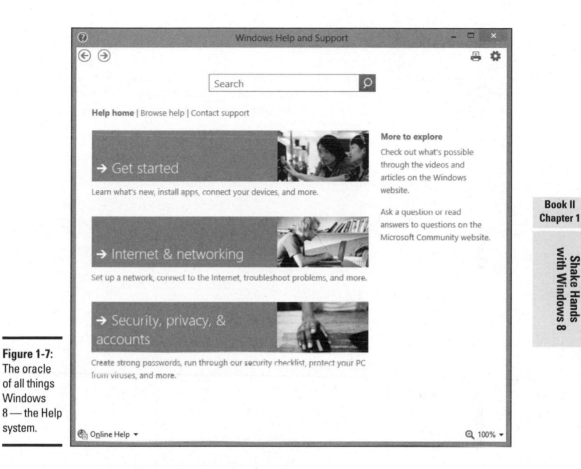

Figure 1-7:
The oracle of all things Windows 8 — the Help system.

Searching for specific help

After the Windows 8 Help and Support window displays, feel free to click any of the *links* (the bolded and underlined words) to display the corresponding topic. However, you usually visit the Help system to search for specific help on a Windows feature or command. To search for a word or phrase within Help, follow these steps:

1. **Click within the Search Help box, at the top of the Windows Help and Support window.**

2. **Type the word or phrase you want to search for and then press Enter.**

The fewer words you enter, the better the chance of getting a match that addresses your topic.

The Help system hums happily to itself for a few seconds and then displays a results page like you see in Figure 1-8. (I searched for the phrase *burning a CD* in this example.)

3. **To display the information in a topic, click the topic name (in the Search Results area).**

Some steps have *links* (look for underlined text), which you can click to open the dialog box or window in question or run the program mentioned in the Help text. (This really makes it easy to fix something, especially when you don't quite know where a particular setting is within the Windows 8 behemoth.) Other search results return *technical articles* — consider them *Tips for Technonerds* — that relate to the topic you found. Technical articles can include bug fixes, workarounds, or just explanations of what precisely is happening when you use a Windows feature.

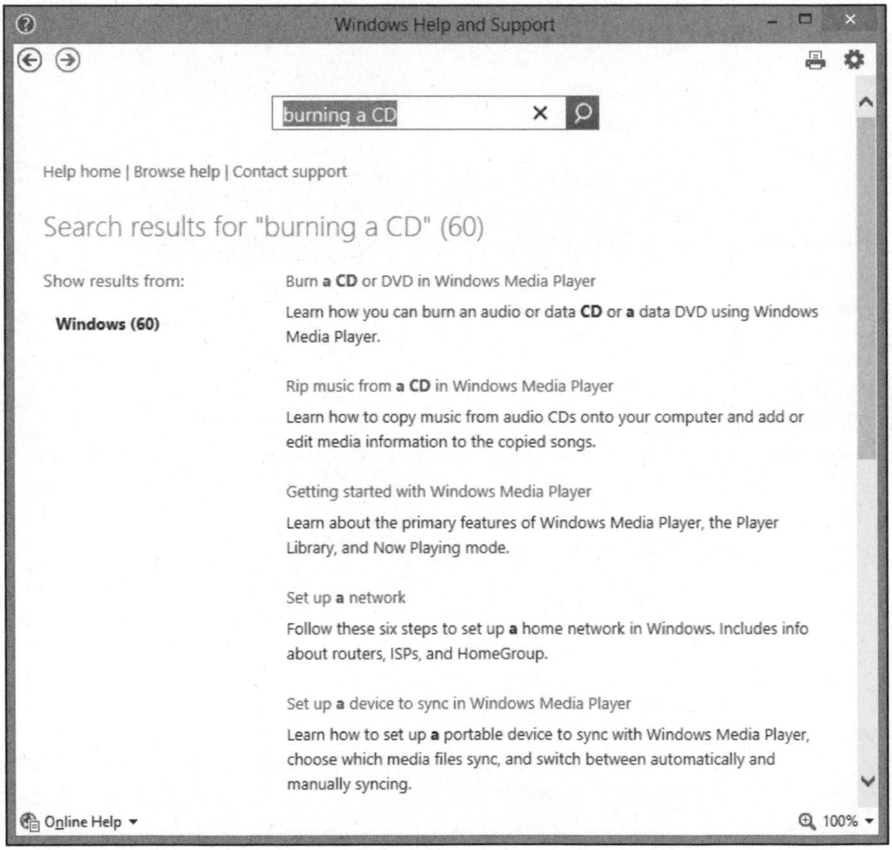

Figure 1-8: The results of a typical search through the Help system.

Windows Help and Support

Help home | Browse help | Contact support

Search results for "burning a CD" (60)

Show results from:

Windows (60)

Burn **a CD** or DVD in Windows Media Player

Learn how you can burn an audio or data **CD** or **a** data DVD using Windows Media Player.

Rip music from **a CD** in Windows Media Player

Learn how to copy music from audio CDs onto your computer and add or edit media information to the copied songs.

Getting started with Windows Media Player

Learn about the primary features of Windows Media Player, the Player Library, and Now Playing mode.

Set up **a** network

Follow these six steps to set up **a** home network in Windows. Includes info about routers, ISPs, and HomeGroup.

Set up **a** device to sync in Windows Media Player

Learn how to set up **a** portable device to sync with Windows Media Player, choose which media files sync, and switch between automatically and manually syncing.

Online Help ▼

🔍 100% ▼

To move backward through Help topics to where you started, click the Back button on the toolbar in the upper-left corner of the Help window.

Yelling for assistance

If you can't find what you're looking for within the Help system, you can turn to Microsoft for direct support. Underneath the Search Help box (refer to Figure 1-7), click the Contact Support link.

If you've lost your Internet connection or you don't have an e-mail address, naturally you can also contact Microsoft for support by telephone — at least for now. (Insert ominous chord here.) The number is always included in your Windows 8 installation documentation.

**Book II
Chapter 1**

**Shake Hands
with Windows 8**

Chapter 2: The Many Windows of Windows

In This Chapter

✔ **Managing windows**

✔ **Recognizing icons**

✔ **Selecting one icon (or many icons)**

✔ **Using toolbars in Windows 8**

Doing things graphically is what Windows 8 is all about. The idea of visual control is at the heart of today's graphical user interfaces (GUIs), like Windows and OS X (and Linux, when it's wearing the right makeup).

In this chapter, I introduce you to the graphical building blocks of Windows 8. Plus, I show you the "antique" keyboard combinations that are even faster than a speeding mouse. (Hey, any power user will tell you that pressing a sequence of two or three keys is often faster than clicking!)

Managing Windows Means Productivity

What's that on the horizon? Oh, boy — it looks like another of those weighty Mark's Maxims:

> **Learn the Zen of the window and become a power user.™**

In this section, you do just that — and your efficiency and speed in Windows 8 will amaze your friends and family. (And that's what it's all really about, right?)

Windows 8 has a helpful feature that displays a short pop-up description of the controls in a window. If this book isn't handy, you can find out the function of a button or control by leaving your cursor sitting motionless on top of the control in question. (Touch-screen and tablet PC owners can usually tap and hold on the control instead.) Interesting trivia fact: The descriptive text that appears is a *tooltip*.

Opening and closing windows

You rarely need to manually open a new window in Windows 8, which is a trademark of good design from the Redmond troop. Windows 8 automatically opens a window when you

+ **Run File Explorer** (as shown in Figure 2-1). Just double-click the Computer icon on your Desktop, or click the File Explorer icon in the taskbar at the bottom of your Desktop. File Explorer is the tool that you use for navigating through the files on your hard drive, copying and moving things from place to place, running programs, and opening documents — for example, using File Explorer, you could open your USB flash drive and load the family reunion photos given to you by your kids.

   File Explorer is your navigation and file management tool. On the other hand, Internet Explorer is a web browser that you'll use to visit sites on the World Wide Web, like www.dummies.com.

+ **Run most Windows applications.** Some programs, however, run in the background or don't automatically create new document windows.

+ **Create a new document in a Windows application, such as Word.**

Figure 2-1: The most common window you'll encounter is the File Explorer window.

By default, the left portion of the File Explorer window — called the *Navigation pane* — contains common locations within Windows 8. You can expand any heading with a right-facing triangle icon next to it; just click the triangle to expand the item (such as a folder or hard drive) and click it again to collapse the item.

You do need to close windows, however, to keep your Desktop tidy and to free system resources for other tasks. To close a window, move your mouse pointer over the *Close button* — the red button with an X in the upper-right corner of the window, as shown in Figure 2-1 — and then click the left mouse button. Alternatively, you can usually choose File⇨Close from the window's menu, or select the File tab and click Close. (You can see the File tab in upcoming Figure 2-2.) From the keyboard, Alt+F4 is typically recognized as well.

Start screen apps can usually be closed by swiping from the top of the screen to the bottom. (This trick also works with a mouse. Make sure your cursor turns into a hand icon at the top of the screen before you drag the mouse down to the bottom of the screen.)

And no worries that you might close a window by accident and lose all your work because a safety net is in place within any well-behaved Windows application (such as Word 2013 or Photoshop, for example): The program first asks you for confirmation before it closes a window containing an unsaved document.

Scrolling windows

Suppose that you're editing a large photograph and you decide to add a title at the bottom — unfortunately, the bottom of the photo is nowhere in view. (In the same vein, you could be using a File Explorer window to navigate a hard drive with dozens of folders, and the folder you want is farther down within that gaggle of folders.) How do you get to the area or the item you want to see?

That's the job of those unsung heroes, your scroll bars (as shown in Figure 2-2). To move through the contents of the window, just click in the area above or below the scroll button or click the up and down buttons at the top and bottom of the scroll bar. (*Note:* If your document is wider than the application window, as it is in Figure 2-2, you see a horizontal scroll bar as well. It works the same way, by just moving the contents of the window to the left or right.)

Most touch-screen and tablet PCs allow you to tap and drag the contents of a window, but you can also tap and drag a scroll button to scroll.

File tab   Scroll button   Scroll bar   Up button

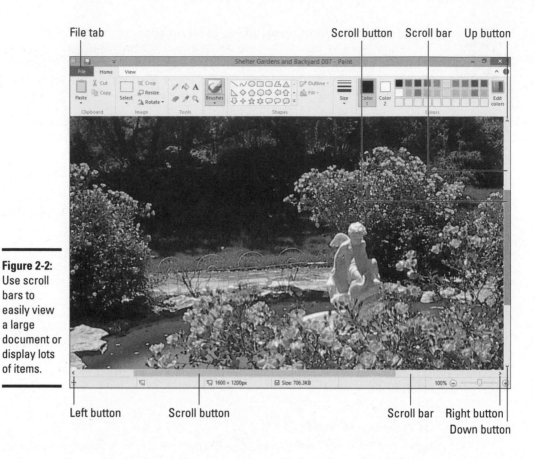

Figure 2-2:
Use scroll
bars to
easily view
a large
document or
display lots
of items.

Left button   Scroll button   Scroll bar   Right button
                                                                  Down button

To really move like the wind within a window (bad pun that I won't repeat),
you can even click the scroll button and drag it. When you drag something,
you first click it — in this case, the scroll button — and then hold down the
mouse button while you move the mouse in the desired direction. (On a
touch-screen or tablet PC, press and hold on the screen while moving
your finger to drag.) You can find more uses for dragging later in this
chapter.

Many applications allow you to scroll through the contents of a window
with your keyboard arrow (navigation) keys or with a scroll wheel on your
mouse. And, pressing the Page Up and Page Down keys should move an
entire page at a time through the contents of a window.

Minimizing and restoring windows

Sometimes you want to keep a window open, but you don't want it full-screen on your Desktop. For example, you might be checking a website in the Desktop version of Internet Explorer and you need to copy a picture into a Word document. How do you move the Internet Explorer window out of your way temporarily without closing it? This is a job for the Minimize button, as shown in Figure 2-3.

Book II
Chapter 2

The Many Windows
of Windows

Close button
Maximize/Restore button
Minimize button

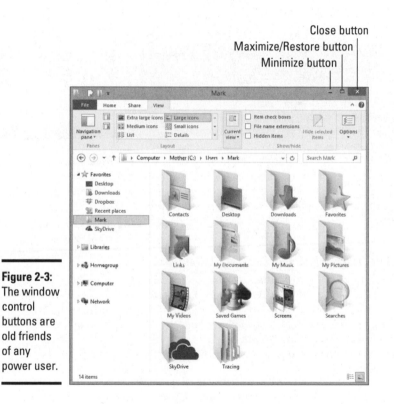

Figure 2-3:
The window
control
buttons are
old friends
of any
power user.

Minimizing a window hides it. Well, more accurately, the window is stored as a button on your taskbar, at the bottom of the screen. To return the window to its original glory, simply click the button on the taskbar. If you have a lot of windows open, the taskbar might sprout its own set of scroll buttons so that you can scroll through the minimized windows within the taskbar. (I tell you more about the taskbar in Chapter 3 of this minibook.)

The taskbar also uses another trick if you have a large number of windows open. Separate windows within a single application are grouped together as a single taskbar button — and, when you hover your cursor over the button, Windows 8 displays each window as a thumbnail. Click the desired thumbnail to select it, as shown in Figure 2-4.

Figure 2-4:
Choosing between multiple Internet Explorer windows from the taskbar.

"So does a program continue to run when it's minimized?" Good question. Most do, but some applications pause when minimized (such as games or video players) and then restart when the window returns to the Desktop.

Maximizing and restoring windows

If you already guessed that maximizing a window is the opposite of minimizing it, pour yourself another soda as a reward! *Maximizing* a window expands it to fill the entire screen, giving you plenty of elbowroom to work with. In fact, applications such as Microsoft Word take advantage of a maximized window by displaying as much of your document as possible, using automatic word wrap (or even displaying multiple pages in one window).

If the window isn't maximized, click the Maximize button once — it's the middle button in the group in the upper-right corner (refer to Figure 2-3). After the window expands, the multitalented Maximize button toggles to the Restore button. When you click the Restore button, the window returns to the original dimensions it had before you clicked the Maximize button, and that doggone button morphs back into the Maximize button again. ("Ethel, make it stop!")

Moving windows

When you need to move a window from one area of your Desktop to another, Windows 8 is there for you. On a typical day, I end up juggling multiple windows like the world's worst circus clown. (Alternatively, you can buy a larger monitor. Yeah, right.)

To move a window to another piece of Desktop real estate, click (or tap) and drag the window's *title bar* — the colored strip at the top of the window that displays the application or document name — and the entire window follows. When the window is in the correct place, release to drop it. (Of course, you can't do this when the window is maximized. Go figure.)

To arrange multiple document windows within an application, choose Window⇨Arrange All, and the document windows line up in an orderly fashion so that you can choose one.

Resizing windows

A window can be resized to different dimensions as necessary — sorry, no triangles or parallelograms, though. Simply move your mouse pointer over the lower-right corner of the window or to one of the sides of the window until the mouse cursor changes to an arrow icon. Then click and drag to move that window in the indicated direction. (As you might expect, you can't resize a window if it's fully maximized. Go figure.)

Switching windows

Although you can easily open 10 or 15 windows within your Windows 8 Desktop, keep in mind that only 1 window at a time is *active*. And, the active window takes precedence, appearing on top of other windows, because it's the window you're viewing, editing, or using. Windows that are open on your Desktop — and not minimized — are *inactive* windows. They're dimmed (or shaded) to indicate that they're offline. (Note, however, that you can still copy or move files to an inactive window, which I demonstrate in Chapter 3 of this minibook.) You can see both the active and inactive window in Figure 2-5; in this case, Internet Explorer owns the lucky active window.

To switch to a different window, you can

✦ Click anywhere within the desired inactive window.

✦ Move your cursor to the taskbar and click an application button or a window button.

✦ Cycle through the open applications by holding down the Alt key and repeatedly pressing Tab until the window you want becomes active.

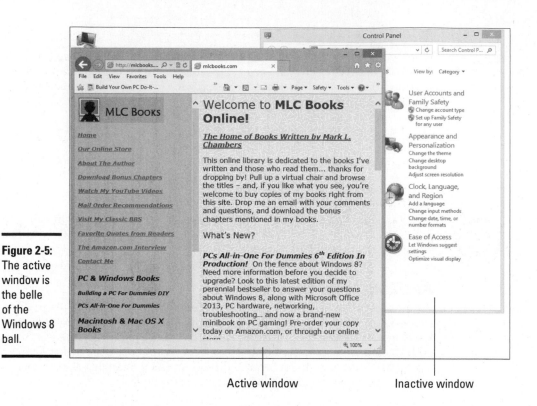

Figure 2-5:
The active
window is
the belle
of the
Windows 8
ball.

Active window　　　　　Inactive window

Note that you can still use a window's Minimize, Maximize/Restore, and Close buttons even when the window is inactive. Also, an application might continue to run while its window is inactive.

A Field Guide to Icons

Now I begin my discussion of Desktop icons with a classic Greek comedy. (Readers familiar with my books will already know about my propensity for vignettes.)

8 and *The Iliad*
(with apologies to Homer)

As the play opens, Hector is tussling with his new installation of Windows 8. He's knee-deep within a File Explorer window that's filled to the brim with icons.

Hector: "I want to run Microsoft Word! Which of these furshlugginer little pictures stands for the program, and which of these are my documents? What do I double-click? *Help!*"

[Enter proud Odysseus, hero of the Trojan War and experienced Windows 8 power user.]

Odysseus: "Do not panic, good Hector. You see, Microsoft Word has its own *program icon,* and each Word document that you create uses the Word *document icon.* The same is true for everything from Excel to Adobe Acrobat."

Hector: "So how do I learn which is which?"

Odysseus: "Read the manual that you got with the application or open an Explorer window and look in the folder where you saved a document from the application. Each software developer creates a unique program and document icon combination, but most of them are pretty self-explanatory."

Hector: "Or I could eschew icons completely by running Word from a Start screen tile, and then I can load the document that I want from Word's File tab, right?"

Odysseus: "That's right, or you can even double-click the document icon itself within that File Explorer window, and it will automatically load Word with that document."

Hector: "Hey, bud, that's in the next chapter. And where's that Trojan horse you promised me?"

Odysseus: "Whoops — busted again. I'm out of here!"

Fin

In this section, I help Hector (and you) by identifying each type of icon and showing some common examples.

Don't be afraid to right-click an icon to see its properties. Mouse owners can put their cursor over the icon in question and press the right mouse button once, which displays a pop-up contextual menu, while touch-enabled PC owners can (usually) tap the icon with two fingers. Click Properties, and you can see which application created a document — or, as Windows 8 calls it, *opens with* — as well as other nifty stuff that I discuss at several points in later parts of this book.

Hardware icons

Only a select few hardware devices have their own icons in Windows 8, but you'll be surprised at which ones do, including rather nebulous things such as network and Internet connections. These hardware icons tend to hang out on your Desktop or in a top-level File Explorer window.

Here's a representative list of hardware that's represented by Windows 8 as icons, many of which are shown in Figure 2-6:

+ **Hard drives**

+ **DVD and Blu-Ray drives**

+ **Printers**

+ **Removable storage,** such as floppy drives and portable Universal Serial Bus (USB) flash drives

+ **External devices,** such as MP3 players and digital cameras

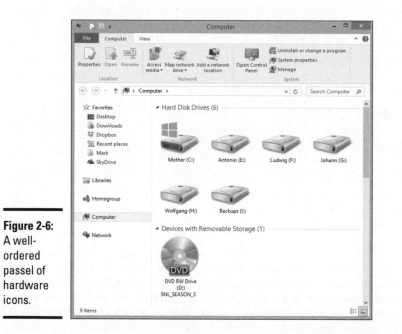

Figure 2-6:
A well-ordered passel of hardware icons.

In general, you can open, activate, or control a hardware device by double-clicking its icon (depending on which type of hardware device it is). Find more on this topic in the appropriate spots later in this minibook.

Program icons

Because you already know about program icons (thanks to Hector and Odysseus), I don't go into much detail here. Double-clicking a program icon runs the application from a File Explorer window or your Desktop, and a single click will suffice from the Start screen or a pinned item on the taskbar.

TIP

You can drag an item to the taskbar and click the Pin to Taskbar pop-up that appears, and that item remains on the taskbar. To open or run the item, just click on the pinned icon in the taskbar.

Figure 2-7 illustrates a number of well-known program icons. (I've made the icons larger so you can see them more clearly — you discover how to do this in Chapter 4 of this minibook.)

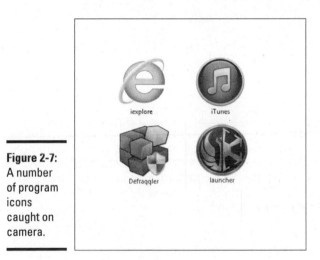

Figure 2-7:
A number
of program
icons
caught on
camera.

File icons

Technically, document icons are a subspecies of *file icons,* which can represent any type of data file on the planet. Windows 8 uses a couple of generic icons to represent files it doesn't recognize, so every file on your system — and I mean *every* file — can be represented by some kind of an icon.

Like it does with a document icon, Windows 8 attempts to open any data file you double-click. If Windows 8 knows the application that created the file, the program runs automatically to display the file. On the other hand, if Windows 8 doesn't recognize the file type, you see a dialog box that looks like Figure 2-8, where you can choose to

✦ Browse for the program that should open the file (by clicking the More Options link).

✦ Search the Windows Store for an app that can open the file.

✦ Select the program that you want to use to load the file from the list shown in the dialog.

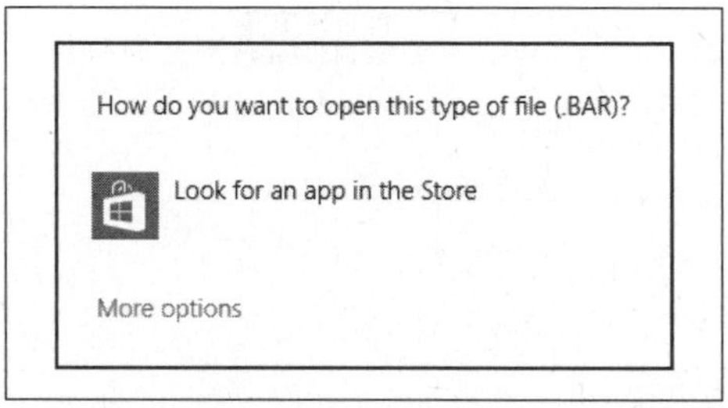

Figure 2-8:
Specify which program Windows 8 should use for this document.

How do you want to open this type of file (.BAR)?

Look for an app in the Store

More options

Folder icons

A *folder* is nothing more than a container to hold and organize other items, which can include both icons and subfolders. All folders use the ubiquitous manila file folder icon. If the folder is empty, the icon looks, well, empty. The icon for a folder that contains files displays miniature thumbnail images of the items it contains, as shown on the right side of Figure 2-9. Chalk up this cool effect to the eye candy in Windows 8.

Shortcut icons

A *shortcut* is represented by a unique icon. Although a shortcut looks much like a regular icon, a thorough examination reveals a curved arrow at the bottom of the image. (The phrase *Shortcut to* might also appear at the end of the icon label.)

Think of a shortcut as a signpost or a link to another item within your Windows 8 system. For instance, you can set up a shortcut to *World of Warcraft* that runs the program just as though you had clicked the program icon directly on the Start screen or had double-clicked the program icon in the File Explorer window.

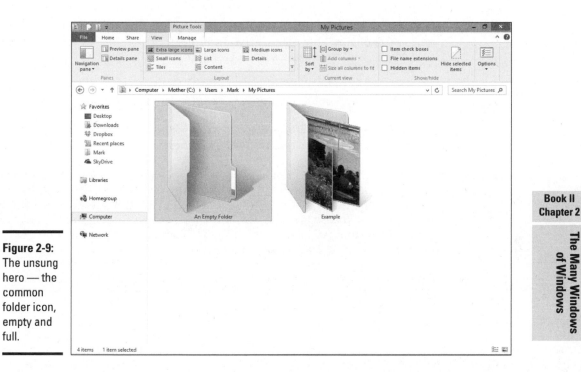

Figure 2-9:
The unsung
hero — the
common
folder icon,
empty and
full.

Because shortcuts take up only a few bytes of hard drive real estate, they
come in handy when you're customizing your Desktop or organizing a folder.
You can set up a program to be run from any folder (without requiring that
you dig down with File Explorer). Too, a shortcut can be easily tossed into
the Recycle Bin after you're finished with it because it's not a part of the
original application.

In fact, many games and applications now offer to add a shortcut to your
Desktop during installation, and I usually take them up on the offer. A
Desktop shortcut is quite convenient, and the software developer knows
that you can delete it quickly and easily, if necessary. If a program doesn't
offer to install a shortcut on your Desktop and you'll be using that program
often, I would recommend manually creating a shortcut on the Desktop
(which I'll cover in Chapter 4 of this minibook).

Because a shortcut is only a link to a program (or folder or even a hardware
device), you can create multiple copies for different locations in your system
and still not waste a tremendous amount of hard drive territory. (A friend
of mine always creates a folder on his Desktop with shortcuts to all the

documents and files relating to his latest project. That way, he can immediately work on anything relating to that project and just delete the folder with the shortcuts after the job is done.)

"But Mark, can't I take matters into my own hands and just move the application?" Let me put out this potential fire with a well-placed Mark's Maxim:

> **Never try to simply copy or move an application that you've installed in Windows 8 from one folder to another.**™

Not only is the application unlikely to work (because it can't find any of its support files), but you also can't use the Programs and Features screen within Control Panel to uninstall the application later! (I tell you more about uninstalling software the *right* way in Chapter 5 of this minibook.) Instead, create a shortcut (which I demonstrate in Chapter 4 of this minibook) and move that shortcut to the desired location.

Figure 2-10 shows off a number of shortcut icons, along with their original source icons.

Figure 2-10:
Shortcut
icons are
an excellent
way to
organize
your stuff.

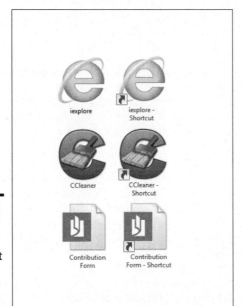

Tile icons

Tile icons work much like other icons, but they're easier to tap with that handy human pointing device, the finger. Tiles generally appear only on the Start screen, but you can also find them lurking in Windows 8 Start screen apps. (*Start Screen app* refers to the full-screen, touch-friendly layout that debuted with Windows 8, like the Weather and News apps.) For example, the Internet Explorer web app uses tiles to display your Favorites, as well as websites you've visited recently.

You can click and drag tiles to any location on the Start screen, and Windows 8 automatically reorganizes the remaining tiles. Right-clicking a tile displays the toolbar, which provides controls for that specific tile (such as unpinning it from the Start screen, changing its size, or toggling the display of live information on or off). Touch-screen owners can change these same tile properties by swiping down from the top of the Start screen.

System icons

The final type of Desktop icon represents a system function or a system location in Windows 8, such as Computer, the Recycle Bin, or the Network. Like other icons, you can use them or right-click them to display a context-sensitive pop-up menu. For example, right-clicking the Recycle Bin displays a menu with a number of choices that directly apply to deleted files.

I discuss these icons and what they represent in various spots throughout this book (especially in Chapter 4 of this minibook).

Book II Chapter 2

The Many Windows of Windows

Selecting Icons

After you become familiar with icons, you might be wondering how you can manipulate them. I go into more detail in the next two chapters of this minibook, but for now, you need to know how to select one or more icons on the Desktop or within a File Explorer window: that is, how to highlight the icon (or icons) that you want to use when performing the next action, such as copying, moving, or deleting the selected icons. (Note that these methods are not used on the Start screen.)

I should note at this point that Windows 8 offers different ways to view the contents of a folder, which I discuss later in Chapter 4 of this very minibook. For example, you can display icons in a list format as well. The methods of selecting icons, however, do not change.

Selecting a single icon

To select a single icon on the Desktop or within File Explorer, click it once — and notice that Windows 8 has highlighted it to indicate that it has been selected.

If you're on the Start screen, you can select one or more tiles by right-clicking them (this automatically displays the Start screen toolbar because you're selecting tiles in order to do something with them). To clear the tiles you've selected, click the Clear Selection icon in the toolbar, or press Esc.

Selecting multiple contiguous icons by dragging

To select a group of icons that are next to each other, click your mouse in a part of the window above and to the left of the first icon, and then drag the mouse down to a spot below and to the right of the last icon you want to select. Any icons within the box are selected and highlighted.

Selecting multiple contiguous icons by clicking

Another method of selecting a group of contiguous icons is to select the first icon in the group by clicking it, holding down the Shift key, and then clicking the last icon you want to select. This method is especially handy when viewing files in List view.

Selecting multiple separated icons by clicking

What if you want to select a number of icons that aren't contiguous? How do you select them? In this case, click the first icon you want to select, hold down the Ctrl key — don't stop holding it down — and then click each additional icon you want to select. After you select everything you need, release the Ctrl key.

To deselect an icon you pick by mistake, click it again.

You must continue holding down the Ctrl key until you finish selecting (and deselecting) what you want.

Using the Toolbar

The final stop in the graphical Windows world — at least in this chapter — is the toolbar. Most Windows applications now use toolbars (or their close cousin, the Ribbon); you can see in Figure 2-1, earlier in this chapter, the

Explorer window has its own Ribbon. Each button in a toolbar or the Ribbon typically replicates one of the application's popular menu commands and performs the same function as though you had selected the menu command.

If you already know how to click a button in Windows, you know how to use a toolbar or the Ribbon: Just move your pointer on top of the desired button and click the left button once. Touch-screen and tablet PC owners, you know the drill: Tap on the desired button once. Whoosh!

However, not all toolbars are stuck at the top of a window. Some applications have toolbars across the top and both sides of the screen, along with — gasp! — floating toolbars that you can click and drag to wherever you like! (As of this writing, the Ribbon has remained steadfast and always appears at the top of the window, but that could change in the future.)

Where am I going with this? Well, I'm suggesting that you read the manual for an application thoroughly because often you find that you can customize that application's toolbars with just the commands you want. Why take up valuable space on that toolbar with a Print button if you don't have a printer? I show you how to customize toolbars in several spots throughout the book, but for now, just enjoy using toolbars because they can save you all kinds of time.

**Book II
Chapter 2**

The Many Windows
of Windows

Chapter 3: Windows 8 Basics

In This Chapter

✔ **Starting and exiting an application**

✔ **Moving, copying, and deleting items**

✔ **Creating new folders and renaming items**

✔ **Recovering valuable stuff from the Recycle Bin**

✔ **Using and configuring the Start screen**

✔ **Working with printers**

✔ **Using and configuring the taskbar**

✔ **Terminating a misbehaving program**

*B*oot camp is over — now it's time to discover some of the more advanced tasks within Windows 8.

For example, no PC owner can ever hope to become a power user without becoming good friends with both the Windows 8 Start screen and taskbar. You need to know how to run programs, whether they're installed and appear on the Start screen or whether you have to track 'em down and run them from your hard drive or optical drive.

Files and folders need to be copied, moved, or removed; deleted files need to be permanently erased (or recovered, in the case of an accident); and new folders need to be created while you're using your PC. You might need to change printer settings, shut down a program that's no longer responding, or locate another computer on your local network with the shared file that you have to copy to your hard drive. All these tasks are basic, yet a surprising number of PC owners are in the dark about them — they still know only one way to close a program, or they aren't aware that you can change the characteristics of a printer by just right-clicking it and choosing Printer Preferences!

That's what this chapter is all about — delving into the different methods of taking care of basic tasks within Windows 8.

Running Applications from the Start Screen

First things first: Windows 8 becomes a lonely place indeed if you can't run any applications. To run a program from the Start screen, follow these steps:

1. **Move your mouse pointer to the upper-right corner of the screen and click the Start icon (which looks like a window pane) on the Charms bar.**

   Or, if you have a keyboard with Windows keys, press one of them to display the Start screen. (Your keyboard probably has two of these critters. Just look on either side of the Alt keys, which are on either side of the spacebar. The Windows keys look like the fluttering Windows flag.)

   Figure 3-1 illustrates the Start screen and the Charms bar. Any applications you recently used typically appear in a group at the right of the Start screen.

Tiles   Charms bar

Figure 3-1: The Start screen and Charms bar — truly a dynamic duo!

2. **To run a recently used application again, click the application tile, and dance around the room because you were able to do things The Convenient Way.**

3. **If the program doesn't appear as a tile, type the first few letters of the program name.**

   Yep, you read that correctly — from the keyboard, there's no need to click the Search icon in the Charms bar (or even open a text box of any kind)! Just start typing the program name, no matter where your cursor is on the Start screen. Windows 8 automatically displays the Search Results pane with any programs with matching names. (Touch-screen PC owners can open the Charms bar and tap the Search charm to select an app.)

4. **Click the application name to run it.**

Running Applications from Your Hard Drive

Often you want to run a program from the forested undergrowth that is your hard drive. Perhaps you downloaded a program from the web or you're running a shareware application that doesn't install itself on the Start screen.

There are two easy ways to display the File Explorer window — the one you use depends on whether you're currently looking at the Start screen or your Windows 8 Desktop.

From the Start screen, follow these steps:

1. **Type the letters fi to start an Apps search.**

2. **Click or tap the File Explorer button that appears in the Search Results pane to open the File Explorer window (behold it in Figure 3-2).**

3. **Double-click the hard drive that contains the program you want to run.**

   If necessary, continue clicking folders and subfolders until you see the application you want. This, good reader, is *navigating,* and I do a lot of navigating in this book!

4. **Double-click the application icon to run it.**

From the Desktop, follow these steps:

1. **Move your cursor to the bottom of the screen and click the File Explorer icon on the taskbar to open the File Explorer window (refer to Figure 3-2).**

2. **Double-click the hard drive that contains the program you want to run.**

Again, you'll likely have to do some navigating to find it.

3. **Double-click the application icon to run it.**

Figure 3-2:
You can always run programs from the File Explorer window.

Running Applications from Your Optical Drive

By default, Windows 8 loves to be helpful. So, usually when you load an application's CD or DVD-ROM into your optical drive to install the program, Windows 8 automatically runs the installation program for you. However, from time to time, you might need to venture onto Planet Optical and run a program directly from a disc. Follow these steps:

1. **Press the button on your optical drive to eject the tray; load the disc (shiny side down) and press the button again to retract the tray.**

   If the application's installation menu appears, just click the Close button or click Exit or Quit to shoo it away.

2. **Open the File Explorer window (as I demonstrated in the previous section).**

3. **Right-click the optical drive that contains the desired application and choose Open (or click the drive once to select it and click Open on the Ribbon at the top of the File Explorer window).**

   If necessary, navigate to the location of the program by double-clicking any folders and subfolders. (See? I told you that you'll be navigating Windows 8 all the time!)

4. **Double-click the application icon to run it.**

Running Applications from a Network Drive

If your PC is connected to a LAN (engineer-speak for a wired or wireless network), you might have access to programs located on other network computers. As my grandfather used to exclaim, "Zounds!" (It's really not magic, though.) Follow these steps:

1. **Display the File Explorer window.**

   Check out the Navigation pane at the left side of the File Explorer window, and you'll see the Network heading, with the network computers you can access displayed below.

2. **Double-click the network folder or hard drive that contains the program you want to run.**

3. **Double-click the application icon to run it.**

Before you imagine a wonderland (or, if you're security-conscious, a nightmare world) where anyone on your network can run any program on your PC, keep in mind these two caveats to running an application over a network:

✦ **You need the proper user access.** The person using the "host" PC must give you proper access to run the program. (This helps prevent others from accessing stuff you don't want them to use.)

✦ **The program must support networking.** Not only does the application need to support network operation, but you may also need a separate user serial number to run it from another PC on the network.

For more information on the ins and outs of networking, visit Chapters 1 and 2 in Book VIII, which cover home networking (and tell them I sent you).

Exiting a Program

After you perform whatever magic you need within an application, I recommend exiting the program. Of course, you can leave it running, like a web browser, but most of the time, you avoid slowing down your PC's performance by closing applications you're not using. (Even when you're not directly using a program, Windows 8 spends processor time and memory keeping it ready for you, as well as maintaining all the eye candy of window frames and shiny 3D buttons.)

To shut down a program, use one of these methods:

✦ **Click the Close button (the big X) in the upper-right corner of the window.**

✦ **Choose File⇨Exit from the program's menu.** If the program is from Microsoft and uses a Ribbon, click the File tab and click Close.

✦ **Swipe downward.** If you're using a touch-sensitive screen, just swipe downward from the top of the screen all the way to the bottom. (Surprisingly, this trick also works with a mouse, but make sure you wait until the cursor turns into a hand icon at the top of the screen before you drag it down.)

✦ **Press Alt+F4.** This one doesn't work on all programs, but many still honor the old Exit keyboard shortcut.

If you haven't saved any open documents and you try to exit an application, most Windows programs prompt you for confirmation so that you don't lose your stuff accidentally — as shown in Figure 3-3, where I'm trying to close a line drawing I've created in Paint without saving it. No, Mark, don't do it!

Where the @#&! is the @#&! Alt+F4 key?

If you're scanning your PC's keyboard in vain for the Alt+F4 key, you should stop now: There's no single key named that way on any keyboard. Instead, Alt+F4 stands for a key *sequence* — it's two keys pressed together. When you see two keys conjoined by a plus sign, press the first key and hold it while pressing the second key. For example, if I tell you to press the sequence Ctrl+C (which copies a selection), I'm asking you to hold down the Ctrl key while you press the C key. After you press the C key, you can release the Ctrl key.

Most Windows 8 shortcut key sequences use one of three keys as the first key: Alt, Shift, or Ctrl. You can press the specified key on either side of the keyboard, so lefties might press the Shift key that's under the Enter key. It's all

gravy to the Big 8. In fact, most PC owners are familiar with the Ctrl+C (copy), Ctrl+X (cut), and Ctrl+V (paste) sequences. (No need to hold down the Shift key or use Caps Lock, a lower-case c, x, or v works just as well.)

Some rare key sequences involve three keys: The first two keys are held down while you press the third one. The most famous three-key sequence, of course, is the infamous Three Finger Salute — the legendary Alt+Ctrl+Delete sequence that would reboot a PC running DOS. In Windows 8, applying the Three Finger Salute displays the Task Manager (which I discuss a bit more later in this chapter), as well as the Lock, Switch User, and Sign Out commands I discuss in Chapter 1.

Figure 3-3:
Don't exit
without
saving.

Putting Your Files in Order

Have you considered how to manage files in Windows 8? Don't worry, the folks in Redmond are one step ahead of you — you can use the File Explorer window to take care of your chores, as you see in this section.

You can find file management alternatives to Windows File Explorer. One of my favorites is Total Commander (shown in Figure 3-4), which has been a popular shareware favorite for many years, and for $44 (US), it's a bargain. Total Commander is list-based, so you see and select from more than the traditional icon view in File Explorer. (I show you how to switch views in Chapter 4 of this minibook.) You can download a copy to try out from www.ghisler.com.

Before you buy software — either shareware or a commercial program — don't forget to check and make sure your new toy is fully compatible with Windows 8, and keep in mind that there's a *big* difference between the 32-bit and 64-bit versions of our favorite operating system. Programs that are written for one version of Windows 8 often refuse to even *install* on the other version!

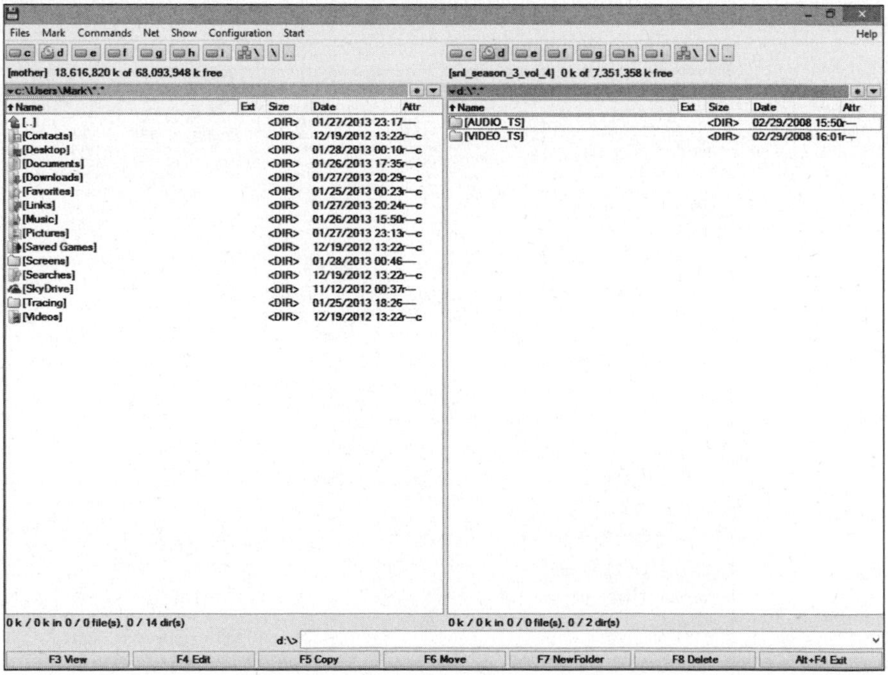

Figure 3-4:
Total Commander is an excellent alternative to File Explorer.

Copying and moving stuff

To copy selected files and folders from one File Explorer window to another — or to the Desktop or to a drive — you can use one of these methods:

✦ **Click the selected items and drag them from one File Explorer window to the destination File Explorer window.** Of course, this method requires you to open two File Explorer windows, but that's life in the Big 8. Also, note that in order to copy from one location on a drive to another location *on the same drive,* you must hold down Ctrl while you drag. Otherwise, Windows 8 assumes that you want to *move* the items instead. (If you're copying something from Drive C to a location on Drive D, you don't have to hold down the Ctrl key.) You can always tell when you're copying something with the mouse because Windows 8 adds a small plus sign (+) to the items while you drag.

✦ **Right-click the selected items and drag them to their destination.** IMHO (short for In My Humble Opinion), this choice is always better than copying with the left mouse button. Why? Well, you don't have to hold down Ctrl — Windows 8 pops up a menu when you release the mouse button and asks whether you want to copy or move the file. It's much more civilized, don't you think?

✦ **Copy and paste the items.** Right-click the items and choose Copy from the pop-up menu, click in the destination File Explorer window, and then right-click and choose Paste. From the keyboard, you can press Ctrl+C to copy or Ctrl+V to paste. (Click the Home tab on the File Explorer Ribbon, and you'll note that Copy and Paste appear as separate buttons there as well. You have Microsoft's permission to use them instead!)

To move selected items, use one of these methods:

✦ **Right-click the selected items and drag them to their destination.** Again, it's my favorite — release the mouse button and choose Move from the pop-up menu that appears.

✦ **Cut and paste the items.** Right-click the items and choose Cut from the pop-up menu, click in the destination Explorer window, and then right-click and choose Paste. From the keyboard, you can press Ctrl+X to cut or Ctrl+V to paste. (The Cut button also appears on the Home tab with its Copy and Paste siblings.)

If you attempt to copy or move a file that has the same name as another file in the target location, Windows 8 prompts you for confirmation before overwriting anything. (Feel free to rename the file and try the operation again.)

Book II Chapter 3

Windows 8 Basics

If you need to reverse direction when navigating — for example, if you click one subfolder too many and now you need to return to the previous folder — don't forget about the Back button in the upper-left area on the File Explorer toolbar (under the Ribbon), which functions just like the Back button in Internet Explorer. You can move forward as well, returning to your original position — just click the Forward button.

Creating a new folder

Creating new folders is the cornerstone to good organization in Windows 8. Dumping everything in your Documents Library folder is a bad idea because it will rapidly resemble a sold-out rock concert (complete with additional files struggling to get in).

To create a new folder within the current location in File Explorer, use one of the following methods:

✦ **Click the New Folder button on the Ribbon's Home tab.** File Explorer adds the new folder icon and also opens a text box underneath it, in which you can type a name for the new folder.

✦ **Right-click any open spot in the File Explorer window and then choose New⇨Folder from the pop-up menu that appears.** Note that I said "open spot" — if you happen to right-click an icon or a control, you see a completely different pop-up menu, so pick an unoccupied parcel of territory.

Deleting stuff with mouse and keyboard

That heading kinda sounds like "Deleting stuff with moose and squirrel," don't you think? (Boy howdy, sometimes I turn into a real laugh riot — usually when I've had very little sleep.) Anyway, if you need to delete unnecessary files or folders from your system, Windows File Explorer can handle that task as well.

Use your mouse to select the items you want to trash, click the Home tab on the Ribbon, and then click the Delete button. Alternatively, you can right-click the selected items and then choose Delete from the pop-up menu that appears. If you're into dragging things, you can drag an item from the Desktop or a File Explorer window and drop it on top of the Recycle Bin on your desktop.

From the keyboard, just select the unwanted items and press Delete. It doesn't get any easier than this, folks.

Deleted stuff is whisked away to the Recycle Bin — but that stuff may not be permanently deleted yet. (Read more on your Recycle Bin later in this chapter.)

Displaying properties

You might want to display an item's Properties dialog box, for a number of reasons:

+ **If it's a shortcut:** You can find the location of the original file.

+ **If it's a folder:** You can see how much total space the folder uses and how many files it contains.

+ **If it's a file:** You'll see the file type, who created it, and when the file was last modified.

+ **If you're displaying a drive's properties:** You can see how much free space the drive has left, or you can scan it for errors and then defragment it. (Read more on scanning and defragmenting in Book IV, Chapter 2.)

**Book II
Chapter 3**

Here's the point: Every item on your Windows 8 Desktop and in a File Explorer window has a Properties panel, and the contents change depending on what the item is. Throughout the rest of this book, I show you how to use the Properties settings for all sorts of items.

To display the properties for an item, right-click it and then choose Properties from the pop-up menu that appears. For example, Figure 3-5 illustrates the properties for my drive C.

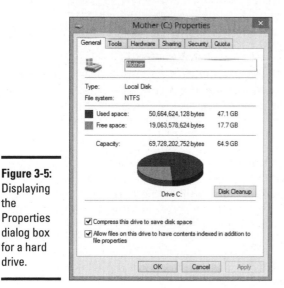

Figure 3-5:
Displaying
the
Properties
dialog box
for a hard
drive.

Renaming items

You have four ways to rename an item in a File Explorer window. Here's the first half of the process (telling Windows which item you want to rename):

+ **Click the item once, pause a second or two, and then click again.** Unfortunately, this method takes a bit of experience to do reliably.

+ **Click the item to select it and then press F2.**

+ **Click the item to select it and then click the Rename button on the Home tab.**

+ **Right-click the item and then choose Rename from the pop-up menu that appears.**

Regardless of which method you use, Windows 8 opens a text entry box with the current name. To delete the current name completely, just type the new name. To use a portion of the original name, click in the text box and use your cursor keys and the Delete key to remove the unwanted characters.

Emptying the Recycle Bin

"Mom, where do we empty the recycled files?" Technonerds still chuckle about "recycled" ones and zeroes, but the Windows 8 Recycle Bin is a popular spot on your Windows 8 Desktop, and you eventually have to empty it. (You can tell whether it's holding deleted items because the icon shows a discarded document in the bin.)

To delete the contents of the Recycle Bin, right-click it and then choose Empty Recycle Bin from the pop-up menu that appears.

Windows eventually deletes older items from the Recycle Bin automatically — or when you use Disk Cleanup. (If you've never used the Disk Cleanup utility, right-click your hard drive icon in File Explorer and click Properties, and then click the Disk Cleanup button in the Properties dialog box.) However, you free up space every time you empty the Recycle Bin, and sometimes that extra space can come in quite handy on a drive that's filled to the brim.

By default, Windows prompts you for confirmation before deleting your trash. If you feel that such clucking is overdoing things and you want to banish this file deletion confirmation, right-click the Recycle Bin and choose Properties to display the settings you see in Figure 3-6. Deselect the Display Delete Confirmation Dialog check box, and then click OK.

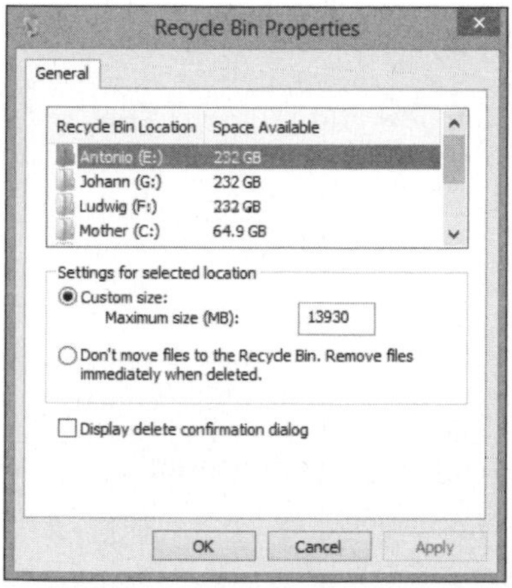

Figure 3-6:
Turning off
that darned
file-deletion
dialog box.

Recycle Bin Properties

General

Recycle Bin Location	Space Available
Antonio (E:)	232 GB
Johann (G:)	232 GB
Ludwig (F:)	232 GB
Mother (C:)	64.9 GB

Settings for selected location
○ Custom size:
    Maximum size (MB): 13930
○ Don't move files to the Recycle Bin. Remove files immediately when deleted.

☐ Display delete confirmation dialog

OK   Cancel   Apply

Recovering Items from the Recycle Bin

Here's a feeling we've all shared from time to time: You suddenly realize that you just dropped your Great American Novel into the Windows 8 Recycle Bin by mistake. (*Hint:* If you back up your files regularly, you won't panic nearly as much as the poor PC owner who has *never* backed up.)

However, there's still a chance that you can recover from your mistake and recover that orphaned Word document from the Recycle Bin! (The quicker you try a rescue after you realize the error, the better; read on to discover why.) Follow these steps:

1. **Double-click the Recycle Bin to display its contents.**

2. **Select the item you want to restore.**

3. **Right-click the item you want to restore and then choose Restore from the pop-up menu that appears (or click the Restore the Selected Item button on the Ribbon's Manage tab).**

The Recycle Bin is useful, but it's not a perfect solution because Windows 8 might use the space occupied on your hard drive by a deleted item to store new data, which makes restoration impossible. That's why I recommend that you restore a deleted item *as soon as possible* — I try to do it immediately after I catch my mistake.

Putting the Start Screen through Its Paces

Ready to disassemble the dazzling new Start screen? That's what this section is all about: helping you gain control of the Start screen and customizing it for your specific needs.

Adding a tile

Your Start screen shows a number of tiles by default — some are placed automatically on the Start screen when you install Windows 8 (like Desktop, News, and Internet Explorer), others are added by applications when you install them (like iTunes and Movie Maker), and you'll also find tiles that display programs that you've recently used.

If you need to name one of those groups on your Start screen, move your cursor to the lower-right corner of the Start screen and tap the minus sign icon that appears — suddenly, your Start screen is miniaturized! You can't click individual tiles in this view, but you can right-click a group of tiles and name them (using the Name Group icon in the toolbar). If you're using a touch-sensitive screen, you can pinch the screen with two fingers to minimize the screen and reverse the action (pulling your fingertips apart) to return the tiles to their normal size.

But what if you want to add a new tile for an application? No problem, just follow these steps:

1. **Press the Win+Q keyboard shortcut (remember, hold down the Windows key and then press Q) to display your Apps list.**

2. **Right-click the application icon you want to add.**

Windows 8 displays the toolbar you see in Figure 3-7 below the Apps list. (Touch-screen users can simply swipe upwards from the bottom of the screen to display the toolbar.)

3. **Click Pin to Start.**

Note that you can also choose to pin the application to your Desktop taskbar as well.

Many Start screen apps from Microsoft allow you to add tiles from within the application as well — for example, you can add a website as a tile from within the Internet Explorer web app.

Book II
Chapter 3

Windows 8
Basics

Figure 3-7:
You can
pin an
application
to your Start
screen from
here.

Deleting a tile

Over time, the Start screen can get so crowded with tiles that you actually have to scroll to see them all. (Or reduce their size, which I talk about next.) Anyway, you can help cut down on that irritating Start screen clutter by removing tiles you no longer need.

To remove a tile from the Start screen, right-click the offending tile, and then click the Unpin from Start icon in the toolbar that appears.

Resizing tiles

Are you wondering why some tiles on the Start screen are larger than others? Typically, it's because they display some sort of information (these are commonly called *live* tiles because they're constantly being updated whenever you're connected to the Internet. The News, Sports, and Weather tiles on the Start screen are live tiles.)

Some tiles on the Start screen can be resized — tiles you use often on touch-screen PCs might benefit from being enlarged, for example. If a tile can be resized, you can right-click it and click either the Smaller or Larger icon in the toolbar at the bottom of the screen.

Choosing a Start screen background and color

The default Windows 8 Start screen background is . . . well . . . nice, but is it really *you*? Because you spend so much time on the Start screen, you may want to personalize it with your own design.

To change the Start screen background and color, just follow these steps:

1. **From the Start screen, press Win+I to display the Settings charm.**

2. **Click the Change PC Settings link at the bottom of the pane.**

3. **Click the Personalize item at the left.**

4. **Click the Start Screen link at the top of the screen.**

   Windows 8 displays the screen you see in Figure 3-8.

5. **Click a design thumbnail to select it.**

   Feel free to browse! The preview shows how your current choice will look.

6. **Click a color combination from the strip.**

7. **When everything is perfect, press the Windows key to return to your new and improved Start screen.**

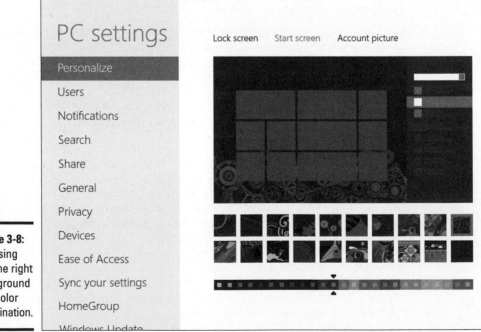

Figure 3-8: Choosing just the right background and color combination.

Choosing an account picture

Tired of being represented by a rounded, anonymous quasi-human figure? You can change your account picture at any time — substitute a photo from your hard drive, or a photo that you've taken with your PC's webcam. From the Start screen, click your account name and picture at the top-right corner of the screen, and then choose Change Account Picture from the menu.

From the Personalize screen that appears, click the Browse button to choose a file from the photos on your system, or click the Camera button to take a photo using any recognized camera device on your system.

Changing system settings

Windows 8 displays a number of often-used system settings on the Charms bar Settings pane, allowing you to change them quickly. These settings include

✦ The network you're connected to

✦ The audio volume

✦ The screen brightness level

✦ The keyboard (both the layout and language you're using, and the virtual keyboard for touch-sensitive PCs)

✦ The notifications you receive (including those that appear on the Lock screen)

✦ The power control

To display the system settings, press Win+I to display the Settings pane on the Charms bar, and then click the desired setting to change it.

Searching for files, apps, and settings

If you've read Chapter 2 of this minibook, you already know that you can search for an application on your system by simply typing the first few letters of the application name while the Start screen is displayed. This neat feature is actually part of the new Windows 8 built-in Search charm functionality. To display the full Search charm from anywhere in Windows 8, move your cursor to the upper-right corner of the screen to display the Charms bar — touch-screen PC owners can swipe from the right edge of the screen toward the left. Now click (or tap) the Search icon (which looks, coincidentally, like a magnifying glass).

TIP

To jump directly to the Search charm from the keyboard, press Win+Q.

The Search charm allows you to search for applications, files (and folders), and even settings you can change. To select which type of search you want to perform, click the three headings under the Search box at the right side of the screen. After you've chosen the type of search, click in the Search box and begin typing — your search words can be part of a filename, the name of an application or setting, or even the name of a song or video clip.

Results of your search are shown in the Search Results pane at the left of the screen, as shown in Figure 3-9.

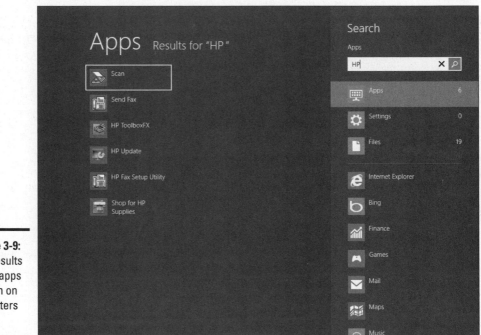

Figure 3-9:
The results
of my apps
search on
the letters
HP.

Adding and Using Printers

Printers are special beasts, and we love them dearly . . . when they work. Typically, the installation software supplied by the manufacturer automatically adds your new printer within Windows 8, and many printers are automatically recognized when you plug them into your PC's USB port — just in case you need to add a printer manually, however, I'll go over the procedure here.

After you've connected the printer and turned it on, follow these steps to manually add it within Windows 8:

1. **From the Start screen, press Win+I.**

2. **Click the Change PC Settings link.**

3. **Click Devices in the list at the left.**

   You'll see the Devices pane shown in Figure 3-10.

4. **Click Add a Device.**

   After a few seconds, your new printer should appear in the list.

5. **Click the printer in the list and click Next.**

6. **Choose whether you want to share your new printer with others on your network and click Next.**

   Windows 8 gives you an opportunity to print a test page.

7. **Click Finish.**

Figure 3-10:
Preparing
to manually
add a
printer to my
system.

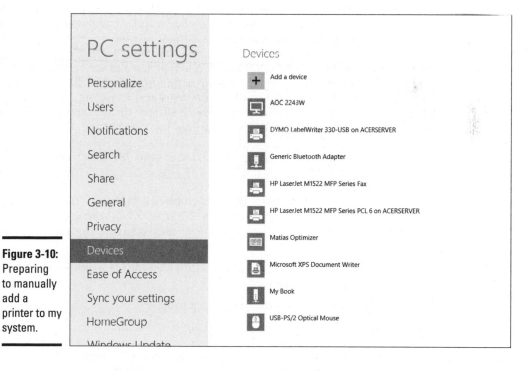

You can also display your printers from the Desktop's Control Panel window — which is also the place for changing the settings provided by your printer manufacturer's Windows 8 driver. For example, you can likely change the print quality, and perhaps you can clean your inkjet's print nozzles or check its ink levels. Follow these steps to display and configure your printers:

1. **From the Desktop, click the File Explorer link in the taskbar.**

2. **Click the Computer item in the Navigation pane at the left of the File Explorer window.**

3. **Click the Open Control Panel button on the Ribbon's Computer tab.**

4. **Click View Devices and Printers in the Hardware and Sound category.**

Now you can right-click a printer icon and then choose Printing Preferences to see what you can change. What you see depends on your printer manufacturer.

You can choose your default printer throughout Windows 8 from the Devices and Printers window as well. Right-click the desired printer and then choose Set as Default Printer. Windows 8 adds a spiffy check mark symbol to the printer's icon to indicate that it's the default printer.

Note that Windows 8 also displays several advanced printer settings in a printer's Properties dialog box, including printer sharing (which I cover in Book VIII) and color management for color printers. To display these settings, right-click the printer icon and choose Printer Properties. Again, what you see varies according to the make and model of printer.

Windows 8 applications are likely to use one of four different methods to print:

✦ **Press Win+K to display the Devices charm and click on the desired printer.** (Note that this method only works with full-screen Start screen apps like the Internet Explorer web app, and only with the currently displayed content.)

✦ **Choose File⇨Print from the application's menu (or from the Ribbon in a Microsoft application).**

✦ **Click the Print icon on the program's toolbar.**

✦ **Press Ctrl+P.**

To display (and control) pending printing jobs, return to the Control Panel's Devices and Printers window. Click a printer to select it and then click the See What's Printing button on the Devices and Printers window toolbar. This action displays a Print Jobs window with details about the pending printer jobs. You can pause all your print jobs on the selected printer by choosing Printer⇨Pause Printing from the Print Jobs window menu; to restart the printer, click the Pause Printing menu item again. (If your printer is on a network, you need Administrator rights to pause all print jobs.)

To pause a single print job, click the job in the Print Jobs window list and then choose Document⇨Pause. To resume printing, click the job in the list and then choose Document⇨Restart.

Handling the Taskbar

Yep, it's yet another Windows 8 control. This time, I'm talking about the *taskbar,* which is that loyal strip of screen real estate that appears at the bottom of the Desktop — or at the side or the top. (Read more on this in a second.) In this section, I tell you more about the often-neglected taskbar.

Switching programs

The primary use of the taskbar — and one that has been around since Windows 95 — is to allow you to easily switch between the windows of the programs you're running. You can switch between programs by clicking your cursor on the taskbar button for the program you want to use.

Shhh . . . there's also another method of switching programs that doesn't use the taskbar — and because we're on the topic, I tell you about it here. You can press Alt Tab to move between the programs you're running. To step through the programs from the Desktop, hold down Alt while you press Tab repeatedly, and you advance through your programs like Tiny Tim tiptoeing through the tulips — when the desired program is highlighted, just lift your fingers.

When you press Alt+Tab from the Start screen, you'll see a strip of thumbnails appear at the left side of the window — each thumbnail represents a program that's running. Click or tap a thumbnail to switch to that program, or hold down Alt while you press Tab repeatedly to move through the thumbnails. You can close a window by right-clicking on the thumbnail and clicking Close on the pop-up menu.

Controlling the notification area

Another item on the taskbar Hit Parade is the *notification area* — that's the far right end of the taskbar, shown in Figure 3-11. Most of these icons represent a program that's running, such as your antivirus program. The Volume icon lives here (which you can click to set your PC's volume or mute sound altogether) as well as network connection icons.

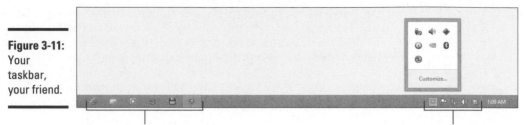

Figure 3-11:
Your
taskbar,
your friend.

Icons pinned to the taskbar   Notification icons

So what did you glean here? ("Bueller? Bueller? Anyone?") Not everything in the notification area is a program; rather, the icons that appear there indicate (or notify you about) programs that are available and events that are happening on your PC. You can, however, right-click most notification icons to display pop-up menus. Typically, the menu allows you to control whichever program or feature the notification icon represents (including the ability to close or exit, if the icon represents a program that's running).

If you see a tiny yellow or red X appear on a notification icon, right-click it immediately to display the program's window, which displays the reasons why you're seeing a warning icon. Typically, you'll see such flags on the Windows 8 Action Center icon — Windows 8 is shooting a flare to warn you that your firewall or virus protection has been limited or disabled. When you have set things right, the warning marker disappears from the notification icon.

If you see an arrow pointing up at the beginning of your notification icons, Windows 8 is hiding the notification icons you haven't used recently. To see these hidden icons, click the arrow.

If you're dissatisfied with the contents of your notification area, right-click in any open space on the taskbar, choose Properties, and click the Taskbar tab. Click the Customize button in the Notification Area section — now you can configure which items you want to appear in the notification area, as shown in Figure 3-12.

Adding icons to the taskbar

Within Windows 8, you can right-click and drag any program icon, file icon, or folder icon down to the taskbar, where Windows 8 displays the Pin to Task Bar bubble — click the bubble to pin the item to the taskbar. From that point on, clicking the icon on the taskbar runs the application, opens the document, or opens the folder.

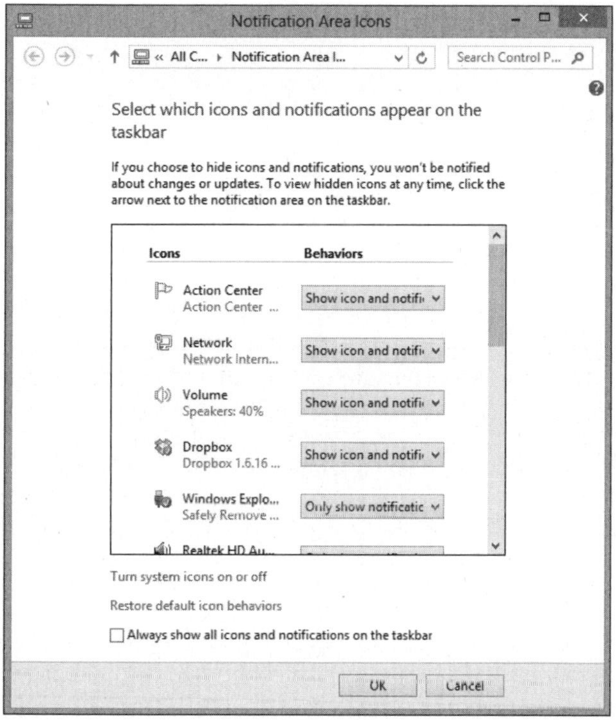

Figure 3-12:
Customizing the notification area settings.

Naturally, space on the taskbar is limited, so I recommend that you add only the programs, folders, and items you use the most.

"Hey, I can't pin anything on the taskbar!" That's probably because the task-bar is *locked,* which prevents anyone (including you) from inadvertently dragging a pinned icon off to the Desktop or from making any changes to the dimensions or location of the taskbar. Right-click anywhere on the taskbar itself (and not on an icon or control), choose Lock the Taskbar to unlock it, and then try again. After you're done arranging the taskbar as you like it, it's a good idea to lock it again.

Configuring the taskbar

Would you rather have your taskbar on the left or right side of the Windows 8 Desktop? How about at the top of the Desktop? No problem. First, make sure that the taskbar is unlocked (see the preceding section); then click in the center of the bar and drag it to any other side of the screen. (Check out Figure 3-13.)

**Book II
Chapter 3**

Windows 8
Basics

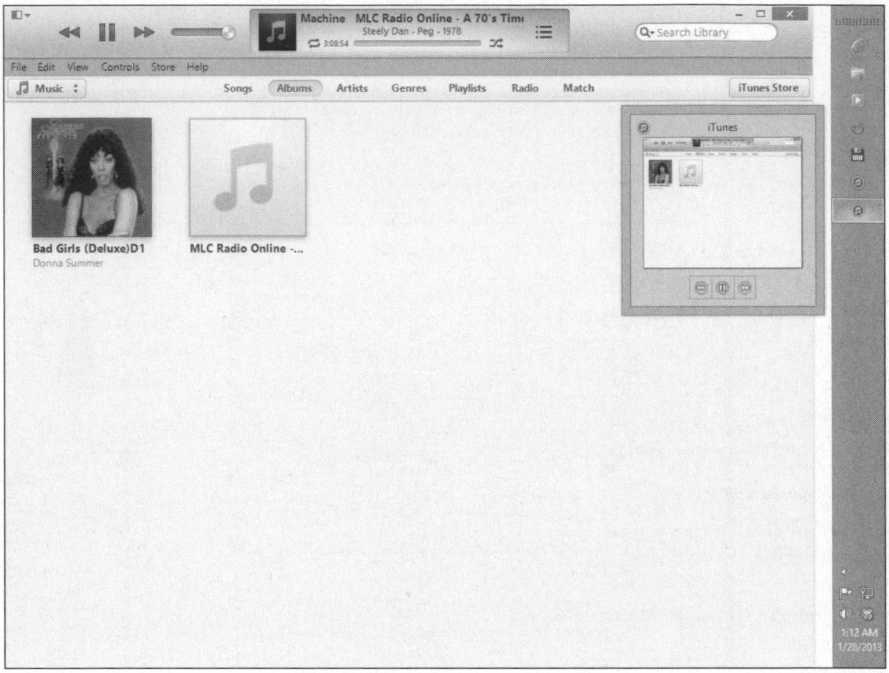

Figure 3-13:
Zounds! For
those who
gravitate to
the right. . . .

While the taskbar is unlocked, you can also expand it by clicking the edge closest to the Desktop (where the thin strip appears) and dragging it up. (Some folks prefer a larger, easier-to-read taskbar.)

Now that you see how easy it is to alter the taskbar, you understand the necessity of locking it! Don't forget to batten down the hatches after you have things just as you want them.

TIP

Even many Windows 8 power users don't know that you can also add toolbars to the taskbar! Right-click any open part of the taskbar, choose Properties, and then click the Toolbars tab. Now you can add extras like an *Address toolbar* (where you can type or copy a web or FTP site and go to that location, right from the taskbar) and a *Desktop toolbar* (which displays the items directly on your Desktop). To remove a toolbar, just click to deselect the check box and then click Apply.

Terminating a Program with Prejudice

Sometimes a program just decides to misbehave. At least things are better in Windows 8 than they were in Windows 98 or Me, where one locked program was likely to lock the entire machine. In the Big 8, you *should* be able to force a nonresponsive program to quit without losing any open files or having to restart your PC — although I always save my files in the other applications, just in case!

To force a locked program to terminate, follow these steps:

1. **Right-click any empty spot on the taskbar and choose Start Task Manager from the pop-up menu to display the Task Manager. (From the Start screen, press Ctrl+Alt+Delete — the old familiar "Three Finger Salute" — and choose Task Manager.)**

2. **Click the Processes tab to display the list shown in Figure 3-14.**

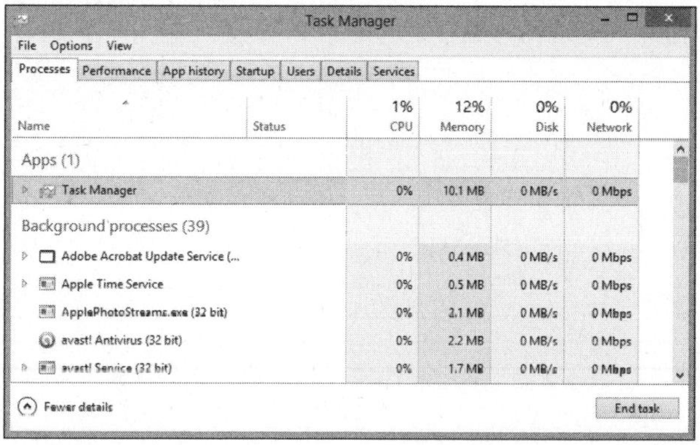

Book II
Chapter 3

Figure 3-14:
Control
the Task
Manager,
and you
control
Windows 8.

3. **Click the name of the application that's causing the problems.**

   It's usually marked as Not Responding in the Status column.

4. **Click the End Task button to initiate the terminate sequence.**

   Note: It might take several seconds for the terminated program to disappear, or you might need to repeat this step two or three times to force termination.

   Sometimes, Windows 8 displays a dialog box saying that the program will not shut down properly. In this case, move on to Step 5.

5. **Click the End Now button.**

   The program disappears from the Applications list.

6. **Click the Close button to close the Task Manager.**

By the way, you can also see who's logged in to your machine — either locally or remotely — from the Task Manager window. Click the Users tab, where you can also disconnect any undesirables.

Those interested in performance should eyeball the Performance tab, which allows you to graphically monitor your CPU and memory usage. The Ethernet display on the Performance tab lets you track your network speeds and the amount of data moving to and from your PC over your LAN connection.

Chapter 4: Advanced Windows 8

In This Chapter

✔ **Customizing your Desktop background**

✔ **Buying apps the Microsoft way**

✔ **Fine-tuning the windows**

✔ **Sharing and syncing stuff**

✔ **Using a HomeGroup**

✔ **Understanding multiuser computing**

✔ **Sending and receiving faxes in Windows 8**

✔ **Playing MP3 files in Media Player**

✔ **Viewing and downloading digital photographs**

✔ **Recording your own data CDs in Windows 8**

✔ **Watching a DVD movie**

I f you're following along in this minibook, you've been a slave to the Microsoft default settings. That might be the status quo for novice Windows 8 users, but if you want to mold Windows 8 into *your* operating system (and thus become a PC power user), you must master the customization features within Windows 8. Just say "No!" to Icons view or that too-familiar Desktop background — add your favorite sound effects from *The Rocky Horror Picture Show* to your Windows 8 experience. (I boot up every morning to the lilting sounds of "The Time Warp," much to the consternation of our family cats.)

This chapter ties together the actions you need to take to transform your PC from a personal computer into a *personal tool* — which, I might add, should be the goal of every hardware manufacturer and software developer, including the Microsoft crowd. In these pages, I do my part: You discover how to optimize your copy of Windows 8 for productivity, share your computer with others in a multiuser environment, sync your portable devices, and send and receive faxes with your PC's fax modem. You'll shop for apps from the Windows Store. I also introduce you to Windows Media Player, which you can use to enjoy all sorts of digital multimedia. And stick around for a brief look at downloading and viewing digital photographs. I even show you how to burn a CD-R with data files from your hard drive — *without* your having to buy an expensive CD recording application!

So, good reader, prepare yourself for the advanced stuff — turn that cookie-cutter machine with its vanilla Windows 8 into your personal, custom-made *muscle PC,* and take it up a notch!

Personalizing Your Desktop

Don't get me wrong — I like the soothing blue-green swirl of the typical Windows 8 Desktop. After a few weeks, though, you say to yourself, "Self, you spent two grand on this system. Why not jazz it up a little bit?" In this section, I show you how to take care of spicing up the look and sound of Windows 8.

Changing the background

First up on the makeover tour is the most popular trick — changing your Desktop background to something more palatable. Windows 8 prefers images in the JPEG and bitmap formats for your Desktop background — personally I use JPEG because the equivalent image in Bitmap format takes up a honking amount of hard drive space!

Follow these steps to select a new background:

1. **Right-click anywhere on the open space of your current Desktop and then choose Personalize from the menu that appears.**

In other words, don't click an icon or a Windows 8 control, such as the taskbar. The Personalization Control Panel window appears.

2. **Click the Desktop Background link at the bottom of the window to display the settings you see in Figure 4-1.**

3. **Open the Picture Location drop-down list to choose a category of images.**

By default, Windows 8 displays the images in the Windows folder, under the category Windows Desktop Backgrounds. To choose a Desktop image from your Windows folder, click the thumbnail image in the list. Windows immediately displays it on your Desktop.

You can load your own image by clicking the Browse button and navigating to the location of the image; then just double-click the image file to load it.

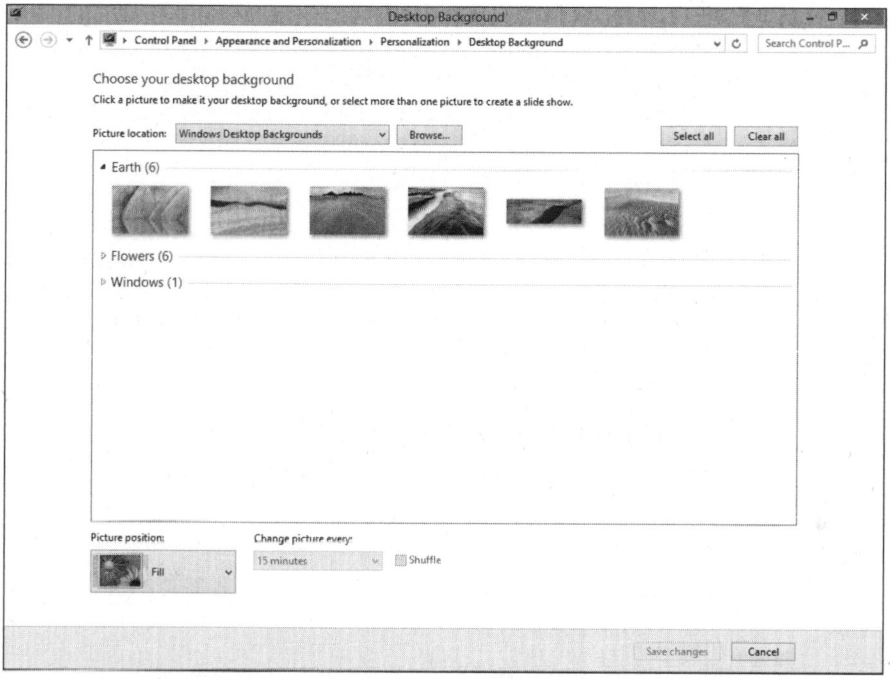

Book II
Chapter 4

Advanced Windows 8

Figure 4-1:
The Desktop
Background
screen
offers
many visual
treats.

4. **To stretch an image that doesn't quite fit across your entire Desktop, click the Picture Position pop-up list and select the Fill item.**

   If the image is too small to fill the Desktop, pick Center to put it in the middle of the Desktop, or Fit to increase the size to match the horizontal or vertical dimensions of your screen. Alternatively, you can choose Stretch to increase the size of the image (kind of like pulling taffy); however, the smaller the image, the more likely that Stretch will distort it to an unacceptable degree. (If you choose Stretch or Fit, don't worry: The original image remains pristine.) If the image is a repeating pattern, choose Tile.

5. **To set the Desktop to a solid color, open the Picture Location drop-down list and choose Solid Colors.**

   Solid colors are an excellent choice for those with less-than-perfect eyesight (like yours truly).

If you like what you see, click OK. If the result would make Andy Warhol cringe, try again.

Select an entire folder full of images, and Windows 8 can cycle through them automatically using the delay you choose from the Change Picture Every drop-down list. You can also right-click the Desktop and choose Next Desktop Background from the menu that appears to immediately jettison the current background image and load a new one from the folder!

Using themes

A Windows 8 *theme* is a package deal: Selecting a theme gives you a background, a color scheme, a screen saver, and sound effects. Themes are available from Microsoft, or you can download themes (of varying quality) from sites all over the web. To choose a theme, follow these steps:

1. **Right-click anywhere on the open space of your Desktop and choose Personalize from the menu that appears.**

2. **Click the desired theme thumbnail.**

   Windows 8 immediately updates your desktop characteristics with the selected theme.

3. **To create a theme of your own based on the current Desktop settings, click the Save Theme link.**

4. **Type a name for the new theme and click Save.**

Care to peruse the latest free themes offered by Microsoft? Click the Get More Themes Online and browse to your heart's content.

Changing system sounds

Windows 8 offers a number of events that can be heralded by system sound files in WAV format. Follow these steps to assign sounds:

1. **Right-click anywhere on the open space of your Desktop and choose Personalize from the menu that appears.**

2. **Click the Sounds link to display the dialog box you see in Figure 4-2.**

3. **To choose an existing sound scheme, open the Sound Scheme drop-down list and choose the scheme you want.**

4. **To assign sounds individually to events, select an event from the Program Events list box and then open the Sound drop-down list to display all sounds installed within Windows 8.**

   To hear a sound, click the Test button. (When you assign a sound to an event, Windows 8 marks that event with a tiny speaker icon.)

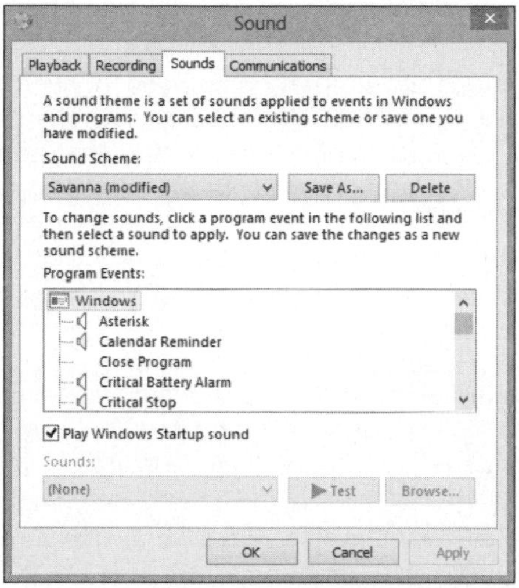

Figure 4-2:
The sounds
of
Windows 8.

5. **You can also use sound files from another folder on your hard drive (as long as they're in WAV format); click the Browse button, navigate to that folder, and then double-click the file to load it.**

   If you create your own custom sound scheme, don't forget to click Save As to save it under a unique name so that you can load it in a flash in the future.

6. **When you're ready to rock, click OK to close the Sound dialog box.**

Downloading Apps from the Windows Store

The Windows Store is the modern alternative to a brick-and-mortar software store — forget the crowds, the checkout lines, and the hassles of storing discs! Instead, you browse the titles from the comfort of your computer chair, and when you buy a program, it's immediately downloaded to your PC and ready to use within minutes. If you purchase an app, you can also download that app to four other PCs as well (for a total of five machines). Plus, the Windows Store remembers what you purchased, allowing you to receive free updates for all of your applications with a single click.

The Windows Store requires an Internet connection . . . but you're not surprised, are you?

To start shopping, click the Store tile on your Start screen. After a moment, you'll see the Store's top-level screen, as shown in Figure 4-3, with the Spotlight group of applications prominently displayed. (Check out that CNN tile.) Note the Top Paid, Top Free, and New Releases tiles displayed next to the Spotlight group — click one to display a list of the most popular paid and free applications, as well as the latest arrivals in the Windows Store.

Is there a number displayed at the corner of your Store tile? If so, that's the number of application updates waiting for you to approve. (More on updating in a page or two.)

Swipe or scroll to see additional groups: Games, Social Apps, Entertainment, Sports, and more. Each group includes the same Top Paid, Top Free, and New Releases tiles. You'll also note that each application tile includes a one- to five-star rating, as well as the price of the app (making it easy to stay within your budget).

Before you begin shopping, take care of the financial business: from the Store's top-level screen, press Win+I to display the Settings panel, and then click Your Account. From the Your Account screen, you can add a payment method for the paid apps you download, as well as select which five PCs running Windows 8 will be able to download the apps you install.

Figure 4-3:
The Windows Store Spotlight group.

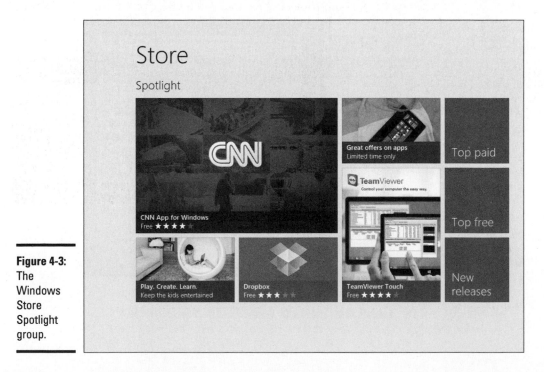

Now the fun begins! Click on a tile to display its overview screen. Figure 4-4 illustrates the overview screen for a favorite game of mine, Robotek — note that the screen includes

✦ **Permission information:** What access to your information and files will this application use? Will it require your location?

✦ **Reviews:** Click the Reviews link at the top of the screen to see the comments and star ratings posted by those who've used the application.

✦ **Details:** Click the Details link at the top of the screen to display the processors and languages supported by the application.

✦ **Age rating:** Each app has a suggested age rating.

✦ **Description and features list:** The program description and a list of its outstanding features.

If you'd like to install the application, click the Install button — otherwise, click the Back arrow at the top-left corner of the overview screen. Installed apps appear as tiles on your Start screen.

Figure 4-4:
Viewing the details for an app before I make a buying decision.

When Windows Store displays an update notification at the top of the screen, just click it to view the available updates. You can specify which apps to update, but I personally update everything!

Switching Views and Sorting Items

Next, allow me to discuss the different views within Windows 8 File Explorer — and how you can switch between them in a flash.

To switch between views in the File Explorer window, click the View tab, and then click one of the buttons in the Layout group. (You can also right-click any open space in the content pane and choose View from the pop-up menu.) Your choices include

+ **Tiles:** Choose this view to make items appear as icons on well-spaced tiles at regular intervals, thus making it easy to click (or tap) an item without running something else accidentally.

+ **Icons:** This view is a traditional favorite, where each item appears as an icon. However, spacing is much tighter than in Tiles view, so longer file-names are often abbreviated (and you must be more careful when click-ing). You can choose four sizes of icons, from small to extra large.

Icon view displays images and video clips as *thumbnails* (pictures), but be warned: Windows 8 can take a significant amount of time to process a folder containing a lot of images, especially on an older machine. In this view, folders contain pictures that are displayed as tiny thumbnails of the images they contain — *sassy* indeed!

+ **List:** Another long-standing favorite, List view features each item arranged in list format — one entry per line. Depending on the window size and the number of files in the current location, Windows 8 might even see fit to arrange your list in columnar format.

+ **Content:** This view provides a "sneak peek" at the content within files and folders, along with the item size and creation or modification date.

+ **Details:** If you like List view but wish you had more information on each item, choose Details view. Again, Details view takes a little more time to display, so expect a delay before you see the statistics — the larger the folder, the longer it takes.

To sort the items in the List or Details views to your particular fancy, click the Sort By button on the View tab. (I find that Name, Type, and Total Size are the most useful.) You can also right-click any open space in the content pane and choose Sort By from the pop-up menu.

You can also elect to group items. Just right-click any open space in the content pane, choose Group By from the menu that appears, and then pick the group criteria.

Don't Forget the Preview Pane!

The default File Explorer window displays the Navigation pane, which allows you to jump directly to your favorite locations throughout your system. This classic "tree" display of the folders on your system dates all the way back to Windows 3.1. (Some things are just too good to change!) You can turn off the display of the Navigation pane from the View tab — click the Navigation Pane button to display the pop-up menu and click the Navigation Pane item.

From within the Navigation pane, click a drive or folder to immediately display its contents. You can also click a right-facing arrow to expand an item or click the tilted arrow next to an item to collapse it again. The File Explorer window is updated automatically with the contents of the drive or folder you're viewing. You can also access network locations and the shared files and printers offered by your HomeGroup. (I'll wax enthusiastic on your HomeGroup later in this chapter.)

You can also add locations to the Navigation pane. Drag a folder from the content pane within any File Explorer window to the Favorites heading within the Navigation pane, and you'll see the Create Link in Favorites label appear. Release the mouse button, and suddenly you can hop there in an instant. *Nice!*

You can also turn on the Preview pane (see Figure 4-5), which I find practically a requirement within File Explorer. The Preview pane provides a thumbnail preview and details on the file or folder you've selected in the Content window — and that includes the ability to play audio and video files without opening them up in Windows Media Player. To turn on the Preview pane, click the View tab on the Ribbon and click the Preview Pane button.

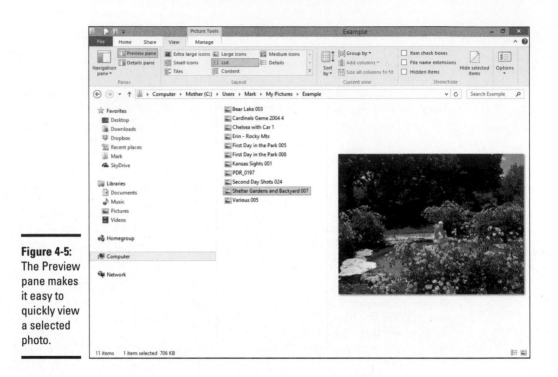

Figure 4-5:
The Preview pane makes it easy to quickly view a selected photo.

What's This Stuff in the My Users Folder?

Windows 8 gives each user a separate account folder (named after your account name), which contains a number of important subfolders, as shown in Figure 4-6. Your account folder appears within the top-level Users folder on your Windows 8 boot drive. For example, it's C:\Users\Mark on my system.

The default subfolders include

✦ **My Pictures:** Images

✦ **My Videos:** Video clips

✦ **My Music:** Digital audio files

✦ **Contacts:** Your list of contact information

✦ **My Documents:** Documents you created with your programs

✦ **Downloads:** Downloaded files

✦ **Desktop:** The contents of your Desktop

✦ **Saved Games:** Your saved files from your games

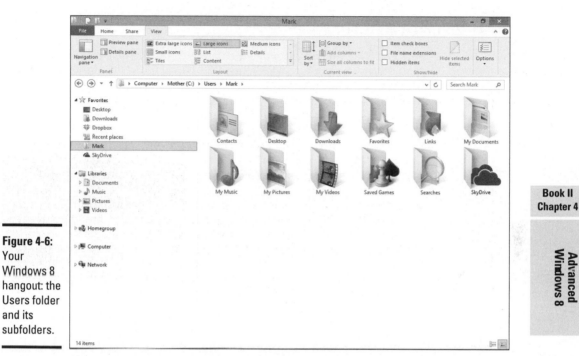

Figure 4-6:
Your
Windows 8
hangout: the
Users folder
and its
subfolders.

Why all the fuss over this standard folder organization? Because the Redmond Gang wants you to use your account subfolders as your center of operations, and most software developers respect the Microsoft standard. Thus, most programs default to saving their documents to the My Documents folder (or another standard subfolder, like My Pictures). In fact, you're likely to accumulate a number of extra subfolders in your Users folder — they've been created automatically by the programs you run.

You can reach these locations in a number of different ways: from the Navigation pane in a File Explorer window, as well as from the Locations list in Save (As) and Open dialog boxes.

You can create as many subfolders within your Users folder as you like, and it's a logical place to keep your stuff (at least on your C drive, where Windows 8 is usually installed).

Each user you create in Windows 8 has a separate set of account folders, so the stuff you see in your My Documents folder *isn't* the same as the stuff Brother Elroy sees in his My Documents folder. (Microsoft makes this easy to remember by prefacing your personal music, pictures, and video collections with the word "My", as in *My Videos*.) What Windows 8 displays is keyed to the active user account.

A Word about Libraries

Check out the Libraries group, which appear in any File Explorer window in your Navigation pane. (See Figure 4-7.) Libraries — first introduced in Windows 7 — make it easier to access documents, music, pictures, and videos. Like a folder, a library contains items, but those items don't necessarily reside in the same place on your system. For example, your Music library might contain MP3 files stored on both an external drive and your internal drive, and your Documents library could contain Excel spreadsheets saved on a USB flash drive. So, in other words, a library is a method of organizing and centralizing all sorts of files and folders "under one roof."

You can easily include any folder in a library. Just navigate to the folder's location in a File Explorer window, right-click that folder, and then hover your cursor over the Include in Library menu item. Windows 8 displays a sub-menu, from which you can choose from the four default libraries. Note, however, that you can also create your own new library from the selected folder by clicking Create New Library on that same sub-menu. Windows 8 creates a library with the same name as the selected folder and adds the contents of the selected folder in the new library automatically.

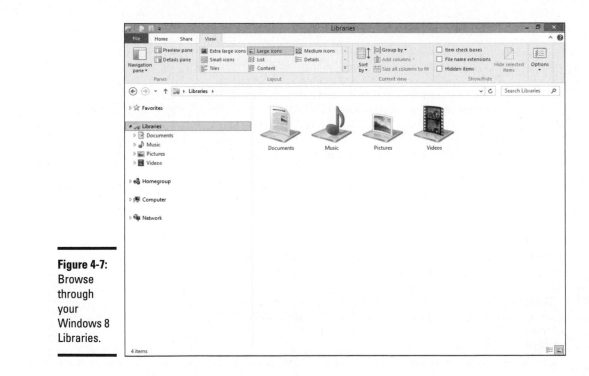

Figure 4-7: Browse through your Windows 8 Libraries.

Share the Documents . . . and Other Stuff

By the way, the contents of your Users account folder are also hidden from other users, so you can't put a document there and expect other users of your PC to be able to reach it. Instead, use the Public folders within the Libraries group. Each of the four default Windows 8 libraries has a separate Public subfolder, like Public Pictures and Public Music.

When you save or copy an item to one of the Public folders, anyone using another account on your PC can open and copy that item. And after you turn on *Public sharing,* anyone on your local network can also access the item.

By default, Windows 8 installs with Public sharing turned off. To turn on the feature and share the contents of these library Public folders among other computers on your network, follow these steps:

1. **In the File Explorer Navigation pane, display one of the Public folders inside a library.**

2. **Right-click the Public folder and choose Share With from the menu that appears; then click Advanced Sharing Settings. See Figure 4-8.**

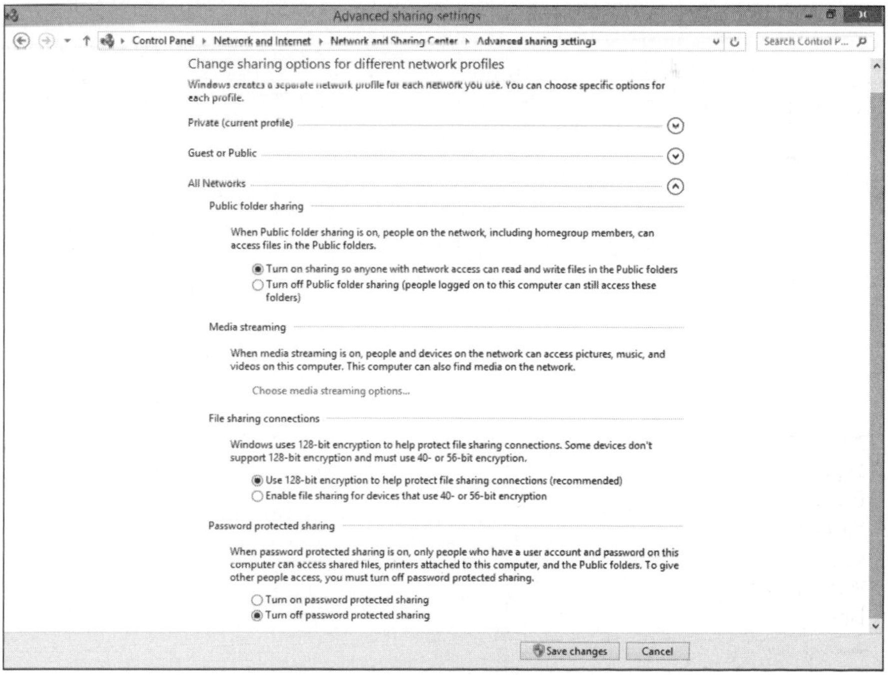

Figure 4-8:
Tell
Windows to
share Public
library
folders.

3. Under the All Networks heading, select the Turn On Sharing so That Anyone with Network Access Can Read and Write Files in the Public Folders radio button.

4. Under the All Networks heading, select the Turn Off Password Protected Sharing radio button.

5. Click the Save Changes button.

Using the Windows 8 Sharing Charm

If you're a dedicated Facebook or Twitter fan, rejoice! The new Windows 8 Sharing charm makes it easier to post photos, videos, and web links with all sorts of social networks, as well as your e-mail.

Within an app, you can display the Share charm at any time by pressing Win+H. (Owners of touch-screen PCs need only swipe from the right edge of the screen to the left to display the Charms bar, and then tap Share.) If there are sharing possibilities for whatever's currently displayed — a website within the Internet Explorer web app, for example — the Sharing pane displays them. (Note that some apps require you to right-click to select a specific item before the Share charm recognizes it. Touch-screen users can swipe downwards from the top of the screen to select items.)

When one or more destinations appear in the Share pane, click the desired destination for the shared item (like the People app for Facebook and Twitter), and Windows 8 creates a post (or text, or e-mail message, or whatever) with that shared item included or attached.

The "forgotten" Devices charm

Perhaps the Windows 8 Devices charm isn't *forgotten* — after all, it is still prominently displayed on the Charms bar, and you can always display it with the Win+K keyboard shortcut — but some PC owners will still never use it.

Why? Well, the answer is simple: In order to use the Devices charm, you have to have a cable or wireless connection between an external device and your PC, and some folks don't use peripherals at all (not even a printer). Some Start screen apps also don't support the Devices charm, so you might see the "Nothing can be sent" message when you try the Devices charm.

However, for those who *do* have devices like smartphones, printers, multiple monitors, or external media streaming units, the Devices pane allows Start screen apps to send content and documents to those devices. The most common example of this is printing from within a Start screen app (such as the Internet Explorer web app) to either a USB or a wireless printer.

The Devices charm works much like the Sharing charm: Simply display the desired content within the Start screen app, and then press Win+K. If the content can be sent to a connected device, it appears in the Devices pane — click the desired destination and configure any settings (like number of copies). Windows 8 does the rest.

Syncing devices with Windows 8

For the first time, you can sign into Windows 8 with either a *local* account (which doesn't require an Internet connection) or your *Microsoft* account. Here's the big advantage to a Microsoft account: If you use it, Windows 8 can store and sync all of your settings, documents, and Windows Store purchases across the Internet with your other PCs, Xbox gaming consoles, and mobile devices that use the same Live account. If you have a reliable broadband Internet connection (or you can typically reach the Internet wherever you are), I recommend that you set up and use your Microsoft account.

If you have more than one device running Windows 8, why not synchronize your data and settings between them? The Big 8 handles everything automatically, but first you must configure your PC:

1. **Press Win+I to display the Settings pane and click Change PC Settings.**

2. **Click the Users item in the list at the left.**

3. **If you're using a local account, click the Switch to a Microsoft Account button and follow the on-screen instructions.**

   You can skip this step if you're already signed in with your Microsoft account. (If you have to set up a Microsoft account, note that you'll be asked to confirm your e-mail address by responding to an e-mail message.)

4. **After you're signed in on your Microsoft account, click the Trust this PC link.**

   You'll be prompted to confirm your identity (even if you just did in Step 3), so you'll once again need to respond to an e-mail message. (Personally, I approve of this, because I'd rather be secure when it comes to my data and my identity!)

5. **Press Win+I to display the Settings pane and click Change PC Settings.**

6. **Click the Sync Your Settings item in the list at the left.**

7. **Click the Sync Settings on this PC switch (shown in Figure 4-9) and make sure it's set to On.**

   If you'd like to fine-tune what's synced between devices, you can also toggle individual settings On and Off from this screen (like Start Screen and Desktop Personalization data). Click a specific settings switch to Off to prevent that type of data from syncing.

You must follow this procedure on each Windows 8 device in order to successfully sync — the device must be trusted, and syncing must be turned On.

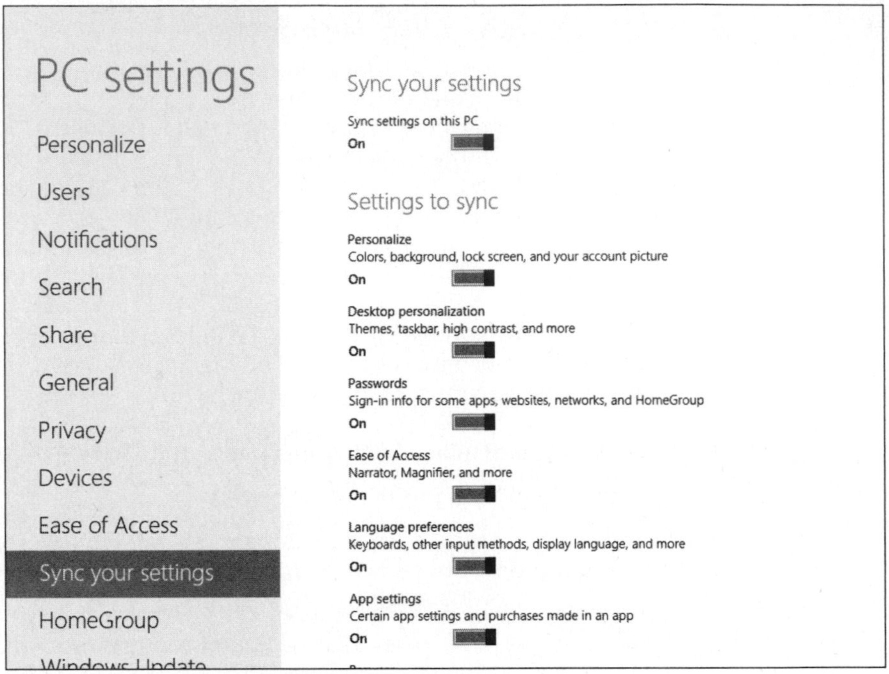

Figure 4-9:
Configuring
Windows 8
Sync
settings.

Using Your HomeGroup

Speaking of sharing, Windows 8 also includes a nifty method of sharing files and printers with other computers on your network — a *HomeGroup*. Microsoft designed this feature to make home networking easier, but it has one somewhat troublesome requirement: Every computer that uses HomeGroup on your network must be running either Windows 7 or 8, so computers running Windows XP or Vista (or your daughter, the maverick, with her iMac) can't join in the fun. (They can network with Windows 8 using old-fashioned workgroups, just not a HomeGroup.)

When you install the first copy of Windows 7 or 8 on a PC on your network, a HomeGroup is automatically created, and any PC running Windows 7 or 8 that joins your network afterward will request your permission to join the existing HomeGroup. (Can't get much more automatic than that!) However, you can always add computers or manage the settings within your HomeGroup from the HomeGroup screen within Control Panel, as shown in Figure 4-10. (I cover the Control Panel in the next chapter, but it's easy to reach: From the Desktop, press the Settings charm key shortcut Win+I, and then click the Control Panel item in the Settings pane.)

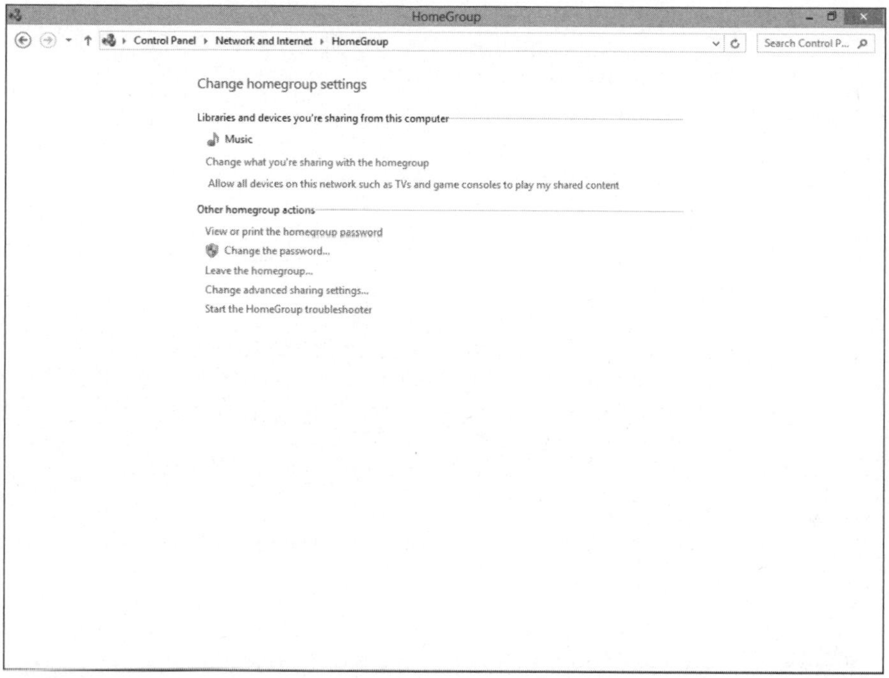

Figure 4-10:
Access
everything
HomeGroup
from the
Control
Panel.

"Wait a second, Mark. If I'm part of a HomeGroup, everyone can share everything I have? Where's the security in that?" Fear not! You can select what you share through your HomeGroup. From the HomeGroup screen in Control Panel, click the Change What You're Sharing with the HomeGroup link, and Windows 8 opens a wizard that allows you to choose which of the four libraries you want to share. (You can also share your local printer and connected devices, if you like.) The same wizard provides you with a password that must be entered on all the other computers that join your HomeGroup.

It's important to keep in mind that Windows 8 is referring to your top-level Libraries (and not just the Public subfolders) when you're selecting which Libraries to share. (In other words, others on your HomeGroup can access not just the contents of your Public Pictures subfolder, but also the contents of the Pictures Library itself.) This is different from sharing without a HomeGroup (as I discussed in the previous section), where only the contents of the Public subfolders within each library are shared.

When you join a HomeGroup, all the other user accounts on your PC also join that HomeGroup automatically.

If you're not using HomeGroup to build your home network, I invite you to the comforting confines of Book VIII, Chapter 2, where I describe how to create a network or connect to an existing network.

Creating a Shortcut

In Chapter 2 of this minibook, I introduce you to shortcuts, and now it's time to create them. Here are two ways to create a shortcut. Both ways begin by right-clicking the icon:

✦ From the pop-up menu that appears, choose Create Shortcut, and Windows 8 does just that — a new shortcut appears in the same folder as the original icon. You can then copy or move the shortcut to another location on your system. You can also choose Send To⇨Desktop (Create Shortcut) to plop a shortcut directly on your Desktop.

✦ Drag the icon where you want to place the shortcut. When you release the mouse button, choose Create Shortcuts Here from the pop-up menu that appears.

Ever wonder where the shortcut's original file is located? To find out, right-click the shortcut, choose Properties from the resulting pop-up menu, and then click the Shortcut tab to display the Target field (see Figure 4-11). The target path points to the original file.

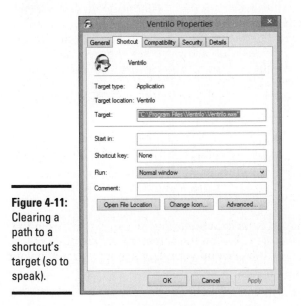

Figure 4-11:
Clearing a path to a shortcut's target (so to speak).

Multiuser Operation For Dummies

Earlier in this chapter, I mention the Public subfolders within each library: where the local users on your PC can share files and folders. That's an example of *multiuser* operation. Unlike a network environment — where multiple computers are connected — a multiuser PC need not be part of a network. Instead, different people use the same PC; each person has his own user account; and Windows 8 keeps track of everyone's Control Panel preferences, File Explorer views, Desktop backgrounds, Favorites, and all the other sundry Windows 8 elements that I show you how to customize in this minibook.

In this section, I discuss how multiple folks can share a single workhorse PC.

Windows 8 offers three different user account levels:

Book II
Chapter 4

Advanced
Windows 8

✦ **Administrator:** The user has full access to Control Panel, can manage other user accounts, and can install programs and hardware. If you're the only person who will use your PC, Windows 8 sets you up with an Administrator account — as it should.

✦ **Standard:** The Standard account user can change the account password, cannot install (or uninstall) hardware and software, and has full control over only those files that she creates. If you're setting up accounts for others and you're less than impressed with their computing skills, by all means give them Standard accounts!

✦ **Guest:** I tell you a tad more about the Guest account in the upcoming section "Be my guest."

Signing in

Your first chore when you sit down to a multiuser PC is to sign in. This step identifies you to Windows 8 and allows the operating system to load and apply all your custom settings.

To switch between a local account and a Microsoft account, press Win+I to display the Settings pane and click Change PC Settings, and then click User in the list at the left and click the Switch to button.

You can sign in to Windows 8 in a number of ways:

✦ **Boot your PC with multiple users active.** Anyone can sign on from the Lock screen — just click anywhere on the screen to display the user account thumbnails, and then click on your user account and type your password.

✦ **Press Ctrl+Alt+Delete.** You can then choose Sign Out to return to the Lock screen.

✦ **Switch users:** Again, press Ctrl+Alt+Delete, and then choose Switch User to allow another person to log on without closing any of your programs. Just make doggone sure that the other user knows not to turn off the PC completely! (Windows 8 helps prevent any tragedies by displaying the message "Signed In" under your user thumbnail on the Sign In screen.) After the switched user completes his session, he should simply sign out using Ctrl+Alt+Delete (so that your programs remain running).

On the Sign In screen, a user must

✦ Click a user account thumbnail to select an account.

✦ Type the correct password — and it had better be spelled correctly. (Case *does* matter.)

Let BitLocker guard your data!

Are you concerned about the security of your data? Although any type of PC could be the target of data theft, laptop owners make the perfect target — it takes only a second for someone to steal an unattended laptop PC, and suddenly your documents and files are in danger. (Even your desktop PC isn't safe because computers are prime targets during a robbery.) If you're running either the Pro or Enterprise version of Windows 8 and you work with sensitive information (or if you just want to keep your Windows Live Mail contacts away from prying eyes), take advantage of Microsoft's BitLocker feature, and encrypt your PC's hard drive! (You can also encrypt a removable drive, such as an external hard drive or a USB flash drive.) With the basic configuration, you must enter a password to unlock your drive and access the contents. Some PCs can also use *transparent encryption* (meaning that after you log on with the correct account password, data is automatically encrypted and decrypted in the background as necessary).

Note that your PC's BIOS must support BitLocker — if your BIOS isn't compatible, Windows 8 lets you know. To encrypt the boot drive (where Windows 8 was installed), you also need a TPM (short for *Trusted Platform Module*) Security device. The TPM is typically built into a laptop's motherboard, or within the circuitry on a hard drive.

To configure BitLocker from the Start screen, display the Search panel and click the Settings button, type **bitlocker** in the Search box, and click the Manage BitLocker button that appears in the Search Results pane. Click the drive you want to encrypt — remember, Windows 8 indicates whether you can't encrypt a particular drive — and then click the Turn On BitLocker link.

If your boot drive supports BitLocker, you can use full transparent mode: Enable only the Automatically Unlock This Drive on This Computer check box (leave the other two disabled). If your boot drive isn't encrypted, enable only the Use a Password to Unlock the Drive check box (and leave the other two disabled).

Be my guest

Before I cast off from Multiuser Land, I should elaborate on the third type of user account: The Guest account is perfect for someone who needs to use your PC right this moment but won't need an account in the future. The Guest account

✦ Doesn't require a password.

✦ Can be toggled on and off when necessary.

✦ Can't be duplicated or deleted — there's only one Guest account.

To turn on the Guest Account from the Start screen, display the Search panel and click the Settings button, type *guest* in the Search box, and click the Turn Guest Account On or Off button that appears in the Search Results pane.

Book II
Chapter 4

**Advanced
Windows 8**

What exactly can a guest do? Basically, the Guest account has the same abilities as a Standard user account: The guest can use your PC, but Windows 8 prevents that person from abusing it.

Fax Me, Please

Yep, I know that many readers are exclaiming, "Hey! I didn't know that Windows 8 could act as a fax machine! That is positively *trick!*" And, indeed it is — all you need is a fax modem, a telephone line, and the instructions in this chapter.

Setting up faxing under Windows 8

You need to configure the fax support within Windows 8 before you tell folks that you're ready to accept calls from their fax machine. Follow these steps to set up your fax-receive service:

1. **From the Start screen, type the words *Windows Fax*, and then click on the Windows Fax and Scan button in the Search Results pane.**

Windows 8 runs the Windows Fax and Scan utility, which you see in Figure 4-12.

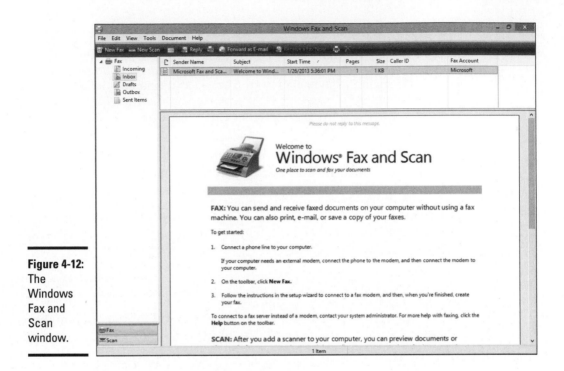

Figure 4-12:
The
Windows
Fax and
Scan
window.

2. **Click the Fax button in the lower-left corner of the window to switch to Fax mode.**

3. **Choose Tools⇨Fax Settings.**

   Whew. Way to bury this thing, Redmond.

4. **Select the Allow the Device to Receive Fax Calls check box.**

   Of course, if you want to send faxes as well, select the Allow the Device to Send Faxes check box.

   Also specify whether

   • You want the fax modem to pick up automatically (after a certain number of rings).

   • You should manually answer incoming fax calls.

5. **Click OK to save your changes.**

To set up your fax send service, click New Fax on the Windows Fax and Scan toolbar, and the utility displays the Fax Setup Wizard, which you see in Figure 4-13. Click Connect to a Fax Modem and follow the instructions to enter your full name, fax number, and company name, as well as your Transmitting Subscriber Identification (TSID) and Called Subscriber Identification (CSID). Usually both the TSID and CSID are simply a combination of your full name (or company name) and your fax phone number.

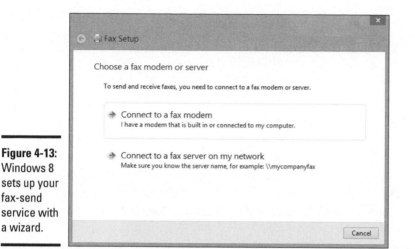

Figure 4-13:
Windows 8
sets up your
fax-send
service with
a wizard.

Sending faxes

If you followed along in the previous two sections, you're now Windows 8–fax-sending-empowered. To send a fax, follow these steps:

1. **In its native application, open (or create) the document you want to fax.**

   For example, fax a Word document from within Word.

2. **Press Ctrl+P to display the Print dialog box (or, within applications like Office 2013, the Print pane).**

3. **Choose the fax device.**

   Click the Printer Properties link to switch between Normal (200×200 dpi) and Draft (200×100 dpi) quality. Draft is quicker, but it's, well, draft quality.

4. **Click Print.**

   Windows 8 launches the Windows Fax and Scan utility and displays a New Fax window.

5. **Type the name of the recipient and the person's fax number. Or, if she's in your Windows Contacts list, click the Contacts button and choose the contact from there.**

6. **(Optional — but highly recommended) Add a cover page:**

   a. *Choose a cover page template from the drop-down list.*

   b. *If you like, add notes in the Cover Page Notes text field.*

7. **Click the Send button.**

If you configure Windows 8 for automatic reception of incoming faxes after a specified number of rings, you really don't have to do anything to receive faxes other than keep your PC running and stay off that telephone line. (See Step 4 in the previous section for the lowdown on how you want the fax call answered.) However, if you specify manual answering for incoming faxes, you have to follow these steps for each incoming fax:

1. **From the Start screen, type the words** *Windows Fax*, **and then click the Windows Fax and Scan button in the Search Results pane to run the program.**

   If you'll be receiving faxes often, I heartily recommend pinning this program to your Start menu or your Desktop toolbar!

2. **When you hear the phone ring, click the Receive a Fax Now button on the toolbar.**

3. **Verify that the incoming fax has been properly detected by watching the Fax Monitor.**

Doing the Multimedia Thing

The final stop on this customization trip concerns multimedia. Windows 8 can be dead boring without liberal doses of digital audio, digital photographs, and DVD movies! In this section, I show you how to enjoy all sorts of digital entertainment as well as how you can record your own CDs from within Windows 8.

Playing your MP3 files

MP3 files are the modern solution to crystal-clear, high-quality music that's

✦ **Standardized and compatible:** MP3 files are supported within every computer operating system these days, along with countless personal music devices, handheld personal digital assistants (PDAs), and palm PCs.

✦ **Easy to create, copy, and share:** Okay, perhaps the music is *too* easily created, copied, and shared — but I'm just reporting on what you *can* do, not involving myself in the ongoing copyright debate over MP3 distribution. (And, like the bumper sticker on the back of my Jeep used to read, "MP3 is not a crime.")

✦ **Easy to record on CD-Rs:** Same copyright argument, same excuse on my part — but it's currently legal to make "compilation discs" of MP3 songs as long as you own the original audio CDs (or bought and downloaded the songs online).

To play MP3 files within Windows 8, double-click an MP3 file within the File Explorer window. Unless you installed an alternative MP3 player (like Apple's iTunes), Windows 8 cranks up Windows Media Player, as shown in Figure 4-14, and begins playing the music immediately. In this case, it's Donna Summer — as long as I'm around, disco will never die!

**Book II
Chapter 4**

**Advanced
Windows 8**

Figure 4-14:
My tunes
sound great
in digital
format!

The familiar controls at the bottom of the Media Player window are shown in Figure 4-14 as well. You can click and drag the progress slider to change your current point in the song. You can also mute or pause the playback from the control strip.

For a complete discussion of MP3 files — including how you can "rip" your own digital music from existing audio CDs — see Book VI, Chapter 2.

Viewing and downloading digital photographs

Digital camera owners, Windows 8 has three features you'll want to try:

✦ **Icon view:** At the beginning of this chapter, I discuss the thumbnail images that appear for images when you're using Icon view within the File Explorer window. As I mention there, it's slower than Tiles, List, or Details views, but if you're sifting through a folder full of digital images and you want to move, copy, or delete some, icon view is the row to hoe. Figure 4-15 illustrates a folder from my digital photograph collection as seen in Large Icons view.

Figure 4-15:
View thumbnail icons of folders stuffed full of media.

✦ **Preview pane:** Don't forget to use the Preview pane within the File Explorer window, as I mention earlier in this chapter. Windows 8 automatically displays a larger preview of a picture when you select it (also shown in Figure 4-15).

✦ **Automatic Import:** The Windows 8 import feature kicks in automatically when you connect your Universal Serial Bus (USB) digital camera to your PC.

You can find much more information on digital cameras and these features in Book VI, Chapter 4.

The disk cognoscenti

If you want to avoid looking like an idiot when talking with a PC power user, listen up. The round, shiny object that you load into your CD-ROM or DVD-ROM drive is a *disc,* ending with a *c* — and not a *disk,* ending with a *k.* The latter word more accurately describes your hard disk (or even one of those ancient irritating floppy disks). Think Latin, think Greek, think *disc*us, think *disc*ography — it's just plain round. Anyone who pretends to be a PC power user and talks oh-so-knowingly about a *CD-ROM disk* or *DVD disk* is a dweeb. Shun them.

Recording your own CDs

Most CD and DVD recorders are accompanied by their own recording programs — like Roxio Creator NXT, from Corel Corporation (www.roxio.com).

However, you can record a data disc within Windows 8 without a separate commercial CD/DVD-recording application. Grab a blank recordable CD or DVD and follow these steps:

1. **Load the blank disc into your recorder.**

   Windows 8 displays a dialog box asking what the heck you want to do with the disc.

2. **Click Burn Files to Disc from the list and then click OK.**

   Windows displays the Burn a Disc dialog box.

3. **Click With a CD/DVD player and click Next.**

   The Mastered format provides the best compatibility with other computers and older versions of Windows. Windows 8 opens a File Explorer window for the recorder.

4. **Select the files you want to record.**

5. **Drag the selected files directly to your optical drive.**

   Nothing has been recorded yet, of course, but we're getting close. Note that Windows 8 indicates the drive is ready with the heading `Files Ready to Be Written` (making it easier to follow what goes where).

6. **Click the Manage tab in the File Explorer Ribbon and click the Finish Burning button.**

7. **Sit back and relax — this step can take some time (anywhere from 5 to 30 minutes, depending on the speed of your drive and the type of media you loaded).**

Watching a DVD movie

To watch a DVD movie in Windows 8 Pro with Media Center, just load the disc. Windows 8 should automatically run Media Center — you might have to choose it on the AutoPlay menu first — and then play the movie. (Note that Windows 8 and Windows 8 Pro without Media Center can't play DVD movies at all.)

You can switch between the window display and a full-screen display by pressing Alt+Enter.

Plus, you get the same familiar set of control buttons that appear at the bottom of the Media Player window. They work for everything from MP3 files to digital video clips to DVDs. Rapture!

Chapter 5: Taking Control of the Control Panel

In This Chapter

✔ Introducing the Control Panel

✔ Setting your PC's date and time

✔ Personalizing Windows 8 just so

✔ Configuring AutoPlay options

✔ Fine-tuning power options

✔ Adjusting your keyboard

✔ Changing mouse settings

✔ Setting Internet options

✔ Removing programs the right way

✔ Configuring user accounts

*P*icture this: You're the engineer on the bridge of the starship Enterprise — the first one, the *real* Enterprise — and Captain James T. Kirk suddenly bellows, "I need more power!" in your direction. Where do you turn? Which panel has the right randomly blinking lights and the right fake switches?

In the Windows 8 galaxy, my friend, you (and Scotty) need go no further than the Control Panel — where all the switches are real! Just about all the check boxes, drop-down lists, and buttons that determine how Windows 8 acts are available from this single screen. And, in this chapter, I show you how to poke a tiny flashlight into the most commonly used Control Panel dialog boxes to fix your starship's shields — whoops — I mean, customize Windows 8 for your needs.

Sorry — like most other first-generation technonerds, I *really* enjoy my *Star Trek*.

The Control Panel at a Glance

Figure 5-1 illustrates the Control Panel top-level window, which you can easily reach from the Start screen — just type the word **control**, and then click the Control Panel button that appears in the Search Results pane.

Some of the same settings I discuss in this chapter are also available in easy-to-use touch-screen form: within the Start screen, press Win+I to display the Settings charm, and then tap Change PC Settings. To select a particular group of settings, tap one of the items on the pane at the left of the screen (shown in Figure 5-2). Although I sometimes use the PC Settings screen elsewhere in this book, the full Control Panel window offers far more options than the limited number of controls you'll find on the PC Settings screen.

The Control Panel window also sports a Search box in the upper-right corner — to search for a specific control (or group of controls), type in one or two words to match the control name or description. To delete the contents of the Search box and start a new search, click the X at the right side of the box.

Figure 5-1: Behold the Control Panel — Settings Central inside Windows 8.

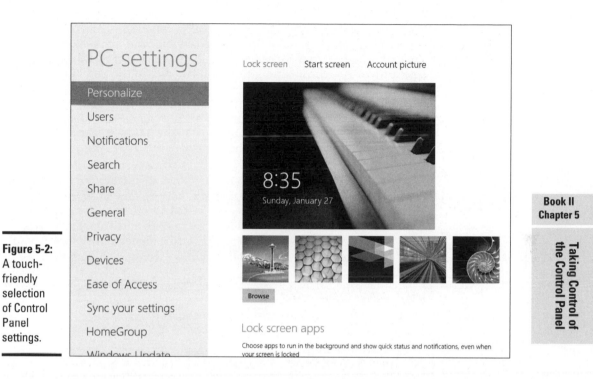

Figure 5-2:
A touch-
friendly
selection
of Control
Panel
settings.

Now a word about *dialog boxes*! (I know, you've been waiting the entire book for this moment.) Anyway, most of the dialog boxes that appear while you're working within Control Panel sport three spiffy buttons: Apply, OK, and Cancel. You probably already know that clicking Cancel closes the dialog box without making any changes — and if you didn't know that, now you do, so you can safely back out of any Control Panel dialog box by just clicking Cancel. Apply and OK do the same thing — any changes you made are saved — but this list describes their two important differences:

✦ **OK:** When you click OK, the dialog box closes, and you can make no more changes to that dialog box. Because many Control Panel dialog boxes have multiple panels (each of which might have a setting that you want to change), it makes sense to click Apply if you need to hang around.

✦ **Apply:** When you click Apply, Windows 8 makes the setting change immediately. Usually, a setting change doesn't do anything obvious right off the bat, but if you're working in the Personalization Panel dialog box, you usually can see which setting changed (like your background or your screen resolution). If you don't like the effect you just wrought, you can easily choose another setting without the hassle of opening the dialog box again.

If you'll be following along with me as I trek through the Control Panel, use the Path box at the top of the Control Panel window to jump immediately back to the main window (or anywhere along the way in the displayed path). To return to a specific location, click that location in the path, just like you would in a File Explorer window. For example, if you're looking at the Desktop Personalization controls, you'll notice that the Path box contains the line *Control Panel➪Appearance and Personalization➪Personalization* — to jump immediately to the main Control Panel window, click the words *Control Panel* at the beginning of the path.

Configuring the Date and Time

The first stop on the Control Panel tour is the Date and Time Properties dialog box, which you reach by clicking Clock, Language, and Region, and then clicking the Date and Time link.

Date and Time tab

Check out its first tab, Date and Time, as shown in Figure 5-3.

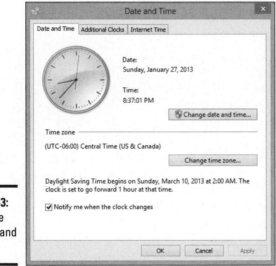

Figure 5-3:
Configure
the date and
time.

Click the Change Date and Time button to use

Book II
Chapter 5

Taking Control of
the Control Panel

✦ **The calendar display:** To select the current day, click it in the calendar display. You can move forward and backward through the months by clicking the arrows on either side of the title.

✦ **The Time clock:** Click the hours:minutes:seconds display and then click the up and down arrows to set the time. (In older versions of Windows, you clicked and dragged the hands of the clock. Someone at Microsoft finally put an end to this analog anachronism in a digital world.)

Click the Change Time Zone button to set your current time zone by using the drop-down list. You can also set Windows 8 to automatically adjust for daylight savings time.

Additional Clocks tab

Windows 8 allows you to display as many as two additional clocks — a real boon for the world traveler who needs to keep tabs on different time zones. You can name each display clock to help keep things straight.

To display all your clocks, as well as a convenient calendar, just click the time display once on the taskbar.

The Internet Time tab

If you have an Internet connection that you use every day — either a dialup or an always-on digital subscriber line (DSL), network, or cable modem connection — you can set Windows 8 to automatically set its own clock by using an Internet time server! Forget about setting the clock manually.

Click the Internet Time tab, and then click the Change Settings button to display the settings you see in Figure 5-4. Select the Synchronize with an Internet Time Server check box and then click the Server drop-down list to select a time server. I prefer the time.nist.gov server because the idea of handing over my PC's time to the Redmond Empire is somewhat unsettling. (Sure, Mark — like they don't already control your waking hours through Windows 8?)

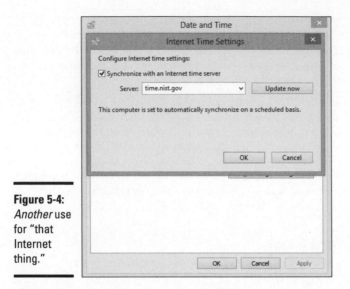

Figure 5-4:
Another use
for "that
Internet
thing."

Changing Personalization Settings

Windows 8 groups a number of settings that used to be in separate
areas into the Personalization settings, shown in Figure 5-5, which you
reach by clicking Appearance and Personalization, and then clicking the
Personalization link. (You can also get to these Desktop settings by right-
clicking any open space on your Windows 8 Desktop and then choosing
Personalize from the pop-up menu that appears.) I hit the major stops along
the road in this section.

Theme

This list offers a number of different color schemes that apply throughout
the Windows 8 Desktop. (The High Contrast schemes may help those who
have trouble reading the screen.) Along with a color scheme, most themes
also contain one or more Desktop backgrounds, a set of sounds, and a
screen saver. (Note that Windows 8 no longer supports the Aero themes that
were featured in Windows Vista and 7.)

These settings affect only the Windows 8 Desktop — to personalize the Start
screen, follow the instructions included in Chapter 3 of this minibook.

Figure 5-5:
The Per-
sonalization
settings
are made
for Desktop
tweakers.

You can also create your own theme with your own elements — simply
choose the Desktop background, window color, sound set, and Screen Saver
that you want (as I show you in the next sections), then save those elements
as a theme for later use! Click the Save Theme link, enter a name for the current theme, and then click Save to seal the deal. You'll see that Windows 8
adds your theme to the My Themes section of the list.

Desktop background

Click Desktop Background to choose a background from the thumbnail list.
To display a folder of backgrounds (and optionally cycle through them automatically), click the Picture Location drop-down list. To enable the random
background feature, click the Change Picture Every drop-down list and
choose the desired delay.

If you want to load your own picture (or a folder of photos), click the Browse
button and then navigate to the location of the image or folder. (Windows 8
automatically updates the preview thumbnails.) Although an image with a
lower resolution can be stretched to fit across your entire Desktop from the
Picture Position control, don't be surprised if it loses quality. Instead, pick
Center to put the image in the middle of the Desktop — or, if the image is a
repeating pattern, choose Tile.

Beware some screen savers

It's *very* easy to write a "bad" screen saver — by that, I mean a screen saver that can slow down or even hang your PC. (Because of their popularity, screen savers are also prime targets for spreading viruses.) Therefore, take care when adding to your system a new screen saver that's not from Microsoft. Your antivirus program should be running (naturally), and you should watch your PC's performance carefully after the screen saver has been running, to make sure that it hasn't caused any problems.

To use a plain-color background, click the Picture Location drop-down list and choose Solid Colors, and then pick your favorite shade.

Sounds

Click Sounds to display the Sound tab within the Sound Control Panel dialog box. You can choose a sound scheme from the drop-down list or create your own scheme by selecting individual programs and events and assigning them your own sound files. Click to select an event in the Program Events list, and then click Browse to locate and select the new sound. You can listen to the selected sound by clicking the Test button.

After you build a new sound scheme, click Save As to save it under a new name, and then you can choose it later from the Sound Scheme drop-down list.

Screen saver

Click Screen Saver to configure these settings:

+ **The screen saver:** Click this drop-down list to choose a Microsoft screen saver or a screen saver that you installed yourself.

+ **Settings:** If the screen saver has any configuration options (like toggling sound effects on or off or increasing the number of flying small appliances on the screen), you can set them by clicking the Settings button.

+ **Preview:** Click this button to see how the selected screen saver will look. To return to the Display dialog box, move your mouse.

Click the up and down arrows to choose the delay period before the screen saver kicks in. You can optionally require your user password to be entered before the screen saver returns you to Windows 8.

Click the Change Power Settings link to display the Power Options settings, which I describe later in this chapter.

Adjusting Display Settings

Choose Control Panel➪Appearance and Personalization➪Display to choose from the following smorgasbord:

✦ **Adjust Resolution:** Click the Adjust Resolution link at the left of the window, and then click the slider and drag it to set a new screen resolution. Click OK to accept the change.

✦ **Refresh Rate:** Click the Change Display Settings link, and then click the Advanced Settings link. From the Display Properties dialog box that appears (see Figure 5-6), click the Monitor tab to set the refresh rate for your monitor. Whenever possible, leave this value set to the default setting — however, if your monitor offers a higher refresh rate than the typical default of 60 Hertz, you may find that the higher refresh rate causes less eyestrain after extended periods at the keyboard. (It takes some experimentation to see how your eyes react.) To check on the refresh rates supported by your monitor, check the monitor's user manual.

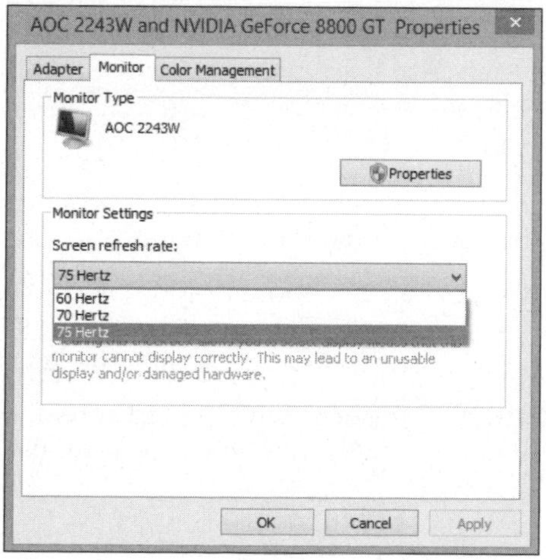

Figure 5-6: Display properties are available on a Windows 8 Desktop near you.

AOC 2243W and NVIDIA GeForce 8800 GT Properties

Adapter | Monitor | Color Management

Monitor Type

AOC 2243W

Properties

Monitor Settings

Screen refresh rate:

75 Hertz

60 Hertz
70 Hertz
75 Hertz

monitor cannot display correctly. This may lead to an unusable display and/or damaged hardware.

OK | Cancel | Apply

If you're having trouble reading smaller text on your Desktop — like icon labels or menu titles — choose Control Panel⇨Appearance and Personalization⇨ Display and choose the Medium or Larger setting. To fine-tune the ClearType text-smoothing feature — which might make text easier to read — choose the Adjust ClearType Text link on the Display window and follow the ClearType Wizard instructions.

Choosing AutoPlay Options

If you need Windows 8 to automatically run a program when you open a certain file, connect a certain device, or load a certain type of media, you can configure that program from the Control Panel. For example, you might like to run your favorite DVD recording program on your PC every time you load a blank disc.

Many Windows programs can automatically set the AutoPlay options for specific media, files, and devices for you — but if a program stubbornly refuses to snap to attention when it should, click Control Panel⇨Hardware and Sound⇨AutoPlay. The window shown in Figure 5-7 enables you to choose a default program for just about any type of file or media, and if any devices (like a digital camera or portable audio player) are registered within Windows 8, they show up at the bottom of the list.

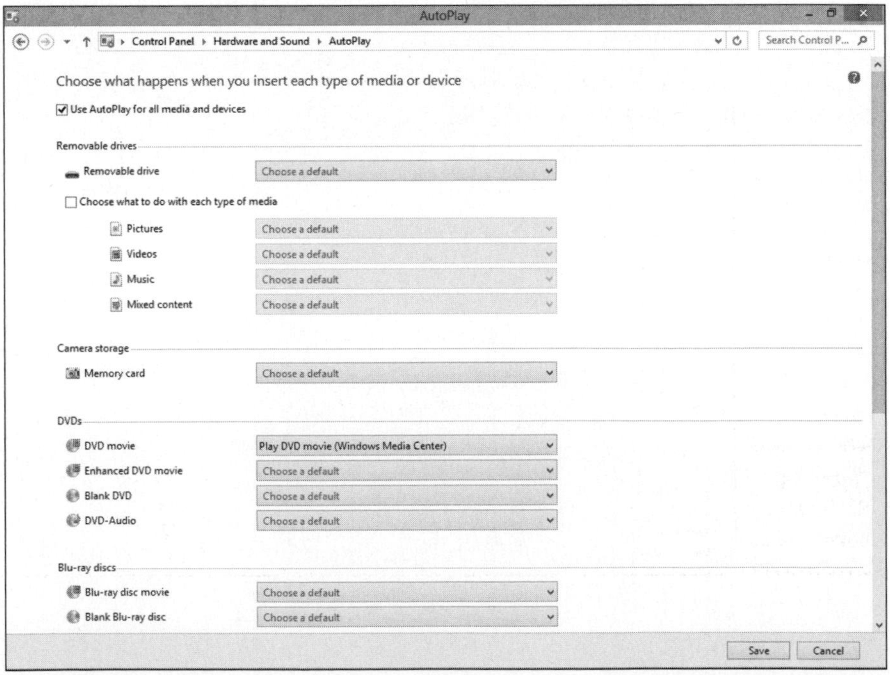

Figure 5-7:
You can easily specify which programs run when you open or load stuff.

Click the drop-down list for the desired media, file type, or device, and choose the option you prefer (including Take No Action, for those moments when you want your PC to remain passive, and Ask Me Every Time, if you often use more than one program for a specific purpose). When everything's set perfectly, click Save.

Adjusting the Power Options

Choose Control Panel⇨System and Security⇨Power Options to display the window you see in Figure 5-8.

The radio buttons in this dialog box allow you to choose a default *power plan,* which controls the steps that your PC takes to conserve power. Power conservation is a handy trick for laptop PC owners but still important for desktop PC owners. Each of the three preferred plans — Balanced (the default), High Performance, and Power Saver — is rated according to its energy savings and the overall performance of your PC while using the plan. (If a preferred plan is hidden, just click the down arrow next to the Show Additional Plans heading to display it.)

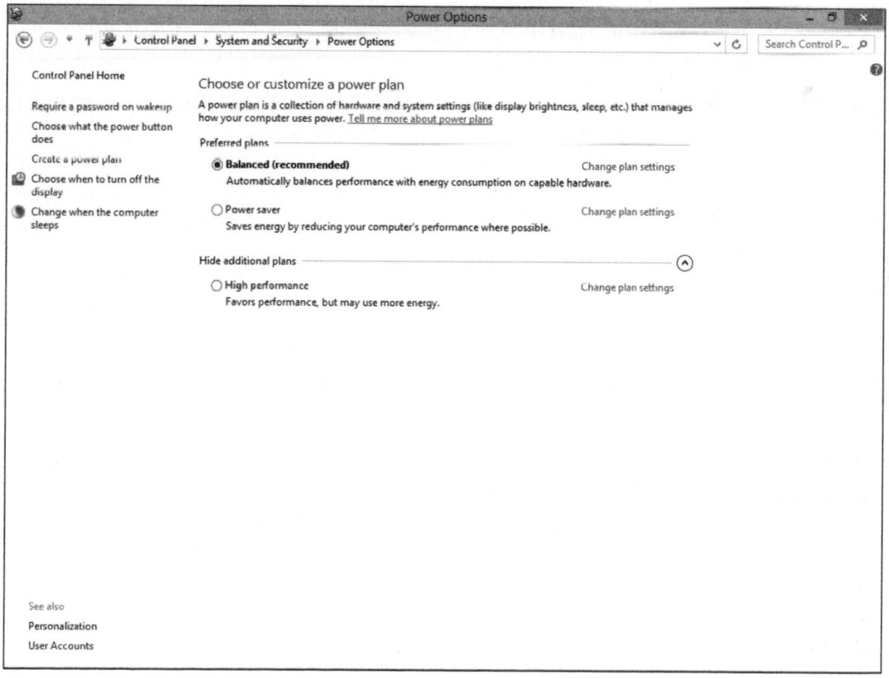

**Book II
Chapter 5**

Taking Control of the Control Panel

Figure 5-8:
Select a
power plan.

To create a completely new power plan for your PC, click the Create a Power Plan link at the left side of the Power Options window. Windows 8 opens a wizard to lead you through the process.

However, you don't have to settle for the default settings! After you decide which of the preferred plans is closest to your needs, click the radio button to select it, and then click the Change Plan Settings link next to the plan to tweak the power options.

The settings include

✦ **Turn Off the Display:** Select the amount of inactivity that Windows 8 waits before switching your monitor to *Standby* mode (where the screen goes blank and the power light usually flashes or turns a different color). The monitor is automatically turned back on when you move your mouse or press a key.

Liquid crystal display (LCD) and light-emitting diode (LED) monitors use less power than traditional cathode ray tube (CRT) models, but you save a surprising amount of money when *any* monitor is switched to standby. In fact, your monitor probably uses more electricity than your PC! Therefore, I always set this value to the smallest amount of time that I can (without the feature becoming a hassle or an inconvenience, where I'm continually having to awaken my screen). For me, this setting is typically 30 minutes.

✦ **Put the Computer to Sleep:** All PCs made in the past several years support *sleep mode,* in which the entire PC (rather than just your monitor and hard drives) switches to low-power mode. Click this drop-down list to select the period of inactivity required to activate sleep mode. Again, mouse or touch-screen activity (or the press of a key on your keyboard) should return your PC to life, with all programs and files intact.

If you need to tweak the operation of your power plan even further, click the Change Plan Settings link, then click the Change Advanced Power Settings link. The settings on this list include

✦ **Turn Off Hard Disk After:** This setting determines the period of inactivity Windows 8 waits before powering-down your hard drive. I know that it sounds dangerous, but this harmless feature saves energy because your hard drives are no longer kept spinning unnecessarily. Like your monitor in sleep mode, a mouse movement or a key press returns your hard drives to active duty.

✦ **Require a Password on Wakeup:** This security feature (shown in the Advanced Settings tab in Figure 5-9) is similar to the screen saver password check box. You can require Windows 8 to prompt for your user password before you're allowed to return from sleep mode. I recommend this setting for anyone who works in an office environment!

✦ **Power Button/Sleep Button Action:** PCs made in the past several years allow you to specify which action Windows 8 should take when you press the power button on your computer: You can opt to shut down the PC, do nothing (think of the wandering fingers of a three-year-old), prompt for the action to take, or switch immediately to sleep or hibernate mode.

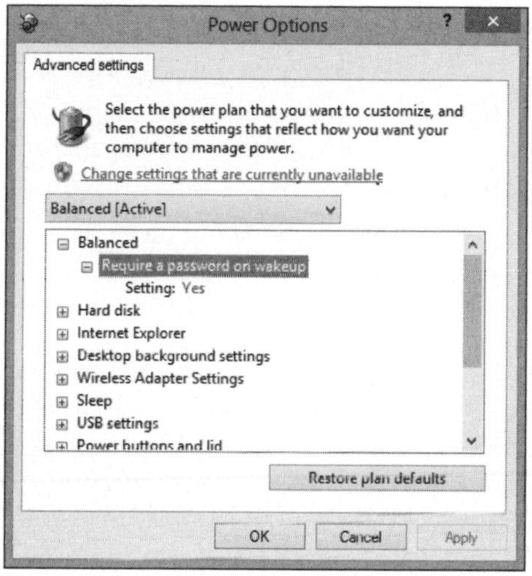

**Book II
Chapter 5**

Taking Control of
the Control Panel

Figure 5-9:
Tweak
your power
options "just
so."

After you choose your advanced power settings, click OK to save the new settings.

Tweaking the Keyboard

You'll have to use the Control Panel window Search box to locate your Keyboard settings because they're not directly available from the default view within the Control Panel window! (Sound of palm hitting forehead.) Click in the Search box and type **keyboard**, and then click the Keyboard link that appears at the top of the results list. Finally you'll gaze upon the wonder that is the Keyboard Properties dialog box, as shown in Figure 5-10. (Note that your keyboard manufacturer's driver may include different tabs that allow you to configure extra buttons.)

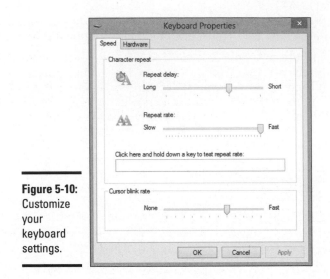

Figure 5-10:
Customize
your
keyboard
settings.

The Speed tab

You can use the settings on this tab to customize your keyboard to fit your preferences:

✦ **Repeat Delay:** Drag this slider to specify how long Windows 8 waits before repeating a character when you hold down a key. (If you're a slower typist and your keys keep repeating, set this slider closer to Long.)

✦ **Repeat Rate:** Drag this slider to set the rate at which characters are repeated when you hold down a key.

To test the repeat delay and repeat rate, click in the test box and hold down a key. You can also specify the rate at which your cursor blinks within programs like Word or Notepad.

The Hardware tab

If you have multiple keyboards (or an input device configured as a keyboard, like some specialized game controllers), you can display the properties of that device (including information about any driver software it requires) or troubleshoot it from this tab.

Adjusting Thy Mouse

The settings you see when you choose Control Panel⇨Hardware and Sound⇨Mouse vary according to the manufacturer of your mouse. For example, my Logitech trackball displays a completely different Mouse Properties dialog box than does a Microsoft mouse because Logitech supplies its own mouse driver.

No matter which pointing device you own, however, you're likely to find the following settings. They might be named slightly differently, but most of them should be there nonetheless:

✦ **Middle button function:** If you're using the manufacturer's mouse driver, you can probably specify which action is produced when you click the middle button on a three-button pointing device. Possibilities include double-clicking, cutting or copying, maximizing or minimizing the active window, or even running a program you specify. (I have mine set as a double-click because it prevents accidental double-clicking with the left button, which sometimes happens when you want to click the left button only once.)

✦ **Pointers:** You can usually either choose a Windows 8 pointer scheme or assign your own pointer symbols. You can also choose graphics directly from your hard drive: Click the pointer action you want to change, and then click the Browse button to "go shopping." (Remember, however, that selecting a picture of your significant other likely does *not* result in a workable mouse pointer! For this reason, most cursor graphics are especially designed for rodent work, and some are even animated.) If you created a new pointer scheme of your own, click Save As to add it to the Scheme drop-down list.

✦ **Mouse trails:** This feature adds a number of trailing pointers when you move your mouse. This trick is quite helpful when you're using a laptop because the mouse pointer is often hard to find on a laptop screen. Visually impaired PC owners might also find this option helpful.

✦ **Scrolling:** If your mouse has a wheel, you can specify how much screen real estate should scroll whenever you move the wheel a notch. (Heck, some mouse wheels even have a vertical scrolling function *and* a horizontal function. Old-timers like me remember when a mouse had just one button (on a Mac) or two buttons (on a PC), and you *liked* it. You had no choice.)

✦ **Acceleration:** If you enable acceleration, your mouse pointer moves faster the farther you move it. This setting is a good idea if you're running your Desktop at a whopping 1600 x 1200 resolution, where the mouse can seem to take forever to get anywhere!

Configuring Internet Options

Next on the Control Panel hit parade is the always fascinating world of Internet Options, which is located in the Network and Internet section of the Control Panel. (Figure 5-11 bares all, including the fact that the dialog box itself is named Internet Properties.) Sit back for the ride, folks, 'cuz this is gonna be a big 'un. (And that's partly because many of the settings that should be tucked away in Internet Explorer are instead dumped here.)

Note that virtually all of the settings I discuss for this dialog box affect only the Desktop version of Internet Explorer — the settings for the Internet Explorer web app are displayed in the Settings charm (which you can view by pressing Win+K within the app).

Figure 5-11: My heavens, what a dialog box! The Internet is a Complex Thing.

The General tab

This tab allows you to set these items:

✦ **Your home page:** In the interest of brevity, you can find a complete discussion of this setting in Book III, Chapter 4.

✦ **Startup:** Use this control to specify whether the Desktop version of Internet Explorer should start with the tabs you had open the last browsing session, or your home page.

✦ **Tabs button:** This dialog box allows you to turn off tabbed browsing altogether. If tabs are enabled, you can also fine-tune their default behavior within the Desktop version of Internet Explorer. Finally, you can specify how the program displays "pop-up" pages received from the websites you visit in a new tab or a new window.

✦ **Browsing history:** The Desktop version of Internet Explorer uses these cache files to speed up the display of pages you've already seen, but after a while, the files can become true hard drive hogs. You can specify which temporary files to delete by clicking the Delete button or simply clicking the Settings button and dragging the file folder disk space slider to 5 or 10MB. (That amount prevents too much waste, and you no longer have to use the Delete button.)

You might be wondering what cookies are doing in the Delete pane. The name has nothing to do with baked goods in this context. Instead, *web cookies* are small files that are saved to your hard drive by your web browser to allow websites to automatically determine who you are. (Ever wonder how Amazon.com always knows that it's you who is visiting? That's because of a cookie.) Most cookies are innocuous (and some sites even require them), but they can be used to store information about you, the sites you visit, and the type of web browser you use. So, if you like, you can click the Cookies and Website Data check box to enable it and wipe 'em out when you click the Delete button.

Again, a lot of this stuff applies only to the Desktop version of Internet Explorer. (In fact, you can get to the same dialog box if you choose Tools⇨Internet Options within the Desktop Internet Explorer.) I discuss the History file in detail in Book III, Chapter 4.

If you'd simply rather allow Internet Explorer to delete your browsing history automatically when you close the program, select the Delete Browsing History on Exit check box. (I recommend this setting.)

✦ **Colors:** Specify the colors you want to use for links (both visited and new), the default text color on web pages, and the default background color on web pages.

✦ **Languages:** Internet Explorer can display text in multiple languages. Click here to select which languages you need or to add extra language packs that you downloaded.

✦ **Fonts:** Specify which fonts are used when a web page doesn't include its own font definition.

✦ **Accessibility:** To force Internet Explorer to use your preferred font style, font color, and font size — no matter what the page is designed to do — click this button. (These features help folks with limited eyesight who have customized their browser font settings.)

**Book II
Chapter 5**

**Taking Control of
the Control Panel**

The Security tab

You see the settings shown in Figure 5-12 on the Security tab:

✦ **The web content zone:** Yep, you can specify different security sites for the Internet as a whole, your local company intranet, and the websites you trust (*and* those you want to restrict). Click an icon to set the security level for that zone. To add sites to the zone you selected, click the Sites button.

✦ **Enable protected mode:** When this check box is enabled, the desktop version of Internet Explorer will warn you when a web page attempts to run external software (a specialty of many spyware programs and viruses). This feature is on by default, and I recommend that it stay that way.

✦ **The security level:** Drag the slider in this section to specify a security level, and Windows 8 displays the actions it will take based on the security level you choose. You can build your own, custom security level by clicking the Custom Level button, or you can return this zone to what Microsoft feels is appropriate by clicking the Default Level button.

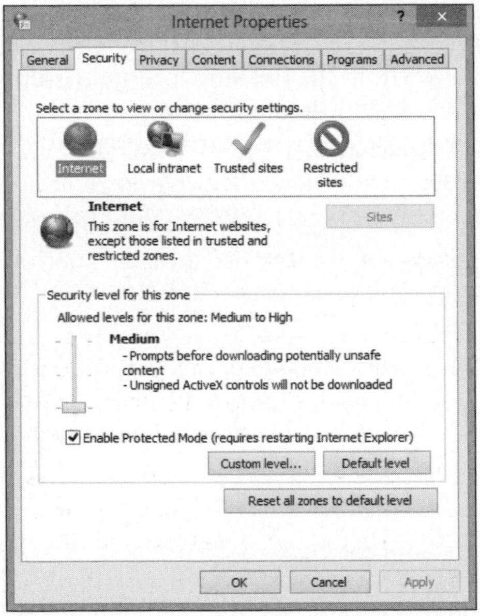

Figure 5-12:
Set your
browser
security
level.

The Privacy tab

The Privacy tab is another "slider" tab, as you see in Figure 5-13. However, the settings you find affect only the Internet zone:

✦ **The privacy level:** Drag the slider to choose an overall privacy setting for the websites you visit. *Note:* This setting also controls the cookies that I mention a bit earlier in this section. Each privacy level is described next to the slider. To import an existing IE privacy preferences file — something that your company might ask you to do — click the Import button. Click the Advanced button to override the cookie handling at the privacy level you chose; you can specify your own cookie handling here.

✦ **Website privacy:** Heck, if you're *really* interested in security, you can even click the Sites button to specify the cookie handling for individual websites! This setting might be just the ticket if a site you like to visit requires you to use its cookies but you eschew cookies otherwise. (Man, that is one ridiculous sentence. Who *named* these things, anyway? Pee Wee Herman?)

✦ **Location:** Some tablet PCs can pinpoint your location, and that location information can be used within some websites (for example, to display where you were when you posted a message). Many folks find this convenient, while many other folks immediately get nervous (especially parents). If you'd prefer to block your location from being used by a website, enable the Never Allow Websites to Request Your Physical Location check box.

✦ **The pop-up blocker:** I hate pop-ups — any red-blooded PC user hates them, too. Pop-up banners and advertisements litter the web like confetti on the fair streets of New Orleans after Mardi Gras; if you select the Turn on Pop-up Blocker check box, however, Windows 8 does a commendable job of blocking these pop-up pests. Click the Settings button to selectively allow the pop-ups you want — some websites use pop-ups to display honest-to-goodness information. You can also view your list of sites where pop-ups are allowed (and change the notification and filter settings).

✦ **InPrivate:** This check box controls how Internet Explorer operates while you're using InPrivate browsing, a feature that doesn't leave any indications of the sites you visit or your activities. No cookies, no history storage, nada. To prevent add-ons from using information during an InPrivate session, select the Disable Toolbars and Extensions check box.

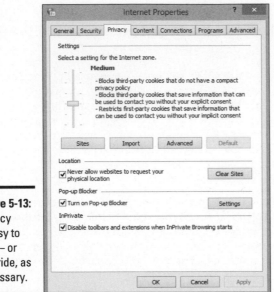

Figure 5-13:
Privacy
is easy to
set — or
override, as
necessary.

The Content tab

Here's a tab that will interest every parent who's concerned about kids surfing the web (hang ten on Figure 5-14). The Content tab settings include

✦ **Family Safety:** If you want to limit the amount of hours a user account is on the Internet, where that user is allowed to go on the web, or even which games and programs that user can run, click the Family Safety button and choose a Standard-level user account that you want to control. (You must be using an Administrator-level account with a password to assign parental controls to another account.)

✦ **Certificates:** These controls allow you to verify your identity to a website; many companies use certificates to ensure the privacy of their intranet data. Certificates can get complex, which is why most normal human beings don't bother with them.

✦ **AutoComplete:** With AutoComplete enabled, Internet Explorer automatically fills out online forms, web addresses, and username-and-password combinations that you previously entered on a site. Click the Settings button to specify which types of data you want filled out. You can also clear your AutoComplete history or clear the passwords in the history.

✦ **Feeds and Web Slices:** Click the Settings button to set an automatic update schedule for your RSS feeds and Web Slices within Internet Explorer.

Figure 5-14:
Control,
filter, and
certify
content to
your heart's
"content."
(Sorry.)

The Connections tab

The settings on this tab can be used to set up a virtual private networking (VPN) connection or a special proxy server configuration; you can also modify your local area network (LAN) Internet connection. Again, this ground is covered in other chapters, so I don't repeat myself here. To wit

✦ Setting up a VPN connection is covered in Book VIII, Chapter 5.

✦ Setting up a network connection to the Internet is covered in Book VIII, Chapter 2.

To set up a proxy configuration, you need several pieces of information from your network system administrator or your Internet service provider's (ISP) technical support department. And, you should set up and use a proxy server only at the ISP's specific request because configuring or using one incorrectly can seriously mess around with your broadband, dial-up and VPN connections. Therefore, leave any proxy settings alone unless you're told to change them. (I do the same thing, so don't feel bad.)

The Programs tab

Figure 5-15 illustrates the Programs tab; from here, you can choose which programs handle your Internet functions.

Of primary importance is a new setting in Windows 8: the Choose How You Open Links drop-down menu, which allows you to specify the default web browsing application system-wide. From this menu, you can elect to open either the web app or Desktop version of Internet Explorer when you click on a link anywhere within Windows 8 (for example, in a Word document or an e-mail message):

✦ If you prefer only to use the familiar face of the Desktop Internet Explorer program, choose Always in Internet Explorer on the Desktop. (Note that you can optionally choose to open website tiles on the Start screen using the Desktop version.)

✦ If you prefer the new Start screen web app version of Internet Explorer, choose Always in Internet Explorer.

The default setting, Let Internet Explorer Decide, essentially dictates that

✦ A link clicked within a Metro app (or a click of the Internet Explorer tile or a website tile on the Start screen) runs the web app.

✦ A click of a website shortcut on the Desktop (or a click of the Internet Explorer icon in the taskbar) runs the Desktop version.

The other controls on this pane include

✦ The program that runs when you edit a web page (HTML Editor)

✦ The default programs that Windows 8 uses for different Internet applications, such as reading and posting Usenet newsgroup messages or talking with someone using a Voice over IP (VoIP) connection (Set Programs)

✦ The types of files that will automatically open Internet Explorer (Set Associations)

Note that a program you install might overwrite these settings.

Click the Manage Add-Ons button to display, manage, and update the add-on programs that add extra functionality to the Desktop version of Internet Explorer. Most add-ons are offered by third-party companies (such as Adobe's PDF "helper" add-on that appears in the Internet Explorer window), but some add-ons are even bestowed upon us by Microsoft itself. You can selectively enable, disable, and update add-ons. You can also select a new default search provider within the Desktop version of Internet Explorer. The default is Bing (no surprise there), but you can add Google or Yahoo! by clicking the Search Providers item in the list at the left of the dialog box.

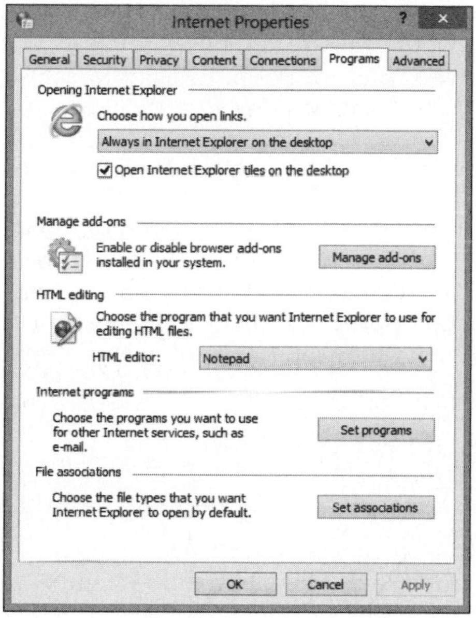

Figure 5-15: So, like, which Internet program does what?

The Advanced tab

The final tab on the Internet Properties dialog box is chock-full of dozens of individual features that you can enable and disable. These settings affect both Internet Explorer and many other Internet applications, so they're often mentioned in program manuals (and in hushed tones around late-night campfires). The options are divided into eight rather nebulous categories; some are a little more self-explanatory than others — like those in the Browsing and Multimedia categories — but most are cryptic. As always, click OK to save your settings.

Because it would take an entire chapter just to explain each setting — and you won't use 99 percent of them unless you're asked to by your ISP, network administrator, or clergy member — I recommend that you check the Windows 8 Help system for information on individual options.

If either version of Internet Explorer no longer opens correctly (or is exhibiting bizarre problems that make the program unusable), click the Reset button to return every Internet Explorer setting to its default state.

Uninstalling and Repairing Programs and Features

Every Windows 8 user should be familiar with the Control Panel window shown in Figure 5-16, because the Programs and Features window is the one truly safe method of uninstalling applications from your system.

(Alternatively, some programs add an Uninstall menu item in their folder; this is fine, too, because it's basically just a different way of starting the same procedure.) To arrive at this scenic spot, click the Uninstall a Program link from the top-level Control Panel window.

Let me reiterate: **Never uninstall an application by simply deleting the program and its folder!** This action can raise all sorts of havoc within Windows 8 — your Windows 8 Registry file (which holds most of the configuration settings for your programs) eventually ends up looking like an army munitions testing ground after a day's work. (And that's A Bad Thing.) In the worst-case scenario, deleting a program folder willy-nilly can even lead to lockups and affect other programs that you didn't even know were distant cousins to the original application.

Follow these steps to remove a program safely:

1. **Display the top-level Control Panel window and then click the Uninstall a Program link.**

(Alternately, you can open a File Explorer window and click on the Computer item in the Navigation pane at the left of the window, and then click on the Uninstall or Change a Program button on the Computer tab.) Regardless of the method you use, after a few seconds, the Programs and Features window appears. You see a list of the programs you installed within Windows 8.

Figure 5-16:
You want to uninstall a program? You talk to me.

Name	Publisher	Installed On	Size	Version
Adobe Reader XI (11.0.01) MUI	Adobe Systems Incorporated	1/13/2013	573 MB	11.0.01
iTunes	Apple Inc.	12/18/2012	189 MB	11.0.1.12
NVIDIA Display Control Panel	NVIDIA Corporation	11/1/2012	135 MB	6.14.12.6141
Safari	Apple Inc.	5/14/2012	104 MB	5.34.57.2
iCloud	Apple Inc.	1/1/2013	81.8 MB	2.1.1.3
QuickTime	Apple Inc.	11/11/2012	73.1 MB	7.73.80.64
Apple Application Support	Apple Inc.	11/29/2012	65.0 MB	2.3.2
Microsoft Silverlight	Microsoft Corporation	5/31/2012	50.6 MB	5.1.10411.0
TweakNow PowerPack 2012	TweakNow.com	4/18/2012	32.5 MB	4.1.0
Star Wars: The Old Republic	Electronic Arts, Inc.	11/1/2012	27.2 MB	1.00
Microsoft SkyDrive	Microsoft Corporation	11/12/2012	25.1 MB	16.4.6013.0910
Apple Mobile Device Support	Apple Inc.	11/29/2012	25.1 MB	6.0.1.3
Malwarebytes Anti-Malware version 1.61.0.1400	Malwarebytes Corporation	4/18/2012	18.0 MB	1.61.0.1400
Microsoft Visual C++ 2010 x86 Redistributable - 10.0...	Microsoft Corporation	11/13/2012	15.0 MB	10.0.40219
Microsoft Visual C++ 2010 x64 Redistributable - 10.0...	Microsoft Corporation	11/13/2012	13.8 MB	10.0.40219
Boot Camp Services	Apple Inc.	4/18/2012	11.0 MB	4.0.4033
Microsoft Visual C++ 2008 Redistributable - x86 9.0.3...	Microsoft Corporation	11/13/2012	10.1 MB	9.0.30729.6161
SnapCrab for Windows 1.1.0	Fenrir Inc.	1/25/2013	8.00 MB	
Ventrilo Client for Windows x64	Flagship Industries, Inc.	1/24/2013	6.66 MB	3.0.8.0
Bing Desktop	Microsoft Corporation	1/1/2013	5.25 MB	1.1.165.0
HP Update	Hewlett-Packard	4/19/2012	3.98 MB	5.003.001.001
Apple Software Update	Apple Inc.	4/18/2012	2.38 MB	2.1.3.127
Bonjour	Apple Inc.	4/18/2012	2.00 MB	3.0.0.10
Microsoft SQL Server 2005 Compact Edition [ENU]	Microsoft Corporation	11/12/2012	1.92 MB	3.1.0000
HP Product Detection	HP	4/18/2012	1.86 MB	11.14.0001
HPSSupply	Hewlett Packard Development ...	4/18/2012	987 KB	2.2.0.0000
Microsoft Visual C++ 2008 Redistributable - x86 9.0.3...	Microsoft Corporation	4/18/2012	596 KB	9.0.30729.4148

Currently installed programs Total size: 1.44 GB
71 programs installed

2. **Click the application entry in the list.**

3. **Click the Uninstall button.**

   This step launches the application's uninstall procedure, which varies according to application and manufacturer.

   If you want to keep an application on your PC but it's acting screwy (displaying error messages about missing files or not running when you try to open an associated document), you can try the Repair function from the Programs and Features window. (If repairing the application doesn't seem to fix it, you probably have to uninstall the program and reinstall it again.) Note that the Repair button doesn't appear for every program.

4. **Follow the onscreen instructions to complete the uninstall process.**

Unfortunately, some uninstall procedures don't remove all files associated with a program. Games, for example, are famous for leaving orphan folders with Save files. Also, if you relocate a shortcut that was placed on your Desktop, that shortcut isn't deleted because it's in a different place. Therefore, I always take a moment to check to make sure that a program folder has been completely dusted after running the uninstall procedure. *After* you officially uninstall the application, you can indeed delete any orphan files or folders from the program that are left on your drive, without fear of toasting your system.

To close the Programs and Features window, click the Close button in the upper-right corner.

Fine-Tuning User Accounts

If you click Control Panel⇨User Accounts and Family Safety⇨User Accounts, you'll discover that the User Accounts window isn't really a typical window. As you can see in Figure 5-17, it's a classy and helpful collection of wizards that features full onscreen instructions for everything you do. (Way to go, Big M!) Therefore, I don't go into step-by-step detail concerning each function, but I do take a moment to list what can be done from these wizards because everyone who shares a machine with others likely needs to perform some type of magic with a user account.

Figure 5-17:
The truly
magnificent
User
Accounts
Control
Panel
Wizard.

From the wizard, you can

✦ Manage an existing account or create a new account (Manage Another Account).

✦ Change your account name (Make Changes to My Account in PC Settings).

✦ Change a pesky password (Make Changes to My Account in PC Settings).

✦ Change the picture associated with an account (Make Changes to My Account in PC Settings).

✦ Turn the Guest account on or off (Manage Another Account).

✦ Enable and configure Family Safety (Manage Another Account).

Book III

The Internet

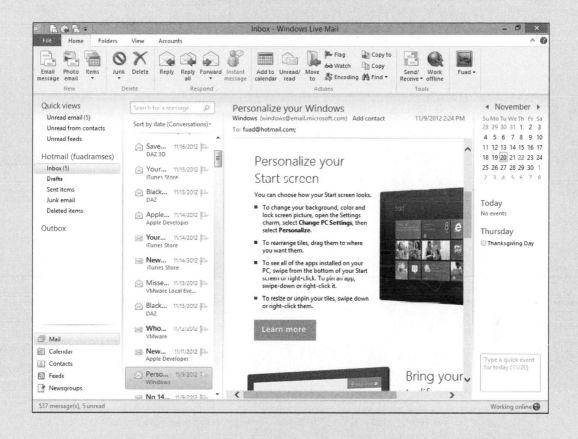

Visit www.dummies.com/extras/pcsaio for more on managing the Windows 8 Firewall.

Contents at a Glance

Chapter 1: Making Sense of the Internet

In This Chapter

- ✓ Defining the Internet
- ✓ Exploring Internet technologies
- ✓ Comparing Internet connection methods
- ✓ Checking your PC's minimum hardware and software requirements

Although the Internet continues to grow and change before our eyes, it seems to be getting more complex rather than simpler to use. Ancient search tools (such as Archie and Gopher) once used to locate stuff before the arrival of the new millennium are practically extinct now, and more everyday uses for the Internet become less exotic seemingly every month: instant messaging, webcams, streaming Internet radio stations, social networking and blogs. Some folks have told me that they're ready to throw their modems out the window and return to the blissfully ignorant days when we all wrote letters with (gasp) paper stamps affixed. (The post office would certainly be happier.)

If you're somewhat wary of the Internet, however, don't give up hope. In this chapter, I explain what's available online, using actual English words of fewer than five letters. (Usually. I might have to hyphenate some of the tech-nonerd terms, however.) If all you do online now is visit sites on the web and communicate through e-mail, you're missing out on a ton of cool activities, and you're likely several years behind the latest Internet technologies. Hey, I live for this stuff.

So, stick with me here to gain a good grasp of what you can do via the Internet and which types of Internet connections are, well, hip and happening. You can then jump to the other chapters within this minibook for in-depth coverage of major Internet applications, such as your web browser and e-mail program.

What's in an address?

So, how does your ISP know where that particular web server is on the network? I don't go into any crush-depth detail here, but here's the quick version. Every computer on the Internet is assigned an address — an *Internet Protocol address,* or IP address — that identifies it to other computers. (This address is technically a Transmission Control Protocol/ Internet Protocol [TCP/IP] address. No glazing over of the eyes yet.) This IP address typically takes the form of four groups of numbers separated by periods, like this example: `192.168.1.100`. (Sophisticated computers keep track of who has which IP address and also which English-language web address, like `www.microsoft.com`, is tied to which IP address.)

See? Like I said, it's beautifully organized chaos, and I'm proud to say that my web server adds three or four additional websites to the billions on the planet!

Exactly What Is the Internet, Anyway?

Many of the PC owners I talk to are convinced that the Internet is a real substance. They're not quite sure whether it's animal, vegetable, or mineral, but they're sure that they either *have it* or *want it* inside their computers. (It's probably a tiny, glowing ball: a cross between Tinker Bell and St. Elmo's fire.)

Seriously, though, you don't need to know what the Internet is in order to use it. From a PC owner's standpoint, you would be correct (in a way) if you said that the Internet begins at the phone connection or the cable modem coaxial cable. Therefore, if you want to skip to the next section and avoid a glance underneath the hood (or if you already read my description of the Internet in another book), be my guest.

Still here? Good. To help you find out a little more about how your PC connects to the online world, Figure 1-1 illustrates the process.

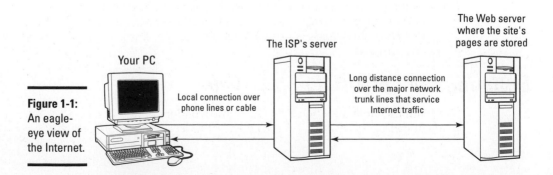

Figure 1-1:
An eagle-
eye view of
the Internet.

Your PC

Local connection over phone lines or cable

The ISP's server

Long distance connection over the major network trunk lines that service Internet traffic

The Web server where the site's pages are stored

Here's a brief description of what happens when you connect to the Internet and visit a website via a web browser:

1. **Your PC connects to an ISP.** *ISP* is the techie slang for *Internet service provider,* a company that gives you access to the Internet proper. (Note that your ISP is not the same as a *web browser* like Internet Explorer — the former is a company that makes money from providing you with an Internet connection, while the latter is a program on your PC that uses your Internet connection to display websites.) Your ISP account usually includes reserved space on its computers for your own website as well as one or two e-mail addresses. This arrangement is analogous to your dialing the telephone for a voice call, using a specific number that connects you to the other party.

2. **Your ISP locates the website across the Internet.** You might hear techie types talk about *pipelines* when they discuss the Internet. Although no physical pipes are involved, the term makes a certain warped sense. In this case, you request a specific website, and your ISP uses its name (its Universal Resource Locator, or URL) to locate the computer it resides on (a *web server*) and then creates a pipeline between your PC and the server. (For example, the URL www.mlcbooks.com leads to my website, which runs on my hard-working server PC in my office.) Here's another example: If you're using an *e-mail client* (a program that sends and receives electronic mail), that client connects to a certain electronic mail server computer across the Internet to transfer your e-mail.

3. **Your computer communicates with the web server.** After you make a connection with a website, a web page is displayed in which you can click links and images to send commands to the web server, which loads other pages or even sends your PC packing to other web servers. (How rude!) This process is much like the result of a voice telephone call: You converse with the other party, using a language that you both understand.

This is the essence of everything you do on the Internet: Computers connect with other computers (no matter where on the planet they might be) and exchange information of various types (e-mail messages, web pages, music, or real-time video signals).

Keep reading to see what you can do when your PC is connected to the Internet. You have the web to explore; you can host your own site and keep journals online; you can keep in touch by e-mail; and more.

Exploring the Potential of the Web

Start with the familiar. When it comes to the wonders of the modern Internet, you just can't get any more mundane and humdrum than the World Wide

Web (now simply referred to as the web). Heck, my kids don't even remember the days when a TV commercial didn't list a company's website or when schoolwork didn't involve an online search. (The endless cycle continues: What did we do before the web? Or microwave ovens? Or air conditioning? Or the telephone? Or a sharpened stick?)

Surf the Web

Visiting websites is as simple as starting your browser (in this case, Internet Explorer, as shown in Figure 1-2), typing a website address in the Address field, and pressing Enter. Boom. (That's my company website, MLC Books Online, which you're welcome to visit at `www.mlcbooks.com`.) Folks surf for all sorts of reasons, including online shopping, research, banking, and various types of fun.

If you're running Windows 8, Internet Explorer 10 is your default browser, and it's already installed! I discuss Internet Explorer (IE) in all its exquisite design in Chapter 4 of this minibook.

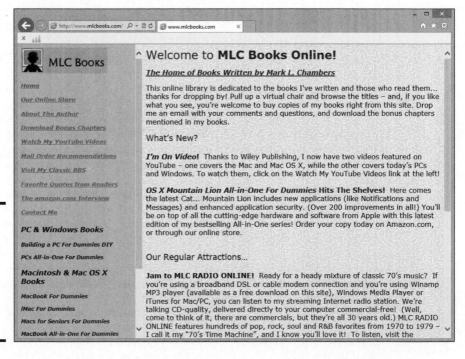

Figure 1-2:
Web browsing is as easy as typing an address or clicking a link.

A website's *extension* (the two- or three-character suffix behind the period) can help you keep track of the major categories of sites. Some common ones are

✦ .com: A commercial or business site

✦ .org: Usually a club, organization, or nonprofit group

✦ .gov: A federal or state government website

Build a website

A-ha! Here are more interesting waters. Despite the somewhat magical tech-nowizard reputation of webmasters and web designers, you can run your own website to support your needs whether it concerns your hobby, your business, or your grandchildren. You need

✦ **A little creative work**

✦ **The proper type of Internet connection,** whether it's an always-on connection (such as cable), a digital subscriber line (DSL), or a network

✦ **The right software,** such as Microsoft Word 2013

Unfortunately, all the intricacies of designing and building Web pages and running a website are beyond the scope of this minibook, but a short stroll through the shelves of your local bookstore provides you with dozens of books devoted completely to the subjects of web design and web server setup. I can personally recommend the excellent books *Building Web Sites All-in-One For Dummies,* 3rd Edition (David Karlins and Doug Sahlin) and *Creating Web Pages All in One For Dummies*, 4th Edition (Richard Wagner; both books from John Wiley & Sons, Inc.).

Blogging

Until a few years ago, I would have thought that blogging was a bread pudding that has gone bad or a B-movie monster. However, now that I run my own web log — *blog,* for short — I'm much more sophisticated. (Can't you tell?)

Blogs, the latest cutting-edge Internet technology in writing a diary, are websites that are updated fairly continually by individuals and crammed full of daily entries, like a journal. Rather than keep your journal private, however, the idea behind a blog is to share your thoughts with anyone who's interested — family members, co-workers, or fellow hobbyists. Blogs usually include the books and music that the person is enjoying as well as links to other sites that the person favors. To create your own site, try Google's Blogger at www.blogger.com.

E-mail and instant messaging

Long before the arrival of the web, the Internet provided a number of truly valuable services — and Internet e-mail is still the most important thing I do online. Avoiding spam like a bullfighter, I can converse with folks planetwide and send them all sorts of stuff as attachments: Microsoft Office documents, programs, web links, and photos, as you can see in Figure 1-3.

Anyone can use Windows Live Mail (under Windows 8, Windows 7, Vista, and XP) to send, receive, and manage e-mail. I think that Windows Live Mail is one of the best free programs that Microsoft has ever produced — and to that end, Chapter 5 of this minibook is dedicated to that program.

If you travel often or you need to check your e-mail on any computer with a web browser, you can use a web-based e-mail account like those offered by Google (www.gmail.com) and Yahoo! Mail (http://mail.yahoo.com). Most web-based e-mail services are free, but you may have to put up with advertisements.

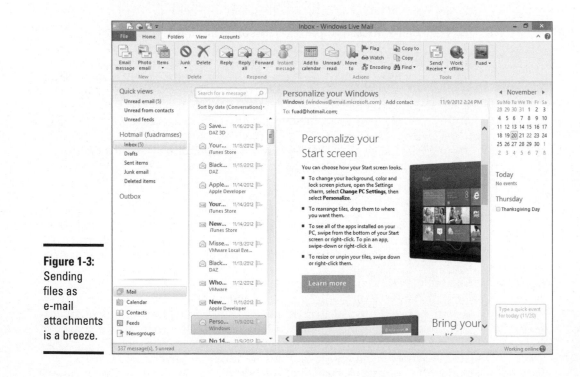

Figure 1-3:
Sending files as e-mail attachments is a breeze.

You can also use applications that allow you to run your own *mailing list,* which is an automated e-mail discussion group, usually concentrating on a specific topic or supporting a specific company or product. Check out MailList Controller 9 at `www.arclab.com/products/amlc` for a good example of a freeware mailing list server.

And e-mail is great, but what if you want to share that gossip *now?* With Skype, you can type your messages to others in real-time — as long as your family and friends are online and available, you can now communicate with them in seconds. (Most folks call this real-time conversation *chatting*, to keep things straight.) Unlike e-mail, with instant messaging, you're sending and receiving messages instantly, in real time, just like texting back and forth on cellphones. (I like to chat while reading the MSN news, as shown in Figure 1-4.)

FTP file transfer

File Transfer Protocol (FTP) is one of the bona fide pillars of the Internet; unlike other antique Internet applications, however, FTP is still alive and doing very well, thank you. You can use FTP to transfer files to and from remote computers; the computer you connect to runs (you guessed it!) an *FTP server.* FTP is great for sending honkin' big files (like 5GB DVD videos) or large numbers of files at a single session.

**Book III
Chapter 1**

Making Sense of the Internet

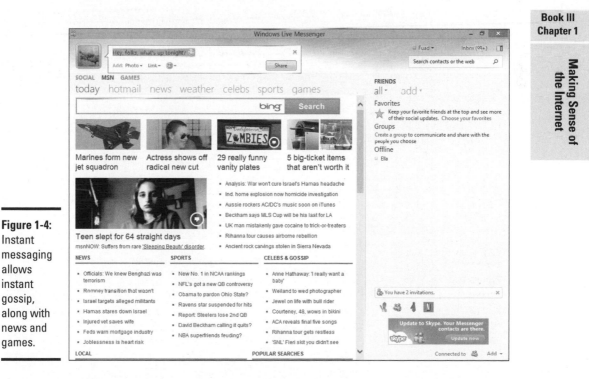

Figure 1-4:
Instant messaging allows instant gossip, along with news and games.

Internet Explorer provides built-in support for FTP transfers, but the IE list of features is definitely on the Spartan side. If you're planning on using FTP often, I recommend that you use a separate application to transfer files. Figure 1-5 illustrates AceFTP 3 Pro, my FTP program of choice. It's a shareware bargain at only $30 US when you download your copy; you can register at the Visicom Media website, `www.visicommedia.com`.

Newsgroups

Think of *newsgroups* as huge discussion boards. Most aren't moderated, and virtually all participants choose to remain anonymous, so opinions and arguments abound.

With that understood, I absolutely *adore* newsgroups! Each newsgroup is dedicated to a certain topic, whether it's Elvis, World War II fighter planes, *The Simpsons,* or something in between. Your ISP usually provides you with access to its newsgroup server when you sign up.

Newsgroups offer more than just the chance to discuss a topic: Many groups are dedicated to certain types of file downloads, so you can share images, sounds, movies, and even programs with others.

Figure 1-5:
Do the FTP thing with AceFTP Pro.

As a first stop before you join the group scene, pick up a copy of my favorite freeware newsreader: Xnews, written by Luu Tran, and available on his website at `http://Xnews.newsguy.com`. You can also try Google Groups at `http://groups.google.com` — it's all web-based, so no additional software is necessary.

Webcams and web videoconferencing

I shouldn't forget one of the cornerstones of web technology that have revolutionized the Internet for soldiers and grandparents alike: the ability to send video from one computer to another by using a webcam. Besides popular services like Skype, companies are now using web *videoconferencing* (where several folks can get together over the Net for a real-time video meeting) on a regular basis.

Now, if you have a high-speed broadband connection such as DSL or cable, you can enjoy a high-resolution video feed that fills that entire high-definition monitor! Who knows? Maybe the large-scale acceptance of web videoconferencing really *has* arrived! Check out the popular Skype videoconferencing application for Windows 8 at `www.skype.com`.

Enjoy digital media over the Internet

If you enjoy music and video as much as I do, this stuff is exciting — streaming Internet radio offers FM-quality (or even CD-quality) stereo music broadcasts that you can tune into with your web browser, Windows Media Player, iTunes, or other MP3 software.

Although you can't capture the music as separate MP3 files, I find Internet radio to be a wonderful resource that I can tune into wherever an Internet connection is handy. Like a video feed, a high-speed Internet connection is a must if you're interested in listening to the higher-quality stations.

In fact, I've run my own station for years! It's MLC Radio, specializing in music from The Era That Will Never Come Again: the 1970s! With a broadband connection, you hear hundreds of classic 1970s hits in 128 Kbps CD-quality stereo; to tune into MLC Radio, visit my website at `www.mlcbooks.com`.

And it's not just your ears that will benefit! Online providers like Netflix (`www.netflix.com`) and Hulu (`www.hulu.com`) make it easy to watch streaming video on your PC (either for a low subscription fee for commercial-free viewing, or for free if you don't mind an advertisement or two). Talk about *sassy!*

**Book III
Chapter 1**

**Making Sense of
the Internet**

Understanding Internet Connections

If you're wondering what DSL stands for or how the speed of a cable modem connection stacks up against your old phone modem, here I discuss each of the common connection types in addition to their pros and cons.

Dialup connections

Once the single most common type of Internet connection, the hoary dialup modem dates back to the days of the early 1980s. Dialup connections use standard telephone lines. In fact, you can consider a dialup connection to be a telephone call between two computers.

✦ **Dialup pros**

- *Simple equipment:* Only a standard voice telephone line and an inexpensive modem

- *Easy access:* Access available anywhere telephone service exists

- *Minimal cost:* A minimal amount for access ($10–$20 US per month: that is, as long as you're calling a local access number — not a long distance toll call)

✦ **Dialup cons**

- *Busy signals:* Busy telephone line (depending on the feature set offered by your modem)

- *Slow speed: Much* slower than any other form of Internet access

- *Reconnection hassles:* Must dial your ISP each time to connect

Dialup access still has its merits, but I wouldn't recommend a dialup connection unless your Internet needs are limited to e-mail and five minutes' worth of browsing per day.

DSL connections

A digital subscriber line (DSL) is one of the two most common high-speed connections. As long as you're within the DSL service area of your telephone provider and your ISP, you can move to DSL.

✦ **DSL pros**

- *Always-on connection:* No dialing necessary for Internet access

- *Fast:* True broadband access speeds (although generally not as fast as cable)

- *Basic equipment:* Uses standard telephone wiring, although you'll need a splitter (shown in Figure 1-6) to separate the PC's data connection from your telephone's analog connection

✦ **DSL cons**

- *Cost:* Usually at least double the cost of a dialup Internet account

- *Cost:* Need to rent or buy a DSL modem, which is more expensive than a familiar dialup modem

- *Limited access:* Might not be available in your area

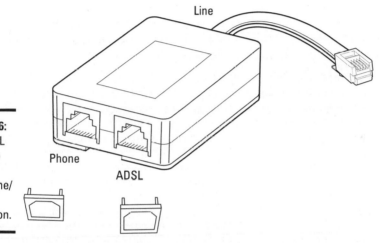

Figure 1-6:
Use a DSL splitter to separate your phone/ Internet connection.

Line

Phone

ADSL

I recommend DSL for anyone who spends more than an hour a night online or who specifically needs faster data transfer.

Cable modem connections

Cable Internet access just plain rocks; it's the other popular broadband connection technology on your block.

✦ **Cable pros**

- *Always-on:* No dialing necessary

- *Very fast:* True broadband access speeds (in most areas, faster than DSL)

- *Simple equipment:* Uses your cable TV coaxial cabling to connect

✦ **Cable cons**

- *Cost:* About twice as expensive as a dialup account

- *More cost:* Need to rent or buy a cable modem

- *ISP limitations:* A limited number of ISP choices accompany cable access (generally, one ISP or none)

Cable access speeds vary according to how many fellow users are connecting to the Internet in your neighborhood: The more people who are connected, the slower your access. (Keep that in mind if you're renting an apartment.) Mind you, the difference might not be significant. I have cable modem access, for example, and because my average connection speed is about one-third faster than the DSL in my area, I still end up with faster surfing and download speeds. Therefore, a bit of checking and speed comparison is in order before you choose between cable and DSL in your area.

I recommend cable for folks who spend more than an hour a night online or who specifically need faster transfers.

Satellite connections

A satellite Internet connection provides transfer speeds comparable with a cable connection, but satellite technology is also (as you might have guessed) usually the most expensive. You usually rent your equipment (an internal adapter card) from your ISP, and the account is also typically more expensive. Bad weather or heavy cloud cover can also slow your connection. However, if you're living in the middle of Alaska and can't get anything other than long distance access to an ISP, the satellite route is likely the way to go.

The latest satellite service uses the satellite antenna to send and receive data. Check with your satellite ISP for information about which type of connection is offered and how much it costs before you sign on the dotted line.

"What Exactly Do I Need?"

Here's the list of minimum requirements to achieve an Internet connection from your PC:

+ **Your PC:** Natch. Windows 8 is preferred in my little chunk of the universe.

+ **An Internet account from a local ISP:** Most larger ISPs offer at least dialup and DSL. If you choose cable or satellite access, your ISP is the company providing the connection.

+ **A modem of one sort or another:** Whether you choose a telephone modem, a DSL or cable modem, or a satellite adapter, you can't just connect a cable to your PC and expect it to work.

+ **A service call (for satellite, cable, or DSL access):** You can connect a telephone modem by yourself, but a service technician has to perform a number of magic tricks if you choose cable or DSL access.

And then there's terrestrial wireless...

Recently, another type of Internet connection has appeared in rural areas where DSL and cable are still hard to get (or completely non-existent): *terrestrial wireless* Internet service providers, or WISPs, can deliver tremendously fast Internet speeds that can out-perform a typical DSL or cable broadband connection. The signal is typically broadcast from a tower or mountaintop, while subscribers use a dish or antenna that's quite similar to a satellite TV dish to receive the signal.

It's important to note that terrestrial wireless service is not the same as the wireless Ethernet networking I discuss later in the book, so you typically can't use your PC's built-in 802.11n Wi-Fi card to receive an Internet connection from a WISP. Also, a terrestrial wireless connection can only travel over relatively short distances (usually less than 50 miles from the WISP tower). A satellite Internet connection, on the other hand, can operate anywhere that offers a clear line of sight to the satellite.

Book III
Chapter 1

Making Sense of the Internet

Chapter 2: Adding an Internet Connection to Windows 8

In This Chapter

✔ Obtaining the right account data

✔ Checking your physical connection

✔ Creating a dialup, DSL, or cable connection in Windows 8

✔ Troubleshooting a faulty Internet connection

Albert Einstein once said, "Imagination is more important than knowledge." When it comes to adding an Internet connection, however, our friend Albert is just plain wrong. (No disrespect intended — Albert was truly a genius.)

You'll find that this chapter is definitely a work of nonfiction — and for good reason. For most PC owners, setting up an analog dialup, satellite, DSL, or cable connection (or "installing the Internet," as I've heard it called) seems to be one of the most daunting tasks possible. And that's a shame because adding an Internet connection is really a simple process. It's just full of all sorts of strange and weird numbers and snippets of data.

With more and more PC owners turning to broadband Internet connections (like cable and DSL), the old-fashioned dialup modem is already preparing to join the other antique hardware in the PC Dinosaur Museum. However, until we *all* have access to broadband connections (and those faster connections become more affordable), this chapter continues to remove the mystery behind all flavors of going online, so that you can get — and stay — online!

Gathering the Account Incantations

Unfortunately, setting up an Internet account is still not a plug-and-play operation, but that's not the fault of Windows 8. Rather, blame it on how the Internet works (which I discuss in Chapter 1 of this minibook) and the information that other computers need to know before they can communicate with your PC. Without the proper setup, you can have the fastest network connection on the planet to your Internet service provider (or ISP), but plugging in your PC provides you with absolutely zip — or, as my dad used to say, "the big diddly-squat."

Don't lose hope! Before you get waist-deep in the Sea of Nervous Tension, let me reassure you that you need to gather only a few MIVs (that's my own abbreviation, short for *Mysterious Internet Values*). Plus, they should all be given to you (for free) by your Internet service provider when you sign up for an Internet account!

If you opt for using a dialup connection instead of broadband, you'll definitely save money — unless accessing your ISP means making a toll or long-distance call from your home phone. Watch out for that gotcha. Perhaps dialup is your only option for going online. After all, not everyone has cable or DSL available where they live (a good time to consider a satellite Internet connection if you can afford the premium price tag). However, if at all possible, I heartily and healthily recommend NOT using a dialup connection. You'll be truly disappointed at the speed at which things *don't* download, such as streaming video and the like.

If dialup is your choice, though, here's a list of the required information you need to set up your Internet access in Windows via a dialup modem:

✦ **Your ISP account name and password:** *Note that this information is often different from your e-mail account username and password.* This is the first troubleshooting question that I ask when folks tell me that they can't connect.

✦ **The local access number provided by your ISP:** Note that many ISPs offer more than one local access number.

✦ **The name of your ISP:** If you have multiple accounts from the same ISP, use more descriptive names, such as *Business account* and *Personal account.*

Now, of course, that's not all the gobbledygook you get from your ISP, but that's all you need to know to handle the steps in this chapter. If you didn't get that gobbledygook, you need to contact your ISP's technical support or help desk by telephone and request it, because you won't be able to connect to the Internet without it.

The rest of the arcane knowledge you receive from your ISP is required later in this minibook, when I cover Windows Mail in Chapter 5 — but after you read this chapter, you'll be a certified technonerd.

If you're using a DSL, satellite, or cable connection to the Internet, you just need your ISP account name and password. If your broadband connection is professionally installed, just hang on to the information in case you have to manually reconfigure your Internet connection because of a hard drive crash, operating system upgrade, or other major change to your system.

Making the Physical Connection

First, make sure that you're plugged in. You've likely heard the horror stories about a recalcitrant PC that stubbornly fails to accept an Internet connection only to find later that the doggone thing simply wasn't hooked up correctly.

Before you delve into the next section, here's a list of the physical connections necessary for each type of Internet access:

✦ **Dialup connection:** Your modem needs to be connected to the telephone wall jack. Most modems are internal (inside your PC case); if you're using an external modem, make sure that it's connected to your PC's Universal Serial Bus (USB) port. (See Book I, Chapter 3 for more on ports.)

✦ **Digital subscriber line (DSL) or cable connection:** Your modem needs to be connected to the telephone wall jack or DSL phone line splitter (for a DSL connection) or your cable TV coax connection (if you're using cable access), and your PC's network card must be connected to the modem with an Ethernet cable. As I mention in Chapter 1 of this minibook, both these Internet technologies are typically installed by a professional, so you shouldn't have to worry about your physical connections. (In fact, if you have a DSL or cable connection, you might not need anything in this chapter because most installation technicians are nice individuals who usually set up the entire shootin' match for you. If you *don't* get a professional installation with your DSL or cable service, don't panic. I'm still going to demonstrate things here!)

✦ **Satellite connection:** Your PC's network card must be connected to the satellite dish's signal box with an Ethernet network cable.

If you had an Internet connection that was working on a previous computer, use the Windows Easy Transfer Wizard to transfer it. From the Charms bar, click Search, choose Apps, and type **Windows Easy** into the Search box. Click the Windows Easy Transfer button that appears in the Results pane.

Creating a New Dialup Connection in Windows 8

If your ISP provided you with complete instructions for setting up your account in Windows 8 — in fact, I would look sideways at the ISP if it didn't — feel free to follow those instructions rather than the steps in this section. Of course, if you didn't get any instructions, you're still covered. (They don't call me Mister Thorough Author for nothing.)

This procedure covers the most common scenario, where

✦ You already signed up for an account with a local ISP.

✦ Your ISP didn't provide a set of detailed instructions (thanks a *heap*).

✦ You're using a dialup modem (either internal or external USB), and it's connected and turned on.

With that said, take a deep breath and follow these steps:

1. **Display the Charms bar and click the Search icon, and then click the Settings button and type** Dialup **into the Search box.**

2. **Click the Set Up a Dial-Up Connection button that appears in the Search results pane to open the Create a Dial-Up Connection Wizard.**

So far, so good, but the screen shown in Figure 2-1 is where some people go astray.

3. **In the Dial-Up Phone Number text box, type the local access number provided by your ISP.**

A local number should be in form xxx-xxxx, like 555-1234. If the number is a toll-free call, don't forget to add the *1-xxx* prefix, as in 1-800-555-1234. On the other hand, if your ISP doesn't provide a local access number and you have to call long distance to connect, **run** (do not walk!) to your telephone and cancel that account! (These days, no one should have to incur long distance charges on top of Internet access. Look for a local ISP instead. Here's a chance to use a telephone book again — remember when they used to be so important?)

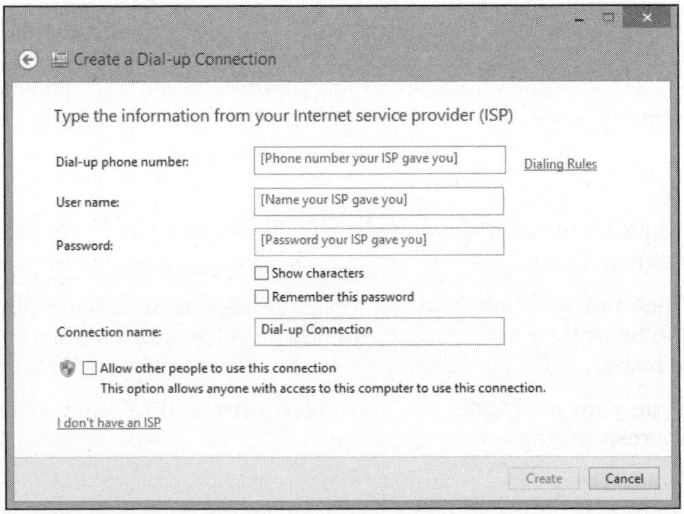

Figure 2-1:
Set up your
ISP account
name and
password
here.

Create a Dial-up Connection

Type the information from your Internet service provider (ISP)

Dial-up phone number:	[Phone number your ISP gave you] Dialing Rules
User name:	[Name your ISP gave you]
Password:	[Password your ISP gave you]
	☐ Show characters
	☐ Remember this password
Connection name:	Dial-up Connection

☐ Allow other people to use this connection
This option allows anyone with access to this computer to use this connection.

I don't have an ISP

Create   Cancel

4. **Type your username and password provided by your ISP into the corresponding boxes.**

   For security, the wizard displays round bullet characters rather than the letters and numbers you type. If you're in a secure location and you prefer to see what you're typing, select the Show Characters check box.

   Security is A Good Thing, as you find out in Chapter 3 of this minibook — therefore, enable the Remember This Password check box *only* if you're not sharing your PC with others and it's in a secure location, like your home. Otherwise, anyone can connect to the Internet automatically using your account, *without* knowing your password!

5. **Type the name of the ISP (or an identifying name that you can remember) into the Connection Name text box.**

   If you're sharing your computer with another person and you don't want them to be able to use this Internet connection from their account, don't select the Allow Other People to Use This Connection check box.

6. **Click Connect.**

   That's it! See — I told you it was (practically) painless.

Creating a New DSL, Satellite, or Cable Connection in Windows 8

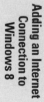

As I mention earlier in this chapter, a DSL, satellite, or cable modem installation might be performed for you or the equipment is accompanied by a detailed set of instructions. Don't forget this important maxim:

> If the manufacturer or your ISP gives you more specific installation instructions than the generic steps that you see here, use those instead!™

It's what I would do. You won't hurt my feelings.

Follow these steps to set up Windows 8 for broadband goodness:

1. **Display the Charms bar and click the Search icon, and then click the Settings button and type** Broadband **into the Search box.**

2. **Click the Set Up a Broadband Connection button that appears in the Search results pane to open the Create a Broadband Connection Wizard.**

3. **Type your username and password provided by your ISP into the corresponding boxes (see Figure 2-2).**

   Again, I recommend that you enable the Remember This Password check box *only* if you're not sharing your PC with others and it's in a secure location. Why allow some elusive, shady character to automatically connect to the Internet with your account?

4. **Type the name of the ISP into the Connection Name text box.**

   Do you want to allow other users of your PC to jump onto the Internet using this connection? If so, click the Allow Other People to Use This Connection check box.

5. **Click Create.**

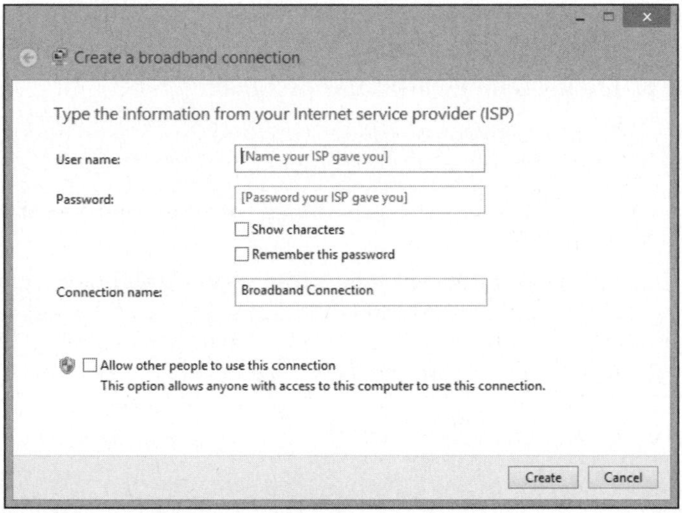

Figure 2-2:
Entering data for a broadband connection.

"Is My Connection Alive?"

The final step in your odyssey is the testing: Have you successfully connected your PC to the Internet? The easiest way to test your work is to run Internet Explorer and try loading a popular site, such as CNN.com or Amazon.com. Type the site name in the Address box and press Enter, and your PC should automatically dial out if you're using a modem. You might not hear the dial tone, but Windows 8 should display a progress dialog box to let you know what's going on. Naturally, a connection using a DSL or cable modem (or a satellite network card) doesn't need to dial out.

If your browser displays the site, you're online! Or, as pilots say, "You're in the pipe, five by five." (I don't know why.)

"My Connection Appears to Be Dead"

If you don't end up clapping your hands in celebration, here are the common troubleshooting tips that I always offer to my consulting customers:

✦ **Check your physical cable connections.** It's always possible that your external modem simply isn't plugged in, connected to your PC, or connected to the phone jack (for a dialup modem or DSL modem) or the cable connector (for a cable or satellite connection). An internal modem needs only a cable from the correct port on the PC to the wall phone jack.

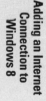

Speaking of correct ports, remember that most analog dialup modems have two ports on the back: One is for the cable running to your wall jack, and the other allows you to plug in a regular telephone to the back of the modem so that you can use your telephone line in the old-fashioned, human-powered manner. Make sure that you plug your phone line from the wall socket into the correct port, which is usually decorated with an icon showing a wall jack.

✦ **(Dialup) Verify the telephone number provided by your ISP.** Pick up your phone and dial the old-fashioned way, using the exact sequence of numbers you entered for the ISP's phone number in Step 4 in the previous section. If you hear the familiar screeching banshee wail of a modem on the other side, you know that the number is correct.

✦ **Double-check the account name and password.** If Windows 8 displays a dialog box saying that your account name or password isn't correct, make sure that you typed your ISP account username and password and *not* your e-mail account username and password. If all appears okay, a call to your ISP's technical support is in order.

Chapter 3: Protecting Your Internet Privacy

In This Chapter

✔ Understanding the risks of the Internet

✔ Using your common sense online

✔ Using the built-in Windows 8 Firewall

✔ Protecting your PC from viruses

"**A**m I *really* taking any risks with my computer or my privacy when I'm online?"

That is one of the most common questions I receive from my readers. I wish that I could assure you that security automatically accompanies the once-unimagined freedom of the Internet — but, unfortunately, the opposite is true. For once, the popular media's perception of computer crime is quite accurate: With your Internet connection comes the possibility of exposure to hackers and con artists.

But just what *can* happen online? How much is hype, and how much is reality? With the right precautions and a little additional hardware and software, you can be reasonably sure that you're well insulated from the bad guys on the Internet! In this chapter, I provide you with everything you need to know — the same recommendations I've made to my clients, friends, and family for more than a decade — to protect *your* privacy online.

What Can Really Happen?

Before I present you with the worst that the Internet can offer, please keep these two important questions in mind:

✦ **Are you a target?** The likely answer is no — and I'm glad to say that's my answer as well. Virtually no private citizen really draws the attention of the serious hackers and other bad guys on the Internet. Hackers would rather attack someone famous, the government, or a corporation than spend their time trying to get a copy of your Word documents, your e-mail, and your Quicken data. (Of course, hackers are getting younger and younger these days, so you might be targeted as a practical joke or juvenile prank. To me, nothing is even remotely humorous about attacking someone else's online personal life — the effect is the same.)

✦ **Are you a tough nut to crack?** Yes! (Or at least you will be after you institute the safeguards in this chapter.) Plenty of "open PCs" are on the Internet, whose owners haven't protected themselves, so (like any car thief) a hacker focuses on the easy mark — or in this case, the "unlocked PC." In fact, with the right protection, it's virtually impossible for a hacker to even detect your presence on the Internet — much less try to invade your privacy — thereby preventing most of the nasty scenarios that I'm about to describe.

Okay, take a deep breath and relax. Here's what *can* happen to you with an Internet connection or a network with a shared Internet connection:

✦ **Someone can try to contact you or the members of your family.** Believe me, there are some truly unpleasant and sleazy individuals who can use all the great communications features of the Internet for the wrong reasons. They can use *Windows Live Messenger* (the instant messaging software provided by Microsoft as a companion to Windows 8), web discussion boards, e-mail, or newsgroups. With common sense and diligence, you can stop these people from communicating with you.

✦ **You can be the target of identity theft.** The con game is alive and well and thriving on the Internet, where your credit card number, address, and personal information should be guarded like the jewels that they are.

✦ **Hackers can turn your PC into an Internet weapon.** If a hacker can gain access to your PC, it can be fooled into participating in attacks against public web servers and File Transfer Protocol (FTP) servers. Denial-of-service (DoS) attacks can actually shut down websites like eBay, Yahoo!, and Amazon.com. In simple English, the hackers manipulate PCs that they have "appropriated" over the Internet to flood these large websites with millions of simultaneous connections and cause the web server to simply "freak out."

✦ **The files on your network can be read or erased.** Woe unto those who run an unprotected network — especially a wireless network, which can be accessed from outside your home or office.

✦ **Your system can be hit with a virus, Trojan, or harmful macro.** Most of us have already heard of the havoc that a virus infection can wreak on your system — deleted files or even empty hard drives.

I told you that it was a grim list — but if all these bad things actually happened to the majority of people who go online, the Internet wouldn't be anywhere as popular and important today as it is. Most of us use our common sense — a most valuable commodity that can help safeguard your Internet presence.

Common Sense Goes a Long Way

Along with common sense comes one of the best of Mark's Maxims, which I hope you immediately commit to memory:

> If something seems like a bad idea online, it probably is.™

You see it happen all the time on the Internet: People give out sensitive (personal and financial) information and communicate with others on a level that they would never do over the telephone or through the mail. Chalk it up to the siren song of the online world and the charms of technology, I guess.

Take a second to review a number of common-sense guidelines that should govern your time online.

Passwords

First, consider the password: It's not an elegant solution to the problem of security, but it has been around since the early days of the online bulletin board systems (or BBSes, for short) in the mid-1980s and early 1990s. No one has found an easier way to protect your identity on the Internet — unless, of course, you want to install fingerprint sensors on everyone's keyboard. (This type of sensor exists right now, but don't hold your breath waiting to see them in common use.)

Here are the guidelines I recommend that you follow when using passwords:

Book III
Chapter 3

Protecting Your
Internet Privacy

✦ **Use random passwords.** I know that using random passwords is a hassle, but they work. Even adding a single number to the end of a word can mean the difference between someone guessing your password and your identity remaining pristine. Some operating systems and online sites recognize the difference between uppercase and lowercase characters, and you can also mix cases to make your passwords even better.

Never use a password that's easily guessed, such as the names of family or friends, or your birthdate.

✦ **Use a different password for each site and server.** If you connect to a dozen systems and need a dozen passwords each night when you're online, it probably isn't feasible — I understand that. However, for the majority of the PC owners online, only three or four passwords are used daily; in that case, using multiple passwords helps keep things as secure as possible.

✦ **Do not write down your passwords.** If you store that sheet of paper or sticky note in a safe, you're okay. A desk drawer, on the other hand, makes that crib sheet a bad idea.

✦ **Don't share passwords.** Or why use them at all? —'Nuff said.

✦ **Don't allow applications to remember your passwords.** Many programs that use the Internet offer the ability to remember the passwords you use online. It's convenient as all get-out, but unless you're guaranteed to be the only person using your account, it's also easy for someone to pose as you within your e-mail or instant messaging applications.

✦ **Use the AutoComplete feature in Internet Explorer sparingly.** Most web browsers can automatically store your personal data for you, but I don't recommend using this feature. I show you how to turn off this feature within Internet Explorer later in this minibook (in Chapter 4).

Of course, your lifestyle might make it easier to skirt some of these recommendations. For example, if you live by yourself, you're already considerably more secure than an office worker surrounded by fellow employees. Just evaluate your own need for security and follow as many of these guidelines as possible. (See there? I can be reasonable.)

Risky behavior

You have to consider a number of online practices that are, sadly, lacking in (you guessed it) plain, common sense. Although you might find it hard to believe, each of these mistakes is committed countless times every day by intelligent individuals (who really should know better). Be sure never to

✦ **Divulge personal information to strangers during online chat.** Chatting is great fun unless the total stranger whom you're chatting with asks for personal information. (Is the person on the other end of this conversation *really* a 17-year-old cheerleader from Omaha?)

✦ **Offer personal information in Internet newsgroups.** This behavior is especially bad. These newsgroups are public discussion areas, and posting anything personal is asking for trouble. (It's no accident that virtually everyone who participates in a newsgroup uses an alias and a fake e-mail address.) Also, these messages remain on newsgroup servers for years, so a single telephone number or e-mail address that you divulge can come back to haunt you years later. After something is posted on a newsgroup, it's there to stay, in the great pile of searchable data that is the Internet. (Try this experiment: Use `www.google.com` to search for your name or an alias that you use on websites and in newsgroups. See how far back that stuff goes?)

✦ **Reply to spam.** Just delete those irritating junk e-mail messages in your Inbox, even if they claim that by replying, you remove your name from their lists. (Yeah, right, and I've got some great oceanfront property in Kansas for you, too.) By replying to spam, you're *verifying* that your e-mail address is correct, and you get double or triple the number of messages overnight.

◆ **Participate in phishing expeditions.** Maybe you're not familiar with the Internet term *phishing*. It refers to the process of attempting to gain your personal information through a combination of an e-mail message tied to a bogus (but official-looking) website. Unfortunately, these criminals are good at creating the impression that you're receiving mail from your bank (or eBay, or Amazon), requesting that you "verify your account information" or "update your user ID and password" by clicking the accompanying link (which opens a page that even looks like the company's website). Always remember that *no self-respecting company will ever request personal information from you through e-mail!* If you're unsure, visit the company's web page (by typing in the bona fide address or using a bookmark) and contact the customer support staff. You may just be able to report an intended crime and help put the bad guys out of the phishing business.

◆ **Allow just *anyone* to access your PC remotely.** Windows 8, Windows 7, and Windows Vista include a remote control feature that allows someone on the Internet to use your PC as though they were sitting at your keyboard. *Do not use this feature unless you're absolutely sure of the person who will control your PC* — such as a technical support representative or your Aunt Harriet. Remember that the person controlling your PC can delete files and open your personal documents at will. (Sobering thought, ain't it?)

◆ **Download files from a site you don't trust.** It's up to you to decide which sites are trustworthy. If you do download something, at least make sure that your computer is protected by a good antivirus scanning program when you run the downloaded program.

◆ **Buy something from an online store without a secure connection.** A reputable online store establishes a secure connection between its web server and your browser. Information is encrypted, so it can't be easily intercepted. (Of course, this statement is especially important when you're entering your credit card information.) If you're using Internet Explorer 10 and a small padlock icon appears on the right side of the address bar at the top of your browser window (and the prefix `https:` appears at the beginning of the site address, as shown in Figure 3-1) then you've got a secure connection. If the connection isn't secure, *don't enter any personal information and don't provide your credit card number* — just find another store that offers a secure connection!

◆ **Open e-mail attachments without using a good antivirus program.** These include executable (or `.exe`) files and Word documents. E-mail attachments are becoming the prime method of distributing viruses. And, because the virus uses the victim's e-mail program to replicate itself, those horrid e-mail booby traps can even originate from your "e-friends and e-family!"

The padlock means your connection is secure.

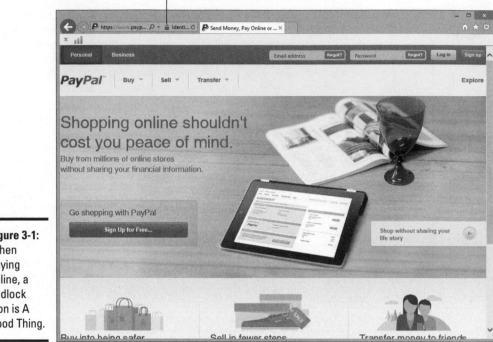

Figure 3-1:
When buying online, a padlock icon is A Good Thing.

Dodging those personal questions

I generally don't provide my real name, age, address, or phone number on most websites. If a website demands this type of personal information and I don't trust the company or organization, I use false information. (Coincidentally, I receive very little spam on my private e-mail account. Go figure.)

I know that providing false information sounds dishonest — and it will anger any webmaster who might be reading this chapter — but why do I have to enter my personal information just to download a demo or use a (supposedly) free service? I'm a webmaster myself, and I don't need that information from casual visitors to my sites! Do some websites sell that contact information to other individuals and companies? (I think you already know the answer to *that* one.)

Naturally, if you're registering a piece of hardware or software or contacting a company's technical support department, providing the required information makes sense — but weigh other queries with care!

E-mail

I mention spam in the previous section. You *can* fight back, you know. Most e-mail applications have their own built-in armor plates, called *filters* or *rules,* which allow you to automatically move junk mail to a separate folder, where it can be quickly perused and tossed at your leisure. I show you how to enable spam protection in Windows Live Mail in Chapter 5 of this minibook.

By the way, get in the habit of at least skimming the Subject lines for probable spam; that way, you can verify that an honest-to-goodness valuable message didn't get accidentally tagged as junk.

Using the Built-in Windows 8 Firewall

Believe me, good people, your firewall *is* your best friend if, for some reason, a serious hacker indeed becomes interested in accessing your PC or your network. A *firewall* is a software application or a separate hardware device (or both) that performs a number of duties:

+ **It masks your PC or network from others on the Internet.** You make it practically impossible for a hacker to locate your PC (much less attack it).

+ **It prevents incoming Internet traffic for the services you specify.** Web and FTP services are two examples, as illustrated so very well by Figure 3-2.

+ **It monitors outgoing traffic and blocks any activity you specify.** Examples are visits to particular websites or any Windows Live Messenger communications.

Book III
Chapter 3

Protecting Your
Internet Privacy

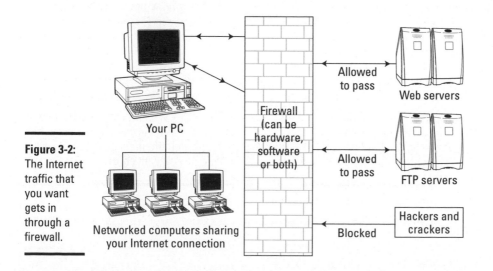

Figure 3-2:
The Internet traffic that you want gets in through a firewall.

Which is better — a hardware or software firewall? That depends on the number of PCs on your network — if you have one — and the level of security you need:

✦ **For a single PC (or a shared Internet connection through Windows 8) with typical home or home office security:** The built-in Windows 8 Firewall is all you need.

✦ **For a network of several PCs — or for any environment where you demand the best security:** Turn to a hardware firewall device. For example, Figure 3-3 illustrates some of the port protection features built into my Internet router.

Device Administration Settings

Main Menu
• OnePage Setup
Advanced
• DHCP Settings
• Access Control
• Virtual Server
• Device Admin
• Status Monitor
• Special App.
• DMZ Host
• RIP
• Static Routing
• PPPoE

Product Name: XRouter Pro

Administrator Password

Password Change: •••••
Password Confirm: •••••
External Admin.: ○ Enable ○ Disable
Block WAN Port Scanning: ○ Yes ○ No
Block WAN Ping Response: ○ Yes ○ No
Reset Device: ○ Yes ○ No
Factory Defaults: ○ Yes ○ No

[Apply] [Undo]

Figure 3-3: My Internet router can be configured to block just about anything.

If you're using an Internet-sharing device (such as an Internet router or switch) that includes NAT, celebrate! NAT stands for *Network Address Translation,* which performs the masking that I mention earlier in this section. Most devices with NAT support also include a hardware firewall. Check the device's manual to be sure.

If you peruse Chapter 2 of this minibook, you know that I recommend enabling the built-in firewall in Windows 8 when you create your Internet connection.

You can easily enable the Windows Firewall, but you need a user account with administrator access to do the job. Follow these steps:

1. **Display the Charms bar, click Search and click Settings, and then type** Firewall **into the Search box.**

2. **Click the Windows Firewall button in the Search results pane.**

3. **Click the Turn Windows Firewall On or Off link at the left side of the window to display the Windows Firewall settings shown in Figure 3-4.**

4. **Select both of the Turn On Windows Firewall radio buttons (Home network *and* Public network locations) to enable or disable the firewall as necessary and then click OK.**

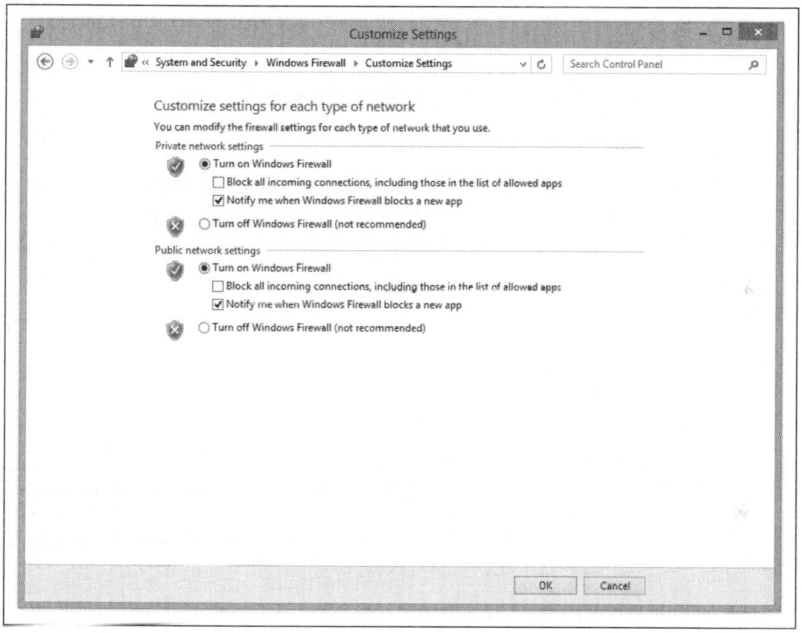

Figure 3-4:
Watch your firewall there, friend.

Book III
Chapter 3

Protecting Your
Internet Privacy

The Windows 8 Firewall is one smart puppy; it shouldn't interfere with any of the Internet activities that a typical home PC owner is likely to try. However, many multiplayer games have trouble sharing your PC with a firewall. If a specific program has problems with the Windows Firewall, check the program's manual to see whether you need to make changes to accommodate a firewall.

Hey, how about a free test of your Windows 8 Firewall? No, pardner, I'm not offering to hack into your system. Instead, I'm inviting you to visit Gibson Research Corporation at www.grc.com, where you can try out ShieldsUP!!. This first-class, *free* online utility checks your Internet connection for a number of entranceways popular with hackers and even gives you advice on how to fine-tune your firewall to close 'em up.

There are third-party firewalls on the market for Windows 8 — for example, Norton Internet Security, from Symantec (www.symantec.com). If you decide to install a new primary firewall, make sure that you follow the instructions provided by the developer carefully to safeguard your PC's security (you may have to disable the Windows 8 Firewall first, for example).

Using Antivirus Software

The last stop on the Internet security tour is a good antivirus program. Windows 8 is the first version of Windows to contain a built-in robust virus protection — Windows Defender has been "beefed up" by Microsoft and can now serve as your primary antivirus protection. However, if you appreciate additional free protection, I recommend that you run a dedicated antivirus program as well.

I'm constantly asked to recommend my favorite antivirus application, so here it is: the well-written avast! Free Antivirus, from AVAST Software. The standard version is free, but you can upgrade with more features by purchasing a subscription. I highly recommend this terrific program. For all the details, visit www.avast.com.)

As I see it, the two most important features of any antivirus program are

✦ **Real-time scanning:** Whatever you run or load, your antivirus program should check it before your PC is exposed. I also appreciate the fact that both Windows Defender and avast! Antivirus check all my Word and Excel documents for dangerous macro viruses. With real-time scanning, the need to check your entire hard drive for viruses is reduced to once every three months or so rather than once every week.

✦ **Automatic and frequent updates:** The best antivirus protection in the known universe isn't worth a plug nickel the moment you stop applying updates. Without updates that contain the latest virus signatures, your antivirus program becomes vulnerable to the newest strain. (A *signature* is a set of characteristics that your antivirus program can use to spot a particular virus.) Therefore, make sure that the antivirus program you choose is updated often and automatically — both Microsoft and AVAST Software excel in providing at least one or two updates a week.

Figure 3-5 illustrates Windows Defender at work.

By the way, avast! Antivirus works inside most e-mail programs (including all versions of Outlook). In fact, the program even checks both the incoming file attachments you receive and the outgoing files you send — just in case.

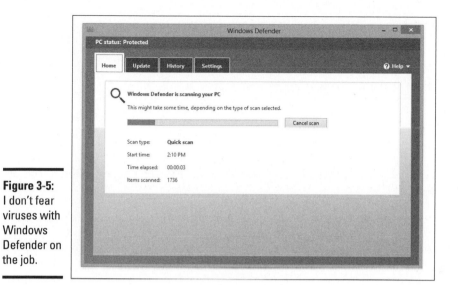

Figure 3-5:
I don't fear
viruses with
Windows
Defender on
the job.

Chapter 4: Cruising the Web with Internet Explorer 10

In This Chapter

↳ **Starting Internet Explorer**

↳ **Introducing the browser window and controls**

↳ **Searching for websites**

↳ **Adding and using Favorites**

↳ **Using tabs like a pro**

↳ **Working with RSS feeds**

↳ **Downloading files**

↳ **Using the History file**

↳ **Printing and saving web pages**

A nd the answer to the unspoken question is, "Yes, you *still* need this chapter, even if you've been using Internet Explorer for the past several years."

You see, Internet Explorer (or almost any web browser) is one of the simplest applications on the planet to use, requiring only three or four buttons to operate most of the necessary functions. Many PC owners I've met don't even know that Internet Explorer offers a ton of additional features to help you organize sites, print pages just-so, and search for the web content you need. Although Internet Explorer 10 is installed with Windows 8, if you're running Windows 7 you can upgrade to Internet Explorer 10 for free. Well done, Microsoft!

In this chapter, I show you the power-user side of Internet Explorer 10 — it's time to supercharge your surfing!

Running Internet Explorer 10

Here are a number of methods you can use to start Internet Explorer 10. (After all, the web has its tentacles in practically everything, right?)

✦ In Windows 8, click the Internet Explorer tile on your Start screen. (In Windows Vista or Windows 7, double-click the IE icon on your Desktop.)

✦ If you've added a website tile to your Start screen, click the tile. (More on how to create a website tile later in the chapter.)

✦ From your Desktop, click the IE button on the Quick Launch portion of the taskbar.

✦ If you're running Bing Desktop, type a word or phrase into the Bing search box and click an item that appears (or press Enter to display the Bing results page).

✦ Click an embedded HTML link in many applications and documents, such as Word and Excel documents or e-mail messages. (This automatically opens the website corresponding to that link.)

The Explorer Window (s) and Basic Controls

Like Windows 8 itself, Internet Explorer 10 now has two faces — one version of the application that's optimized for touch screen and tablet PCs, and one version that's more familiar and has more features (and, in my opinion, is better-suited to mouse control). The window you see depends on how you run the program.

The new Internet Explorer 10 web app is shown in Figure 4-1. You reach this version of Internet Explorer by tapping or clicking the Internet Explorer tile on the Start screen. As you can see, the Address bar and a minimum number of controls appear at the bottom of the window, which always occupies the entire screen. (Throughout this chapter, I refer to this program as the web app.)

You can't run plug-ins in the web app, which may prevent you from visiting some sites or viewing some content. The web app does have the popular Flash player built-in, however.

Figure 4-2 illustrates the more familiar Desktop version of Internet Explorer 10, which you reach from the Desktop taskbar — move your mouse down to display the taskbar, and then click the Internet Explorer icon. Like older versions of Internet Explorer, the Desktop version can run in windowed mode and minimized.

Because more features are available in the Desktop version, I'll focus on that version for most of this chapter. (Luckily, both versions of Internet Explorer 10 use similar controls — just far less of them for the web app.) Don't worry: When the web app handles things differently, I'll make sure to mention it!

Content window

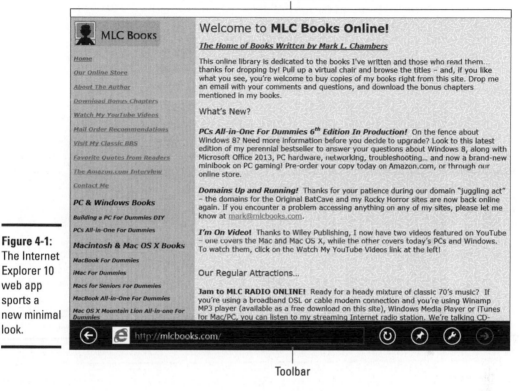

Figure 4-1:
The Internet
Explorer 10
web app
sports a
new minimal
look.

Toolbar

You can click or tap in either version of Internet Explorer 10, so don't feel
that you *have* to use gestures in the web app — it's just easier because the
web app was designed for touch screen operation. Conversely, you can tap
within the Desktop version of Internet Explorer as well, but it may be harder
to use that way.

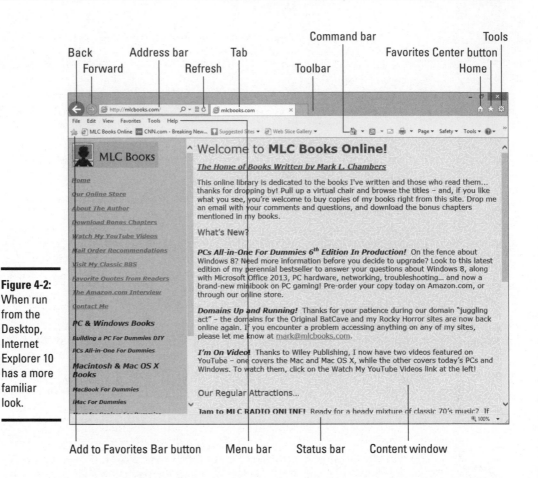

Figure 4-2:
When run from the Desktop, Internet Explorer 10 has a more familiar look.

After Internet Explorer unveils itself in all its stately grandeur, note the following major controls and important spots (refer to Figures 4-1 and 4-2):

✦ **The Address bar:** Here's where you type (or paste) the URLs for websites. From the Desktop version, you can click the drop-down list to see the addresses you recently visited — the web app displays a strip of frequently-visited and favorite websites when you begin tapping. Click a site to return to it with a minimum of fuss. You can also enter a word or phrase in the Address bar, and Internet Explorer searches the web for sites containing that text.

The all-important Secure Sockets Layer (SSL) encryption icon appears on the Address bar, next to the website's address. If you do a lot of online shopping, you see this tiny padlock icon whenever you're entering your personal data or credit card number; it indicates that the site you're visiting is *secure,* which means that the encrypted information you're typing can't be intercepted by hackers. (Secure site addresses also begin with the "https://" prefix, instead of just "http://".)

By default, Internet Explorer 10 uses Bing as your web search provider, but you can also switch to other popular providers like Google and Yahoo!. From the Desktop version, click the Tools icon on the toolbar (it looks like a gear), and then click Internet Options on the pop-up menu that appears. Click the Programs tab, and then click the Manage Add-Ons button; from the Manage Add-Ons dialog box, you can add or change search providers.

✦ **The toolbars:** The toolbar display in both versions includes a number of pop-up menu buttons, which I discuss in detail throughout this chapter. Within the Desktop version, the toolbar also displays any tabbed web pages you might have collected in your travels.

✦ **The Menu bar:** Although it's hidden by default, I personally like the "antique" Internet Explorer Menu bar, so I leave it displayed. These menus make it easier to reach some of the more advanced features within the Desktop version. To display the Menu bar, right-click the window title bar (the strip of color at the top of the window) and click Menu bar on the menu that appears. To hide the Menu bar, repeat the process.

✦ **The Command bar:** The Command bar includes buttons that let you add or change your Home page, view and subscribe to RSS feeds, read mail using Live Mail, and print web pages. To display the Command bar, right-click the window title bar and click Command bar on the menu that appears. To hide the Command bar, repeat the process.

The Help window within the Desktop version of Internet Explorer can be displayed from the Menu bar or the Command bar, or you can press F1.

✦ **The Favorites Center:** You'll find this configurable panel very convenient, but it's only available in the Desktop version of Internet Explorer 10. It can be toggled between displaying all sorts of information, including your Favorites, your surfing history, and your RSS feeds. To display the Favorites Center, you can choose the Favorites Center button on the toolbar (it carries a star icon) and then choose the panel you want to see, or you can press the shortcut key combinations that I provide in the following section, "More buttons for your buck". To banish the Favorites Center from the Internet Explorer window, click the Favorites Center button again.

You can resize the width of the Favorites Center by hovering your mouse pointer over the left edge of the bar until it turns into a double-arrow cursor. Then click and drag the separator to the desired spot.

✦ **Content window:** Believe it or not, the Internet Explorer window shows you web content, too (among all the other stuff). Clicking or tapping an underlined or graphical link in the Content window whisks you somewhere else (either within the same site or on a completely different website). Other Windows-style controls, such as drop-down lists and text entry boxes, can also be displayed and used as part of your surfing. It all depends on the webmaster who designed the page you're viewing — or the webmistress, as the case may be.

One of my favorite keyboard shortcuts in the Desktop version is Ctrl+N, which opens a new Internet Explorer window with the current page loaded. Opening a new window comes in handy when you suddenly need to compare the contents of two web pages because you can navigate to the second page without disturbing the first, and the two windows can be resized to allow a direct comparison. Alternatively, you can open a website in a new tab, which I discuss later in this chapter.

✦ **Status bar:** Last and smallest — but certainly not the least — the Internet Explorer Status bar (available in the Desktop version) displays information about the page you're viewing. If you rest your mouse pointer on a link or photo on a web page, the status bar displays information about that item. Use the Zoom level menu on the right side of the Status bar to zoom out or zoom in on a page within the Content window — a helpful feature if you prefer to zoom in to relieve tired eyes after a long night of web surfing!

If your Desktop Internet Explorer window doesn't have a Status bar, right-click the window title bar and click Status bar. Note that this is also how you can display (or hide) the Menu bar, Command bar, and Favorites bar.

The web app can also display the address for a link or photo: tap and hold (or hover, if you're using a mouse) on the item to display a box with the address.

More buttons for your buck

Just in case you were never properly introduced to the control buttons in Internet Explorer 10, they include

✦ **Back:** With a click or tap of the Back button, Internet Explorer returns to the last page you visited, and each subsequent use of the Back button takes you one more page back. You can also press Alt+← on your keyboard to move backward. If you're using a touchscreen PC, you can flick to the right across the screen.

✦ **Forward:** If you click Back, you need a way to return, right? Click the Forward button to go to the next page (or pages) where you originally were, in forward order. From the keyboard, you can press Alt+→ to move forward. If you're using a touchscreen PC, you can flick to the left across the screen.

If you notice that the Back button is disabled (grayed out), you haven't visited at least two sites yet. If the Forward button is disabled, you haven't used the Back button yet. (Little did we all know that Internet Explorer had a PhD in quantum physics.)

Mouse users can click to move forward and back in the web app as well — hover your cursor over the middle left or middle right edge of the screen to display ghostly Back and Forward buttons!

✦ **Refresh:** Clicking the Refresh button (the curly arrow to the right of the Address field) reloads the contents of the current web page, which allows the web server to update the page with any new information. (This button is helpful for connections to news sites, like CNN.com.) You can press F5 to refresh as well.

✦ **Stop:** This option is wonderfully self-explanatory. If a page is loading, the Refresh button turns into a Stop button (which looks like an X), and you can click it to cancel a page from loading. Pressing Esc does the same job from the keyboard.

✦ **Add to Favorites bar:** Click this button to add the current site to the Favorites bar (which appears right next to the button). (Note that the Favorites bar must be enabled for this button to appear.)

✦ **Favorites Center:** Click the Favorites Center button to display the Favorites Center (available only in the Desktop version), or press Alt+C. (Again, I tell you more about Favorites later in this chapter.)

✦ **Suggested Sites:** If you've turned on your Favorites bar in the Desktop version, you can click this button to display suggested sites you might enjoy based upon the sites you visit most often. (Favorites appear in the web app when you begin typing in the Address bar.) To turn on Suggested Sites, display the Favorites Center and click the Turn On Suggested Sites button at the bottom of the Favorites Center.

✦ **Web Slice Gallery:** If you've turned on your Favorites bar in the Desktop version, this list displays the Web Slices you've selected from web pages with updated content. (You'll find more about Web Slices in the sidebar titled "What the heck is a Web Slice?" later in this chapter.)

✦ **RSS Feeds:** If you've turned on your Command bar in the Desktop version, clicking this button displays any RSS feeds available from the current site. (If that sounds like Greek, don't worry: I cover RSS feeds later in this chapter, in the sidebar "Lean, fast, and mean — that's RSS.") Click the small arrow next to the RSS Feeds button to display (and choose from) the major feed headings.

✦ **Read Mail:** If you've installed Windows Live Mail 2012 on your PC, you can click this button to jump directly to the Mail window.

✦ **Tabs:** These nifty controls make it easy to peruse multiple websites — you can click or tap a tab to immediately switch to that site in the Content window. I cover tabs in more detail later in this chapter.

✦ **Pin Site:** Offered only on the web app version, a click on this button pins a tile for the current web page on your Windows 8 Start screen.

**Book III
Chapter 4**

Cruising the Web
with Internet
Explorer 10

✦ **Home:** Click this button (available only in the Desktop version) to immediately jump to your home page. Mine is `mlcbooks.com`, for example, which makes a trip to my company home page always one click away. From the keyboard, press Alt+Home.

✦ **Tools/Page Tools:** Within the Desktop version, the items on this toolbar menu button (which bears a gear icon) allow you to switch to a full-screen display, delete your history file (which indicates where you've been in past browsing sessions), save a web page to disk, print, and find text on the page. Within the web app, the Page Tools button allows you to find text on the page and download Windows 8 apps for the current site (if the site offers one).

✦ **Help:** If the Help button (which bears a white question mark in a blue circle) doesn't appear on your Command bar, don't panic — just click the double right arrows that appear next to the Tools button, to display "the rest of the Command bar!" (Yep, this is what happens when you have too many buttons in too little space.) Anyway, you find on the Help menu all the high-quality online help you've come to expect from Microsoft.

 To display a short one- or two-word description of an Address bar or control button, just leave your mouse pointer motionless over the button for a second or two.

"The Story of Little URL"

Every web-touring saga begins with the *URL* — short for Uniform Resource Locator — that identifies every website on the planet. It's commonly called a *web address* because a URL is as unique as a traditional mailing address.

Most URLs begin with the now-oh-so-darn-ubiquitous `www.` prefix. However, Internet Explorer doesn't require that you type the triple-w when you're entering a new web address to visit. For example, if you just type **cnn.com** on the Address bar and then press Enter, Internet Explorer automatically adds the `www.` prefix for you. You get to visit CNN.com and save four characters of typing to boot. Also, you never need to type the `http://` portion of the URL because Internet Explorer always tries to load an address as a website unless you specifically indicate that you're trying to connect to a File Transfer Protocol (FTP) site by using the `ftp://` prefix.

Also, you might have noticed recently that a number of sites no longer even use the triple-w. Therefore, don't assume that a URL starts with `www.` or else you might not be able to load the page. Instead, always enter the URL exactly as it's given to you.

Finding a home page

I always encourage everyone on the planet to choose their own home page. If you're continually returning to the same spot on the web, you'll find that your home page can significantly speed up your surfing, which is why I use my site mlcbooks.com as my home page. Many PC owners prefer Google or their ISP's home page, or even CNN.com if you're a newshound. From within the Desktop version of Internet Explorer 10, follow these steps:

1. **Navigate to the page you want to use as your home page.**

2. **Click the Tools button and choose Internet Options from the pop-up menu to display the dialog box you see in Figure 4-3.**

3. **Click or tap the Use Current button.**

4. **Click OK to save your changes and return to the browser window.**

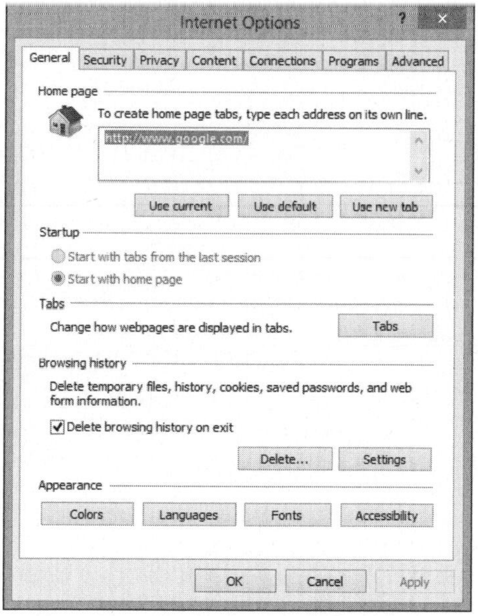

Figure 4-3: There's no place like home (page).

Book III
Chapter 4

Cruising the Web with Internet Explorer 10

If the Command bar is displayed, you can also click the drop-down arrow next to the Home button on the Command bar and choose the Add or Change Home Page menu option.

Navigating the Web

Earlier in this chapter, I talk about how you can visit a site by typing or pasting a URL directly into the Address bar and pressing Enter. Both versions of Internet Explorer 10 automatically show you any sites with a matching address while you type the URL. If you already visited the site, just press Enter when you see the proper address appear, or click a site that appears from your history or Favorites list. (The web app displays these as tile strips, labeled Frequent and Favorites.) If you're using the web app, results appear as you type, and you can tap a button in the Results pane to jump directly to that site.

However, here are other methods of navigating to a new site:

✦ **Click or tap a link** within another web page.

✦ **Click the Home button,** which displays your home page (Desktop version only).

✦ **Click a web link** in a document, an e-mail message, or an application.

✦ **Click an HTML file** from File Explorer.

✦ **Click a suggested site** from the Suggested Sites menu (Desktop version only).

✦ **Click a Web Slice** from the Web Slice Gallery (Desktop version only).

✦ **Click a Favorite** within the Favorites Center or on the Favorites bar (Desktop version only).

In this section, I tell you more about Favorites, and I fill you in on that most pleasant of creatures, the tab.

Simplifying surfing with Favorites

After you select a web page as a Favorite, you can easily reach that site quickly (and without a forest of sticky notes appearing all over your monitor). To add a Favorite, display the page you want within Internet Explorer and use one of these methods:

✦ **Click the Add to Favorites bar button on the toolbar (Desktop version only).** The Desktop version adds the site instantly to the Favorites bar for easy access.

✦ **Click the Pin button on the toolbar (web app only).** Tap Add to Favorites from the menu that appears.

What the heck is a Web Slice?

A *Web Slice* is a rather nutty name for a very cool feature in Internet Explorer 10. Web designers can mark content that updates often as a *Web Slice*—for example, the scores section on your favorite sports site, or the movie listings at your local theater. Instead of manually visiting the same site several times a day to check for new content, you can use a Web Slice to notify you automatically when the page has been updated!

You must first turn on the Web Slice feature before you can use it. Click the Tools button in the toolbar and click Internet Options, then click the Content tab. Click the Settings button in the Feeds and Web Slices section, then click the Turn On In Page Web Slice Discovery check box to enable it. Click OK to return to the

Internet Options dialog box, then click OK again to return to Internet Explorer.

If a Web Slice is available on a specific site, the Web Slice icon appears in your Desktop version toolbar, and it also pops up when you move your mouse over the "sliceable" section of the page. (The icon looks like a white double-arrow in a green square, at least to me.) You can click the icon in the toolbar to add the content to your Favorites bar. When Internet Explorer highlights the Web Slice in the Favorites bar, you've got new content! Click the button to preview the change, and click the preview pop-up to return to that website.

Unfortunately, every time I see the words *Web Slice,* I think of apple pie! Someone at Microsoft needs to consider a new name.

✦ **Press the Ctrl+D keyboard shortcut.** This method displays the dialog box you see in Figure 4-4. Type a new name (if necessary), click the Create In drop-down list to select the location or Favorites folder where you want to store the entry, and then click Add.

✦ **Right-click anywhere on a web page and choose Add to Favorites from the menu that appears (Desktop version only).**

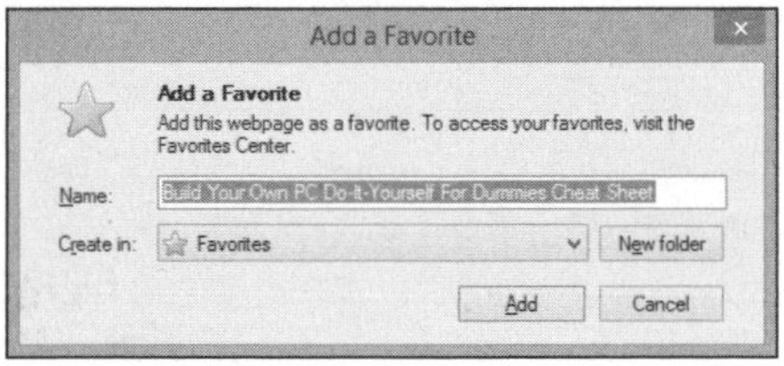

Figure 4-4: Add a web page as a Favorite within the Desktop version.

After you set up your Favorites, using them is simplicity itself:

✦ From the Favorites Center, click the Favorite you want to visit (Desktop version only).

✦ From the Favorites bar, click the Favorite you want to visit (Desktop version only).

✦ If you displayed the Menu bar (as I discuss earlier in this chapter, in the section "More buttons for your buck"), click the Favorites menu and then click the Favorite you want.

✦ Click on the Favorite you want to visit from the Favorites tile strip (web app only).

When you add a number of Favorites, you find them easier to use if you spend a moment to organize them. Follow these steps within the Desktop version:

1. **Click the Favorites Center button, click the down arrow next to the Add to Favorites button, and then choose Organize Favorites from the menu to display the Organize Favorites dialog box. (See Figure 4-5.)**

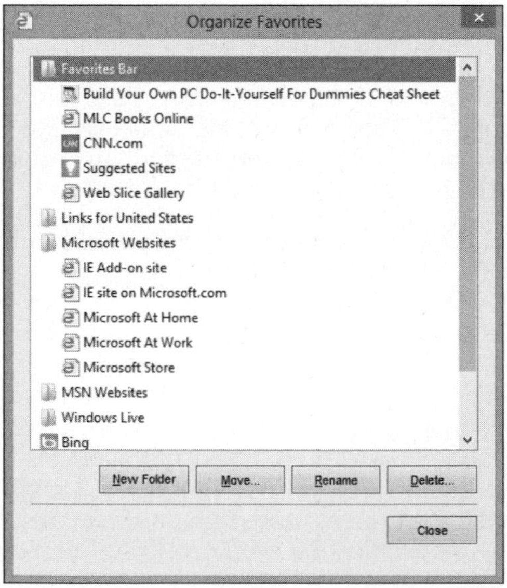

Figure 4-5:
Organize
your
Favorites
any way you
like.

2. **Click the New Folder button to add a new folder, which appears on the Favorites menu on the Menu bar and in the Favorites Center.**

3. **To move a Favorite into a folder, select a Favorite, click the Move button, select the destination folder, and then click OK.**

   Alternatively, you can just drag the Favorite into the desired folder.

4. **To rename a Favorite, select a Favorite, click the Rename button, type the new name, and then press Enter.**

5. **To delete a Favorite, click to select the offending Favorite and then click the Delete button.**

6. **When you're done organizing your Favorites, click the Close button to return to the browser window.**

To change the order of the Favorites from the Organize Favorites dialog box, just click and drag a Favorite to its new spot and release the mouse button to drop it.

If the URL for a Favorite changes — because the site moved to another domain and changed addresses, for example — the Favorite will no longer work. However, it's easy to fix! To modify the URL that's connected to a Favorite from within the Desktop version, right-click the Favorite and then choose Properties (from the contextual menu that appears) to display the Properties dialog box, which you see in Figure 4-6. Click the Web Document tab, type (or paste) the new address into the URL text box, and then click OK to return to the web.

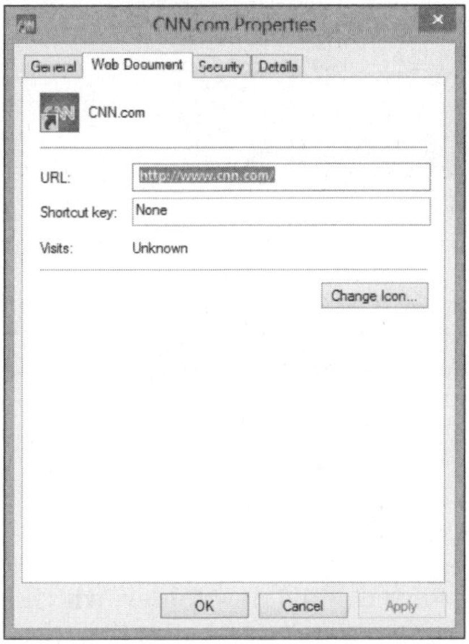

**Book III
Chapter 4**

**Cruising the Web
with Internet
Explorer 10**

Figure 4-6:
Change a
Favorite's
URL here.

Adding a web tile to your Start screen

If you visit a website often, it's smart to add that site to your Windows 8 Start screen as a web tile. From within the web app, follow these steps:

1. **Navigate to the screen you want to add.**

2. **Tap or click the Pin button.**

3. **Choose Pin to Start from the pop-up menu.**

4. **Click in the Tile Name box and type a new name, as shown in Figure 4-7.**

5. **Tap the Pin to Start button.**

Figure 4-7: Pinning a web tile to my Start screen.

Searching for the hay in the needlestack

To search for a specific website among the billions on the planet, use the Address box. Follow these steps:

1. **Click within the Address box, or press Ctrl+E to jump directly there.**

2. **Type a complete sentence — as short and lucid as possible — into the box and then press Enter.**

    Any matches that Internet Explorer finds appear in the Content window.

3. **Click or tap a page link to view that page.**

I use this feature a lot. Figure 4-8 shows the result of my attempt to find Elvis in the Desktop version.

Figure 4-8: You can search for The King from the Address bar.

Book III
Chapter 4

Cruising the Web
with Internet
Explorer 10

Doing the Tab thing

It's time to talk about *tabs* — and I don't mean the word processing tab that we've all gotten to know from the ancient typewriter (and the modern word processor). Instead, think of the tabs in Internet Explorer like the familiar tabs on file folders, which make it easier for you to locate a particular folder in a filing cabinet.

The Internet Explorer tabbed browsing system allows you to display (and organize) multiple web pages at one time. For example, if you're doing a bit of comparison shopping for a new piece of hardware between different online stores, tabs are ideal. Kids of all ages also appreciate tabs while researching because more than one page can remain open — within the same window — while they continue to search the web.

To open a new, blank tab within the Desktop version, click the empty tab on the toolbar (which looks like a square) or press Ctrl+T. You can also open a link on a web page on a new tab: Hold down the Ctrl key as you click the link — if you don't hold down Ctrl, things revert to business as usual, and Internet Explorer replaces the contents of the window with the new page. (You can also right-click on the link and choose Open in New Tab.)

If you're using a mouse or trackball, you may be able to open a link as a new tab by clicking with the wheel button (depending on your button configuration).

To open a new tab within the web app, right-click with your mouse (or swipe downwards from the top of the window) to display the Tabs strip at the top of the screen, and then click on the plus sign icon at the right side of the Tabs strip. You can also press Ctrl+T.

Switching between tabs in the Desktop version is as easy as clicking to select a tab on the toolbar. To switch between tabs in the web app, display the Tabs strip, and then click on the desired tab. (The active tab has a blue border.)

If you build a group of tabs that you want to return to often — perhaps your favorite stock pages or news pages — click the Favorites Center button, click the down arrow next to the Add to Favorites button, and choose Add Current Tabs to Favorites. The group is created as a separate folder in the Favorites Center. Click the right-arrow button next to the folder name to load your tab group. *Sweet!*

Lean, fast, and mean — that's RSS

Well, maybe not; RSS isn't *mean* — after all, I don't want you to be afraid of RSS (RDF Site Summary or Really Simple Syndication) pages! Internet Explorer 10 supports RSS feeds, which display updated information using a shortened list format, rather like a newspaper headline, without unnecessary graphics or silly advertisements. You can tell when a website has an RSS feed available because Internet Explorer plays a sound and the RSS button on the Command bar changes color. (When you click the RSS icon, the web address usually switches to an address with an RSS prefix — another indication that you're not in Kansas reading HTML pages anymore.)

To display more information about a news item on an RSS page, click the item headline. Internet Explorer opens the corresponding web page — yep, once again you're back in the world of HTML — and you can read the full story. To return to the RSS feed, click the Back button on the Address bar. Naturally, RSS feed pages can be saved as Favorites.

You can sort your RSS display from the sort fields on the right side of the page, but Internet Explorer 10 also provides a number of feed settings within the Internet Options dialog box. Click Tools and choose Internet Options from the menu; then click the Content tab and click the Settings button in the Feed section of the pane. You can set Internet Explorer to check regularly for updated RSS headlines — and of course, you can also check for updates manually by reloading the RSS page, just like you would check any other web page. You can also specify that Internet Explorer mark feed content as Read after you view it to help separate the stuff you've read from the stuff you haven't absorbed yet.

Oh, I shan't forget to mention the RSS feed gadget available from the Windows 7 Sidebar. It's one of the three default gadgets that appear the first time you invoke the Sidebar.

Downloading Files

Downloading files is a simple operation, indeed. When you click or tap a download link within a web page, both versions of Internet Explorer 10 automatically download the file to your hard drive. You're given the option of saving the file to your Downloads folder or opening/running the file immediately after the download.

However, note this catch: Unless you're running an antivirus program that checks your downloaded files, you might be receiving a malignant virus rather than a bona fide treasure. That's why Internet Explorer warns you of potential danger when you click a download link that includes an executable program.

How best to handle this situation? Here are my recommendations:

✦ **If you're using an antivirus program, such as avast! Free Antivirus or McAfee VirusScan, go ahead and click Run.** These programs can check the file when you run it.

✦ **If you're not using an antivirus program, click Save.** After you save the file to disk, don't run it until you close any open applications and disconnect from the Internet. However, I *much* prefer that you download a free copy of avast! Free Antivirus from www.avast.com. An unprotected PC is a perfect target for viruses from downloaded files or e-mail attachments.

✦ If you're not using an antivirus program that checks downloads, **do not click Run unless you're downloading a patch or update from the Microsoft website (or another well-known site you trust).** Executing the download from your drive is always a better idea than doing it on the fly.

Here's a pickle. You see an image that you want to download from a website, but it's not really a file that's set up for downloading — instead, it's part of the web page itself. No problem: Just right-click the image you want and then choose Save Picture As (or, in the web app, Save to Picture Library) from the menu that appears. If you're running the Desktop version of Internet Explorer, the program prompts you for the location where you want to save the file. Within the Desktop version, you can also choose Print Picture or instantly make the picture become your Windows Desktop background by choosing Set as Background. (Unfortunately, Internet Explorer can't make a small picture look good across your entire Desktop — or convert a low-resolution shot into a better-quality background — so use this feature only with larger, high-resolution pictures.)

Not all downloaded files can be run immediately. Many sites *compress,* or archive, their download files by using the *Zip* standard, which saves time when downloading (because the compression reduces the file size) and saves hassle (because multiple files are archived into a single file). Zip archives end, predictably enough, with the extension .zip. To *restore* the archive, or decompress it, just double-click it within File Explorer.

Keeping Track of Where You've Been

Bet you didn't know that you were building a history when you tour the web. But what happens if you need to return to a site that you visited an hour ago and you don't remember the URL or how you got there?

Don't worry. Within the Desktop version, the History list of the Favorites Center (see Figure 4-9) makes it easy to retrace your virtual steps. To display the History list, click the Favorites Center button and then click the History tab (or press Ctrl+H). You can immediately return to any page in the list by clicking it.

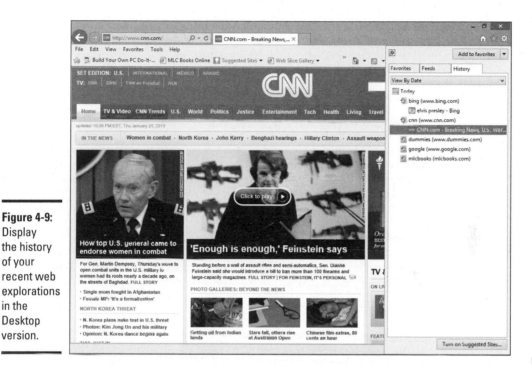

Figure 4-9:
Display
the history
of your
recent web
explorations
in the
Desktop
version.

Book III
Chapter 4

Cruising the Web
with Internet
Explorer 10

Within the web app, your history appears as a simplified strip of tiles above the Address bar, under the title Frequent.

Note that the Desktop version of Internet Explorer keeps track of your history on a site-by-site basis, with all the pages on each site grouped in a single folder. However, you can also display the History list by using other sort criteria. Just click the View by Date drop-down button, and you can specify a sort order based on the date visited, the sites you visited most often, and the sites in the order you visited them today.

You can also search for a specific word or phrase within the History list. Click the View by Date button and then click the Search History menu item — now you can type that word or phrase in the Search For text box. Click the Search Now button to display any sites that contain matching text in the page title.

If you're somewhat leery of even keeping a history file, run the Desktop version of Internet Explorer, click Tools and choose Internet Options from the menu. From the General tab of the Internet Options dialog box, click the Delete button in the Browsing History section. Now you can click the Delete button to immediately delete the current contents of the History list. To specify how many days IE should keep the History list, return to the General tab and click Settings in the Browsing History section. Set the Days to Keep

Pages in History to zero, and Internet Explorer then disables the History list altogether. (Alternatively, enable the Delete Browsing History on Exit check box on the General tab, and Internet Explorer 10 will delete your history automatically each time you close the program.)

Printing and Saving Web Pages

From time to time, you want a printed copy of the content on a web page. Or, you might want to save the page itself, complete with all its content, graphics, and links, to a set of files on your hard drive. In this section, I serve you these two palatable options.

Putting the web in print

I *could* say that printing a web page using the Desktop version is as simple as clicking the Print button on the Command bar (or pressing Ctrl+P), and technically, I would be right. But there's really more to it than that — specifically, the Options tab in the Print dialog box, as shown in Figure 4-10.

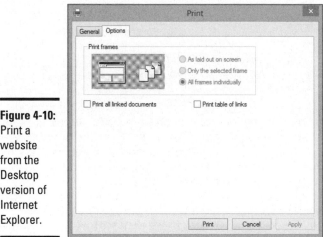

Figure 4-10:
Print a website from the Desktop version of Internet Explorer.

If the page you're printing uses *frames* — a method of putting different panels on a web page, each with its own content — you can choose to print the page in three different ways:

✦ **As Laid Out on Screen:** The entire web page is printed.

✦ **Only the Selected Frame:** Only the contents of the active frame on the page are printed. You can usually activate a frame by clicking within it or by using a scroll bar within the desired frame.

✦ **All Frames Individually:** The contents of each frame are printed separately.

"Yo, Adrian! Who typed that?"

If Internet Explorer suddenly starts completing website addresses and fields within online forms — like your name, your address, or even your password — don't panic. There's no reason to call Ghostbusters. You're seeing the Internet Explorer *AutoComplete* feature, which automatically fills out online forms, web addresses, and username-and-password combinations that you previously entered on a site.

This feature is all friendly and downright convenient, but what if you're more interested in privacy or security? No problem. You can toggle AutoComplete off for certain types of data, or you can turn it off completely. Within the Desktop version, click the Tools button and choose Internet Options from the menu to display the Internet Options dialog box, and then click the Content tab. Click the AutoComplete Settings button to specify which types of data you want filled out. If you're already nervous, click the Delete AutoComplete History button to wipe away any AutoComplete data for online forms and passwords.

By default, the Desktop version of Internet Explorer 10 prints only the current page. However, you can print the current page and any documents it links to, by selecting the Print All Linked Documents check box. This choice is a good one if you want to print the contents of a website with multiple pages.

You can also choose to print an index of links that appear on the page you're printing. This index is a handy tool when the printed page has a large number of links that lead to other documents you might need. Select the Print Table of Links check box to enable this feature.

Saving the best (for last)

Occasionally I run across a page that I want to save in its entirety because I need to view it offline while I'm traveling or when a large number of images accompanies the page. The Desktop version of Internet Explorer makes it easy to save a displayed web page as a set of files on your hard drive. Simply follow these steps:

1. **Click the Page button on the Command bar and choose Save As from the menu (or simply press Ctrl+S) to display the special Save Webpage dialog box, which you see in Figure 4-11.**

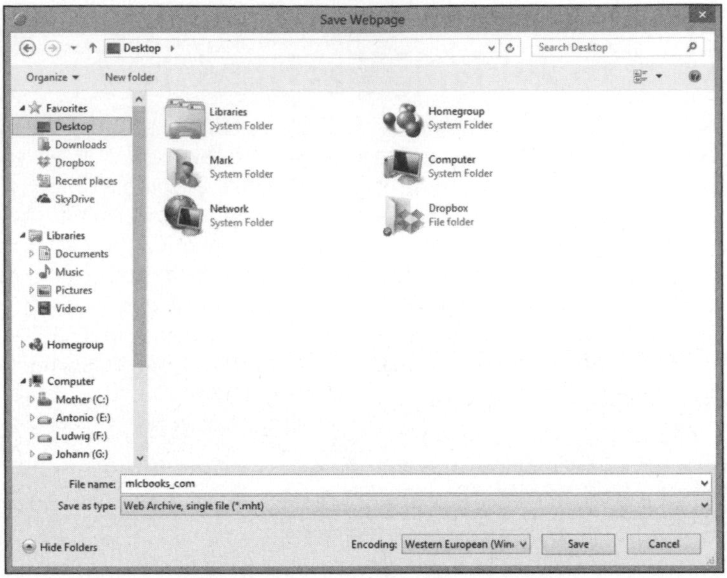

Figure 4-11:
Preparing
to save a
web page to
disk.

2. **Type a name for the saved page in the File Name text box and then navigate to the desired location on your PC.**

3. **Click the Save as Type drop-down list and choose Web Archive, Single File.**

This is my favorite option, where the program stores the entire kit and caboodle so that you can display the page from the file just as it appeared online.

Generally, I don't recommend choosing Web Page, HTML Only, or Text File because you're likely to end up with either a partial page of text or a bunch of meaningless HTML commands.

4. **Click Save to begin the download process.**

Internet Explorer creates an MHT file that you can double-click to display the page, which contains all images and documents from the original page.

Chapter 5: Harnessing Your E-Mail

In This Chapter

✔ Touring the Windows Live Mail window

✔ Configuring your e-mail account

✔ Receiving, reading, and replying to mail

✔ Composing and sending a new message

✔ Sending and receiving e-mail attachments

✔ Blocking that dastardly spam

✔ Using the Contacts list

E-mail rules the Internet roost. Sure, the web gets a lot of attention, but which single service provided by the Internet would cause the most chaos if it were interrupted? That's right — the lowly Internet e-mail message that invites you to lunch or informs you of a new baby (or brings you junk advertising that promises to refinance your home at 2%). Without e-mail, most of today's business world would be left stricken — and you wouldn't get those blonde jokes in your inbox every morning. The mind reels — the soul cries out for more Diet Coke at the very thought.

Because of the mind-boggling importance of e-mail, Microsoft put a lot of work into designing a truly first-class e-mail application for Windows 8. And it's free! You don't get some of the truly powerful features of Outlook 2013, but as an e-mail application, Windows Live Mail can stand proudly on its own. You can download Windows Live Mail as part of the free Windows Essentials 2012 package at `http://download.live.com`.

In this chapter, I describe how you can keep track of your e-mail messages, your contacts, and your identities in Windows Live Mail. You discover how to ward off junk mail messages and how to attach Aunt Gertrude's Big Bang Brownie recipe to the next e-mail you send (for the brownie lovers on your Contacts list).

And even if you use a different e-mail program — meaning, what you see onscreen will look a little different — the concepts are the same.

Introducing the Mail Window

Before you venture into the world of Internet communications, get familiar with the controls of the Live Mail window; click the Windows Live Mail tile on your Start screen, and then catch the hoopla in Figure 5-1.

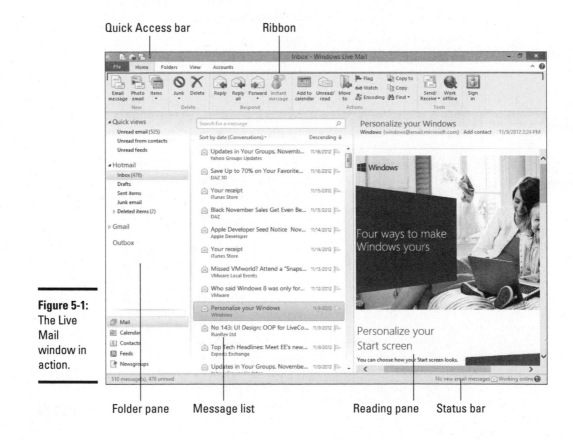

Quick Access bar   Ribbon

Figure 5-1: The Live Mail window in action.

Folder pane   Message list   Reading pane   Status bar

These controls include

✦ **Ribbon:** From this standard Windows Ribbon — also used in other Windows Essentials applications, as well as the Office 2013 suite — click a tab to display the items in that group, and then click a menu item to perform that action.

✦ **Quick Access bar:** Click a Quick Access bar button to perform the same function as the corresponding Ribbon button — by default, you can choose New Message, Reply, and Update All. You can customize the bar by adding and removing buttons. Just click the down arrow button at the right side of the bar and then click the buttons that you want to add from the drop-down menu, as shown in Figure 5-2. (A check mark appears next to the active buttons.) Conversely, to remove a toolbar button, click the button name in the menu to banish the check mark.

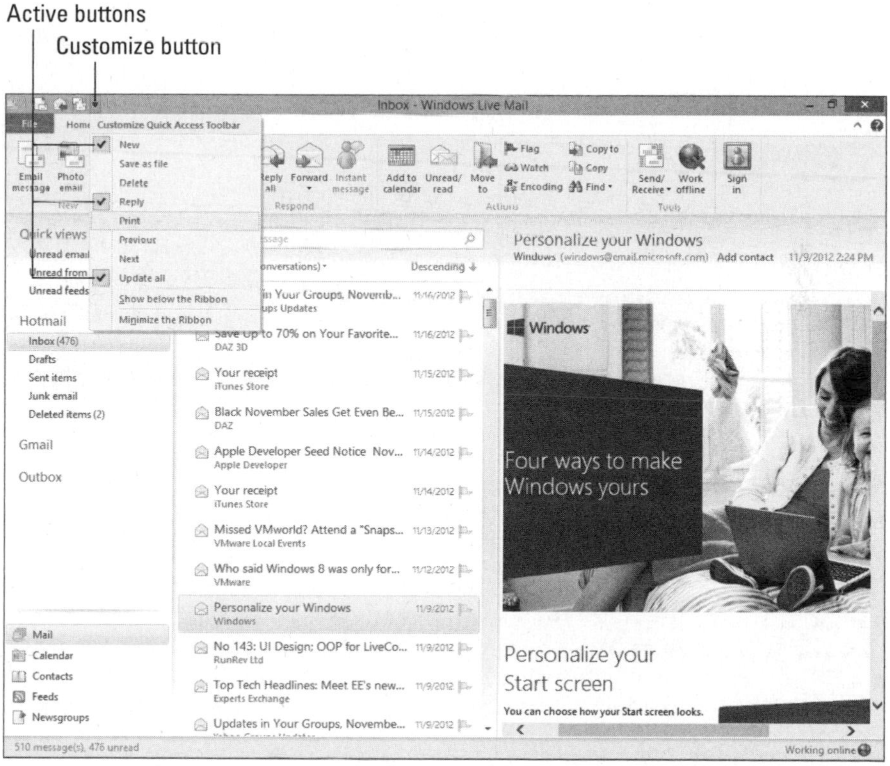

Active buttons

Customize button

Figure 5-2: Make changes to the Windows Live Mail Quick Access bar here.

Book III Chapter 5

Harnessing Your E-Mail

✦ **Folder pane:** Click any storage folder link in the tree display to display the contents of that folder. You can also switch between e-mail accounts as well as display your unread e-mail in the blink of an eye by clicking a Quick View entry in the Folder pane.

To add a new folder to the Folder list, right-click any folder in the list and then choose New Folder from the pop-up menu that appears. Live Mail displays the Create Folder dialog box (see Figure 5-3), where you can type a name for your new folder and select the existing folder that will act as its "parent." Click OK, and the new folder appears in the Folder list.

Create Folder ☒

Folder name:

	OK
	Cancel

Select the folder in which to create the new folder:

Hotmail
  Inbox
  Drafts
  Sent items
· Junk email
  Deleted items
    POP

Gmail
  Inbox
  [Gmail]
    All Mail

Figure 5-3:
Add a new
folder to the
Folder list.

✦ **Message list:** Messages in the selected folder are displayed in list form in the Message list.

✦ **Reading pane:** Clicking a message in the Message list displays it in the Reading pane (without the hassle of opening the message in a separate window). After all, we are a people interested in convenience, are we not?

The Message list and Reading pane are highly configurable little beasties. Click the View tab on the Ribbon to display the window layout settings in the Layout group, and then click the Message List or Reading Pane buttons to display a pop-up menu (Figure 5-4). You can hide the Reading pane, or you can display it below or next to the Message list. You can also toggle the display of the messages in the Message list using one or two lines.

Figure 5-4:
Fix your
window
layout
"just so."

✦ **Status bar:** Last — and pretty much least — is our old friend, the humble Status bar. Here, you can see basic totals on the number of read and unread messages and also your online/offline status. (The program is typically offline if you're not connected to the Internet.) It also shows you when Windows Live Mail is sending and receiving mail. To display or hide the Status bar, click the View tab on the Ribbon and click the Status bar button in the Layout group.

You can easily adjust the size of any section of the Live Mail window: Move your mouse pointer over the divider bar that you want to move until it turns into opposing arrows and then drag to relocate the bar.

Setting Up Your Mailbox

Even the mightiest barrage of e-mail begins with a single step. Okay, two steps at first because you have to start Windows Live Mail initially — but then, mind you, you're down to a single step! I'm talking about adding at least one e-mail mailbox account to your Mail configuration because without a mailbox account, you get diddly-squat.

To create a mailbox account, follow these steps:

1. **Click the Accounts tab on the Ribbon.**

2. **Click the Email button to display the New Email Accounts wizard (Figure 5-5).**

No, it's not that Gandalf guy. Even the Dark Lords of Redmond couldn't afford that kind of talent. This is a simple, hard-working Windows Live Mail wizard.

Figure 5-5:
Creating
a new
account
with
zest and
panache.

[Screenshot: Windows Live Mail — Add your email accounts]

Add your email accounts

If you have a Windows Live ID, sign in now. If not, you can create one later.
Sign in to Windows Live

Email address:

someone@example.com

Get a Windows Live email address

Password:

☑ Remember this password

Display name for your sent messages:

Example: John Doe

☐ Make this my default email account
☐ Manually configure server settings

Most email accounts work with Windows Live Mail
including

Hotmail
Gmail
and many others.

Cancel   Next

3. **In the Add an E-mail Account window, type the e-mail address and password that your Internet service provider (ISP) gave you.**

Make sure that you're entering your *e-mail name* and *password,* which are not necessarily the same as your account logon name and password that you use to connect to the Internet. (If you don't have this information, contact your ISP's technical support or help desk and request it.)

4. **Type your name as you want it to be displayed when you send messages.**

Like Outlook 2013, Live Mail can almost always automatically configure your e-mail settings. However, if your ISP or network system administrator requires you to enter your incoming (POP3) server and outgoing (SMTP) server addresses, select the Manually Configure Server Settings check box. Check with your ISP for the steps you'll need to take.

If you have multiple accounts in Live Mail, you can specify this account as the default for sending and receiving mail. Just select the Set This Account as the Default Mail Account check box.

5. **Click Next.**

If verification was successful, the wizard displays a confirmation.

6. **Click Finish.**

   Your new e-mail account appears in the Folder pane. Note that the name of the account refers to the ISP through which the e-mail is received — Hotmail, for example, if you have a Hotmail account. If you've previously created folders within the account you've added, Live Mail may prompt you for permission to download the folders and the messages they contain.

You can change the ISP settings on an e-mail account at any time. Right-click the account in the list and then click the Properties button to display the Mail Properties dialog box, which you see in Figure 5-6. Most of this stuff never changes, but occasionally an ISP changes the name of an e-mail server or sets up new security measures that require a change on your end.

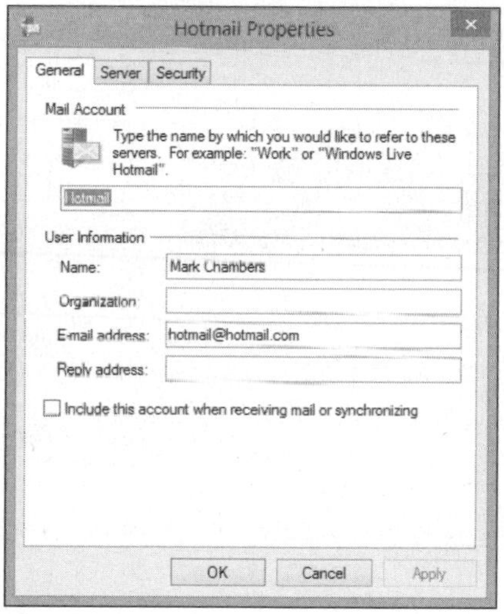

Figure 5-6:
Edit mail
account
properties
at any time.

> **Hotmail Properties**
>
> General | Server | Security
>
> **Mail Account**
>
> Type the name by which you would like to refer to these servers. For example: "Work" or "Windows Live Hotmail".
>
> Hotmail
>
> **User Information**
>
> Name: Mark Chambers
>
> Organization:
>
> E-mail address: hotmail@hotmail.com
>
> Reply address:
>
> ☐ Include this account when receiving mail or synchronizing
>
> OK | Cancel | Apply

The Three R's: Receiving, Reading, and Replying

Time to get to it! You've got mail! All the fun things (or tedium) that come along with paper snail mail are just the same as in the electronic world. Read along to see how similar they are.

Receiving e-mail

Time to check your e-mail? Windows Live Mail checks automatically each time you run the program, but you can always check manually by clicking the Update All button on the Quick Access bar (or the Send/Receive button on the Home tab). Your received e-mail appears in your Inbox, which you can display by clicking the Inbox header in the Folders pane, and new messages show up as bolded entries in the Message list.

Reading e-mail

To read an e-mail, just double-click a message to open it. (Unread messages display a closed envelope icon, while messages you've read display an open envelope icon.) Mail displays the message in its own, separate window (as shown in Figure 5-7), complete with a separate (smaller) Ribbon.

Figure 5-7:
Reading an
incoming
message.

If the Reading pane is active, you can scan a message by clicking it once in the Message list (or by using the up- and down-arrow keys to move through the Message list). As soon as you scan or read a message, it's marked as read, and the bolding on the message heading in the list disappears. (If you need to restore the Reading pane to its full glory, click the View tab on the Ribbon and click the Reading pane button.)

If you encounter a message from someone who's not in your Contacts list and you want to add that sender, right-click the message in the Message list and then choose Add Sender to Contacts from the pop-up menu that appears. Read more about the Contacts list in the upcoming section, "Working with Your Contacts."

Replying to and forwarding e-mail

To reply to a message, follow these steps:

1. **Click a message in the Message list to select it, and then click the Reply button on the Quick Access bar (or press Ctrl+R).**

   If you're reading an open message in its own window, click the Reply button on the window's Ribbon. You can also click the Reply All button to send your reply to others who also received the message (including those who were copied; more on that in a bit).

   A Reply window appears (feast on Figure 5-8) with the insertion cursor at the top of the message box. The text of the original message is included under the original header, and Live Mail has already filled in the To field with the name of the person who sent the original e-mail.

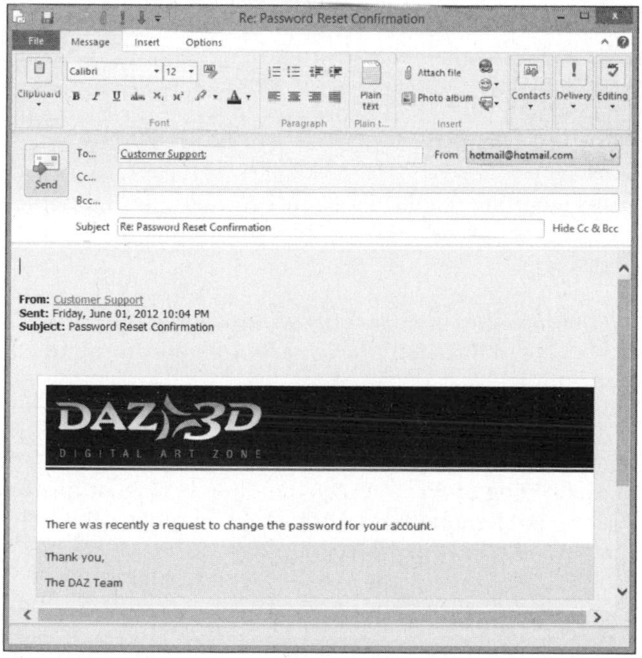

Figure 5-8:
Sometimes a simple reply works just fine.

2. **Although Mail has already inserted the prefix Re in front of the original subject line, you can click in the Subject box and type a new subject, if necessary.**

3. **Type your message in the message box.**

4. **Click Send.**

You can also choose to *forward* a message, allowing you to add a comment to the body of the original message before you send it to new recipients. To forward a message, click the Forward button rather than the Reply or Reply All button. Forwarding a message also sends any attachments that accompanied the original message, which doesn't happen when you reply.

Messages you send are deposited in your Sent Items folder. You can peruse them at any time if your memory needs refreshing.

To Bcc, or not to Bcc

When you want to reply to, forward, or even create a new message to more than one person — and you want recipients other than those available from Reply All, if applicable — use the carbon (Cc) or blind carbon (Bcc) copy feature.

If you send standard Cc copies of your message, each recipient can see who else received the message — and even add the e-mail addresses of the other folks to their Windows Contacts lists. A *Bcc* is a message sent to more than one person in which the e-mail addresses of some recipients are intentionally hidden.

In some cases, sending regular Cc copies can be a serious breach of privacy. Other than the extra privacy, Bcc addresses are handled in the same manner as Cc addresses.

One look at the new message or reply windows, though, and it's apparent that Windows Live Mail doesn't have carbon copies or blind carbon copies. Tell me that's not true!

Carbon dating

Talk about your carbon footprint. The "carbon" part of Cc and Bcc harkens back to the previous millennium, when people used typewriters (look it up) and paper with sheets of carbon paper between to create copies. Much less noxious than a ditto machine (look that up, too).

All is not lost. Live Mail does indeed offer Cc and Bcc features. To expose the Cc/Bcc Easter egg while creating or replying to a message, click the Show Cc & Bcc link at the right side of the Subject box. There they are! (You'll have to click the link each time you need to use the Cc or Bcc feature.)

Here's how simple it is to send a Cc or Bcc message:

1. **Click the Show Cc & Bcc link (if necessary), click in the Cc or Bcc box, as appropriate, and then type recipients' addresses manually. (Note that you must separate recipient names with a semicolon.)**

Alternatively, click the Cc or Bcc button (next to the corresponding text fields) to choose names from your Windows Contacts list (as shown in Figure 5-9). Then click OK to return to the message window.

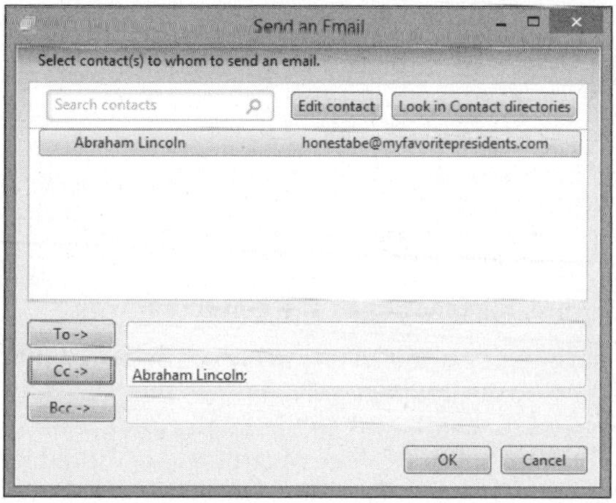

Figure 5-9:
Extract addresses from your Contacts list.

2. **Click in the message box (if necessary) and type the contents of your message.**

3. **When you're ready to send your message, click the Send button to usher it on its way immediately (or press Alt+S from the keyboard).**

E-mail housekeeping: Deleting and filing

No one likes housework. (Well, maybe some people.) Still, if you don't keep up on keeping things tidy, piles of stuff, well, pile up. Same thing applies to e-mail, which can multiply faster than coat hangers in the hall closet. Take a minute here and there to file away important messages as well as throw away the chaff.

To delete a message that you no longer need from any folder, click the message in the Message list and then press Delete or click the Delete button on the Ribbon. The messages are deposited in your Deleted Items folder and can be retrieved, if necessary.

To move a message from one folder to another, click the folder where the message currently resides, and then drag the message icon from the Message list to the new folder.

Creating and Sending E-Mail

Time to create a new e-mail (that is, not reply to or forward a message that came to to you). Regardless of whether your message is going to someone who's in your Contacts list or not (more on that in a bit), it's a snap.

After you've created a message, it appears in your Outbox in the Folder list at the left of the window.

1. **Click the New button on the Quick Access bar. (Or simply press Ctrl+N.)**

Live Mail opens the New Message window, which you see in Figure 5-10.

2. **Click in the To box and then type the e-mail address.**

You can add carbon copy and blind carbon copy recipients by clicking in the Cc and Bcc boxes, respectively. If these fields aren't there, then click the Show Cc & Bcc link next to the Subject line. Read all about this earlier in "To Bcc, or not Bcc." And, of course, you could add the recipient name from your Contacts list; more on that in a bit.

3. **Click in the Subject field, type the subject for this message, and then press Tab to move to the message editing box.**

4. **Type the text of your message; if it's set as an HTML message, apply any formatting you want to the text.**

Read more about this in the section, "Formatting a message."

5. **Ready to ship it? You have the same options available as you have when replying to a message:**

- Click Send to send it immediately.

- Click the File tab on the New Message window Ribbon and click Save (or press Ctrl+S) to save it in your Drafts folder. (Read about drafts in "Creating and sending a draft.")

- Click the File tab on the New Message window Ribbon and click Save as File. Mail displays the Save Message As dialog box, where you can select the destination and name for the file.

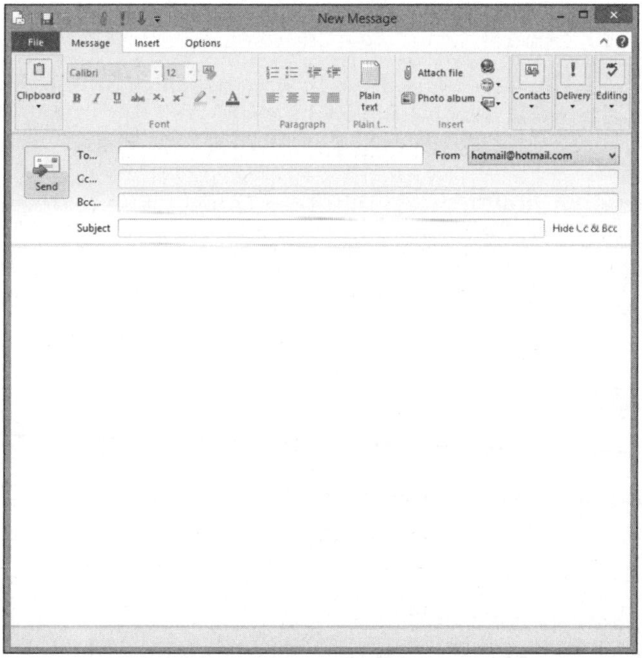

Figure 5-10:
Say, isn't that a New Message window?

Formatting a message

To spice up your message text, click and drag across it (*select* it) and then apply formatting (such as bold or italic) from the Font section of the Message tab. You can also add attachments from the Message tab. (Use the procedure that I outline in the upcoming section "Sending and Receiving File Attachments.")

If the Font section of the Message tab is disabled, you're writing your e-mail message in plain text. Click the Rich Text (HTML) button on the Message tab, and all your formatting controls are then available. However, I'm personally not a big fan of rich text messages: Not all e-mail programs handle Rich

Text (HTML) messages properly, especially older e-mail applications. Plus, rich text messages are much larger than plain text messages and can take longer to send and receive.

Creating and sending a draft

If you want to reply to or create a message but delay sending it, save the message in *draft* form.

1. **Reply to, forward, or create a message.**

2. **Click the File tab on the Ribbon, and then click Save (which automatically closes the New Message window).**

   The message appears in your Drafts folder.

3. **To send the draft message, click the Drafts folder to open it, double-click the message to open it, and then click Send.**

That's the nub of creating and sending a basic e-mail. Keep reading for the next level of e-mail wizardry.

Message tricks and tips

Here are a few more advanced things you can do in Windows Live Mail:

✦ **Add an attachment (or more than one).**

Find more on this topic in the upcoming section, "Sending and Receiving File Attachments."

✦ **Check the spelling in your message.**

a. *Select the text of your message.*

b. *Click the Spelling button on the Message tab (which carries the letters ABC and a blue check mark).*

   Live Mail underlines possible spelling errors automatically. If you get the urge to check for yourself and go the spell-check route, Windows Mail opens the dialog box shown in Figure 5-11.

   • *To substitute the boo-boo word (Not in Dictionary field) to the Change To suggestion:* Click the Change button.

   • *To substitute the wrong word to something in the Suggestions list:* Click the suggestion you want and then click the Change button. If you mangled the word several times in the same message, click the Change All button instead.

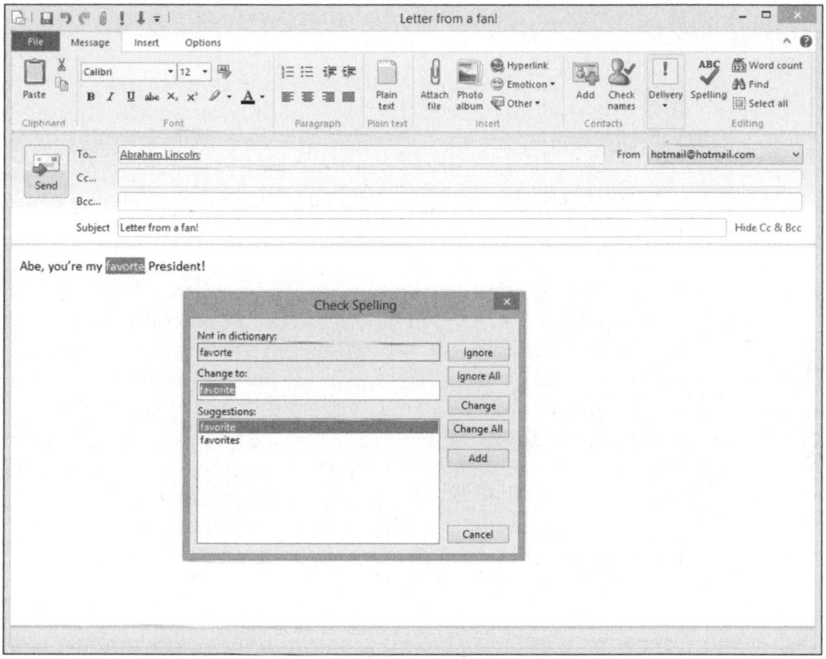

Letter from a fan!

File   Message   Insert   Options

Paste | Calibri 12 | B I U abe x₂ x² 🖉 A ▾ | ☰ ☰ 🛱 🛱 ☰ ☰ ☰ ☰ | Plain text | Attach file | Photo album | 🔗 Hyperlink 🙂 Emoticon ▾ 🔲 Other ▾ | Add | Check names | ! Delivery | ABC Spelling | 🗮 Word count 🔍 Find ☑ Select all
Clipboard | Font | Paragraph | Plain text | Insert | Contacts | Editing

Send | To... Abraham Lincoln; | From hotmail@hotmail.com
Cc...
Bcc...
Subject | Letter from a fan! | Hide Cc & Bcc

Abe, you're my favorte President!

Check Spelling

Not in dictionary:
favorte

Change to:
favorite

Suggestions:
favorite
favorites

Ignore
Ignore All
Change
Change All
Add
Cancel

Figure 5-11:
Speelling
iz ophten
sumwatt
himportunt.

Did you spell *thakamology* correctly? You can always choose to ignore the flag (click the Ignore button) or ignore all occurrences (click Ignore All) to avoid further unnecessary nagging during a spell check. If you use *thakamology* quite a bit in your messages — and who doesn't? — click Add to add the word to the Windows Live Mail dictionary, and the program shan't bother you again.

✦ **Flag as high importance.** If the message deserves immediate attention — "Help, Mom, I'm stuck in Vienna with no cash!" — click High Importance on the Message tab.

This step doesn't send the message any faster, nor does it travel with any extra gusto. However, it shows up with a priority flag in the recipient's e-mail application.

✦ **Verify that a message has been read.** Click the Message tab, and then click the Read Receipt check box to enable it.

Note: This *does not guarantee* that you receive notice when the message has been read. The recipient is prompted for confirmation beforehand, so a read receipt can be canceled.

Sending and Receiving File Attachments

Why limit your messages to a silly message box? Break out of the box with file attachments! Just about any type of file can be attached to a message, and you can save that file to your hard drive from within the read message window. (Yes, that includes most files sent to you by your friends with those funky Macintosh and Linux computers, as well as all sorts of tablet and smartphone devices!)

Unfortunately, some file attachments that you might receive should be *immediately* cast out. I'm speaking, naturally, about e-mail viruses and macros with a homicidal bent, which are becoming as common these days as the generic junk mail messages you receive every day. Luckily, you can use an antivirus program like avast! Free Antivirus (www.avast.com/) that automatically scans attachments for any dangerous programs before you use them. *Never open an attachment without proper antivirus protection!* That includes attached files that you receive from folks whom you know and trust! (They could unknowingly be hosting a virus themselves — some of these bugs are even smart enough to replicate themselves by enclosing copies of themselves in innocuous-looking messages!)

With that stern admonishment in mind, here's how you can add an attachment to your outgoing message:

1. **Reply to a message or compose a new message.**

2. **Click the Attach File button on the Message tab to display the Open dialog box, as shown in Figure 5-12.**

3. **Navigate to the location of the file(s) you want to attach; then click the first filename to select it.**

   To add more than one file from the same folder, hold down the Ctrl key while you click.

4. **Click the Open button to add the files to the message.**

   Mail displays attached files in the Attach box within the header area of the message dialog box.

When you receive an e-mail message with an attachment, a paper clip icon is displayed next to the message entry in the Message list.

Figure 5-12:
Attaching a file to your message.

To download an attachment from an incoming message

1. **Right-click the file attachment in the header.**

2. **Choose Save As to select a spot on your system to store the file.**

3. **Navigate to the desired location and click Save.**

You can't send the kitchen sink as an e-mail attachment, so don't get carried away trying to send hundreds of photos or the like. It takes a very long time to download big files over a dial-up connection — yes, a number of folks still use telephone modems — and all Internet service providers limit the size of a message and all its attachments. This limit usually rejects any message over 20MB or so in total size. (The exact limit is determined by both your Internet e-mail server and the recipient's e-mail server.) Therefore, I recommend limiting your total attachment size to 10MB or less. You can easily tell when your attachments are too doggone big: Either your ISP's mail server or the recipient's mail server sends you an error message saying that your original e-mail is undeliverable.

Spam: 1 Hate 1t — Truly 1 Do!

Is there anyone on the planet who actually *opens* a message promising instant hair regrowth? Or a once-in-a-lifetime investment opportunity?

**Book III
Chapter 5**

Harnessing Your
E-Mail

Or some sort of illicit physical offer that you neither want nor need? Why does junk mail exist? Aren't these spam-slingers just wasting their time?

Good questions, all. For some reason, though, junk mail continues to accumulate on your Internet doorstep. Not even the government can stop it — something about that pesky Bill of Rights — but you can sure doggone reduce the flow of spam to a trickle by using the mail-blocking feature within Windows Live Mail.

When you receive a junk mail message from someone, right-click it in the Message list and then choose Junk E-Mail⇨Add Sender to Blocked Sender List from the pop-up menu that appears. Live Mail displays a confirmation dialog box to let you know that the offending sender has been added to your Blocked Sender list and that the message has been moved to your Junk E-Mail folder.

Use this method to block all messages from a specific e-mail address. Any mail you receive from that source is then dumped directly into your Deleted Items folder. (You can still look at it there, of course, just to verify that the proper trash was picked up.)

However, nefarious junk mail villains can still get around a blocked-sender list by changing their sending addresses: For example, `imajerk@justan example.com` suddenly becomes `hahastillhere@justanexample.com` or something similar.

Does this mean that you have to continue to suffer? Not in the least, good Internet citizen! You can also block an entire *domain name,* which is the part of an e-mail address that follows the @ sign, like `spamtwit.com` in `bonehead@spamtwit.com`. That way, no matter which silly username they try, Live Mail still throws straight into the trash anything they send. To block an entire domain name, just right-click the offending message in the Message list and choose Junk E-Mail⇨Add Sender's Domain to Blocked Sender List, to knock them out completely.

If you add an address or an entire domain to your blocked list by accident, you can return that address or domain to good standing. Click the Junk E-Mail folder in the Folder pane to display its contents in the Message list. Then right-click the message and choose Junk E-mail⇨Add Sender to Safe Sender List. To restore the message to your inbox, right-click the message and choose Junk E-Mail⇨Mark as Not Junk. Mail whisks the forgiven message back to the Inbox automatically.

If you get a message from an obvious spam tycoon who includes a line about how you can oh-so-conveniently "unsubscribe" from his mailing list, *don't do it!* This scam is designed to verify that your e-mail address is valid; if you unsubscribe, you end up with a regular tidal wave of junk mail. Better to add his e-mail address (or the entire domain) to the Blocked list.

Working with Your Contacts

The Contacts list in Live Mail is usually all most folks need for 99 percent of their workdays. I explain earlier in this chapter how you can add contacts by simply right-clicking the author's e-mail address in a message; that's the most common action to take.

However, you can reach the Windows Contacts list proper from within Live Mail. Just click the Contacts button at the lower left of the window, and the Windows Live Contacts window appears (behold Figure 5-13).

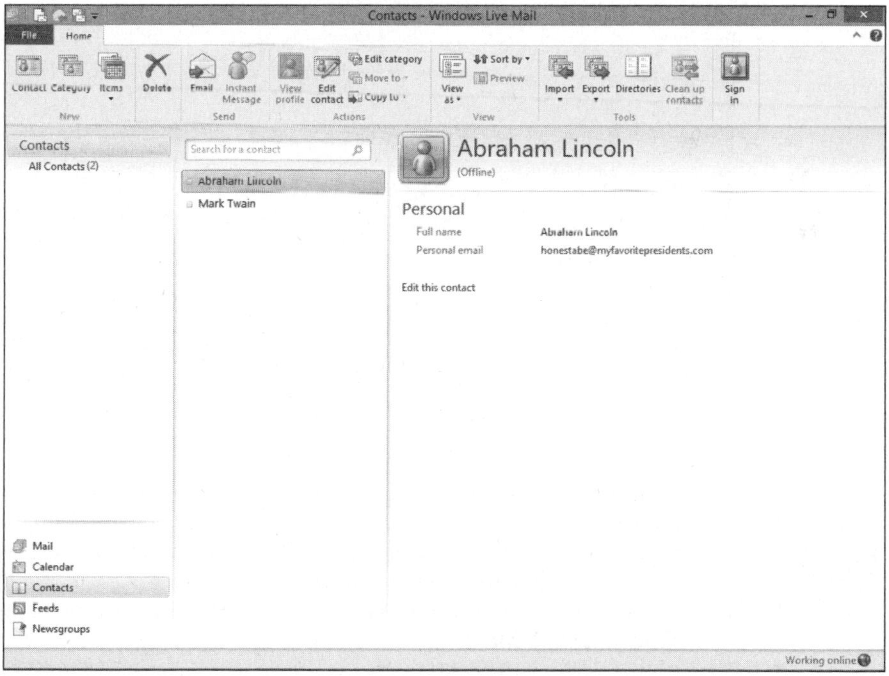

Figure 5-13: Feel free to open the Windows Contacts list from within Mail.

Book III
Chapter 5

Harnessing Your E-Mail

From this window, you can

✦ **Create a new contact.** Click the Contact button on the Home tab; the Contact list displays the Add a Contact dialog box, as shown in Figure 5-14. Click in each field that you need to complete to add the contact's information. To display additional fields for categories (like Personal and Work information), click the corresponding button in the list on the left. To save your new contact, click the Add Contact button.

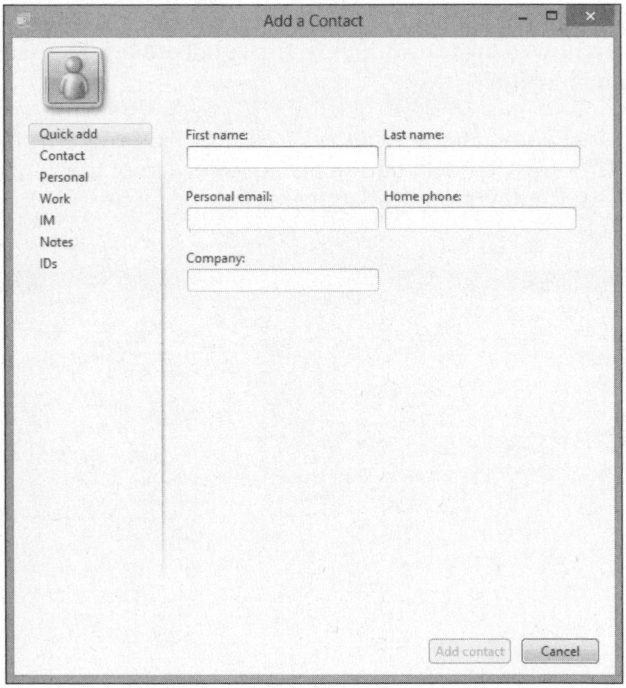

Figure 5-14:
Add a new
contact.

✦ **Edit an existing contact.** Click the contact name that you want to edit in the list, and then click Edit Contact from the pop-up menu that appears to display the Edit Contact dialog box, which includes all the fields you originally saw when you created the contact. You can click in any field to either change existing data or add new information. To save your changes, click Save.

✦ **Send an e-mail message.** Click the contact name that you want to edit in the list, and then click New E-Mail on the pop-up menu. You return to the Windows Live Mail window, where you find a New Message window (already addressed to the contact, naturally).

✦ **Import contact data.** Import vCard information for a contact. A *vCard* is a small text file that contains all the contact information for one or more people in a standard format that you can pass around to others like a virtual business *Card.* (Cute, eh?) To import, click Import on the Home tab and then click the correct format from the pop-up menu; for example, vCards use vCard (VCF file) format. Windows prompts you for the location of the import file.

Windows Live Mail can also import contacts stored in a Windows Address Book format file (which ends in the .wab extension) and a simple list of comma-separated values (ending in the .csv extension).

✦ **Export a vCard file.** To export one or more contacts in vCard format, select the contact record (or records) that you want to export and then click the Export button on the Home tab. From the pop-up menu that appears, choose Business Card (.VCF), and then navigate to the spot where you want to save the file. Click OK to create the vCard file, which you can then send as an attachment in e-mail messages or place on your website for others to download.

Book IV
PC Troubleshooting and Maintenance

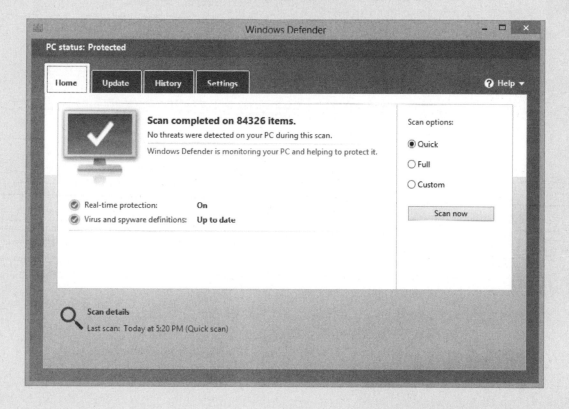

Contents at a Glance

Chapter 1: Easy PC Troubleshooting

In This Chapter

- ✔ Taking a moment to relax
- ✔ Troubleshooting your hardware and software
- ✔ Using System Recovery options
- ✔ Reinstalling Windows 8
- ✔ Locating troubleshooting help

I *hate* my Rubik's cube. I've never been able to solve the silly thing, and it just sits on my desk, taunting me and driving me to distraction until I grab it and make another futile attempt to match up all those squares. (Perhaps I'm in need of cube therapy.) What really gets me, though, is how my 21-year-old daughter can pick up that same cube, spend 45 seconds turning it in some wizard way, and then drop the solved puzzle and move on to something different. Geez! Why is such a difficult thing so easy for some people to do?

Troubleshooting Windows 8 has the same frustrating effect on most PC owners. You sit, staring at the keyboard and wondering why your operating system no longer works right and how you can fix it. Often, the solution is to call a friend or family member who can help — or, in the worst case, pack up the entire heap and take it to a computer shop where technotypes smile that mysterious little smile and fix your problem in 45 seconds. And then charge you an arm and a leg.

This chapter is here to help *you* tackle your Windows 8 troubleshooting puzzle. It might take more than 45 seconds, but you'll feel an enormous sense of accomplishment. Plus you might avoid lightening your wallet.

Relax and Breathe Easy

Here's the first step in Mark's Troubleshooting Procedure: When the going gets tough, the techs relax. That's right, I said *relax*. Even though Windows 8 — or your PC in general — is acting crazy, keep these important points in mind:

✦ **Never blame yourself.** Even the most nimble-fingered computer programmer or hardware technician can make a mistake. (Heck, I've heard
that even His Billness makes them every so often.) Accidents eventually happen — and, as with poorly written software or viruses, the fault
might not even be yours anyway. Don't treat yourself to a guilt trip.

✦ **Remember your backup.** As long as you take my advice throughout this
book (ahem! *back up your data!*), you won't lose your life's work — or
even last week's grocery list.

✦ **This, too, shall pass.** Even when hardware and software fail, you *can* find
the problem. Remember that the problem is only temporary — and certainly not unsolvable. (Not even my Rubik's cube is impossible to solve.)
You *can* get your PC back.

✦ **Help is available.** Besides friends and family, PC user group members,
and resources you can find on the Internet, you can always turn to the
tech experts at your local computer store for professional help at a
price. (But wouldn't it feel gratifying if you could fix it yourself?)

Yes, a Windows Remote Assistance option is available from the
Windows 8 Start screen — this feature allows a trusted friend or family
member to take remote control of your PC to help fix the problem.
However, remember these two caveats: First, the person to whom you
give remote control over your entire computer had better be *doggone*
trustworthy, so this option isn't the one to explore if a neighbor's mis-
chievous kid says, "I can fix that, easy." Also, if Windows 8 is the cause
of the problem (especially if your network is down or you can't get an
Internet connection), Remote Assistance isn't likely to work anyway.
With that said, if you have a close friend who's also a technowizard,
you can start a Remote Assistance session from the Charms bar: Click
Search, click Settings, and type **Remote** in the Search box. Click the
Invite Someone to Connect to Your PC and Help You, or click Offer to
Help Someone Else button in the Search results pane to display the
Windows Remote Assistance wizard.

And, a final tip while you're preparing to troubleshoot:

✦ **Your PC is *not* against you.** The troubleshooting process is *not* a battle
between you, your hardware, and your software. Many folks tell me that
they find it quite easy to personalize the anger they feel and direct it
toward that inanimate hunk of metal, plastic, and silicon. Stay calm, and
remember this important Mark's Maxim:

**Don't take out your frustration on your PC (no matter how uncoopera-
tive it seems).**™

To illustrate this last point, here's an honest-to-goodness true story that I love to tell. In the days of DOS, before Plug and Play or automatic configurations within Windows, adding a Small Computer System Interface (SCSI) adapter card and even just one SCSI device to your PC was a feat on the order of Hercules cleaning the Augean stables. An old friend of mine — who was quite handy with a screwdriver and normally well versed in PC hardware — spent more than *six continuous hours* attempting to install a used SCSI card and a SCSI hard drive in his 386 PC. He didn't curse, and he didn't scream. I'll never forget the look of utter peace on his face when he good-naturedly clamped the recalcitrant card in his metal vise and proceeded to melt the SCSI adapter with his portable torch.

He uses Windows these days, of course — but he never has forgiven the SCSI interface standard.

The Troubleshooting Process, Step by Step

It's time for the star of our show: Mark's Step-by-Step Windows 8 Troubleshooting Procedure! Note that this process doesn't center completely on software because it's often hard to tell at the beginning whether the problem at hand is caused by Windows 8 or by your PC's hardware.

Follow these steps:

1. **Simply shut down Windows 8.**

Many folks often don't have to move past this first step. Believe it or not, a simple shutdown solves a good 25 percent of the temporary glitches you might encounter, such as a frozen mouse or a locked-up PC resulting from a power failure. Shutting down works because it resets all your PC's hardware — and Windows 8 itself — and returns everything to normal. (By the way, if you can't reach the Start screen or the Power button on the Settings charm because your PC is locked up tight or the mouse doesn't move anymore, you have every right to get tough with your PC. First, try delivering the classic Windows "Three Finger Salute" by pressing the Ctrl+Alt+Del keys simultaneously, which displays a menu that includes commands for signing out and the Task Manager. If that doesn't work, it's time to get really ugly: Press and hold your power button until your PC turns itself off. Don't unplug your PC directly — always press and hold the power button instead!)

Always check for hard drive errors after you're forced to shut down Windows 8 by simply turning off your PC. For instructions on how to scan your drives for errors, see Chapter 2 of this minibook.

2. **If you restart your PC and the problem continues, double-check all cables leading to your PC.**

Yes, I know this sounds ridiculous, but I'll bet you your next paycheck that they do this step on nuclear submarines, too. You might not have problems with your AC power cord, for example, but it's quite easy to accidentally unplug other connectors from your PC — like your keyboard or network or external devices, such as your modem and printer. If you recently moved your PC or bumped against it, loose connections are prime suspects for all sorts of mischief.

If you just replaced a cable and one of your peripherals (like a printer) is now an expensive doorstop (or your network suddenly no longer recognizes your PC), try a spare cable that you know works. Although bad cables are rare, they do happen. (Bad Ethernet cables have been known to cause insomnia.)

3. **If all your cables are shipshape, your next mission is to sit — and *think*.**

Take a moment to consider any software or hardware you recently installed that might be causing (or contributing to) the problem. I always install new hardware or software one piece at a time because then I can easily tell which new addition is wreaking havoc. A PC that was originally chugging along nicely can suddenly turn rogue with one seemingly innocent change. (Note that this also includes any program or operating system updates, patches, or upgrades you might have just applied.)

I also use System Restore points liberally when installing new stuff. Find more on the System Restore utility in Chapter 2 of this minibook.

4. **Still no go? Time to shut down and remove any offending external devices — such as an external hard drive that's dead in the water — to see whether your PC suddenly returns to normal.**

If so, that peripheral is your prime suspect, so try it on another PC to determine whether the device is still working. Also try using another cable. If the peripheral works fine on another PC, your problem lies in either the device driver or the device configuration that you set up in Windows 8. Check the manual for the device, reinstall the device driver (make sure to visit the manufacturer's website for the latest driver first), and — if all else fails — contact the manufacturer's technical support team.

5. **Uninstall any programs that are misbehaving or locking up Windows 8 and then reinstall them.**

   After you reinstall — but *before* you apply a patch or an upgrade — try using the application to see whether it still exhibits the problem. If not, the software developer has (as Desi so eloquently put it) "some 'splainin' to do." Visit the developer's website and check for information about compatibility, especially with Windows 8 and Service Pack patches, which often wreak havoc on unprepared software.

6. **If you recently made changes in the Control Panel, the System Properties dialog box, or any networking dialog boxes, take a moment to revisit those settings and verify that they're still correct.**

   Unfortunately, anyone can easily and accidentally change a setting within one of the Control Panel screens. To make sure that you don't disturb something, just click Cancel if everything looks okay.

7. **If you're still having problems, check your hard drives (see Figure 1-1).**

   Use the procedure I demonstrate in Chapter 2 of this minibook to verify that your drives are free from disk errors.

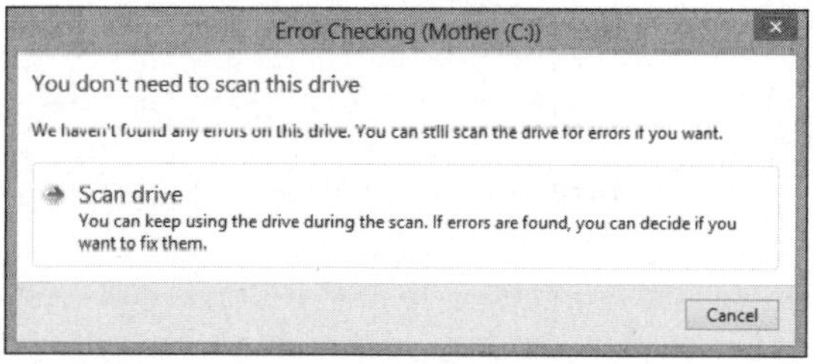

Figure 1-1: Check your hard drive often for errors.

8. **Scan your hard drives and any removable disks.**

   I talk about antivirus software throughout this book; on all of my Windows 8 machines, I use avast! Antivirus Home Edition, from AVAST Software (www.avast.com/), as shown in Figure 1-2.

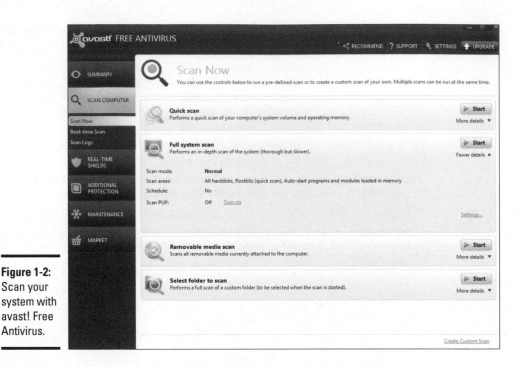

Figure 1-2:
Scan your
system with
avast! Free
Antivirus.

Each time you run a scan, take a second to make sure that you're using the latest antivirus signature data file from the developer's website. (If you're using avast!, the program automatically checks for updated virus data files.)

9. **Verify that you're still connected to and receiving packets from your home or office network — or, if you're using a broadband connection, your cable modem or digital subscriber line (DSL):**

   a. *From the Charms bar, click Search and click Settings; then type Network into the Search box. Click the Network and Sharing Center button in the Search results pane.*

   b. *Check to make sure that each connection is displayed, without any red X marks, which indicate disabled broken connections.*

   If your network is down, Windows 8 has a nasty habit of slowing to a crawl when you open files or use Windows Explorer — and many applications that expect a network connection as their divine right can lock up tighter than Fort Knox. Don't forget to berate your network administrator or tech staff — boy, they just *love* it when you do that!

10. **If you're using a shareware or freeware screen saver, realize that a slew of badly written screen savers, readily available for download on the Internet, can take Windows 8 on a permanent vacation.**

    To test whether your favorite Care Bears screen saver is causing those intermittent lockups, follow these steps:

    a. *Right-click your Desktop, choose Personalize, and then click the Screen Saver link.*

    b. *Choose None and then click OK.*

    c. *Reboot and use your PC for a day without any screen saver — or choose one of the Windows 8 screen savers provided by Microsoft, which are proved stable.*

11. **Check whether another user with Administrator access might have changed the write-protect status of your applications or your documents.**

    This step is for those who share a PC with other users by taking advantage of the multiuser features built in to Windows 8.

    This is usually the case when Word complains that it doesn't have the rights to open a document you were working on yesterday. Have a user with an Administrator account log in and verify the permissions on your applications and document files. (I tell you more about this topic in Book II, Chapter 4.)

12. **Even if you can boot in Safe mode, first try the Windows 8 System Configuration utility (see Figure 1-3), which can help you diagnose where the trouble lies in your boot process.**

    a. *To display the settings from the Charms bar, click the Search button and click Apps, and then type **msconfig** into the Search box. Click the System Configuration button that appears in the Search results pane to display the System Configuration utility.*

    Note that you can try a *Diagnostic Startup* (which offers more functionality than Safe mode), or you can choose *Selective Startup* and specify which boot steps to enable.

    b. *After you choose your boot options, click OK and then reboot Windows 8.*

**Book IV
Chapter 1**

Easy PC
Troubleshooting

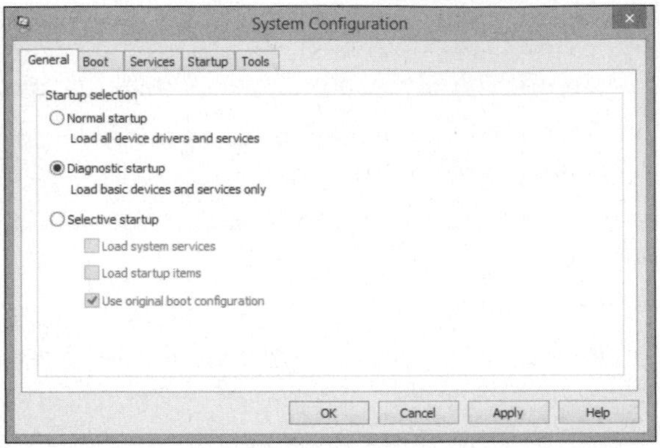

Figure 1-3:
Try a selective startup with the System Configuration utility.

To disable just one startup program, click the Startup tab and click the Open Task Manager link, which displays the Task Manager's Startup pane. Right-click the offending application and choose Disable. Then it's a breeze to troubleshoot problems you encounter when installing new software that loads automatically during the boot process. You can repeat this process to disable more than one startup item. If Windows 8 suddenly boots correctly and your problem appears to be solved, immediately uninstall the program that you last disabled and contact the software developer's technical support.

13. **If you're still with me, it's time to get serious with your hardware and display Device Manager (see Figure 1-4), as I describe in Chapter 2 of this minibook.**

Make sure that Windows 8 hasn't flagged any of your hardware devices as either disabled or not working; if a component is flagged with an exclamation point, a little investigation might well turn up the solution to the problem.

At this point, you've exhausted most of the easier troubleshooting chores and fixes you can perform. It's time to get drastic.

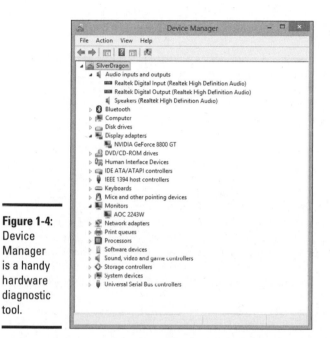

Figure 1-4:
Device
Manager
is a handy
hardware
diagnostic
tool.

Safe mode to the rescue

If your PC is locking up before you even have a chance to click anything on the Start screen (or it freezes before your Start screen even appears), it becomes nearly impossible to get far enough to fix anything. Although you can boot from the Windows 8 installation disc, your choices are severely limited. Even when you know what needs to be done (like a specific driver file needs to be deleted or a device needs removed in Device Manager), the old witticism remains true: "You can't get there from here."

Luckily, Windows 8 maintains an old friend from the days of Windows 95 and Windows 98:

Safe mode, the alternative boot-up mode where device drivers are disabled (generally a very good thing if your PC is experiencing bad karma) and you again have access to Windows Explorer and basic Windows 8 functionality. Although Safe mode isn't always available — sometimes Windows 8 is so badly obfuscated that even Safe mode doesn't work — it's a valuable addition to your troubleshooting toolbox.

If your PC is in the midst of a breakdown and you can't reach Windows, find in-depth Safe mode coverage in Chapter 2 of this minibook.

Drastic Things That You Won't Do Often

As I say at the beginning of this minibook, Windows 8 (like Windows 7 and Vista before it) is much harder to crash than previous versions of Windows. In fact, it even attempts to automatically fix system files that are corrupted by other programs, by using the *Windows File Protection* feature. However, the folks in Redmond can do only so much to armor-plate their favorite son. You might end up with a PC that makes even the most dedicated PC technicians shake their heads in defeat — and if that happens, it's time to read this section.

Using System Recovery Options

As I mention earlier in this chapter, I take full advantage of the Windows 8 System Restore utility. But if your PC is in truly bad shape and you can't run the System Restore program, your next step is likely to run the Windows 8 *System Recovery Options,* which you can activate from your Windows 8 installation DVD, from the PC Settings screen, or during the boot cycle:

✦ If your computer has System Recovery Options preinstalled — as many PCs from major manufacturers do — it's one of the options available when you press and hold F8 just before Windows 8 begins loading (before you see the Windows logo).

✦ If you can display the Charms bar, click the Settings button and click the Change PC Settings link to display the PC Settings screen. Click General in the list at the left and then click the Restart Now button in the Advanced Startup section in the right pane.

✦ If the System Recovery Options weren't preinstalled on your PC, you need to use your Windows 8 Installation disc. Load the disc in your DVD drive and reboot, and then press any key during the boot process to start Windows 8 from the DVD.

Click Troubleshoot and click Advanced Options to display your System Recovery options. Besides System Restore, they include

✦ **Automatic Repair:** A basic replacement of critical system files, Startup Repair is helpful if the data on your PC's hard drive was damaged by viruses or your Windows 8 system files have been corrupted by a disk error. Always try Automatic Repair before you turn to System Image Recovery (or the procedures in the next section).

✦ **System Image Recovery:** You can choose to restore your entire hard drive from a backup image, as I discuss in Chapter 2 of this minibook.

✦ **Command Prompt:** For those familiar with the DOS command line, you can perform simple file management and run command-line programs.

✦ **Startup Settings:** If you need to restart your PC in Safe mode, click the Startup Settings button and then select Restart.

Refreshing, resetting, and reinstalling

If your entire operating system is in serious jeopardy — that is, it doesn't boot or it locks up every single time you use it as soon as your mouse cursor appears — you can *refresh* Windows (without losing any of your files) or *reset* your entire PC (which deletes all your files and restores most of the Windows 8 system files). You can also choose to fully reinstall Windows 8 directly from the installation disc.

If you created a System Image file (*before* your system began exhibiting problems), you should always use the System Image Recovery feature on the Advanced Options screen to completely restore your PC before turning to any of these more drastic options. Your System Image file can restore your PC to *exactly* the way it was — a refresh, reset, or reinstall always requires some amount of work on your part to bring things back to normal.

Naturally, you'll want to try refreshing Windows 8 first. (If you think that sounds somewhat absurd at first, so do I.) With a simple refresh, Windows keeps your documents, programs, and apps, but *not* any settings — this means you'll likely need to reconfigure your programs when Windows is running again. Unfortunately, not every critical Windows 8 problem can be solved with a refresh — if your PC continues to display the same problems after a refresh, you'll have to consider resetting or reinstalling Windows 8.

The next step is a reset, which (as I mention above) essentially returns your PC to a "vanilla" Windows 8 system — you'll lose all of your personal files, apps, and programs, but resetting has a much higher chance of success in fixing a badly damaged Windows 8 installation. If that doesn't work, it's time to consider a full reinstall of Windows 8.

So-called learned people in the world swear up and down that you should never, *never* reinstall Windows. Mention such a drastic step to these self-appointed experts, and they immediately start whooping, "There's no reason to do it, and you might possibly launch a thermonuclear warhead at Nepal if you diddle with a single setting. Just suffer! After all, it's Windows 8 — enjoy the eye candy."

Well, good reader, I'm here to tell you the honest truth. You certainly *won't* be resetting or reinstalling Windows 8 every weekend, but only as a last resort (after you try the System Recovery Options, attempt to restore from your System Image backup, and consult with the techs at your local computer repair shop). However, in some situations (like the two I just mentioned), resetting or reinstalling your operating system might solve your problem.

Manually back up whatever personal files you can from your system before resetting or reinstalling Windows 8. (Perhaps use Safe mode, which I mention earlier in this chapter.)

If your PC came equipped with a System Restore disc, note that using a manufacturer's System Restore disc isn't the same as resetting or reinstalling Windows 8! When you use the manufacturer's System Restore disc, your hard drive is probably erased and reformatted and the hard drive restored to the exact condition it was in the first time you booted your PC. All your files, applications, and settings are gone, and you have to set up all your multiuser accounts as well! If there's no other way, and refreshing or resetting Windows 8 doesn't do the trick, please make certain that every file you want to save has been safely stored on a CD-R or DVD-R (or a much roomier external hard drive backup unit) before you use the System Restore disc.

If you received (or bought) a bona fide Windows 8 installation disc, you can also reinstall Windows directly from the disc. Follow the instructions that accompanied the disc to install Windows 8. You can choose to keep settings, personal files, and apps when prompted, or throw all caution to the wind and just keep your personal files. (Naturally, keeping just your personal files has a greater chance of fixing whatever's wrong because it may be a corrupted setting that's causing the trouble in the first place.)

If you reinstall, here are a few tricks that I want to mention first:

✦ **You need the same product key.** If Windows 8 came preinstalled on your PC, you should find the product key on an official-looking sticker somewhere on the PC's case.

✦ **You have to reactivate Windows 8.** Remember how you had to activate Windows 8 when you first installed it or first started your new PC? *Activation* is the Microsoft antipiracy protection scheme; luckily, the folks in Redmond have made allowances for catastrophe and allow you to reactivate a legitimate copy of Windows 8.

✦ **You lose all your System Restore points.** Of course, if you can't get to them, they don't do much good — but I wanted to mention the loss, anyway.

Once again, the best-laid plans of mice and trackballs (sorry about that) can go awry, but as long as you backed up your personal files and important documents, you *will* persevere (even if you have to format the drive, reinstall from scratch, and manually reload your files and applications)!

HELP!: Additional Troubleshooting Resources

If you have a Windows 8 troubleshooting question, you might be able to make a phone call to your local computer shop for a quick answer — even after the warranty expires — but most folks I know turn more often to the source. After all, Microsoft built the doggone thing.

In this final section, I discuss the three troubleshooting resources offered by Mother Microsoft. (And one option doesn't even require the Internet.)

The Windows 8 Help system

I show you how to use the Help system in the first chapter of Book II. (See, I told you I like to plan ahead.) But I also want to point out that the Microsoft Knowledge Base entries you find in Help (which, to no one's surprise, are pulled directly from the Microsoft Knowledge Base website) are particularly valuable when you're troubleshooting problems with Windows 8.

Microsoft tech support

Microsoft offers both online and telephone technical support, using real human beings. This type of support is probably the most valuable trouble-shooting resource around, along with the technical support you receive from the manufacturer when you buy your PC. Because all Microsoft products have different telephone support numbers, check your Windows 8 documentation for the proper number to call.

The Microsoft website

Of course, you can also always find Microsoft online (if you can still get online with the trouble you're encountering) at www.microsoft.com/. The Microsoft website is stuffed full of information, and each product typically has its own home page.

Chapter 2: Maintaining Windows 8

In This Chapter

✔ Scanning your hard drives for errors

✔ Defragmenting to speed up your PC

✔ Backing up your files in Windows 8

✔ Using System Restore

✔ Using Safe Mode in Windows 8

✔ Taking Windows Update for a ride

Maintenance. It's important, and you've got to do it — so why not make it *exciting?* Rather than consider it dull preventive care, think of the pit crew around an Indy car, and . . . well, on second thought, that might be a stretch. Anyway, you gotta do it.

You might not find this chapter overly exciting, but if you regularly follow the procedures you find here, I guarantee that you'll be happy with the performance and stability of your PC running Windows 8. And who knows? Maybe that Indy pit crew job will materialize someday. (Even if it doesn't, you'll have the smoothest-running PC on the block, and that counts for a lot.)

Device Manager: The Hardware Tool

The first stop on your maintenance tour is the Windows 8 Device Manager, which I recommend that you check at least once per month. *Device Manager* is essentially a status window that displays the operating status of each of the hardware devices in your PC as well as the peripherals connected to it. With one glance, you can see any hardware device that Windows has marked as a troublemaker, and locating trouble is the first step in solving it.

Now, don't panic at the idea of rooting around in your hardware. In fact, the idea of a hardware conflict is easy to understand. Just about every hardware device in your PC needs a unique pathway to be able to communicate with the CPU and other devices. For instance, your Ethernet network card must be able to send and receive data to and from the Internet without getting spurious stuff that's meant for your printer. (Imagine the fun you would have if your hard drive and your DVD-ROM drive kept exchanging data by accident. Harrumph.)

Luckily, Windows 8 does an excellent job of allocating hardware resources and routing data betwixt everything, especially if you're using Universal Serial Bus (USB) and other peripherals. However, sharing problems still crop up from time to time with older hardware that might not have up-to-date drivers. (A *driver* is a program that tells Windows 8 how to communicate with and use a specific hardware device.) Device Manager can not only display which devices are causing trouble, but also help you update the drivers for that device.

Follow these steps to use Device Manager in Windows 8:

1. **Display the Charms bar and click the Search icon, and then click the Settings button and type** Device Manager **into the Search box.**

2. **Click the Device Manager button that appears in the Search results pane to open the Device Manager window, which you see in Figure 2-1.**

   If a device in the Device Manager window is marked with a yellow exclamation point or a red check mark, it might be in conflict with another device, which in turn might also be marked by a yellow exclamation point.

   Disabling a device (in effect, turning it off temporarily) marks that device with a gray arrow pointing down — PC techs sometimes disable devices while troubleshooting to help them track down a problem. To enable a device again within Device Manager, right-click it and choose Enable from the menu that appears.

   If nothing is flagged, skip to Step 5 — Windows 8 has given your hardware the all-clear!

   You might also find helpful information in the Device Status display:

   • *If a Driver tab appears in the device's Properties dialog box:* Try updating your system with the latest driver for the device. (Go to Step 4.) This strategy often fixes things right away.

   • *If no Driver tab exists:* Scurry on to Step 5.

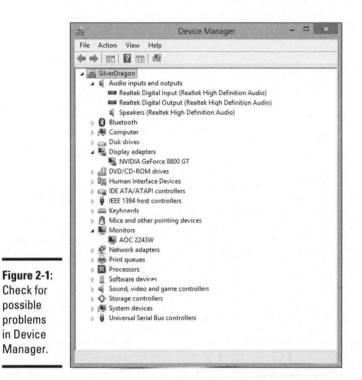

Figure 2-1:
Check for
possible
problems
in Device
Manager.

3. **To check for possible conflicts with a particular piece of hardware, right-click the marked device and then choose Properties from the pop-up menu that appears to display its settings.**

   Figure 2-2 shows properties for my graphics card.

4. **Click the Driver tab and then click the Update Driver button to run the Update Driver Software Wizard.**

   The wizard leads you through the process of checking for a new driver online or from a CD-ROM supplied by the manufacturer.

   Don't forget to check the manufacturer's website for drivers.

5. **Click OK to return to the Device Manager dialog box and then click the Close button in the Device Manager window.**

   If you made changes, Windows 8 prompts you for confirmation before rebooting your PC.

**Book IV
Chapter 2**

**Maintaining
Windows 8**

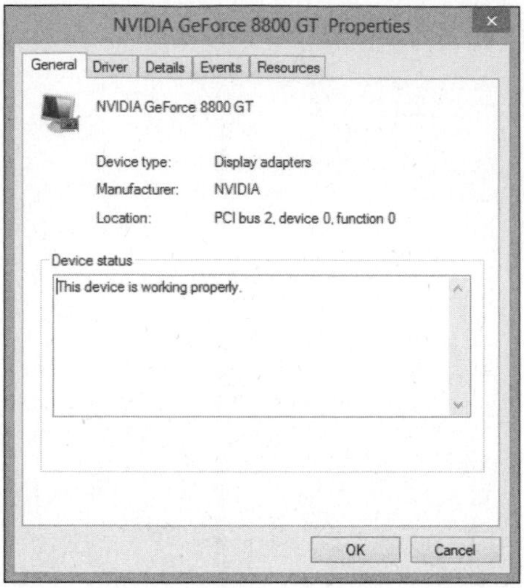

Figure 2-2:
Display the
settings for
a specific
hardware
device.

[Screenshot caption: NVIDIA GeForce 8800 GT Properties window showing tabs General, Driver, Details, Events, Resources. Device type: Display adapters; Manufacturer: NVIDIA; Location: PCI bus 2, device 0, function 0. Device status: This device is working properly.]

Checking Your Hard Drives in Windows 8

Let me clear up two common misconceptions concerning hard drives:

✦ **Hard drives don't malfunction.** Oh, yes, they do. Even if you've never
had a hard drive crash, you've likely heard about them. Even so, today's
hard drives are generally so reliable and so long lasting that folks often
forget. Hard drive errors can be *physical* (the drive's hardware malfunc-
tions) or *logical* (the error is in the format or the data stored on the
drive). If your PC is caught by a power failure and file corruption occurs,
you're the victim of a logical file error.

This misconception has grown even stronger with the growing popularity of SSDs (short for *solid-state drive*). An SSD has no moving parts —
in essence, it uses much the same technology as a USB flash drive —
so many PC owners figure that they don't need to back up the data
on their SSD because it will last "practically forever." Unfortunately,
an SSD still has an operational life, and when that drive fails, it still
takes your data with it — just like its older magnetic hard-drive
brethren.

✦ **Errors are immediately noticeable.** Most logical errors don't cause
your PC to crash, and they might not affect files that you're currently
using, so they often go unnoticed. (They share this trait with computer

viruses, which use stealth to hide themselves.) Over time, logical errors can cause real damage to your files and documents, so catching them quickly is vital.

For these reasons, scanning your PC's hard drives often (both internal and external) for potential problems is important. Windows 8 automatically scans each hard drive on your system on a regular basis, but you can manually scan a drive at any time — for example, immediately after a power failure or an AUI (my acronym —, it stands for *Accidental Unplugging Incident)*. Microsoft makes this task easy in Windows 8 by providing an error-checking feature that you can reach from a hard drive's Properties panel. (For you crotchety Windows old-timers, think *ScanDisk.*)

Follow these steps to scan a hard drive for errors:

1. **Click the Desktop tile on your Start screen, and click the File Explorer icon in the taskbar.**

2. **Click the Computer entry in the sidebar at the left of the Computer window.**

3. **Right-click the hard drive you want to scan, choose Properties from the pop-up menu that appears, and then click the Tools tab to display the buttons you see in Figure 2-3.**

Figure 2-3:
Microsoft hides these programs away, but power users know where they are.

4. **Click the Check button to display the Error Checking dialog box, shown in Figure 2-4.**

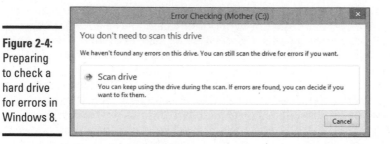

Error Checking (Mother (C:))

You don't need to scan this drive

We haven't found any errors on this drive. You can still scan the drive for errors if you want.

→ Scan drive
You can keep using the drive during the scan. If errors are found, you can decide if you want to fix them.

Cancel

5. **Click Scan Drive.**

In Windows 8, you can continue to work on other tasks while your hard drive is scanned — this process can take some time, depending on the capacity of the drive and the number of files and folders it contains. I recommend that you use this feature once every six months to a year on each drive in your system.

After the scan has completed, Windows 8 informs you of the results and prompts you for confirmation if a reboot is necessary to fix any problems. (Windows 8 automatically completes the repairs during the boot process.)

Defragmenting Just Plain Rocks

Another program that you can reach from any hard drive's Properties dialog box is Disk Defragmenter. I admit that it's a strange name, but returning file fragments to their proper places can significantly increase your hard drive's performance. (Technonerds call it "running a defrag." *Très* nerd.)

So what the heck are fragmented files? Here's the straight skinny: Each time you delete or move files from one spot on your PC to the other, you open up sections of your hard drive so that new files can be stored there. When you're ready to save a file, however, it might not fit into any single open area on your hard drive, so Windows 8 saves the file in pieces, or *segments,* across several open sections.

Suppose that you're downloading a 300MB game demo, but your hard drive doesn't have 300MB of contiguous open space handy. Windows 8 decides to save 50MB in one spot, 120MB in another, and the rest in a third open space. When you decide to install the demo and run the file, Windows 8 automatically pulls the right data from these different spots on your hard drive and reassembles the pieces into the original file. (I bet you didn't know all that was happening when that little green light blinks on and off, but then, the Eight can be a mysterious beast.)

Of course, this assembly process takes more time if the file has been broken into more pieces. And when your drive is extremely fragmented with little segments of thousands of files that Windows 8 has to keep track of, your hard drive performance really starts to suffer. Fragmentation slows down everything, and Windows 8 has to work harder every time you open or save a file.

The Windows 8 Disk Defragmenter restores the files on your drive to smooth, unbroken data storage territory. (Think of the *Bonanza* spread, but with ones and zeroes rather than cattle.) Figure 2-5 illustrates your drive before you run Disk Defragmenter, and Figure 2-6 shows your drive afterward. The program reads fragmented files, combines those nomadic segments, and then saves the defragmented file back to the disk. Outstanding!

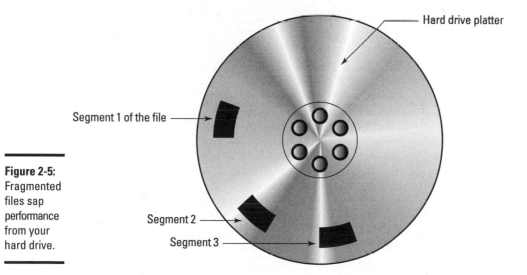

Figure 2-5: Fragmented files sap performance from your hard drive.

Microsoft recommends that you do *not* defragment solid-state drives (SSDs), and I agree completely. (An *SSD* is a super-fast hard drive that actually has no moving parts and uses memory chips, much like a USB flash drive.) You'll get no appreciable performance gain from defragmenting a solid-state drive — in fact, the defragmenting process can actually shorten the operational life of your SSD. If you're uncertain as to whether a drive on your PC is magnetic or solid-state, check the Media Type listed next to the drives in Step 1 of the following list: A drive listed as a hard-disk drive is safe to defragment, whereas a drive listed as a solid-state drive or SSD should not be defragmented.

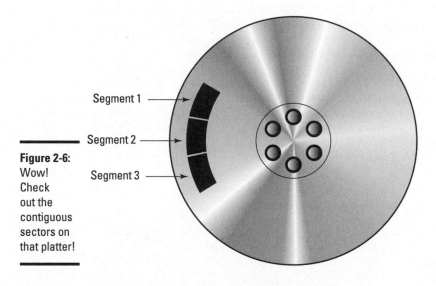

Segment 1

Segment 2

Segment 3

Figure 2-6: Wow! Check out the contiguous sectors on that platter!

Although Windows 8 does automatically defragment your drive, I still recommend manually defragmenting your hard drives once every three months — a manual defragment is more efficient and more comprehensive than the automatic defragmenting that Windows 8 performs. If you do defragment your drive manually, do it when you're not using your PC (because the process takes much less time to finish that way). Most PC owners defragment at nights or on weekends. Make sure you close any other programs or apps that you have running before you start the defrag.

As I mention above, you can run the Disk Defragmenter from the same hard drive Properties dialog box that I discuss in "Checking Your Hard Drives in

Windows 8," earlier in this chapter. Follow Steps 1 through 3 in the previous section to display the tools shown in Figure 2-3 and then follow these additional steps:

1. **Click the Optimize button to open the Optimize Drives window, which you see in Figure 2-7.**

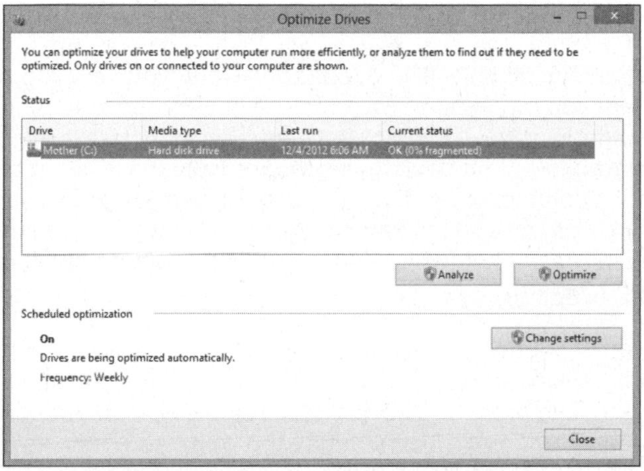

Figure 2-7: Defragmentation is like a bowl of granola for your PC.

2. **(Optional) To schedule Disk Defragmenter to run automatically, click the Change Settings button and then select the Run on a Schedule (Recommended) check box; click the drop-down lists to set the schedule and then click OK to save your schedule.**

3. **To run a defragment manually, click the drive you want to defragment in the list and then click Optimize.**

Defragmenting a hard drive takes time, and the larger the drive the longer the process will take — a typical 1TB drive requires at least two to three hours to complete a defragment session and perhaps even longer, depending on how badly the drive is fragmented.

Be Smart: Back Up Your Stuff

In this third part of your hard drive triple-header, I talk about how you can back up your hard drive to safeguard your data against future calamity. I don't lecture you here — oh, what the heck, yes I *will* — *DO IT*.

**Book IV
Chapter 2**

**Maintaining
Windows 8**

All smart PC owners take the trouble to save their stuff. Back up regularly, and someday (maybe years from now) you'll send me an e-mail message at mark@mlcbooks.com with the subject "Thanks, Mark, My Backup Saved My Tail!" Then we can both celebrate that you did the smart thing. I've received literally hundreds of those messages since the first edition of this book was printed — so *DO IT.*

How often is often enough when it comes to backing up your data? The answer depends completely on how often your data changes. The idea is to back up often enough so that you always have a recent copy of your important files close by. If you wait too long to freshen your backup, you find that you spend far too much time restoring the changes you made between backups. For example, a small business or home office with a large, continually changing database might back up anywhere from every night to every three days. (If you decide that you have to back up every night, you might want to consider a commercial backup solution that can be automated.) On the other hand, a typical home PC might require a backup only once per week or even once per month.

If you would rather not use the Windows 8 backup features, either buy a commercial backup application or consider copying your most important files to a USB flash drive or DVD-RW disc regularly — including the contents of your Documents folder. You still have to reinstall Windows 8 and your major applications if you have a crash or your computer is stolen, but at least the irreplaceable stuff is safe.

If you use DVD media, I recommend that you use rewriteable DVDs as your backup media. You'll save a considerable amount by erasing the older backup files you no longer need (instead of spending money on write-once DVD-R discs).

Along with USB flash drives and DVDs, you can back up to

✦ **A tape drive supported by Windows 8.**

✦ **External cartridge media.**

✦ **Online backup sites like Carbonite** (www.carbonite.com).

✦ **A network folder.** This uses space on your network's file server or another PC's hard drive on your network.

✦ **An external hard drive that's especially made for backups.** Nothing works as fast as another hard drive!

It may seem like somewhat of a misnomer, but Windows 8 performs backups from within the Windows 7 File Recovery window. (I guess Windows 7 did such a good job at backups, the folks at Microsoft decided not to upset the apple cart.) Anyway, follow these steps:

1. **Display the Charms bar and click the Search icon, and then click the Settings button and type** Back Up **into the Search box.**

2. **Click the Windows 7 File Recovery button that appears in the Search results pane to open the File Recovery window.**

> You also see the Create a System Image link within the Windows 7 File Recovery window. This is a method of backing up your *entire* Windows 8 system — in other words, a full system image allows you to restore your entire system rather than just your documents and files, so you don't have to reinstall any apps or programs later. Click the Create a System Image link to create an image file, and the wizard leads you through the process. It's important to note, however, that a full image backup takes far longer and uses many more discs (or a larger chunk of hard drive or network real estate) than the file backup I lead you through in this section.

3. **Click the Set Up Backup link to display the first screen of the Set Up Backup Wizard, shown in Figure 2-8.**

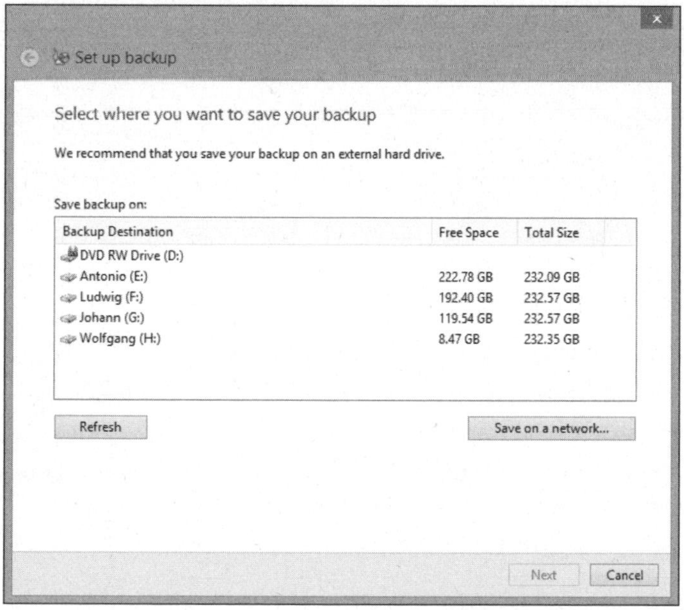

Figure 2-8:
I'm in good hands with the Set Up Backup Wizard.

**Book IV
Chapter 2**

**Maintaining
Windows 8**

4. **Select the destination media for your backup (a hard drive, a CD/DVD/Blu-Ray drive you select from the drop-down list, or a network location you choose with the Save on a Network button) and then click Next to continue.**

5. **Click Let Windows Choose to allow Windows to select which files to back up, or Let Me Choose to specify the target files yourself; click Next to continue.**

   The default setting is Let Windows Choose, and it normally results in the fastest backup (using the fewest discs, if you're using your optical drive).

   Windows 8 sets up a regular backup schedule for you, no matter which type of backup you choose.

   If you do decide to select your own files, you see the dialog box shown in Figure 2-9. Decisions, decisions. To expand the tree and show subfolders, click the triangle to the left of an entry. To choose a file or folder, click the check box next to it. When you've selected all the files and folders you want to include, click Next.

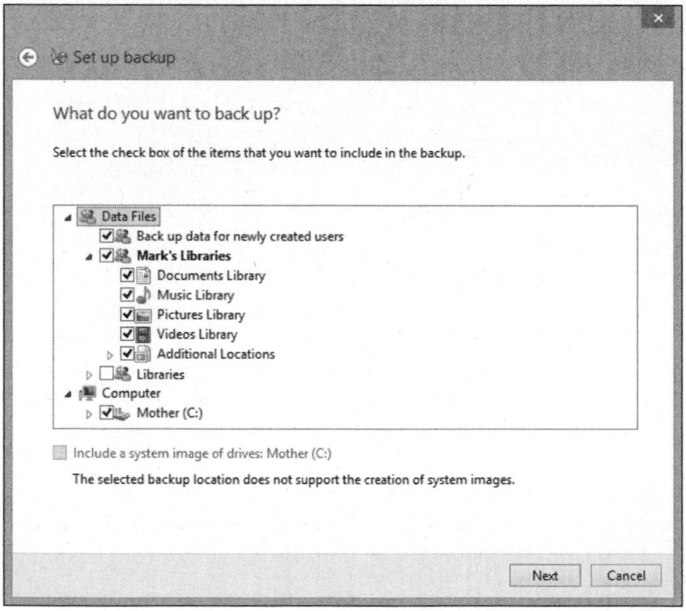

Figure 2-9:
Choose the files you want to back up.

[Screenshot: Set up backup dialog]

Set up backup

What do you want to back up?

Select the check box of the items that you want to include in the backup.

- ▲ ☑ Data Files
  - ☑ Back up data for newly created users
  - ▲ ☑ **Mark's Libraries**
    - ☑ Documents Library
    - ☑ Music Library
    - ☑ Pictures Library
    - ☑ Videos Library
    - ▷ ☑ Additional Locations
  - ▷ ☐ Libraries
- ▲ 🖳 Computer
  - ▷ ☑ Mother (C:)

☐ Include a system image of drives: Mother (C:)

The selected backup location does not support the creation of system images.

[Next] [Cancel]

TIP

If you have enough space on your backup device, you may also be able to create a system image as well by selecting the Include a System Image check box. This virtually guarantees that you'll be able to restore individual files and folders (in case something's deleted by accident, or erased by a virus) or the entire contents of the target drive (in case your hard drive fails completely). Note that only certain types of destination media support the creation of a system image — the wizard alerts you in Step 4 above if the destination media you select doesn't support the inclusion of a system image.

6. **Windows 8 chooses a default schedule time for future backups. If necessary, click the Change Schedule link and specify a different schedule using the three drop-down lists you see in Figure 2-10; then click OK to return to the confirmation screen.**

Figure 2-10: Creating an automated backup schedule. You rock!

> **Set up backup**
>
> How often do you want to back up?
>
> Files that have changed and new files that have been created since your last backup will be added to your backup according to the schedule you set below.
>
> ☑ Run backup on a schedule (recommended)
>
> How often: Weekly
>
> What day: Sunday
>
> What time: 7:00 PM
>
> OK   Cancel

It's easy to change the date and time for your backup if they aren't acceptable — for instance, if your PC is in an office environment and won't be turned on at the default time.

Your PC must be turned on for a scheduled backup to run, and the appropriate media must be present (or connected and powered on)!

7. **Click Save Settings and Run Backup.**

Sit back and enjoy the peace of mind as the backup process begins — but don't forget to feed your PC the media it needs (if necessary) during the backup process.

If you scheduled an *unattended* backup, you have to choose either a hard drive with enough capacity to store all your stuff or a network location to store your backup. Why? Well, no one will be around to load more media if your backup takes more than one blank disc!

To restore from a backup you made, load the backup media, follow Steps 1 and 2 in the previous procedure to display the Windows 7 File Recovery window and then click either Restore Files and Folders (if you used the Let Windows Choose option) or Restore System Settings or Your Computer (if you created a system image). The wizard leads you through the restore process — don't forget to breathe a sigh of relief!

Safeguarding Your System with System Restore

Remember when you were a kid and you held your fingers crossed behind your back when you made a promise? A "take-back" was a big deal back then. And even though you're all grown now, Windows 8 gives you the chance to say "I take it back!" if an installation goes awry.

This helpful feature is *System Restore.* It lets you set *restore points* (think of them as snapshots of your important system files), which you can return to whenever the Big Eight experiences problems. Most folks turn to System Restore if the installation of new hardware or software causes instability in Windows 8; I've also used it when a system file was accidentally erased or altered. Note that System Restore can recover only your Windows 8 *system* files, so if you accidentally trash Aunt Harriet's prized family brownie recipe, you're still out of luck — it's time to turn to your backup that you created in the previous section.

Windows 8 automatically saves restore points regularly, but you can follow these steps to manually create a restore point as a safety net — for example, if you're about to install a new device. (You should only create a restore point if your PC is behaving itself and acting normally.)

After you apply a restore point, Windows 8 must reboot. Therefore, I recommend closing down any applications that you have running with open documents *before* you run the System Restore Wizard.

Follow these steps to create a new restore point:

1. **Display the Charms bar and click the Search icon, and then click the Settings button and type** System Restore **into the Search box.**

2. **Click the Create a Restore Point button that appears in the Search results pane to display the settings you see in Figure 2-11.**

3. **Click the Create button.**

4. **In the following wizard window, type a name in the Description box — something like** Windows 8 before adding new video card — **and then click the Create button.**

   Windows 8 displays a confirmation message indicating that the restore point has been successfully saved. Click OK to acknowledge your success.

5. **Click OK to return to your Desktop.**

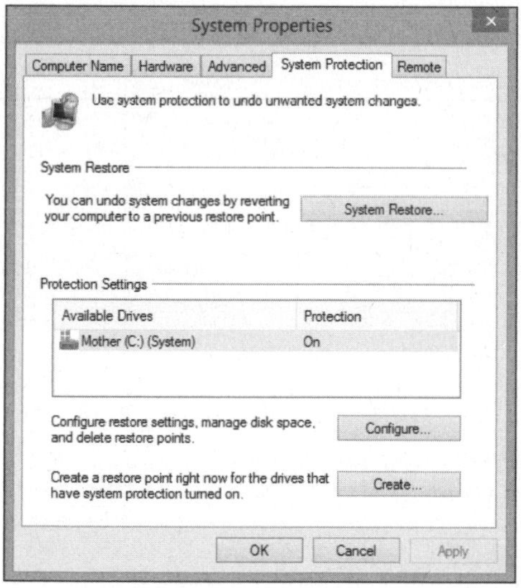

Figure 2-11:
You can create a system restore point at any time.

If you need to use a restore point to recover from a calamity, follow these steps:

1. **Display the Charms bar and click the Search icon, and then click the Settings button and type** System Restore **into the Search box.**

2. **Click the Create a Restore Point button that appears in the Search results pane.**

3. **Click the System Restore button to run the System Restore Wizard; then click Next on the introductory screen.**

4. **Click to select a restore point from the list (see Figure 2-12) — before you encountered your current problem, naturally — and click Next to continue.**

   Windows 8 displays a confirmation message with information about the point you chose.

5. **Click Finish to apply the restore point.**

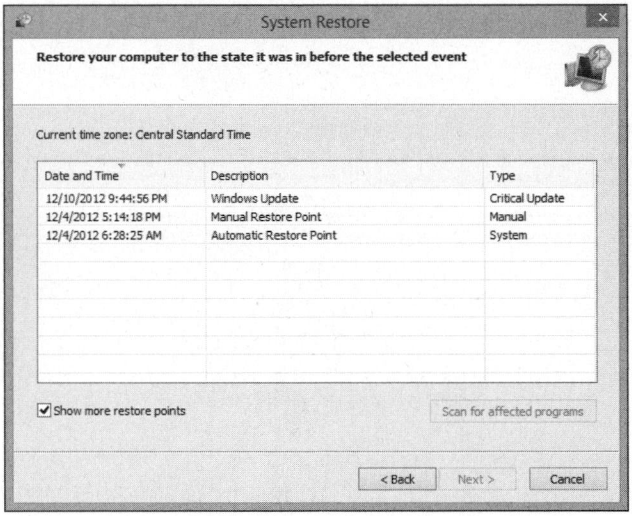

	System Restore	✕

Restore your computer to the state it was in before the selected event

Current time zone: Central Standard Time

Date and Time	Description	Type
12/10/2012 9:44:56 PM	Windows Update	Critical Update
12/4/2012 5:14:18 PM	Manual Restore Point	Manual
12/4/2012 6:28:25 AM	Automatic Restore Point	System

☑ Show more restore points   Scan for affected programs

< Back   Next >   Cancel

Figure 2-12: Selecting a restore point from my "collection."

Have at Thee, Foul Virus!

One of the first book chapters I ever wrote concerned viruses — that was way back in 1992, in the days before Windows when DOS was king.

I recommended a number of antivirus applications (only one has survived to this day: McAfee VirusScan) and a number of guidelines to help readers avoid viral infection. Unfortunately, many folks ignored viruses back then and paid the price later.

Viruses are much harder to ignore these days. The number of viruses now circulating has jumped dramatically, and you read about viral attacks continually in your newspaper and on your favorite news websites. Luckily, antivirus software has stayed current with "infection technology." In fact, the good guys are now out in front, and I'm happy to report that it's now child's play to surround Windows 8 with a protective antiviral wall.

How easy? Just use my two-fold defense: Use Windows Defender (which I cover in the next section), and install the latest version of avast! Free Antivirus (www.avast.com/), shown in Figure 2-13. Finally, sit back and watch the viruses beat themselves to deletion trying to reach your system. Unlike the antivirus software of 1992, when you had to scan for viruses from the DOS command line once a day, everything now works in real time. Although you can (and should) still scan your entire system manually once every six months or so, your antivirus program monitors every document you open and every program you run in the interim. It's *fun* to open your e-mail and see viral-laden spam identified and killed *before* you even open the message.

A good antivirus program covers the entry points used by viruses to reach your PC, including

+ Your e-mail

+ Programs you download or receive on disk or CD from others

+ Office documents that might contain dangerous macros

However, here's one important task that you must never take for granted, and it's definitely a Mark's Maxim:

Keep your antivirus data files up to date, or you're toast.™

This step is so important that antivirus programs can now automatically update their data files without your help! (As long as your PC can connect to the Internet, anyway.) Why? Well, without the latest data files, your antivirus software is out of date, and the latest viruses can attack your system undetected.

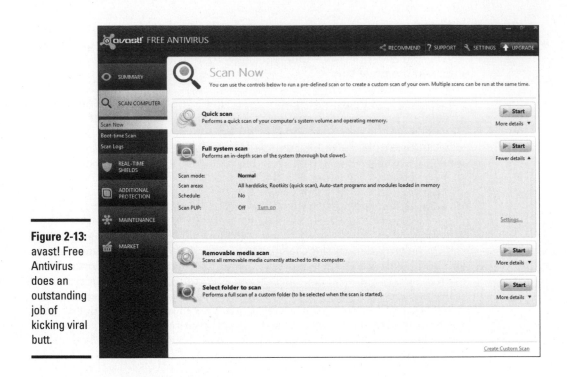

Figure 2-13:
avast! Free
Antivirus
does an
outstanding
job of
kicking viral
butt.

Using Windows Defender

Microsoft dislikes the word *malicious* as much as you do — hence the folks in Redmond included Windows Defender to help you eliminate both viruses and spyware throughout your system. (If you're not familiar with the term, *spyware* is software that is designed to collect personal information that you enter through your browser, e-mail, and even IM applications. It's Nasty Stuff, and if your PC is afflicted with a number of them you'll actually see your computer's performance drop significantly. They should be terminated quickly and with prejudice.)

Windows Defender offers more limited protection against viruses than a dedicated antivirus program does. (Hence my recommendation that you use both Windows Defender and avast! Free Antivirus in the previous section.) *Remember, your PC needs full-time antivirus protection, and in this author's opinion, that means using a third-party application along with Windows Defender.*

You can run Windows Defender at any time from the Start screen — type **Windows Defender** and click the Windows Defender button in the Search results pane. From the Windows Defender screen (shown in Figure 2-14), click the Scan Now button to start a manual scan. However, Windows Defender works best when it's set to automatically run in real time. To make sure that Windows Defender is working full-time for you, follow these steps:

1. **Display the Windows Defender screen, as shown in Figure 2-14.**

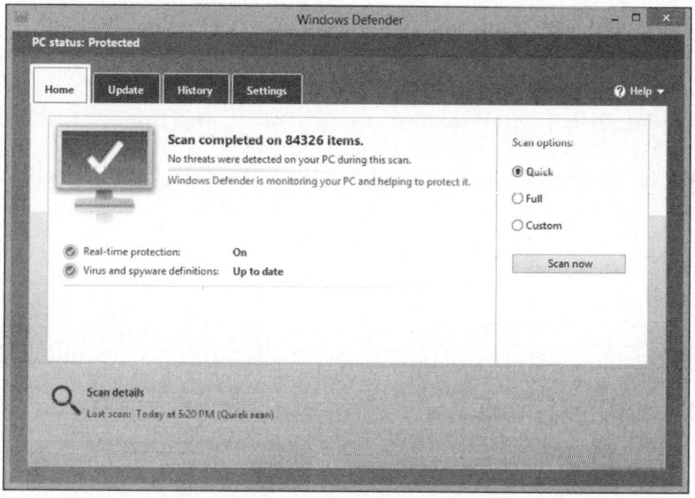

Figure 2-14:
Windows
Defender
is your
weapon
against
spyware.

2. **Click the Settings tab and then click the Real-Time Protection item in the list at the left.**

3. **Select the Turn On Real-Time Protection (Recommended) check box to enable it.**

4. **Click Save Changes.**

If Windows Defender does recognize a virus or spyware attack, it asks for confirmation before deleting the malicious intruder. (I think Microsoft does this so that you can share in the visceral pleasure of zapping these malicious bad guys!)

**Book IV
Chapter 2**

Maintaining
Windows 8

Using Safe Mode

Ninety-nine percent of the time when you boot Windows 8, you're talking on the phone or pouring another Diet Coke or looking through your (paper) junk mail. That's because 8 requires no help when it's running normally. You just press your PC's power button and wait.

However, if your PC isn't working correctly, you might that perennial favorite among PC technicians everywhere: Windows *Safe mode*. Think of Safe mode as generic "vanilla" Windows 8. If a hardware device conflict is locking up your PC, or if a driver that you recently installed or updated is causing Windows to crash, you can use Safe mode to run Windows 8 in a stripped-down mode.

In Safe mode, external devices can't be used, and much of the functionality that's available with your internal hardware is also disabled. For example, you immediately notice that your fancy video card is using the lowest resolution possible (typically 800 x 600 or 1024 x 768) — but at least you can move or delete files and use File Explorer.

To use Safe mode, reboot your PC and hold down the Shift key and press the F8 key right after you see text on the screen. (This is before the Windows banner screen appears, so you have only a second or two.) Click See Advanced Repair Options from the Recovery screen and then click the Troubleshoot button.

If you can still display the Charms bar within Windows, here's an easier method of reaching the Troubleshoot button: Click the Settings icon and then you can hold down the Shift key while choosing Power⇨Restart. Click the Troubleshoot button on the screen that appears and then continue with the rest of the steps I cover below.

On the Troubleshoot screen, click Advanced Options and then click Startup Settings on the Advanced Options screen. Finally, you've reached the end of the Yellow Brick Road, and you can simply click Restart to reboot your PC and display the Startup Settings screen.

Press 4 for standard Safe mode. Besides the lower screen resolution, you'll note that Windows 8 displays *Safe Mode* at all four corners of the screen, and opens the Help window with a description of Safe mode and how you can use it. As I mention before, you won't be able to use any external peripherals or the advanced features of your PC, but at least you can manage files and troubleshoot what's wrong with your system.

You also notice two other specialized forms of Safe mode on the Startup Settings screen:

✦ **Safe mode with networking:** Press 5, and Windows 8 loads network drivers and services so that you can log on to your network. If you need to copy files from a network server or copy your latest documents to a network drive for safekeeping (just in case), this Safe mode is the one to use. (Networking is disabled altogether in standard Safe mode.)

✦ **Safe mode with command prompt:** Press 6, and Windows 8 loads in Safe mode but reverts to that cryptic DOS-like command prompt. This option should be used only at the request of a tech support person — unless, of course, you're an ancient DOS-using dinosaur like I am.

Using Windows Update

Windows Update is a gas. It automatically searches for Windows 8 patches and upgrades from Microsoft and then applies them while you relax. This feature is A Good Thing because any piece of software as complex and powerful as Windows 8 needs frequent patching (especially because every hacker on the planet wants a piece of Microsoft). The two methods of using Update are to either leave it completely to Windows 8 or run Windows Update manually.

The fully automatic way

The Big Eight can take care of virtually the entire update process in the background so that you're not bothered with it. Windows Update is set to run automatically by default, so there's nothing you need to do.

The (somewhat) manual way

You can also run Windows Update at any time. Perhaps you've heard of an important patch that Microsoft has just released or you just want to impress your spouse. For whatever reason, make sure you're logged in as an Administration user, and follow these steps:

1. **Display the Charms bar and click the Search icon, and then click the Settings button and type** Windows Update **into the Search box.**

2. **Click the Windows Update button that appears in the Search results pane.**

3. **Click the Check for Updates Now button, shown in Figure 2-15.**

If updates are found, Windows Update informs you how many are pending and takes care of installing them automatically at the next restart.

Oh, and while we're here, make sure you enable the Give Me Updates for Other Microsoft Products When I Update Windows check box — that way, Windows Update will also download and install updates for other Microsoft programs (such as Office 2013).

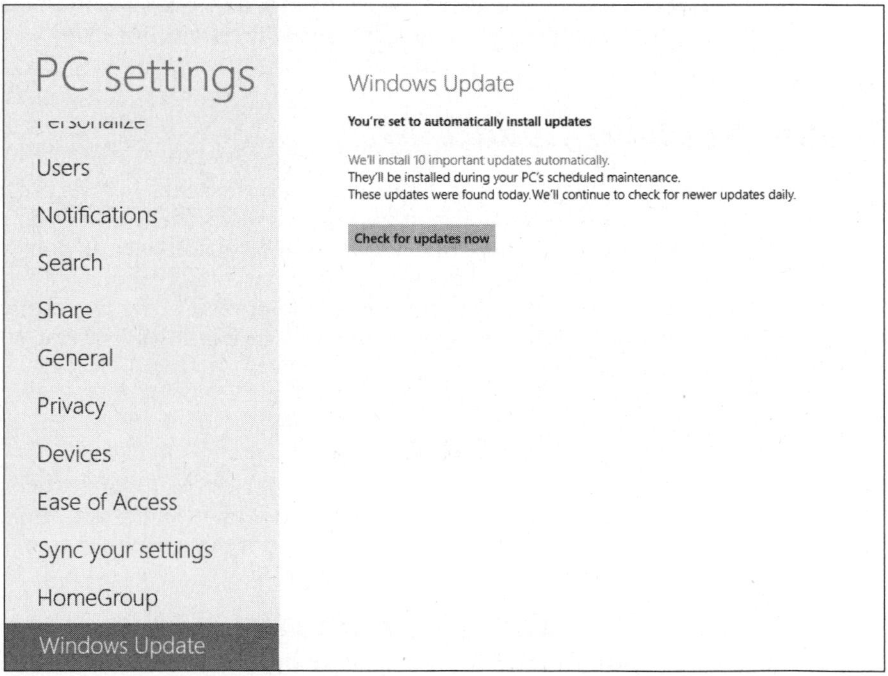

Figure 2-15: Set Windows Update for automatic operation.

Tweaking Windows Update

Note that Windows Update also has three other settings for important updates — you can display the settings for Windows Update by typing **Windows Update** in the Charms bar and clicking the Turn Automatic Updating On and Off button that appears.

Using the drop-down list box in the Important Updates section, you can set Windows 8 to

✔ **Download updates but let you choose whether to install them:** You can decide whether to install each update. (A Notify icon appears in the notification area on the taskbar.) To install the updates that Windows 8 has downloaded, click the Notify icon.

✔ **Check for Updates without automatically downloading or installing them:** (Again, Windows 8 displays an icon in the notification area.) To download and install the updates, click the Notify icon.

✔ **Turn off Automatic Updating completely.**

Naturally, I recommend setting Windows 8 to Install Updates Automatically — however, if you're running an older PC and you would rather not slow it down with all that hidden background activity (or if you're using a dialup connection), you can follow The Manual Path.

Chapter 3: Maintaining Your Hardware

In This Chapter

- ✔ Moving your PC the right way
- ✔ Dusting your PC
- ✔ Keeping cables under control
- ✔ Cleaning your monitor and scanner
- ✔ Freshening your mouse and keyboard
- ✔ Practicing printer maintenance

With the right credit card balance, anyone can buy a supercharged $2,000 (U.S.) PC — but *maintaining* that expensive equipment is another kettle of fish altogether. Although your PC's case might appear to be a closed environment, its fans draw in dust while they're cooling things — and what about peripherals, such as your printer and scanner, which are always more exposed to dust, dirt, and contaminants? The only desktop PC I've encountered that doesn't need regular maintenance is the model that you can buy in *The Sims* franchise.

In this chapter, I cover the basic cleaning and maintenance necessary to keep your hardware in top shape — long enough for it to become a seriously outdated antique! (And that's coming from the proud owner of antique computers, including two Radio Shack and three Atari 8-bit systems.)

When Should You Move Your PC?

Counter to popular myth, even a desktop PC can go mobile whenever it wants. Of course, you can't stow it with your other carry-on items on a plane, but if you've been challenged to a multiplayer network game at someone's apartment or you're moving to a new home, you'll find that your PC *enjoys* chaperoned trips (rather like a dog, without the tongue out the window).

Ready for one of my Maxims? (Get your highlighter out, if you like.) When you're ready, consider these guidelines that you should follow when moving your PC:

✦ **Never move your PC until it's completely powered down.** In this case, *move* means any movement whatsoever (even nudging your PC's case a few inches across your Desktop to dust). Hearken to this particularly important Mark's Maxim:

> **Never move your desktop PC if it is running.™**

Even laptop computers and external hard drives shouldn't be jolted or jerked around while they're running. Many PCs have only a handful of moving parts, such as fans, DVD recorders, and hard drives — but brother, any movement while the latter two are still spinning carries the possibility that you can shorten the drive's operational life. Always give your PC at least ten seconds after it shuts down before you pick it up.

✦ **Never set your PC upright in a seat or on the floor of your car.** We've all seen the videos of crash test dummies — and your beloved digital friend doesn't have a car seat in case you come to a sudden stop. You can use seatbelts to secure your PC in a vehicle, but I think it's just easier to lay your PC's case flat on the floor of your vehicle. The same also goes for your monitor, which is also dangerous (for itself and your head) when airborne for short distances.

✦ **Use your towel.** If your PC has to ride on top of a surface that might scratch your case, wrap your PC in a towel or blanket to protect its finish. (Fans of the *Hitchhiker's Guide to the Galaxy* series know what I'm on about.)

Avoiding Dust Bunnies

Think I'm kidding? Dust bunnies are *real* — and they seem to reproduce as fast as their namesakes, too. Thanks to your trusty can of techno-nerd compressed air, however, you can banish that dust from your PC and get back to work or play.

Here's a checklist of what to do:

✦ **Open and dust your desktop PC at least once a year.** Consider it a birthday present for your computer. Unscrew or unlatch your PC's case and use a can of compressed air (available at any office supply store) to blow any accumulated dust from the motherboard, adapter cards, and cables. If allowed to accumulate, that dust can act as a comfy heat-retaining blanket over your PC's circuitry, and overheated components have a significantly shorter lifespan. (For proof, check out the fans at the back of your PC's case and the fan on top of the processor. Heat is the enemy.)

✦ **Remove dust that's settled on the fan blades.** Speaking of fans, use your compressed air to get rid of any additional dust on fan blades and within air intake holes. To properly ventilate and cool your PC, these openings need to be free of dust bunnies.

✦ **Wipe down your PC case and your monitor with a clean, dry cloth every few months.** Don't *ever* use household solvents to clean your PC's case; instead, use special antistatic cleaning solutions and cloths made just for cleaning computer hardware. You can readily find these at your local computer shop or office supply store.

If you have a stain that won't come off your PC's case, even when you use an antistatic cleaning cloth, try my secret weapon: Armor All protectant (which you've probably been using on your car's rubber and vinyl for years!). Apply a small amount of Armor All to that cloth and try again.

✦ **Avoid eating near your PC.** I know; it's difficult not to snack while you're on the Internet, but at least be diligent about cleaning up afterward — and *never* park anything liquid anywhere near your computer!

✦ **Keep your workspace clean and open.** Surrounding your PC with papers and knickknacks might optimize your desktop space (or at least help you feel more human around an inhuman boss), but you contribute to the accumulation of dust inside your computer. And in the worst case, you block the flow of air. I try to leave at least six inches of free space around the base of my PC at all times.

Book IV Chapter 3

Maintaining Your Hardware

If your PC must be located in a dusty environment, consider using an air cleaner and ionizer unit. I use one in my office, and I find significantly less dust to clean from my PC every year.

Watching Your Cables

With the popularity of external Universal Serial Bus (USB), eSATA, Thunderbolt, and FireWire peripherals these days, the forest of cables sprouting from the back of your PC can look like Medusa on a bad hair day. Normally, this isn't a problem — until you decide to move your PC or you want to repair or upgrade an internal component. Talk about the Gordian knot!

Here's a list of tips for keeping your cables under control:

✦ **Use ties to combine and route cables.** I'm a big fan of the reusable Velcro cable tie strips that you can find at your local office supply store. With these ties, you can easily combine cables that are heading in the same direction into a more manageable group. You can also fasten these cable ties to the underside of your desk or behind furniture to keep network and power cables hidden and out of danger.

✦ **Label your cables!** Sure, you can determine the source and destination of some cables at a glance (for example, network cables are pretty easy to spot), but what about your USB printer and scanner, which both use the same type of cable? If you must move your PC or unplug cables regularly, avoid the ritual of tracking each cable to its source by doing what techs and computer shops do: Use a label machine to identify the tip of each cable with the peripheral name.

✦ **Tighten those connectors.** "Gee, my monitor was working last night. What gives?" If you didn't use the knobs on either side of the video cable connector to tighten things down, small shifts in position over time could make cables work loose.

✦ **Check your cables for damage periodically.** I have two cats — or, I should say, they have me. Does a cat have you? How about a dog? If so, don't be surprised to find a chewed cable one morning — and pray that it isn't a power cable. (I keep all animals away from my office for this reason — not to mention the mess that a shedding dog can leave around your PC.) Of course, cables can also be damaged by bending or stretching them, so I recommend checking each cable at least once a year; I combine this ritual with my PC's yearly cleaning.

Cleaning Monitors and Scanners

Most PC owners are aware that they should keep the viewing surfaces of their monitors and scanners clean — but beware, because you can do more harm than good if you don't know what you're doing. Here are the guidelines that I recommend you follow when working with monitor screens and scanner glass:

✦ **Abrasives are taboo!** Even some household glass cleaners — which you might think could be trusted — can scratch the glass in your monitor or flatbed scanner when used with a rag or paper towel. With a scanner, small scratches can mean real trouble because a scratch can easily show up in your images at higher resolutions. Therefore, I recommend that you use only a dry, soft photographer's lens cloth (which doesn't scratch) or lens cloths with alcohol that are made specifically for monitors and scanners.

✦ **Never spray liquids onto a flatbed scanner or an LCD monitor.** If liquid gets under the surface, you could end up with condensation on the inside of the scanner when you use it. Again, a dry photographer's lens cloth is a good choice, or a premoistened lens cloth, which doesn't carry enough alcohol to do any harm. (I launch into scanners full-scale in Book VI, Chapter 1.)

✦ **Monitors should never be opened.** *Never* take the cover off any type of monitor, even if it needs cleaning. Why? Well, your PC's monitor is one of the two components of your system that carry enough voltage to seriously hurt you. (The other one is your PC's power supply.) If your monitor needs to be serviced or cleaned on the inside, take it to your local computer shop.

✦ **Use a cover for your scanner.** Scanners are somewhat different from most external peripherals. They don't generate any heat while they're on (unlike an external hard drive), and most of us use a scanner only once or twice a week. Therefore, your scanner is a perfect candidate for a cover that keeps it clean and dust-free — and by no small coincidence, you can find this type of cover at your local office supply store.

Cleaning Your Mouse and Keyboard

"Natasha, why we must clean Moose and Squirrel?" (Sorry, I couldn't help it.) Mice and keyboards get *grimy* — *fast* — because your PC's keyboard and pointing device are continually in use, and they get pawed by human hands. (Of course, you could always wear surgical gloves, but what about your kids?)

Never fear. Here's a list of guidelines that help you keep your pointing device and keyboard clean and working:

✦ **Buy an optical mouse or trackball.** (You'll thank me.) If you're still using an old-style mouse with a ball — how very 1980s — clean it once a month as well. Unscrew the retaining ring on the bottom, remove

**Book IV
Chapter 3**

Maintaining
Your Hardware

the mouse ball, and use a cotton-tipped swab dipped in tape-cleaning alcohol (which is 90+ proof and leaves no residue) to clean the rollers inside. Also, make sure that your mousepad is clean and dust-free to prolong the life of your rodent. (Chapter 1 of this minibook talks trackball.)

An optical mouse or a trackball doesn't need to be cleaned anywhere near as often (if ever) — that's why I keep crowing about them.

✦ **Do the Keyboard Shake!** No, it's not a new dance craze, but it is the best method of cleaning accumulated gunk from your keyboard, and I recommend doing it at least once per month. Turn your keyboard upside down and shake it vigorously back and forth; prepare to be amazed (or grossed out, especially if the whole family uses your PC).

A number of manufacturers sell swabs premoistened with alcohol that work great for cleaning keys, and there are dusting contrivances especially made for keyboards that can help keep your keyboard pristine.

✦ **Find *another* use for your compressed air.** Your keyboard can collect debris that can't be shaken free. If so, using compressed air will likely blow it free (unless it's alive and well dug-in, but I haven't encountered anything like that in my travels so far).

Cleaning and Maintaining Your Printer

It's time to consider a peripheral that not only needs cleaning, but can also contribute mightily to its own mess. If you've ever had to clean up spilled laser printer toner, I think you know what I mean. Printers have all the necessary features that make them prime targets for regular maintenance:

✦ They're open to the outside world.

✦ They're stuffed full of complex moving parts.

✦ They're continually running out of ink or toner.

✦ They act as magnets for dust.

In this section, I show you how to clean and maintain yon printing instrument.

Cleaning laser printers

Your laser printer contains a mortal enemy — *toner,* the insidious stuff that seems to have a diabolical mind of its own. Luckily, most cartridges are at least partially sealed, and only older models of laser printers can produce a really nasty Three Mile Island–level spill. If any toner escapes, however, you quickly find that the very fine powder is sensitive to static charges and immediately heads to every corner of your printer. Those nooks and crannies can be a real pain to clean. And because toner can permanently stain clothing and carpet — *and* it's harmful to pets and kids — you should be doubly careful to keep toner inside the cartridge, where it belongs.

Therefore, please take the time to completely read the instructions for your specific laser printer before you install that first toner cartridge. Also, avoid shaking the cartridge unless the manufacturer recommends a particular motion to help distribute the toner evenly.

If you spill toner, head to your local office supply store for toner clean-up cloths. These handy wipes contain a chemical that attracts toner and keeps it on the cloth. Oh, and don't use warm or hot water to wash toner off your hands — toner can literally melt and adhere to your skin!

Never attempt to clean the interior of your laser printer while it's on! Laser technology uses very high temperatures to bond toner to paper, so you could be subject to serious burns if you're not careful. I always make sure that a laser printer has been off for at least 30 minutes before I clean or service it. For the same reasons, you should *always* follow the specific instructions for your brand and model of laser printer while cleaning its interior!

Changing inkjet cartridges

Here are two methods of determining when you need to change the cartridges in your inkjet printer:

+ **The automatic route:** Most inkjet printers now on the market have onscreen alerts that appear whenever the ink level of the cartridge is low. Or, as you see in Figure 3-1, your printer might display the amount of ink remaining in a cartridge. (This trick is very valuable indeed, especially with a large print job looming.)

+ **The "Man, I can barely read this page!" method:** If you have an older inkjet printer, you might not receive any warning about the ink levels in your cartridges — but when they're empty, pardner, you'll know.

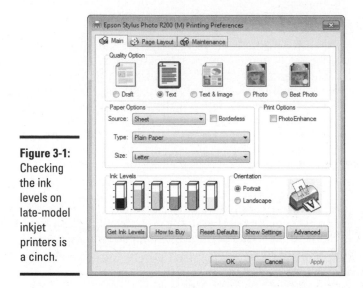

Figure 3-1:
Checking the ink levels on late-model inkjet printers is a cinch.

After you know that you need to change your cartridges, however, the general procedure is the same for virtually every inkjet printer I've ever encountered:

1. **Open the top of your printer.**

   This step causes most inkjet printer models to politely center the carriage, to provide you access to the cartridges. Or there might be a button to press that centers the carriage.

2. **After you have access to the cartridges, you may be required to turn off your printer.**

   Check your printer's manual to see if you should switch off your printer before replacing the ink cartridges.

3. **Lift or turn the latches holding the ink cartridge in place.**

   Most inkjet printers have at least two cartridges — one for black and one for color — so make sure that you're working with the right cartridge before you remove it.

4. **Remove the used cartridge.**

   At this point, you can opt to refill the cartridge (I discuss the pros and cons of refilling later in this chapter) or replace with a new one.

5. **Load the full cartridge, and fasten the latch to hold it down.**

6. **Turn your printer back on, and close the lid.**

Before you count the job done, print a short one-page document as a test — it's always a good idea to run a test page to make sure that the cartridge swap went well!

Windows 8 offers a pretty comprehensive printer troubleshooting wizard as well — from the Charms bar, click Search, click the Settings button, and then type **Printer** into the Search box. Click the Find and Fix Printing Problems button in the Search results pane to start the printer troubleshooting wizard.

Calibrating your printer

This maintenance task is reserved only for inkjet printer owners. (My, aren't we lucky?) *Calibration* refers to the proper alignment of the inkjet cartridge nozzles to both the paper and each other; without a properly calibrated printer, your print quality degrades over time. This is usually the problem when folks complain that lines appear fuzzy in artwork or when colored areas in printed images start or stop before they should.

If you hear a professional photographer or graphic artist talk about color calibration, that's something completely different; *color calibration* is the process of color matching between the colors that appear on your monitor and the colors produced by your printer. Most of us never need that level of precise color, and most inkjet printers now allow you to make changes to the hue and saturation of your prints by simply dragging a slider in the program installed by the manufacturer. But if you need to perform a full color calibration, check your printer's manual for more information about using Windows color profiles.

Your printer probably automatically calibrates itself when you first load a new cartridge, so I recommend that you calibrate either three months after installing a new cartridge or when you notice that your print quality is suffering — whichever comes first. (Of course, the period varies according to how often you use your printer and the length of your average printed document.)

Each brand (and sometimes each model) of printer has different onscreen controls for calibrating output, but you should be able to access them from the software you installed when you set up your printer. Check your printer manual for the location of the calibration controls (probably within a separate application that you can run to display your printer's maintenance toolbox).

Follow the onscreen directions for your specific printer, and have a couple of pieces of plain paper handy.

Book IV
Chapter 3

Maintaining
Your Hardware

Cleaning inkjet cartridges

Here's another fun task limited to just inkjet owners. I usually clean my inkjet cartridge nozzles about once every three months or whenever the output from my printer suddenly starts showing streaks of horizontal white lines. (As you probably can guess, the nozzles control the placement and amount of each droplet of ink.) The good news is that you don't need a bucket and a scrub brush for this chore; instead, your printer can take care of cleaning its own cartridges (with your approval, of course).

A new inkjet cartridge provides your printer a brand-new set of nozzles, so you should restart that three-month period when you change cartridges. However, if you refill an inkjet cartridge — which I discuss in the next section — you should clean the cartridge nozzles immediately after the refilled cartridge has been reinstalled.

Like the calibration controls I discuss in the preceding section, the location of your printer's cartridge-cleaning controls is likely displayed by the software you installed with your printer.

Figure 3-2 illustrates the cleaning controls for my Epson inkjet printer. I just click the Head Cleaning button and wait about a minute, and I'm done.

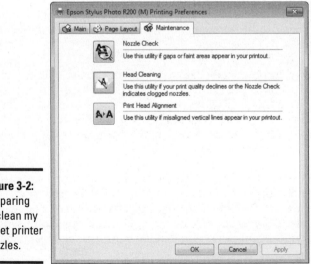

Figure 3-2:
Preparing to clean my inkjet printer nozzles.

Refilling inkjet cartridges

I'll be honest with you: I don't refill inkjet cartridges, and I don't recommend that you do, either. The only real advantage to refilling cartridges is the money you save over buying a new cartridge. As a fellow inkjet owner myself, I feel your pain when you're standing in the checkout line at Walmart with a $40 cartridge in your hand.

However, here are the reasons why I buy new cartridges — consider these the facts that you *won't* see when that refill-kit TV commercial appears for the umpteenth time:

✦ **Mess:** Even if you're experienced at refilling an ink cartridge, there's a good chance that you'll end up with a toxic spill. Make sure that you cover your work surface with a plastic sheet, and don't wear anything formal.

✦ **Substandard ink:** One of the reasons why ink refills are cheaper is that the quality of the ink used in the refill kits is usually never as good as the ink in a new cartridge. That second-rate ink can cause color changes or uneven coverage and might also end up taking longer to dry (resulting in Smear City).

✦ **Nozzle hassle:** I mention cleaning cartridge nozzles in the previous section. Unfortunately, those nozzles aren't meant to be reused, and refilling a cartridge can result in clogs. You have to clean your cartridges far more often, and the quality of your printer's output might drop appreciably over time when you use a refilled cartridge.

Thus, my decision and my recommendation: Let someone else suffer below-par print quality by refilling their used cartridges.

Book V
Office 2013

Visit www.dummies.com/extras/pcsaio for tips on saving Office files to SkyDrive.

Contents at a Glance

Chapter 1: Introducing Office 2013

In This Chapter

- ✔ Working with Word
- ✔ Using Excel
- ✔ Creating with PowerPoint
- ✔ Keeping track of data with Access
- ✔ Managing information with Outlook
- ✔ Working with the Office Clipboard
- ✔ Using the Office Help system

Introducing Microsoft Office 2013 is a little like introducing Beethoven's *Fifth Symphony*: We're all familiar with Office, we all think that it's a true work of art, and we all wish that we had the royalties (or, in this case, the mound of cash generated by licensing).

That familiarity might be your ticket to skipping this chapter. For instance, most PC power users need no overview of Office; they know what it can do, what the different applications are used for, and how to access the Office Help system. Heck, chances are good that you're already using at least Word or Excel every day or that you already rely on Outlook to handle your e-mail and personal contacts.

But, just like the intricacies of Beethoven's masterpiece, there's a ton of substance to absorb within Office 2013 (along with a new look and feel to the toolbar and the rest of the user interface). Perhaps you've used only Word and you want to know what the rest of the stuff you paid for can do. Or, maybe you're brand new to the PC scene and you just bought Office 2013. For folks who need a formal introduction to the rest of this minibook, I present to you this chapter — it provides a little information on each Office application so that you can pursue the more in-depth information in the later chapters.

The Components of Office 2013

Office 2013 is a suite of productivity applications, designed to help you easily produce a wide range of documents, crunch numbers, and communicate online, covering most of the tasks that you need to accomplish in a home or office environment. In this section, I describe each major Office 2013 application and provide you with an idea of what you can accomplish with each.

Note that you may also receive a number of companion applications, depending on the version of Office 2013 that you buy. The following table shows what apps come with which version of Office 2013. These apps include OneNote, Publisher, InfoPath, and Lync. For a complete description of everything and all the arcane productivity possibilities within Office 2013, I heartily recommend *Office 2013 All-in-One For Dummies* by Peter Weverka (John Wiley & Sons, Inc.). (To prove just how monolithic Office 2013 can be, that book is as big as this one!)

Application	Home and Business	Professional
Word	Yes	Yes
Excel	Yes	Yes
PowerPoint	Yes	Yes
Outlook	Yes	Yes
OneNote	Yes	Yes
Access	No	Yes
Publisher	No	Yes

Word 2013

Microsoft Word, the world's best-selling word processor for Windows, is an institution these days. (You want to know just how ancient I really am? Your author remembers using the first DOS-based version of Word.) Think of Word as the foundation of Office 2013. You can see a typical Word window in Figure 1-1. Word is suitable for creating any kind of document, from a simple one-page letter to a book-length manuscript. Word also includes features designed for creating scientific, academic, and technical documents, as well as powerful collaborative tools for workgroups.

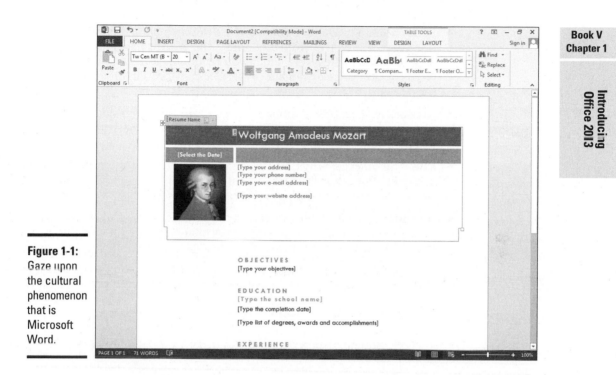

Figure 1-1:
Gaze upon
the cultural
phenomenon
that is
Microsoft
Word.

Other important features that set Word apart include

✦ **Complete control over all levels of document formatting:** This includes
the appearance of everything in a Word document, from the character
level to the entire manuscript. (Believe me: Word can handle a book this
size without batting an eyelash.)

✦ **Sophisticated tables:** Gotta have 'em, and Word delivers — complete
with a wide array of sorting, numbering, shading, and border options.

✦ **Collaboration tools:** If you share editing chores on documents with
other people, you'll welcome the ability to highlight or use revision
marks. (This trick enables Word to track any changes with colored
text to show who did what and when. As a writer who works with
editors, I can attest that the "why" factor can prove a bit more nebulous.) You can also compare two Word documents, add comments,
and implement a basic version-control system. Word documents can
be write-protected as well (to keep unnecessary fingers away from
your work).

✦ **Spell-checking:** Whether you use the default spelling dictionary or create your own custom dictionary, the Word spell-checking feature can be a lifesaver. And, if you're looking for exactly the right word (or utterance or remark or exclamation), you'll flip over the thesaurus.

✦ **Artwork and graphical tools:** Sure, you can use clip art, but you can also draw your own graphics or even add all sorts of 3D effects to titles, sidebars, and callouts.

✦ **Powerful macros:** Why type the same stuff or format the same text over and over? With Word's macro feature, you can automate all sorts of repetitive tasks — and it's easy to record a macro, too.

✦ **Printing:** Word can zoom or scale your printed pages and even collate longer documents. With plug-ins like Adobe Acrobat, you can also produce PDF files from within Word.

✦ **Advanced search and replace:** You can find and replace just about anything in a Word document. It even has an option to search phonetically, or you can search according to specific formatting. ("Hey, Earl, how can we find every italicized word in this 50-page list?")

For a more complete overview of Word, skip to the next chapter of this minibook.

Excel 2013

Microsoft Excel (see a window example in Figure 1-2) is much more than just a spreadsheet application. It's a regular jack-of-all-trades in the Office 2013 lineup, handling everything from a simple family budget to complex statistical and financial forecasting. Excel really comes into its own when a worksheet is linked with data in other Office documents.

Excel offers support for

✦ **Lists:** Excel can generate (and automatically update) lists as you need them, or you can use the complete set of list tools to build your own from scratch.

✦ **Smart tags:** These tags are used to embed and link to all sorts of external data from within your worksheet — contacts, stock quotes, e-mail messages, and more.

✦ **Charts and reports:** If your data needs to be charted, or you need to generate reports to your exact specifications, look no further than Excel!

✦ **Forms:** Offices all around the world rely on Excel for building customized forms. You can print them or complete them on-screen and save
the worksheet for later use.

✦ **Formulas:** Excel provides task-based examples for common formulas
and even includes an error-checking option that checks for potential
problems with the formulas you create.

✦ **Functions:** You can use the predefined functions provided by Excel or
use the recommendations provided by the Function Wizard. Excel even
pops up the arguments for a function when you enter it!

Read through Book V, Chapter 3 for more on this handy application.

PowerPoint 2013

Slide-based and PC-based presentations used to be a business-only proposi-
tion, but many schools teach kids how to create their own presentations
as part of their class work. PowerPoint, illustrated in Figure 1-3, is the king
of the PC presentation applications, with dozens of predesigned templates
and styles to help you deliver professional results. Plus, you can easily
build a standalone, self-running presentation or a manual presentation.
Presentations can be shared online as well.

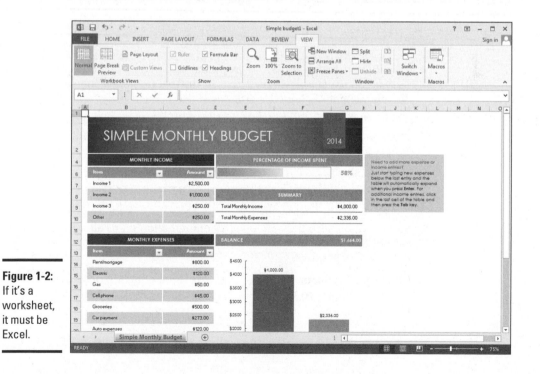

Figure 1-2:
If it's a
worksheet,
it must be
Excel.

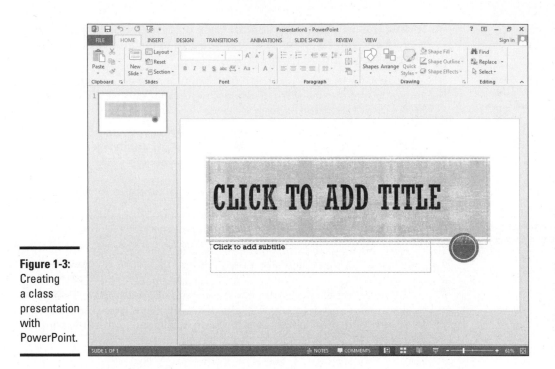

Figure 1-3:
Creating
a class
presentation
with
PowerPoint.

Highlights of PowerPoint include

✦ **Easy-to-use design tools:** No graphical design experience is necessary when using PowerPoint. Even a normal human being can handle the placement of elements. Master slides make it easy to apply global changes across your entire presentation, too.

✦ **Presentation print preview:** Check out your entire presentation before you print a single slide. And, you can check out different layouts for notes pages and handouts.

✦ **Notes and handouts:** Use PowerPoint to easily produce notes for your reference or handouts that you can print for members of your audience.

✦ **Support for multiple screens:** With multiple monitors, you can display a special Presenter view during your presentations. This separate display gives you easier control over the sequence of your slides and makes it easy to track the elapsed time.

✦ **Animation and transition effects:** Keep your audience interested in your message with animation on your slides and transitions between major sections.

✦ **Graphics control:** You can rotate or flip images, use the automatic layout feature to adjust the design when you insert objects, and display a grid when aligning elements on your slides.

For more on PowerPoint, see Book V, Chapter 4.

Access 2013

Access is the unsung hero of Office 2013 — if it's included in your edition. (I've encountered a number of experienced Office users who have never even *heard* of Access because they never used the Professional edition of Office.) However, when you tell folks what they can do with Access, they quickly become its most fervent supporters. You can create a database in just a few minutes, complete with reports, charts, and even web pages that display data on demand. It's a helpful way to store whatever data is important to you — without requiring a degree in software engineering.

Top features of Access include

✦ **Sophisticated error checking and validation:** Let Access double-check the data that's entered. You cut down on human error and help ensure the accuracy of your database.

✦ **Connection with SQL servers:** If your business uses large-scale, corporate-level Structured Query Language (SQL) database applications, you can use Access to pull that information into your own database projects.

✦ **Database encryption:** If you need to keep your databases secure, Access can encrypt the entire file automatically each time you use it.

✦ **Customized queries and reports:** What's the use of keeping a database if you can't view that data intelligently? Define relationships that help define trends or predict problems.

✦ **Web reports and database access:** Offer data from your Access files to others on your office intranet (or to anyone who connects to your website).

✦ **Forms:** Build professional-looking data entry and special input dialog boxes that can collect information and act on that data automatically. (Hey, you're a database programmer now!)

Hone your database magic skills with Access in Book V, Chapter 5.

Outlook 2013

Ah, Outlook — no other single application has done so much for so many. (I know it's done a lot for my organization.) Outlook 2013 is a combination of an e-mail manager and a *PIM* (a rather ridiculous acronym that stands for *p*ersonal *i*nformation *m*anager), which keeps track of your contacts and your schedule. The full-blown Outlook 2013 that ships with Office 2013 includes

✦ **Contact tracking,** which ties all Office documents and e-mail associated with a contact

✦ **An event calendar, complete with daily/weekly/monthly views and an Outlook Today page to sum up today's chores**

✦ **Appointment reminders,** which appear on-screen at the time you specify, to ensure that you don't miss The Big Date

Some of the top Outlook features include

✦ **Group scheduling:** Not only can Outlook handle your personal calendar but you can also participate in a shared common schedule with others in your workgroup.

✦ **A truly awesome Find function:** Imagine being able to search all your e-mail messages, all your appointments, and all your scheduled tasks for the word *pickle* — well, for whatever *you* want, naturally.

✦ **Calendar coloring:** Mom always said, "If it's color coded, it's easier and faster to use." Evidently, the folks in Redmond agree because you can assign colors to appointments.

✦ **Support for Outlook.com (formerly Hotmail) accounts:** If you use the Microsoft Outlook.com web-based e-mail service, Outlook can retrieve those messages for you.

✦ **Mailbox cleanup options:** It's a messy job, but you've got to do it — or do you? Outlook can automatically archive older messages, or you can manually clean your inbox according to the message date or size.

✦ **On-screen reminders:** Let Outlook prompt you to attend that meeting or make that phone call. You can set reminders with an audible alarm or keep things quiet with an on-screen notification dialog box.

Discover how to stay in touch (and organized) with Outlook in Book V, Chapter 6.

Putting the Office Clipboard to Work

The *Office Clipboard* (shown in Figure 1-4, as it appears in Word) is essentially a supercharged version of the standard Windows Clipboard. It's specially designed to hold, display, and paste multiple items from one or more Office documents. For example, you can copy a text string from Access, an amount from an Excel spreadsheet, a contact name from Outlook, and even a company logo graphic from PowerPoint — and then copy all those items into a Word document.

Although the Office Clipboard functions are always available from the Home tab, you can also display the Office Clipboard task pane at any time within Word, PowerPoint, Excel, or Access by choosing the Home tab and clicking the Clipboard expansion icon. If you'd like to display the Clipboard task pane at all times, click the Options pop-up menu button that appears at the bottom of the pane and click the Show Office Clipboard automatically item to enable it.

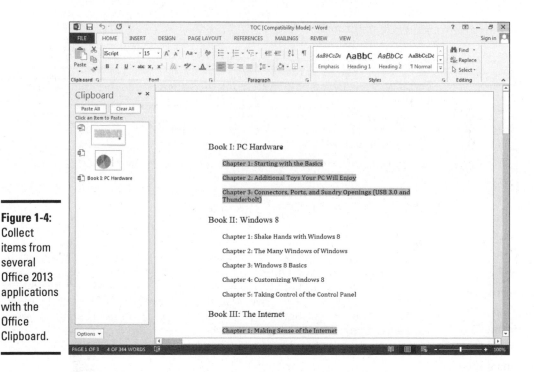

Figure 1-4:
Collect items from several Office 2013 applications with the Office Clipboard.

When you display the Office Clipboard, anything you copy from the Edit menu (or with the Ctrl+C shortcut) is added to it in addition to the system Clipboard. After the copied material is on the Office Clipboard, you can right-click items to selectively paste or delete them (which you can't do from the other Clipboard). To paste all items at once, click the Paste All button in the task pane; to clear everything in one fell swoop, click the Clear All button.

Note that any items you add to the Office Clipboard stay there until you close all Office applications, and they aren't affected by the single item stored on the Windows 8 Clipboard. Now, *that*, my friends, is handy.

Using the Office Help System

No introduction to Microsoft Office 2013 would be complete without information on the excellent Office Help system, as shown in Figure 1-5. Believe me: The Help system is *especially* helpful in Excel and Access. For example, it can save your derrière when you need assistance with a complex formula or function in Excel!

Displaying the Help system

To display the Office Help system for the Office application you're using, you can

✦ Click the question mark icon (upper right of the application window; refer to Figure 1-4).

✦ Press F1.

The Help controls of justice

Need help with a specific feature in an Office 2013 application? Click in the Search Online Help box and type a short, specific question in honest-to-goodness English — or a choice keyword or two — and press Enter (or click the Search button, which looks like a magnifying glass) to display links to matching Help topics. Underlined hyperlinks display additional information if you click them. (You can specify additional resources to search by clicking the buttons at the bottom of the scrolling list of Help topics, such as templates, images, and the Office Store.)

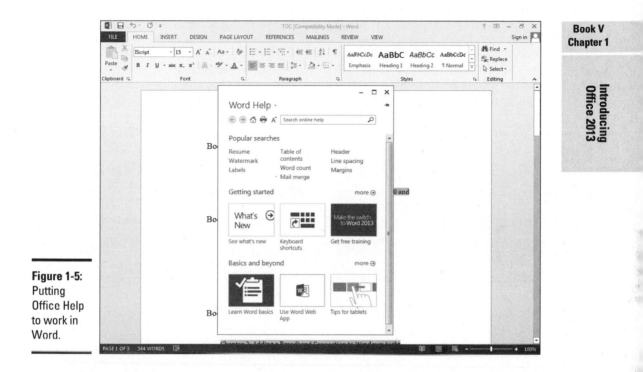

Figure 1-5:
Putting
Office Help
to work in
Word.

Click the Home button on the Help window toolbar to return to the top-level Help screen.

Click the Forward and Back buttons to retrace your steps forwards and backwards through the Help screens you've viewed — these buttons work just like the Forward and Back buttons in Internet Explorer.

Click the attractive Print icon on the Help window toolbar to print the current contents of the Help window.

Chapter 2: Using Word

In This Chapter

- ✔ Starting Word
- ✔ Changing views in Word
- ✔ Typing and editing text
- ✔ Using Find and Replace
- ✔ Creating tables
- ✔ Setting tabs and margins
- ✔ Formatting your document
- ✔ Printing in Word
- ✔ Building web pages in Word

*I*t's time to dive into Word (specifically, Word 2013), which is probably one of the top five most-used applications on the face of this planet. I first used Word when it was a character-based DOS program, well before the arrival of Windows. (Yes, it's that old. And so am I.) Even then, it was easy to use and produced flawless printed pages — which, in my opinion, are the two all-important requirements for any word processor.

Word is now the cornerstone of most PC-based word processing; it's versatile enough to perform equally well for everything from a kid's homework to the most professional-looking yearly report. Therefore, this chapter starts with the basics — key shortcuts and the different views you can use in Word — and ends up delving into more advanced topics, such as collaborative features and web page creation. If you're familiar with Word 2010, take heart: You'll be in calm waters, as the program's core features haven't changed much.

One note about this chapter (and the others in this Office minibook): As Popeye might say, "It ain't quite completes." A casual walk through any computer bookstore will convince you that a dozen 400-page books *completely* concentrate on Word (or Excel or PowerPoint or Access), so you don't find tons o' advanced features or tons o' complex tips in these 30-or-so pages. However, what you *will* find is good, solid coverage of the most commonly used Word features, and that's enough to take care of the vast majority of common documents you might require.

Running Word

Enough talk! To start Word, use one of the following methods:

✦ Double-click a Word document within the File Explorer window or on your Desktop.

This is the only method for opening Word and an existing document at the same time. The next method opens Word and displays the Template window instead. With Word open, to find an existing document, choose File➪Open and then use the resulting Open dialog box to browse to the Word document you want.

Word 2013 offers a new pop-up bookmark box that appears on the right margin when you open an existing document — the program is smart enough to remember where you left off reading the last time! To return to that spot immediately, just click on the bookmark box itself.

✦ On the Start screen, type **Word** (remember, you don't have to click within any box or text field on the Start screen to perform an Apps search). Click the Word 2013 button that appears.

As an author, I use Word more than any other application on the planet — except, perhaps, for *World of Warcraft.* Anyway, if you use Word every hour of your business day, add it to your Start screen, like I did. With the Start screen displayed, press Win+Q shortcut to display your Apps screen. Right-click the Word 2013 app and click Pin to Start on the button strip that appears at the bottom of the screen. *Voilà!* Now you can summon Word with a single click from the Start screen.

The Elements of Word

If Word isn't open yet, go ahead and run the Grand Dame now. After Word has churned its way onto the screen, you'll see the Template window, which offers a number of thumbnails. You can click one of these thumbnails to choose a template as the starting point for a new document. There's also a list of recent documents you've opened along the left side of the Template window, allowing you to open a document you've worked on in the recent past with a single click.

To find a specific type of template, click within the Search Online Templates box at the top and type a keyword (*invitation*, for example). Word displays templates with matching names and descriptions. To open a document that's not on the Recent list and not among the template thumbnails, click the Open Other Documents link that appears at the bottom of the Recent list.

When you create a new document or open an existing document, you'll see the program's window, which should look like the one shown in Figure 2-1.

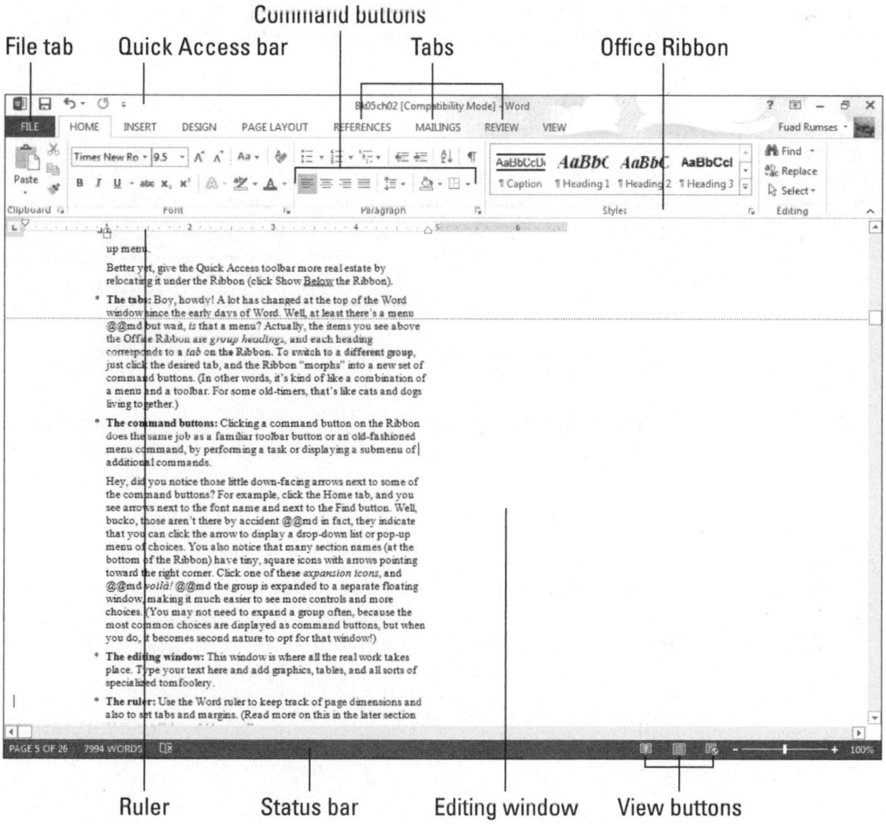

Figure 2-1:
One application to rule them all: the mighty Microsoft Word 2013.

Command buttons

File tab   Quick Access bar   Tabs   Office Ribbon

Ruler   Status bar   Editing window   View buttons

Although you probably know most of the guests invited to the party, you find some surprises if you used previous versions of Word. Here's a quick rundown of who showed up:

✦ **The File tab:** It's blue and hard to miss, and it was designed that way. Click the File tab to access most of the commands you used to associate with the File menu, like New, Open, Save, and Print. (Some call this the *Backstage* view. Theatrics, I say.) Figure 2-17 at the end of this chapter illustrates the Print pane within the File screen. You also find new headings like Share, Export, and Info, each of which offers a subset of commands that appear in the area to the right of the pane. The recent files you created and opened appear on the File tab's Open pane. The Options command allows you to configure global settings within Word.

✦ **The Office Ribbon:** The Ribbon, introduced in Office 2007, is a dynamic, composite, tabbed toolbar. Unlike on an old-fashioned static toolbar, the command buttons you see change according to the group tab you click. (Tabs and command buttons? Read farther down these bullets, please.)

At least you can regain the screen real estate claimed by the Ribbon. Look for the Ribbon Display Options menu at the top-right corner of the screen (to the right of the Help button's question mark icon) and click it to select one of the three options. Click Auto-Hide, and the Ribbon completely disappears (to temporarily restore it, click at the top of the Word window). In Show Tabs mode, all you see are the group names and tabs; if you click a group name, the Ribbon reappears temporarily while you're using the command buttons. To restore the Ribbon to its original, pristine state, click the Ribbon Display Options menu again and click Show Tabs and Commands.

✦ **The Quick Access bar:** Call it a toolbar if you will (and that's generous), but Microsoft wants you to associate this group of buttons above the File tab like pinned tiles on the Windows 8 Start screen.

To add or delete buttons from the Quick Access bar — which is helpful for often-accessed tools, or to reduce tab-hopping — click the down-arrow button to the right of the bar to display a pop-up menu. There, you can toggle the display of the most common command buttons. You can choose from a larger selection of command buttons by choosing More Commands from the pop-up menu.

Better yet, give the Quick Access bar more real estate by relocating it under the Ribbon (click Show Below the Ribbon).

✦ **The tabs:** Boy, howdy! A lot has changed at the top of the Word window since the early days of Word. Well, at least there's a menu — but wait, *is* that a menu? Actually, the items you see above the Office Ribbon are *group headings,* and each heading corresponds to a *tab* on the Ribbon. To switch to a different group, just click the desired tab, and the Ribbon "morphs" into a new set of command buttons. (In other words, it's kind of like a combination of a menu and a toolbar. For some old-timers, that's like cats and dogs living together.)

✦ **The command buttons:** Clicking a command button on the Ribbon does the same job as a familiar toolbar button or an old-fashioned menu command, by performing a task or displaying a submenu of additional commands.

Hey, did you notice those little down-facing arrows next to some of the command buttons? For example, click the Home tab, and you see arrows next to the font name and next to the Find button. Well, bucko, those aren't there by accident — in fact, they indicate that you can click the arrow to display a drop-down list or pop-up menu of choices. You also notice that many section names (at the bottom of the Ribbon) have tiny, square icons with arrows pointing toward the right corner. Click one of these *expansion icons,* and — *voilà!* — the group is expanded to a separate floating window, making it much easier to see more controls and more choices. (You may not need to expand a group often because the most common choices are displayed as command buttons, but when you do, it becomes second nature to opt for that window!)

✦ **The editing window:** This window is where all the real work takes place. Type your text here and add graphics, tables, and all sorts of specialized tomfoolery.

✦ **The ruler:** Use the Word ruler to keep track of page dimensions and also to set tabs and margins. (Read more on this in the later section "Adjusting Tabs and Margins.")

✦ **The status bar:** You find all sorts of statistics on the status bar at the bottom of the Word screen, including the number of pages in your document and the number of words in the document. (To customize the status bar, just right-click it; a pop-up menu appears, allowing you to toggle the display of items on and off.) Also, you can use the buttons to the right side of the status bar to change the view mode and zoom level. Come to think of it. . . .

A Word about Views

Speaking of views, Word can display your document in more than just one mundane way. You can switch between views by clicking the View tab on the Ribbon and then clicking the desired view in the Views group, or you can click the view buttons on the right side of the status bar. Take a gander at this selection of views.

Draft view

Draft view is your plain vanilla, default viewing mode (refer to Figure 2-1). However, I find Draft view to be the quickest to use when I'm typing or when I'm editing an existing document. Note that you can't choose Draft view from the status bar — instead, click View on the Ribbon and select it from the Views group at the left side of the Ribbon.

What you see in Draft view definitely might *not* be what you get when you print, so switch to Web Layout or Print Layout view to edit the final appearance of a document. And use Print Preview (choose File⇨Print) to check the appearance of the printed pages before you send them to the Monster of Toner.

Outline view

In Outline view (check it out in Figure 2-2), the structure of your document is the important thing, much like the outlining you learned in grade school. Outline view allows you to change and rearrange the sections of your entire document (except that this time, you get to use a click of the mouse rather than that doggone eraser). You'll find controls under the Outlining tab that allow you to promote and demote headings, move selected text up and down within the outline, and expand and collapse headings. As with Draft view, you'll have to click the View tab on the Ribbon to choose Outline view.

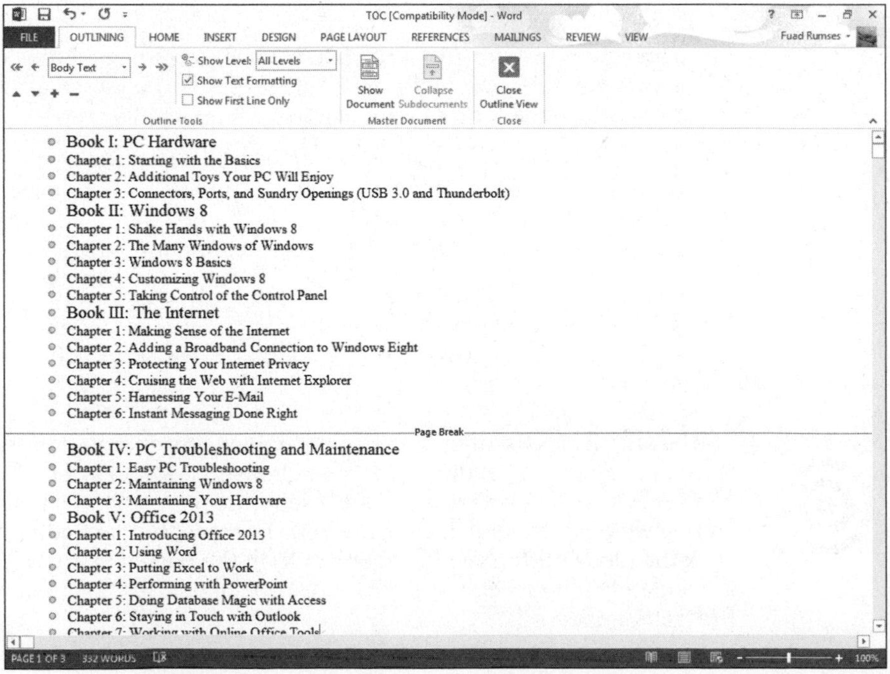

Figure 2-2:
Hey, an outline that I really *like,* for a change!

Word 2013 introduces a new Expand and Collapse feature that makes it easier to concentrate on specific headings while reading or writing — and you don't need to be in Outline view to use it. Move your cursor over a heading in your document, and you'll see a tiny blue triangle appear; click to expand or collapse that heading. Note that Word automatically expands all headings again when you close the document.

Print Layout view

I recommend switching to Print Layout view when you need to design the look of your page because you can easily work with page elements, such as columns and graphics, by clicking and dragging them from place to place. (You can also click most elements and drag their borders to new locations.) If you're familiar with desktop publishing programs like Adobe InDesign, you'll feel right at home in Print Layout view. Click the second tiny button in the view icons on the status bar to switch to Print Layout view.

Web Layout view

Of course, there's the Internet side of things. In Web Layout view, Word adds any background you specify, places images where they will appear in a web browser, and wraps the text to fit the window size. You can use this view to design a document that's saved later as a web page. Click the third button in the view group on the status bar to use Web Layout view.

Reading view

Reading view is specially designed to make your document easy to read onscreen. (Call this view the E-Book Special, if you like.) Pages appear side-by-side, like a book, and the page is automatically sized to fit virtually the entire application window. (Note that the page does *not* appear this way when it's printed!) Word also turns on Microsoft's ClearType font–smoothing feature, to help make the text easier on the eyes — and personally, I think it works. You can't edit text in Read view — the Highlighter feature is still active, however, making it easier to quickly highlight sections of longer documents. Click the first button in the view group on the status bar — which looks like an open book — to use Reading view; to return to the previous view, press Esc or click the View tab and choose Edit Document.

The Navigation pane offers major convenience for moving quickly through large documents in Reading view. Just choose View and select the Navigation Pane check box to have Word open a separate pane on the left side of the editing window (as shown in Figure 2-3). To close the Navigation pane, just click the Close button (which bears an X) in the pane's title bar. You can move immediately to any heading within your document by clicking it within the Navigation pane.

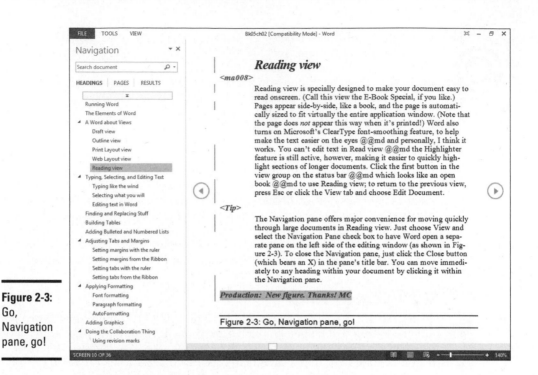

Figure 2-3:
Go,
Navigation
pane, go!

Typing, Selecting, and Editing Text

Ready to start your first foray into the editing window? In this section, I discuss the three all-important things that you do most often during your Word session: type new text, select existing text, and edit existing text.

Typing like the wind

Okay, I know this seems like a no-brainer — and typing in Word is indeed simple. First, locate the insertion cursor (which looks like a blinking bar) where you want in the editing window (by clicking the mouse pointer, which looks like a tiny I-beam, or by using the movement keyboard shortcuts listed in Table 2-1). Tickle the ivories to enter your text.

Press Insert (on the keyboard) to toggle *Overwrite mode,* in which the new characters you type overwrite any existing text; to return to *Insert mode,* in which new characters are inserted at the cursor point, press the Insert key again.

Table 2-1	Movement Shortcut Keys in Word
Key	*Where It Moves the Cursor*
Left arrow (←)	One character to the left
Right arrow (→)	One character to the right
Up arrow (↑)	To the preceding line
Down arrow (↓)	To the next line
Ctrl+←	One word to the left
Ctrl+→	One word to the right
Ctrl+↑	One paragraph up
Ctrl+↓	One paragraph down
Page Up	Up one screen
Page Down	Down one screen
End	To the end of the current line
Home	To the beginning of the current line
Ctrl+Page Up	To the top of the previous page
Ctrl+Page Down	To the top of the next page
Ctrl+Home	To the beginning of the document
Ctrl+End	To the end of the document

Selecting what you will

My father always used to say, "Nothing is perfect the first time around" — and a Word document is no exception. However, don't break out the Liquid Paper for your screen! Instead, use the mouse to select text or graphics by clicking and dragging the I-beam cursor across the text you want to change or format, or use the selection keyboard shortcuts provided so conveniently by Table 2-2.

To select a word, just double-click it; to select a graphic, click it once. To select a chunk of text (even several pages worth), click to place the insertion cursor at the start of the text you want to highlight and then hold down Shift while you click at the end of the desired text.

Table 2-2	Selection Shortcut Keys in Word
Key	*What It Selects*
Shift+A	Entire document
Shift+←	One character to the left of the cursor
Shift+→	One character to the right of the cursor
Shift+↑	Characters to the previous line
Shift+↓	Characters to the next line
Shift+End	Characters to the end of the current line
Shift+Home	Characters to the beginning of the current line
Shift+Page Down	Characters to the next screen
Shift+Page Up	Characters to the previous screen
Ctrl+Shift+←	Characters to the beginning of the word
Ctrl+Shift+→	Characters to the end of the word
Ctrl+Shift+↑	Characters to the beginning of the current paragraph
Ctrl+Shift+↓	Characters to the end of the current paragraph
Ctrl+Shift+Home	Characters to the beginning of the document
Ctrl+Shift+End	Characters to the end of the document

Editing text in Word

After you select the text and graphics you want to change, you can then pick an action (either from the Ribbon or by right-clicking) or use one of the editing keyboard shortcuts shown in Table 2-3.

Table 2-3	Editing Shortcut Keys in Word
Key	*What It Does*
Any character	Replaces the selected text
Delete	Deletes the selected text and graphics
Ctrl+X	Cuts the selection and adds it to the Clipboard (or the Office Clipboard, if it's displayed)
Ctrl+C	Copies the selection to the Clipboard (or the Office Clipboard, if it's displayed)
Ctrl+V	Replaces the selection with the contents of the Clipboard

If you're not familiar with the Office Clipboard and its features, read more about it in Chapter 1 of this minibook.

Finding and Replacing Stuff

I don't know about you, but manually tracking down every single occurrence of the word *salacious* in my Word documents is not my idea of fun! (Okay, perhaps not *salacious* — substitute your own most common word.) Anyway, Word provides you with the dynamic duo of Find and Replace, which ensures that no word or phrase in your document can escape your all-seeing eye.

To perform a Find or Replace operation, follow these steps:

1. **Click the Home tab and then click Replace (in the Editing group). (From the keyboard, press Ctrl+H.)**

   The Find and Replace dialog box appears, which you can see in Figure 2-4. Note that this dialog box floats above the Word window. And, unlike with other active dialog boxes, you can continue to click, select, and type in the Word window while the Find and Replace dialog box is open.

   If you opt for Find instead of Replace (also in the Home↪Editing group), Word eschews the Find and Replace dialog box and displays the Navigation pane instead, complete with a search text box ready for you to enter the text you're looking for.

   For this example, I'll stick with the Find and Replace dialog box.

2. **Type the word or phrase that you need to locate or change in the Find What text field.**

   If you've already run a search for the same target string earlier, click the down arrow next to the box and select it from the drop-down list.

3. **To replace any matches with something new, type the word or phrase that you want to substitute in the Replace With text field.**

   Again, if you already used the new value to replace something earlier in this writing session, just click the down arrow and choose a value from the drop-down list.

   Click More and then click the Special button to display a pop-up menu of special and nonprinting characters that you can insert at the cursor position in the Find What or Replace With boxes. For instance, if you need to search for (or replace using) a graphic, a Tab character, or a caret character, you can pick it from the Special button menu.

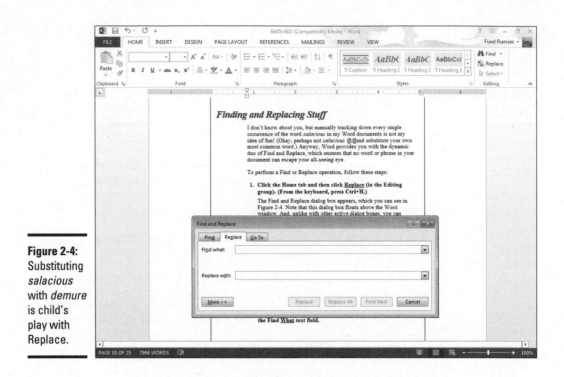

Figure 2-4:
Substituting
salacious
with *demure*
is child's
play with
Replace.

4. **To find the next occurrence, click the Find Next button; to replace the next occurrence, click the Replace button.**

   You can also click the Replace All button to locate and replace all occurrences of the word or phrase. However, I recommend clicking Replace one time first, just to make sure that you're indeed matching what you think! If the correct word or phrase is replaced, click Replace All to finish the job.

   You can immediately use Undo after any Word action goes awry. In this case, if you suddenly find that you replaced every *the* in your document with *thee* by accident, choose the Undo button on the Quick Access bar or use the Ctrl+Z keyboard shortcut.

5. **If you used Find Next or Replace in Step 4, Word selects the next occurrence.**

   You can continue your Find or Replace activities, or you can click Cancel if you're done.

That's the mundane side of Find and Replace. However, if you click the More button at the bottom of the Find and Replace dialog box (which toggles the More button to Less), you see all sorts of interesting options that can help you fine-tune your search, including

✦ **Match Case:** By default, Find and Replace are case-insensitive toys — select this check box to make capitalization matter, allowing you to differentiate between *Ford* (the automaker) and *ford* (the action of crossing a river or stream).

✦ **Find Whole Words Only:** When this check box is deselected, Word matches portions of a word, which comes in handy when changing tenses, prefixes, or suffixes. To force Word to match only the exact string you entered, select this check box.

✦ **Use Wildcards:** A throwback to the days of DOS, *wildcards* allow you to search for specific combinations of letters or numbers in your target strings. Unix folks call this *pattern matching.* (Check the Word Help system for a complete list of wildcards.)

✦ **Sounds Like:** If you know what the target word sounds like but you can't spell it, select the Sounds Like check box, and Word locates matching words that sound the same. For example, *role* matches *roll.*

✦ **Find All Word Forms:** Select this check box to locate all forms of the target noun or verb — tenses, plurals, and such. Trick, indeed!

To perform a search based on any sort of formatting (such as character or paragraph formatting or a specific language within your document), click the Format button and then select the appropriate type of formatting from the pop-up menu that appears.

Building Tables

Tables are great for displaying, well, tabular information. (Stunning stuff, Mark.) But that information need not be uniform, and you can add all sorts of eye candy (like shading and different types of borders).

Follow these steps to add a standard table to your Word document:

1. **Click within your document to place the insertion cursor in the desired spot for the table.**

2. **Choose Insert⇨Table to display the pop-up menu you see in Figure 2-5.**

   For a simple table, just move your mouse pointer over the grid to "mark" the number of rows and columns to insert, and then press the mouse button. Now you can skip to Step 5.

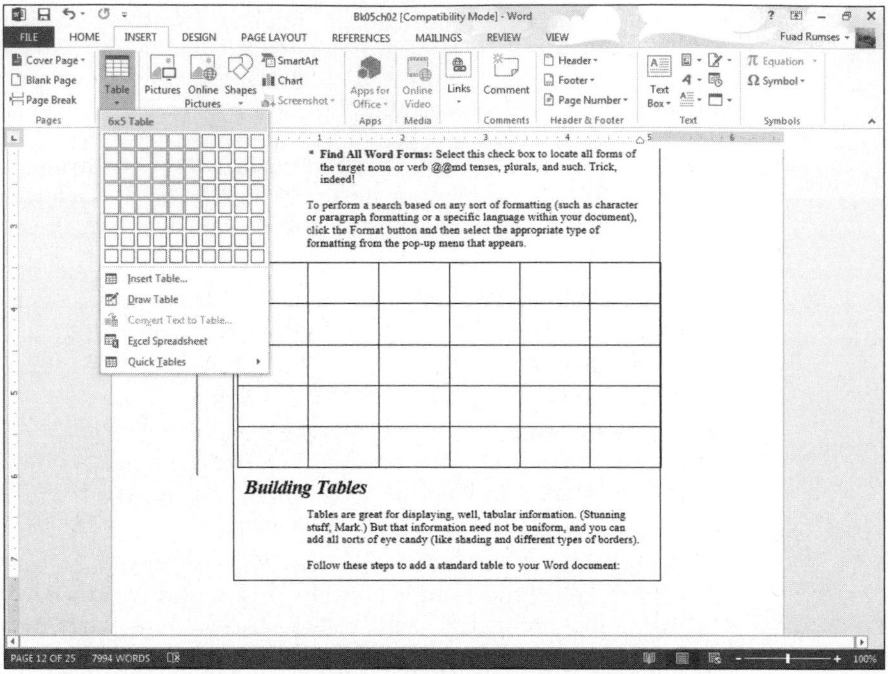

Figure 2-5:
Inserting a table into a Word document, using the grid.

If you need more control over your table characteristics, choose Insert Table from the same pop-up menu to display the Insert Table dialog box. Click in the Number of Columns text box and type the number of columns you need in the table, and then click in the Number of Rows text box and type the number of rows you need in the table.

3. **Select the AutoFit Behavior option that you prefer from the Insert Table dialog box.**

   The default, Fixed Column Width, is fine if all the values that the table will hold will be uniform in length; however, I recommend that you choose AutoFit to Contents if you need to save space in your document or if certain values are far longer than others. If you're creating a web page, select AutoFit to Window.

4. **Click OK in the Insert Table dialog box to create the basic table structure, as shown in Figure 2-6.**

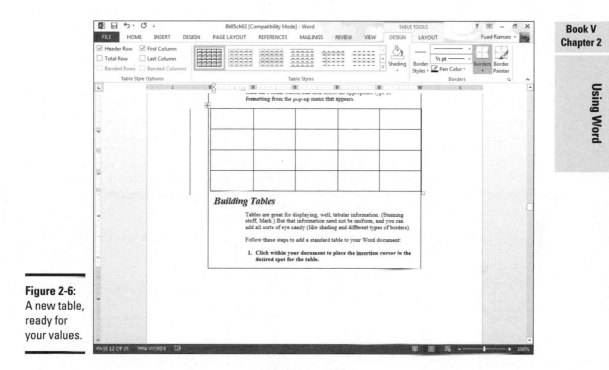

Figure 2-6:
A new table,
ready for
your values.

5. Click in each cell and type the value.

You can apply the same formatting attributes to the text in a table cell,
too. For example, I select the top row of a table and then press Ctrl+B to
create bold column headings.

This procedure provides you with a basic table. Select the table itself and
right-click it, and then choose Border Styles from the pop-up menu that
appears (or click the Design tab on the Ribbon, which appears when you
select the table). You'll be amazed at all the fun fashions you can use to dec-
orate that simple frame! For example, you can change the type, width, and
color of the border. Click the Shading button on the Design tab and choose
your own colors, shading, and patterns (either for the entire table or just for
the cells you select). With the table selected, you can also click the Layout
tab on the Ribbon, where you can tinker with table specifics or add new
rows and columns — I'm all for convenience!

Adding Bulleted and Numbered Lists

Creating bullets and numbered lists automatically in Word is a cinch. Follow these steps:

1. **Click anywhere within the paragraph you want to format.**

2. **Click the Home tab.**

3. **In the Paragraph group, click the drop-down arrow button next to the Bullets button (at the top left of the Paragraph group) to view the available bullet formats or the drop-down arrow button next to the Numbering button to view the available numbering formats.**

   Figure 2-7 illustrates the Bullet Library pop-up menu.

4. **Click the type of bullet or number formatting you want to apply to the paragraph.**

   To apply the same format again to another paragraph, simply click the Bullets or Numbering button — no need to choose the same format again!

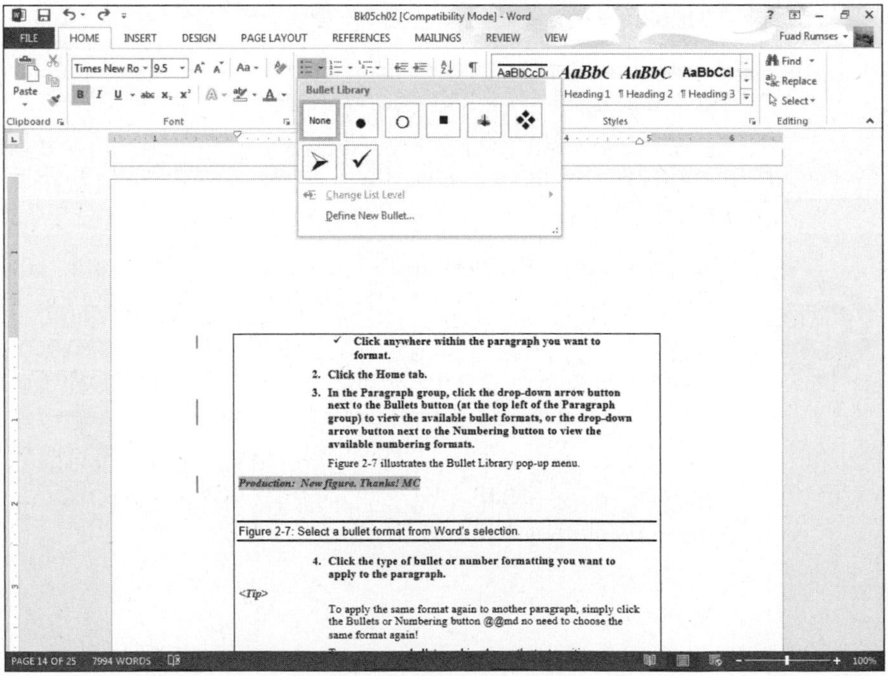

Figure 2-7:
Select a
bullet format
from Word's
selection.

To use your own bullet graphic, change the text positions, or use a character from a favorite font, and click the Define New Bullet item at the bottom of the Bullets pop-up menu. (Naturally, the same goes for the Define New Number Format item at the bottom of the Numbering pop-up menu.) Figure 2-8 illustrates the Define New Bullet dialog box that appears.

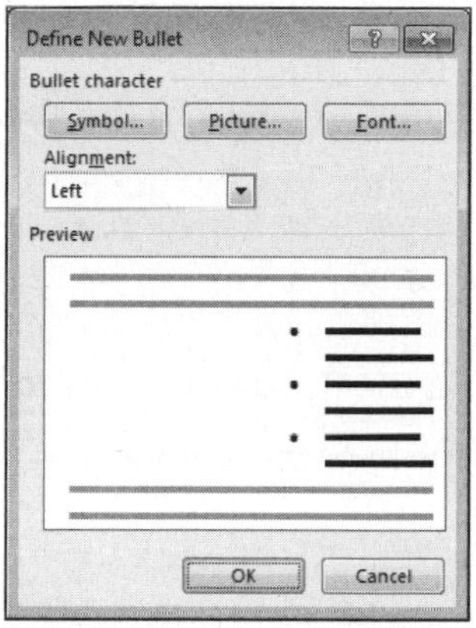

Figure 2-8:
Customize your bullets here.

You can also use the Multilevel List button and corresponding pop-up Library menu in the Paragraph section to create lists, and the Decrease Indent and Increase Indent buttons (which hang out in the same area) to alter the position of the text by a tab stop each time you click them.

Adjusting Tabs and Margins

Call them throwbacks to your typewriter days, but tabs and margins are still with us. After all, these two settings are largely responsible for the appearance of your pages — and how much text and graphics each page can hold.

Word respects these two elders by providing multiple methods of setting tabs and margins; in this section, I show you how to configure tabs and margins by using both your mouse and your keyboard.

Setting margins with the ruler

Follow these steps to set up margins by using Word's horizontal and vertical rulers:

1. **Change to Print Layout view (click the Print Layout button on the status bar or click the View tab and choose Print Layout).**

2. **If the ruler isn't visible, click the View tab and select the Ruler check box to enable it.**

3. **Move your mouse cursor over the end of either of the shaded bars on the ruler.**

   These bars indicate the current margin, and the mouse pointer turns into a twin-arrow cursor to indicate that the bar can be moved (as shown with the right margin in Figure 2-9).

4. **Click and drag the arrow cursor in the desired direction.**

5. **Release the mouse button to set the new margin value.**

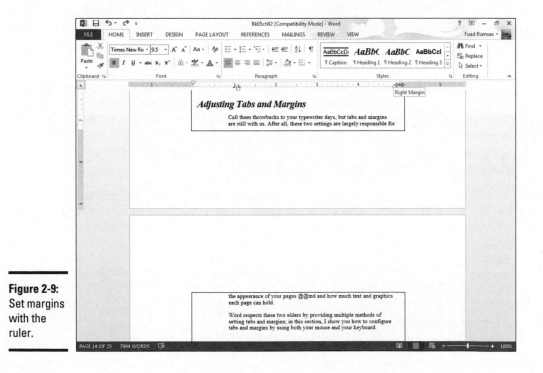

Figure 2-9: Set margins with the ruler.

Setting margins from the Ribbon

Follow these steps to set margins from the Page Layout tab of the Ribbon:

1. **Click the Page Layout tab on the Ribbon and then click the expansion icon of the Page Setup group to display the Page Setup dialog box, which you see in Figure 2-10.**

2. **Click in the appropriate Margins text box (for the margin you want to change) and then type the desired value in inches.**

3. **Click the arrow of the Apply To drop-down list and then select Whole Document.**

   To apply margin changes to just a part of the document, select some text before opening the Page Setup dialog box and then choose Selected Text from the Apply To drop-down list. If you want the margin change to apply to the remainder of the document starting at the current position of the insertion cursor, choose This Point Forward instead.

4. **Click OK to save your changes and return to your document.**

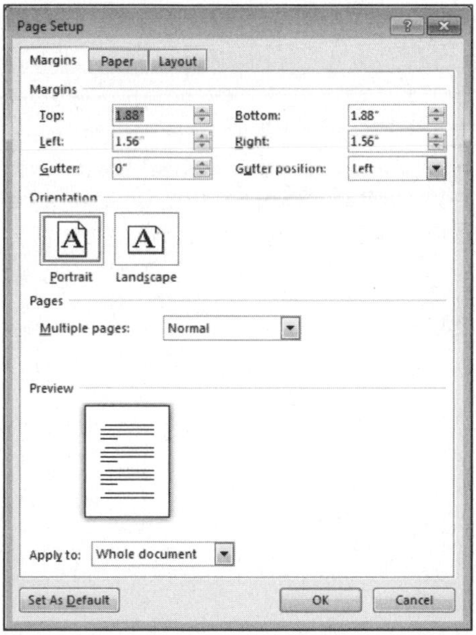

Figure 2-10:
Setting margins from the Ribbon.

Setting tabs with the ruler

Word offers several different types of tabs, including left, center, right, and decimal- or bar-aligned. To add a tab stop with the ruler, follow these steps:

1. **Click anywhere within the paragraph where you want to place the tab.**

2. **Click the Tab button in the upper-left corner of the editing window. The button appears on the left side of the ruler (looks like a capital *L* in a square) — until you select the type of tab you need.**

   To check the current tab type, just leave your mouse pointer hovering on top of the Tab button until the tooltip description appears.

3. **Click the spot on the ruler where you want to place the tab.**

To help you keep track of your tab, Word automatically adds a tab stop mark (it looks like the old-fashioned tab pointer on your trusty manual Olivet type-writer) on the ruler.

Setting tabs from the Ribbon

Follow these steps to set a tab stop from the Page Layout tab of the Ribbon:

1. **Click the Page Layout tab on the Ribbon.**

2. **Click the Paragraph group expansion icon and then click the Tabs button at the bottom of the Paragraph dialog box to open the Tabs dialog box, shown in Figure 2-11.**

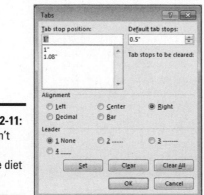

Figure 2-11: Hey, isn't Tab an antique diet cola?

3. **Click in the Tab Stop Position field and then type the position of the new tab stop in inches.**

4. **Select an Alignment option.**

5. **To add a leader to the new tab stop, select one of the Leader selections.**

 A *leader* is a character that's used to fill the open space that normally appears when you press the Tab key. Leader characters are often used in a table of contents, telephone list, or restaurant menu.

 Word sets the default tab stops to every half inch; to choose a new default value for tab stops, click in the Default Tab Stops field and type the new value (in inches).

6. **Click the Set button to set the new tab.**

7. **To clear a tab stop, click the tab stop that you want to remove within the list on the left and then click Clear.**

 Or you can clear all tab stops in one fell swoop by clicking the Clear All button.

8. **Click OK to return to your document.**

Applying Formatting

Word offers a number of different formatting commands. At its lowest level, you can manually format individual characters by changing their attributes. At its highest level, you can set Word to automatically format your document while you type! In this section, I describe how to fine-tune your formatting.

Font formatting

You probably already know the trio of attributes that I like to call The Big Three:

✦ **Bold:** Press Ctrl+B to add emphasis to the selected text.

✦ *Italic:* Press Ctrl+I to italicize the selected text.

✦ <u>Underline:</u> Press Ctrl+U to underline the selected text.

Of course, each of The Big Three is represented by a separate button on the Ribbon — specifically, the Font group of the Home tab (**B**, *I*, and <u>U</u>). But there's a heck of a lot more font formatting where that came from — you can also add these attributes to selected text:

✦ **The font family:** (No relation to the Addams Family.) Click the expansion icon for the Font group to display the Font dialog box, which you see in Figure 2-12; then click the font name you want to use. (Alternatively, click the Font drop-down list in the Font section. This way, you're treated to a visual preview of each font installed on your PC.)

Figure 2-12:
The Font dialog box is a busy metropolitan location.

✦ **The size:** Click to select a font size (in points) from the Size list or type the size you want directly into the Size text box.

✦ **The color:** You can click the Font Color drop-down list to choose the latest fashion color for your text.

✦ **The standard effects:** Select check boxes in the Effects section to enable effects, and Word automatically updates the Preview window with the results.

✦ **The spacing:** Click the Advanced tab and then choose the amount of space between characters, or you can raise or lower the characters by the amount that you specify. Word shows you the fruit of your labor in the Preview window.

Note that you don't need to select text to use font formatting. If no text is specifically selected, Word simply applies your font changes to any new text you type at the current location of the insertion cursor.

Paragraph formatting

Word is a consistent machine. And, as you might expect, formatting a paragraph is quite similar to formatting individual characters. Note, however, that not every separate text element on a page is a true paragraph; to qualify, the text block must end with a paragraph mark, which is represented by that weird backward *P* symbol, our friend, the pilcrow (¶).

Because Word normally hides formatting marks (like pilcrows), you probably don't see any paragraph marks in your document unless you specifically tell Word to display them. You can do this by clicking the Home tab and clicking the Show/Hide command button at the upper right of the Paragraph group (which brazenly carries that same funky backward-P paragraph mark). Personally, I like to be able to see where my paragraphs come to a halt because I do quite a bit of formatting on manuscripts (and it makes a great difference whether you select a paragraph *with* or *without* the paragraph mark)!

Commonly used paragraph formatting attributes include

+ **Alignment:** Click the Home tab and then click the expansion icon of the Paragraph group to display the Paragraph dialog box, which you see in Figure 2-13. Click the Alignment drop-down list box, and you see that Word can align text to the left or right margin or center the paragraph on the page. You can also choose to *justify* a paragraph, which adds extra spacing to stretch each full line in the paragraph from the left to the right margin.

+ **Indentation:** As I show you in the earlier section, "Adding Bulleted and Numbered Lists," you can automatically add bullets and line numbers to your text. From the Paragraph dialog box, you can specify the amount to indent the selected paragraph as well as which kind of indent to use.

+ **Spacing:** Click the Line Spacing drop-down list box in the Paragraph dialog box to choose double spacing or to specify a precise line spacing of your own choosing. This is also the place where you can add extra space before or after a paragraph.

These commands are also conveniently located as command buttons in the Paragraph group of the Home tab.

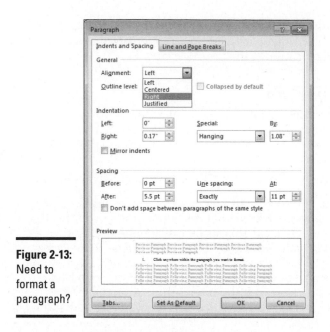

Figure 2-13:
Need to
format a
paragraph?

AutoFormatting

Before I leave the fair shores of formatting, I want to mention a well-known "either you love it or you hate it" feature. I'm talking about the Word *AutoFormat* feature, which — true to its name — automatically recognizes what it feels should be formatted and then takes care of the task for you — whether you want it to or not. To illustrate: If you type an asterisk at the beginning of a line and press Enter at the end, AutoFormat figures, "Oh, that crazy human actually wants a bulleted list item" and thus formats the paragraph with an indent and a bullet character and then adds another bullet for your next item. The same thing happens with numbered lists, too. Try typing **1.** at the beginning of the line and pressing Enter, just to see the results.

Don't get me wrong: If you're a newcomer to Word or you don't need precise control over the formatting in your document, AutoFormat can be a true timesaver and a big help. (Pause.) However, if you *do* need that precise formatting control, AutoFormat suddenly becomes a nightmare when you're forced to helplessly watch Word do what it *thinks* is right.

Therefore, here's how to disable AutoFormat — which is on by default — just in case you find it nerve-wracking rather than helpful:

1. **Click the File tab and then click the Options button at the bottom of the menu.**

2. **Click the Proofing heading on the left and then click the AutoCorrect Options button.**

3. **Click the AutoFormat as You Type tab to display the settings shown in Figure 2-14.**

4. **To completely disable AutoFormatting while you type, deselect all check boxes and then click OK.**

   Note that you can still run AutoFormat on your entire document at once at any time — it just takes a little work because you have to add an AutoFormat button to the Quick Access bar (as I discuss at the beginning of this chapter).

5. **Click OK to save your changes.**

(You can bet that I didn't use AutoFormat to create this numbered list, either. Harrumph.)

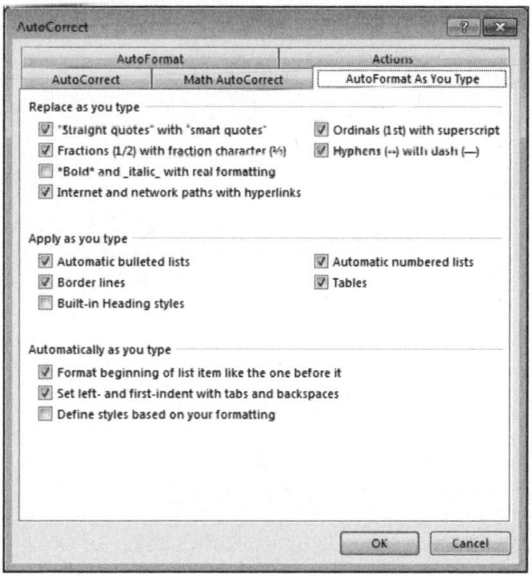

Figure 2-14:
No, Word!
Bad
AutoFormat!
No biscuit!

Adding Graphics

You have a number of different ways to add graphics to your Word document. After you click in the desired spot (which moves the insertion cursor to that point in your document), use one of the following methods:

✦ **Paste it from the Clipboard.** If you copied a graphic to your Windows or the Office Clipboard (which I discuss in Chapter 1 of this minibook), you can paste it to the current cursor location.

✦ **Insert it from a file.** If the graphic is stored on your hard drive, click the Insert tab and click the Pictures command button in the Illustrations group. Word displays the familiar Insert Picture dialog box, from where you can navigate to the location of the image. Click once on the filename to select it and then click the Insert button.

✦ **Insert a clip art image.** Click the Insert tab and click the Online Pictures command button in the Illustrations group to display the Insert Pictures dialog box. Type a keyword in the Office.com Clip Art text box and press Enter to display thumbnail images of any matching clip art. As you can see in Figure 2-15, I'm not the only person who loves Halloween!

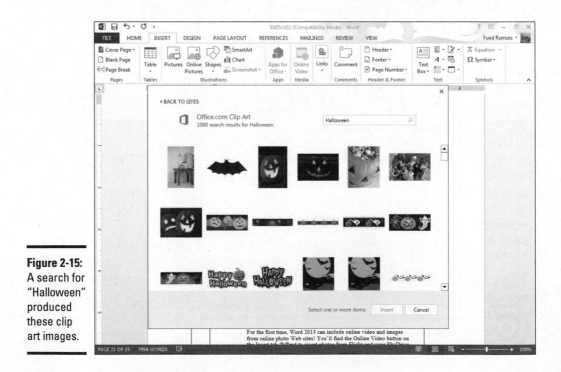

Figure 2-15: A search for "Halloween" produced these clip art images.

For the first time, Word 2013 can include online video and images from online photo websites! You'll find the Online Video button on the Insert tab — to insert photos from Flickr and your SkyDrive, click the Online Pictures button on the Insert tab. (Note that you must be logged in with your Microsoft Office online account to access online pictures.)

Doing the Collaboration Thing

Word includes several features for managing collaborative documents — keeping things straight about who revised what or perhaps adding comments and highlighting to indicate where changes are necessary.

Need to share the information in your Word document with data-mining or database applications? You'll be happy to learn that Word 2013 can save a document in Word XML (Extensible Markup Language) format using the standard Save As command (on the File tab). Choose Word XML Document from the Save as Type drop-down list.

Using revision marks

If several editors have their hands in a single document, revision marks are the only way to go. Everyone can make changes (Word assigns different colors to each editor), and those changes can be reviewed and applied (or discarded) individually, or you can accept or revert all changes at once.

To use revision marks, click the Review tab and click the Track Changes command button. Now you've told Word to track anything that anyone does within the document. Nothing appears to happen — at least, that is, until you make any change to the document. Continue typing or editing as you like. Word formats with a unique color the changes you make, underlining them to make things easier to see. Deleted text and graphics are shown with the strikethrough attribute.

When you're ready to review the revision marks in a document, click the Review tab again to display all your revision tools. Click either the Accept button (which carries a blue check mark) or Reject button (which bears a red X), and you move through your document. (For just a second, you feel like you have the ol' Caesar thumb — you know, the one that Caesar gets to use in any gladiator movie.)

Just in case you don't quite have the power of Caesar, you can always save the revised document under another filename before you decide for or against the edits. (Even a Roman emperor could use a little insurance.)

To accept in one fell swoop all changes made with revision marks, click the down arrow under the Accept button to display the drop-down list and then click Accept All Changes in Document. To toss out all those silly edits, click the arrow underneath the Reject Change button and then choose Reject All Changes in Document. The *nerve* of some people, tampering with perfection!

Using comments

In this section, we take a look at *comments,* which allow anyone to flag a document without directly changing its contents. To add a Comment, select the text you want to comment on and then click the New Comment button on that now-familiar Reviewing tab.

In Print Layout view, Word displays a color marker at the word or point where you made the comment and displays a comment bubble, which you see on the right side of Figure 2-16 in the markup area. The insertion cursor is also automatically relocated in the Comment bubble, so you can type your comment text, which is marked with the name of who added the comment as well as when (date and time). When you're done, click anywhere in the editing window to continue.

When you're ready to review comments, you can

✦ Review the comments in a document by using the Next Comment and Previous Comment buttons in the Comments group of the Review tab. (They appear next to the New Comment button.)

✦ Hover your mouse pointer on top of the highlighted comment marker in the text.

✦ Double-click the shaded header in the markup area, which automatically switches Word into Print Layout view and displays the comment.

Word 2013 allows collaborators to reply to comments, allowing discussions about the comments that can be read by others.

Of course, you can't "apply" a comment, but you can delete those that offend. Just click anywhere in the commented text and then click the Delete Comment button — which bears a red X — on the Review tab (or just right-click the Comment marker in the text and then choose Delete Comment from the pop-up menu that appears).

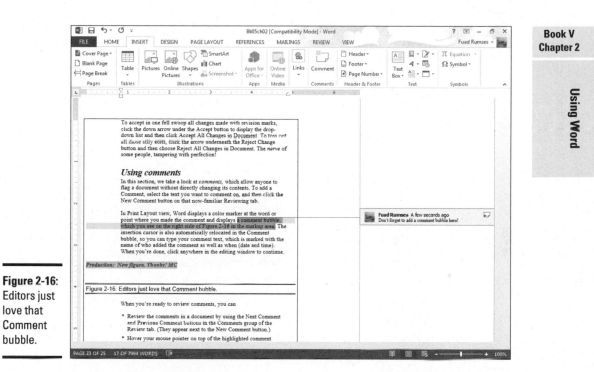

Figure 2-16:
Editors just
love that
Comment
bubble.

Using highlighting

Ever wish that you could turn back the editing clock to paper and those classy neon yellow highlighter markers you used in school? Fear not: Word can take you there. Follow these steps to highlight text in your documents:

1. **Click the Home tab on the Ribbon and then click the Text Highlight Color button (in the Font group). (It looks like a fat, smelly marker with the letters *a* and *b* perched on top.)**

   • *To select a color:* Click the down arrow next to the Highlight button and then click a color.

   • *To erase previous highlighting:* Click None.

2. **Select the text to highlight.**

3. **When you're done highlighting, turn off the feature by clicking the Highlight button again.**

Alternatively, you can first select the text that you want to be highlighted and then click the Highlight button. The Highlight button also appears on the pop-up menu when you right-click selected text.

Printing Your Document

Word offers you two different ways to print an open document:

✦ **Choose File⇨Print.** The Print pane, which you see in Figure 2-17, gives you full control over what gets printed and which printer you use — including the number of copies and the option to print only part of the document. (To display the printer-specific options supported by the printer's Windows 8 software driver, click the Printer Properties link.)

✦ **Press Ctrl+P.** This method also displays the Print pane.

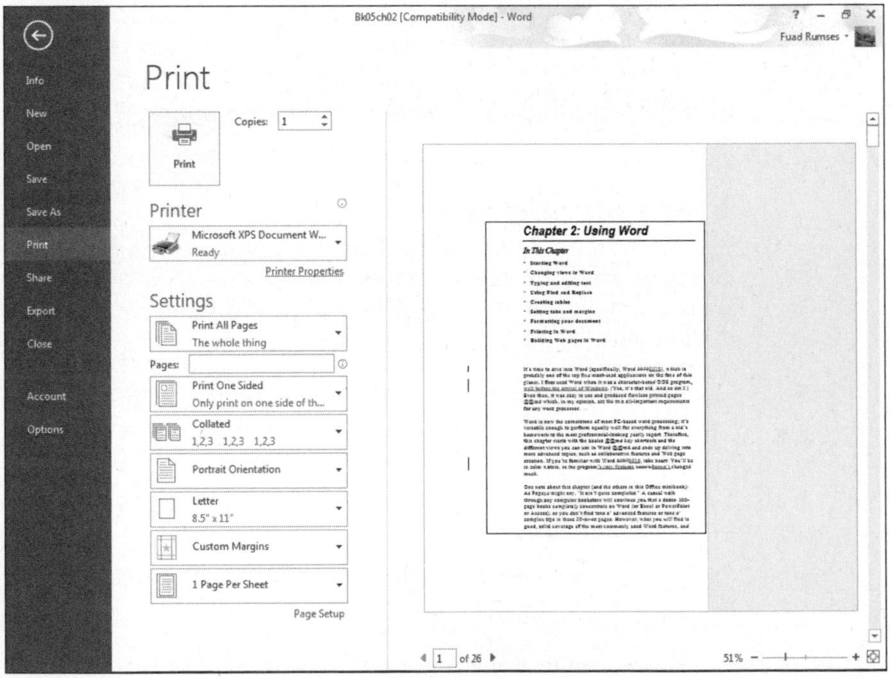

Figure 2-17:
The Word
Print pane.

Creating Web Pages with Word

In a pinch, Word even can step in as a serviceable web page creation tool! After you create a document, follow these steps to turn that document into a web page:

1. **Click the File tab and choose Save As; then click the Browse button.**

2. **Click the Save as Type pop-up menu and choose Web Page.**

3. **Click the Change Title button, type a title for this page, and click OK.**

4. **Navigate to the spot where you want to save the file and then type a new filename for the page.**

   You don't need to add a HyperText Markup Language (HTML) extension because Word does it automatically.

5. **Click Save.**

   Word creates an HTML page and a separate folder that contains any graphics necessary to display the page; all you have to do is move both to your web server.

Because some of the advanced formatting you can use in Word doesn't translate at all to a web page, the application does the best job it can. But at least you can rely on Word to produce a web page that loads in virtually every browser on the planet.

Chapter 3: Putting Excel to Work

In This Chapter

✓ Running Excel

✓ Presenting the Excel window

✓ Typing, selecting, and editing cell text

✓ Handling numbers and dates

✓ Manipulating rows and columns

✓ Formatting cells in Excel

✓ Understanding Excel formulas

✓ Inserting graphics and charts

✓ Linking cell values

✓ Adding headers and footers

✓ Printing worksheets

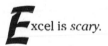xcel is *scary*.

There, I said it. Most Office 2013 users know that Excel is one doggone powerful and versatile tool, but it has a reputation for being difficult to learn. (Not to mention all those strange, foreign-looking formulas and functions — heck, I can barely remember my long division. And don't even get me started on my kid's math homework.)

In this chapter, however, I can help you with that common Excel-phobia that grips the novice who runs Excel for the first time. I show you the basics of selecting cells and entering cell values, manipulating rows and columns, formatting numbers and dates, and adding graphics. And yes — believe it or not — I get you started on the road to understanding and using formulas to calculate the values you need. After all, that's the real power behind Excel — plugging in values to see what happens.

As Thomas Edison, a personal hero of mine, *never* said, "After Excel formulas are your friends, the world is your oyster." (Then again, he certainly *could* have said it, and perhaps no one was around to write it down. Yeah, that's it.)

Running Excel

You can start the number-cruncher that is Excel in any of the following ways:

✦ On the Start screen, simply type **Excel** and click the Excel 2013 button that appears.

✦ Double-click an Excel document in File Explorer or on your Desktop.

✦ If you added an Excel tile to your Windows 8 Start screen, click it.

✦ Press Win+R, type **excel** in the Run dialog box that appears, and then press Enter. (That's assuming that your keyboard is equipped with Windows keys, which look like the waving Windows flags and are located on either side of the spacebar.)

Waltzing Around the Excel Window

If you open Excel itself (instead of an existing Excel document), you'll see the Template window, complete with thumbnails of online templates that can get you started quickly. Click a thumbnail, and Excel opens a new workbook with that template as a starting point. You can also click a workbook you've used recently in the list along the left side of the Template window to open it immediately.

Click within the Search Online Templates box at the top and type a keyword like *budget* to display templates with matching names and descriptions.

As for the Excel main window (as shown in Figure 3-1) itself? Unfortunately, this window has one immediate drawback, and Microsoft has never really been able to address it: Excel simply looks complex from the moment you start it! However, don't be intimidated by all those cells. When you take a second look, the familiar Office controls are still there.

File tab   Quick Access bar   Formula bar   Office Ribbon

Sheet tab   Status bar   Editing window

Figure 3-1:
The Excel
2013 main
window.
Glorious!

Although you know most of the screen controls by heart, here's a refresher:

✦ **File tab:** The File tab includes many familiar menu items you'll immediately recognize like Open, Save, and Print. Recent documents you created and opened appear on the File tab menu, and you find an Options item that leads to global settings you can change that affect all of Excel.

✦ **Quick Access bar:** By default, this group of buttons next to the File tab includes Save, Undo, and Redo commands, but you can click the Customize button next to the Quick Access bar to add or remove command buttons.

✦ **Office Ribbon:** No, it's not a toolbar, but it does have buttons — and they change when you click a group tab at the top of the Ribbon.

Note that Excel includes a unique field called the *Formula bar* underneath the Ribbon, where you can type a formula for a cell or view a formula that's already associated with the selected cell. (More on formulas later in this chapter.)

✦ **Editing window:** Each individual square in the editing window is a *cell,* which can hold text, numbers, tables, and graphics.

✦ **Sheet tabs:** These nifty tabs at the bottom of the editing window allow you to jump among worksheets and charts in the Excel window. Just click a tab to switch to that worksheet.

✦ **Status bar:** The Excel status bar displays information about calculations and the contents of cells.

Before I launch into a discussion of cells, however, let me clear up a common misunderstanding among novice Excel users concerning the difference between a workbook and a worksheet:

✦ **Workbook:** A *workbook* acts just like a file folder in a filing cabinet, storing all the worksheets required for a single project. Because a workbook acts as the container for worksheets, it's the file you're working with when you create a new project or when you load and save in Excel (and is featured in the task pane for that reason). In Excel 2013, each workbook has its own separate window.

✦ **Worksheet:** A *worksheet* is what you use to enter data, graphics, and charts. You can create a new worksheet inside the current workbook at any time. To switch worksheets in the current workbook, use the sheet tabs.

Selecting, Entering, and Editing Cell Data

As I mention earlier, a *cell* is one individual block within a worksheet, and it can hold a number of elements:

✦ Numeric values

✦ Text

✦ Graphics

✦ Formulas and functions (used to calculate new values)

In this section, I show you how to select one or more cells, enter data into a cell, and edit existing cell data.

Filling a cell to the top

To enter data in a cell, just click it and begin typing. The cell changes into a data entry box, as shown in Figure 3-2. After you're done entering data, press Enter (to move one cell down) or Tab (to move one cell to the right). See there — I told you it was easier than it looks, didn't I?

Later in this chapter, I discuss the Formula bar, which is another method of entering stuff — in this case, a formula — in a cell.

Moving around the worksheet

An Excel worksheet can grow to absolutely momentous proportions. And even at the highest screen resolutions, you're still limited to using the same on-screen space as in any other Office document. Therefore, your scroll bars are *very* important controls in Excel; use them often and in good health.

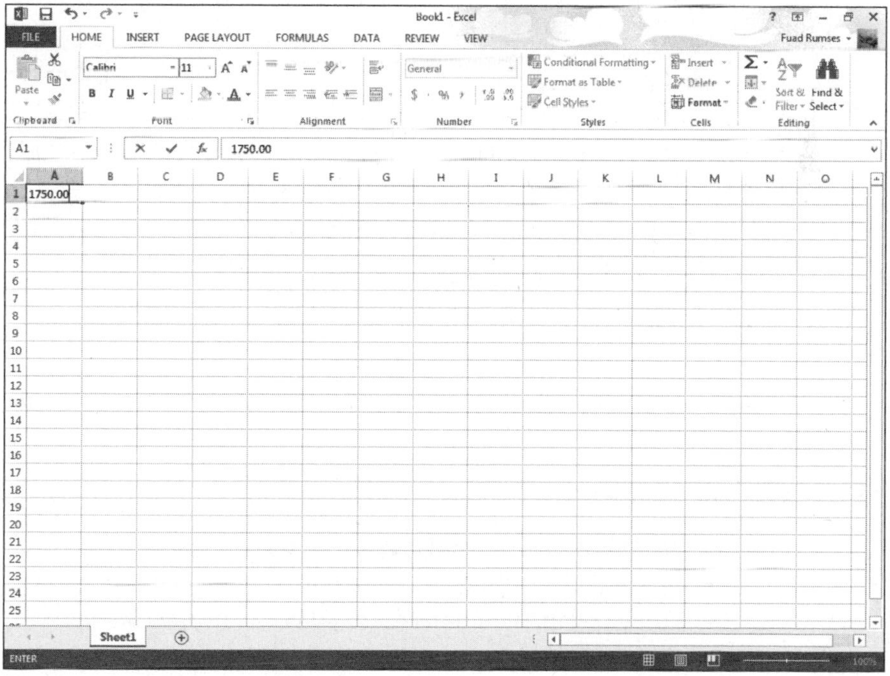

Figure 3-2:
To enter data into a cell, just click and type.

You can also use a number of keys and keyboard shortcuts to get to the right place in your worksheet, as shown in Table 3-1.

Table 3-1	Movement Shortcut Keys in Excel
Key	*Movement*
Left arrow (←)	Moves the cursor one cell to the left
Right arrow (→)	Moves the cursor one cell to the right
Up arrow (↑)	Moves the cursor one cell up
Down arrow (↓)	Moves the cursor one cell down
Home	Moves the cursor to the beginning of the current row
Ctrl+Home	Moves the cursor to the beginning of the active worksheet
Ctrl+End	Moves the cursor to the last cell in the worksheet
Page Down	Moves down one screen
Page Up	Moves up one screen
Alt+Page Down	Moves one screen to the right
Alt+Page Up	Moves one screen to the left
Enter	Moves the cursor one cell down (also works within a selection)
Tab	Moves the cursor one cell to the right (also works within a selection)
Shift+Enter	Moves the cursor one cell up (also works within a selection)
Shift+Tab	Moves the cursor one cell to the left (also works within a selection)
Ctrl+arrow key	Moves the cursor to the corresponding edge of any range containing data

Selecting cells the easy way

This section talks about selecting one or more cells, which you do before performing an action on the entire group. You can use the following mouse actions to select cells in Excel:

✦ **To select a *single* cell:** Just click it.

✦ **To select a *range* of multiple adjacent cells:** Click a cell at any corner of the desired cells and then drag the mouse in the desired direction.

✦ **To select *multiple nonadjacent* cells:** Hold down Ctrl while you click them.

✦ **To select a *column* of cells:** Click the alphabetic heading button at the top of the column.

✦ **To select a *row* of cells:** Click the numeric heading button to the left of the row, or press and hold Shift while pressing the arrow keys.

You can also select a graphic by clicking it once. Table 3-2 illustrates how to select cells from the keyboard.

Table 3-2	Cell Selection Shortcut Keys in Excel
Key	*What It Selects*
Ctrl+spacebar	All cells in the current column
Shift+spacebar	All cells in the current row
Ctrl+A	All cells in a worksheet
Shift+←	One cell or column to the left (depending on the current selection)
Shift+→	One cell or column to the right (depending on the current selection)
Shift+↑	One cell or row above (depending on the current selection)
Shift+↓	One cell or row below (depending on the current selection)

Of course, you can also use your mouse or keyboard to select existing data in a cell:

✦ **With your mouse, double-click the cell, and it again changes into a text-editing box.** You can then click and drag to select characters for editing, just like you do in Word.

✦ **With your mouse, click to select the cell and then click the Formula bar to edit the contents.** I discuss the Formula bar in more detail later in the chapter.

✦ **From the keyboard, select a cell and then press F2.** You can use the keys and shortcuts shown in Table 3-2 to select the contents for editing.

Editing cell contents

After you select some data, you can choose an action from the toolbars or the menu system, or use one of the editing keyboard shortcuts (also shown in Table 3-3).

Table 3-3	Cell Editing Shortcut Keys in Excel
Key	*What It Does*
Shift+←	Selects one character to the left of the cursor
Shift+→	Selects one character to the right of the cursor
Shift+End	Selects characters to the end of the text
Shift+Home	Selects characters to the beginning of the text
Any character	Replaces the selected text
Alt+Enter	Starts a new line within the same cell
Delete	Deletes the selected text or the character to the right of the insertion cursor
Ctrl+Delete	Deletes the text to the end of the line
Ctrl+X	Cuts the selection and adds it in the Clipboard (or the Office Clipboard)
Ctrl+C	Copies the selection to the Clipboard (or the Office Clipboard)
Ctrl+V	Replaces the selection with the contents of the Clipboard
Esc	Cancels the edits made to a cell

Working with Numbers and Dates

Excel includes the font formatting basics on the Office Ribbon Home tab — which I cover in a bit — but you also need to familiarize yourself with a different type of formatting that's unique to spreadsheet, statistical, and financial applications. It's called *number formatting,* and it controls the appearance of all sorts of numbers, including

✦ Dollar amounts

✦ Dates

✦ Times

✦ Telephone numbers

✦ Zip codes

✦ Social Security numbers

The characteristics that specify a particular number format include

✦ The number of decimal places that appear

✦ The notation that represents negative numbers (a minus sign or parentheses)

✦ Whether a comma placeholder separator appears in the numbers

✦ Whether a number carries a dollar sign or a percent sign

Excel provides a whopping 11 different number-formatting categories. Or, if you like, you can go a little wild and create your own custom format that can be applied whenever necessary.

To specify a number format, follow these steps:

1. **Select the cells that you want to format.**

2. **Click the *expansion icon* — the little square with an arrow emerging from the lower-right corner — next to the Number group heading of the Home tab.**

Alternatively, keyboard types can simply press Ctrl+1 (the number 1). Either way, you see the Format Cells dialog box, which you see in Figure 3-3.

By default, Excel uses the General format for cells, which basically means that they have no specialized number format.

3. **On the Number tab, click the formatting category you need. For example, if you're working with dates, click Date.**

Excel displays the different format types for the category you select as well as a sample of how the formatted numbers will appear.

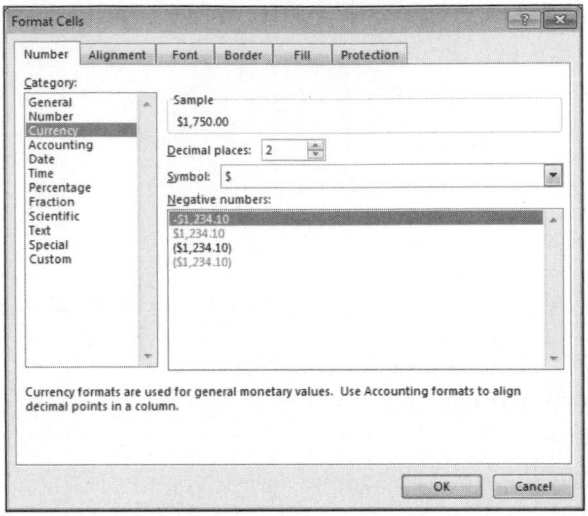

Figure 3-3:
Apply
number
formats to
selected
cells.

4. **If you need number formatting for a specific geographic location, click the Locale drop-down list (if applicable) and pick the right spot on the planet.**

   This field only appears with the Date, Time, and Special categories.

5. **Click the type of formatting you need from the Type list.**

   Again, this field might not appear for some format types.

6. **Click OK to apply the formatting and return to your worksheet.**

By the way, the General number format often works for a simple whole number. Excel displays up to 11 digits, but a decimal counts as a digit; for example, the numeral *11.11* counts as five digits. Excel then uses scientific notation for values more than 11 digits (or those too big to fit in the cell). I don't know about you, but my puny budget doesn't even *begin* to strain 11 digits.

Working with Rows and Columns

I won't lie to you: Every Excel worksheet is a haven for rows and columns. (No big surprise there.) However, you're definitely not constrained to the default arrangement of cells, and you can even insert rows and columns in an existing worksheet, if necessary. In this section, I show you how to take charge of your troops.

Resizing rows and columns

Changing the dimensions of any row or column is easy — and often a requirement when adding a longer line of text or when you need to display multiple lines of text in a cell.

To resize, follow these steps:

1. **Move the mouse pointer on top of either divider line at the desired row or column heading.**

   The mouse pointer turns into a bar with opposing arrows to indicate that you're in the right spot.

2. **Click and drag to reposition the dividing line (see how this looks in Figure 3-4).**

   To make the job easier, Excel displays a pop-up menu that tells you the new height (for rows) or width (for columns).

3. **Release the mouse button when the row or column is at the desired dimension.**

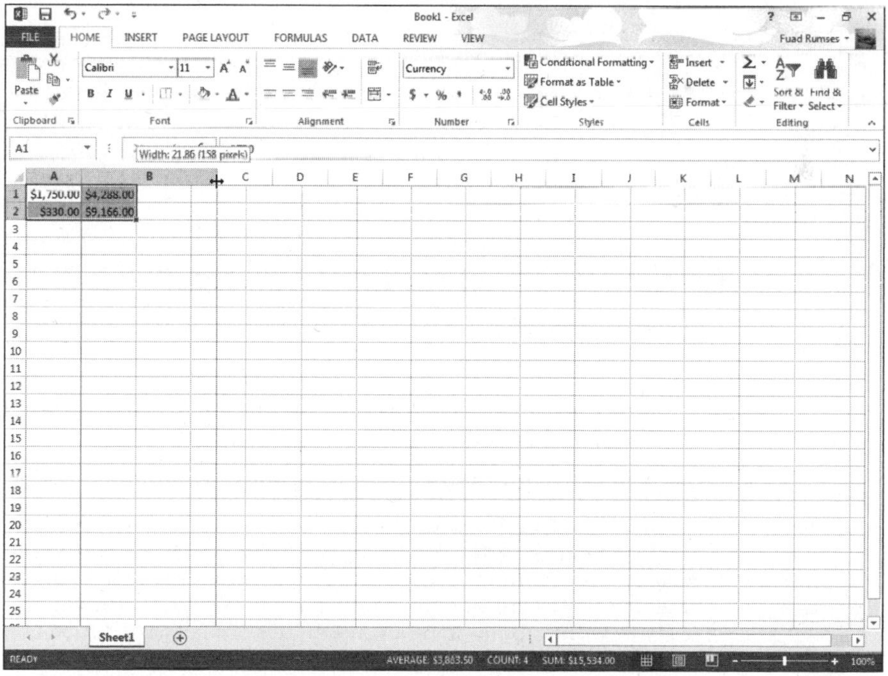

Figure 3-4:
Resizing rows and columns is a cinch.

Inserting blank cells

You can plug new blank cells into a worksheet at any point. Follow these steps:

1. **Select a range of cells.**

   Note: You have to select the same number of cells that you want to insert. For example, if you want to insert two cells at a point in your worksheet, you should select two cells at that location.

2. **Click the Home tab on the Ribbon, click the down arrow below the Insert button in the Cells group, and choose Insert Cells.**

   Excel displays the Insert dialog box, as shown in Figure 3-5.

3. **Choose which direction the selected cells move by selecting either the Shift Cells Right or the Shift Cells Down radio button.**

   Alternatively, select the Entire Row or the Entire Column radio button to shift the row or column, respectively, containing the selected cells.

4. **Click OK.**

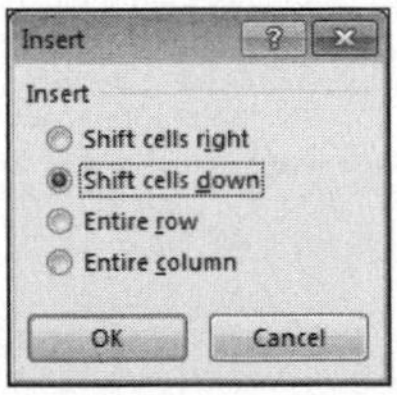

Figure 3-5:
Preparing
to insert a
passel o'
cells.

Insert	?	✕
Insert		
○ Shift cells right		
◉ Shift cells down		
○ Entire row		
○ Entire column		
OK	Cancel	

Inserting cells from the Clipboard

You can also insert cells with what you cut or copied from another spot. Follow these steps:

1. **Cut or copy the desired cells by using the keyboard shortcuts Ctrl+X or Ctrl+C, respectively.**

2. **Select the cell in the upper-left corner of the desired location.**

3. **Click the Home tab on the Ribbon, click the down arrow below the Insert button in the Cells group, and choose Insert Cut (or Copied) Cells.**

   These menu items appear immediately after you cut or copy cells.

   Excel displays the Insert Paste dialog box (see Figure 3-6).

4. **Select either the Shift Cells Right or the Shift Cells Down radio button to determine in which direction Excel moves the adjoining cells.**

5. **Click OK.**

Figure 3-6:
Inserting
cells that
I copied.

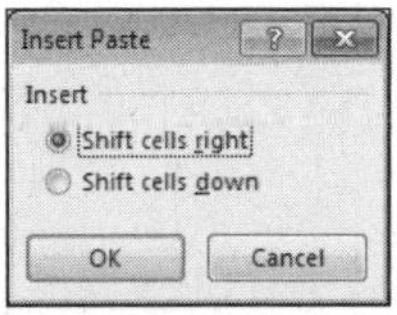

Inserting rows and columns

To insert one or more rows or columns in your worksheet, follow these steps:

1. **Click any cell in the row below (or the column to the right) of the desired spot.**

   Inserting multiple rows or columns works just like inserting multiple cells: You need to select the same number of rows or columns that you want to insert.

2. **To insert rows, click the Home tab on the Ribbon, click the down arrow below the Insert button in the Cells group, and then choose Insert Sheet Rows.**

3. **To insert columns, click the down arrow below the Insert button in the Cells group and choose Insert Sheet Columns.**

Formatting in Excel

Excel includes the standard font formatting that you expect from an Office application, but you also find that you can modify a number of unique attributes for cells, rows, and columns. In this section, I explore the basic formatting tricks you can pull.

Font formatting

Like in Word, you can easily apply the Big Three font attributes from either the toolbar or a keyboard shortcut:

✦ **Bold:** Press Ctrl+B to add emphasis to a selected cell's contents.

✦ *Italic:* Press Ctrl+I to italicize a selected cell's contents.

✦ <u>Underline:</u> Press Ctrl+U to underline a selected cell's contents.

To apply other font attributes to selected cells, click the expansion icon next to the Font section heading of the Home tab to display the Format Cells dialog box. Excel displays the standard font settings you see in Figure 3-7 — they include the font family, size, color, and standard effects.

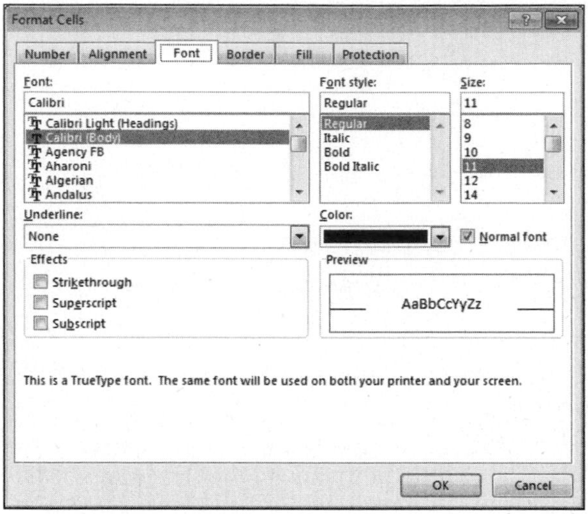

Figure 3-7:
Excel provides all sorts of font fun.

Cell alignment

Click the Alignment tab of the Format Cells dialog box, and you see the settings shown in Figure 3-8.

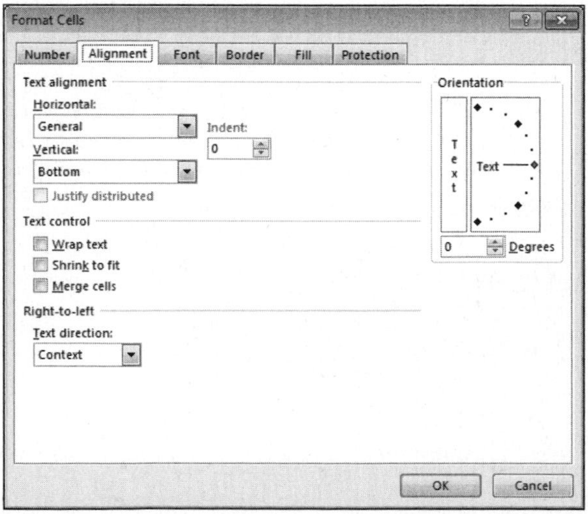

Figure 3-8:
Modify the alignment attributes of selected cells here.

In this dialog box, you can

✦ Change the horizontal and vertical alignment of the characters in selected cells.

✦ Specify the indent for the contents of a cell.

✦ Modify the orientation of cells by clicking and dragging the Orientation control. (Hey, dig those crazy angles!)

✦ Choose to wrap text to fit cell dimensions or shrink the text to fit the size of the cell.

✦ Change the right-to-left or left-to-right direction of text in the cell.

Unless you specify otherwise, Excel always aligns numbers, dates, and times to the right edge of a cell. Negative numbers are preceded by a minus sign or are enclosed with parentheses; a single period is recognized as a decimal point. By default, text is displayed as left aligned within a cell.

Changing borders and shading

Need to add a kick to certain cells to make them stand out, like a heading or a total? Click the Border tab of the Format Cells dialog box to display the settings shown in Figure 3-9.

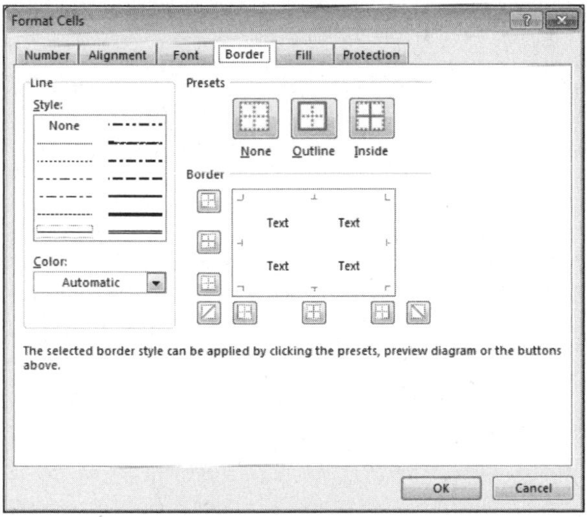

Figure 3-9:
Doggone
it. That cell
needs a
border.

From this tab, you can

✦ Choose a line style and color.

✦ Specify no border, a standard outline border, or an inside grid.

✦ Design a custom border by using the buttons. (Excel displays the effects of your work in the Border preview window.)

Open the Color drop-down list to display the familiar color selector you see in Figure 3-10. You can choose a color from the palette, or click More Colors and go a little wild by creating your own custom color.

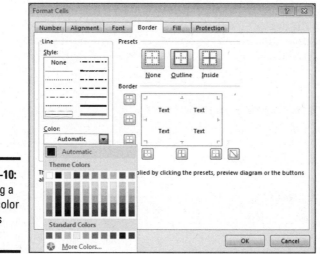

Figure 3-10: Selecting a border color is child's play.

To quickly and easily change the appearance of a selection, click the Home tab and click one of the predefined Style command buttons in the Styles group. To display all the available styles at once, click the More button at the lower-right corner of the Styles group (which looks like a down arrow). You'll find titles, headings, and all sorts of common styles like my two favorites: Bad and Good!

The Basics of Excel Formulas

Okay, talking about spreadsheet formulas might give you the creeps. (I know that it's not a favorite topic around my dinner table.) However, it's important to understand how to enter formulas correctly in Excel, or else you end up with a lot of cells stuffed full of data and nothing else.

A single cell in a worksheet can hold

+ **Constants:** Text or numbers that you type into a cell
+ **Formulas:** Calculations based on the contents of specific cells and ranges of cells

Formulas in Excel start with an equal sign (=), so they're easy to spot. Also, a formula typically includes a cell reference, like F3 (which stands for the current value in the cell located at column F, row 3).

Examples of simple formulas include

+ **=A1–125** instructs Excel to subtract 125 from the value in cell A1.
+ **=C9/B4** instructs Excel to divide the value in cell C9 by the value in cell B4.

See? All that math you studied was worth it! Formulas always include at least one operator, which in the previous examples are the minus sign (–) and the division sign (/).

Excel calculates formulas in sequence from left to right, following the equal sign (just like you and I were taught in school). However, you might need to force a calculation to be performed out of order within a formula, and you can do it with parentheses. To illustrate, I expand on the original example:

=50*(A1–125)

Without the parentheses, the contents of cell A1 would be multiplied by 50 first, and then 125 would be subtracted from that total. With the parentheses, however, Excel first subtracts 125 from the value in A1 and then multiplies that total by 50.

To insert a formula in a cell, follow these steps:

1. **Click in the cell that should hold the formula.**

   It also displays the calculated value, so this is usually the cell that displays a total or the final value.

2. **Type an equal sign (=) to alert Excel that you're going to enter a formula.**

3. **Type the remainder of the formula and then press Enter.**

You can also click your mouse pointer in the Formula bar and enter the formula there. As you can see in Figure 3-11, the Formula bar always displays any formula that you enter in the selected cell.

If you change a number in a cell that's used in a formula, the value of the cell containing the formula is automatically changed to reflect the new number. Suppose that I add the formula

   =A1+B1

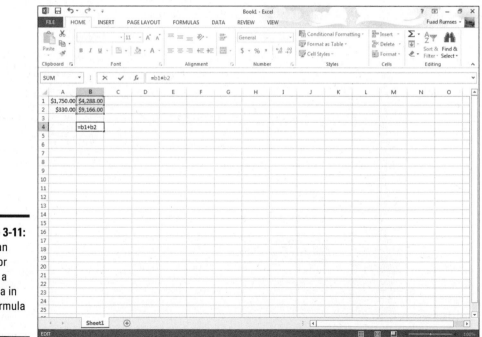

Figure 3-11:
You can enter or check a formula in the Formula Bar.

in cell C1 of my trusty worksheet. If I put the number 1 in cell A1 and the number 5 in cell B1, cell C1 shows — anyone? Yes, you there — that's right! Cell C1 contains the number 6. However, if I change the number in A1 to 3, C1 is automatically updated with the number 8 because the formula now calculates 3 + 5 and returns the number 8.

With just the simple basics I outline in this section, you can build a home budget or a mortgage calculator. But then again, why not use the built-in templates provided by Excel? Click the File tab and then click New to open the window you see in Figure 3-12.

Click one of the categories under the Search for Online Templates text box. (You need an Internet connection, of course.) You can choose from dozens of templates for all sorts of Excel projects online — all free, ready for your downloading pleasure. After you locate the apple of your template eye, double-click the template thumbnail to download the template and create a new worksheet, complete with snappy formatting, predesigned formulas, and built-in instructions!

Figure 3-12:
Save time
with Excel
templates.

For example, you find all sorts of task-oriented Excel templates that were specifically created to help with chores, such as

✦ Remodeling your kitchen

✦ Maintaining a checkbook register

✦ Tracking stock values and quotes

✦ Billing clients and customers

✦ Keeping an allergy log

✦ Planning a baby shower

✦ Generating a grocery list

I told you that this program was versatile!

To search for a specific template — did someone say *baseball scorecard*, as shown in Figure 3-12? Click in the Search for Online Templates box and type a keyword or phrase to match. (Refer to Figure 3-12.)

Excel also offers another important resource that you can use when pondering formulas: the Excel Help system. It's but a click away, compliments of the question mark icon in the upper-right corner of the window. To search for a specific need — such as calculating the days remaining before a date — type a short question or phrase into the Search Online Help text box, like **budget totals**, and then press Enter. To see the list of commonly used formulas, click the Formulas link on the top-level Popular Searches category list.

Of course, formulas (and their siblings, *functions,* which are predefined formulas that use arguments taken from cell values) can get *very* hairy *very* quickly. (There's a lot more to do with a powerful spreadsheet than just add two numbers.) Because I have limited elbow room here, I must move on. However, I can recommend the best-selling and oh-so-very complete *Microsoft Excel 2013 Bible*, by John Walkenbach (John Wiley & Sons, Inc.), for an all-out tour of everything Excel.

Working with Graphics in Excel

Your worksheets aren't limited to text. As in any other Office 2013 application, you can import pictures with aplomb. Click the cell at the upper-left corner of where the graphic should be located, and then

✦ **Paste it from the Clipboard.** After you copy an image into the Clipboard by pressing Ctrl+C, you can press Ctrl+V to paste the graphic into your worksheet from your Windows or Office Clipboard.

✦ **Insert it from a file.** To insert a graphic file from your hard drive, click the Insert tab on the Ribbon and click the Pictures button. Navigate to the location of the image and click the filename once to select it and then click the Insert button.

✦ **Insert a clip art image.** Click the Insert tab on the Ribbon and click the Online Pictures button, and then click the Search Office.com text box and type a keyword. Click Search to display thumbnail images of any matching clip art. When you find the image you're looking for, click it and click Insert to insert it into your worksheet.

As you can see in Figure 3-13, Excel doesn't give a hoot about limiting an inserted graphic to specific cells, rows, or columns. Just use the resizing handles around the border of the image (also visible in Figure 3-13) to change the dimensions of the image. Click and drag a handle to expand or contract the image. To move the image, click in the middle of the image and drag it any which way.

Figure 3-13:
No rows or columns can hold this tiger!

Besides Office.com clip art, Excel 2013 offers the ability to search Bing for images from the Online Pictures button on the Insert tab — and if you're logged in to your Microsoft account, you can choose from images you've stored in your SkyDrive, or photos you've uploaded to Flickr and other services.

Adding a Chart

Another hit among the Excel crowd is the *chart,* which can present your precious data in the easy-to-digest fashion that we all crave in our digi-frenetic, Internet-straddled, talking-head world. (Easy, Mark. Sorry about that.)

Social commentary aside, you have two choices for displaying charts:

✦ **A separate *chart sheet* within the current workbook:** Your chart gets its own fantabulous tab — pun gleefully intended, seeing as how I'm strung out on Diet Coke — and you can display it at any time, just like any other worksheet.

✦ **An *embedded object* within a worksheet:** The chart acts like a picture to be relocated and resized, just like any other graphic.

No matter which type of chart you decide to use, your journey begins with the Excel Chart Wizard. Follow these steps to add a chart:

1. **Select the cells containing the data you want to include in the chart (with column and row labels, if you created any).**

2. **Click the Insert tab, and then click the expansion icon of the Charts group. Click the All Charts tab, and Excel displays the Insert Chart dialog box, which you see in Figure 3-14.**

Here's another new feature in Excel 2013: If Excel can identify the data you've selected, the program offers recommended chart types that it feels will best present the data visually. (If you don't care for the recommended charts, just click on the All Charts tab.)

3. **Click the desired chart type from the list on the left.**

The wizard updates the subtype thumbnails on the right. (No need to stick with the boring column, bar, or line chart — try a cone or pyramid or even a radar chart!)

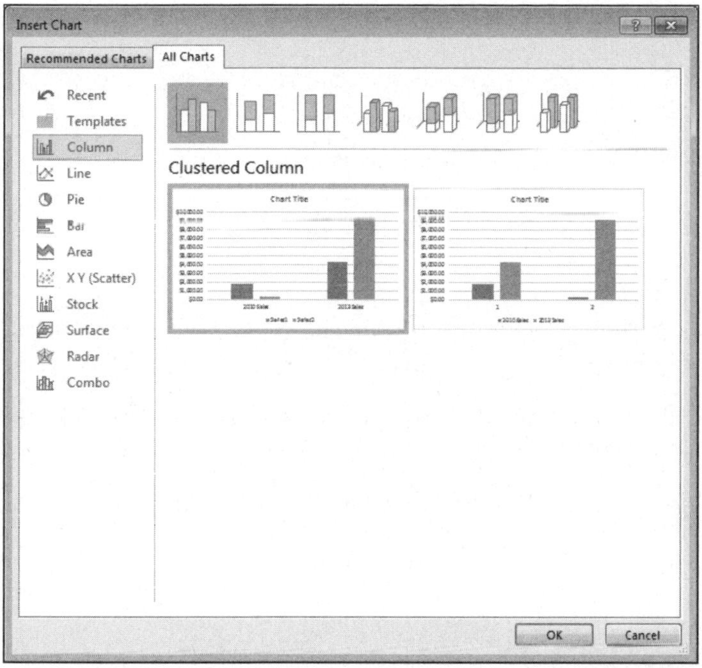

Insert Chart

Recommended Charts | All Charts

- Recent
- Templates
- **Column**
- Line
- Pie
- Bar
- Area
- X Y (Scatter)
- Stock
- Surface
- Radar
- Combo

Clustered Column

Chart Title

Chart Title

OK   Cancel

Figure 3-14:
The Insert
Chart dialog
box struts
its stuff.

You can always change the chart type at any time — just right-click the chart and choose Change Chart Type from the pop-up menu.

4. **Click OK to embed the chart as a graphic in your worksheet.**

Whoa! Check out what happened to the Ribbon: Excel adds two new tabs, grouped under the Chart Tools "super" tab. (See upcoming Figure 3-16.)

- *Design tab:* Click to select a color scheme using the thumbnails here.

If you want to create a chart sheet rather than an embedded chart, click the Move Chart button on the Design tab to display the Move Chart dialog box (Figure 3-15). You can name your chart sheet or even switch a chart sheet back into an embedded chart.

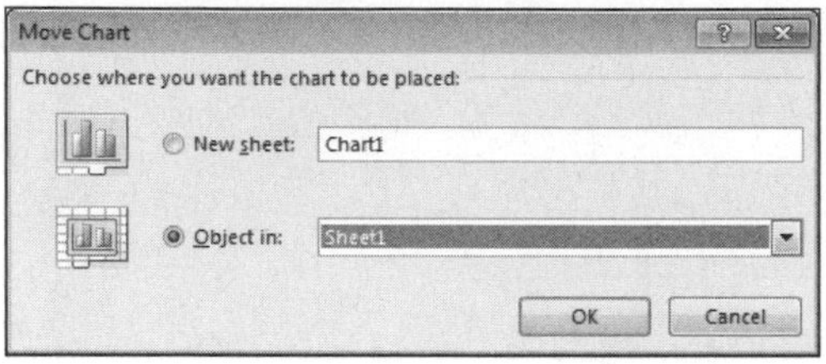

Figure 3-15:
Will that
chart be
embedded
or on a
separate
chart sheet?

- *Format tab:* Adjust the shapes of your chart elements.

    You can use fills and effects to jazz up elements as well.

5. When the chart is finished, click outside the chart to return to your worksheet.

Figure 3-16 illustrates an embedded sheet I created within a worksheet.

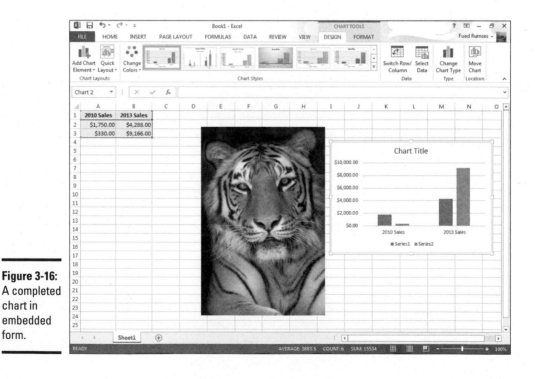

Figure 3-16:
A completed
chart in
embedded
form.

Linking Cells

Another powerful feature that's a big favorite with Excel power users is the ability to link values. That is, when one value changes in one of the cells, it's automatically updated when you display the other cell! For example, if cell A1 is linked to cell E3 on the same worksheet, whatever value you place in cell A1 automatically appears in cell E3.

To create a link between cells on the same worksheet, follow these steps:

1. **Select the cell that contains the data you want to link to another cell.**

2. **Press Ctrl+C.**

3. **Click the cell that you want to link to and then press Ctrl+V to paste the value.**

    Excel displays a pop-up icon next to the cell when you press Ctrl+V.

4. **Click the pop-up icon to display the menu and then select the Paste Link button in the bottom row.**

Adding Headers and Footers

When printing a worksheet, headers and footers can contain quite a bit of valuable identifying information. And that's from someone who has waded through a year's supply of printed personnel worksheets from a midsize company.

To add headers and footers to the active worksheet, follow these steps:

1. **Click the Page Layout tab and then click the expansion icon of the Sheet Options group.**

2. **Click the Header/Footer tab of the Page Setup dialog box to display the settings you see in Figure 3-17.**

3. **Click the Header drop-down list and choose a predesigned header.**

4. **Click the Footer drop-down list and choose a footer.**

5. **Click OK to save your changes and return to the worksheet.**

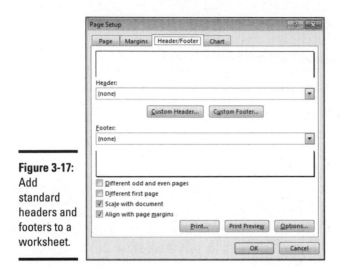

Figure 3-17:
Add standard headers and footers to a worksheet.

Click the Custom Header or the Custom Footer button to get all artistic and design your own header or footer format. (Check it out in Figure 3-18.) Click to place the insertion cursor in the proper section — the left, center, or right section of the design — and then click the template buttons to insert the preformatted elements that you want to add, like the time or date. (You can also type your own text rather than use a template.) When your header or footer is set up as you like, click OK to return to the Page Setup dialog box.

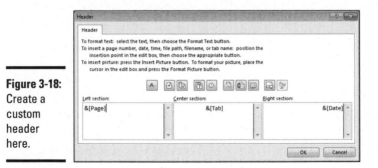

Figure 3-18:
Create a custom header here.

Printing Your Worksheets

When you're ready to print the active worksheet in Excel, click the File Tab and click Print for a preview. From there, you can select from multiple printers, print multiple copies, or print only specific pages from the worksheet. Click the Printer Properties link to set any printer-specific options supported by the printer's Windows 8 software driver.

To print with the cell grid, click the Page Layout tab — under the Sheet Options section, and select the Print Gridlines check box. (You can also choose to turn off the row and column headings from this section.)

To print just the contents of certain cells in your worksheet, select the cells first before you display the Print settings and then click the Print Active Sheets button. Click the Print Selection entry in the pop-up menu that appears.

After you're satisfied that you'll get what you expect, use one of these methods to start the printing process:

✦ **Choose File⇨Print and click the Print button.**

✦ **Press Ctrl+P.** This method also displays the Print settings, just as if you had chosen Print from the File tab.

Chapter 4: Performing with PowerPoint

In This Chapter

- ✔ Working with the PowerPoint window
- ✔ Changing views in PowerPoint
- ✔ Importing and inserting slides
- ✔ Adding text and graphics
- ✔ Using templates and schemes
- ✔ Adding movies and sound to slides
- ✔ Creating a slide show
- ✔ Choosing transitions between slides
- ✔ Using Package for CD
- ✔ Printing in PowerPoint

*N*eed a slide show? How about a set of professional-looking transparencies for that overhead projector? Have no fear; Microsoft Office PowerPoint 2013 is here! PowerPoint has always been easy to use — including a slew of graphically gorgeous templates to use; and the ability to add movies, and transitions, and CD-quality audio; and — whoops, I'm getting a little ahead of myself.

In this chapter, I provide you with the basics of PowerPoint to show you how to accomplish the most common tasks. If you're brand-spanking-new to the program, you see how to spice up that blank slide with text and graphics, and I also show you the power-user keyboard shortcuts to use in PowerPoint. If you're already familiar with the PowerPoint window, you also find out how to create a package for CD and add all sorts of spiffy transitions to your slide shows.

Naturally, I can't provide The Last Word on PowerPoint 2013 in the space I have — there's too much power to cover in a few dozen pages, if you'll forgive my pun — but I can heartily recommend *Microsoft PowerPoint 2013 For Dummies,* by Doug Lowe (John Wiley & Sons, Inc.), if you need a comprehensive guide.

Getting Your Bearings in PowerPoint

You can run PowerPoint in a number of different ways:

✦ From the Start screen, type **Power** and click the Microsoft PowerPoint 2013 button that appears. (No need to use the Charms bar if you're searching for an application.)

✦ Click the shortcut on your Windows 8 Start screen if you pinned the program there.

✦ Double-click a PowerPoint project file within a File Explorer window or on your Desktop.

When you first run PowerPoint (without opening an existing PowerPoint presentation), the program displays the Template window. From here, you can click on one of the template thumbnails available online. When you click a thumbnail, PowerPoint creates a new blank presentation file, complete with the theme's layout and fonts, so you're ready to start work. If you've been working on a presentation already, click the file in the Recent list along the left side of the Template window to open it immediately. To open another presentation not listed under Recent, click the Open Other Presentations link at the bottom.

You can also search for PowerPoint templates and themes online. Click within the Search Online Templates and Themes box at the top and type a keyword to match descriptions or names.

It's show time! The application's main window looks remarkably simple (as shown in Figure 4-1), especially when you contrast it with the rather frightening appearance of Excel 2013. You quickly find, however, that this program is no pushover. The digital-and-silicon equivalent of an '05 Dodge Magnum is lurking behind the curtain! (Yep, I'm extremely proud of my family muscle car.)

File tab   Quick Access bar   Office Ribbon

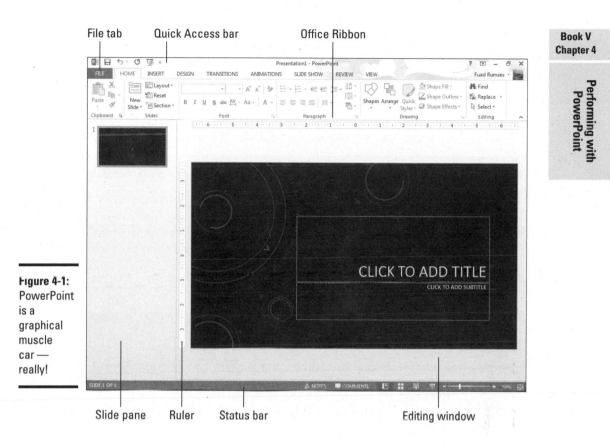

Figure 4-1:
PowerPoint
is a
graphical
muscle
car —
really!

Slide pane   Ruler   Status bar   Editing window

In lieu of formal introductions, here's a quick guide to what you see on-screen:

✦ **File tab:** Like in the other Office 2013 programs, the PowerPoint File tab holds most of the commands you associate with that outdated File menu. It also displays the recent presentations you created and opened, as well as an Options link (where you can make changes to the global settings that dictate how PowerPoint behaves).

✦ **Quick Access bar:** Another now-familiar old friend, the Quick Access bar sports Save, Undo, and Repeat buttons. To tweak the bar, click the Customize button next to the Quick Access bar — you can add or remove command buttons to your heart's content.

✦ **Office Ribbon:** The Office Ribbon displays command buttons that change when you click a group tab at the top of the Ribbon.

✦ **Editing window:** You design your slides here, adding graphics and text, and moving slide elements around the layout guide. The editing window also does double duty in other view modes, which I discuss in a bit.

✦ **Ruler:** Get a grip on dimensions. You can also use the ruler as a guide when placing objects on your slides. The Ruler check box appears on the View tab.

✦ **Slide and Outline panes:** In Normal view, the Slide pane displays numbered thumbnail display of the slides in your presentation. Click the View tab and switch to Outline view to display the text on each slide in outline format on the Outline pane. The Slide pane helps you navigate quickly — you can simply click a thumbnail to jump to that slide. The Outline pane helps you organize your presentation.

You can also click the vertical scroll bar in the editing window to move through the slides in your presentation.

✦ **Status bar:** Like other Office applications, PowerPoint has one of these, too. It displays information about your current view as well as information relating to the selected slide or pane.

Each pane within the PowerPoint window can be adjusted. For example, if you don't need the Slide pane at the moment, move the mouse pointer over the border between the Slide pane and the editing window until it turns into those nifty opposing arrows, and then click and drag to enlarge the editing window.

Changing Views

You can view the PowerPoint application window in a number of different views. In this section, I give you the details on the ones you use most often.

Normal view

Normal view, which is the default in PowerPoint, is the best view for adding and editing text and graphic objects. You can display your slides in Normal view by clicking the View tab on the Ribbon and clicking the Normal button. (Alternatively, click the Normal button on the right side of the PowerPoint status bar. 'Nuff said.)

Need to see what your elegant color slides will look like when printed on a monochrome laser printer? Click that very same View tab, and then click the Grayscale command button in the Color/Grayscale group (or go monochrome crazy and click the stark Black and White command button). When you and Toto are done, return to the Land of Oz by choosing the Color command button from the same group.

Slide Sorter view

Figure 4-2 illustrates Slide Sorter view, where the slides in your presentation are arranged in a larger, easier-to-see format. It's not just the scenery that's important, however: You can also click and drag thumbnails to move them and reorder the flow of your presentation. You can also right-click a slide to delete it or to add a completely new slide (a helpful feature when you've forgotten to include something).

To switch to Slide Sorter view, click the View tab on the Ribbon and then click the Slide Sorter button in the Presentation Views group. From the status bar, click the Slide Sorter button.

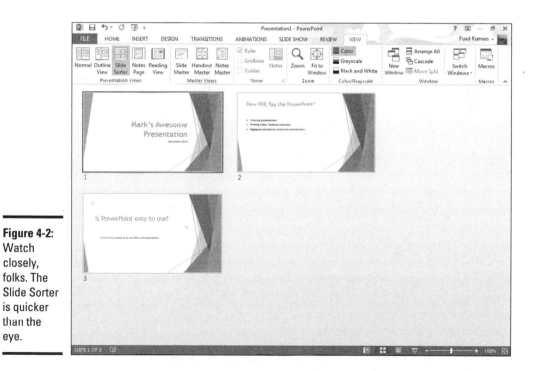

Figure 4-2:
Watch closely, folks. The Slide Sorter is quicker than the eye.

Notes Page view

Click the View tab and then click the Notes button to view a full-size layout for your Notes pages (which I discuss later in this chapter), as shown in Figure 4-3. The top portion of the Notes page contains the corresponding slide from your presentation. From this view, you can edit the text in your Notes pages just like you edit the text boxes in your slides (as opposed to the Notes pane, which is somewhat cramped if you have a large number of notes to enter for a slide).

Reading view

Reading view is a good choice for presenting on your laptop's screen, instead of on a projector or larger display. You'll see the presentation in a window rather than full-screen. Previous and Next buttons appear on the status bar, allowing you to page through your presentation quickly.

To use Reading view, click the View tab and then click the Reading View button, or click the Reading View button at the right side of the status bar.

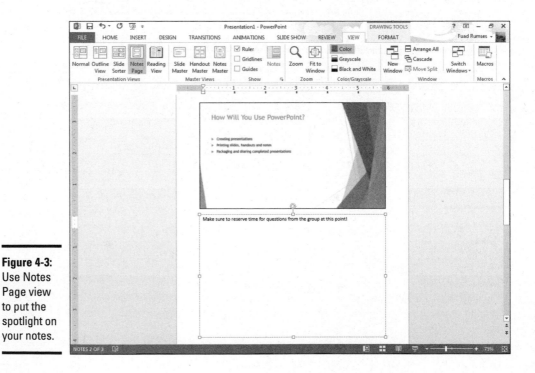

Figure 4-3: Use Notes Page view to put the spotlight on your notes.

Outline view

Outline view in PowerPoint corresponds closely to Outline view within Word — PowerPoint replaces the Slides pane with the Outline pane at the left side of the window, making it easy for you to drag headers and cut, copy, and paste text. Press Enter to create a new slide.

You can invoke Outline view by clicking the View tab and then clicking the Outline View button.

Slide Show

Oh, no — this is not your Aunt Harriet's idea of a slide show. ("Enough with the beach pictures, Harry!") Instead, this one displays a PowerPoint slide show using the slides from the open presentation. I cover slide shows later in this chapter, in the section "Building and Running a Slide Show," so hang tight.

To activate Slide Show, click the Slide Show button on the status bar. (Note that this runs the show from the current slide, so you don't see any preceding slides.) You can also click the Slide Show tab and choose to start the slide show at the current slide or from the beginning of the presentation.

Creating Slides

As a personal favor to you, PowerPoint creates a new, blank first slide each time you start the program, or each time you create a new presentation by choosing File⇨New.

To add a new slide to a presentation, follow these steps:

1. **If you already have a number of slides in the presentation, click an existing slide in the Slide pane.**

   The new slide is inserted after the selected slide.

   If you have only one slide, the new slide is appended at the end. Go figure.

2. **Click the Home tab and click the down arrow at the bottom of the New Slide button to display the pop-up menu, which displays the various types of slides you can add.**

   I prefer this method because you can click a layout that most closely fits your needs for the new slide. Heck, you can also press Ctrl+M. (Microsoft and its options!)

   PowerPoint adds the new slide to the Slide pane and displays it in the editing window.

   Note: Each slide is given a sequential number as you add it, which comes in handy, such as when you want to print only certain slides.

Do you have existing slides in your presentation that you want to use as the model for new slides? No problem! Rather than create blank slides from scratch, PowerPoint allows you to duplicate one or more existing slides. Click the slide(s) you want to duplicate in the Slide pane (hold down Ctrl while clicking to select multiple slides), right-click them, and then choose the Duplicate Slide menu item. After the new slides appear, you can move them individually within the Outline or Slide panes by dragging them to their new home. (And when the slides are moved, they're automatically renumbered. *Sweet.*)

If you need to axe a slide, right-click it in the Slide pane and then choose Delete Slide from the contextual menu that appears. It's a goner. Again, renumbering is automatic.

To temporarily hide a slide, right-click it in the Slide pane and choose Hide Slide — you'll note that the slide number appears with a slash, and the slide won't appear in your presentation. This is A Good Thing for quickly lengthening or shortening a presentation by hiding or displaying additional material (I call them "hints 'n' tips" slides) without having to insert and delete slides manually. To restore the slide to your presentation, right-click it again in the Slide pane and click Hide Slide again.

Inserting slides

If you have another PowerPoint presentation with one or more slides that you need for your current project, you can insert them by following these steps:

1. **Click a slide in the Slide pane where the inserted slides should appear.**

   An inserted slide appears *after* the slide you click in the Slide pane.

2. **Click the Home tab and click the down arrow under the New Slide button, and then click Reuse Slides to display the Reuse Slides pane, which you see in Figure 4-4.**

3. **Click the Browse button and choose Browse File.**

   PowerPoint displays a standard Windows Browse dialog box.

4. **Navigate to the folder containing the existing PowerPoint presentation, click the file to select it, and then click Open.**

   Thumbnails of the slides in the existing presentation appear in the Reuse Slides pane.

5. **Click Insert All to insert all the slides in the file.**

6. **To pick a single slide, click the thumbnail representing the desired slide.**

7. **Click the Close button in the Reuse Slides pane to return to your presentation.**

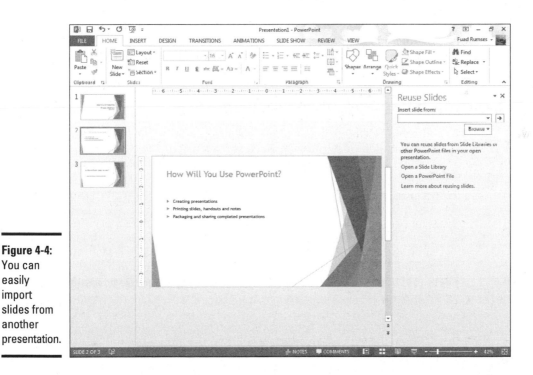

Figure 4-4:
You can easily import slides from another presentation.

Inserting a document

You can also insert the contents of a Word document directly into your slides as an outline. This option is useful for those who need to pull the text for a presentation from an existing document, like a student who needs to provide both a written assignment and a PowerPoint presentation on the same material.

Follow these steps to insert a document:

1. **Click a slide in the Slides pane (where the inserted text should appear) to select it.**

2. **Click the Home tab and click the down arrow under the New Slide button, and then click Slides from Outline.**

3. **Navigate to the location of the document and then click the filename to highlight it.**

4. **Click the Open button.**

Naturally, you get the best results if the document you're inserting is formatted in outline form (with a hierarchy of headings), but I find that PowerPoint does a surprisingly good job importing just about any kind of Word document.

Typing, Selecting, and Editing Text

After you create a blank slide — or insert slides from an existing PowerPoint presentation or perhaps insert text from a Word document — you're ready to type and edit text. Luckily, this section is about exactly that topic.

Adding text

You probably already noticed the huge Click to Add XX prompts all over your slides. Reminds me a little of *Alice in Wonderland*, with little slides running around your feet bearing signs that read "Click Me!" Anyway, things couldn't get much easier. Just click the text, and PowerPoint erases it and displays an insertion cursor just like the one in Microsoft Word (see Figure 4-5).

While you type, the text is updated on the thumbnail in the Slide pane, and the text is also displayed in the Outline pane if you're in Outline view.

You can also edit text in a slide directly from Outline view. Click in the Outline pane that appears and drag to select the text you want to change, and then type to replace it.

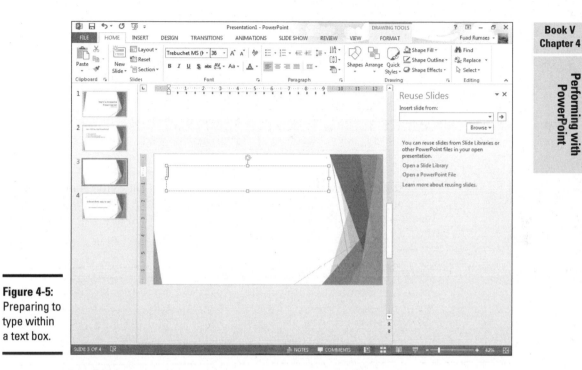

Figure 4-5:
Preparing to
type within
a text box.

Moving within text fields

Table 4-1 provides the movement shortcuts you can use while typing text in
a PowerPoint field.

Table 4-1	Text Field Movement Keys in PowerPoint
Key	*Where It Moves the Cursor*
Left arrow (←)	One character to the left
Right arrow (→)	One character to the right
Up arrow (↑)	To the preceding line
Down arrow (↓)	To the next line
End	To the end of the current line
Home	To the beginning of the current line
Ctrl+←	One word to the left
Ctrl+→	One word to the right
Ctrl+↑	One paragraph up

(continued)

Table 4-1 *(continued)*

Key	*Where It Moves the Cursor*
Ctrl+↓	One paragraph down
Ctrl+Home	To the beginning of the text box
Ctrl+End	To the end of the text box
Ctrl+Return	To the next title or body text entry box

To switch between titles or body text entry boxes with your mouse, click once on the box you want to edit. You can add a text box by clicking the Insert tab on the Ribbon and choosing the Text Box command button from the Text group.

Selecting text and objects

After you enter text-editing mode, you have a number of keyboard shortcuts at your disposal for selecting text that needs to be changed. Table 4-2 provides these selection keys as well as selection shortcuts for slide objects.

Table 4-2	**Text Field and Object Selection Keys in PowerPoint**
Key	*What It Selects*
Shift+←	One character to the left of the cursor
Shift+→	One character to the right of the cursor
Shift+↑	Characters to the previous line
Shift+↓	Characters to the next line
Ctrl+Shift+←	Characters to the beginning of the word
Ctrl+Shift+→	Characters to the end of the word
Tab	The next object
Shift+Tab	The previous object
Ctrl+A	All objects, slides, or text (depending on your view)

You can also get the mouse into the selection act: Double-click a word in a text box to select it, and you can select multiple objects on a slide by holding down Shift and then clicking each object.

Editing text

From the keyboard, you can use the shortcuts shown in Table 4-3 to play Frankenstein with the contents of a text box.

Table 4-3	Text Field Selection Keys in PowerPoint
Key	*What It Does*
Any character	Replaces the selected text
Enter	Starts a new line
Delete	Deletes the selected text or object
Ctrl+X	Deletes the selection and adds it in the Clipboard (or the Office Clipboard)
Ctrl+C	Copies the selection to the Clipboard (or the Office Clipboard)
Ctrl+V	Replaces the selection with contents of the Clipboard (or the Office Clipboard)

You can click the Home tab and click the expansion icon next to the Font group name (it looks like a square with a tiny arrow in the lower-right corner) to display the Font dialog box, as shown in Figure 4-6). From there, you can add all sorts of attributes, change the font family or font size, and determine the color of the text. The Font section of the Home tab provides many of these same commands in convenient mouse-click form.

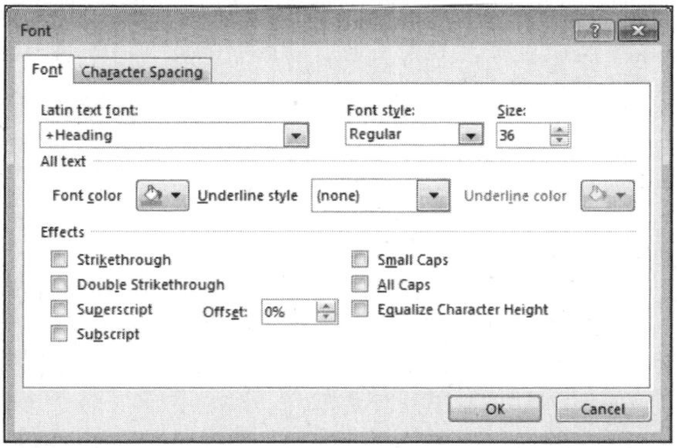

Figure 4-6: Change font attributes in PowerPoint.

Moving slide elements

Naturally, the elements on your slide — text boxes and graphics — aren't embedded in cement. You can use your mouse or the keyboard to move these elements to a different location around the slide:

✦ **To move an element with the mouse:** Click the object to select it (you get that funky, four-direction cursor again) and then drag it to the desired spot. (For text boxes, click the frame. For graphics, click in the center of the image.)

✦ **To move an element with the keyboard:** Press the Tab key to cycle through the elements on the slide. After an item is selected, press the arrow keys to move it. This feature is useful when you need fine control over the placement of an object, but remember *not* to click a text object. That puts you in Edit mode, and as you can read in earlier parts of this section, the cursor keys have different uses when you're editing.

Installing Graphics in Your Slides

No good presentation is complete without a dog or a pony. Don't ask me why — I just work here. Add graphics to your slides to capture (and securely hold) your audience's attention. From my personal experience of watching many a boring presentation (thankfully, not my own), I can tell you that a pure-text presentation will have your audience heading for a restroom break in less than five minutes.

Follow these steps to add a graphic from your hard drive to a slide (or, if you're using Notes Page view, to your Notes page for the slide):

1. **Click to select a slide in the Slide pane.**

2. **Click the Insert tab and click Pictures in the Images group.**

PowerPoint displays — you guessed it — the Insert Picture dialog box.

3. **Navigate to the folder where the image is stored and click that file to select it.**

4. **Click the Insert button.**

The image can be resized by clicking and dragging any of the square handles arranged around the edges (check out the guitar graphic in Figure 4-7), or you can drag the entire image by clicking in its center and dragging the graphic to its new home.

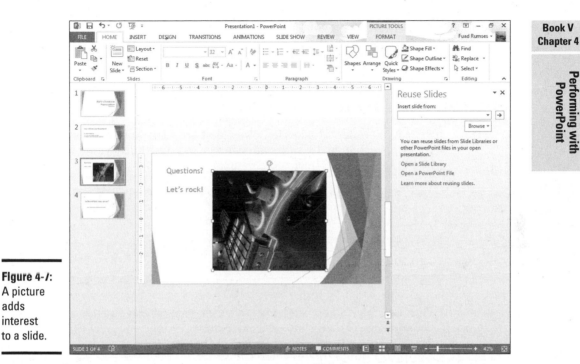

Figure 4-7:
A picture
adds
interest
to a slide.

If you're inserting an image that might be updated later — for example, a graphic of your company's stock price — click the down arrow next to the Insert button in the Insert Picture dialog box and then click Link to File instead, which automatically reloads the image from disk each time you display the slide in PowerPoint.

As always, an image can be pasted into your slide from either the Windows Clipboard or the Office Clipboard. And yes, our old friend, the Insert Pictures dialog box, is also available in PowerPoint! (Again, this is the beauty of an application suite.) To insert clip art, click the Insert tab and click the Online Pictures command button. Click in the Search Office.com box and type a word or phrase, and then click the Search button (which looks like a tiny magnifying glass). Double-click the thumbnail to insert the desired graphic.

Didn't find the right image within the Office.com Clip Art library? Click in the Search Bing box instead (which also appears in the Insert Pictures dialog box) — Bing displays images from all across the Internet that match your search criteria.

If you sign in with your Microsoft account before you add media, you can also access both photos and video clips from your SkyDrive and popular online media storage sites like Flickr.

Applying a Theme

Repeat after me: "Themes in PowerPoint are *sassy* things." That's because a theme can change the entire appearance of your slides with just a click or two of the mouse. Themes can control

✦ The position of the objects on your slides

✦ The background design

✦ The fonts and formatting used in text objects

✦ Animation effects

✦ The color scheme

Plus, a theme can be used at any time — even when you have an entire presentation's worth of slides already built!

To apply a theme, follow these steps:

1. **Select the slides that will use your theme in the Slides pane.**

2. **Click the Design tab.**

   PowerPoint opens the Ribbon group you see in Figure 4-8.

3. **Choose the type of theme you want to apply from the thumbnails in the Themes group.**

   To make a change to the theme's colors, fonts, or graphical effects, click the Variants command button (noted in Figure 4-8) to the right of the thumbnail list.

4. **Apply the theme.**

   • *To apply the template or scheme to all slides in your presentation:* Right-click the theme thumbnail and choose Apply to All Slides.

   • *To apply the template or scheme to only the selected slides in your presentation:* Right-click the theme thumbnail and choose Apply to Selected Slides.

PowerPoint immediately updates your presentation with the new theme (like the spiffy one shown in Figure 4-9), so you can either approve or disapprove on the spot. Feel free to try on all sorts of new looks. Microsoft doesn't charge you for the privilege (at least for now).

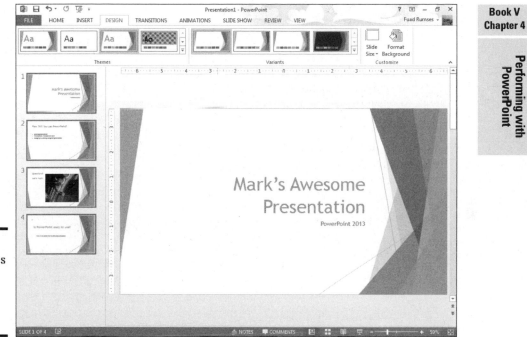

Figure 4-8:
The Themes group dominates the Design tab.

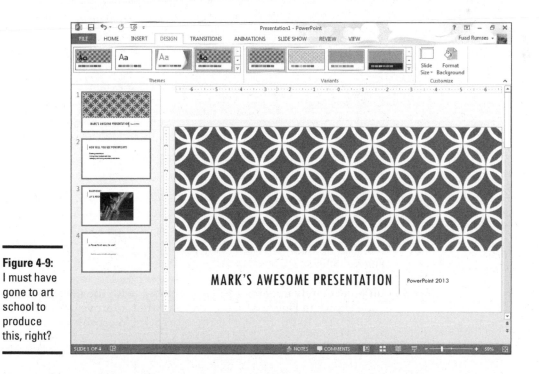

Figure 4-9:
I must have gone to art school to produce this, right?

Entering Notes

Notes are a handy tool, allowing you to jot down reminders and information about a slide (without those notes appearing on the slide itself). Many folks also print the contents of the Notes pane as handouts; I show you how to print them later in this chapter.

Although PowerPoint has support for more formal handouts, I find that the printed Notes pages (which, as I mention earlier, also boast the images of the slides in your presentation) work just fine for distribution to your audience.

To enter notes, just click in the Notes pane and begin typing (check out Figure 4-10). Or, you can paste text directly into the pane. If you like, you can also edit the notes for a slide from Notes Page view, as I describe earlier in this chapter. To add graphics to your Notes page, you must use Notes Page view — and note that any graphics you add in Notes Page view aren't visible in Normal view. To enlarge the Notes pane while in Normal view, as I did in Figure 4-10, click the divider at the top of the Notes pane and drag it upward.

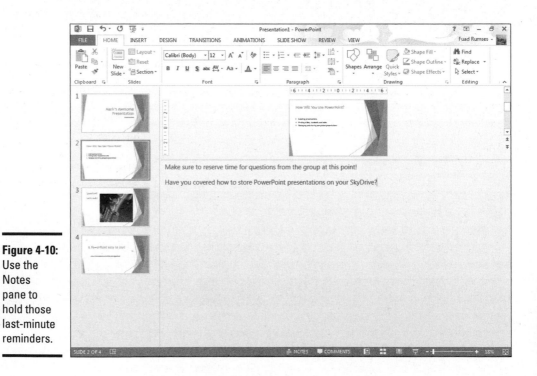

Figure 4-10:
Use the Notes pane to hold those last-minute reminders.

Using Movies and Sound

PowerPoint allows you to add video clips and audio to your slides. Naturally, these don't work well with presentations that use transparencies (no surprise there), but you'll like the effect if you use a laptop screen, monitor, or a projector!

To add multimedia to a slide from your hard drive, follow these steps:

1. **Click to select a slide in the Slide pane.**

2. **Click the Insert tab on the Ribbon and click either the Video or Audio pop-up menu in the Media section.**

3. **Click either Video on My PC or Audio on My PC to display the ubiquitous, all-knowing Insert Video (see Figure 4-11) or Insert Audio dialog box, respectively.**

   If you've signed on to your Microsoft account and you click Online Video or Online Audio instead, you'll see a dialog box similar to the Insert Picture dialog box I discussed in the earlier section on inserting graphics. With video, you can search the Internet with Bing, or add an HTML embed code (popular with YouTube and other online streaming sites). Online audio is drawn from Office.com.

4. **Navigate to the folder where the media is stored and then click the file to select it.**

5. **Click the Insert button.**

Figure 4-11: PowerPoint can play a clip or sound automatically or by your leave.

Figure 4-12 illustrates both a video and an audio clip inserted into a slide. The video or sound icon appears on your slide like any other object. To play the video or audio clip within the editing window, click the clip and click the Play button in the frame. You can pause the clip by clicking the Pause button.

Although a video object can be moved and resized just like a graphic, don't be surprised if expanding it by a large amount causes it to turn *jaggy* (rough-edged). Video clips (and even images in JPEG, bitmap, or TIFF format) are created at a fixed dimension, and they might not look that good when stretched like taffy.

What's that, Bunkie? You say you have no video or audio handy on your hard drive to use in your presentation, but you saved the perfect thing on your SkyDrive? No problem! If you sign in with your Microsoft account before you add media — and then choose Online Video or Online Audio, as in the previous Step 3 — you can access both audio and video clips from your SkyDrive. There's your multimedia goodness, ready for adding to your presentation!

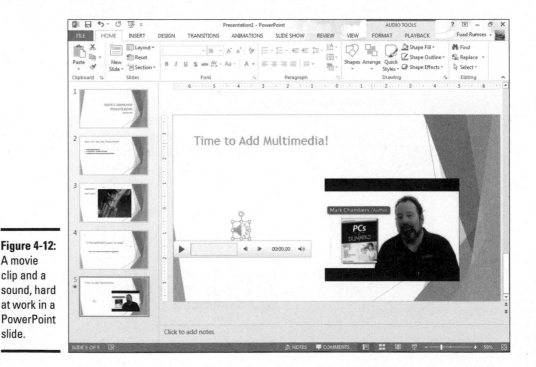

Figure 4-12: A movie clip and a sound, hard at work in a PowerPoint slide.

Building and Running a Slide Show

As I mention earlier in this chapter, you can choose to view your presentation as a slide show whenever you like. Follow these steps to run your own show:

1. **Choose Slide Show on the Ribbon and click From Beginning, click the Slide Show View button on the status bar, or press F5.**

PowerPoint takes control, switches to a full-screen display, and shows the current slide in the presentation.

2. **Click the mouse button or press N (or Enter, or the right-arrow key) to move to the next slide.**

To move backward to the previous slide, press P (or Backspace or the left-arrow key).

3. **Click the mouse button on the final screen in your presentation to return to the PowerPoint window, or press Esc at any time to exit.**

That's the basic method of running a slide show. However, PowerPoint also allows you to build a self-running show that needs no intervention — and you can even choose to limit user input, which is a good feature in case strange fingers hit the keyboard.

To create a self-running show from the open presentation, follow these steps:

1. **Click the Slide Show tab and click Set Up Slide Show to display the Set Up Show dialog box, which you see in Figure 4-13.**

2. **Select the Browsed at a Kiosk (Full Screen) radio button.**

In *kiosk mode,* there are no controls or visible windows, and the slide show fills the entire screen.

3. **Choose the slides you want to display.**

- *To show them all:* Select the All radio button.

- *To show a selection of slides:* Select the From/To radio button and then enter the starting and ending slide numbers in the appropriate fields; you can type the numbers directly in the boxes or use the up and down buttons next to each box.

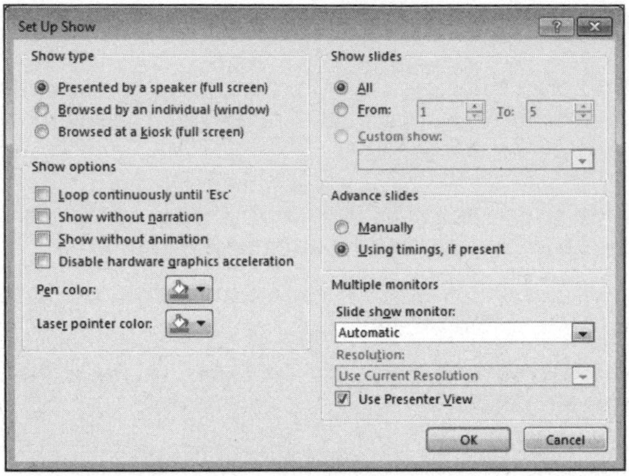

Figure 4-13:
Preparing a
self-running
slide show.

4. **Select the Using Timings, If Present radio button.**

This step sets the slide show to advance slides automatically. Viewers can also click the mouse button to advance to the next slide, but everything else is disabled in Kiosk mode except the Esc key, which closes the show.

5. **Select the Loop Continuously Until 'Esc' check box.**

Your slide show repeats endlessly until the Esc key is pressed. (Sorry, gotta have *some* way of ending the show, but you can always hide the keyboard.)

6. **Click OK to save your changes.**

To run your show, click the Slide Show tab and click the From Beginning command button in the Start Slide Show section. I list in Table 4-4 the basic slide show control keys that you can use during a presentation.

Table 4-4	Slide Show Control Keys in PowerPoint
Key	*What It Does*
slide number+Enter	Jumps to a specific slide
W	Toggles the display of a white screen
B	Toggles the display of a black screen
S	Stops or restarts an automatic slide show
Shift+F10	Displays a shortcut menu

Key	What It Does
Ctrl+Shift+B	Starts the slide show from the current slide
Ctrl+U	Hides on-screen controls and pointer in 15 seconds
Ctrl+H	Hides on-screen controls and pointer immediately
F1	Displays the slide show control list

Making a Transition 'twixt Slides

One way that you can add a little life to a long slide show is with the inclusion of *transitions,* which are animated effects that occur between slides. However, remember that a little goes a long way when it comes to transitions. You want your audience to pay attention to the content in your presentation and not gawk at the visual spectacle of your transitions. Less is more.

To add transitions to your slide show, follow these steps:

1. **Switch to either Normal or Slide Sorter view.**

    I find this task much easier in Slide Sorter view.

2. **If you want to apply a transition to selected slides, highlight all the slides to be preceded by the same transition.**

3. **Click the Transitions tab to select a transition from the scrolling list.**

    PowerPoint plays a quick preview of the transition, allowing you to choose another if your director's instincts weren't right the first time.

4. **Click the Duration list in the Ribbon box to choose the speed of the effect in seconds.**

    PowerPoint again previews the animation when you select a different speed.

5. **To add sound to the transition, click the Sound drop-down list to see your choices.**

    (I gotta admit that the typewriter and the applause sounds are favorites of mine, but you have to address the audience — the CEO of your company might not approve.) To play the sound continuously until the next slide that has another sound is ready, select the Loop Until Next Sound item at the end of the Transition Sound menu. Click the transition thumbnail again to hear the sound.

6. **Decide whether the slide should advance with a mouse click (the default) or advance automatically after a delay period you set.**

   Enable both, and you get the best of both worlds: A click works; otherwise, the slide advances automatically.

7. **To apply the same transition to all slides in your show, click the Apply to All command button.**

Using Package for CD

I know, I know — "Using Package for CD" sounds *really* weird. (Even the naming professionals in Redmond can shrug their shoulders from time to time.) Anyway, you can use the PowerPoint *Package Presentation for CD* feature to package a PowerPoint presentation to run on another Windows PC.

"But what if my good friend doesn't have a copy of Microsoft PowerPoint installed?" Good question, and Microsoft has the answer: By default, a copy of the free PowerPoint Viewer is included in your packaged presentation!

To create a Package for CD, follow these steps:

1. **Open the presentation file you want to package.**

2. **If you want to save the file to removable media (like a USB flash drive or a blank CD) rather than to a folder on your system, load the media into the drive.**

3. **From the File tab, choose Export and click Package Presentation for CD. Then click the Package for CD button to display the dialog box you see in Figure 4-14.**

4. **Type a descriptive name in the Name the CD field.**

5. **If you need to add multiple presentations to a single CD, click the Add button.**

   This step opens an Open dialog box, allowing you to locate and select the other presentations.

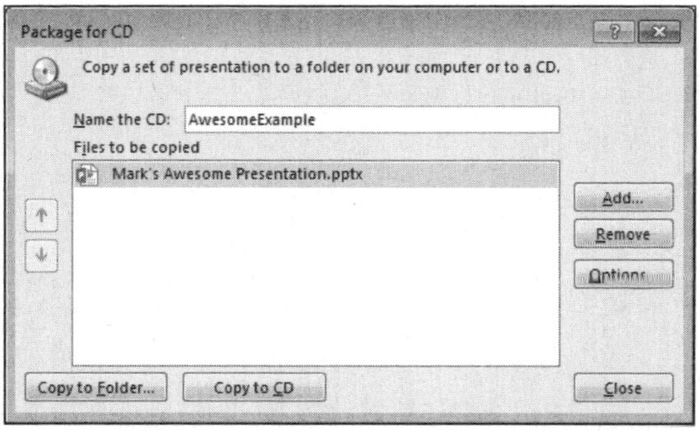

Package for CD

Copy a set of presentation to a folder on your computer or to a CD.

Name the CD: AwesomeExample

Files to be copied

Mark's Awesome Presentation.pptx

Add...

Remove

Options

Copy to Folder...   Copy to CD   Close

Figure 4-14:
Proparing
to package
things up.

6. **If you included any even slightly unusual fonts in your package,
   click Options and select the Embedded TrueType fonts check box
   to include them in your package.**

   I mention linked graphics earlier, in the section "Installing Graphics
   in Your Slides." If you package a presentation that displays linked
   graphics, those images either have to be on the destination PC (and
   in the same exact folder structure) or you have to include them in
   your package file. Otherwise, the graphics don't show up in those
   slides.

   Take it from someone who has done a lot of work with printing shops
   and publication houses of all sizes: Assume nothing and *always* include
   linked files! (That's why both check boxes are selected by default.)
   However, you're also assuming that the destination PC has the same
   fonts. To make absolutely sure that your presentation can be viewed on
   any PC running Windows, I recommend that you also select the Embed
   TrueType Fonts check box.

7. **Click the Copy to Folder button to specify the target location on
   your hard drive or an external USB drive for the package. Or,
   click the Copy to CD button to burn the files to a CD-R or CD-RW
   disc.**

   If you update your presentation, you must repeat this process again to
   repackage it. However, you can save it on the same CD-RW disc or in the
   same folder, and PowerPoint prompts you for permission to overwrite the
   original package.

   Naturally, there arc other ways to present that don't involve your presence! You can also share a PowerPoint presentation that you've saved to
   your SkyDrive. From the File tab, click Share, and then click Invite People.
   Click the Save to Cloud button, and then follow the on-screen steps to invite

others and make your online presentation. To create a standalone video from your presentation (which you can in turn burn to disc, e-mail, or upload to an online site like YouTube), click Export and click Create a Video. You can also create a PDF of your presentation from the Export screen.

Printing Your Document

The final stop on the PowerPoint tour is the Print function. In addition to printing slides, you can print several other types of documents, including your Notes pages and any handouts you created.

Don't forget that PowerPoint displays Print Preview to verify how things look before you print. (Click that looming File tab, and then choose Print.)

To print the slides from the entire presentation by using the default settings, you can simply click the File tab, click Print, and click the Print button. However, if you press Ctrl+P (or pause on the Print pane first), PowerPoint offers you quite a bit of control over what gets printed and how it looks, as you can see in Figure 4-15.

Figure 4-15: Preparing to print in PowerPoint 2013.

From the Print pane, you can choose

+ The printer to use

+ The number of copies

+ The documents to print (from the Full Page Slides drop-down list)

+ Color, black and white, or grayscale (from the Color drop-down list)

+ Whether to surround your slides and Notes pages with a frame (the Frame Slides item at the bottom of the Full Page Slides list)

+ Whether to print the entire presentation, specific slides, or a range of slides (from the Print All Slides drop-down list)

As I mention in other Office chapters in this minibook, your printer's software driver might offer additional settings. To display these settings, click the Printer Properties link next to the Printer drop-down list.

Chapter 5: Doing Database Magic with Access

In This Chapter

- ✔ Starting Access
- ✔ Touring the Access window
- ✔ Creating tables
- ✔ Creating forms
- ✔ Printing your data

*W*hat? You never used Access? Don't sweat it: There's a good reason why Microsoft Office Access 2013 isn't everyone's bag of potato chips. Much like Excel, Access can be more complex and harder than the average application for the novice to use — hence, the relative obscurity of Access compared with Office applications like Word and PowerPoint. (Based on what I see in my appearances at user group meetings and in mail from my readers, Access has far less of a following than the "superstars" of Office.)

However, Microsoft has done its best to help bring Access to the home PC owner. Wizards abound, and the Access Help system is one of the most extensive in the Office 2013 suite. (It's no coincidence that the other stand-out in the Help system is Microsoft Excel.) I'm happy to report that you can easily take care of basic Access chores — like building tables and forms — without having to have a degree in particle physics. In this chapter, I introduce you to those basics and show you how to keep track of really important data — like your collection of porcelain chicken planters.

If you're interested in taking the plunge and trying everything that Access has to offer, I can heartily recommend the more comprehensive book *Access 2013 For Dummies,* by Laurie Ulrich Fuller and Ken Cook (John Wiley & Sons, Inc.). She has the elbow room to cover Access from one end of the Ribbon to the other.

Running Access

You can use any of the following methods to start Access:

✦ On the Start screen, type **Access** and click the Access 2013 button that appears.

✦ Double-click an Access database or project file.

✦ If you've added an Access tile to your Start screen, click the tile.

If you're opening the program for the first time, Access automatically displays the Templates screen (which you normally reach from the New menu item on the File tab). Yep, free stuff! You'll find an abundance of high-quality, predesigned templates grouped by category available from Microsoft.

Figure 5-1 illustrates the settings on the Templates screen — you can click a thumbnail to create a new database using that template as a starting point, or click in the Search for Online Templates box to search for specific keywords.

Figure 5-1:
You can
create
a new
database
from the
Templates
screen.

A Quick Tour of the Access Window

After you choose a template and open a new blank database, the initial Access 2013 window, shown in Figure 5-2, looks somewhat empty. That's because the idea behind Access is to accept, store, display, and edit information in a free-form manner — and you can create your own look-and-feel for the program.

Here's a quick rundown of the elements within the Access window:

✦ **File tab:** Click the showy File tab to access file and global commands, like New, Open, Save, and Print. (You can also sign in to your Microsoft account from the Account menu item.) The recent databases you created and opened appear on the Open menu's Recent list, and the Options button takes you to your global Access program settings.

✦ **Ribbon:** The Ribbon might look like a toolbar, but it changes to offer different command buttons when you click a tab. (Access is somewhat lean on tabs compared with the other Office 2013 programs, but there's plenty of power there.)

✦ **Quick Access bar:** This group of buttons next to the Office Button acts like the Quick Launch buttons on the Windows 8 taskbar, and they can be customized easily.

To add or delete buttons from the Quick Access bar, click the arrow button to the right of the bar to display a pop-up menu from which you can toggle the display of the most common command buttons. You can choose from a larger selection of command buttons by choosing More Commands from the pop-up menu, or even relocate the Quick Access bar under the Ribbon by clicking Show below the Ribbon.

✦ **Editing window:** In Access, the editing window is more of a container for the tables you create as well as other windows and displays. However, I used that name already for Word, Excel, and PowerPoint, and I'm not going to stop now.

✦ **Navigation pane:** Although the Navigation pane can be collapsed (by clicking on the double-arrow button), it never completely disappears, and it hangs out on the left side of the editing window. Look to the Navigation pane when you want to create and edit database objects (such as tables, queries, and forms, which I discuss in a bit).

✦ **Status bar:** In Access, the status bar allows you to switch between Datasheet and Design views. In addition, it displays the current status of your Num Lock, Caps Lock, and Scroll Lock keys; and also provides simple help messages and information about database fields. It's not exciting stuff, but such is the life of a status bar.

File tab   Quick Access bar   Office Ribbon

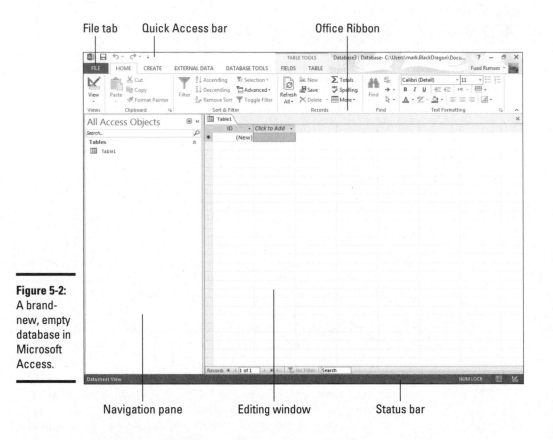

Figure 5-2:
A brand-
new, empty
database in
Microsoft
Access.

Navigation pane   Editing window   Status bar

Creating Access Tables

Tables in Access are interesting database beasties: They look like the
tables that I discuss in the earlier Word chapter of this minibook, but they
store information as *fields* (or individual pieces of data, like your telephone
number) within *records* (each record contains all the fields describing one
person, place, or thing). Tables are the building blocks of an Access database. A name and an address of a customer, for example, might make up a
record; the customer's first and last name, street address, city, state, and ZIP
code are all fields within that record.

A table uses Datasheet view, which organizes fields as columns. Records
appear as rows.

Note that the database you created already has one blank table — you can switch between tables in a database by clicking the table tabs at the top of the editing window. (Note that these tabs are below the Ribbon, so I'm not talking about the Table tab on the Ribbon here.)

To open an existing database that you recently used, click the File tab and then click Recent to select a database file in the list.

To create a new table, just click the Create tab on the Ribbon and then click the Table button. Access adds another blank table to your database file.

The new table you created now shows up in the Navigation pane as a second item. (Check it out in Figure 5-3.) You can open it to enter additional records (or view or edit existing records) at any time by clicking it within the Navigation pane.

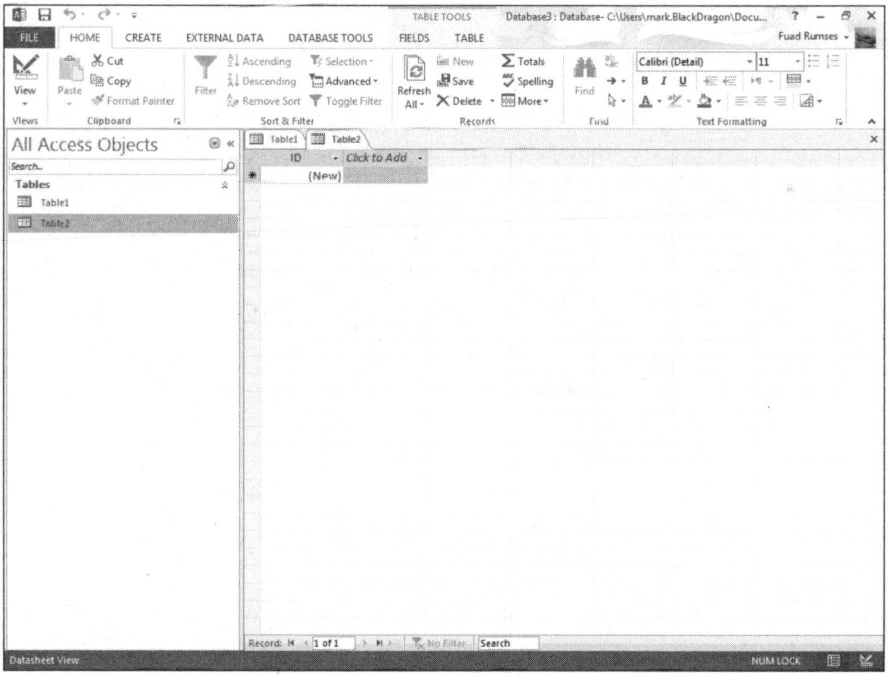

Figure 5-3:
Admiring my new table in the Navigation pane.

To delete a table, you must first close it by clicking the Close button (X) at the upper-right corner of the editing window. (Note that this is *not* the Access window Close button, which is at the top corner of the Access window itself. See Figure 5-3.) If you decide not to save the changes made to the table, it disappears immediately. If you saved the table earlier, however, just right-click it in the Navigation pane and then click Delete. Access prompts you for confirmation before trashing the table. (It had better. That confirmation dialog box has saved my rump many, many times.)

I describe how to enter data directly into a table a little later in this chapter. First, I delve into creating a form with the Form Wizard.

Creating a Form with the Wizard

Creating your own form is important because it simplifies your database for normal human beings. By using forms, anyone can enter data into your database, even if they're not familiar with the database creation process or if they have little experience with Access.

By default, all forms are saved as separate tabs in the Datasheet window, and they also appear in the Navigation pane, under the corresponding Table entry. You can enter data into a table by clicking the corresponding Datasheet tab or by clicking the form entry in the Navigation pane. Forms are also used to display existing data in a table. For example, if I only want to find out the length of the film *Alien* from my DVD database, I can just display the record for that film within the form.

You can easily create a custom form for a database table by using the Form Wizard. Follow these steps to build your own form:

1. **Click the Create tab and click Form Wizard.**

 The first screen of the Form Wizard appears, as illustrated in Figure 5-4.

2. **From the Tables/Queries drop-down list, choose the table that will be linked to this form.**

 To specify the fields that appear in the form — not all need be included, of course — click in the Available Fields list each field you want to include in the form, and then click the single right arrow. (You can click the double right arrow to add all fields in the table.) When you click each field, it moves to the Selected Fields box.

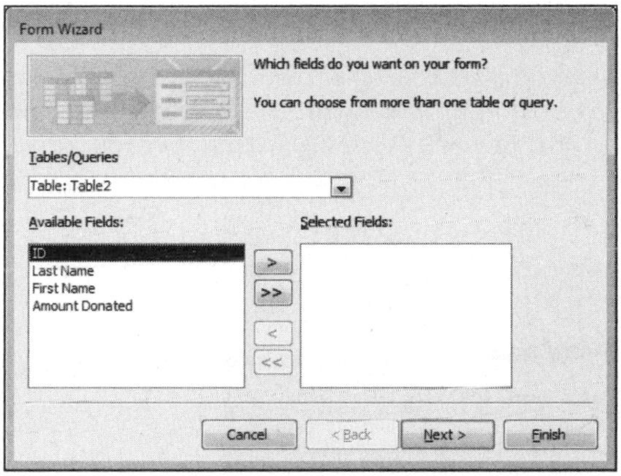

Figure 5-4:
You can
build a
new form
easily with
the Form
Wizard.

To remove a field from the Selected Fields list, click the field name you
don't want and then click the single left arrow; to empty your field list
and start all over again, click the double left arrow.

3. **When the Selected Fields list on the right has the fields you need,
   click Next to continue.**

   From the wizard screen shown in Figure 5-5, you can select from a
   number of predesigned formats, including the Datasheet layout (which
   looks quite similar to Excel) and the standard Columnar layout that
   Access uses when it generates a form automatically. (Personally, most of
   my forms use Justified layout, which I think presents a more pleasing —
   and somewhat more familiar — look to the human eye.)

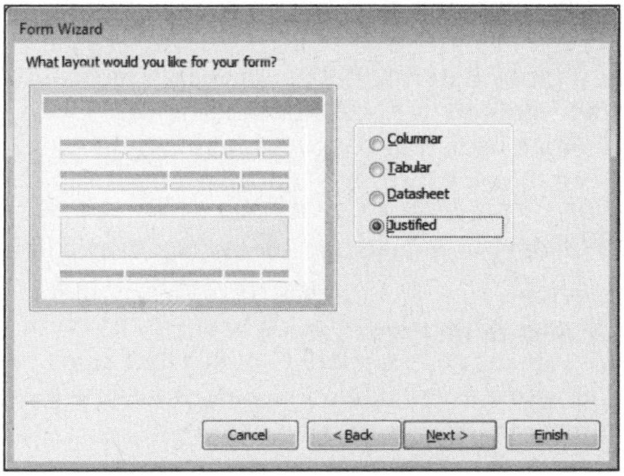

Figure 5-5:
It's time to
choose a
layout for
your new
form.

4. **Select the layout you need and then click Next to continue.**

The final Form Wizard screen, as shown in Figure 5-6, prompts you for a descriptive title for your new form. You can choose to open the form immediately to add records or view existing records, or you can edit the design of the form.

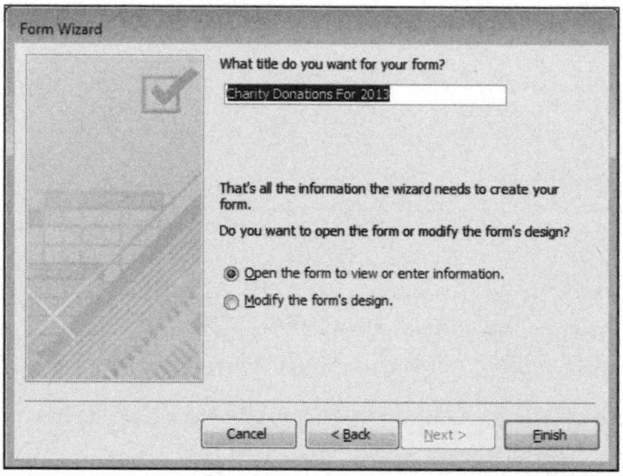

Figure 5-6:
You're nearly finished building your Access form.

Form Wizard	

What title do you want for your form?

Charity Donations For 2013

That's all the information the wizard needs to create your form.

Do you want to open the form or modify the form's design?

⦿ Open the form to view or enter information.

○ Modify the form's design.

Cancel   < Back   Next >   Finish

5. **Click Finish to close the wizard.**

To delete a form you no longer need, first click the Close button in the upper-right corner of the Editing window to close the form, click the form in the Navigation pane, and then press Delete. You're prompted for confirmation before the file is deleted. *Note:* Deleting a form doesn't delete any data from your tables.

So how do you use a form? Entering data is probably more intuitive within a form than any other method in Access because a form looks so doggone much like an online form that you would encounter on a website. The instructions you need to use a form are just this simple:

✦ **To enter data:** Click your mouse pointer in the desired field and then type.

✦ **To move to the next field:** Press Tab.

✦ **To move to the previous field:** Press Shift+Tab.

✦ **To close the form and save your data:** Click the Close button in the upper-right corner of the form.

If a field has the value (AutoNumber), it indicates that the field is automatically incremented when you close the form. For example, if the previous record had a 5 in that field, the next record you add automatically uses a value of 6 in the field.

Access uses the Record box for moving between records — it's in the lower-left corner of the editing window, which displays the current record number. To navigate between records, use the navigation buttons around the Record box, as shown in Figure 5-7:

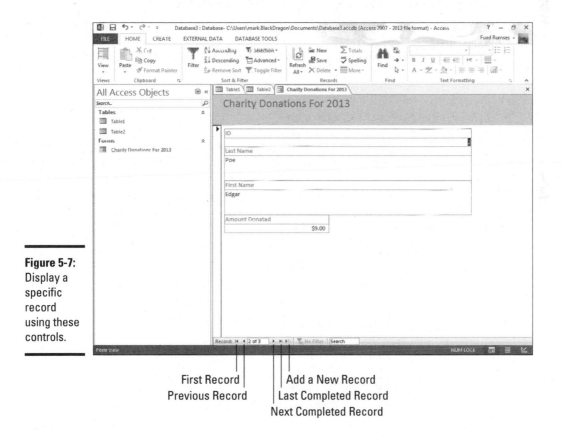

Figure 5-7:
Display a
specific
record
using these
controls.

First Record
Previous Record

Add a New Record
Last Completed Record
Next Completed Record

✦ Click the arrow pointing to the bar at the left to move to the first record in the table.

✦ Click the arrow pointing to the left to move to the previous record.

✦ Click the arrow pointing to the right to move to the next completed record.

✦ Click the arrow pointing to the bar at the right to move to the last completed record in the table.

✦ Click the far right arrow to move to the end of the table and add a new record.

Entering and Editing Fields Manually

I admit that I get pretty enthusiastic about forms: They're easy for computer novices to use, and they look quite professional. However, you can view, enter, and edit your data directly from the table itself, using Datasheet view. And, because the table displays many records at a time in rows, it's often faster than using a form.

Follow these steps to enter or edit a field value in a table:

1. **Select the record that you want to enter or change by either clicking it with the mouse or pressing the Tab/Shift+Tab combination to move to it.**

2. **Type the new data value; depending on the data format, you might have to select the contents with your mouse (or the Shift+arrow keys) and the original value first.**

   Access displays a pencil icon to the far left of the record to indicate that you made a change to the record.

3. **If you're entering data in a new record, press Tab to move to the next field.**

4. **Click within any other record to save the new values.**

5. **To edit another record, begin again at Step 1.**

Each time you enter a value in the empty record at the bottom of the window, Access automatically adds a new, empty record; however, if you create a new record by mistake, just press Esc to cancel your edits.

Printing Your Data

Before you decide to put your data on paper, I always recommend that you use the Print Preview feature. Just click the File tab, click Print and then choose Print Preview. Many times I've been thankful that I checked first to verify that what I expected to print was actually what was going to appear on the hard copy!

Access can print from just about any view, no matter what's being displayed. When you're ready to print, choose one of these three methods:

✦ **Click the File tab, choose Print, and then click the Quick Print button.** The contents of the active window are immediately printed with the current settings.

✦ **Click the File tab, choose Print and click Print again.** Although this takes longer than a Quick Print, you can elect to print just selected pages (or the selected records in a datasheet window). You can also select from multiple printers or specify multiple copies from the Print screen. If you need to change any printer-specific options supported by the printer's Windows 8 software driver, click the Properties button. When you're ready, click OK.

✦ **Press Ctrl+P.** This method also displays the Print dialog box.

Chapter 6: Staying in Touch with Outlook

In This Chapter

✓ Running Outlook

✓ Introducing the Outlook window

✓ Setting up your Outlook e-mail account

✓ Reading and replying to incoming mail

✓ Sending messages

✓ Adding file attachments to messages

✓ Entering contacts

✓ Creating appointments

✓ Using the Outlook Today screen

✓ Printing within Outlook

*I*f you didn't install Outlook 2013, *run* — do not dawdle — to your bookshelf and grab your Office 2013 DVD. You see, you need it in order to install Outlook. It's that good, and — in my opinion — using just about anything else is strictly second best. (No offense to those other electronic mail applications; it's just that Outlook can organize just about everything in your life better than any other program I've ever used — without becoming confusing or complex.) Naturally, Outlook has the same look and feel as the rest of its Office 2013 brethren.

In this chapter, I provide you with the basics you need to use Outlook as your comprehensive e-mail, address book, and calendar application. You attach files, read messages, make appointments, and send blind carbon copies in no time at all. I also mention a number of tips that I've found helpful in my experience with Outlook.

For a complete discussion of everything that Outlook 2013 can do and store, you obviously need more than just a single chapter. And I can't recommend a better book than *Outlook 2013 For Dummies,* by Bill Dyszel (John Wiley & Sons, Inc.).

Running Outlook

You can start Outlook by using any of the following methods:

✦ If you added Outlook to your Desktop Quick Launch bar or your Windows 8 Start screen (which I definitely recommend), click the icon.

✦ From the Windows 8 Start screen, type **Outlook** and click the Outlook 2013 button that appears. (No unnecessary text boxes or Search buttons — just start typing at the Start screen to display matching applications!)

✦ Press a Windows key while holding down R (Win+R) to bring up the Run dialog box; type **outlook** in the Open text box and then press Enter.

Look for the two Windows keys on your keyboard; they reside in the same stratosphere as your spacebar and Alt keys. If ya got 'em (and you probably do), they bear the waving Windows flag.

Elements of the Outlook Window

Figure 6-1 illustrates the Outlook window in all its glory.

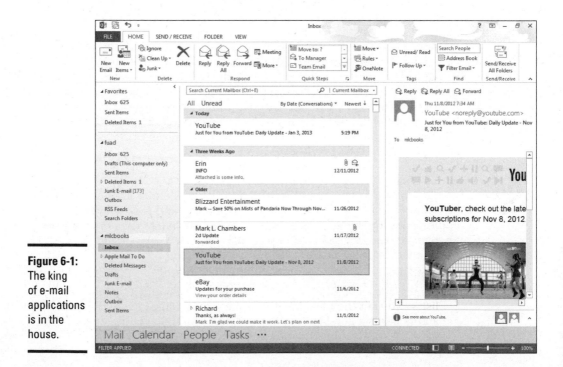

Figure 6-1: The king of e-mail applications is in the house.

Here's a quick rundown of the elements within the Outlook window:

✦ **File tab:** The File tab is your direct connection to the functions that used to appear on the File menu in previous versions of Outlook. From here, you can open files, import data from other programs, print data, and edit your account settings. You can also configure global Outlook settings from the Options menu item.

✦ **Ribbon:** Outlook sports the same familiar Ribbon across the top of the window as the other Office programs. The contents of this Ribbon change with the tab you select.

✦ **Tabs:** Clicking a tab changes the content of the Outlook Ribbon, displaying command buttons specific for that tab.

✦ **Command buttons:** Like the toolbars of old, a click on one of these buttons performs a function within Outlook. You'll notice that some of these buttons also have a downward or sideways-facing arrow, which you can click to display a pop up menu of choices corresponding to the button.

✦ **Folder pane:** The top of this pane includes a tree display, where you can select an Outlook folder. Just click to select a folder, and the contents are displayed in the Message list. You can use the strip of buttons at the bottom to jump between different views and functions within Outlook. For example, you can immediately switch to your Outlook Calendar view, or you can click the People button to check a telephone number from your Contacts list. (I'm not sure why the button doesn't read *Contacts* instead of *People*. It's a mystery.)

✦ **Message list:** Here are displayed messages of the current folder; however, in other views (like Contacts or Tasks view), the contents change to match the data you're displaying.

✦ **Reading pane:** If you click a message in the Message list, the contents are displayed in the Reading pane. This is a neat way to see what's contained in the message without opening the message in a separate window.

TIP

If the Reading pane doesn't appear on your screen, click the View tab and click the arrow next to the Reading Pane button in the Layout group. Then click either Bottom or Right to specify where the Reading pane should appear.

Virtually any pane can be resized in Outlook. Move your mouse pointer over the divider bar until it turns into opposing arrows and then drag to relocate the bar.

✦ **Status bar:** The Outlook status bar typically displays the total number of messages in a folder or the total number of contacts in your Contacts list — you get the idea. (Don't get me wrong: I appreciate the totals. The status bar is a good soldier in the fight to hold down RIE, or runaway inbox expansion — but that's about it.)

Configuring Your Mail Account

First things first. When you initially launch Outlook 2013, you see an Outlook 2013 Startup Wizard. The prompts and on-screen help are self-explanatory, but the information you're asked for is also covered in this section (because the Startup Wizard sets up your first mail account). With that in mind, I recommend that you refer to this section if you need a dash of clarity while running the Startup Wizard.

"But Mark, I have more than one e-mail account!" No worries, good reader. Adding a mail account within Outlook involves — surprise! — a wizard. (I think that someone in Redmond got the message that Wizards are A Good Thing.)

Although Outlook 2013 and Windows Live Mail both handle your e-mail, Outlook 2013 is far superior in features and functionality. If you have both on your PC, take my advice and use Outlook 2013 . . . you'll thank me later!

Follow these steps to add an Internet e-mail account within Outlook:

1. **From the File tab, click Info. Then click the Account Settings button and choose Account Settings from the pop-up menu. (Whew!)**

   Outlook displays the dialog box you see in Figure 6-2.

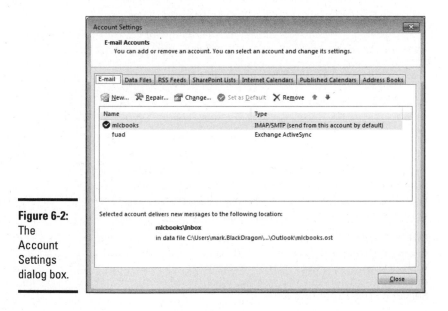

Figure 6-2:
The Account Settings dialog box.

2. Click the New button on the E-Mail tab toolbar.

The Add Account Wizard appears, as shown in Figure 6-3. (Note that you can also change an existing account from the toolbar.)

Outlook 2013 can automatically set up most e-mail accounts for you. For virtually all home PC owners, that's a POP3 server, which is the common choice with most dialup and digital subscriber line (DSL) or cable Internet service providers (ISP's). (Enough abbreviations for one sentence?) You can also set up a separate account for a web-based server (like Hotmail or Gmail). For these steps, we'll do things automatically.

TIP

If you're connecting to an office e-mail server, check with your network administrator to determine the manual settings you'll need to enter — in fact, if that august personage has created a set of Outlook account setup instructions for your office network, feel free to deviate happily from this procedure and follow those steps instead!

3. Click the E-Mail Account radio button and click Next.

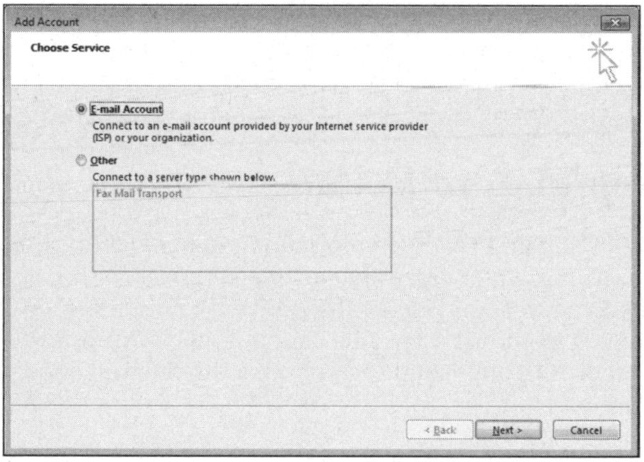

Figure 6-3:
Provide
Outlook 2013
with your
account
information,
and it does
the rest!

4. Type your name into the Your Name box and then type the e-mail address supplied by your ISP into the E-mail Address box. Finally, type your e-mail account password into the Password box and then retype it to confirm your spelling.

Check the documentation provided by your ISP for information like your e-mail address and password — if you can't find it, a call to your ISP's technical support line is in order. If you're manually entering your ISP or company's server information, click the Manual Setup or Additional Server Types radio button.

5. **Click Next.**

    Outlook attempts to connect to the specified server and download a sample message.

    Any errors are reported at the bottom of the dialog box. If you misspelled your password, you can correct it and retry the connection. The wizard reports success after the connection has been made and the message downloaded.

6. **Click Finish to close the wizard.**

    Note that your new account has been added to the list in the Account Settings dialog box.

To remove an account or to specify a new account as the default, click the account in the list to select it, and then click the Remove or Set as Default buttons on the E-Mail tab's toolbar.

If you rely heavily on Outlook to store all your important information, I beseech you — even more than usual — to *back up your doggone hard drive!* You might be able to re-create most of your résumé, but how about every single telephone number that you ever stored in Contacts or every single e-mail message you ever received? Do it. *Back up. Do it!*

Reading and Replying to E-Mail

Naturally, receiving and reading your incoming mail is the primary thrust behind Outlook, and you can easily check all your accounts at once. Click the Send/Receive tab and click Send/Receive All Folders — or press F9. (To send and receive from just a specific account, click the Send/Receive tab, click Send/Receive Groups, and then choose the desired account from the resulting pop-up menu.)

Oh, joy! "You've got mail" — and it's not a chunk of worthless spam that you want to immediately delete. (Read more on eradicating spam later in this chapter.) New messages appear as bolded entries in the Message pane; double-click the message to open it in a message window (as shown in Figure 6-4).

Wait a second! There are our friends, the Ribbon and tabs! Yep, they appear within the Reading and Replying windows. Note, however, that the Ribbon is limited to two tabs in the Reading window (and six in the Reply window), and the File tab is really necessary only for file functions, such as saving a draft message, moving messages to a different folder, resending messages, and printing message contents.

Figure 6-4:
Read a
message
in its own
window.

If you would rather scan your mail, click the message once, and it's shown in the Reading pane. (If the Reading pane is missing, click View and click the Reading Pane button; then select the location where the Reading pane should appear. If you're not interested in previewing your mail, this option is a good one to toggle off because you see much more of the Message list that way.)

By default, Outlook uses a Usenet or newsgroup format, where the messages are arranged in a conversational style rather than by the date you received them. (This style of display is also called *threading*, where a message is followed by all its replies in linear order.) You can disable this format:

1. **Click the View tab.**

2. **Click the Show as Conversations check box to disable it.**

3. **When prompted by Outlook, specify whether you want to turn off threading for all mailboxes or just the currently selected folder.**

To add the author of an incoming message to your Contacts list, right-click the person's e-mail address in the From field (while the message is displayed in a message window) and then choose Add to Outlook Contacts from the contextual menu that appears. (More about adding Outlook contacts later in this chapter.)

Does one of your incoming messages deserve a pithy reply? (Otherwise called "returning a piece of flaming e-mail" — all in fun, of course.) If so, follow these steps to reply to it:

1. **Click to select a message in the Message pane list, click the Home tab, and then click the Reply button.**

   If the message is already open in its own window, click the Reply button within the message window.

   Was the original message addressed to additional folks besides yourself? If so, you can send your reply to everyone who received a carbon copy of the original message by clicking the Reply All button (rather than Reply) on either the Home tab or the message window Ribbon.

   Outlook opens the Reply window, as shown in Figure 6-5, with the insertion cursor already hanging out at the top of the message. Outlook includes the text of the original message, too — just look underneath the separator line to see the original message. The To field is already completed, filled with the name of the person who sent the original e-mail.

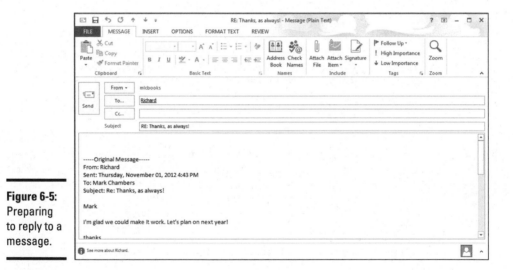

Figure 6-5:
Preparing
to reply to a
message.

   Notice that Outlook automatically adds the prefix *RE:* to the beginning of the original subject line, but feel free to click in the Subject box and type a new subject if you like.

2. **(Optional) To send copies of the reply to other individuals, click once in the Cc box and enter addresses manually (separated by semicolons) or click the Cc button to select names from your Outlook Contacts list. See Figure 6-6.**

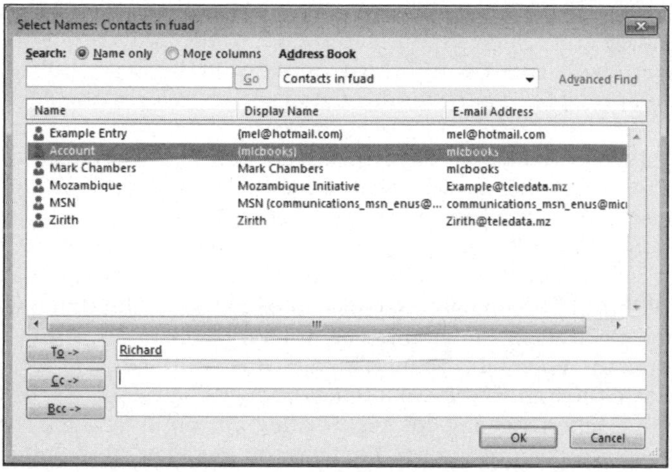

Figure 6-6:
Selecting names from my Outlook Contacts list for carbon copies.

The text of the original message is included. If necessary, you can delete it manually to preserve that all-important privacy.

"Hey, can't I send *blind* carbon copies too?" (That's where the recipients of copies don't see the others who have also received a copy.) You surely can, but for some strange reason, Outlook hides the Bcc field in the Reply header unless there's already a Bcc recipient. To add a Bcc recipient, click the To or Cc button to display the Select Names dialog box. Click the contacts you want to include and click the Bcc button to add them directly into the Bcc box. (You can also type or paste addresses into the Bcc box.)

3. **Go ahead — type like the wind! After you enter the text of your message (and format it, if you like, by using the familiar formatting controls in the Basic Text group of the Message tab), you can add attachments.**

   I cover attachments later in this chapter, in the section wittily titled, "Using File Attachments."

4. **When all is in readiness, click the Send button to send your message immediately.**

To save a draft of the message without sending it immediately, click the File tab, click Save, and then close the Reply window. The message appears in your Drafts folder within the Folder pane; to send it later, click the Drafts folder to show a list of the documents in it, double-click the message to open it, and then click Send.

To save a copy of a message or reply in text or HTML format, click the File tab and click Save As.

You can also forward a message, allowing you to add a comment to the body of the original message before you send it to the new recipient. To forward a message, click the Forward button rather than the Reply button. Then sally forth, following the instructions I detail within this section.

Could you use some help prioritizing the messages that need replies? That's where the Outlook Follow Up feature comes in handy. Check out the column at the far right of the Message list that contains a ghostly outline of a pennant. (If you don't see the Flag column, you may have to hide the Reading Pane from the View tab by clicking the down arrow under the Reading Pane button. The Flag column can also be shown or hidden using the Show Columns dialog box, which you can open by clicking the Add Columns button on the View tab.) Right-click the Flag column for a particular message to indicate the importance of a timely reply. When you need to prioritize your inbox, click the Flag column heading button. When you're done with a message, you can right-click the Flag column again and choose Clear Flag from the pop-up menu. *Sublime!*

Composing and Sending Messages

Sometimes a reply just isn't enough; instead, you need to stir up trouble by initiating the e-mail conversation. To compose and send a new message, follow these steps:

1. **Click the New Email command button on the Home tab or press Ctrl+N.**

Outlook displays the new message window you see in Figure 6-7.

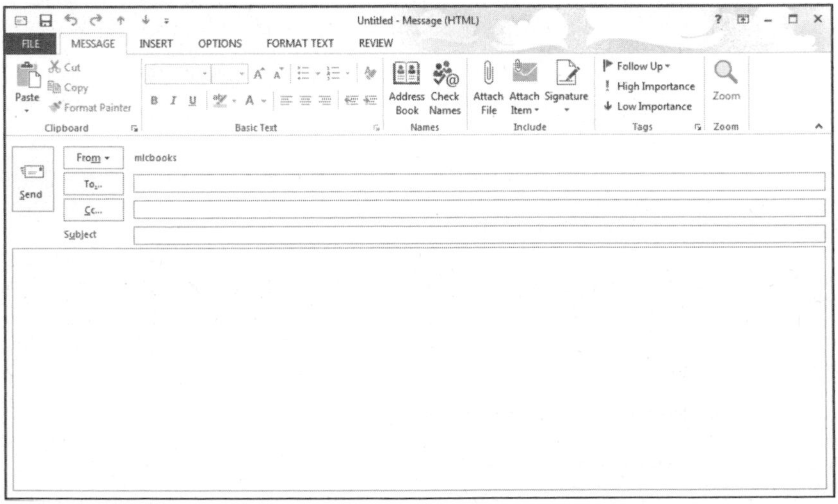

Figure 6-7:
Creating a new message begins here.

2. **Address your message.**

   - *If the recipient for this message isn't in your Contacts list:* Click in the To box and type the e-mail address. (Or, if it's on the Clipboard, you can paste the address by using the Ctrl+V shortcut.)

   - *If you have the recipient for this message in your Contacts list:* Click the To button and then choose the person from the Select Names dialog box that appears. You can also add carbon copies and blind carbon copies from this dialog box.

   Click OK to return to the new message window.

3. **Click in the Subject field, type the subject for this message, and then press Tab to move to the message editing box.**

4. **Type the text of your message and apply any desired formatting to the text.**

   Select the text, and then either right click the selection or use the controls on the Message tab in the Basic Text group to format the text just the way you like.

5. **Add any attachments.**

   Use the procedure that I show you in the next section.

6. **Send the message.**

   - *Now:* Click the Send button to send the message immediately.

   - *Later:* Alternatively, click the File tab inside the new message window and then click Save to save the message in your Drafts folder, as I explain in the preceding section.

     The ability to save your e-mail messages is a truly neat feature, especially if you're composing messages offline on your laptop without an Internet connection. You can turn that idle time spent waiting in the airport into productive time. When you get back to your home or office and your Internet connection, send each message as I describe earlier.

Using File Attachments

Time now to turn your attention to file attachments. You can include all sorts of files with your e-mail messages, such as

+ Office documents

+ Pictures, sound clips, and *short* video clips

+ Programs and data files

If the recipient of your message is using Outlook (or another popular e-mail application), she should be able to save and use the files you send just as though they had been stored on a USB flash drive or a disc.

Attaching files and sending them to your friends with Macintosh and Linux computers is a useful way to swap documents that can be read on multiple platforms (like a Word document, for example).

ISPs place a ceiling on the size of an individual message — and that includes any attachments. How much is too much? The typical limit is under 10MB for a single message, but the exact limit is determined by both your Internet e-mail server and the recipient's e-mail server. With this in mind, another Mark's Maxim appears:

> Never send a 300MB video clip to your best friend as an e-mail attachment and expect it to arrive in one piece.™

You know that you exceeded the maximum message size if you receive an error message from either server that declares your original e-mail to be undeliverable. The *noive* of some people! Nyuk.

Here's how to send an attachment:

1. **Reply to a message or compose a new message.**

2. **Click the Message tab on the reply or new message window Ribbon, and then click the Attach File button in the Include group.**

   Outlook displays the Insert File dialog box.

3. **Navigate to the location of the files you want to attach and then click each one.**

   For multiple files, hold down Ctrl while you click.

4. **Click Insert to add the files to the message.**

   Attached files appear in the Attached header area of the message dialog box (see Figure 6-8).

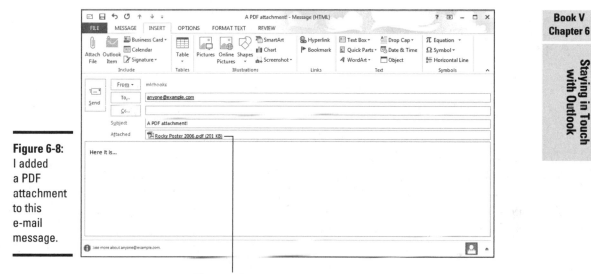

Figure 6-8:
I added
a PDF
attachment
to this
e-mail
message.

The attachment

If someone sends you an attached file, right-click the file attachment in
the header and choose Save As from the pop-up menu that appears; then
browse to select a spot on your system where the file will be stored.

Repeat after me: "Mark, I promise never to run an attached file unless I
manually scan it — or unless my anti-virus scanning software has already
scanned it automatically!" E-mail viruses and malicious macros are wide-
spread these days, and running any attachment (even one from someone
you know) without protection is just asking for trouble.

Keeping Track of Your Contacts

Enough with the e-mail! Outlook can also take care of your contacts like any
other good personal information manager (PIM). To display your contacts,
click the People button on the button strip below the Folder pane or press
Ctrl+3. The Contacts window appears, as shown in Figure 6-9.

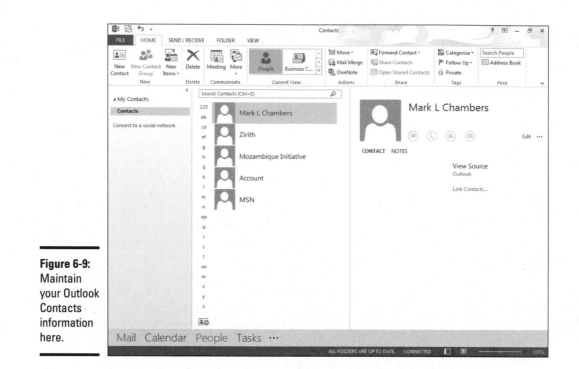

Figure 6-9:
Maintain
your Outlook
Contacts
information
here.

To jump directly to a specific first letter of a contact's last name, click the desired letter on the button strip down the left side of the Contacts screen.

So what can one do with a contact? Of course, half the value of the Contacts window is the ability to simply store your address book information in an organized central location, but you can also

✦ Create a new e-mail message to that contact.

✦ Set up an appointment or a meeting request with that contact.

✦ Set a new task for that contact.

All these sundry actions are available when you right-click any contact entry displayed in the Contacts window.

Entering a contact

To enter a new contact from the Contacts window, follow these steps:

1. **Press Ctrl+N or choose New Contact from the Home tab.**

Outlook displays the Contact window, which you see in Figure 6-10.

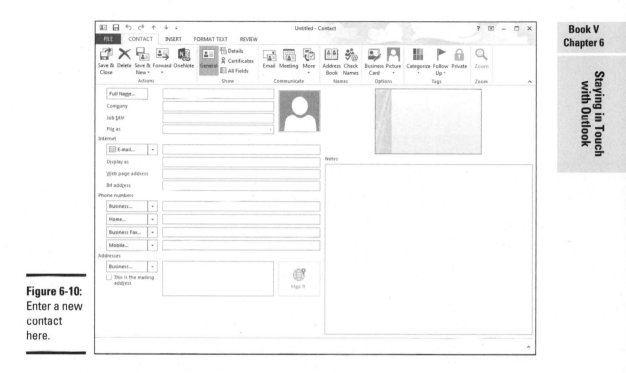

Figure 6-10:
Enter a new
contact
here.

2. **Click in the appropriate field to enter information such as the person's
   telephone numbers, job title, address, and web page address.**

   Entry is completely free-form; the only fields that I recommend you
   should always enter are the person's name and e-mail address. As you
   complete fields, you'll note the information appears in the business card
   display at the right side of the window. Click in the Notes box at the
   right side of the window and type any comments or notes that you want
   to save for this contact.

   To add a photo of the contact from your hard drive, click the Picture
   button and choose Add Picture.

   If a field has a down-arrow button next to it, you can click the button to
   display additional fields of the same type. For example, click the down
   arrow next to the Business Phone field, and you can click to display the
   person's pager or home fax machine number. (Each field you complete
   is marked with a check mark in the drop-down list.)

3. **To display additional fields, click the Details button on the Contact
   tab; from this panel, you can enter the person's birthday and anniver-
   sary, spouse's name, and other such data.**

4. **After you enter all the data for a contact, click the Contact tab and
   then click Save & Close.**

Editing a contact

You can easily add new information to an existing contact or even edit the data you already entered: Just double-click a contact entry in the Contacts window. Outlook opens the same window that you used to enter the contact information. Of course, the data that you already added to the contact is still there, but everything can be edited if necessary, and you can add new data.

To close the window and save the updated information, click the Save & Close button again.

Using the Outlook Calendar

If I told you that Outlook is also a full-featured calendar program, would you believe me? Yep, this program is a regular Swiss Army knife! To display the Calendar, click the Calendar button below the Folder pane or press Ctrl+2. Figure 6-11 illustrates the Calendar window.

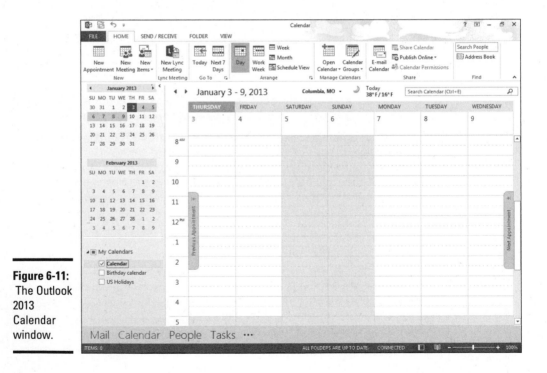

Figure 6-11: The Outlook 2013 Calendar window.

Click the Home tab and then the appropriate button in the Arrange group to display the different Calendar periods, which are highlighted within the Calendar window. From these views, you can set appointments that will appear on your Calendar:

✦ **Day:** A single day.

✦ **Work Week:** A five-day work week.

✦ **Week:** A full, seven-day week, beginning on Sunday and ending on Saturday.

✦ **Month:** An entire month.

✦ **Schedule View:** Your current calendar view is presented in a horizontal arrangement, making it easier to schedule appointments that don't overlap (like mine always seem to do).

Creating an appointment

To create a new appointment for your Calendar from the Calendar window, follow these steps:

1. **Press Ctrl+N or choose New Appointment from the Home tab.**

Outlook displays the Appointment window, as shown in Figure 6-12.

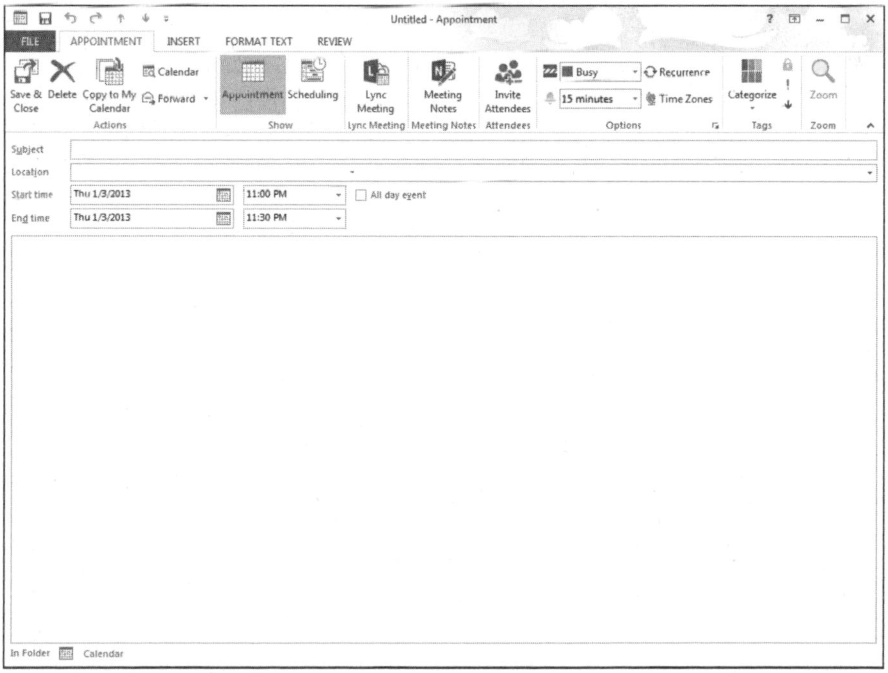

Figure 6-12: It's time to add a new Outlook appointment.

2. **Type a descriptive subject for the appointment, press Tab, and then type the location for the meeting.**

   To use a location you used previously, open the Location drop-down list and select it from the list.

3. **Set the start and end times for the meeting.**

   a. *Start:* Click the Start Time drop-down list, choose the date for the appointment, and then click the start time.

   b. *End:* Likewise, click the End Time drop-down lists and set the ending date and time for the appointment.

   c. *All day:* If the appointment lasts all day, select the All Day Event check box, and Outlook disables the End Date and Time fields.

4. **(Optional) If you need a reminder from Outlook before the appointment, click the Reminder drop-down list in the Options group of the Appointment tab. Choose the length of time you need to reach your appointment after the reminder appears.**

   You can also set an audible reminder from the Reminder Sound item at the bottom of the Reminder drop-down list, choosing an alarm sound to play as a little added "encouragement."

5. **From the Show As list in the Options group, choose a status for the appointment.**

   The appointment status shows up in your Calendar as a shaded or colored block.

   By default, Outlook uses Busy as the status for a new appointment.

6. **Click in the Notes box at the bottom half of the Appointment window and type any free-form comments or notes that you want to associate with this meeting.**

7. **Click the Categorize button on the Appointment tab to assign a category to this appointment.**

   Click the All Categories item at the bottom of the list to display the Color Categories dialog box, as shown in Figure 6-13.

   You can assign multiple categories to an appointment.

8. **After everything is set, click the Save & Close button on the Ribbon to add the appointment to your Calendar.**

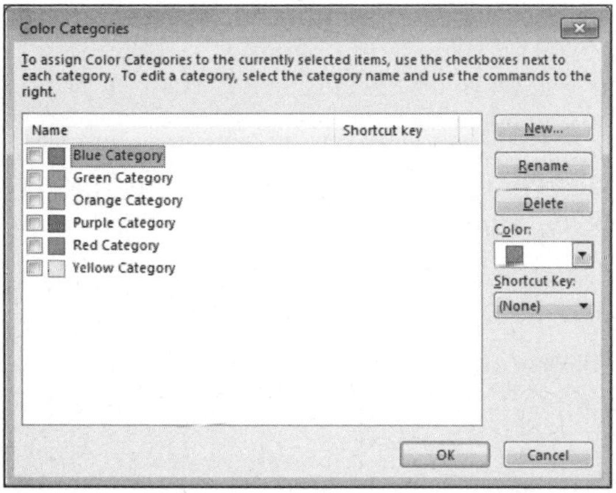

Figure 6-13:
Categories help you organize your appointments.

Displaying today's appointments in Outlook

To view your daily appointments and summarize your entire existence each morning — pretty cool when you think about it — display the Calendar window and click the Today button on the Home tab. Outlook displays everything that's happening today arranged on a single screen. This, folks, is a neat trick, and I use this view throughout my workday.

To display the specifics about an appointment or task, double-click the item.

Printing within Outlook

Believe it or not, you can print just about any data from Outlook in its native form — and considering the wide variety of information stored within Outlook's copious environs, that's quite a feat. Depending on the current view and the selected item (items), you can print anything from the contents of an e-mail message to your appointment schedule and your Contacts list — the printed output varies according to the module you're currently using, like Contacts or Calendar.

Like with the other Office 2013 applications, I strongly recommend that you pause long enough to preview the printed copy. When you're displaying the view you need within Outlook (and you've selected any specific items to print), you can view how things will look by clicking the File tab and clicking Print.

Remember how I just finished crowing about how great the Today view is? And here we are talking about printing. Hmmm . . . what better way to print a reminder of what you need to do during the day than by printing the Today screen? It's your entire day on one sheet of paper.

So you're satisfied with the preview — but don't forget the powerful settings available from the Print screen! From here, you can set the page style, print multiple copies, select the target printer (including network printers), and select a range of pages to print. Figure 6-14 illustrates the Print screen when you print from within the Calendar screen. To set any printer-specific options provided by your printer's driver, click the Print Options button. After you set the printer options you need, click Print.

From anywhere within Outlook, you can jump directly to the Print screen by pressing Ctrl+P.

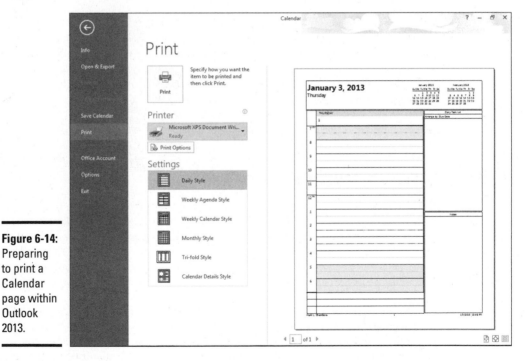

Figure 6-14: Preparing to print a Calendar page within Outlook 2013.

Chapter 7: Working with SkyDrive

*I*n the ancient days at the turn of this century, Microsoft Office stayed put on your hard drive. Sure, you could share documents with others through e-mail or scoot documents around on your office network, but you *certainly* didn't create or save stuff online!

Enter that most intangible feature that has revolutionized document sharing: the cloud! Office 2013 includes support for the Microsoft SkyDrive online storage system, which offers anyone with a Microsoft account a whopping 7GB of space. Oh, and did I mention that you can access the files stored on your SkyDrive anywhere in the world? If you have an Internet connection, you're online with SkyDrive — it's that simple.

In this chapter, I demonstrate how you can use SkyDrive to store your Office documents and how you can customize your online storage for your needs. Get ready to live the carefree life of hardware independence!

Answers to Your Online Storage Queries

Before I delve into creating and using a SkyDrive, I want to answer some common questions I've often received from readers about online storage:

✦ **Is my stuff safe?** The answer is a definite yes; Microsoft maintains the servers where your data is stored, and backs them up on a regular basis. I'd venture to say that the data you store on your SkyDrive is as safe as your physical hard drive — in fact, if you don't back up your hard drive at all, your SkyDrive is already *much* safer. Just locate an Internet connection you can use, and your data is within reach at all times!

✦ **What can I store online?** Although SkyDrive is designed for easy use with Office documents, Microsoft allows you to store just about any type of file online (as long as it's legal). This also makes SkyDrive a great choice for simple file backups, allowing you to keep copies of your truly invaluable files online in case of catastrophe. Initially, a SkyDrive account can store up to 7GB of data, but you can purchase 20GB, 50GB, or 100GB of additional storage space for $10, $25, or $50 a year, respectively.

✦ **Is my stuff private?** Again, I'm going to wax enthusiastic about Microsoft's implementation of online storage. The company has taken great pains to ensure that your data remains secure from prying eyes.

✦ **How much will it cost me?** A number of online storage sites on the web will charge you for territory, but I'm happy to say that the initial 7GB of SkyDrive storage is free to all Windows Live members.

✦ **Can I save and load Office documents directly to and from SkyDrive?** Not only can you, but Microsoft is actively encouraging you to do just that (by making your SkyDrive a default destination in the Save and Open screens within Office applications).

✦ **How fast is the transfer?** Online storage is nowhere near as fast as the dedicated hard drive inside your PC. However, most Office documents and photographs of reasonable size should transfer within a few seconds. Naturally, the faster the Internet connection you're using, the faster SkyDrive will work.

So what do you need to use SkyDrive? Here's a list of Microsoft's requirements at this writing:

✦ **Windows Vista or later (as well as Mac OS X Lion and later)**

✦ **A broadband Internet connection**

✦ **A Windows Live account**

   If you're already using the Windows Essentials suite of online tools (or you have a Hotmail account), you've already set up your account, and you can use that username and password. Otherwise, visit `https://home.live.com` and click Sign Up.

Signing In to SkyDrive

Ready to join the SkyDrive revolution? Good; fire up Internet Explorer and visit `https://skydrive.live.com`. In the Sign In window (as shown in Figure 7-1), type your Microsoft account ID and password and then click Sign In.

Here we are with the old battle betwixt security on one hand and convenience on the other. If you'll be using SkyDrive from a secure location (like your home) and you're the only one using the PC, feel free to select the Keep Me Signed In check box. If you're in a public place, using a laptop, or sharing your PC with others, however, I *strongly* recommend that you don't enable the Keep Me Signed In check box.

Figure 7-1:
Sign in for
Microsoft
SkyDrive
online
storage.

Figure 7-2 illustrates the main SkyDrive screen, with the following important items you should note:

✦ **Files link:** Click this link to display all folders within your SkyDrive (whether you used them recently or not).

✦ **Recent docs list:** This group of folder icons represents the SkyDrive folders you used within the last few sessions.

✦ **Space remaining:** You can always check the amount of space remaining in your SkyDrive using this meter.

✦ **Manage storage:** Click this link to subscribe for additional storage space or to control who can add a people tag (which leads to your profile) to photos that include you.

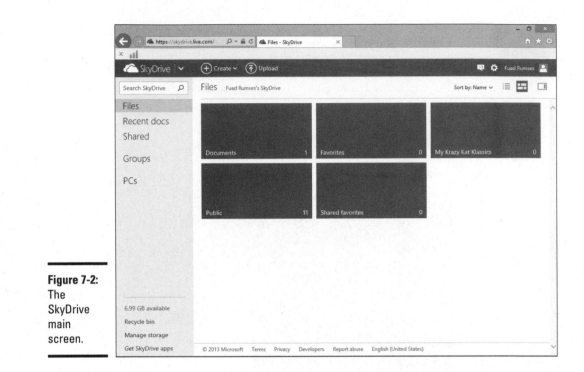

Figure 7-2:
The
SkyDrive
main
screen.

Marking Your Own Territory and Adding Files

The default folder names are essentially self explanatory: The contents of Documents are for your eyes only, for example, and the Public folder can be accessed by anyone through your Windows Live profile. I'm a customizing kind of guy myself, though, and I'll bet you'd prefer to create your own top-level folders within SkyDrive, with names like "My Krazy Kat Klassics" and "Important Stuff." (I know I did.)

To organize your SkyDrive to your liking, follow these steps from the main SkyDrive screen to create a new folder:

1. **Click Create and click Folder from the menu that appears.**

SkyDrive displays a new folder tile (or folder link), as shown in Figure 7-3.

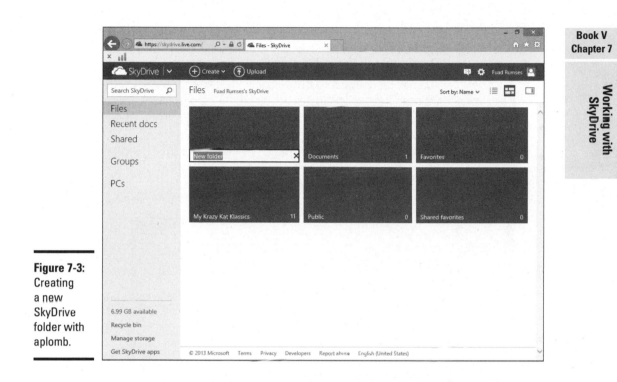

Figure 7-3:
Creating
a new
SkyDrive
folder with
aplomb.

2. **Type a descriptive name into the Name text box and press Enter.**

   This creates a folder with the default security settings.

3. **Right-click the folder you've just created and choose Share from the menu that appears.**

4. **Choose how to share the contents of your new folder.**

   You can send an e-mail to those lucky folks (Send Email), or post a link on Facebook, Twitter, or LinkedIn. Click Get a Link to create a link with two security levels that you can insert into a web page or e-mail message manually: a View Only link and a View and Edit link. (Visitors have to use the link you provide to access the folder.) You can also choose to make the contents of this folder completely public — click Get a Link and click the Make Public button, and anyone can search for and view the contents of this folder.

5. **Click Done to continue.**

6. **If you'd like to immediately add files to your new folder, click the Upload button on the toolbar and select the desired files using the Choose File to Upload dialog box, as shown in Figure 7-4.**

You can also drag and drop files from a File Explorer window into the square. The maximum size for each file upload using a web browser is 300MB, but you can upload files of up to 2GB in size using the SkyDrive application.

Uploading may take some time, depending on the speed of your Internet connection, so do not close or navigate away from the Upload screen until the completion message appears.

Figure 7-4:
Adding
files to your
SkyDrive.

To add files to an existing folder, click the folder from the main SkyDrive screen to open it and then click the Upload button. SkyDrive returns you to the Choose File to Upload dialog, ready for you to select files.

Office anywhere!

From the folder contents screen, you can also create a new Office document. Click Create and choose the document type you want to create, which automatically opens the corresponding web-based version of Word, Excel, PowerPoint, or OneNote. Whoa, wait a second, *what just happened here?*

Welcome to Microsoft's new direction: web-based Office applications, which are an integral part of Microsoft's Office Web Apps suite. Consider these new applications the "lite" version of the familiar (and far more powerful) hard drive–based Office programs. With these online versions of your Office applications, you can work anywhere there's an Internet connection (even if the PC you're using doesn't have Office installed)! Friends and neighbors, it doesn't get much cooler than that.

If you right-click a document icon within one of your SkyDrive folders and choose Properties, a sidebar appears that displays the file's information, as well as a description that you can add. To open the existing document from the folder screen using the web application, just click the icon. To retrieve the file and save a local copy on the PC's hard drive, right-click the document icon and choose Download.

Although the web-based Office applications have nowhere near the features and options that I discuss in earlier chapters in this minibook, they do allow basic editing with controls that usually mirror the full version as closely as possible. Plus, the web-based applications create, open, and save documents in the standard office formats (`.docx` for Word, for example), so you can conveniently work with your files on either platform.

Oh, did I mention that Microsoft has made these web-based Office applications completely free to everyone with a Microsoft account? Time to celebrate, PC owners!

Saving Files within Office Applications

As I mention in the nearby sidebar, "Office anywhere!" you can click an Office document in a SkyDrive folder to edit it within the corresponding web-based application.

"Well that's great, Mark, but I want to save a file to my SkyDrive from within my traditional hard drive-based Office program!" No problem, good reader; just follow these steps:

1. **Click the File tab in Word, Excel, PowerPoint, or OneNote (Microsoft's note-taking and collaboration tool, also part of Office).**

2. **Click Save As.**

3. **Click SkyDrive.**

   If you haven't used SkyDrive so far in this computing session, you're prompted to enter your Microsoft account login information.

4. **Click the destination SkyDrive folder (or click Browse to select a SkyDrive folder).**

   After a moment, you see a standard File Save dialog box where you can enter a filename and pick a document format.

5. **Click Save.**

   You might experience a bit of "busy time" as your Office application uploads the file to your SkyDrive.

Book VI

Fun with Movies, Music, and Photos

Contents at a Glance

Chapter 1: Scanning with Gusto

In This Chapter

- Understanding scanner technology
- Shopping for a flatbed scanner
- Acquiring an image
- Rotating and cropping your scans
- Scanning guidelines to follow
- Handling copyrighted material

A scanner might rank as one of the most versatile pieces of hardware that you can slap onto your PC. With an investment of anywhere from $75 to $400 (U.S.), you can add the ability to copy and fax printed documents (with a modem and a printer, of course), create digital images from all sorts of materials, and even use optical character recognition (OCR) to read text from documents directly into your PC's word processing application.

What's inexpensive isn't always easy to use, however. You have to choose among different types of scanners that use different types of connections to your PC — and to produce the best results, you need at least an introduction to the basics of scanning. You also need the skinny on cleaning a scanner, deciding on an image format, and handling copyrighted material. In this chapter, I provide you an introduction to the basics of scanning.

By the way, if you're planning to copy your face — or any other body part — you don't need to read this chapter. Just visit your local copy center or stay a little late at the office. (Oh, and be discreet.)

What Happens inside a Scanner?

I can't say that it's Party Central inside your scanner; in fact, most popular scanners now on the market have very few moving parts. Plus you don't really have to know how your scanner does its job in order to use one, so you can skip to the next section with a clear conscience.

Still with me? Then read on to discover how this magic box can turn a printed document into a digital image. Check out Figure 1-1.

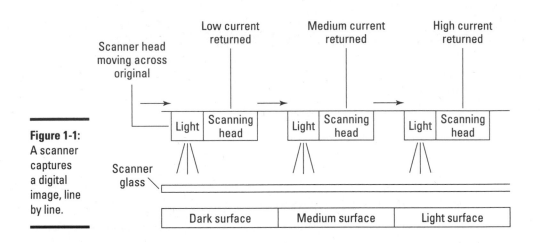

Figure 1-1:
A scanner
captures
a digital
image, line
by line.

Here's how it works:

1. The scanner's sensor (an array of photosensitive cells) moves one line across the material you're scanning. (In some scanners, the material moves past a fixed sensor; this concept gets important pretty soon.) The sensor is paired with a strong light source that illuminates whatever you're scanning.

2. As the sensor moves past the original, each cell sends a level of current corresponding to one dot (a *pixel)* of the reflected light from the material. For example, scanning the white part of a printed page results in a far different signal from scanning the black text on the same page.

3. Your scanner's electronic brain (tiny as it is) collects all the signals from each pixel, resulting in a digital picture of one line of the original.

4. The scanner sends the data from the scanned line to your PC.

5. The sensor (or the material) advances one line, and the entire process begins again at Step 1.

I often compare this process with taking a digital photograph of each line of your document and then laboriously pasting those separate images together in an image editing program. Luckily, you don't have to do the hard work: Your PC collects each line sent by the scanner and builds the document for you, usually while you watch. Technology is grand that way.

Your Friend, the Flatbed

I present the Mark's Maxim for this page:

Buy a *flatbed* scanner.[tm]

Figure 1-2 illustrates a flatbed scanner preparing to do its duty; note that the top lifts up, just like a copy machine. The sensor head moves in a flatbed scanner while the material you're scanning remains motionless on top of the scanning glass. (In a second, you discover why a motionless original is A Good Thing.)

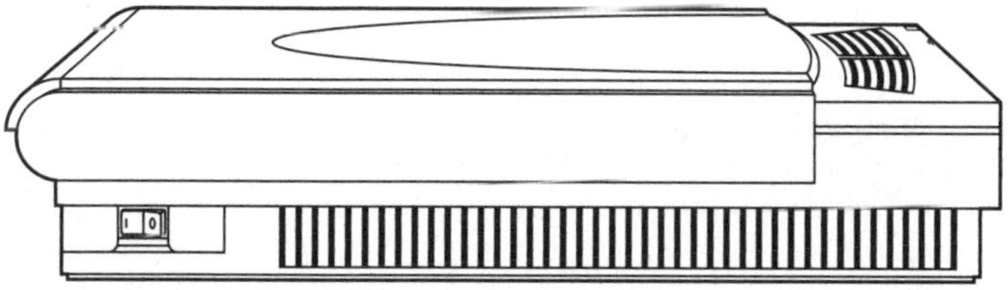

Figure 1-2: Nothing pleases like a flatbed scanner.

Comparatively, with a sheet-fed scanner, the material you're scanning moves through a system of rollers while the sensor remains stationary. Printer manufacturers often use sheet-fed scanning hardware in all-in-one, or *multifunction,* devices, which combine the functionality of a printer, a scanner, a fax machine, and a copy machine in one svelte case. (Some multifunction devices even sport both a flatbed scanner and a sheet-feed option, so you get the best of both worlds.) Gotta be honest, though; I don't recommend sheet-fed scanners. And before all you owners of sheet-fed scanners out there In PC Land begin reaching critical mass and flooding my e-mail inbox, let me attest to the single major advantage to sheet-fed scanners, like the one you see in Figure 1-3: They take up far less space. (I know this from personal experience because I've used both sheet-fed and flatbed scanners in my office.)

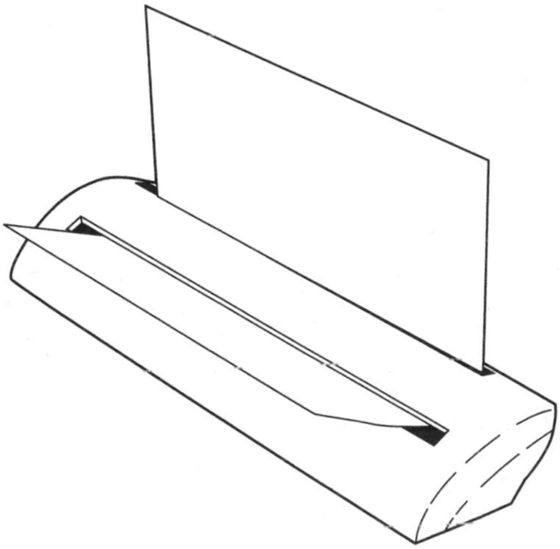

Figure 1-3: A sheet-fed scanner looks much like a fax machine.

"Okay, Mark, I'll 'byte': If I can save valuable desktop space with a sheet-fed scanner, why are you such a diehard supporter of flatbed models?" Dear reader, here are the top three reasons why you should pick a flatbed:

✦ **They deliver a better-quality scan.** Because the original material remains fixed in a flatbed (compared with the moving original in a sheet-fed), you have less chance of shifting, which allows a flatbed to deliver a better scan with more detail.

✦ **They're versatile.** If an original can fit on top of the flatbed's glass, you can scan it — pages from a book, small items such as business cards, or even items such as clothing. With a sheet-fed scanner, you're limited to paper documents, and you have to use a clear plastic sleeve to hold those business cards. (Many sheet-fed scanners don't even accept small items.)

Sheet-fed owners: Keep those documents as pristine as possible, meaning no torn edges, no staples, and no brittle or fragile antique documents that could suddenly decompose inside the hard-to-reach areas of your machine.

✦ **They have fewer moving parts.** Sheet-fed scanners can easily jam if the original document doesn't feed correctly, and I've found them less reliable over the long run than flatbed models because sheet-fed scanners require more cleaning and adjustment.

If you already invested in a sheet-fed model, don't despair; there's no reason to scrap your hardware. However, you have to limit yourself somewhat in your material — unless, of course, you don't mind cutting pages from books and magazines to scan them.

Other specialized types of scanners are lurking in the shadows these days:

✦ **Negative scanners:** These expensive models are especially designed to produce the best possible scans from film negatives. They do nothing else, so versatility isn't their claim to fame. (Read about how to scan film in a bit.)

✦ **Business card scanners:** Again, the name says it all. These portable scanners capture images and information from standard-size business cards. They're often used in conjunction with laptop or netbook computers.

✦ **Pen scanners:** A pen scanner captures only a single line of text at once, but it's easy to carry around and can be used with a laptop computer and OCR software to read text from documents into a word processing application. (The wand scanner, a close relative to the pen scanner, works in a similar fashion — however, it can capture an entire page as you sweep it across the sheet.)

Popular Scanner Features

Here's a list of the minimum features I typically recommend for home or home office use when you're shopping for a flatbed scanner:

✦ **A minimum flatbed optical resolution of 4800 x 9600:** Without delving too deeply into the details of scanner *resolution* — the number of pixels your scanner can capture — you should reject any flatbed scanner that offers less than 4800 x 9600 dots per inch (dpi) and any sheet-fed scanner with less than 600 x 1200 dpi. Note that you should be checking the *optical* (also often called *hardware* or *raw*) resolution and not any resolution figure that's *enhanced* or *interpolated.* Those fancy words just indicate that the scanner's software is adding extra dots in the image. I call them *faux pixels* because they aren't read from the original. Just ignore any enhanced or interpolated resolution figures when shopping for a scanner.

✦ **Single-pass operation:** If a scanner can capture all the color data that it needs in one pass, it takes less time (and introduces less room for registration error) than a scanner that must make three passes across the same original. —'Nuff said.

✦ **One-button operation:** Most scanners now offer one or more buttons that can automatically take care of common tasks. For example, one button might scan the original and create an e-mail message with the scanned image as an attachment, and another might scan the original and automatically print a copy on your system printer. I'm all about convenience.

✦ **A minimum of 42-bit color:** The higher the bit value, the more colors your scanner can capture. Ignore any scanner that can't produce at least 42-bit color; heck, many scanners can now produce up to 96-bit color!

✦ **A film adapter:** Whether it's optional or included with the scanner, the ability to add a film adapter allows you to scan film negatives and slides (positives) with much better results.

✦ **USB or FireWire connection:** Choose a scanner that uses either a Universal Serial Bus (USB) 2.0/3.0 connection or a FireWire connection. Of course, your PC needs the prerequisite ports, as I explain in Book I, Chapter 3.

Basic Scanning with Windows Photo Gallery

Scanner manufacturers ship a bewildering number of different capture (or *acquisition)* programs with their hardware, so there's no single proper way to scan an original. However, scanners that comply with the TWAIN standard can be controlled from within popular image editors such as Adobe

Photoshop. *TWAIN,* for you acronym nuts, is not an acronym — it refers to the line "and never the twain shall meet," from that Kipling guy. (Many folks think that TWAIN means *technology without an interesting name.* It doesn't.)

Now that you've been properly introduced, here's the important part you'll be tested on: Devices that are TWAIN-compatible are operating system–independent, meaning that these devices are interchangeable among Windows, Macintosh, and Linux. Any TWAIN-compatible hardware device can work with any TWAIN-compatible image editor or software application — pretty *sassy,* no?

Acquiring the image

In this section, I demonstrate how to use a typical USB Hewlett-Packard scanner within Windows Photo Gallery, which you can pick up as a free add-on for Windows 8 (as part of the Windows Essentials suite) at `http://download.live.com`. If you follow along with this procedure, you end up with an image that you can edit within a program like Photoshop, convert to another format, or simply save to your hard drive. (Of course, your scanner will also include the manufacturer's software, which likely includes at least a basic image editing program. It's up to you which editing program you choose.)

Assuming that you have the Windows Essentials suite loaded on your computer, follow these steps:

1. **Display the Start screen and type** Photo**, and then click the Photo Gallery button that appears in the Apps Search results pane.**

   If you've added a Photo Gallery tile to your Start screen, you can also click the tile. No matter how you get there, the main program window, shown in Figure 1-4, appears.

2. **Click the Home tab, and click the Import button in the New group.**

3. **Click the entry for your scanner and then click the Import button.**

   At this point, Photo Gallery invokes the scanner's TWAIN driver, so the resulting dialog box will be different for every manufacturer — however, the important controls should be evident if you explore a bit.

4. **Click the Start a New Scan button (or whatever it's called within your scanner's controls).**

   Your scanner should rumble to life, and eventually the dialog box produces a thumbnail image of the original.

**Book VI
Chapter 1**

Scanning with Gusto

Figure 1-4:
The Photo
Gallery main
window.

**5. If you're satisfied with the dimensions of the image and the automatic
settings chosen by your scanning software, click the Send the Scan
Now button.**

The result appears as a new image within Photo Gallery, ready for you to
edit and experiment to your heart's content.

However, if you need to fine-tune the image before sending it to Photo
Gallery in Step 5, here are the common settings that you can change in most
scanner drivers, along with what you accomplish:

✦ **Output type:** This setting controls which type of image file the scan
produces. Typically, you want a color photograph in 24-bit (or 16.7 mil-
lion) colors, but other choices might include a web image at 256 colors,
a grayscale image (what most folks think of as "black and white"), a true
black-and-white–only drawing, or simple text (optimized for reading with
an OCR program). Generally, use JPG format for smaller file sizes and
TIFF format when archival storage and highest quality are important.

✦ **Image boundaries:** Use this feature to click and drag the boundaries of the scanned image. For example, I recommend moving the scanned image border inside any extraneous material on the edges of the original, such as text that surrounds a picture you want from a magazine page. When you reduce the size of the actual scan, your image file is smaller and the scanner takes less time to do its job — plus you can save a step by cropping that extraneous part of the image now instead of later within your image editing program.

If your scanning program includes an auto-edge detection feature, use that option, and you'll likely eliminate most of this fine-tuning.

✦ **Image scale:** You can use the original image size, or you can scale the scanned image by a specified percentage. Also, most drivers allow you to set the width or height of the scanned image in inches, and the software automatically calculates the proper proportion change for the other dimension.

✦ **dpi (or resolution):** A setting of 150 to 300 dpi is usually fine for scanning photographs or documents, but if you're planning to enlarge an image with a lot of detail, you might want to specify a higher resolution. However, this significantly increases the size of the finished image file.

Rotating and cropping images

After the scanned image is safely in your image editor (either Windows Photo Gallery or the editing software provided by your scanner's manufacturer), you're free to have fun — fixing problems big and small, removing portions of the image that you don't want, or even zooming in to view and change individual pixels.

Although a complete discussion of image editing is far too in-depth a subject for this chapter — in fact, you can find dozens of books on Photoshop and other high-octane image editing programs — I want to cover the two most common procedures required for most scanned images:

✦ **Rotation:** An image that's literally standing on end or displayed upside-down needs to be *rotated* (turned).

✦ **Cropping:** An image with too much extraneous background needs to be *cropped* (trimmed). Cropping an image can significantly cut down its file size.

To rotate an image within Photo Gallery, follow these steps:

1. **Scan an image into Photo Gallery, or if the image already appears within Photo Gallery, click it to select it.**

Read how in the previous section.

2. **Click the Rotate Clockwise or Rotate Counter-clockwise button in the Home tab's Manage group.**

   Photo Gallery rotates the entire photo in the desired direction by 90 degrees.

If you only to need to straighten a photo — not rotate it a full 90 degrees — use the Straighten feature of the Editing tab, which I discuss next.

To crop a scanned image inside Photo Gallery, follow these steps:

1. **Double-click the desired thumbnail.**

   Photo Gallery opens the image for editing and displays the Edit tab on the Ribbon, as shown in Figure 1-5.

2. **Click the Crop button within the Adjustments group.**

   On your image, Photo Gallery displays a highlighted crop box, as shown in Figure 1-5. The edges of the box are marked with tiny boxes called *handles.* The area inside the box is the portion of the photo that will remain after the cropping is complete.

3. **Click and drag any handle to resize the crop box to the desired size.**

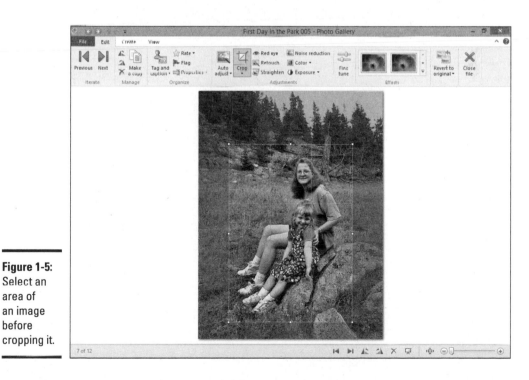

Figure 1-5:
Select an area of an image before cropping it.

4. **To select a specific proportion (like 16 x 9 for use in a widescreen slideshow), click the arrow below the Crop button to display the drop-down menu, and move your cursor over the Proportion item to select the desired ratio.**

   To set your own proportions for the cropped image, opt for the Custom proportion.

5. **Click the arrow below the Crop button, and click Apply to remove everything outside the selection box; see the results in Figure 1-6.**

Other simplified photo editing tools available on the Ribbon include Red Eye, Retouch, Straighten, Noise Reduction, Color, Exposure, and the Effects thumbnails. These are rudimentary tools, though. You'll always have much more control and creativity in a beefy photo editing app like PaintShop Pro X5 or Photoshop.

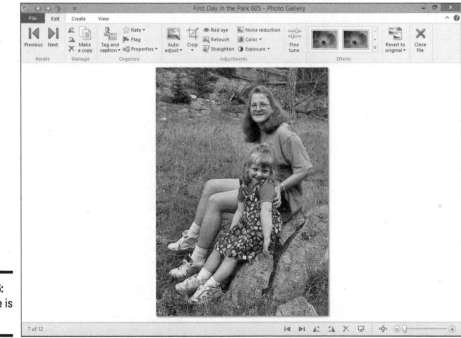

Figure 1-6:
The image is cropped.

If you make a mistake, you can always click the Undo button in the Quick Access bar (at the top-left corner of the Photo Gallery window) to cancel the last action you performed. To back out of all changes and revert the image to its pristine original form, click the Revert to Original button at the right side of the Ribbon.

To close the image when you're finished with editing, click the Close File button — the thumbnails (and the original Ribbon) return.

Scanning Do's and Don'ts

Today's scanning software helps make the scanning process easier than it was just a few years ago, but here are some tried-and-true guidelines to follow for the best results from your hardware:

Do

✦ **Work with the largest possible original.** The larger the original, the better-quality image you're likely to get. (Sure, you can scan a postage stamp, but use a higher dpi setting so that you have enough pixels to enlarge the image later.)

✦ **Clean your scanner glass with the right material.** Never spray glass cleaner directly on the glass: Too much liquid on the glass can leak under the surface, causing condensation later. Instead, use a soft photographer's lens cloth or a monitor wipe moistened with alcohol, which evaporates quickly. I clean my scanner glass at least once weekly.

✦ **Add as much memory to your PC as you can afford.** The more memory you add, the easier and faster your PC can handle larger scans. Remember that some of those scanned images might end up being 50MB (or even more). Also, any image editor performs much better with additional memory. If you're using Photoshop regularly, for example, I recommend a minimum of 4GB. Memory, my friend, is cheap.

✦ **Keep your scanner drivers up to date.** As with other hardware devices that I mention throughout this book, check your scanner manufacturer's website often for updates to your scanning software and for Windows drivers.

Don't

✦ **Overwrite your original scan.** If you're experimenting with a scanned image — for example, if you're applying filters or changing the color balance for an artistic effect — keep the original as is. (Instead, create a copy of the file to work with within File Explorer.) After you apply changes in an image editor and save those changes, you usually can't backtrack to the quality of the original image.

✦ **Place heavy objects on your scanner's glass.** Believe it or not, I've heard horror stories of people trying to scan bricks and rocks — usually trying to capture a particular color or pattern for an e-mail attachment or a web graphic. Besides the possibility of a cracked or a broken scanner glass, rough or pointed objects can cause scratches that show up in your images.

Paper clips and staples are Public Enemy #1 for your scanner. Remove them before you place your original!

+ **Use outdated or specialized image formats.** For example, PC owners should avoid Microsoft Paint (MSP) images. (I like to call these little-known and less-recognized formats by a single collective acronym *WIF*, which stands for *w*eird *i*mage *f*ormat.) My point is simple: By using one of the major image formats (TIFF, JPEG, or BMP), you give others a better chance to load and work with your scanned images.

Those Irritating (Or Invaluable) Copyrights

Of course, copyrights aren't so doggone irritating if you happen to be the creator of a work of digital art (whether it's a photograph, a painting, or a poem). As an author, I'm personally all for copyrights. However, as a scanner owner, you might find yourself walking a legal tightrope without a pole when you decide to include scanned material in your own documents.

Like I said, I'm an author — *not a lawyer!* (I do know some great lawyer jokes, but that's not the same as a law degree.) Therefore, before I describe some common myths about copyright law, let me say that you should *always* consult a knowledgeable copyright/intellectual properties lawyer. These guidelines are here to help, but they're not a substitute for bona fide legal advice.

With that well-worded disclaimer in mind, here's a selection of the most common fallacies concerning copyrighted material:

+ **"I got it off the Internet, so it must be in the public domain."** Wrong. It doesn't matter where you got a creative work — from the Internet, a publication, or even off the wall of a subway tunnel. If you use anything that you didn't create completely by yourself, you need permission from the author.

+ **"I added a line and some shading to this scanned image, so now it's mine."** Embellishing an original work does *not* make it yours. (After all, I can add an extra line of lyrics to any Beatles song that you can name, but that doesn't give me the copyright to "Eight Days a Week.")

+ **"This photograph didn't carry a copyright mark, so the scan is my original work."** Nope. An original work, whether a document, a photograph, or a scribble on a napkin, doesn't need any mark (although a copyright mark does reinforce your copyright claim). In the legal world, a copyright is bestowed automatically in most cases as soon as the creator completes the work.

✦ **"This project is not-for-profit, so I can include this artwork."** This one *might* be true, but only if you're using something from a clipart collection or royalty-free photograph archive that gives you specific rights to use intellectual property in your work. Otherwise, it doesn't matter whether your work is for profit or nonprofit — a copyright applies to the original work in either case.

✦ **"Why, the very act of scanning this photograph gives me the copyright."** I don't hear this one often. Evidently, by creating a digital copy, these folks think that they can magically acquire the copyright. (Sound of palm slapping forehead.) Why didn't I think of that strategy before? Oh, yes, now I remember — it's *not true*. Simply changing the form of a work doesn't release the creator's copyright.

✦ **"This artwork was drawn 100 years ago — the copyright doesn't apply to me."** Before you assume that a copyright has expired on a work, check with a copyright lawyer. Descendants of the original copyright owner might now own the rights to the work.

**Book VI
Chapter 1**

Scanning with
Gusto

Chapter 2: Dude, MP3 Rocks!

In This Chapter

↙ **Understanding the MP3 format**

↙ **Ripping MP3 files from an audio CD**

↙ **Playing MP3 files**

↙ **Downloading MP3 music to your MP3 player**

↙ **Comparing other audio formats with MP3**

↙ **Burning audio CDs from MP3 files**

Can you name one or two truly revolutionary technologies that have arrived in the past 20 years? Perhaps CD-ROMs and DVD-ROMs, cell-phones, or *Oprah?* (Okay, that last one was a deliberate attempt at humor.) Anyway, historians often claim that no person can accurately point to a world-changing technology in his lifetime because we just don't have the perspective to recognize its importance when it happens.

Well, guess what? MP3 is here in your lifetime; it absolutely rocks, and, my friend, it is *indeed* one of those revolutionary technologies. You can quote me on this, with a Mark's Maxim I coined several years ago that made me a visionary (who wears glasses):

> **The creation and distribution of digital music will permanently change everything in the recording industry, including the career of every musician on the planet.**™

To be honest, that wasn't really such an earth-shattering prediction — in fact, it's already happening! In this chapter, I tell you what's so incredibly cool about MP3 digital music and how you can create your own MP3s.

And yes, MP3 is legal when used correctly. Sorry, Big Brother Music.

An MP3 Primer

First, what is a furshlugginer MP3, anyway? Things can get really technical really fast here, and that's not what this book is about — therefore, here's my definition of the MP3 process for Normal Human Beings:

When you create (or *rip*) an MP3 (short for MPEG-1 Layer 3) file, you're capturing (or *sampling*) an analog sound recording and saving that audio in digital form.

Clear as mud? Here's another way to think of it: MP3 files store music and audio in the same fashion that music is stored on an audio CD — as a string of *binary* characters. It's all zeroes and ones, but your PC — and Macs and MP3 players and even many personal electronic devices, such as smartphones, car CD players, and portable stereos — can decode that binary information and re-create it as the original analog signal.

Note that just about any CD- or DVD-ROM drive — including the read-only variety — can rip tracks, so you don't need a CD or DVD recorder to do the job. The process is technically called *digital audio extraction,* but you and I call it *ripping.*

Here are more parallels between audio CDs and MP3 files:

✦ A typical MP3 file corresponds to a single track on an audio CD (which makes sense because virtually all MP3s are ripped directly from audio CDs).

✦ MP3 files offer the same audio quality as audio CDs.

✦ Like the tracks on an audio CD, MP3 files can contain information about the song title and artist, as well as the album art.

✦ Like the music on an audio CD, the quality of an MP3 recording stays pristine no matter how many copies of that MP3 file you make. Because an MP3 is digital, it suffers no degradation when you make additional copies of it.

✦ A series of MP3 files can be recorded (or burned) onto a blank CD-R, creating a new audio CD. You can even burn MP3 files from many different CDs to produce your own compilation discs.

Because an MP3 file is just another data file to your PC, you can do many of the same things with an MP3 file that you can do with other digital media files (such as an image from your digital camera). For example, you can

✦ **Send 'em.** Send smaller MP3s as e-mail attachments — generally, most ISPs allow you to send 5 or 10MB (total) of attachments for a message.

✦ **Offer 'em.** Allow MP3 files to be downloaded from your website or File Transfer Protocol (FTP) server. (You must have legal ownership of the file to be able to offer it for downloading. A good example would be an independent recording artist allowing others to download her music for free.)

✦ **Save 'em.** Save MP3 files to removable media, like CDs, DVDs, and USB flash drives.

Of course, this very portability is a double-edged sword because it makes MP3 music easy to copy — which, under copyright law, is a synonym for *steal*. I discuss what you can and can't legally do with your MP3 files in a sidebar toward the end of the chapter.

The audio quality of an MP3 file is determined by the *bit rate* at which it's *sampled* (a fancy engineering term for *recorded*). The higher the bit rate, the better the sound file (and the larger the size of the physical MP3 file itself, which makes sense). Table 2-1 lists some common bit rates for different types of MP3 files; anything more than 128 Kbps is actually better than the quality of audio CD tracks.

Table 2-1	Bit Rates for MP3 Files
Quality Level	*Bit Rate*
Audiobook	48 Kbps
FM stereo	64 Kbps
Near CD	96 Kbps
Audio CD	128 Kbps
Audiophile	160/192/256/320 Kbps

Ripping Your Own MP3 Files

To demonstrate just how easily you can rip MP3 files from an audio CD, I'll choose one from my collection at random — hmmm, how about comedy legend Steve Martin and his classic 1977 album *Let's Get Small?* — and then extract a set of MP3 files that I can listen to with my MP3 player.

For this demonstration, I'll use the Microsoft tool of choice for ripping MP3 files on the PC: Windows Media Player 12, which is built into Windows 7 and 8! PC owners using Windows Vista and XP can run version 11 of Windows Media Player, which you can find at

```
www.microsoft.com/windows/windowsmedia/player/
    previousversions.aspx
```

I have also installed Windows Media Center, which is available as an upgrade to Windows 8 Pro. If you want to watch DVD movies on your PC (as well as enjoy the full range of features available in Windows Media Player 12), I highly recommend you invest in this upgrade.

Here's the first inkling of the copyright controversy, which I wade into at the end of this chapter: You can legally rip MP3 files *only from audio CDs you bought for yourself!* If you rip songs from a friend's CD — or even an audio CD that you borrowed from the public library — you're violating copyright law. (In this case, I own this audio CD, so I can legally create MP3 files from it for my own personal use. However, I can't give those MP3 files to anyone else, or else I'm in violation of copyright law.)

Now that Perry Mason has had his say, follow these steps to create your own MP3 files from an audio CD:

1. **From your Desktop, click the Windows Media Player icon in the Quick Launch bar.**

2. **From the Start screen, click the Windows Media Player tile, or type Media and click the Windows Media Player button that appears in the Apps Search results pane.**

Media Player displays the main window you see in Figure 2-1.

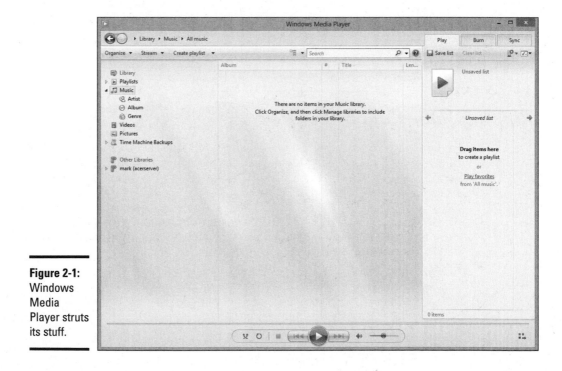

Figure 2-1:
Windows Media Player struts its stuff.

3. **Load the audio CD with the music you want to rip into your drive.**

   Media Player automatically connects to the Internet and retrieves the track names and album cover. The program displays the CD information in the window (see Figure 2-2) and begins to play the CD. Because I don't want to listen to the disc right now, I click the Stop button (the square) on the control strip at the bottom of the window.

Figure 2-2:
Media
Player auto-
matically
plays an
audio CD.

4. **Before you extract any tracks, you should first configure the MP3 settings within Media Player. Click the Rip Settings button in the toolbar at the top of the window.**

   (If the Rip Settings button doesn't appear, there's not enough space to display the entire toolbar — click the double arrow next to the Rip CD button in the toolbar to display the additional toolbar commands.)

5. **From the menu that opens, choose Format and then choose MP3 Format.**

   In this case, I want my MP3 tracks for my iPod player (instead of the default, which is Microsoft's Windows Media Audio or WMA format).

6. **Click the Rip Settings button again; choose Audio Quality and then choose 128 Kbps from the list.**

   Typically, CD-quality (128 Kbps) is the best choice for ripping MP3 music with Windows Media Player unless you prefer audiophile sampling rates with higher quality. (Remember, though, that higher bit rates result in larger MP3 files.)

7. **Mark the tracks you want to rip.**

   By default, Media Player automatically rips all tracks on the disc. However, if you don't want to rip all the tracks, you can select individual songs from the track list. Click the check box next to a track to select or deselect it.

8. **Click the Rip CD button on the toolbar.**

   The completed MP3 files are placed in a separate folder within your Music folder, complete with the artist name and album title. Media Player also adds the tracks to your Media Player Library, which you can display by clicking the Music entry in the Navigation pane at the left side of the Media Player window.

Listening to Your Stuff

After you've ridden the digital wave of the future and ripped a number of MP3 files, you're ready to enjoy them. Here are a number of different ways to listen to MP3s on your PC using Windows 8:

✦ **Double-click an MP3 file.** Double-clicking an MP3 file on your Desktop or within File Explorer loads the program associated with MP3 audio on your system. By default, this program is Windows Media Player, but if you installed another MP3 player — such as the excellent Apple digital audio player iTunes (`www.apple.com/itunes`, shown in Figure 2-3) — Windows plays the file with that program instead.

✦ **Right-click an MP3 file and choose Play from the menu that appears.**

✦ **Run Windows Media Player.** As I mention earlier, you can always display the tracks you added to your collection by clicking the Music entry in the Navigation pane on the left of the window. To play a specific song, double-click it in the track list. You can also switch between displaying songs by artist, album, and genre.

Figure 2-3:
Another
MP3
favorite,
iTunes from
Apple, hard
at work.

If Windows 8 is using the wrong application to play MP3 files — for example, you installed iTunes but you want Windows Media Player to run when you double-click an MP3 file — it's time to change the association for the file. Right-click the MP3 file within File Explorer, choose Open With from the menu that appears, and then choose Choose Default Program to display the Open With dialog box, which you see in Figure 2-4. Make sure that the Use This App for All .MP3 Files check box is selected and then click the application with which you want to play your MP3 files.

To skip to the previous and next tracks, click the Previous and Next buttons on the Media Player control strip at the bottom of the window — huge surprise there, right?

MP3s are easy to pause while you're retrieving your toaster pastry or pouring another soda. Just click the Pause button to pause the audio and click it again to restart the playback.

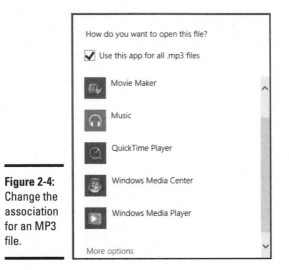

Figure 2-4:
Change the
association
for an MP3
file.

You can also create a group of songs — a *playlist* — and return to that group at any time in the future (a great feature if you like to match your music to your mood). To create a playlist, click the Create Playlist button on the toolbar. Media Player adds a new unnamed entry under the Playlists heading at the left of the window, ready for you to type a descriptive name. Press Enter to save your name and create the playlist.

Now you can add songs to your new playlist: Click the Music header at the left of the window to display your song collection and then click and drag track names from your library to the playlist entry in the Navigation pane. You can drag as many tracks as you like, and you can click and drag the track titles within your playlist to rearrange them! To load that playlist in the future, just click the playlist name in the Navigation pane.

Internet radio arrives

Wait — there's more! Digital audio players like iTunes can now open up an entirely new world of music: broadcasts of Internet radio stations! Computer technomusic jocks call this method of delivery *Internet audio streaming*.

You can tune in to an Internet radio station from a sponsoring website (like my favorite, SHOUTcast, at www.shoutcast.com). As with everything else on the Internet, you enjoy better quality and have less trouble if you have a broadband DSL or cable connection, but even dialup Internet users can take advantage of Internet radio. To try out a station, visit my website at www.mlcbooks.com/ and follow the instructions you find there to connect to *MLC Radio*. I specialize in classic hits from 1970–1979, delivered commercial-free (and in CD-quality stereo, if you have a broadband connection).

Downloading to an MP3 Player

Here's another significantly cool thing that your PC can do for you: Download MP3 files to your personal MP3 player for your portable listening pleasure. For example, I use my iPod, which has 80GB of storage, a built-in 12-hour battery, and a very fast USB 2.0 connection. (Although PC owners might not like it, the iPod is another masterpiece of design from our friends at Apple Computer, `www.apple.com`. Luckily, the iPod works on the PC as well when using the Apple iTunes player.) I heartily recommend the iPod sweet machine as the best MP3 player now on the market. In fact, iTunes automatically downloads and synchronizes your music on both your PC and your iPod, so there's really not much else to say.

But wait — what if you don't have an iPod? If you're using one of the many MP3 player models supported within Windows Media Player, you're still in good shape! However, you may have to install a specific driver or plug-in for your player (these files are supplied by your MP3 player manufacturer, so follow the instructions provided by the installation program to add them to your system).

When any drivers or plug-ins are installed, follow the steps in the previous section to add MP3 tracks to your playlist (or to load an existing playlist).

To download the songs in your current Media Player playlist to your MP3 player, follow these steps:

1. **Plug your MP3 player into the USB or FireWire port.**

   Windows should automatically recognize that you plugged in the device.

2. **Click the Sync tab at the top right of the window.**

   Media Player should recognize your device and display the sync list. Drag and drop individual tracks or complete playlists to the sync list.

3. **Click the Start Sync button.**

4. **After the copying process is complete, unplug your player and jam!**

Using Other Sound Formats

I would be remiss if I didn't mention some of the other sampled sound formats out there on the Internet (and sometimes swapped between PC owners). However, the MP3 format is now so popular for music that these other formats have been reduced to storing Windows sound effects and such. Some sound editors can convert audio between different formats, but if you're working with music, you can't lose with MP3.

WAV format

The Microsoft Windows Audio/Video (WAV) audio format is the standard format used by Windows for playing sound effects, and it's also used in games and on the web. Your browser should recognize and play WAV audio files like a familiar old friend. Although WAV files can be recorded at audio CD quality — and therefore can be used to record music — MP3 files offer the same (or better) quality and are much smaller (*megabytes* smaller) in comparison. All versions of Windows since Windows 95 have included a simple sound recorder that can capture WAV files by using a microphone plugged into your PC.

WMA format

Not to be outdone by MP3, Microsoft developed the WMA (Windows Media Audio) format as a contender for the Best Digital Audio Format crown. Indeed, WMA files are as high in quality as MP3 files, and WMA audio can be recorded in multichannel 5.1 Surround sound. However, I don't see the challenger from Redmond usurping MP3 any time soon. For once, I think that the open standard is stronger than any proprietary standard that Microsoft attempts to enforce. For example, many current MP3 players don't recognize or support WMA tracks — and portable MP3 players sure don't need Surround sound. Plus the built-in DRM protection (short for Digital Rights Management) severely limits what you can do with your WMA tracks — you may not be able to burn an audio CD with your WMA-format music, for example, or play that track on another PC.

AAC format

Apple's entry into the digital audio format wars is higher in quality and smaller in size than MP3, so it makes a good choice for squeezing the largest number of songs into your MP3 player (as long as it supports AAC, like the iPod). Any music you download from the iTunes Store is in AAC format. Note, however, that Windows Media Player doesn't support AAC.

AU format

The Audio Unix (AU) format was introduced by Sun Microsystems, so (as you would expect) it's a popular standard for systems running Unix and Linux. AU audio files are typically of lower quality than MP3 files, but they're even smaller in size, making them popular on many websites. Luckily, both Internet Explorer and Firefox can play AU files with ease.

AIFF format

At one time, Apple used the Audio Interchange File Format (AIFF) as standard equipment within its operating systems, including music files. However, these days, the Cupertino Crew has switched wholeheartedly and completely to AAC, so AIFF has already started down the road once taken by the dinosaurs. (OS X still recognizes AIFF files for sound effects, but that's about it.) Although AIFF files can be recorded at CD quality, they're simply huge, so don't expect to find them on the web or on your personal MP3 player.

MIDI format

Musical Instrument Digital Interface (MIDI) files aren't digital audio but instead are directions on how to play a song — kind of like how a program is a set of directions that tells your computer how to accomplish a task. Your PC or a MIDI instrument (like a MIDI keyboard) can read a MIDI file and play back the song. As you might guess, however, MIDI music really doesn't sound like the digitally sampled sound you get from an MP3 or WMA file. I discuss MIDI support when I cover upgrading your sound card in Book VII, Chapter 5.

Burning Audio CDs from MP3 Files

Return with me (or just come along) to the multitalented Windows Media Player so that I can demonstrate how to burn your own audio CDs from your MP3 collection. The resulting disc is a perfect match for any home or car CD player and can also be played in your PC's CD or DVD drive.

To record an audio CD from MP3 files, follow these steps:

1. **Click the Burn tab at the top right of the window.**

2. **Drag tracks and playlists to the burn list.**

Figure 2-5 shows a burn list that I created.

3. **Load a blank CD-R into your recorder.**

Only certain audio CD players can read a CD-RW (rewriteable disc), so always use write-once CD-R media for true compatibility with all audio CD players.

4. **Click the Start Burn button — and sit back and relax while your new disc is recorded.**

Figure 2-5:
Selecting
songs to
burn to an
audio CD
with Media
Player.

Of course, not everyone follows these rules to the letter. As a matter of fact, I don't know any folks who spend their nights tossing and turning because they ripped tracks from *Johnny Cash at Folsom Prison*. However, it's my duty to make sure that you know the legal ramifications of The Rip Thing. End of story.

I got the music in me — illegally?

"Okay, Mark, everything that I've read in this chapter is cool beyond belief — now, what's this you're telling me? My MP3 (or WMA, or AAC) collection might be *illegal?*" It's possible — it all depends on where you obtained the original audio CDs! Here's the rule: If you didn't buy the audio CD and you don't own it, you can't legally rip any audio. Period. (Naturally, if you purchase and download music from an online store like Amazon or iTunes, that music is also legal for you to own.)

The reasoning behind this copyright law is similar to the law governing the duplication of computer programs, where only the owner is generally allowed to copy a piece of commercial software. By law, any copy of a program that you make is to be used for backup purposes; you can't give that copy to anyone else, and it can't be loaded on anyone else's PC.

Likewise, you can create all the MP3 files from your own audio CDs that you like, and you can listen to them with your personal MP3 player — but you can't give those MP3 files to anyone else. You also can't distribute them over the web or Internet newsgroups, and you can't give one of your *Best of Slim Whitman* compilation CDs to your friend.

Music publishers have considered (and tried to implement) a number of different copy protection–schemes that can help safeguard audio CDs from wanton ripping; as I mention earlier, WMA and AAC formats can include copy protection. Only the future will determine just how successful these schemes will be, but it's already common knowledge that many consumers will simply not purchase music if it's copy-protected. (In addition, you know how tricky those hackers can be. It's likely that any copy protection will be broken sooner or later.)

Chapter 3: Making Movies with Your PC

In This Chapter

↙ **Adding and importing clips and photos**

↙ **Assembling a movie**

↙ **Adding transitions**

↙ **Using special effects**

↙ **Adding a soundtrack**

↙ **Using titles**

↙ **Previewing your movie**

↙ **Saving and recording the finished film**

Have you long harbored the urge to make your own film? You pick the subject — from your kid's kindergarten graduation to a science fiction action flick worthy of James Cameron himself. You edit your footage, add professional-looking transitions and special effects, and even set the mood with a custom soundtrack recorded on your aunt's antique Hammond organ. Ladies and gentlemen, this is the definition of *sweet* — and it's all made possible by your PC. (For the full effect, buy a canvas director's chair and a megaphone.)

In this chapter, I demonstrate how you can use footage from your digital video (DV) camcorder — or, with the right equipment, even the footage you recorded on tape — to produce your own film. Your finished work of visual art can be stored on your hard drive for use on your web pages (and for later recording to a DVD using third-party software).

Getting the Lowdown on Windows Movie Maker

My filmmaking tool of choice is Windows Movie Maker, as shown in Figure 3-1. The program is available for free as part of the Windows Essentials suite, which you can download at `http://download.live.com`. Movie Maker runs like a well-oiled machine under Vista, Windows 7, and Windows 8.

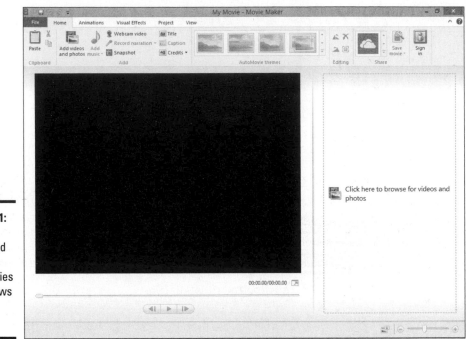

Click here to browse for videos and photos

Figure 3-1:
It's easy
to edit and
enhance
your movies
in Windows
Movie
Maker.

After you install Movie Maker, you can run it from the Windows 8 Start screen by simply typing movie and clicking the Movie Maker button that appears in the Apps Search result pane.

Take a moment to examine the Movie Maker main window, and you'll see the three major controls you use:

✦ **Ribbon:** Like the Office 2013 applications, Movie Maker includes this powerful collection of command buttons, which changes to reflect the tab you select.

✦ **Player window:** It sounds self-explanatory, and (for a change) it is. The Player window allows you to play back and view your movie within Movie Maker while you're working on it.

✦ **Storyboard:** If you're familiar with the concept of *storyboarding* in cinematography — where sketches of scenes are arranged to create a paper mock-up of the film — you probably already guessed that you use this section of the window to add and reorder items that you import from your hard drive. And you're right. These media clips are the building blocks of your finished movie.

Rounding Up Clips and Images

First things first. Movie Maker might not directly import video clips from some camcorders! Instead, depending on the camcorder you're using, you might need to run the software that came with your camcorder to import your video clips to your hard drive.

After you import your clips, however, Movie Maker does allow you to import digital photographs and use them anywhere you like within your movie — even directly from your scanner or your digital camera. Digital cameras that also take video might allow you to directly import video clips as well.

To import video clips or photos that are saved to your hard drive, follow these steps:

Book VI
Chapter 3

Making Movies with Your PC

1. **Open an Explorer window.**

2. **Navigate to the location of the video or photograph that you want to add.**

3. **Drag it to the storyboard pane within the Movie Maker window.**

To add video clips and photos from your hard drive via the Ribbon, click the Add Videos and Photos command button to display a standard Open dialog; select the desired items and then click Open. Movie Maker supports a very wide range of common video, audio, and image formats — at the time of this writing, however, there's no support for DivX video clips, and any media you add can't be copy-protected with Digital Rights Management (DRM).

Video clips appear as a filmstrip, and photos appear as individual snapshots. (Movie Maker can produce slide show movies from photos, so it's not necessary to add video to a project.)

Never the TWAIN shall meet

TWAIN. You're probably saying to yourself, "Self, that's the most ridiculous acronym yet." Well, it sounds silly — many folks think that the acronym stands for *technology without an interesting name.* However, in this case TWAIN is not an acronym at all; it refers to the famous poem by Kipling, *The Ballad of East and West,* which includes the line "and never the twain shall meet." It makes sense, considering that the TWAIN standard helps make sure that your scanner, camcorder, digital camera and software (like Movie Maker) can work together. Never let it be said that technotypes don't have occasional flashes of wry literary humor!

By the way, if you're not completely acronym-happy by now, visit VERA, the Virtual Entity of Relevant Acronyms, no less — on the web at `http://cgi.snafu.de/ohei/user-cgi-bin/veramain-e.cgi`, and you can discover the true meaning of computer-related acronyms to your heart's content.

Besides importing from your hard drive, here are other ways to import video and audio clips:

✦ **Download them.** Any still images or and sample video clips you download from the web are suitable for use in Movie Maker (as long as they're legal for you to use and the format is recognized by Movie Maker). As I mentioned before, video clips with DRM protection can't be used in Movie Maker.

✦ **Acquire clips and photos from your camcorder, scanner, or camera.** If your camcorder, scanner, or digital camera is TWAIN compatible, O Happy Day! (Find out more in the sidebar, "Never the TWAIN shall meet.")

   a. Connect your hardware.

   b. Click the blue File tab on the Ribbon.

   c. Click Import from Device and then click OK to import items to Photo Gallery.

As shown in Figure 3-2, Movie Maker prompts you to select the image source from the available TWAIN-compatible hardware devices. Again, the process varies according to the hardware you're using, but if you're experienced with scanning or downloading images, you're in familiar waters. After the photos and video clips have been imported into Photo Gallery, you can drag and drop them into Movie Maker, or use the Add Videos and Photos button on the Home tab.

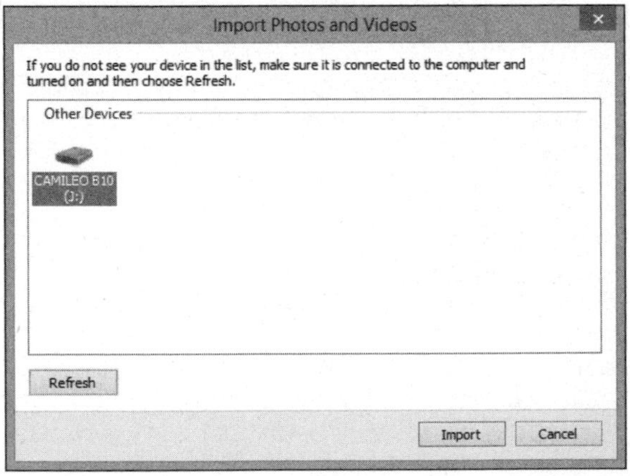

Figure 3-2:
Putting
TWAIN
to work,
importing
video and
photos.

Building Your First Movie

After you import all the pieces of your new film, it's time to grab your megaphone and start creating. You start by adding items in the linear Storyboard window, which you use to literally assemble your movie, moving from left to right.

I like to map out the general flow of my film on paper — even as a simple list of scenes, titles, and images — before I start creating it. However, Movie Maker makes editing so easy that many folks can simply build a film on the fly, following their inspiration where it takes them. Go figure.

Anyway, when you're ready for the real work, add all the video clips and photos you want to use. Figure 3-3 illustrates the first photo and video clip that I added to my film.

When you have multiple items in the Storyboard pane, you can change their order by clicking and dragging an item from one media square to the desired media square.

**Book VI
Chapter 3**

**Making Movies
with Your PC**

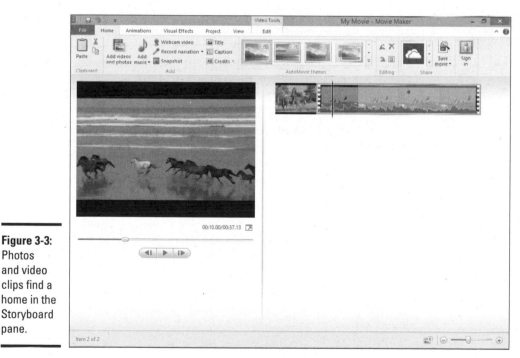

Figure 3-3:
Photos
and video
clips find a
home in the
Storyboard
pane.

If you decide against using a clip or photo, delete it from the Storyboard pane by right-clicking the item on the strip and then choosing Remove from the pop-up menu that appears.

To trash all the media you added within the Storyboard pane and start completely over, right-click any item on the strip and choose Select All from the menu that appears. Then right-click again and choose Remove from the menu that appears.

Adding Transitions without Breaking a Sweat

Imagine a film that cuts directly from scene to scene with fade-ins, fade-outs, dissolves, or wipes. These are all types of *transitions* — and without transitions, your movie ends up moving at a frantic pace. (I call it *jarring the audience;* most horror films are shot with few transitions.) Of course, this might be your intention with some projects, but it's not likely to be your goal with most films you make. In this section, I demonstrate how to add transitions to your film.

Transitions can be placed within the Storyboard pane only after you add at least one video clip or still image. After the pane contains at least one item, follow these steps:

1. **Click the Animations tab to display the list of transitions, as shown in Figure 3-4. (Click the More drop-down list button, which bears a horizontal line over a downward-facing arrow, to display additional transition effects.)**

2. **Click the item in the Storyboard pane that should follow the transition.**

   If you need to place a transition between a photo followed by a video clip, for example, click the video clip to select it.

3. **Click a transition from the Ribbon to select it.**

   Movie Maker has a cool feature to help you decide which transition you want to use: Hover your cursor over a transition in the list, and the item animates in the Player window to demonstrate how the transition will appear onscreen.

   To add the same transition throughout your movie, right-click any item in the Storyboard pane and choose Select All. Then click on the desired transition.

Figure 3-4:
Add
transitions
to tie your
clips and
photos
together.

4. **To delete a transition you added to the strip, click the following item again and click the "blank" No Transition button at the far left of the Transition group.**

    Or, to get radical, right-click any item and choose Select All, and then click the No Transition button to remove all transitions in your film with one fell swoop.

As you experiment with transitions, you begin to understand where your movie needs them to link together scenes and still images, as well as where you can simply cut from one item to the next. One cardinal rule of filmmaking is to maintain the focus of your audience on your message: Too many transitions are distracting.

Adding Special Effects without Paying George Lucas

Ready to take your creativity up a notch? Click the Visual Effects tab to display the Effects group you see in Figure 3-5. From there, you can add special visual effects throughout your film.

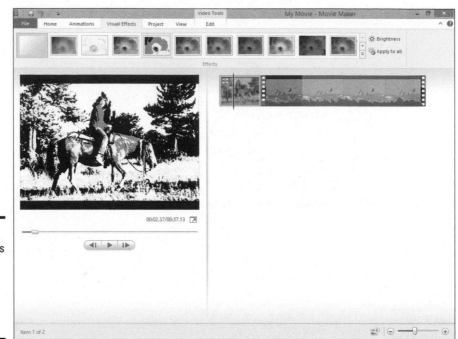

Figure 3-5:
Add all sorts
of visual
bells and
whistles
using
Effects.

When most of us think about special effects in the movies, *Star Wars* and *Harry Potter* come to mind: light-sabers, flying brooms, and invisibility cloaks. (I really, *really* want one of those cloaks.) However, in the world of video editing, an *effect* is a special visual appearance that you add to the video. For example, Movie Maker allows you to

✦ Flip your movie's vertical alignment.

✦ Change color footage to black and white.

✦ Rotate your entire movie 360 degrees.

✦ Turn your movie into an animated charcoal drawing.

Maybe these effects aren't appropriate for your sister's wedding video, but when the subject of your movie is fun and games or when you want to create a new film *noir* masterpiece in stark black-and-white, effects are just the ticket. (Horrible pun intended.)

To experiment with effects, simply click the desired item in the Storyboard pane to select it. Or, throw caution utterly to the wind: Right-click any item and then click Select All to apply the effect to your entire movie. Now click any effect thumbnail on the Ribbon and gauge the results.

Again, you can delete an effect on an item (or on your entire film) by select-ing whatever needs fixing and clicking the "blank" No Effect button at the left side of the Effects group. How 'bout them apples, Mr. Hitchcock?

Adding Sound

What movie is complete without a stirring soundtrack? For example, would the zombies in *Return of the Living Dead* have been anywhere near as scary without that punk rock playing in the background? Or, how about the sig-nature scary chord you heard every time you saw any body part from the monster in *Creature from the Black Lagoon*? With Movie Maker, it's easy to add music to your movie.

Book VI
Chapter 3

**Making Movies
with Your PC**

If a video clip already contains audio, you don't have to add anything. However, you can still overlay — or, as videoheads call it, *dub* — extra music or sound effects, which play along with the audio from the clip.

Movie Maker program accepts audio in MP3 and Microsoft WAV formats. (Just don't forget those pesky copyrights, and add only what you're legally allowed to add.)

To add a soundtrack, follow these steps:

1. **Click the Home tab.**

2. **Click the Add Music command button and click Add Music on the pop-up menu.**

   You'll note that you can also add audio from AudioMicro, the Free Music Archive, and Vimeo — they all appear under the Find New Music Online heading.

3. **Navigate to the desired audio, select it, and then click Open.**

After you add music to your movie, it appears as a named "strip" over the items in the Storyboard. To delete the musical score, just click this strip and press the Delete key.

You can also add your own narration track to your movie — click the Record Narration button on the Home tab. The Record and Stop buttons work just like that old cassette recorder that's accumulating dust in your closet.

You've Just Gotta Have Titles!

In movie jargon, *titles* can be anything from the opening titles of your film to the ending credits. With Movie Maker, you can open your film with impressive titles that fill the screen, or you can thank your brother for being the best boy, grip, or gaffer. (I have no earthly idea what those exalted individuals do, but they must be pretty important.)

To add a title, click the item that the title should precede, click the Home tab, and click the Title button. As you can see in Figure 3-6, the Player window turns into a text field where you type your title. To save your changes, simply click in any open space within the Storyboard pane.

Heck, Movie Maker can end your film with professional-looking credits as well! Click the down arrow next to the Credits button on the Home tab, and you can choose which credits item you want to add to the end of the movie. The credits item works just like a title item, so it only takes a few seconds to thank your director (remember, that's you).

Don't forget to add effects to your titles and credits! When you select your title or credits item, the Ribbon includes a number of different animated effects to choose from — click the Format tab and then click an effect button to check out the result.

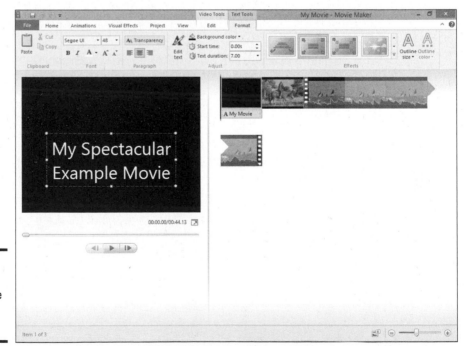

Figure 3-6:
No movie is complete without titles.

Previewing Your Oscar-Winning Work

Okay, I know you're itching to see what your next masterpiece looks like. Lucky for you, Movie Maker allows you to preview your work at any time. Of course, your Storyboard strip must contain at least one video clip or still image, or else you have nothing to preview.

✦ **To view the entire film from beginning to end:**

    a. *Click the slider under the Player window and drag it all the way to the left.*

    b. *Click the familiar Play button.*

✦ **To preview the film from another point:**

    a. *Drag the slider to the desired point*

    b. *Click the Play button.*

When you click Play, Movie Maker displays a black vertical line (commonly called a *scrubber bar*) across the items in the Storyboard pane. The program also displays the total duration of the selected clip (or the entire movie) as well as the elapsed time.

Saving and Sharing Before Traveling to Cannes

I think that Cannes is somewhere in France — or perhaps Belgium. Anyway, it's a big thing among filmmaking legends like you and me, so you want at least one copy of your finished masterwork to carry along with you. Luckily, Movie Maker allows you to save your films in a number of different formats, e-mail them, or even share them on YouTube — which I cover in this last section. (You'll see many of these same commands on the Home tab in the Sharing group.)

You can always save your work in progress. To save a project that you're working on to your hard drive for later, click the File tab and choose Save Project. Windows opens the familiar Save As dialog box, where you can specify a location and a filename.

After your project is completed, here are two methods you can use to produce a finished movie.

Creating a digital video file

If you simply want to watch your film on your PC monitor or other device, this option is best. Just don't forget that it can take several hundred megabytes or more of space to store a single movie. Follow these steps:

1. **Click the File tab and click Save Movie.**

2. **Choose the quality or destination from the submenu that appears.**

   You can choose between several different resolutions, including high-definition, widescreen, or standard TV. Note that you can also prepare the movie for use with a mobile phone or as an e-mail attachment.

3. **Choose a location and type a name; then click Save.**

Sharing your masterpiece on YouTube

Talk about convenience! Movie Maker automatically formats your movie for optimum viewing on YouTube and then sends it there for you. If you have an existing account on YouTube, simply follow these steps:

1. **Click the Home tab and click the YouTube button in the Share group.**

2. **Choose the resolution of your movie.**

   Movie Maker displays a dialog box where you can enter your YouTube username and password. (You must also sign into your Microsoft account if you haven't already.)

3. **Click Sign In.**

   After Movie Maker logs you in, you're given the chance to enter a name and description, and then the film is uploaded for you. See you at the Oscars!

Chapter 4: I'm Okay, You're a Digital Camera

In This Chapter

✔ Understanding digital camera technology

✔ Evaluating the advantages of digital photography

✔ Buying extras (besides your camera)

✔ Composing photographs for better results

✔ Organizing your images

✔ Downloading your images

✔ Using Windows Live Photo Gallery

I'll be the first to assure you that I'm no Ansel Adams, yet I've been capturing moments and memories on film for most of my life, and I've slowly worked my way into what most folks would deem semiprofessional photography. (I can shoot a decent portrait, I take on a commission from time to time, and I have a reasonably well-stuffed camera bag.)

Does that mean I'm loaded down with expensive 35mm cameras and a dozen different varieties of film? Definitely not! I've never been darkroom material, and film photography no longer excites me. These days, I work entirely with *digital* cameras, which don't use traditional film. Why digital? My entire portfolio of digital photos — which would easily fill several dozen traditional bound photo albums — fits comfortably on two DVDs. I can display those photographs on practically any PC or print hard copies that are almost impossible to tell from film prints. I don't spend a dime on film processing, either — and when you take 10 to 20 images per day, that savings really adds up.

I spend this chapter introducing you to the world of digital photography. You discover how a digital camera works, why it's better in many respects than a film camera, and how to move to your PC the images you take with your camera. If you're interested in shooting better pictures, I also cover a number of well-worn basic rules used by professional photographers all over the world. You also discover how to download images from your digital camera (by using the features built into Windows 8) and how to catalog your photographs (thus making it easier to locate a specific image).

How Does a Digital Camera Work?

A common misconception surrounds today's digital cameras: Because these cameras don't use film and because they produce pictures as data files, many folks think that digital cameras must use a radically different method of capturing images. Actually, your family film camera and that power-hungry, battery-munching digital camera you got for Christmas are remarkably similar in most respects.

As you see in Figure 4-1, a film camera has a shutter that opens for a set amount of time (usually a fraction of a second), admitting light into the body of the camera through at least one lens. (Of course, that lens can be adjusted to bring other objects at other distances into focus, or different lenses can be tacked on.) Figure 4-2 illustrates (up to this point, anyway) that your film camera and its digital brethren work exactly the same.

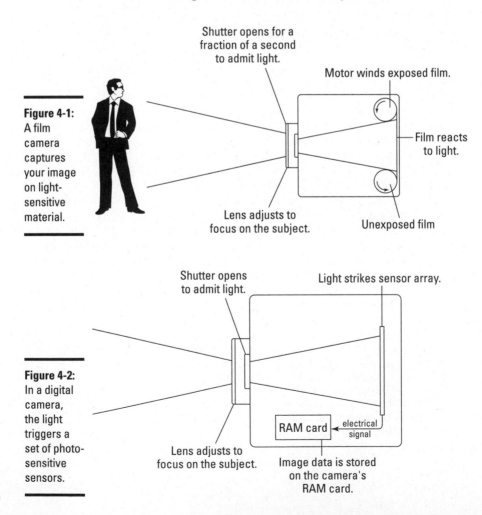

Figure 4-1: A film camera captures your image on light-sensitive material.

Shutter opens for a fraction of a second to admit light.

Motor winds exposed film.

Film reacts to light.

Lens adjusts to focus on the subject.

Unexposed film

Figure 4-2: In a digital camera, the light triggers a set of photo-sensitive sensors.

Shutter opens to admit light.

Light strikes sensor array.

RAM card ← electrical signal

Lens adjusts to focus on the subject.

Image data is stored on the camera's RAM card.

The big difference is the method that each of these two types of cameras uses to record that incoming light. To wit:

✦ A **film camera** uses a strip of light-sensitive celluloid coated with silver halide, which retains the image. The film must later be developed, and the negatives and positives that are produced can be used (reproduced, usually on photographic paper) to make copies of the photograph.

✦ A **digital camera,** on the other hand, uses a grid (or an *array)* of photo-sensors to record the incoming pattern of light. Each sensor returns an electrical current when it's struck by the incoming light. Because the amount of current that's returned varies with the amount of light, your digital camera's electronic innards can combine the different current levels into a composite pattern of data that represents the incoming light — in other words, an image in the form of a binary file.

**Book VI
Chapter 4**

**I'm Okay, You're a
Digital Camera**

If you've read some of my other books on CD/DVD recording, photography, and scanning, you already know about *binary,* which is the common language shared by all computers. Although your eye can't see any image in the midst of all those ones and zeroes, your computer can display them as a photograph — and print the image, if you like, or send it to your Aunt Harriet in Boise as an e-mail attachment.

"Wait a second, Mark. How does the image file get to my computer?" That's a very good question; naturally, no one wants to carry a PC around just to shoot a photograph. Most digital cameras store the image file until you can *transfer* (download) it to your computer — other digital cameras (and many smartphones) can now directly transfer the photos you take to your PC, or even Facebook or Flickr wirelessly!

Different types of cameras use different methods of storing the image files:

✦ **RAM cards:** *Random access memory (RAM) cards* (the most common storage method) are removable memory cards that function much like the memory modules used in a USB flash drive. Some memory cards are proprietary, but some cards are interchangeable with netbooks, smartphones, and tablet PCs. The most popular types of media include CompactFlash, SmartMedia, and Memory Stick cards, generally ranging from 512MB to 128GB of storage. When the card is full of images, you either download the images from the card (presumably to your PC) to free up space or eject it and "reload" with a spare, empty card.

✦ **Hard drives:** Yep, you read right — some cameras have their own onboard hard drives, and others use tiny removable hard drives that are roughly the same size as RAM cards. Naturally, these little beauties can easily store hundreds of gigabytes of your images. (Geez, I'm old enough to remember when a full-size computer hard drive couldn't store that much.)

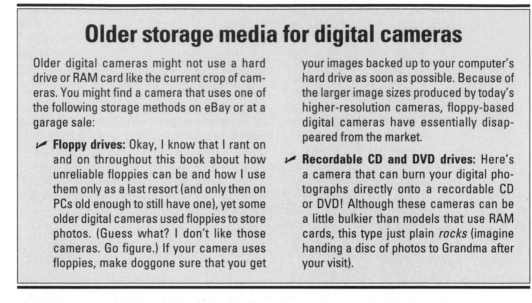

Older storage media for digital cameras

Older digital cameras might not use a hard drive or RAM card like the current crop of cameras. You might find a camera that uses one of the following storage methods on eBay or at a garage sale:

✔ **Floppy drives:** Okay, I know that I rant on and on throughout this book about how unreliable floppies can be and how I use them only as a last resort (and only then on PCs old enough to still have one), yet some older digital cameras used floppies to store photos. (Guess what? I don't like those cameras. Go figure.) If your camera uses floppies, make doggone sure that you get

your images backed up to your computer's hard drive as soon as possible. Because of the larger image sizes produced by today's higher-resolution cameras, floppy-based digital cameras have essentially disappeared from the market.

✔ **Recordable CD and DVD drives:** Here's a camera that can burn your digital photographs directly onto a recordable CD or DVD! Although these cameras can be a little bulkier than models that use RAM cards, this type just plain *rocks* (imagine handing a disc of photos to Grandma after your visit).

If you're wondering approximately how many images you can fit onto a specific RAM card, remember that most 10- to 16-megapixel (MP) cameras now produce images of about 2 to 6 megabytes (MB) at their highest-quality mode.

The Pros and Cons of Digital Photography

I mention earlier in this chapter that I switched completely from my 35mm single lens reflex (SLR) cameras to a (rapidly expanding) collection of digital cameras. However, there's a lot more to like about the digital revolution than just cutting the expenses of film and processing. Here are some other advantages:

✦ **Digital photos and prints are versatile.** The digital photographs that you take can be enclosed in e-mail messages, burned as CD or DVD slide shows, or displayed as your PC's Windows Desktop and screen saver. Of course, you can also print them, and with today's special inkjet papers, your images can end up on items like greeting cards and T-shirt transfers.

If you're interested in producing prints from your digital photographs in the shortest time possible, check out one of the latest inkjet printers that can directly accept memory cards from your digital camera. Heck, with one of these inkjet marvels, you don't need a PC. Many of these printers can even rotate and resize images and perform simple editing on their own.

✦ **Look, Ma, no developing!** With a digital camera, you have practically instant access to your photographs. Save yourself the trip to the photo store — even a one-hour photo lab can't match the three minutes that it takes to connect your camera to your PC (with a Universal Serial Bus [USB] cable) and download your images to your hard drive. (And you avoid the ravages of a misaligned development machine or a clumsy operator.)

✦ **Extra digital information is no charge.** Even if you never set your VCR player's clock, you'll want to set your digital camera's date and time correctly — that's because today's cameras save quite a bit of information with every shot you take. This information is called *metadata,* and along with the date and time the shot was taken, you'll also likely find information about the make and model of the camera, as well as the settings that were used. Some cameras (especially those built into smartphones like Apple's iPhone) can even include GPS data, so you'll know where you were when you took the photo! Windows 8 File Explorer can display much of this data In the Preview pane when you click a photo thumbnail.

✦ **Editing is easy with your PC.** Imagine everything that can go wrong with a picture: a bad exposure, a case of red eye, or perhaps a tree sprouting from someone's head. With a digital photograph, you can reduce or eliminate these problems; with the proper editing, a bad picture becomes mediocre, and a good picture can become a work of art. *Bonus:* With the right software, you can add all sorts of special effects as well, like text balloons and sepia tones.

✦ **You can manage your photographs on location.** Imagine being able to review a shot as soon as it's taken. With a traditional film camera, you're stuck with what you take, and you don't see the results until that roll of film has been developed. A digital camera, however, gives you the freedom to *manage* your images. For example, you can view each image on a memory card and delete the ones you don't need, to free up space. Using the camera's liquid crystal diode (LCD) screen also allows you to review a photograph as soon as you take it. Don't like the way a particular photograph turned out? If you review each shot as soon as you snap it — which I always do — you can try to retake most pictures immediately! (Of course, this feature doesn't help you if the UFO has already zipped over the horizon, but it's darned handy on vacation.)

Virtually all digital cameras on the market these days can also do double duty as simple video camcorders — at least for anywhere from 30 seconds to several minutes — using the *movie mode* feature. Virtually all cameras with movie mode can record audio along with the video; the length of time you can record depends on the amount of storage available, so a digital camera with a 4GB memory card can capture many more seconds of video than a camera with only a 2GB memory card.

However, all is not perfect in the digital world — not yet, at least. Film cameras aren't doomed to share the fate of the dinosaurs because traditional film photography still has these advantages over digital photography:

✦ **Film cameras are still less expensive.** Although digital cameras have dropped considerably in price over the past few years, film cameras still provide better resolution and image quality for a lower initial price. In fact, at the time of this writing, most film cameras less than $20 (U.S.) can still take a better-quality photograph than most digital cameras selling for less than $150. Of course, if you're willing to spend more, you narrow the quality gap, and these days it's much easier to find an 8MP camera that can produce film quality. Because digital camera prices continue to drop, an entry-level digital camera will eventually be able to take a shot that's as good as a film camera.

How can you tell which digital cameras produce better images? While shopping for a digital camera, keep the camera's *megapixel rating* in mind — that's the number of *pixels* (individual dots) in an image that the camera can capture. Here's another Mark's Maxim to keep handy:

> **The higher the megapixel value, the better the image quality, the more expensive the camera, and the larger the photographs that you can print.**™

As a rule, a 6–8MP camera is suitable for most casual photography, but amateur photographers will prefer at least a 10MP camera.

✦ **Film cameras are better at capturing motion.** Older consumer digital cameras in the 3–4MP range still have trouble taking shots of subjects in motion, such as at sporting events. (It's because of the longer delay required for those photosensitive sensors to capture the image.) However, current higher-megapixel digital cameras are much better at *motion* (stop action) photography — most high-end digital cameras can shoot photos in burst mode, one exposure following another within less than a second.

✦ **Man, do those digital cameras use the juice!** Unlike a film camera, a digital camera relies on battery power for *everything,* including that power-hungry LCD display. If you're in the middle of shooting a wedding and you haven't packed a spare set of batteries, you have my condolences. A film camera is far less demanding of its batteries.

As you might have already guessed, many photographers have chosen to carry both traditional film and digital cameras, which allows them to use whatever best fits the circumstances (depending on the subject and the level of control they need on location). For me, the long-term savings and convenience of my digital cameras — and the ability to review my photographs as soon as they're taken — makes them the better choice.

So what can you do with digital photographs? A heck of a lot more than a film print, that's for sure (at least on your PC and in the online world)! Common fun that you can have with digital images includes

✦ **Printing 'em:** Today's inkjet printers can produce a hard copy on all sorts of media (everything from plain paper to blank business cards and CD/DVD labels), but naturally you get the best results on those expensive sheets of glossy photo paper.

✦ **Using them on your personal or business website:** Jazz up your web pages with images from your camera.

✦ **Sending them as e-mail attachments:** I get a big kick out of sending photos through e-mail! As long as you add a total of less than 5 to 10MB of images to an e-mail message, the recipient should receive them with no problem. (And then the attached files can be viewed, printed, or saved to the recipient's hard drive.)

✦ **Creating slide shows:** Check your camera's software documentation to see whether you can create a slide show on your hard drive (or on a CD/DVD disc) to show off your digital photographs. (I also demonstrate how to use Movie Maker [part of the Windows Essentials suite of free applications] to create a slide show in Chapter 3 of this very minibook!)

✦ **Using them in craft projects:** Plaster your digital photographs on T-shirt transfers, buttons, greeting cards, and all sorts of crafts.

Digital Camera Extras to Covet

No one gets a pizza with just sauce, and the extras are important in photography, too. If you take a large number of photographs or you're interested in producing the best results from your camera, consider adding these extras to your camera bag.

External card readers

As I mention earlier, virtually all modern digital cameras connect to your computer via a USB 2.0 cable to transfer pictures. The downside is that you can't take more shots until the downloading process is complete. If you're in a hurry or if convenience is important, buy an external card reader that takes care of the downloading chores for you. Simply pop the card into the reader (which in turn connects to your PC's USB port) and load a backup memory card into your camera, and you're ready to return to the action.

External card readers are also the best solution if you have an older digital camera that connects to a USB 1.*x* port. Because an older USB 1.*x* connection is as slow as watching paint dry, you can speed things up considerably by ejecting the memory card from your camera and pushing those pictures to your PC through a much faster USB 2.0 connection. An external reader is cheap, too, usually running less than $30. (I use this solution for the oldest digital cameras in my collection.)

Rechargeable batteries

Gotta have 'em. I'm not kidding. You'll literally end up declaring bankruptcy if you use your digital camera often with single-use batteries. For example, one of my older 3MP cameras can totally exhaust four AA alkaline batteries after one session of 20 photographs.

Here are the three major types of rechargeable batteries to choose among:

✦ **Nickel-cadmium (NiCad):** *NiCad* batteries are the cheapest type and are available in standard sizes, but they drain quickly and take longer to recharge.

✦ **Nickel-metal-hydride (NiMH):** *NiMH* rechargeable batteries provide the middle of the road between higher cost and longer life; they take less time to recharge than NiCad batteries, and they last longer, but they're not as expensive as Li-Ion batteries.

✦ **Lithium-ion (Li-Ion):** These batteries are the best available. They provide more sustained power over a longer period than either of the other types, but they're the most expensive.

Just as I recommend an extra memory card, I also recommend carrying a spare set of charged batteries in your camera bag. The Boy Scouts are right on this one: Be prepared.

Lenses

Like their film brethren, most medium-price and higher-end digital cameras can use external (add-on) lenses. Although your digital camera is likely to have several zoom levels (both digital and optical), photographers use a number of specialized lenses in specific situations. For example, consider these common extra lenses:

✦ **Telephoto:** Using a *telephoto* lens provides you tremendous long-distance magnification, but you don't have to be James Bond or a tabloid *paparazzo* to use one. For example, wildlife and sports photographers use telephoto lenses to capture subjects from a distance. (Referees tend to get surly when you stray on the field just to photograph the quarterback.)

✦ **Macro:** These lenses are specially designed for extreme close-up work; with a *macro* lens, you can capture images at a distance of a few inches. (They're great for making your fiancée's engagement ring look much, much bigger.)

✦ **Wide angle:** A *wide angle* lens can capture a larger area — what photographers call the *field of view* — at the expense of detail and the possibility of adding linear distortion. These lenses are often used for scenic or architectural photographs.

Don't forget a decent lens cap and a photographer's lens-cleaning cloth to help prevent scratches on those expensive lenses!

Tripods

When most people think of tripods, they think of unwieldy, 5-foot-tall gantries suitable for launching the Saturn V. Yes, some tripods meet those requirements, but they're absolutely required for low-light, time-lapse, and professional portrait photography.

My camera bag also stows two other platforms that are much smaller:

✦ **Mini-tripod:** My Ambico mini-tripod can hold my cameras anywhere from 2 to 4 inches above the table. I use it in concert with my macro lens for shooting my scale models from a realistic perspective. The GorillaPod (http://joby.com/gorillapod/original) is another popular mini-tripod I'd recommend.

✦ **Monopod:** My collapsible monopod (which looks just like a walking stick) can hold the camera steady for quick shots on just about any surface. It also works great when you trip over exposed roots in the forest — but you didn't hear me admit to that. I should also note that many museums (and government buildings and churches) do not allow monopods because of security considerations.

Although a tripod isn't a requirement for the casual photographer, you'll find yourself wishing for one quickly if you move to more serious amateur photography. They sell tripods at your local megamart for a reason.

The Lazy Man's Guide to Composing Photographs

If you want to remain firmly in the point-and-shoot casual photography crowd, you can comfortably skip any discussion of *composition* — that's the process (most call it an art) of aligning your subject and compensating for the available light at your location. Composition isn't a requirement for simple snapshots, but if you're going to create true visual art, you need the time to prepare your subject, your viewing angle, and your lighting.

In fact, what if I told you that composing a shot can result in less cropping and editing time on your computer — and that you end up taking better photographs? If you follow the tips that I provide in this section, I can just about guarantee that you'll discover at least one FRP in every set of images that you download! (*FRP,* coined by my favorite journalism instructor at LSU, means *first-rate photo* — the kind of photograph that you'll be proud to display on your wall.) The photograph examples in this chapter are taken from my personal FRP collection.

And despite what you might have heard about composing photographs, it takes only a few seconds before each shot to make a difference. Take it from me — with practice, you'll compose your shots automatically!

The rule of thirds

The *rule of thirds* is the foundation of good composition for most photographers. Applying this guideline helps draw the eye toward multiple subjects or to the focus of interest while maintaining balance within the frame. To use the rule of thirds, simply split the frame in your viewfinder into nine equal areas, as shown in Figure 4-3, "Time Tunnel." Align your subject (subjects) and the surroundings (where possible) along either

+ A line crossing the frame
+ One of the intersections where two lines meet

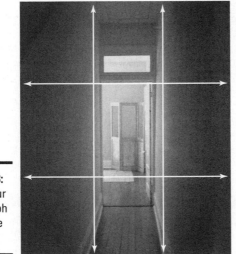

Figure 4-3:
Divide your
photograph
by the rule
of thirds.

TIP

The rule of thirds works exceptionally well when taking photographs of landscapes or architecture, as you can see in Figure 4-4. This photograph, "View from Hoover Dam," uses the rule to draw the viewer's eye along the river until it disappears around the bend. (Bet you never knew that Mother Nature was a shutterbug, right?)

Figure 4-4:
The movement of water flows closely along one line and ends at an intersection.

That's all there is to it. If you take a moment to examine the composition of the photographs in your favorite magazines, you see this time-tested classic rule followed over and over.

The rule of asymmetry

The second rule of composition often used in photography, the *rule of asymmetry,* presents the subject against a number of minor subjects as well as the background. Asymmetrical composition revolves around a relationship that you build between the major subject and either one or more minor subjects or the background itself. Following this rule, you merge different combinations of the three basic shapes — the square, the circle, and the triangle — to form a new outline or contour.

To illustrate, take the still life shown in Figure 4-5, "Cultures." Here, I mix a light circular shape (the instrument) with strong rectangles (the skis). I find that an asymmetrical composition works better when you feature a sharp contrast level between light and dark elements or between strong color patterns and shadows.

Figure 4-5:
Add interest with a classic asymmetrical composition.

I always make it a point to experiment with different camera angles — for instance, moving to the side or below the subject, as in "Warbird" (see Figure 4-6). Of course, sometimes you don't have the luxury of extra time to try something different, but I think that you'll like the results. (And remember, you're not wasting any film.)

Here's a list of exposure do's and don'ts for those who want to compose with light:

Do

✦ Make use of existing light when possible, if you can disable your camera's flash. Natural lighting can really "make" the photo.

✦ Use a tripod (or brace your camera if possible) when taking photographs without flash, which requires a longer exposure time to capture the image.

✦ Use your PC's image editor — such as Adobe Photoshop Elements — to enhance the contrast for underexposed shots. You can also change the hue and saturation levels for the colors in a photograph with your image editor. In Chapter 1 of this minibook, I cover some of the basics within Windows Essentials Photo Gallery, such as cropping and rotating images, converting images to different formats, and saving them to disc.

Don't

+ Attempt to photograph your subject through a sheet of glass or plastic if you're using a flash. Also don't pose your subject against a reflective background — you create *hotspots* or flash reflections.

+ Use a flash if your subject is illuminated internally or with spotlights, such as a neon sign or a statue at night.

Figure 4-6:
Experiment with unusual camera angles.

Shadows can add a tremendous visual impact, as shown in a favorite FRP of mine, "French Quarter Staircase," in Figure 4-7. In this case, I needed no additional light, but I'm not above using an isolated spot *flood* (light source) to cast the shadow effect I want. Even a flashlight can do the job in a pinch.

Figure 4-7:
Remember that shadows can be your friend.

Organizing Your Pictures

If you would rather not stare at a meaningless collection of filenames, here are some tricks you can use to help you locate a photograph that you stored on your hard drive or a DVD full of images. First, organize your photos into folders based on the date, location, or subject of your photographs. Also, use the long-filename support in Windows 8 to better describe your photo-graph. After all, you can more easily visualize `Goats Grazing Outside Nepalese Village.jpg` than `nepgoats.jpg`.

To take your organization a step further, use an image-cataloging program. For many PC owners, Windows Photo Gallery is all that's needed, but more powerful applications out there that offer more features. ACDSee 15 from ACD Systems (`www.acdsee.com`) is a good example. ACDSee 15 offers the tools you need to perform simple image editing to boot. At $50, this program is an invaluable tool for any amateur photographer.

Downloading Your Images

Before you launch into the downloading process, make sure to take care of those dull prerequisites:

✦ Make sure that you installed any software that came with your digital camera or card reader; this ensures that any drivers are installed before you connect. (It's always a good idea to check the camera manufacturer's website to see whether a new set of drivers has been released for Windows 8.)

✦ Connect the cable that came with your camera (or your external card reader) to the corresponding port on your PC — which is very likely your PC's USB port. If you're using an internal card reader (a special slot built into the front of your PC) or an external card reader — eject the memory card from your camera and load it into the slot in the card reader (as shown in the card reader's documentation).

✦ If you're connecting your digital camera directly to your PC and it has an AC adapter, make sure that you plug the camera into the AC adapter first; this can save you an hour of recharge time!

Although most digital cameras come with their own software, Windows 8 offers Windows Photo Gallery (part of the Windows Essentials application suite, which is free from Microsoft). Personally, I've always felt that if your camera comes with its own downloading software, it's a better idea to use that program instead, but at least Photo Gallery can likely do the job alone in a pinch. After you've downloaded and installed the Windows Essentials suite, type **Photo** at the Start screen and click the Photo Gallery button that appears, and then click the Import button at the far left of the Photo Gallery Ribbon to display the Import Photos and Videos dialog box you see in Figure 4-8.

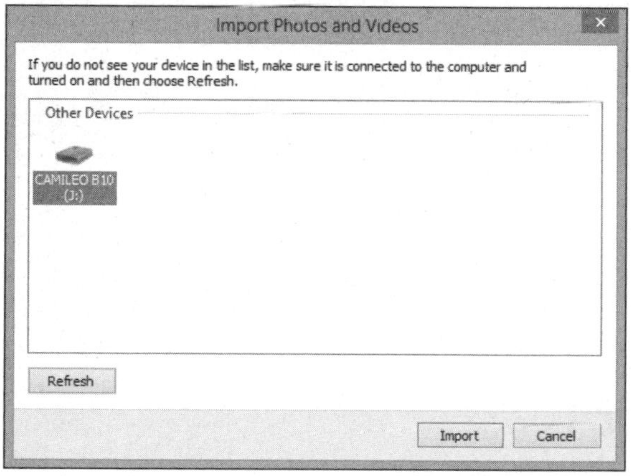

**Book VI
Chapter 4**

I'm Okay, You're a
Digital Camera

Figure 4-8:
Let Photo
Gallery
help you
download
images
from your
camera.

Import Photos and Videos

If you do not see your device in the list, make sure it is connected to the computer and turned on and then choose Refresh.

Other Devices

CAMILEO B10
(J:)

Refresh

Import   Cancel

To complete the download process, just click your camera, card reader, or USB flash drive in the list, and click Import. To select only specific photos and videos, click the Review, Organize and Group Items to Import radio button and then click Next. Each photo or video is represented by a thumbnail, and you can select or deselect items to import with the check box next to each thumbnail.

Click the Import All New Items Now radio button and click Next to import everything in one fell swoop, without viewing thumbnails beforehand. Photo Gallery uses the name you enter to title the images and videos as they're imported. For example, if you enter the tag **Fun Photos**, the filenames are `Fun Photos 001.jpg`, `Fun Photos 002.jpg`, and so on.

After the import is complete, you see the Windows Photo Gallery main window, shown in Figure 4-9. Photo Gallery highlights the new folder you just imported in the source list at the left for you — click the heading, and the photos you just downloaded appear in the pane on the right side of the window. To view a larger version of a thumbnail, hover your mouse cursor over the photo.

Figure 4-9:
Windows Photo Gallery is a great place to organize your imported photos.

Follow these steps to manipulate images within Photo Gallery:

✦ **To rotate an image:** Click to highlight a photograph and then click either of the rotate buttons within the Manage group on the Ribbon's Home tab.

Each click of the Rotate Left or Rotate Right button rotates the image 90 degrees in that direction.

✦ **To select a group of images:** Hold down the Ctrl key while you click or drag a selection box around the desired photos. You can also select a thumbnail by clicking the Next and Previous buttons.

✦ **To delete an image from your imported photos:** Click the thumbnail to select it and then click the Delete button on the Ribbon.

✦ **To display your imported photos in a full-screen slide show:** Click the Slide Show button, and select the desired effect or transition from the menu that appears.

To exit the slide show at any time, press the Esc key.

✦ **To view another collection of images:** Click to select an entry in the source list, to the left of the Photo Gallery window.

To assign a star rating, tag a photo, add a caption, or change the information for a photo, use the buttons in the Organize group on the Home tab.

After the images are transferred, you can unplug your camera's USB cable. Now you can have all sorts of fun sharing, tweaking and creating with your photos and videos!

✦ Click the Edit tab on the Ribbon to edit a selected image by fixing exposure and color levels or by cropping the stuff you don't want.

✦ Click the Home tab to send selected images as e-mail attachments, or share photos or videos on your SkyDrive, Facebook, YouTube, and other services.

✦ Click the File tab and click Print to send your selections to your system printer.

✦ Click the Create tab to automatically create a collage with selected photos, order prints, or create a blog post.

✦ Click the Find tab to locate items taken on a specific date, by rating, or by people you've tagged.

Book VII
Upgrading and Supercharging

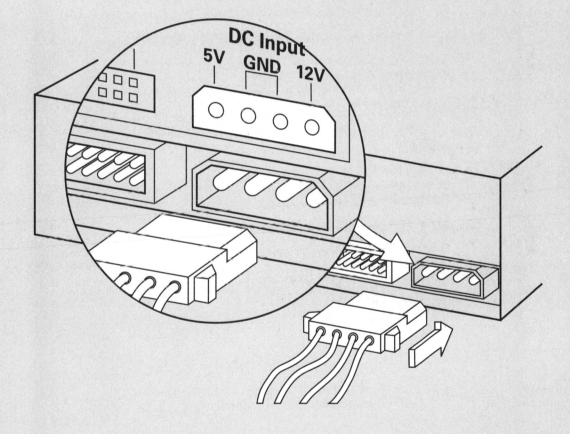

Visit www.dummies.com/extras/pcsaio for tips on upgrading your PC.

Contents at a Glance

Chapter 1: Determining What to Upgrade

In This Chapter

✓ Knowing when to upgrade your CPU and motherboard

✓ Figuring out whether you need additional memory

✓ Determining whether you need extra ports

✓ Considering a hard drive upgrade

✓ Evaluating a CD/DVD recorder or a tape backup drive

✓ Deciding on audio and video improvements

M y father always said, "Son, never take a long trip without a road map handy." This is why our old family Plymouth had six metric tons of paper maps for every state in the Union stuffed into the glove compartment, ready to be pulled out just in case we went astray. (Now I just use my handy GPS unit — progress marches on.)

Consider this introductory chapter a road map to upgrading your PC: what you can do, what you should add or replace, and what your benefits will be after the dust has cleared. After you read this PC upgrade primer, you can easily determine what you need to upgrade, and you can jump to the proper chapter within this minibook to find the specifics.

One note before you jump in: Upgrading your PC is not a difficult job! All it requires is

✦ The courage to remove your computer's case. (Believe me, you'll get used to it.)

✦ The ability to follow step-by-step instructions.

✦ Basic skills with a screwdriver.

With these requirements in mind, read on to determine what you need in order to turn your PC back into a hot rod.

Making Performance Upgrades: CPU, Motherboard, and Memory

I cordoned off the upgrades in this section into a separate category that I call *performance upgrades:* They give your PC an overall performance boost that affects all programs you run, including Windows itself.

Upgrading your CPU and motherboard

Simply put, a *central processing unit (CPU)* is the brain of your PC. A significant upgrade to your CPU usually results in more than just replacing the CPU chip itself. For example, if you decide to upgrade from an older Intel Core 2 Duo processor to the quad-core Intel i7 3.4 GHz CPU, your PC's motherboard certainly needs to be replaced as well (as will the RAM memory modules). The *motherboard* is the largest circuit board in your computer's case, shown in Figure 1-1 — it holds the CPU and memory modules and all the rest of the electronics — so this is probably one of the most technically demanding upgrades you can make.

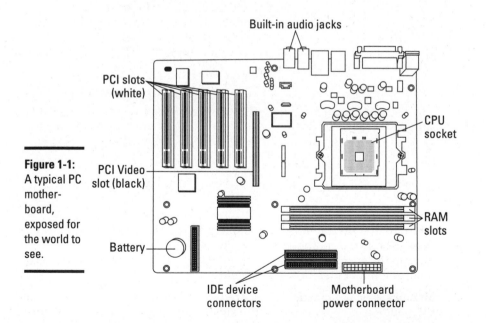

Figure 1-1: A typical PC motherboard, exposed for the world to see.

Naturally, replacing your computer's brain with the next generation of chip results in faster performance. How much faster depends on the speed of the chip — which is usually specified in megahertz (MHz) or gigahertz (GHz) — and on whether you're skipping a generation. This list describes two upgrade examples:

✦ **From a Core i5 3.0 GHz processor to a Core i5 3.4 GHz processor:** This upgrade results in a speed increase. And, because the chip generation may remain the same, you probably can use your current motherboard. However, the performance increase might not be significant enough to be noticeable in many of your programs. (You're not really advancing very far.)

✦ **From a Celeron 2.2 GHz processor to the same Core i5 3.4 GHz:** This upgrade, on the other hand, changes your plodding plowhorse into Shadowfax (the uberstallion from Tolkien's *The Lord of the Rings*). You're not only installing a CPU that's much faster but also upgrading from single-core Celeron technology to *quad-core* technology — and the tasks that you perform now will finish in a fraction of the time.

Hence, this Mark's Maxim:

> **Upgrade your CPU and motherboard only when you're either moving to a new generation of processor or when you're at least doubling the speed of your current CPU.™**

Anything less is a waste of time and effort (unless the CPU fairy dropped a new chip on your pillow for free).

Adding memory

I'll be honest: Adding memory (*random access memory,* or *RAM*) is my favorite performance upgrade, and I recommend adding memory far more often than I recommend upgrading a CPU/motherboard combo. Here's why:

✦ **Memory packs performance punch.** Any PC tech will tell you that dollar for dollar, adding memory results in a far more significant performance boost than simply upgrading your processor by a few megahertz. Windows uses every *bit* of that additional memory (bad techno-nerd pun intended there), and everything your PC does is done faster.

✦ **Memory is cheap.** I'm talkin' really, *really* cheap. Most folks can now afford to max out their memory capacity. (The total that you can add depends on your motherboard, so check with the PC manufacturer or look up the specifications for your motherboard to determine the maximum amount of memory you can add.)

✦ **Memory is easy to install.** Compared with upgrading a motherboard and CPU, adding memory is one of the simplest upgrade tasks you can perform in the bowels of your machine.

Here's the prerequisite Mark's Maxim for memory:

**Book VII
Chapter 1**

Determining What
to Upgrade

If you're looking for an easy and inexpensive performance boost, add memory to your PC before embarking on a CPU and motherboard upgrade. ™

'Nuff said.

Expansion Upgrades: eSATA, USB 3.0, Thunderbolt, and FireWire

Consider adding ports to an older PC — what I call *expansion upgrades*. Although adding or upgrading ports doesn't speed up your computer, you can connect a wider range of external devices.

Like the RAM upgrade that I discuss earlier in this chapter, adding Universal Serial Bus (USB 3.0), eSATA, Thunderbolt, or FireWire ports to your PC is a relatively easy upgrade. All you do is remove the cover from your PC and add an adapter card to one of the open slots on your motherboard (Figure 1-2). Remember, this is how the original cadre of IBM engineers — the ones who designed the architecture of the first PCs and sat in those squeaky nerd chairs — intended for you to add functionality to your computer, so it's practically a walk in the park.

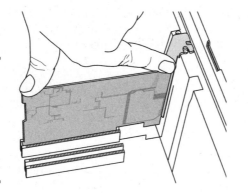

Figure 1-2:
Adding a port adapter card expands your PC's connectivity.

I discuss eSATA, USB 3.0, Thunderbolt, and FireWire ports in-depth in Chapter 4 of this minibook.

If you've decided to swap your PC's old motherboard with a new model, always shop for the fastest and widest range of built-in ports you can afford. Look for a motherboard with a minimum of built-in eSATA and USB 3.0 ports (and add Thunderbolt and FireWire ports to that list if you think you might need to connect those types of peripherals to your PC in the future). This saves you the hassle of adding an expansion card later to a nearly-new motherboard, just to add a specific type of port!

If you already have USB, Thunderbolt, or FireWire ports on your PC and you simply run out of connections (for example, you have two USB ports and you're using one for your printer and one for your webcam), you don't need to add another set of ports. Instead, you just need a USB or FireWire *hub,* a nifty little device that plugs into one of those ports and turns it into four or eight additional ports! (Think of the familiar AC extension cord, which plugs into one of your wall power sockets and allows you to plug in three or four cords.)

Making Storage Upgrades: Internal and External Drives

Why limit yourself to the sorry patch of digital real estate that originally shipped with your PC? I'm talking about your PC's original hard drive, or perhaps a slower, older DVD recorder. Upgrading these devices is a *storage upgrade* because you use these devices to permanently store (or record) data for later use.

Hard drives and DVD/Blu-Ray recorders are both continually dropping in price (and adding extra capacity and features), which is fortuitous because today's operating systems and applications tend to take up more and more hard drive space. Therefore, it's only natural that most serious PC users will eventually decide to add a second drive (or replace their existing drives with new units).

Adding a hard drive

The majority of today's PCs use Serial ATA (or SATA) hard drives, which can be mounted *internally* (within your PC's case) or *externally* (by connecting to a USB, Thunderbolt, or FireWire port). You'll also encounter older Integrated Drive Electronics (IDE, sometimes called PATA) hard drives, which are fast disappearing from today's PCs — they're significantly slower than SATA drives and harder to configure. Finally, some high-performance machines can use external SATA drives by connecting to an eSATA port.

Here's how to tell which type of drive you should choose:

+ **Internal:** Choose an internal drive if you don't mind opening your PC's case and installing a new drive. (I show you how later, in Chapter 3 within this very minibook.) Internal drives are significantly cheaper than external drives and are somewhat faster than external FireWire or USB 3.0 drives. Finally, you won't use any more of your precious desktop space.

+ **External:** Choose an external drive if you would rather not open your computer or if you have no available hard drive bays left in your computer's case. (Don't laugh — techno-types can fill up even the largest tower case with all sorts of devices.) External hard drives can be shared among computers that have the same ports, and you can simply unplug an external drive and carry it with you. (How's that for security?)

Adding a recorder

DVD recorders have been around for years, and they're equally attractive as internal drives or external devices. Today's eSATA, FireWire, and USB recorders are almost as blazing fast as their internal brethren! Therefore, as long as you have an eSATA, USB, or FireWire port, you now have the same choice that I describe with hard drives: Either stick it in your machine or leave it outside. It works like a charm either way.

The new generation of recordable Blu-Ray drives can hold 30 or 50GB on a single disc, and prices have dropped drastically on Blu-Ray drives! Blu-Ray drives can also read and record standard DVD discs. Therefore, before you invest in a simple DVD recorder, consider buying a rewriteable Blu-Ray drive instead.

Making Sound and Video Upgrades: Sound and Video Cards

To finish my road map of PC upgrades, consider the hottest video and audio cards now on the market. There are more reasons than just gaming to add or upgrade your PC's eyes and ears: For example, maybe you want to move up to a sound card with Dolby Surround sound support or perhaps a video card with video capture capability. Like the addition of high-speed ports, these upgrades are pretty simple: Just take the case off your PC, remove your current sound or video adapter card, and plug the replacement card in its place.

Before I jump into a discussion of these cards, I should note that most motherboards now have built-in sound (and/or video) hardware on the motherboard rather than on separate adapter cards. If your motherboard has either a built-in video card or sound card, you should be able to disable the onboard hardware so that you can add your upgrade card. Typically, you must either display your PC's Basic Input/Output System (BIOS) and disable the onboard hardware from there or move a jumper on the motherboard. Read your motherboard user manual to discover which avenue to take.

Sound cards on parade

A number of specialized sound cards are available for the discriminating audio connoisseur — which, no doubt, you are. Consider these gems:

✦ **A MIDI card:** If you're a musician that's invested in a MIDI keyboard or instrument, a sound card with MIDI ports makes it easy to compose music on your instrument and record it on your PC, or, conversely, play your MIDI instrument automatically from your PC! A typical sound card with MIDI support can set you back anywhere from $100–$200 US), but you'll find the convenience of MIDI well worth the cost.

✦ **A 24-bit card:** For the absolute best in audio reproduction, pick up a card that can produce 24-bit audio (that's 192 KHz, for you audioheads), which is far superior to the sound produced by virtually all audio CD players. Many high-end sound cards also support DVD audio or feature front-panel controls that fit in an open drive bay (whipped cream and cherry on the sundae). Expect to pay a prime price for one of these cards, usually in the $75–$100 range.

✦ **A Surround sound card:** These cards are specifically designed for 3-D environmental audio within games and for full support for Dolby Surround sound as you watch DVD movies on your PC. Naturally, you need more than two mundane speakers from a discount store to enjoy the full effect — which is why a premium set of speakers is usually included with these cards. Look for these cards to set you back around $50.

Deciding which video card is right for you

When you think about upgrading a video card, please do not — I repeat, *do not* — just think "gamers only." A number of specialized video cards on the market have nothing to do with games. (Okay, I admit it: Gamers like myself do indeed love video cards.) Here's a cross section of what's available:

✦ **A gamer's card:** The latest 3D video cards (equipped with chipsets from NVIDIA and ATI) simply kick serious tail, no matter whether your favorite games involve mowing down Nazis, building a civilization one stone at a time, or matching wits with your computer over a chess board. If you haven't seen the realistic 3D figures that these cards can produce, visit your local mall's Maze o' Wires store (you know what I mean) and ask a salesperson to crank up the latest game. Of course, Windows displays ho-hum applications faster with one of these cards as well. Most 3D gaming cards also offer dual monitor support so that you can run two monitors side-by-side for a really big desktop.

These high-end, 3D cards run tremendously hot — after all, they're practically separate computers — so they usually have a fan (or two) already installed on the card. However, if you're planning to install the card in an older PC, I recommend having at least two fans installed in your case — that's one for the power supply (which is standard equipment) and at least one larger auxiliary fan (to help circulate air to all those hot components). Unfortunately, most "pizza box" and "shoe box" cases don't have the necessary fans on-board to handle a cutting-edge video card.

✦ **An MPEG card:** These cards are specifically designed for encoding and decoding Motion Picture Experts Group (MPEG) digital video (usually from a DVD, but hardware MPEG support is also very useful for doing serious video editing on your PC). The idea is simple: Let the card, rather than your PC's processor, do the video grunt work, and everyone is happier. High-end video cards specially designed for digital video editing are significantly more expensive than video cards meant for home and gamer machines.

✦ **A capture card:** You use this popular video upgrade card to capture an incoming analog video signal and convert it to digital video. For example, you can connect your VCR or older analog VHS-C camcorder to the card, convert the signal to digital video, and then record DVD backups of your home movies. If you can display it on your TV, you should be able to capture it with one of these toys.

Chapter 2: Adding RAM to Your Hot Rod

*W*hat's not to like about a memory upgrade? As I discuss in the previous chapter, the *dinero* required for extra random access memory (RAM) is a mere pittance compared with a new CPU (or CPU-and-motherboard combination). Plus, RAM is easy to install, requiring only that you remove your PC's case and plug in the modules. Your PC should recognize additional RAM immediately, with no silly drivers required. Also, additional RAM makes everything run faster in Windows — both the applications you run and the operating system itself.

"Mark," you say, "there's *got* to be a hitch *somewhere*." In fact, there are two: you have so many different types of RAM modules to choose from, and your motherboard can only accept a certain amount of RAM. Read this chapter before you buy RAM modules, and keep these pages handy when you add new memory or upgrade your existing memory.

Defining the Different Types of RAM

To begin this primer on memory, review the different types of RAM available for PCs made within the past five years or so.

Before I begin: If you're considering installing a new motherboard and CPU on an older PC, double-check that the new motherboard will use the same RAM type and speed as your current motherboard. (Visit each manufacturer's website to compare the specifications for your existing motherboard and the new toy, or refer to the documentation for both motherboards.) If not, the RAM that you add won't do you any good when you upgrade your motherboard. If you have your eye on a significant motherboard/CPU swap in the near future, I definitely recommend upgrading the motherboard, CPU, *and* RAM all at once. For example, the memory modules that work with an older Athlon 64 X2 PC aren't likely to work with a faster AMD Phenom II X6 motherboard. In a case like this, I recommend ordering a *populated* motherboard, complete with a preinstalled CPU and the amount of RAM you specify.

DDR

Double data rate (DDR) modules were the first 168-pin standard Dual Inline Memory Modules (DIMMs) available for PCs; they're commonly used on older Pentium and Athlon computers running Windows XP. The *double* in the DDR name is significant because a DDR module effectively doubles the speed of the module, compared with older Synchronous Dynamic Random Access Memory (SDRAM) memory. Also, DDR memory is assigned a speed rating as part of its name, so it's commonly listed as DDR266 or PC2100 (for the 133 MHz speed versions) and DDR333 or PC2700 (for the 166 MHz version). As you might guess, the faster the access speed, the better the performance. The speed rating that you should choose is determined by the memory speeds that your motherboard supports. DDR memory modules have one notch on the connector and two notches on each side of the module.

DDR2

DDR2 modules doubled the data transfer rate between RAM and mother-board, but they basically look the same. These days, DDR2 modules are most often found on lower-cost PCs running Windows Vista and Windows 7.

DDR3

Here's a good question: Which new memory specification is fast replacing DDR2? "Gee, Mark, *could* it be DDR3?" That's right: DDR3 modules provide the best performance around, suitable for PCs running Windows 7 and 8. DDR3 modules were once significantly more expensive than their older DDR2 brethren, but DDR3 modules are now the most common type of RAM on mid-range and high-end PCs. DDR3 modules are available in capacities up to 8GB.

RDRAM

Rambus (RDRAM) modules are much faster (and also more expensive) than standard DDR modules. In fact, until the arrival of DDR2 and DDR3 memory, RDRAM was the memory standard of choice for high-speed PCs. DDR3 has now crept up from behind and taken the coveted title of First Place Performer, and RDRAM is slowly disappearing from the market.

SDRAM

SDRAM (sometimes called SyncDRAM) took the form of standard 168-pin DIMMs. These modules were standard equipment on most Pentium III and some older Pentium 4 machines. SyncDRAM ran at an access speed of 133

MHz, which is too doggone slow for today's fast processors. SDRAM memory modules sport two notches in the bottom and only one notch on each side.

If you're planning to add memory to a motherboard that uses SDRAM modules, I strongly urge you to instead upgrade the Big Three: motherboard, CPU, and memory. (I don't intend to offend, but I'll be blunt: Your PC is so far behind the performance of new models that it just isn't worth adding SDRAM memory to your older motherboard. Plus, SDRAM memory is now much harder to find and is getting *more* expensive over time. Just chalk that up to the price of running antique hardware.)

Figuring Out Which Type of RAM to Buy

Here are two methods to determine which type of memory modules your current motherboard requires and which memory speeds it can handle:

+ **Check the specs.** Refer to the motherboard manual. Or, if you purchased your PC from a manufacturer, check the documentation that accompanied the computer. If you don't have any manuals (think "used PC"), visit the company's website for memory compatibility information or specifications so you don't have to open your PC's case until you're ready to install the new RAM modules.

+ **Check the existing modules.** If you can't find any documentation, specifications, or data on the web concerning your PC's RAM modules, it's time to remove the case from your computer. (See how in the step-by-step procedure at the end of this chapter.) Look for the memory slots on your motherboard; DDR, DDR2, and DDR3 modules look like the ones shown in Figure 2-1. (*Note:* You might have more than one module already installed on your PC.) Your RAM modules might also have a descriptive label (which allows you to read the specifics without taking anything out). However, more likely, you'll have to remove one and take it to your local computer shop. Use the instructions later in this chapter to remove a module; then protect the module in an empty CD-ROM jewel case when you take it for identification. The good techs, when presented with the module, should be able to tell you which memory type and speed you're using.

Figure 2-1:
A DDR/
DDR2/DDR3
DIMM.

Deciding How Much RAM Is Enough

As I mentioned at the beginning of this chapter, every motherboard has a maximum amount of memory it can support. You can install the maximum amount by filling up all the motherboard's memory banks (sockets) with modules of the right type.

It's time for another Mark's Maxim:

> **Whenever possible, buy RAM modules of the same brand at the same time from the same dealer.**™

This advice ensures that you're spared any compatibility problems when you install the modules.

Theoretically, any RAM module of the same type and speed *should* work with any other brand of RAM, but I date back to the earlier days of PCs when using memory chips from different manufacturers resulted in errors and a locked computer. In fact, I still hear tales of compatibility problems, even in our new, improved, fresher-smelling world.

However, not everyone can afford to take their PC's memory to the max — even with today's prices, buying dozens of gigabytes of fast DDR3 RAM modules can set you back. Therefore, the following table illustrates my recommendations for the minimum amount of RAM that you need in order to run the different versions of the Windows operating system comfortably on your PC. ("Comfortably" means *my* opinion of decent performance, perhaps with Microsoft Word running. Of course, memory-hungry applications such as Adobe Photoshop run their best only with plenty of memory elbow room to spare, so consider this the *absolute* minimum.)

Windows XP	Windows Vista	Windows 7	Windows 8
512MB	1GB	2GB	4GB

You might notice that my recommendations sometimes don't jibe with Brother Bill's — that's because the folks in Redmond literally mean *the least you can get away with* when mentioning minimum memory requirements. For example, with 1GB of RAM, Windows 7 is slower to awaken than my kids on a school day. Personally, I like to *use* my computer and not wait half an hour for a scanned image to load.

Using ReadyBoost

Do you happen to have a high-capacity USB 2.0 or USB 3.0 flash drive — say, a 1GB to 16GB model — lying around doing nothing? If you're running Windows Vista, Windows 7, or Windows 0, you can use the ReadyBoost feature to magically use that solid-state external storage to speed up your PC!

To use ReadyBoost, just plug your USB flash drive into one of your PC's USB 2.0 or USB 3.0 ports. Windows displays a ReadyBoost option in the AutoPlay dialog box that appears; choose the ReadyBoost entry and Windows prompts you for the amount of space on the drive that you want to allocate to ReadyBoost. (A minimum of 1GB of free space is required, but if you're not using the rest of the drive, throw caution utterly to the wind and use the entire thing!) Windows keeps ReadyBoost turned on until you eject the USB drive or reboot your PC.

Note that ReadyBoost doesn't run with most older 1.*x* USB flash drives because the memory those drives use is too slow — hence the need for a USB 2.0 or USB 3.0 flash drive.

Installing Extra RAM

If you're ready to install your new RAM upgrade, follow these steps to install a typical DDR/DDR2/DDR3 module:

1. **Cover your work surface with several sheets of newspaper (to protect your case).**

2. **Power down your PC, unplug it from its power source, and place it on top of the newspaper.**

3. **Remove the PC's case.**

   Most PC cases are held on with two or three screws; just remove the screws and slide the case off. (Don't forget to stash those screws in a safe place.) Other cases are hinged, often with a lock. If you're unsure how to remove your PC's case, check the manual that accompanied your computer.

4. **Touch the metal chassis of your case to dissipate any static electricity on your body.**

   An electrical charge can send your new RAM modules to Frisco — permanently.

5. **Locate the DIMM slots.**

   Check the motherboard manual, which should have a schematic diagram that helps you locate the slots. Typically, the RAM modules are found close to the CPU, in the center or in one corner of the motherboard.

6. **Turn your PC's chassis so that the DIMM slots are facing you (as shown in Figure 2-2) and make sure that the two levers on the side of the socket are extended.**

Figure 2-2: Align the DDR/DDR2/DDR3 module with its socket.

Note that the notches cut into the connectors on the bottom of the memory module match the spacers in the sockets themselves, so you can't install your modules the wrong way. (Smart thinking there.)

7. **Align the connector on the bottom of the module with the socket and push down with light pressure to seat the module.**

8. **While you push down, the levers on each side of the socket should move toward the center, as shown in Figure 2-3, until they click in place.**

Figure 2-3: Hey, those levers just clicked into place!

After you correctly install the module, the two levers should be tightly flush against the sides of the memory module to hold it securely.

9. **Slide the cover back on your PC and secure it.**

10. **Move your PC back to its place of honor and plug it in.**

11. **Restart your computer and prepare to enjoy a faster PC!**

**Book VII
Chapter 2**

Adding RAM to
Your Hot Rod

Chapter 3: Adding Hard Drive Territory to Your System

In This Chapter

✔ **Understanding virtual memory**

✔ **Selecting the proper drive**

✔ **Choosing an internal or external drive**

✔ **Adding a second internal drive**

ere's what I call the *Elbowroom Hypothesis:* Both mankind and his computer tools will expand to fill whatever room they're given. If you're bent on becoming a PC power user, I can assure you — in fact, I can downright *guarantee* you — that the largest hard drive you can buy today will eventually be filled in the future. As you discover in this chapter, even Windows 8 itself demands a chunk of hard drive territory — when you install it *and* when it's running. Hence the explosion in hard drive capacities over the past ten years or so.

Luckily, you can upgrade your PC's hard drive with ease by either connecting an external drive or upgrading your current internal hard drive. Alternatively, you can simply cast yourself to the four winds with abandon and keep your current internal drive and add a second drive. This chapter is your road map.

The Tale of Virtual Memory

"Wait a furshlugginer minute here, Mark — you cover memory upgrades in Chapter 2 of this very minibook. Why bring it up now?" Good question, and the answer lies in the fact that the pseudo-RAM called *virtual memory* actually exists on your hard drive rather than as memory modules on your motherboard.

Hard drives in ancient times

I'm old enough to remember when a 1GB hard drive was an unheard-of dream. Heck, I still have the first hard drive I ever owned in my wild single years: a huge RadioShack 15MB (yes, you read it right, *15 whopping megabytes*) disk system that I used with my TRS-80 Model IV. (Oh, did I mention that those 15 megs of storage cost me more than $1,000 US in 1983 and that the drive is about the size of a typical modern PC case?) I use it as a combination monitor stand, conversation piece, and possible proof of past visits by extraterrestrials.

If you're totally confused, here's the explanation: Modern operating systems (Windows 8/7/Vista/XP, Mac OS X, Unix, and Linux) all use the virtual memory trick to feed your applications the memory they need. Suppose that your PC has only 2GB of random access memory (RAM) installed, but you just ran Photoshop and demanded that it load two 500MB high-resolution digital images. If Windows were limited to using only your computer's *physical* RAM (the memory modules you installed on your PC's motherboard), you would be up a creek because Windows 8 requires a minimum of around 500MB of memory itself, and Photoshop takes a significant chunk of memory to run. On top of all that, you'd be loading 1GB of data! Considering the size of today's documents and the amount of RAM needed by memory-hungry mega-applications, your 2GB PC literally couldn't do its job. And, don't forget that you'd probably be running more than one application at a time. What's a computer to do?

As you can see in Figure 3-1, Windows turns to your hard drive for help. It uses a portion of the empty space on your hard drive to temporarily hold the data that would otherwise be held in your computer's memory. In this case, your hardworking silicon warrior uses 2GB of hard drive space, so the total memory available within Windows (using both 2GB of physical memory and 2GB of virtual memory) is now 4GB, providing more elbowroom to work with. Your programs don't know that they're using virtual memory — Windows takes care of everything behind the scenes, so Photoshop thinks that you have 4GB of physical memory.

Now that you understand how virtual memory works, commit this Mark's Maxim to memory:

Always leave enough empty hard drive space for Windows to use as virtual memory!™

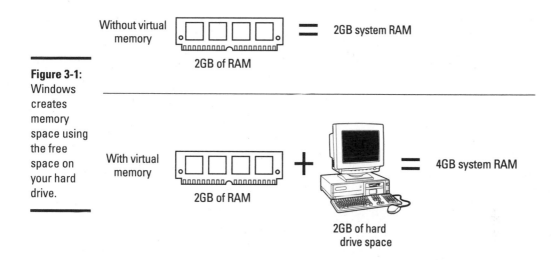

Figure 3-1:
Windows creates memory space using the free space on your hard drive.

Without virtual memory — 2GB of RAM = 2GB system RAM

With virtual memory — 2GB of RAM + 2GB of hard drive space = 4GB system RAM

How much is enough? I try to leave at least 25GB or 30GB free on the C: drive at all times on my Windows 8 machines. (Your C: drive is typically the hard drive that Windows 8 boots from. To check how much space it has remaining, display your Desktop and click on the File Explorer icon on the taskbar, and then right-click on the drive you want to check and choose Properties.) A PC that runs out of hard drive space is a terrible thing to see; applications start to lock up, you might lose any changes you made to open files, and Windows begins displaying pitiful error messages begging you to close some of your open application windows (or even restart).

 Also, note that virtual memory is always — and I mean *always* — slower than true physical memory. After all, that data has to be written to and read from your hard drive rather than from superfast memory modules. This is why I'm a proponent of adding as much RAM to your PC as possible; the more memory that you add, the less likely that Windows needs to resort to virtual memory.

 PC techs call your computer's use of virtual memory *drive thrashing* because Windows must continually write data to, read data from, and erase data from your hard drive. When you run out of physical memory, the hard drive activity light on the front of your machine never seems to go out. And yes, if you're wondering, all that activity shortens the life of your hard drive over time.

Recognizing a Well-Dressed Hard Drive

When you decide to take the plunge and add storage space, reading this section helps you shop by separating the good specifications from the gobbledygook.

Today's PCs use Enhanced Integrated Drive Electronics (EIDE, also called PATA) or Serial ATA (SATA) hard drives. Although a PC can use an internal Small Computer System Interface (SCSI) hard drive, anyone using expensive and complex SCSI hardware is already a PC power user and can probably skip this chapter without a second glance.

Size definitely matters

Virtually all EIDE and SATA drives on the market today are 3½" format, which means that they can fit within a typical floppy drive/hard drive combo bay of your computer's case. Unfortunately, some mini-tower cases have only one or two of these 3½" bays.

Therefore, if you're planning to park that 3½" drive within a much larger 5¼" bay (the kind used with DVD and Blu-Ray drives), you need a metal framework called a *drive cage kit.* In effect, the hard drive is mounted into the drive cage, which in turn is mounted in the PC's 5¼" bay. Most drives don't come with a drive cage kit (check first, of course), so you need to buy one at your computer shop. (They usually run about $10 US.)

How fast is your access?

When you see a drive's *access* (or *seek*) time listed, that's the amount of time (in milliseconds; ms) that it takes the drive to read or write data. Naturally, a lower access time is desirable — and usually somewhat more expensive. Drives with access times less than 7 ms are usually at the top of their price range, especially when the drive in question has a higher revolutions per minute (rpm) rating.

What does rpm have to do with hard drives?

In the world of personal computers, just like in the world of the Indy 500, the abbreviation *rpm* means *r*evolutions *p*er *m*inute. (However, I'm counting the revolutions that the magnetic disk platter turns inside the drive.) And, with a refreshing constancy, a higher-rpm hard drive means better performance, just like a beefier engine's rpm means greater speed in auto racing.

Most of today's EIDE and SATA drives fall into one of three ranges:

✦ **5,400 rpm:** These drives are standard equipment on most older PCs and can also be found on low-cost Intel Celeron and AMD Sempron computers.

As reliable as vanilla ice cream, one of these drives gets the job done — but don't expect whipped cream and a cherry.

+ **7,200 rpm:** This is the standard rpm rating for most consumer hard drives on today's market — the increased rpm leads to better performance because files load faster and Windows runs faster on a 7,200 rpm drive.

+ **10,000 rpm:** Lucky dog! These "sports car" hard drives are found on today's high-performance PCs. You pay a bit more, but a 10,000 rpm SATA drive can really speed up your disk-intensive applications (and Windows 8 itself).

I heartily recommend that you select a 7,200 rpm or 10,000 rpm drive when upgrading any PC or buying a new one. The significantly faster read/write performance on one of these drives peps up your entire system.

Internal versus External Storage

I address the idea of internal and external peripherals in a number of places elsewhere in this book, so I don't go into a crazy amount of detail here. Suffice it to say that I recommend using an internal hard drive whenever

+ You don't need to share the drive among multiple computers, or take your drive with you while traveling.

+ Your PC has an additional open drive bay, or you're willing to upgrade the existing drive.

+ You want to save money.

As you might expect, with those criteria, I usually push internal hard drives on both my unsuspecting consulting customers and on myself. Figure 3-2 shows the curvaceous rear end of a typical modern hard drive. (Well, at least it *looks* curvaceous to a techno-nerd like me.)

Don't get me wrong: External drives are neat toys, and they're perfect for backups and media storage (like your photo and MP3 music collections). However, they cost significantly more than their internal counterparts, and you lose some of your precious desk space accommodating them. Most external drives also have their own power cords, so you have to pull another AC wall socket out of your magician's hat. If you really do need an external drive and you want to save yourself the hassle, consider a drive that's powered over a Universal Serial Bus (USB) or FireWire connection, which means no additional power cable worries. For under $100 (US), you can pick up one of my favorite USB-powered external drives, the Western Digital My Passport 1TB with USB 3.0 connection, at www.newegg.com.

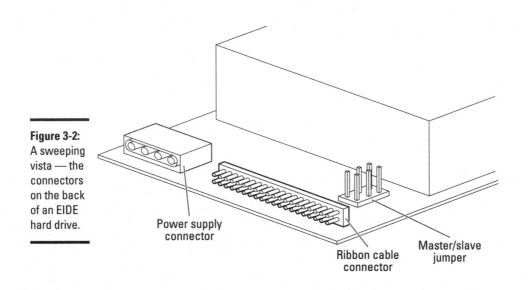

Figure 3-2:
A sweeping
vista — the
connectors
on the back
of an EIDE
hard drive.

Power supply
connector

Ribbon cable
connector

Master/slave
jumper

If someone tries to give you a USB 1.*x* hard drive — or, heaven forbid, you're thinking of buying a used USB 1.*x* hard drive — I beg you *not* to do it! The first generation of USB drives was ridiculously slow. In other words, your kids are likely to graduate from college before you finish transferring a single gigabyte's worth of data from that drive to your PC. Keep a safe distance from that tired drive and call your local antique hardware shelter.

Adding a Second Internal Hard Drive

For most current PC owners, the easiest method of adding more hard drive space is to add a second hard drive to their systems. I cite three very good reasons for this:

✦ **No backup is required.** Of course, *you should be backing up your current hard drive anyway.* (If not, shut this book immediately and back up your drive!) Adding a second drive eliminates the setup that you have to perform if you upgrade your current drive because you don't have to restore the current contents of your old drive to the new drive.

✦ **Most PCs have at least one open drive bay.** Unless your computer is already stuffed to the gills, you should have enough room to add a second hard drive. If it *is* stuffed to the gills, you either have to upgrade the current drive or add an external FireWire, eSATA (external SATA), Thunderbolt, or USB 2.0/3.0 drive. For more information about these external connections, visit Chapter 4 in this minibook.

✦ **It's like . . . well . . . more for less.** Rather than replace an existing 500GB drive with a 1TB drive — and end up with only 500GB more room — I always find it more attractive to leave the original drive as is and add that second drive, resulting in the full 1TB that you paid for. (***Remember:*** You *will* eventually use that space. Trust me.)

Are you girded and ready for battle? Because there are actually more steps involved in the installation of an EIDE drive, I cover that here (but, as I mention in the sidebar, the steps for a SATA drive installation are much the same).

Follow this procedure to add a second internal EIDE hard drive to your current system:

1. **Cover your work surface with several sheets of newspaper.**

2. **Turn off your PC, unplug it, and place it on top of the newspaper.**

3. **Remove the case screws and slide off the case, putting the screws aside in a glass or wooden bowl or cup.**

If you're unsure how to remove your PC's case, check the manual that accompanied your computer.

4. **Touch the metal chassis of the computer to dissipate any static electricity.**

5. **Verify the jumper settings on the back of your original drive, as shown in Figure 3-3. If necessary, change the existing drive to *multiple drives, master unit* (or just *master*) by moving the jumper to the indicated pins.**

Remember, if you're installing a SATA drive, you won't need to worry about jumpers! Just skip to Step 7.

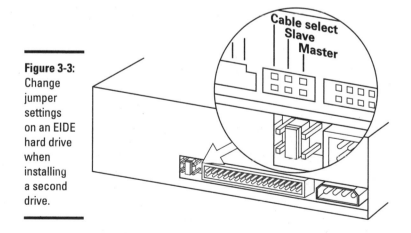

Figure 3-3: Change jumper settings on an EIDE hard drive when installing a second drive.

Serial ATA is in the house

Although EIDE was once the most popular hard drive interface for new PCs, serial ATA has finally surpassed EIDE and now appears more often. That's because a SATA connection allows significantly faster data transfer rates (in English: SATA is faster than EIDE) and there are no jumpers to set for a SATA drive. (Skip to the steps on adding a second internal hard drive for more on jumpers.) The installation of the physical drive is the same as I outline here for an EIDE drive; then simply plug in the data cable from your motherboard (it goes on only one way) and the power cable from your PC's power supply, and the drive is ready for action.

In fact, virtually all the latest motherboards on the market have both EIDE (sometimes called PATA, short for Parallel ATA) and SATA connectors onboard. You can mix and match and use both or work only with the faster SATA connections.

Jumpers are the tiny plastic and metal shunts that you use to configure hard drives and CD/DVD drives.

Jumper

Your jumper configuration is probably different from the one shown in Figure 3-3. Most EIDE hard drive manufacturers now print the jumper settings on the tops of hard drives. If the settings aren't printed on the drive, you can refer to the drive's manual or visit the manufacturer's website and look up the settings there. If all this seems a little exotic, the terms really aren't risqué; *master* means primary (and if you have at least one drive, there must be a master device), and *slave* means secondary. Other than that, the devices are treated the same way by your PC.

6. Set the jumpers on the back of the new drive for *multiple drives, slave unit* (often listed as just *slave*).

7. If your new drive needs a drive cage to fit into the desired bay, use the screws supplied by the drive manufacturer to attach the cage rails to both sides of your drive.

For more on drive cage kits, see the earlier section "Size definitely matters."

8. **Slide the drive into the selected bay from the front (or inside) of the case, and make sure that the end with the connectors goes in first and that the exposed circuitry of the drive is on the bottom.**

9. **Slide the hard drive back and forth in the drive bay until the screw holes in the side of the bay are aligned with the screw holes on the side of the drive (or on the drive cage rails).**

10. **Tighten down the drive to the side of the bay with the screws that came with the drive (or your cage kit), as illustrated in Figure 3-4.**

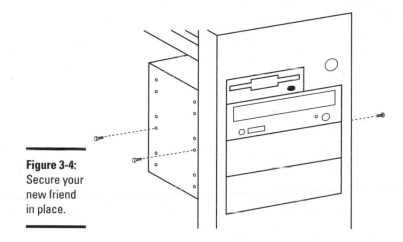

Figure 3-4: Secure your new friend in place.

11. **Choose an unused power connector and plug it in, and make sure that the connector is firmly seated (see Figure 3-5).**

Joyfully, there's only one way to connect a power cable to a hard drive — the right way.

12. **Plug the other connector from the hard drive cable into the back of the drive and make sure that the cable is firmly seated.**

Note that both EIDE hard drives use the same cable, so you might need to unplug the original drive from the cable and switch connectors. Don't worry: It doesn't matter which connector goes to which drive as long as the jumpers are correctly set. (Multiple SATA drives do not use the same cable, as each SATA drive is individually connected to the motherboard.)

Check for a blocked hole in the cable connector, which should align with a missing pin on the drive's connector. This alignment trick, called *keying,* helps ensure that you're installing the cable right side up. However, don't panic if the cable isn't keyed: Remember that the wire with the red or black marking on the cable is always Wire 1 and that it should align with Pin 1 on the drive's connector (see Figure 3-6).

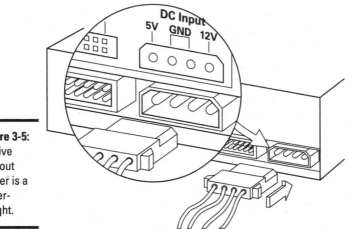

Figure 3-5:
A drive without power is a paper-weight.

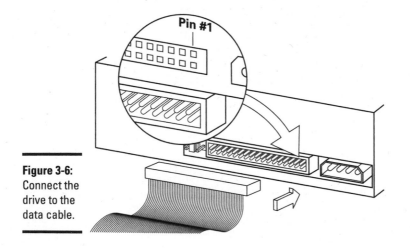

Figure 3-6:
Connect the drive to the data cable.

13. Replace the cover on your PC and tighten its screws.

14. Plug your PC back in and turn it on.

15. Run the drive formatting utility that accompanied your new drive to prepare it for use.

Chapter 4: Partying with USB, FireWire, Thunderbolt, and eSATA

In This Chapter

✓ **Comparing flavors of USB**

✓ **Using FireWire for high-end fun**

✓ **Putting eSATA to work**

✓ **Adding a Thunderbolt device**

✓ **Extending your system with a hub**

✓ **Adding a port card**

*I*n the days of the early IBM PCs, practically every device that you added was *internal* (stored within the computer case). Because so few peripherals existed that you could add to your system, this situation really wasn't a problem. Back in the day, the parallel port took care of the printer (if you could afford one), and as the modem grew in importance, it took up residence with the serial port.

Today, however, PC cases have shrunk. When it comes to size, I can't tell the difference between many new desktops and my kid's PlayStation. And, less internal room means more need for external stuff. Also, because of the huge increase in the number of portable devices you can add to your computer, those toys are naturally designed to be external, such as digital cameras, MP3 players, smartphones, and the like. The days of the PC as a monolith are over.

So what's a poor CPU to do? Enter the star ports of the digital age: Universal Serial Bus (USB) and FireWire, along with the up-and-coming eSATA and Thunderbolt. Talk about *sassy:* They're fast, they offer plug-and-play convenience, and they don't hassle you with arcane errors or strange settings. Plus, you can use them to connect practically everything but the kitchen sink to your computer simultaneously.

In this chapter, I share the joy as we party together with these four ports.

A Tale of Four Fine Ports

Even the original IBM PC had ports — that's because the designers of that first digital beast knew that not everything would fit inside the computer's case. The first example of a piece of "outside" hardware was the computer printer, but soon others appeared: Modems, mice, joysticks, drawing pads, and an entire pantheon of other toys started demanding ports.

Today's machines typically offer at least one of the Big Four ports (and depending on the price tag, perhaps three or even all four). In this section, we'll compare and contrast USB, FireWire, Thunderbolt, and eSATA ports.

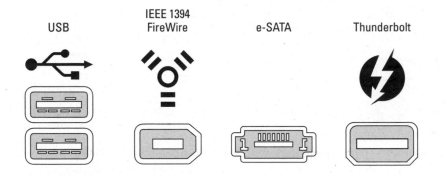

Comparing USB ports

You might think that all USB ports are the same, but they're not. In the beginning, only USB 1.*x* was available. Sure, USB 1.*x* was a fine little port (easy to use and requiring no configuration) but only a few times faster than an old-fashioned serial connection. (To be honest, a FireWire device wipes the floor with the first generation of USB devices when it comes to speed. You can read more about FireWire shortly.) Around the turn of the millennium, the list of peripherals that really required 400 Mbps of transfer speed was limited to digital video (DV) camcorders and external audio/visual (AV) hard drives used by video professionals. Today, that list has expanded:

+ **Digital cameras:** They produce images with bigger file sizes.

+ **High-resolution scanners:** These devices need to churn out images with 500MB of pixels (or, incredibly, more than that).

+ **External, high-speed DVD and Blu-Ray recorders:** Don't even dream of recording a DVD over a USB 1.*x* connection.

+ **MP3 players:** These include my favorite, the Apple iPod.

Comparing speeds of popular PC ports

Check out the following table to see just what a dramatic jump that USB, FireWire, Thunderbolt, and eSATA made in connection speed over the standard PC serial port.

Port	Year Appeared on PCs	Transfer Speed (in Megabits per Second)
PC serial	1981	Less than 1 Mbps
PC parallel	1981	1 Mbps
USB (version 1.1)	1996	12 Mbps
FireWire 400 (version A)	1996	400 Mbps
USB (version 2.0)	2001	480 Mbps
FireWire 800 (version B)	2003	800 Mbps
eSATA	2005	1500 Mbps
USB (version 3.0)	2010	5 Gbps (5,000 Mbps)
Thunderbolt	2011	10 Gbps (10,000 Mbps)

Book VII
Chapter 4

Partying with
USB, FireWire,
Thunderbolt, and
eSATA

Enter USB 2.0, currently the most common variety of USB connection. This generation of port ups the ante, delivering 480 Mbps, which handily tops the original FireWire specification, version A. And because it's backward compatible with older USB 1.1 devices, you don't have to start all over with your USB hardware, and cables will still work no matter which version of the port your PC uses. (Sometimes, change is not A Good Thing.) Of course, only those peripherals that support the USB 2.0 standard can take advantage of the warp speed increase. The fastest USB standard, USB 3.0, offers yet another huge jump in raw speed, and is also backward compatible with USB 1.1 and 2.0 hardware. However, USB 3.0 devices may be somewhat more expensive than their USB 2.0 brethren. (Naturally, if your PC supports only USB 2.0, there's no reason to invest in USB 3.0 hardware — however, a USB 3.0 adapter card is a great inexpensive upgrade for your PC.)

"Hey, Gladys, the external USB drive isn't getting any power. And I've got it plugged in and everything!" Of course, that drive might not be plugged into the wall socket for AC power — an easy troubleshooting task — but if you're using a USB device that's powered through the USB port itself, the problem might be more insidious. Some USB ports don't provide the full power support called for by the USB standard because they're designed only for connecting mice, keyboards, and joysticks. As a workaround, try plugging that USB drive into another PC's USB port (or a powered USB hub, which I discuss later in this chapter) to see whether it wakes up. If it does, try plugging it into another USB port in a different location on your PC.

The two flavors of FireWire

Not to be outdone, the FireWire 800 version B port — which can pump 800 Mbps between your PC and an external device — began showing up on Macs in the first months of 2003. This port is now available for any power-user PC. If your PC doesn't have one and you have FireWire 800 devices you need to connect, you can add a FireWire 800 port to your current machine with a port adapter card.

Unfortunately, unlike USB, the FireWire 800 connector is a different shape from the FireWire 400 connector. To connect a FireWire 400 device to a FireWire 800 port, you'll need an inexpensive go-between adapter. No biggie.

IEEE 1394 is the techie name for FireWire. You might come across this term in your computer and peripheral travels.

Although USB 3.0, Thunderbolt, and eSATA all leave FireWire far behind in terms of transfer speed, there are two reasons why the FireWire standard is still in use:

✦ **Device support:** FireWire has been around since 1996 on most DV equipment, so it's a well-recognized standard. (If you're using older video hardware, FireWire is the common denominator.)

✦ **Control over connection:** Ignore the engineer-speak. Basically, this feature allows you to control your FireWire device from your PC. For example, if you have a DV camcorder with a FireWire port, you can control your camcorder from your keyboard. Just click Play within your editing software, and your camera jumps into action just as though you had pressed the Play button on the DV camcorder itself. Although USB can send a basic signal or two to the device (for instance, a command to erase an image from your digital camera), it's nowhere near as sophisticated as the control over your connection that's possible with a FireWire connection.

Putting internal on the outside with eSATA

eSATA is another popular connection standard for high-performance external hard drives. Although less-known (and quite a bit slower) than USB 3.0, eSATA is appearing more often these days on consumer-level PCs. (Of course, if you want to leap into the fray right now, you can add an eSATA adapter card to your existing PC!) You'll find plenty of eSATA peripherals available, waiting for the port to appear on more computers — if you think that sounds like the state USB 2.0 was in a decade ago, you'd be correct. Like USB and FireWire, eSATA is plug and play.

Essentially, an eSATA port acts as an extension of your PC's internal Serial ATA hard drive controller, making it ideal for external storage (think applications like video editing and high-speed backups). For example, I use my eSATA drive as both a backup drive and a storage center for my digital video clips.

eSATA is often used with RAID *drive arrays*, which are external cases with multiple hard drives connected together. With a RAID array, data transfer speeds are significantly increased — think multiple drives reading data simultaneously. (Or, if you prefer, you can set up a RAID array that features automatic redundancy, which safeguards your data even if one of your hard drives fails!) Neat stuff indeed.

The power user port of choice: Thunderbolt

This section ends with a bang! (I couldn't resist.) I'm talking Thunderbolt, the latest port on the block — and again, like USB and FireWire, appearing first on Macs and then on PCs. Thunderbolt ports offer downright incredible transfer speeds: the newcomer is literally more than *12 times faster* than FireWire 800, and *twice* as fast as USB 3.0 technology.

The downside? There are but two — Thunderbolt peripherals are some of the most expensive computer devices you can buy at the time of this writing, and very few consumer PCs offer a built-in Thunderbolt port (so you'll almost certainly have to add a Thunderbolt port using an adapter card).

Ah, but Thunderbolt is also versatile — it even supports a direct high-definition connection between your PC and your HDMI flat-screen TV, or a superfast high-resolution Thunderbolt monitor. A single plug and play Thunderbolt port can handle up to six peripherals through daisy-chaining, including a mixture of high-resolution displays and devices like hard drives and Blu-Ray recorders.

Or Do You Just Need a Hub?

A technician friend of mine has a great T-shirt with the logo "Got ports?" If your PC already has FireWire or USB ports but they're already all taken, you don't need to install an adapter card to provide your computer with additional portage. (Of course, you can eject one of those devices and unplug it each time whenever you want to connect your digital camera, but that might involve turning your PC around and navigating through the nest of cables on the back.)

**Book VII
Chapter 4**

Partying with
USB, FireWire,
Thunderbolt, and
eSATA

PC power users eschew such hassles. Instead, buy a *hub,* which is a splitter box that turns one USB or FireWire port into multiple ports, as shown in Figure 4-1. (***Note:*** Don't confuse a USB/FireWire hub with a *network* hub, which is an entirely different beast.) Although using a hub fills a port, you gain four, six, or eight ports in the bargain (depending on the hub), and everything stays as convenient and plug-and-play as before. (It's engineering that's both simple and *sassy.*) A *powered* USB hub is a better choice than an unpowered hub because it can provide the AC current that many USB devices require to run.

Figure 4-1:
Power users
love USB
hubs.

Don't forget to check whether a peripheral has one (or more) daisy-chaining ports on the back that will allow you to connect another device. You can tell that a device is designed for daisy-chaining by checking whether it sports two ports of the same type (like a scanner that has two USB ports). If so, you should be able to daisy-chain additional devices. A series of daisy-chained devices will likely help you avoid buying a USB or FireWire hub because everything is still linked to one physical USB or FireWire port on your PC.

By using these methods, you can theoretically plug 63 devices into one FireWire port, 6 devices into one Thunderbolt port, and 127 devices into one USB port. Heck, not even James Bond can stack gadgets that high!

Installing a Port Card

Here's where the original modular design of the IBM PC (all those many, many moons ago) comes in handy. If your computer didn't come with eSATA, Thunderbolt, or FireWire ports, you'll find that adding new ports to your PC is as simple as plugging an adapter card into a slot in the back of your motherboard. A typical eSATA card costs around $50 US and gives you two eSATA ports. Follow these steps to do it the right way — once!

1. **Cover your work surface with several sheets of newspaper.**

2. **Turn off your PC, unplug it, and place it on top of the newspaper.**

3. **Remove the case screws and slide the case off, and put the screws aside in a bowl or cup.**

If you're unsure how to remove your PC's case, check the manual that accompanied your computer.

4. **To dissipate any static electricity, touch a metal surface before you handle your new adapter card or touch any circuitry inside the case.**

Yes, I know I keep haranguing you about static electricity — but it's important. I typically touch the metal chassis of the computer.

5. **Locate an adapter card slot of the proper length at the back of your computer case.**

You want to use a Peripheral Component Interconnect (PCI) slot, which is the standard adapter card connector in today's PCs. See Figure 4-2.

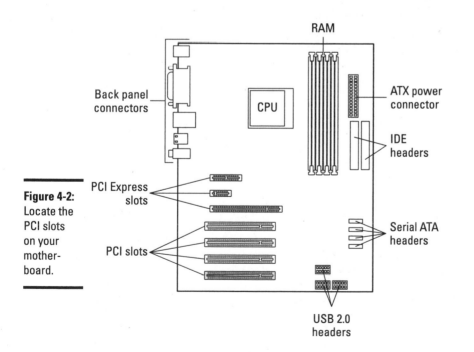

Figure 4-2:
Locate the PCI slots on your mother-board.

Book VII
Chapter 4

Partying with
USB, FireWire,
Thunderbolt, and
eSATA

6. **Remove the screw and the metal slot cover at the back of the case, as shown in Figure 4-3.**

   Because you don't need these items again, put them in your spare parts box.

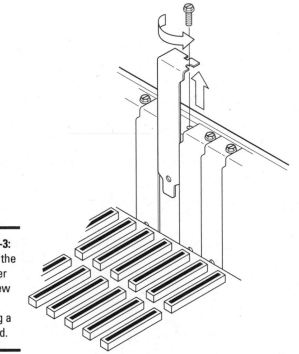

Figure 4-3: Remove the slot cover and screw before installing a new card.

7. **Pick up your port card by its top corners, and line up the connector on the bottom of the card with the slot on the motherboard.**

   The card's metal bracket should align with the open area created when you remove the slot cover from the back of your PC.

   Never try to force a connector into a slot designed for another type of card! For example, PCI Express video cards have different types of connectors, and they don't accept PCI cards. If you need help determining the location of your PCI card slots, check your motherboard manual.

8. **After the connector is aligned correctly (as shown in Figure 4-4), apply even pressure to the top of the card and push it down into the slot until the bracket is resting against the case.**

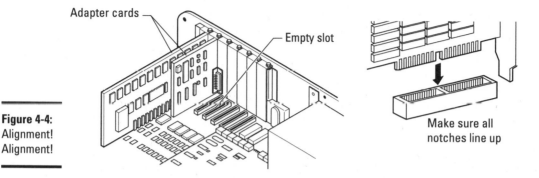

Adapter cards

Empty slot

Make sure all
notches line up

Figure 4-4:
Alignment!
Alignment!

9. Place the screw in the corresponding hole in the bracket and tighten it.

10. Place the cover back on your PC and replace the screws that you saved from Step 3.

11. Plug your PC back in and turn it on.

12. Run the installation disc that came with your port card or load the driver disc when prompted by Windows.

Don't forget to check the manufacturer's website for new Windows 8-specific drivers!

Book VII
Chapter 4

Partying with
USB, FireWire,
Thunderbolt, and
eSATA

Chapter 5: Pumping Up Your Sound and Video

In This Chapter

🖝 Selecting a sound card

🖝 Upgrading your video card

🖝 Installing your new toys

*T*echnology has advanced so much that (at last!) we've reached the point where the personal computer lives up to all that personal entertainment hoopla. You know — the idea that your PC is at the center of your gaming, audio, and TV environment. Or, as I've been putting it for the past couple of years (as another one of Mark's Maxims):

One box to rule them all and in the den to find them.™

(Man, I *love* that one. That's T-shirt material.)

However, putting your PC at the center of your digital lifestyle is a bit difficult if you're still stuck with a subpar sound card or if your computer's video card is more than two or three years old. Look at what you're missing out on: Closing your eyes and enjoying Dolby Surround sound with better than CD-quality audio, watching TV with TiVo-style control on your PC's crystal-clear LCD monitor, connecting your high-definition TV to your PC using an HDMI cable, listening to streaming Internet radio and playing online games where you can behead a super-realistic, 3D orc with extreme prejudice. This, ladies and gentlemen, is a good time to be alive!

If your system needs an audiovisual upgrade, you'll find what you need to know right here.

Sound Card Features to Covet

The first stop on your audiovisual upgrade tour is your PC's sound card (naturally). Shoppers, in this section, I show you what to look for when comparing sound cards.

3D spatial imaging

Most PC owners think of 3D sound as purely a gamer's feature, but nothing could be further from the truth. Sure, today's games are even more fun when you can use your ears as well as your eyes to locate your enemy, but 3D sound comes in handy when you're listening to audio CDs, watching movies, or playing digital audio files from your hard drive. With audio files and music, 3D spatial imaging can add an auditorium or concert hall effect, where the stereo separation is enhanced.

Surround sound support

With a Dolby Surround sound card and the right speakers, your PC can deliver Dolby Surround sound while you're listening to audio CDs or watching DVD movies using your PC. (For me, the biggest hassle wasn't the extra cost or upgrading my PC's sound card: It was finding the space for all five speakers around my already crowded computer desk!)

High-end Surround sound cards, such as the X-Fi Xtreme Audio card from Creative Labs, can deliver Dolby Digital 7.1 Surround sound, 24-bit/192 KHz audio playback (far superior in quality than even a commercial audio CD), and 3D imaging for your games — and all for about $50 (US) from most web stores. Life is truly good.

Figure 5-1 illustrates an old friend to any PC audiophile: A *subwoofer* adds realistic, deep subsonic bass to not only your music but also your games. A subwoofer is an important part of any 5.1 (or better) Surround sound system. Whether you're experiencing the grinding of tank treads or launching a Hellfire missile, a subwoofer provides the necessary sonic punch. Most subwoofers should be placed on the floor, where the vibration isn't a factor.

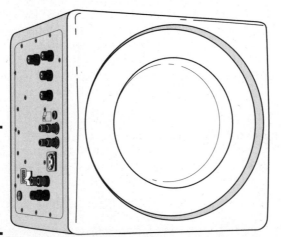

Figure 5-1:
All hail your subwoofer, King of the PC Speaker System.

MP3 encoding support

Although I discuss MP3 files in detail in Book VI, Chapter 2, I want to mention them here because anyone who's heavily into MP3 digital audio will really appreciate a sound card with built-in MP3 encoding and digital effects. That MP3 hardware feature relieves your PC's processor from the job of ripping and playing MP3 files so that you can rip music while you edit a digital photograph in Photoshop with nary a drop in performance. No stuttering audio or long delays, especially on older PCs.

Many hardware MP3 sound cards also allow you to introduce to the MP3 files you create the same concert hall environmental effect that I mention earlier in this chapter. (Now your garage band can claim to have played Carnegie Hall.)

SP/DIF ports

If you'd like to connect your PC to a home theater system, make sure the card you select offers this port — it provides the best possible digital connection (and therefore the maximum quality audio signal) based upon the source.

Game and FireWire ports

Many sound cards are equipped with a little something extra: a FireWire port or a joystick/gamepad port, which was once a dear friend of any PC game player (because it used to be the only way to hook up joysticks and external game controllers). Lately, most PC controllers have switched to the Universal Serial Bus (USB) port, but it's still a plus for a sound card to include a game port. Older game peripherals — many joysticks and flight throttles — don't work with USB, so it's a legacy thing. (Chapter 4 of this minibook delivers the goods on FireWire.)

MIDI ports

Before I move on, I have to address musicians and their Musical Instrument Digital Interface (MIDI) ports. You can use a sound card with standard MIDI ports to connect synthesizers and many different electronic musical instruments, such as drums and keyboards, to your computer. Most MIDI instruments now feature a USB port as well.

With a MIDI instrument connected, your computer can play MIDI music files on the instrument, or you can play the instrument and record the music as a MIDI file on your computer. Note, however, that today's sound cards can play MIDI music files without attaching instruments, so you don't have to buy a card with built-in MIDI ports just to play MIDI music files.

Shopping for a Monster Graphics Card

Having a terrific graphics card isn't all about blasting aliens to kingdom come. A fast 3D video card can speed up the display of digital video and even the operating system eye candy provided by Windows 7 and 8. In this section, I clue you in on what to look for when considering a video card upgrade.

Just say, "PCI Express"

Although today's video cards look like any other typical adapter cards, they usually fit only into a dedicated PCI Express video card slot, so check your motherboard manual or PC manual to make sure that your machine will accept a PCI Express video card. However, after you install a PCI Express video card, you enjoy the fastest possible video performance; if you're a hard-core gamer, I strongly recommend that any new machine you build or buy be equipped with a PCI Express video slot! (In fact, most high-performance motherboards now include a second — or even third — PCI Express slot, allowing you to use multiple video cards to catapult your gaming performance through the roof!

Rate the performance of a particular card while you're shopping by checking the box or the manufacturer's website for benchmark results that you can use to compare with other cards. Try the popular benchmark program 3DMark 11 ($20, from www.futuremark.com). You can also run games like Borderlands 2 or Call of Duty: Black Ops 2 and compare the maximum frames per second (fps) that the card can display. (The higher the frame rate, the better.) You can also find up-to-date reviews of the latest cards and video chipsets at Tom's Hardware on the web at www.tomshardware.com.

Exploring the differences between chipsets

You won't find many differences among *chipsets,* which are the separate graphics processing unit (GPU) "brains" that power today's top 3D video cards. Allow me to explain: The two major players in the PC video card chipset battle are

✦ **NVIDIA:** The cutting-edge crew at NVIDIA (www.nvidia.com) has produced some of the fastest video cards for the PC in recent years — currently, they offer the GeForce series of processors.

✦ **AMD:** ATI Technologies is now a division of AMD (www.amd.com), but the company has been producing popular video chipsets for well over a decade now, including the current AMD Radeon line of performance graphics processors.

Here's the payoff for you, the consumer: The fastest offerings from either company deliver more performance than PC gamers are likely to need for at least six months. However, a powerful video card also appeals to videographers and photographers who demand super–high-resolution images — Photoshop, Lightroom, and Premiere are perfect examples of programs that will take everything your card has and then some, especially on multiple-monitor setups.

Other video card features that you'll want

Naturally, you can evaluate more than just chipsets and connectors when comparing video cards. Keep an eye out for these features and specifications while you shop:

✦ **Onboard random access memory (RAM):** Like your motherboard, your video card carries its own supply of memory. Today's cards typically have anywhere from 128MB to 2GB of memory. Again, the general rule is to buy a card with as much onboard RAM as possible. More RAM equals higher resolutions, more colors onscreen and the best special effects.

✦ **Driver and standards support:** Any PC video card should fully support the Microsoft DirectX video standards — now at DirectX 11.0 for Windows 7 and 8 (or DirectX 10.0 for Windows Vista). Gamers will also appreciate robust *OpenGL* support (an open video standard that's becoming very popular in 3D action games). Support for these standards should be listed on the product's box.

✦ **Maximum resolution:** The higher the resolution a card can produce, the more your monitor can display at once — and not just in games, but documents, digital photographs, and your Windows Desktop. For example, I like to write manuscripts at a resolution of 1152 x 864 rather than 1024 x 768 because I can see more of the page in Microsoft Word without scrolling. Today's cards can reach truly epic resolutions, such as 2560 x 1600; personally, however, I don't work at such stratospheric resolutions often because a few hours of work usually leaves me with eyestrain (and possibly a headache).

The maximum resolution you can display on your system also depends on the monitor you're using. Therefore, if you upgrade to the latest video card but you're still using an old clunker of a monitor with a maximum resolution of 1024 x 768, you're stuck there. (Time to invest in a new display.) For more about your monitor, see Book I, Chapter 1.

✦ **Video capture and TV output:** A card with these features can create digital video footage from an analog TV signal (that's the *video capture* part) and transfer the image you see on your monitor to a TV, VCR, or camcorder (the *TV output* part). If you want to create video CDs or DVDs from your home movies on VHS tape, spend a little extra on a video capture/TV output card.

✦ **TV tuner:** A card with a built-in TV tuner can turn your PC into a TV set, including giving you the ability to pause and replay programs on the fly (like how a TiVo unit works with a regular TV). You can use a traditional high-definition digital TV antenna or connect the card to your cable or satellite system, as shown in Figure 5-2. Just don't let your boss know that the new video card that the company bought gives you the ability to watch your favorite soaps in a window on your Desktop . . . you're supposed to be working.

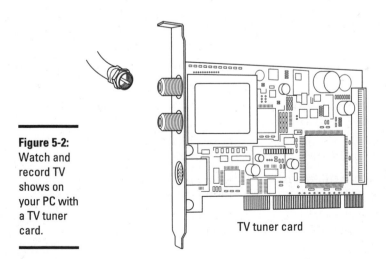

Figure 5-2:
Watch and record TV shows on your PC with a TV tuner card.

TV tuner card

✦ **Multiple monitor support:** Most new video cards allow you to connect two monitors to one card. This is considered a must-have for video editing and 3D or CAD work, and hardcore gamers crave that extra real estate as well. You can either see two separate Desktops or make the two monitors into a seamless Desktop. Imagine the size of your Windows workspace when it's spread across two displays!

✦ **MPEG hardware support:** Finally, I describe digital video — which, as you can read about in earlier chapters of this book, is typically stored in MPEG, AVI, or MOV formats. (The most popular is the MPEG format.) Without the *compression* that these video formats offer (which shrinks the size of the digital video file), you would never squeeze a full-length movie on a single DVD. Although your PC can use software to *encode* (create a compressed MPEG file) and *decode* (read a compressed MPEG file) MPEG files on your hard drive or DVDs, a video card with built-in encoding and decoding features can really speed up the process. This hardware support is particularly valuable if you're going to do serious video editing on your PC because you cut down the amount of time required to save your movies to disk.

Installing Sound and Video Cards

Installing a sound card or video card is much like adding any other adapter card to your PC. If you're installing a sound card, make sure that you connect the audio cable from your DVD-ROM/Blu-Ray drive (see Step 5 in the following step list); if you're installing a video card, make sure that you pick the right PCI Express slot (see Step 7).

**Book VII
Chapter 5**

**Pumping Up Your
Sound and Video**

Follow these steps:

1. **Cover your work surface with several sheets of newspaper.**

2. **Shut down your PC, unplug it from all external connections, and place it on top of the newspaper.**

3. **Remove the screws on the back (or sides) of the case and slide the case off, saving the screws for later.**

Find a bowl (glass or wood; not plastic or metal) to sequester your screws. Nothing worse than a runaway, AWOL screw.

4. **To dissipate static electricity, touch a metal surface before handling any cards or touching your PC's motherboard.**

For example, touch the PC's metal chassis. I shudder to think of what I'll do if anyone develops a fiberglass computer.

To you, it's just a momentary shock. To your PC hardware, however, that static electricity can zap components into oblivion! *Always* ground yourself by touching a metal surface before handling any hardware, including adapter cards and memory modules!

5. **If you're installing a new sound card, check for a thin audio cable connected from your old sound card (or a connector on the motherboard, if your PC has an integrated sound card) to your DVD-ROM or Blu-Ray drive; if your existing sound card has such a cable, disconnect the cable from the old sound card or motherboard connector.**

6. **Remove the screw holding the adapter card you're upgrading, and pull upward to remove it.**

Don't forget to put the screw in your spare parts box and put the old adapter card in an antistatic bag for safekeeping. (I use the bag left behind by the new card.)

Some video card slots have plastic tabs that act as a locking mechanism. Just bend the tab gently with your finger, and you should be able to remove the existing card.

7. **Locate the adapter card slot that matches the card you're installing.**

A PCI Express video adapter requires a dedicated PCI Express 16 slot. (See Figure 5-3.) On the other hand, a standard PCI sound card should fit in any open PCI slot. Naturally, if the upgrade card uses the same type of slot as the card that it's replacing, use the empty slot you just opened up.

Figure 5-3:
Locate the
PCI Express
slot.

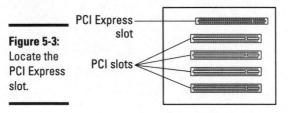

8. **Pick up the adapter card by its top corners and line up the bottom connector on the card with the slot on the motherboard, as shown in Figure 5-4.**

Make sure that the card's metal bracket aligns properly with the opening in the back of the PC.

9. **After the card is aligned, apply even pressure to the top of the card and push it down into the slot.**

10. **Place the screw in the corresponding hole in the bracket and tighten it.**

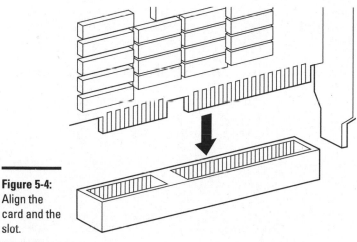

Figure 5-4:
Align the card and the slot.

**Book VII
Chapter 5**

Pumping Up Your
Sound and Video

11. **If you're installing a sound card and you disconnected an audio cable from the old card (or a connector on the motherboard), reconnect the cable from your drive to the new card.**

Check the manual for the card to determine where the optical drive audio connector is located; this is a standard connector, so it should be easy to track down.

12. **If you've installed a video card with a TV tuner, connect the cable from your satellite or cable box to the card (refer to Figure 5-2).**

13. **Place the cover back on your PC and replace the screws that you saved from Step 3.**

14. **Plug your PC back in, reconnect all those cables, and turn it on.**

For video cards, you should immediately be able to gauge the success of your work — if there's an image on your monitor, the installation was a success! However, don't be alarmed if the resolution is completely wrong, and don't adjust your monitor yet — Windows will likely be able to return to your previous resolution once you install the drivers for your new card.

15. **Run the installation disc that came with your upgrade card or load the driver disc when prompted by Windows.**

For sound cards, you'll likely hear nothing until you install your new card's drivers. Reboot after the installation is complete, and listen for Windows to make sure it greets you with its welcome sound. You can also run Windows Media Player and play an MP3 file to verify things are working. Your sound card should also come with an audio configuration program that you can use to test and fine-tune your new ear candy — check your documentation to see what free stuff you got, and where it was installed!

These steps should do it for you. If you need a little more help, I heartily recommend my profusely illustrated book, *Build Your Own PC Do-It-Yourself For Dummies* (published by John Wiley & Sons, Inc.), for detailed instructions and even more photos to see this upgrade in process. My book even has a companion DVD with the same steps, so you can see me do this live!

Book VIII
Home Networking

Visit www.dummies.com/extras/pcsaio for more on creating a VPN connection in Windows 8.

Contents at a Glance

Chapter 1: Do I Really Need a Network?

In This Chapter

✔ Evaluating the advantages of a network

✔ Connecting to other computers and devices

✔ Selecting networking hardware and software

Networking is neat stuff: The ability to copy or edit a document that's on another computer halfway down the hall is invaluable, whether that hallway is in a business or your own home. (Even a home office like mine, where six computers constantly vie for my attention in the same room, benefits from a network. Although the computers are only a few feet apart, moving 60GB worth of data between them would be no small feat without a common network connection.)

However, not everyone with multiple computers *needs* a network. For example, if you don't often exchange information between your computers, you can get by using a "sneaker net" or a simple USB flash drive. However, if you regularly need to share files, applications, and an Internet connection, you'll want a network. (I think you know which course of action I usually recommend. After all, look at the rest of this chapter and this minibook!)

Here, I cover what a network can do for you, which hardware and software you need, and how much work is involved. Later chapters in this minibook fill in the blanks (and compare the pros and cons of wired versus wireless), but after you read this introduction, you'll know whether a network is worth your effort.

Discovering the Advantages of a Network

If you've never used a network to link multiple computers, you might not realize which applications are network ready. Here's a quick list of the most common uses for a network.

File transfer

There's no faster method of moving files between computers than a network connection. And network file transfers are *transparent* to the person making the transfer, which means that you don't have to do anything special to transfer files between computers on a network. You can just drag and drop files as usual or use your favorite file management application to copy or move files between computers on the network, and Windows acts like you would expect. I like the Total Commander file management tool, as shown in Figure 1-1. To try out this excellent piece of shareware, visit `www.ghisler.com`. With Total Commander, it's a cinch to compare the contents of two different drives or folders, and the list display format can pack the maximum possible number of filenames onto your monitor. Copying or moving files 'twixt the panes is as simple as selecting and clicking a button.

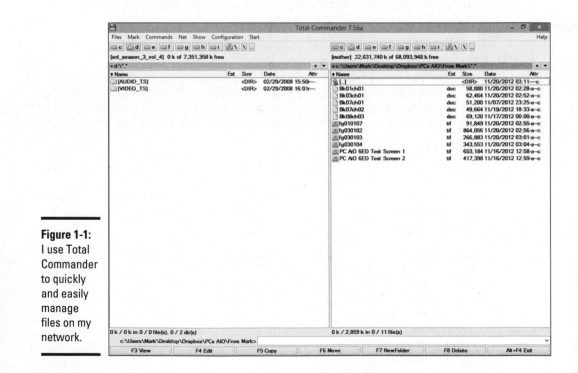

Figure 1-1:
I use Total Commander to quickly and easily manage files on my network.

However, you certainly don't want just *anyone* transferring files to and from your PC — or, for that matter, even accessing your PC over the network. To help preserve security, Windows 8, 7, Vista, and XP make certain that only the users and PCs with the proper rights can transfer files over your network. I discuss network security in greater detail in Chapter 5 of this very minibook.

If you're running more than one PC with Windows 7 or 8 on your network, you can also take advantage of the HomeGroup feature, which helps automate the configuration of a secure file and printer-sharing network. It takes only a few clicks of the mouse to take advantage of HomeGroup, and I show you how in Book II, Chapter 4.

Sharing that-there Internet

Another popular networking benefit is the ability of one computer to share a single Internet connection with all other computers on a network. Typically, this arrangement works best with a broadband connection technology like a digital subscriber line (DSL) or cable, but it's possible with a dialup connection as well.

You can share a connection by using one of these methods:

+ **Software:** Use the built-in Internet Connection Sharing within Windows 8, as I demonstrate in Chapter 4 of this minibook.

+ **Hardware:** Add an Internet sharing device (such as a network router), which usually comes with other features, such as a built-in firewall. I cover hardware Internet sharing in Chapter 4 of this minibook.

One word: Games!

What's that you're saying, Bunky? You're tired of predictable computer opponents in your favorite games? Hordes of enemies in that zombie game that you can handle in your sleep? How about timid enemy monsters that don't attack you or ambush your character in Borderlands 2 (as shown in Figure 1-2)?

Well, forget those lazy "artificial intelligence" tactics because in network *multiplayer mode,* you fight real human beings — the treacherous, backstabbing kind (which, oddly enough, usually turn out to be your best friends). Whenever possible, I try to attend *LAN parties,* get-togethers where multiplayer games are the featured attractions. Your host might have all the PCs and network hardware necessary for 8 or 16 people, but I usually bring my desktop or laptop computer so that I can sit down and plug in with a minimum of effort.

Figure 1-2:
A favorite
multiplayer
network
game,
Border-
lands 2.

Shared documents and applications

Of course, a document that's handed from person to person on a CD or flash drive is technically shared, but is that really a convenient method of working on a document together? (To this day, PC hardware technicians and software developers call this antiquated kind of foot-based transfer a *sneakernet.*) Anyway, forget wearing out your shoe leather just to hand off a document for the next person's comments — today's office workgroup relies on the company network to share documents and common applications the *right* way!

After you network your computers, any PC on your network can copy or open a document on another computer: that is, *if* the owner of the PC being accessed has been granted the proper rights to that file or to the folder where it's stored. For example, say you have a Word document that others need to edit, but you want to keep it on your hard drive: You can move that document to a shared folder. Others on the network can open the document within Word from their computers, just as though it were on their local machines.

And, if that's not *sassy* enough, consider the fact that Bob over in accounting (or your daughter in her bedroom) might be using an application that you don't have. If that application has been written for network use, you can run it on your computer remotely over the network! This type of program is a *shared application,* and it's the neatest thing since sliced cheese.

Read the details on both shared documents and shared applications in Chapter 2 of this minibook.

What Can I Connect To?

A surprising number of objects on the planet have network ports or wireless network cards. Here's a list of the network-savvy stuff I've used:

✦ **Other PCs:** The most common connection on a Windows network is to other PCs — some of which are standard desktop and notebook PCs, and others which are specialized network *servers* that perform only one task. (One example is a *file server,* which is used like a mega-hard drive that everyone on the network can access.) A PC running Windows 8 makes a great dedicated media server, storing your digital photographs, music, and video within networked "easy reach" — any other computer on your network can access those files quickly and conveniently.

Although HomeGroup is a great way to configure your network if *all* of your PCs are running Windows 7 or 8, other PCs on your network running Windows XP or Windows Vista can still become part of the family! Windows 8 networking is backward-compatible with older versions of Windows.

✦ **Macintosh and Linux computers:** Your network need not be a snobby Windows-only country club; invite the neighbors to join in! Macs running Mac OS X can easily plug right in with a minimum of fuss, as can those Linux folks with the beards and suspenders. Of course, you can't run a Mac program on a PC, but — and this is a winner — many applications are available in versions for both operating systems, and they can share the same document! The best examples are Microsoft Office and Adobe Photoshop, which are available in both Mac and PC versions. Word and Excel on both operating systems can open and edit the same Office documents.

Speaking of Mac OS X, I'm also the proud father of the *OS X Mountain Lion All-in-One For Dummies* (John Wiley & Sons, Inc.). And, yes, I really do own both PCs and Macs, and I take advantage of both operating systems' offerings on my same office network. Anyway, if you find this tome helpful and you know a Mac owner who's using OS X Mountain Lion, please drop 'em a line and recommend the OSXMLAIOFD! (How's *that* for an abbreviation?)

✦ Cell phones and **Personal digital assistants (PDAs):** With the right adapter, your cell phone, Palm handheld, or Pocket PC can join in the fun.

✦ **Shared network hardware:** Some shared hardware actually resides within a PC on the network (like an internal hard drive or DVD-ROM drive that you selected to be "visible" and accessible on the network); other network hardware devices work as standalone units (like an Internet sharing device, which is a box by itself).

✦ **Network printers:** Finally, a shared network printer can be connected to a PC on the network. Or, if you have enough pocket change, you can buy a standalone network printer that has its own network card.

Of course, this list is incomplete because it's constantly growing, but suffice it to say that a network usually includes more than just a smattering of desktop and laptop PCs.

What Hardware Do I Need?

The hardware basics that you need for a simple network include

✦ **A network adapter card or PC card:** Each computer on your network requires either a network adapter card (for a desktop) or a PC card (for a laptop). These cards can accept either a wired connection or a wireless connection. Naturally, if your desktop or laptop has wired or wireless hardware built in, you don't need to add a card — instead, smile quietly to yourself in a contented and smug manner. If you have to shop for a wired or wireless adapter for your PC, however, I don't leave you stranded: Chapters 2 and 3 in this minibook discuss what you need.

Naturally, the adapter card you buy will come with installation instructions — but if you'd like a hands-on guide while elbow-deep in your computer, my best-selling book *Build Your Own PC Do-It-Yourself For Dummies* (John Wiley & Sons, Inc.) illustrates the installation process (along with many other hardware chores you encounter throughout this book)!

✦ **A network router or switch:** I describe these black boxes in depth in Chapter 2 of this minibook. For now, I'll just say that they allow you to connect multiple computers to the same network. Some routers and switches are wireless, so no cables are necessary.

✦ **Cabling:** If you're not going the wireless route, you need an Ethernet cable for each computer you add to the network. Again, more on this in Chapter 2 of this minibook.

The hardware that I list here would be used in a standard Ethernet network, but remember that other types of network technologies might use your home's AC wiring or telephone jacks (which I cover in Chapter 3 of this mini-book). You can also network two computers by using special Universal Serial Bus (USB) and FireWire cables although they're no substitute for the convenience and compatibility of an Ethernet network; they're simply for transferring files in a single session.

You might be able to buy all these hardware toys in a single box — *a network kit* — which is a great choice for a home or small-office network with four or fewer PCs. (Plus, the documentation is typically pretty well written.)

What Software Do 1 Need?

If each of your PCs will be running any version of Windows 98 or later, you have all the operating system software you need for a home network. (Thanks, Microsoft!) However, you might also need

+ **Drivers for your network adapter card or PC card:** The manufacturer of your network card provides you with the drivers that Windows needs during installation, but don't forget to check the manufacturer's website for updated drivers.

+ **Network management software:** The administrator of a larger network (I consider a network of ten or more computers to be a *larger* network) will likely buy extra software to monitor network traffic and optimize network hardware although the extra software isn't necessary for a simple network.

+ **Network-ready applications:** As I mention earlier in this chapter, network applications can include productivity suites (such as Office), fax software, and workgroup applications (such as Lotus Notes) that provide a common calendar and e-mail system.

Chapter 2: Ethernet to the Rescue

In This Chapter

✔ **Understanding how Ethernet works**

✔ **Gathering the various pieces o' hardware**

✔ **Considering cables**

✔ **Configuring Windows 7 for your network**

✔ **Putting shared folders to work**

✔ **Configuring a network printer**

✔ **Connecting a switch to the Internet**

✔ **Troubleshooting your network**

This is it, my friend: the chapter with the bravado and the chutzpah to show you how to set up a home- or small-office wired network in Windows 8! Setting up a network gives you many benefits, including saving money by sharing resources (such as printers and an Internet connection) and the added convenience of file sharing.

You'll find that a *working* network (note that I stress the word *working*) quickly becomes as essential as Tabasco sauce or [insert name of your favorite condiment here]. By the way, if you find the word *working* to be more elusive than you first expected, I include a section at the end of this chapter that highlights common problems experienced by folks running their own network — as well as several possible solutions for each one, of course.

After your network is purring as smoothly as the proverbial kitten, you'll walk proudly to the closest person on the planet and proclaim proudly, "I am . . . a *network administrator!*" (Feel free to throw confetti or have a T-shirt made. If you like, send me an e-mail message at mark@mlcbooks.com — use the subject line "Ohmygoodnessitworks" — and we can celebrate together.)

A Quickie Ethernet Primer

No, don't close this book! Of all the supposed technowizard technologies connected with PCs, Ethernet networking is the easiest to master. Windows has come a long way in taming the home networking beast. Sure, you used to need a gold medal in the Tech Olympics to install a small home network, but that was in the days of DOS and Windows 3.1. We've come a long way, baby.

In fact, Ethernet has been around since the days of stone-tipped spears. As the first widely used network structure, it's still the most popular structure for homes as well as offices with around 25 PCs or fewer. Sure, faster networking designs exist these days, but old faithful Ethernet is also the cheapest to set up and maintain, and it's directly supported within all flavors of Windows.

So how does Ethernet work? Surprisingly, it's much like ham radio. A PC that wants to share data (as in moving or copying a file or sending and receiving stuff from the Internet) broadcasts that data across the network cabling in discrete bursts called *packets*. Each packet is marked with an address (much like how an e-mail message always has a To address) of the receiving computer.

When the PC with the matching address receives the packet across the network (along with tons of other packets bound for other locations), it processes the packet; other computers simply ignore any packets that aren't addressed to them. Figure 2-1 represents an Ethernet network at its best.

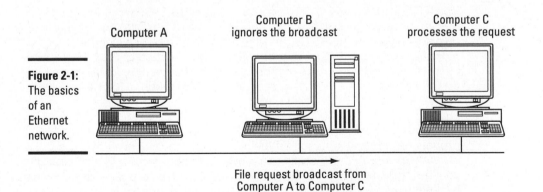

Figure 2-1: The basics of an Ethernet network.

Computer A

Computer B ignores the broadcast

Computer C processes the request

File request broadcast from Computer A to Computer C

This process sounds just nifty, but here's the catch: If two computers on your network try to broadcast packets at the same time, a network collision occurs, and everything stops until one computer successfully gets its data across the network. Collisions slow down the transfer of data, and that's why Ethernet networks are slower than other types of networks. (Of course, you see far fewer conflicts with fewer machines, so if you have only 4 PCs on your network, you typically get great performance. Only when 25 PCs are all trying to talk to each other at one time do conflicts start slowing things down dramatically.)

The first step when installing a small network is to create a chart that lists which computers need to be connected and where they are, plus the approximate distances between all the players. Because of the size limitations of this chapter, I can't provide you with a complete discussion of how to plan the cabling for your network — that's a book in itself. In fact, that book is *Networking All-in-One For Dummies*, 5th Edition, written by Doug Lowe (John Wiley & Sons, Inc.), which expands on all the basics I mention in this chapter.

The Hardware You Need

One benefit of Ethernet networks is their simplicity. You don't need a degree in Advanced Thakamology to install your network, and (because today's PCs come equipped with built-in Ethernet ports) you can put four PCs in a simple Ethernet network for the cost of a few cables.

In this section, I discuss the basic hardware requirements of any small Ethernet network.

Cables

In books I've written that cover Ethernet networking, I discuss two different kinds of cabling that connect computer to computer (or computer to network device):

✦ **Coaxial (coax):** The same type of cable that's used to connect your TV to your cable box. Coax is thick stuff and not easily routed or hidden. Also, each end of a coax Ethernet network must have a terminator to mark the end of the network circuit, which is a hassle (a small one, granted, but a hassle nonetheless).

✦ **Twisted pair:** Looks almost exactly like telephone wire or the cable that runs between a PC's dialup modem and the telephone wall jack. Twisted pair is easier to hide and much easier to route. (Figure 2-2 illustrates the connector — an RJ-45 connector — for a twisted pair cable.) The downside to using a twisted pair Ethernet network is that you need a *switch,* which acts as a central connection point. (See how it's used in Figure 2-3.) However, twisted pair cabling is much cheaper overall than coaxial cable.

Figure 2-2:
Most network techs think this RJ-45 connector is rather attractive.

RJ-45

I used to cover coax cabling, but in this book, I cover only twisted pair cabling. It's by far less expensive and easier to install, which makes it the most popular standard — and that explains why Ethernet networks that use coaxial cabling are rapidly disappearing from the face of the globe. In fact, you have to go out of your way to find a late-model network interface card (NIC) that has a coax connector on it. (As the MCP said so eloquently in the classic movie *Tron,* "End of line.")

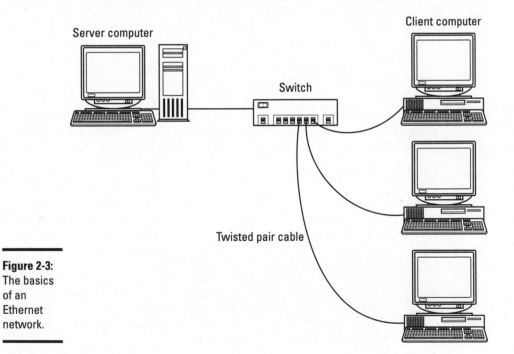

Server computer

Client computer

Switch

Twisted pair cable

Figure 2-3:
The basics of an Ethernet network.

If you would rather eschew cables altogether (well, almost altogether), consider a wireless network. Although it's a bit slower, you have freedom of movement undreamed of by the wired crowd. Heck, you could even throw caution utterly to the wind and get a wireless switch or router that can provide both wired *and* wireless connections. (In fact, alternative wired networks can use your home or office's existing telephone or AC power lines. No, really!) I cover all these marvels of wireless (or almost wireless) networking in Chapter 3 of this minibook.

Switches

As I mention earlier in this chapter, a *switch* is essentially just an overgrown connection box, linking (via cabling) each computer on your network to all other network computers and peripherals, like a printer. It's about as visually interesting as a shoebox. (There's not much need to include a picture in this chapter. Imagine the most boring, nondescript box that you can, add a few lights and several RJ-45 jacks, and that's a switch.) On the inside, a switch prevents those dastardly collisions that I discuss earlier in this chapter. In effect, a switch narrows the broadcast of a packet to only the PC that needs it.

Most Internet sharing devices and routers designed to work with broadband connections have built-in switches — just keep in mind that you need some sort of switch for a twisted pair network. Switches are pretty inexpensive — how much you pay depends on how many ports the switch provides, ranging from about $50–$200 US.

Switches have virtually replaced the earlier, less-efficient Ethernet hub. Always choose a switch over an Ethernet hub. (I mention hubs in case you run across one whilst scavenging or encounter one on eBay.)

NICs

You need a *network interface card* (NIC) for each computer on your network. If your desktop or laptop PC doesn't have a built-in NIC, an internal adapter card is probably the best choice, but installing a NIC doesn't necessarily have to involve opening your PC's case. You can get a Personal Computer Memory Card International Association (PCMCIA; or PC Card) NIC for your laptop, and other network adapters can be connected through a Universal Serial Bus (USB) port. However, you probably don't need to buy a separate NIC for your PC because virtually all PCs now include built-in network connectors. (Check your PC's manual or look for a port labeled Ethernet 10/100 or Network on the back of the computer.)

Book VIII Chapter 2

Ethernet to the Rescue

NICs are rated by the speed of the network. Most home networks use a 10/100 NIC (which means that your network can operate at either 10 Mbps or 100 Mbps), which sets you back about $25–$30 US. The third speed — Gigabit Ethernet — runs at a whopping 1000 Mbps, but you might not need that much throughput unless you regularly transfer huge multigigabyte files betwixt computers. (Gigabit hardware used to be as expensive as a meeting with a good lawyer, but prices for this faster equipment are now on a par with 10/100 hardware.) Well-known Ethernet device manufacturers include D-Link, NETGEAR, and Linksys.

When shopping for your card, check the manufacturer's website and verify the drivers the card uses. The card should support at least Windows XP, Vista, and 7/8. (For me, the value of a NIC lies in direct proportion to its compatibility.) Also, check how often those drivers are updated; a two-year-old driver is not a good sign. In general, most manufacturers display certification statements (both on the box and on the company's website) guaranteeing that a NIC will work with specific operating systems.

Doing the Cable Dance

You have far fewer hassles when installing a twisted pair network as opposed to a coaxial network, as I mention earlier in this chapter. But even when you consider that the cables are easier to handle, I still make — from experience — a number of time-tested recommendations. You should always

✦ **Draft someone to help.** If you're wiring a small office, enlist the help of a steadfast friend (as a gofer, general cable handyperson, and sympathetic ear).

✦ **Buy premade cables!** Building a cable yourself is like cutting a diamond yourself: It can be done, but you had better be experienced or else you'll ruin a perfectly good, well, length of cable. Plus, first-timers can very easily create a cable that *appears* to be correct but doesn't work or that introduces all sorts of spurious problems later on that will be practically impossible to track down. (Can you say "electrical short"? I knew you could.) Instead, do what I do (and what everyone else who has already built one or two small networks does): Walk into your local computer store or online web shop and buy premade cables in the lengths you need.

✦ **Buy extra cables.** Having a few spares never hurts. Hey, they're cheap. And buying cables that are at least a foot or two longer than what you think you'll need is a wise idea.

+ **Test a cable before installing it.** Of course, you can buy a twisted pair cable tester (usually called a *remote cable tester*), but for those with lives outside of networking, simply connect the cable between your switch and a laptop to check it.

+ **Consider pets!** Does Fluffy spend time in your home office unattended? Then prepare for the likelihood of chewed network cabling. (This can *really* test the relationship between pet and person.) To avoid these moments, use cable ties and anchors to run your Ethernet cabling underneath desktops and above the floor level whenever possible.

+ **Avoid exposed cable.** Make sure that your cables are well out of reach of clumsy feet. Also, never cover a cable with tape or a rug where it can become a victim of foot traffic. The stress on the connectors and the wear from contact will destroy even the best cable over time and will likely result in eventual network errors.

Don't forget that a switch is a powered device, so it needs to be located close to an AC outlet.

Building a home? Now is the time to consider running your Ethernet cabling, at the same time your telephone cabling and AC wiring is installed. (Go with Gigabit Ethernet Cat6 cabling, and you'll thank me later.)

Configuring Windows 8 for Your Network

After your NICs are installed, the cabling is in place, and everything's plugged in, you're ready to flip that big Frankenstein-style leaf switch and start networking — and that's done from within Windows 8. In this section, I discuss what every home "network administrator" should know.

Your network allows you to share files and printers with other computers using the network, but it can also be configured to share an Internet connection with those computers. What you decide to share is up to you, as the administrator of your network. (I cover sharing your Internet connection in Chapter 4 of this minibook.)

Ah, sweet DHCP

You know, few acronyms in the computer world make me genuinely smile every time I see them. There's BBS (bulletin board system), of course. TWAIN (which most people think means *technology without an interesting name*) isn't even an acronym! It refers to a poem by Kipling; you know, "and never the twain shall meet." (It's not often that I get to quote Kipling.) But in networking, folks hold a fond spot in their hearts for *DHCP,* which stands for Dynamic Host Configuration Protocol.

What's so uplifting about a networking standard? It's the *dynamic* part. You see, DHCP was developed to automatically assign Internet Protocol (IP) addresses to the computers on your network. A computer's *IP address* is the address I mention at the beginning of the chapter: It's a unique number that identifies the specific PC on the network.

In days of yore, whoever set up a network had to keep track of which IP addresses were assigned to which computers. If a number was assigned twice, all sorts of carnage broke loose (at least on those two machines). A device with DHCP, such as an Internet sharing device or a PC acting as an Internet connection server, automatically assigns a number whenever needed.

If you're already using an Internet sharing device (such as a cable modem or digital subscriber line [DSL] Internet router that has DHCP built in) or a switch with DHCP built in and a connection port for your modem, you need to follow the steps in that device's manual. That's because you don't need a PC to act as the DHCP host for your network. I cover Internet connection sharing in Chapter 4 of this minibook.

Setting up the host

To set up a network under Windows 8 using DHCP and a shared Internet connection — where your DSL or cable modem connects directly to the PC — you need to configure settings on that PC. (That lucky computer becomes your Internet *host,* providing the DHCP functionality for your network. The other computers that connect to the host are *clients.*)

If your host PC is using a NIC to connect to a DSL or cable modem (as most do) and the switch *doesn't* accept a direct connection to your modem, *you need a second NIC installed in that computer* so that you can connect it to the switch! (Take a break and read the section "Using a Standard Switch with a Cable or DSL Modem," toward the end of this chapter, before you proceed. I explain things there.)

Ready to go? Follow these steps:

1. **Display the Charms bar, click Search and then click Settings. Type** Network **into the Search box.**

   Make certain you're using an Administrator-level user account, so that you'll have full rights to set things up. (Simply log in using the account that you used to install Windows 8, and you'll be using an Administrator account.)

2. **Click the Network and Sharing Center button in the Search results pane to display the window you see in Figure 2-4.**

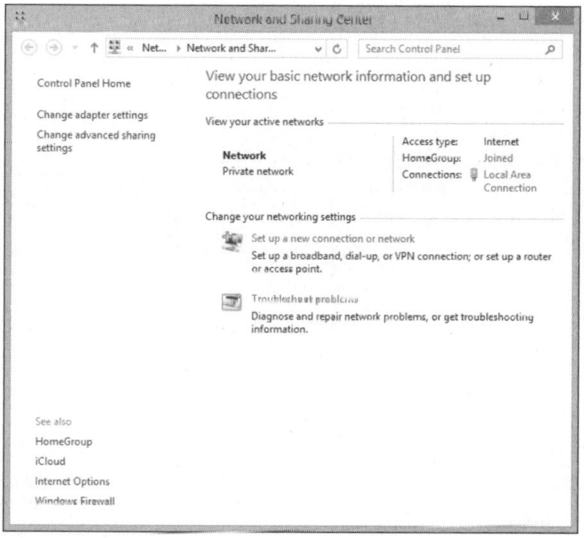

Figure 2-4: Displaying the existing network connection on my host PC.

Make sure that all networking hardware has been installed, connected, and turned on.

3. **Click the Connections link for your Internet connection.**

   Typically, this reads *Ethernet.* Windows 8 displays the Status dialog box for your Internet connection.

4. **Click the Properties button.**

5. **Click the Sharing tab.**

   To see the Sharing tab, you'll need a second NIC, as I explain above. Figure 2-5 illustrates the Sharing tab.

6. **Select the Allow Other Network Users to Connect through This Computer's Internet connection check box.**

   To maintain control of your shared Internet connection on the host PC, click the Allow Other Network Users to Control or Disable the Shared Internet Connection check box to disable it. If you leave this check box enabled, client PCs will be able to turn off your shared Internet connection — something you generally don't want.

Book VIII Chapter 2

Ethernet to the Rescue

7. **Click OK to save your changes, and then click Close on the Status dialog box.**

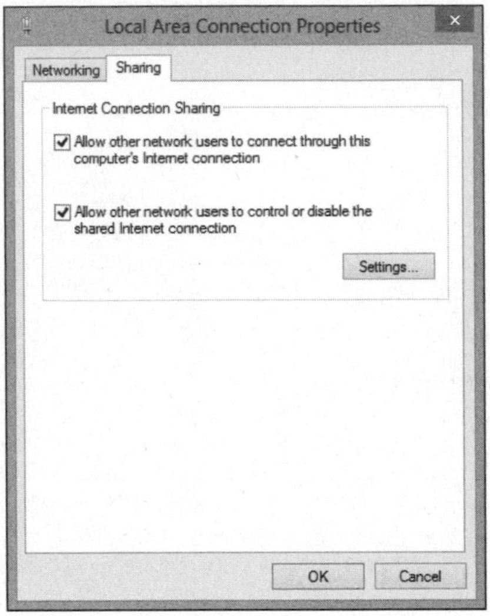

Figure 2-5:
The Sharing tab displays the Internet Sharing check box.

Setting up the clients

After the host is configured, it's ready to accept connections from the other computers on your network. However, you also have to configure each of those PCs as network clients. Yep, that's where the buzz phrase *client/server* comes from. The good news is that you use your friend the Network and Sharing Center again, and the process is pretty similar.

Again, make sure that the host computer is connected to the Internet, and reboot each of the client PCs before continuing. Then follow these steps on each PC running Windows 8 that needs to join the network crowd:

1. **Display the Charms bar, click Search, and then click Settings. Type** Network **into the Search box.**

   Again, be sure you're using an Administrator-level user account.

2. **Click the Network and Sharing Center button in the Search results pane to display the Network and Sharing Center window.**

3. **Click the Local Area Connection link for this client PC to display the Status dialog box, and then click the Properties button.**

   Windows 8 displays the Properties dialog box for your network connection.

4. **If the Internet Protocol Version 4 (TCP/IPv4) entry appears in the item list, click it to select it, and then click the Properties button to display the settings you see in Figure 2-6.**

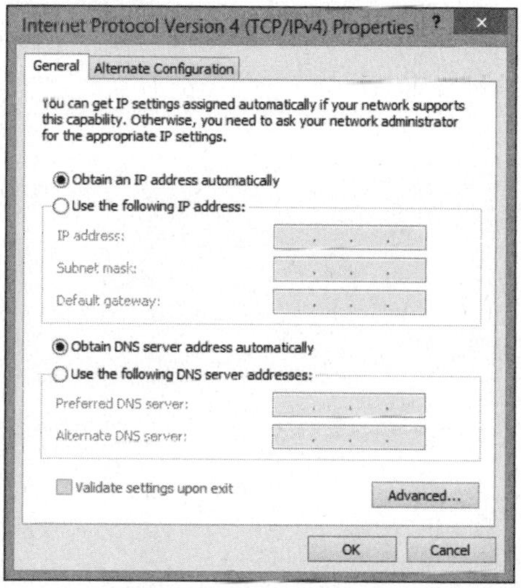

Figure 2-6: Configuring a client PC for that DHCP goodness.

5. **Select the Obtain an IP Address Automatically radio button.**

6. **Select the Obtain DNS Server Address Automatically radio button.**

7. **Click OK to save your changes.**

8. **If the Internet Protocol Version 6 (TCP/IPv6) entry appears in the item list, click it to select it and click Properties.**

9. **Select the Obtain an IP Address Automatically radio button.**

10. **Select the Obtain DNS Server Address Automatically radio button.**

11. **Click OK to save your changes.**

12. **Click OK in the Properties dialog box to return to the Connections window.**

13. **Click Close and restart the client PC.**

When it completes the boot process, the added client PC should be a member of your network family. Now you can proceed to the next client PC and repeat the procedure.

Browsing the neighborhood

After you set up your network, you can easily see which other PCs are available. Windows 8 power users call this activity *browsing* your network, where you saunter around and admire what's connected. From the Charms bar, click Search and click Settings, and then type **Network** into the Search box. Click the View Network Computers and Devices button that appears in the Search results pane to display each of the computers and recognized devices in your networked surroundings (as shown in Figure 2-7).

Figure 2-7:
The
Windows
8 Network
window.

 Whoops! I can hear all sorts of irate Windows 8 faithful growling in irritation, especially if you're working on a large home or office network with a number of different types of computers sharing resources. "Is that a (gasp) *Macintosh* that I see in my network?" That's right. As long as other computers conform to standard Ethernet protocols and have been recognized by the host PC (or DHCP device), they show up. (This includes PCs running Linux, Macs running Mac OS X, and Unix machines.)

 "Wait! Where's Boopsie?" Well, if the client PC that you named Boopsie has been turned on *after* you opened the Network window, it doesn't show up. To see it, right-click any empty spot within the Network window and choose Refresh from the menu that appears, which rescans the network and updates the window's contents. (Whatever moved you to name a PC *Boopsie,* anyway? Are you a Doonesbury fan like I am?)

To display available folders and devices on each computer, simply double-click the computer icon to open it. Note that you might be greeted by a login dialog box; for example, I sometimes see one because I set up my media server as a *secure* (or *closed*) system, and I have to supply my username and password to my account *on that computer.* (If you set up your clients with the procedure in the preceding section, you shouldn't need a login to access their stuff — unless, of course, that computer's user has specifically configured Windows 8 to require a login.) If you've set up your account on a PC without a password (or you remove your password later from the User Accounts screen in Control Panel), that PC is essentially an *open* system.

Windows 8 automatically adds shared printers and displays them in the Network window — just double-click the name of the computer that the printer is attached to, and it appears (along with any shared files or drives). However, you can also manually add a new shared network printer to your Network window. Click Network at the top of the Network window toolbar to display the Add Devices and Printers button — click the button to run the Add a Device Wizard, which guides you through the steps.

Sharing folders and documents

"Mark, what controls what I can and can't see when browsing the network?" Now you've entered The Sharing Zone, where time and space have no meaning. What *does* matter are the shared files and folders that you set up on each computer in your network.

Sharing something across the network allows other computers to see it when browsing. (Note that network sharing is very different from sharing a local file among users of the same PC, which I cover in Book II, Chapter 4.)

Windows 8 takes the safe and conservative approach by default: Nothing is shared across a network until specifically set. (To be honest, I prefer that route over defaulting to a completely open machine.) However, you can share a folder and all its contents by following these steps:

1. **Click the File Explorer icon on your Desktop taskbar to open the Explorer window; then navigate to the folder's location.**

2. **Right-click the folder and then choose Share With from the menu that appears.**

3. **To share a folder — allowing full read/write access with your Homegroup — choose the Homegroup (View and Edit) entry.**

You can choose the Homegroup (View) entry from the menu if you want to allow others in your Homegroup to open and read files, but not make any changes to them.

4. To share the folder with only certain users (instead of everyone in your Homegroup), choose the Specific People entry.

You see the settings shown in Figure 2-8. Type the username to select an individual user to whom you're granting sharing privileges. You can click the Permission Level pop-up menu to set the read or read/write access to the folder and its contents. Then click the Share button to return to the Explorer window.

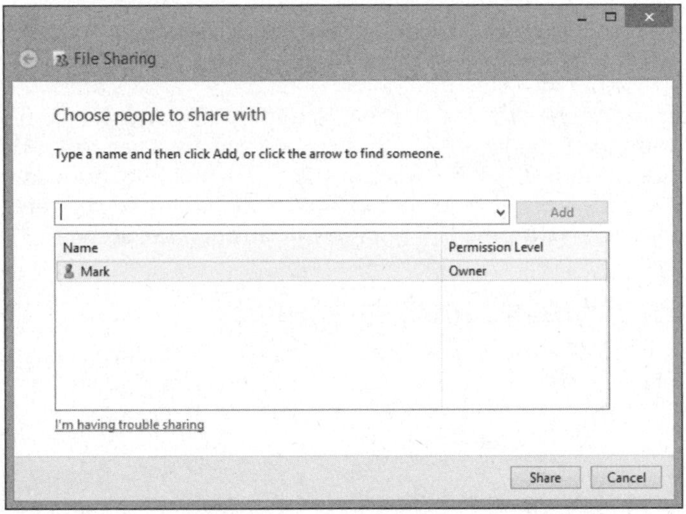

Figure 2-8:
Mark a
folder as
shared
among
specific
users.

> **File Sharing**
>
> Choose people to share with
>
> Type a name and then click Add, or click the arrow to find someone.
>
> [   ] ▾   [Add]
>
> | Name | Permission Level |
> | --- | --- |
> | 👤 Mark | Owner |
>
> I'm having trouble sharing
>
> [Share] [Cancel]

Windows 8 provides convenient links for e-mailing the location of your shared files and folders, or you can choose to copy the links into the Clipboard for pasting later into a document (like a Word document).

You can also share a drive in the same fashion, but Microsoft cautions against it — and so do I. You should assign only one shared folder on each drive on each computer in your network.

When you share a folder, you place everything in that folder on the network. Therefore, if there's even one item (either a document or a subfolder) that you don't want to distribute with others inside a folder, *do not share that folder!*

After a folder is enabled with read/write access, its contents can be opened, saved, moved, or copied, including from within the File Open, Save, and Browse dialog boxes, which are common throughout Windows 8 and your applications. That's the neat thing: Everything works normally across the network by using the same functionality that I cover in Book II.

Printing across the Network

Although sharing an Internet connection is one of the prime advantages of using a network these days, one other resource has been shared across networks now for decades: the network printer. (Read all about Internet connection sharing in Chapter 4 of this minibook.) And, any printer connected to any PC on your network can be used by any other PC, which is a real boon when your office has only one large-format inkjet and only one color laser printer.

You can follow one of four avenues for network printing:

✦ **Hook up the printer to a PC so that it acts as a printer server.** As long as the printer receives only moderate use and it's in an open area, this option can work. (If the PC is in a private office, don't even think about it. You'll drive the occupant smackers.)

✦ **Set up a separate PC as a simple print server.** This is the traditional solution for high-traffic printers that need a central location. The client PC is basically just a doorman, existing only to queue print jobs for the connected printer. Expensive but efficient.

✦ **Buy a network printer box.** This standalone device is essentially an Ethernet card with a slightly more intelligent brain, and it provides the same functionality as a print server.

✦ **Buy a printer with onboard Ethernet network support.** Sure, it's more expensive, but a network-ready printer is *the* most elegant solution.

If you choose one of the latter two methods — either a network printer box or a network-ready printer — you have to follow the manufacturer's specific instructions to set things up. However, if you decide to use a client PC to provide printing services, Windows 8 makes it simpler than ever: Any printer connected to your PC is automatically shared with your Homegroup! You'll find all the details about creating and managing a Homegroup in Book II, Chapter 4.

Using a Standard Switch with a Cable or DSL Modem

I discuss Internet sharing devices earlier in this chapter, and they're covered in detail in Chapter 4 of this minibook. Most have built-in switches, virtually all of them have DHCP support, and they have ports that allow a direct connection to your cable or DSL modem. That's great: In fact, as I mention earlier in this chapter, you don't even need a host PC in that case. Feel free to prance about.

What if your switch *doesn't* have a connection point (typically called a *wide area network* [WAN] port or *uplink* port) for your DSL or cable modem? That's the situation I mention earlier, where your host PC needs two NICs, and you have to set your PC up using both cards.

To do this, connect your hardware and cables so that

+ The cable or DSL modem is connected to one of the NICs on the host PC. (It should already be configured this way, so it's no big deal.)

+ The other NIC on the host PC is connected to one of the ports on the switch.

+ The client PCs on the network are connected to the switch.

Now follow the procedure that I provide earlier (in the section titled, "Setting up the host") for setting up the host PC and the client PCs, and all should function like butter.

Troubleshooting Your Network

I sure hope you're reading this section for fun — or because you thirst for knowledge, or just to be thorough. Why? Well, unfortunately, a misbehaving network can leave even the best techs with a four-bell headache. Every network is a mass of differing hardware, software, and data, all of which must work well in concert before you can send or receive a single packet.

Windows 8 does the best job it can to automate the process, and you can pretty much assume that late-model hardware is compatible. But if you have one bad cable or one faulty NIC driver, your state-of-the-art network becomes a family of dead cables and a little box with no lights. (Sounds like my last attempt at outdoor Christmas decorations.)

In this section, I provide the most common solutions to the most common problems.

Windows 8 doesn't recognize my NIC

Man, talk about starting with a problem from Step One! That's my kind of luck. Anyway, here are the possible problems and descriptions of their fixes:

+ **An incompatible driver:** NIC drivers are legendary for their fickle behavior. Unlike some printers that allow you to use the same driver for Windows Vista and Windows 7/8, a network interface card simply demands the proper driver, or it doesn't work. Period. Reinstall the driver from the manufacturer's media (and make sure that you select the correct operating system version). If that doesn't work (and you still have access to the Internet on another computer), download the manufacturer's latest driver for your operating system from the company's website. (To download a driver, you must have access to another, working PC, and you might need a USB flash drive or a CD-R to install them.) Oh, by the way: You might have to uninstall the NIC and then reinstall it to reload the driver. Such fun.

✦ **A faulty NIC:** This is a definite possibility. If you have a NIC that you know is working, replace the misbehaving card (along with its drivers) to see whether the problem is solved.

✦ **A hardware conflict:** This problem is quite rare under Windows Vista and 7/8, but it can still happen. Use Device Manager to check whether Windows is having problems getting everyone to play nicely together; I demonstrate how to do this in Book II, Chapter 5.

No lights show up on my network card(s) or switch

This is classic stuff. It's not the most comforting thing to hear, but then again, it's good to know that others have been here before you. (To be precise, *I* have. I used to handle network problem calls at a major hospital.) Anyway, a lack of lights indicates that you're not getting a signal, which suggests a number of possible hardware problems:

✦ **Your cable is faulty.** An improperly made cable can short out and cause everything to come to a crashing halt. This is a likely culprit if all the other client PCs have illuminated signal lights and the switch's lights are lit. (If the computer store sold you a special *crossover* cable, march right back in and demand a standard twisted pair cable; crossover cables are meant to hook together two computers directly via their network ports. Unfortunately, it's hard to tell the difference with just your eyes unless you see the word *crossover* printed on the cable.)

✦ **Your NIC or switch is faulty.** If either has gone off the deep end, it needs to be replaced. If other client PCs are working, you can remove a working NIC from one of them and use it to test your switch.

✦ **Your switch isn't powered on.** (Whoops! — no need for embarrassment.) A switch needs AC power to operate.

✦ **You're using the WAN/uplink port.** This is a special port on your switch, as I explain in the previous section; it doesn't work for a client PC connection.

Nothing shows up when 1 browse

Just plain nasty. If everything seemed to go well when you set up your host PC and your client PCs but you still come up empty when you browse, here are the possibilities (and my recommended troubleshooting tips):

✦ **Client PCs are powered down.** Simple but effective. Boot up a client PC and then refresh the Network window — right-click at any empty spot in the window and choose Refresh from the menu. *The client should now be visible.*

✦ **A piece of hardware is faulty.** I use this term because any piece of your networking hardware might be experiencing problems, and you wouldn't be able to browse. See what I mean about the four-bell headache? Anyway, make sure that *all* your NICs and your switch have lighted activity/signal lights.

✦ **No network resources are shared.** Remember that Windows 8 doesn't share diddly by default, so when you first browse your Network window, it's likely to be absolutely blank (or, if you try to open a networked computer, nothing is there). After you create or join a Homegroup, however, your Network window will soon be crowded.

1 can't connect (or print) to a shared printer

I saved the best for last because this problem is usually much easier to solve (apart from the obvious, such as running out of paper, ink, or toner). Try these stress relievers:

✦ **The printer is powered down.** I wish I had a dime for every time someone complained that they couldn't connect to Fred's printer, only to find that Fred was out of the office and (ahem) his PC (and the specific printer in question) was turned off. (Sound of hand slapping forehead.)

✦ **The printer isn't actually shared.** Yep, you guessed it; this is the other hot potato. Make sure that the shared printer hasn't been disabled (either accidentally or on purpose).

✦ **You have faulty NIC or cables.** Again, check the NIC for the PC that's connected to the printer. The easiest thing to do is to see whether you can browse or work with shared files on that PC. If not, there's a good chance that either the NIC or the twisted pair cable is giving you problems.

✦ **The printer has been placed offline.** Some printers have an Online/Offline button. If a printer like this is offline, the printer goes comatose and doesn't respond.

Chapter 3: Going Wireless

In This Chapter

✔ **Comparing wireless and wired networks**

✔ **Comparing wireless standards**

✔ **Using existing telephone and AC wiring**

✔ **Making a wireless connection under Windows 8**

*W*elcome to the future: a world where network cables are on display in museums and your PCs can wirelessly access your home or office network from 100 feet away. Fast, convenient, and (most of all) as secure as a wired network, the wireless network of years to come will even bring other types of devices under its umbrella, such as cellphones, netbook and tablet PCs, and personal digital assistants (PDAs), just to name a few.

Hang on a second. Now that I think about it, all that stuff is available *now*! Wireless networks are rapidly overtaking traditional wired networks in homes and small offices. Even companies with extensive wired networks have added wireless access points (WAPs) for the laptop crowd, just to be hip.

In this chapter, I show you how wireless networking works, what's available, and how you can set up a wireless network under Windows 8.

Understanding Wireless Networking

In a sense, wireless networking isn't as revolutionary as you might think. In fact, it operates in the same manner as the standard wired Ethernet configuration, which I discuss in Chapter 2 of this minibook, complete with packets, collisions, and all the hoo-hah that accompanies networking. Of course, the method of transmitting and receiving packets is different when you're using wireless networking; instead of being sent over a wire, the packets are broadcast through the air like radio signals.

(However, you can't use your wireless network hardware to run a pirate radio station. Sorry about that, matey. Arrgh.)

Comparing wireless with wired

Other than the transmission method, here are the only three major differences between a wired network and its wireless sibling:

✦ **Speed:** *Wireless connections are slower.* This is the big 'un as well as the big reason why most larger networks still depend on wired Ethernet for the bulk of their connections. Even the fastest current wireless technology can pump data at only around 300 Mbps (and that figure would require perfect conditions, so you're more likely to end up with anywhere from 150 to 200 Mbps), but any run-of-the-mill wired network can easily deliver a steady 100 Mbps. Heck, the faster wired networks can hit gigabit (1000 Mbps) speeds! In fact, they can use fiber optic cabling rather than plain copper wire cabling to hit even faster speeds.

✦ **Semolians:** *Wireless hardware is more expensive.* Depending on the standard supported by your wireless hardware (read more about standards in the next section), you pay significantly more for wireless hardware than you do for 10/100 Mbps wired hardware.

✦ **Stuff:** *Wireless networks require no hubs or switches.* Most wireless base stations and WAPs (wireless access points, which I describe in a moment) can provide connections for up to 253 simultaneous users, so a larger wireless network (with 50 PCs or more) requires far less hardware and upkeep than a wired network that can handle the same number of computers.

Do you want to impress your network administrator? (Of course — don't we all? If you run your own home or small-office network, you can impress a hardware-savvy friend instead.) Use the technonerd buzzwords for network transmission technologies and refer to your wireless network as an *unguided* network — as opposed to a *guided* (wired) network.

Naturally, you can add a *wireless access point* — or, as it's commonly called, a *WAP* — to your wired network, which gives you the best of both worlds. Figure 3-1 illustrates a typical WAP device, which brings 802.11n wireless connectivity to an existing wired network; this baby runs about $75 US. Many WAP units require two physical connections: one to your wired Ethernet network (naturally) and a Universal Serial Bus (USB) connection to the computer that controls it. You can also share your Internet connection with a dual router, which has both wired and wireless hardware built in (as I discuss in Chapter 4 of this minibook).

Keeping track of the standards involved

Like any other evolving PC technology, wireless networking suffers from competition between different standards — and, of course, some are compatible with others, but others are not. Readers of my other books are already acquainted with my overwhelming love for strange names and obfuscating acronyms in the PC world — *not.* Unfortunately, wireless networking has a handful of the most confusing names in the entire PC world, so make sure that you have a bottle of aspirin handy.

Figure 3-1:
A typical WAP for your LAN. (Try to keep a straight faco when you say it.)

Here, in one easy-to-consume section, is the lowdown on the different wireless standards as well as which ones you should consider and which ones you should eschew.

The original standard: 802.11b

Commonly called *Wi-Fi* (short for *wireless fidelity*), the first 802.11b wireless base station (AirPort) was introduced by Apple Computer in 1999 — a fact that the good folks at Cupertino have been gloating over ever since. Wi-Fi supports a maximum transfer rate of 11 Mbps, which is just a little faster than the slowest 10 Mbps wired Ethernet standard in common use.

Distance is important in the wireless world, of course. It's one thing to be able to use your laptop on your network from across the room but yet another thing entirely to use it in your backyard. Although 802.11b devices are rated at a maximum distance of 300 feet from the base station, that figure is about as realistic as an African wildebeest wearing a hula skirt appearing in your living room. This idea of "theoretical top speed" also applies to "high-speed" dialup modems, which practically never delivered the top speed that the manufacturer listed on the box. From experience, I can tell you that you can count on 150 feet — and even fewer if a number of intervening walls stand between you and your network or if you're a victim of interference.

A word about USB wireless connections

You can connect a desktop PC to a wireless network without even using an internal adapter card. Just use a *USB wireless adapter,* which uses a USB connection to your PC as a path for wireless network data packets. Hey, that USB is amazing, isn't it? (Note that this toy isn't the same as a simple USB cable network, which allows PCs to share files and printers over USB cabling.) The remote PC gets all the benefits of a wireless Ethernet connection.

As you can read in Book VII, Chapter 4, you'll need a USB 2.0 wireless adapter to deliver the 54 Mbps top speed of an 802.11g connection or the 300 Mbps top speed of 802.11n — an older

USB 1.1 port won't work. (Personally, I think that USB 2.0 is an example of overkill in this scenario. After all, you're moving either 54 or 300 Mbps over a connection that can reach as high as 480 Mbps! I guess having bandwidth to spare is better than not having enough.)

Anyway, an external USB wireless adapter is an excellent way to add "temporary wireless" to a PC in your home or office. Many of these external adapters can also be used to make a printer a standalone wireless device, so you can place your printer in a central location that's convenient for everyone.

Oh, didn't I mention the interference? The 802.11b networking uses the 2.4 GHz broadcasting spectrum, which unfortunately is used by a horde of everyday household devices, including cellular phones, cordless phones, Bluetooth devices (which I cover in a bit), and even microwave ovens. Therefore, 802.11b wireless networks can slow down significantly because of interference from other devices. It's unlikely that your entire wireless network will shut down completely, but you will *definitely* be able to tell when your teenage daughter is using your cordless phone.

The misfit: 802.11a

Why is 802.11a such a misfit, and why did I list it after 802.11b? Well, you'll love this:

+ **The numbering is wrong.** Believe it or not, 802.11a is a faster connection than 802.11b. (If you're wondering why this select group of engineers decided to number successive standards in *reverse* order, it's because the 802.11a standard was actually approved *before* the 802.11b standard. Don't ask me, I just try to explain this stuff.)

+ **It has a shorter range.** Although 802.11a is officially rated at 150 feet under perfect conditions, in the real world, it can reach a distance of only 60 to 70 feet — your wireless world shrinks even further.

✦ **It doesn't play well with others.** Because 802.11a is completely incompatible with both 802.11b and 802.11g, you're effectively limited to 802.11a equipment. (And there's not all that much out there.)

So why did folks develop 802.11a, anyway? It has two advantages:

✦ **Speedy:** The first speed demon in wireless networking, 802.11a delivers up to 54 Mbps (more than five times as fast as 802.11b).

✦ **Different broadcasting spectrum:** The 802.11a standard uses the 5 GHz spectrum, which prevents it from working in the 2.4 GHz range needed by 802.11b (hence the incompatibility). Because there's a lot less activity around most homes and offices in the 5 GHz spectrum, you get less interference and a better chance of achieving the best reception.

Here's the bottom line: Avoid 802.11a hardware completely, and you'll be much happier!

The mainstream: 802.11g

I know you're probably saying to yourself, "Self, I sure wish someone would get off their duff and produce a standard that is compatible with 802.11b *and* provides speeds as fast as 802.11a." Good news: Your wish has been heard! The 802.11g wireless standard does precisely that, combining the best of both worlds. At the time of this writing, 802.11g is still the most common wireless standard in use.

If you (or your company) have already invested in 802.11b wireless hardware, you can continue to use it on an 802.11g network. Naturally, you don't get 54 Mbps, but at least it works at 11 Mbps. New 802.11g hardware will transfer packets at that magic 54 Mbps — well, that's the top speed, anyway, but good luck in getting that kind of performance outside a laboratory.

The downside? Aw, jeez, we're back to the 2.4 GHz spectrum again, so once again your buddy in the next cubicle who loves microwave popcorn will introduce interference. It just goes to show you that nothing's perfect — except, perhaps, a 1964 Cadillac two-door coupe (when I can get it started, that is).

Raising the bar to 802.11n

Technology marches on, and now you can wave goodbye — eventually — to even 802.11g and 54 Mbps. Let me introduce the latest wireless standard from IEEE: 802.11n. Most third-party manufacturers have already standardized on 802.11n wireless equipment. In fact, if you're buying a cutting-edge desktop or laptop with wireless hardware built-in, it's likely 802.11n (or easily upgraded to 802.11n later).

Book VIII Chapter 3

Going Wireless

Why the hubbub? Oh, I forgot to mention that 802.11n can deliver throughput in excess of 300 Mbps! Don't bet your house that you get that kind of speed, though — like the other members of the 802.11 family, it's likely to be a theoretical maximum speed. As I mention earlier, look to 150–200 Mbps as a more likely speed.

Here's another feature you'll appreciate, especially if you have older wireless hardware: 802.11n networking equipment works with *all* members of the 802.11 family, including the black sheep 802.11a. Compatibility is A Good Thing, but note that to get the absolute best performance from your wireless network, *all* your hardware should be 802.11n. Otherwise, things slow down for the older standards.

You can't go wrong with the 802.11n standard: Think superfast wireless connections in your household or office.

The strangely named: Bluetooth

Okay now, here's a wireless standard name that sounds like some scriptwriter or concept artist in Hollywood was working overtime — but at least it breaks the 802.11*x* mold. Unlike the other four standards, Bluetooth isn't designed for full-scale wireless Ethernet networking. Instead, it was developed in 1995 as a specialized wireless technology for short distances to be used with cellphones, PDAs, laptops, palmtops, printers, and other external devices. The maximum distance for a Bluetooth network is anywhere from 30 to 300 feet, depending on your hardware.

The Bluetooth wave is even supposed to reach household appliances, like your TV and your stereo system. I'm sure there's a Bluetooth toaster out there. If you've seen it, drop me a line at `mark@mlcbooks.com` and tell me all about it.

Anyway, unlike the other standards I discuss here, Bluetooth requires very little power to use (befitting its design, which concentrates on battery-operated devices). It's also painfully slow compared with 802.11b — only about 1 Mbps — but that's not supposed to affect the small fry as much as it would your desktop PC. No base station is required for Bluetooth communications between devices. For example, after your laptop gets within 30 feet of your cellphone, they can update each other's telephone number directories. Eerie.

Oh, and Bluetooth also uses the — you guessed it — 2.4 GHz spectrum, so it conflicts with existing 802.11b and 802.11g networks! (The airwaves are getting so overpopulated that tin cans and string are starting to look attractive again.)

Table 3-1 compares wireless networking standards.

Table 3-1		Wireless Standards on Parade	
Standard	*Top Transfer Speed*	*Max Distance*	*Compatibility*
802.11b	11 Mbps	300 feet	802.11g, 802.11n
802.11a	54 Mbps	150 feet	802.11n
802.11g	54 Mbps	150 feet	802.11b, 802.11n
802.11n	300 Mbps	250 feet	802.11b, 802.11a, 802.11g
Bluetooth	1 Mbps	30 feet	None

You can buy an external wireless antenna for your base station or WAP. An 802.11n directional antenna typically costs about $40 or $50 US, and it can boost your existing signal quality as well as extend the range of your wireless network into every nook and cranny of your home or office. Check the documentation that came with your wireless base station or WAP to see whether it can accept an external antenna.

AC and phoneline networking

Although wireless hardware has become quite popular over the past several years, here's another alternative to a traditional wired network: You can also build a network by using either existing standard AC power wiring (a *powerline* network) or telephone wiring (a *phoneline* network) in your home.

If running packets across your AC power lines sounds a little dangerous, let me put your fears to rest: Both these alternative wired networks have been around for several years — longer, in fact, than 802.11b — and they're perfectly safe. (If you're wondering, you can continue to use your telephone or your AC appliances with no changes.) The advantages of an alternative wired network over a wired or wireless network are clear:

✦ **No wires — at least, no Cat 5 or 6 cables:** Your home or office is already set up with all the "cabling" you need, and you likely have "ports" in every room.

✦ **Better security than a wireless network:** Although a wireless network can be made quite secure — I describe how to do this in the next section — you're still beaming a signal that might be picked up outside, in the street. On the other hand, the network packets transferred over a phoneline network or an AC network stay within the building and are practically impossible for anyone outside to intercept.

✦ **Easy to install:** A wireless network might be the easiest to install, but a phoneline network or an AC network is still much easier to set up than a traditional wired network.

Book VIII
Chapter 3

Going Wireless

Using SideShow gadgets

Hey, Windows Vista and 7 users: Got your gadgets goin' on? In case you haven't used the SideShow feature yet, I had better explain. A *gadget* is a small add-on application running on an external device (like a cellphone, multimedia remote control, or PDA) that retrieves data wirelessly from your PC. The external device has a screen that can display information, like a program listing from Windows Media Center or your e-mail Inbox or a web page. (See the following figure.)

Here's the kicker: SideShow works even if your PC is in sleep mode, or *turned off completely!* Now that's pretty slick, wouldn't you agree? This magic trick is easy if you set Windows Vista or Windows 7 to automatically wake your computer to update and transfer information to your devices. SideShow devices can connect to your PC by using Bluetooth, standard wireless Ethernet, or even a USB cable connection. Of course, you need a PC and external devices that are all Vista/7 SideShow–compatible.

Gadget applications are configured from within the Vista/7 Control Panel, using the Windows SideShow settings — make sure that the Set My Computer to Wake Automatically radio button is selected, and select the Automatically Wake My Computer check box to set up your Vista/7 "wake-up call." You can also assign a PIN (personal identification number) that gadgets must supply to receive data, which helps keep your PC secure.

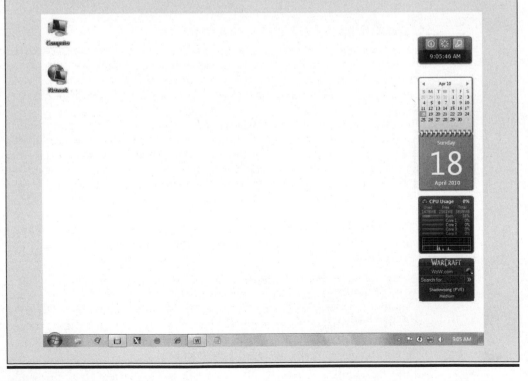

So, why aren't phoneline and powerline networks more popular? Unfortunately, compared with wireless, both these network solutions leave much to be desired:

✦ **Slower than wireless:** The latest phoneline standard (from HomePNA, at www.homepna.org) delivers approximately 128 Mbps, whereas the HomePlug powerline standard (www.homeplug.org) is rated at only about 14 Mbps. The raw file-transfer speed of an 802.11n network wipes the floor with either alternative wired network.

✦ **Less convenient than wireless:** Even though you don't have to string Ethernet cabling all over your office, your networked PCs and peripherals are still tied down to certain areas (around either your telephone jacks or your AC power sockets). A wireless connection works wherever you are as long as you're in range.

✦ **Connect fewer computers:** A wireless network can accept twice as many users (or standalone network devices) as either a phoneline or powerline network.

When readers ask me to recommend a network solution for their homes or small offices, I almost always recommend either a traditional wired gigabit (Cat 6) network, for the fastest speeds and the best security, or a wireless network, which offers convenience and easy installation. The drawbacks of phoneline and powerline networks (along with the explosive popularity of wireless hardware) will likely doom them to gradual extinction.

Using Wireless Hardware in Windows 8

After you install your wireless base station or WAP, you're ready to configure your PC for use on your network. (Of course, if your PC already has built-in wireless Ethernet hardware, you can skip this installation frippery completely. Meet me at the section titled "After the Installation" to continue.)

Preparing to install

Before you begin the installation of an internal adapter card, make sure that you

✦ **Read the manual.** Even if you already installed an adapter card in your PC, take a few minutes to check the documentation that shipped with the card. Here's a Mark's Maxim to live by:

It's better to know about a "gotcha" before you install.™

✦ **Gather the Big Four.** Find a Phillips screwdriver, a plastic bowl to hold any spare parts, a good light source, and some sort of static-free cover for your work surface. (Newspaper always works well if I'm away from my workbench.)

✦ **Ground yourself.** After you remove the cover from your PC, touch the metal chassis of your computer to dissipate any static electricity that's stowing away on your body before it can cause damage to the card.

All manufacturers of wireless adapter cards (for desktops) and wireless PC Cards (for laptops) include their own installation and setup programs — which also create the necessary wireless connection automatically within Windows — so I don't go into the gory details here. However, the next section provides you with some suggestions that will help with the installation, no matter which type of card you're using.

After the installation

During the setup of new hardware (or the configuration of built-in hardware), keep these points in mind:

✦ **Choose between ad hoc and infrastructure.** You might be prompted to choose between ad hoc and infrastructure mode. In most cases, you want to choose *infrastructure* mode (where your laptop and PC workstations connect by using a base station or wireless access point) rather than *ad hoc* (where the devices talk directly to each other on a specific channel number that you determine, just like the CB radio days of old, without a base station or WAP). *Note:* If you're trying to connect your wireless device to your existing wired network, you must use infrastructure mode.

✦ **Check your WPA/WPA2 encryption.** When prompted for WPA/WPA2 information, use the highest level that the PC card supports. WPA2 is designed to automatically fall back to the encryption level used by your base station or WAP.

✦ **Assign your own passwords!** Base stations, wireless routers, and WAPs use an administrator name and password to identify you, and often this information even allows remote control. (Read that term as *hacker banquet.*) Therefore, you should *always* assign your own administrator name and password while configuring your wireless network!

✦ **Check your SSID.** You need an SSID (short for Service Set Identifier) that matches the SSID used by your base station or WAP. *Remember:* Change the SSID to the unique value that you used on your base station or WAP. For the best level of security, *don't* use the default SSID!

✦ **Keep your drivers and firmware current.** I sound like a broken record, but check for the latest drivers and firmware updates from the manufacturer's website every time you install new hardware — including wireless networking hardware.

Making the connection

Microsoft recommends that your wireless base station or WAP broadcast the SSID, as long as you're using WPA/WPA2 encryption in infrastructure mode. I heartily agree: This makes everything easier and more automatic, as long as you select an SSID of your own. (Yep, I'm saying it again: *Don't* use the default SSID, or else you'll leave a security hole in your wireless network.)

With a broadcasted SSID, connecting is as easy as plugging your wireless network card into your laptop — of course, with built-in wireless hardware, you don't need to do a thing. Windows XP, Vista, Windows 7, and Windows 8 automatically search for and connect to your network. (The first time you connect, you'll be prompted to choose your network and provide the proper password.) If you're using a desktop PC with a wireless card, this same process occurs when you log in to Windows. (See? I told you it was easy.) You see on the taskbar a notification icon letting you know that the connection has been made as well as how strong the signal is.

Chapter 4: Sharing Your Internet Connection

In This Chapter

✔ **Understanding the advantages of connection sharing**

✔ **Sharing your connection by using Windows 8**

✔ **Using a wired hardware sharing device**

✔ **Using a wireless hardware sharing device**

A high-speed Internet connection is a thing of beauty, especially when it's shared with everyone in your home or office over your network. After your network is set up and running smoothly, consider whether you want to share that connection through hardware or software as well as what sort of security you need in order to protect everyone on your network.

In this chapter, I discuss all the possibilities and show you how to set up Internet connection sharing within Windows 8.

Why Share Your Internet Connection?

"Don't I need a separate Internet connection for each PC on my network?" Actually, you just answered your own question: The network you installed allows for all sorts of data communications between PCs, including the ability to plug in to a shared Internet connection.

I should note here that it is indeed technically possible to share a dialup Internet connection by using the software connection-sharing feature in Windows 8. However, I don't think that you'll be satisfied with the results. (Sorry — it doesn't provide enough horsepower to handle more than one computer, and even then browsing the web is as slow as molasses.) Therefore, I assume for the rest of this chapter that you're already using a digital subscriber line (DSL), a cable modem Internet connection, or a satellite connection.

Here's a list of benefits that help explain why Internet connection sharing — whether through the software built into Windows 8 or a dedicated hardware device — is so doggone popular these days:

✦ **Cost effective:** As long as your Internet service provider (ISP) allows you to share your broadband connection, you save a bundle over the cost of adding completely separate connections for multiple machines in your home or office. (Naturally, this is the major benefit.)

✦ **Convenient:** With a shared Internet connection, other PCs on your network are easy to configure, and each one is as content as a sleeping cat. Each PC on your network operates just as though it were directly connected to the Internet, and the computers on the network can all do their own thing on the Internet simultaneously.

✦ **Centralized security:** With a *firewall* in place — either running on the PC (if you're sharing through software) or on the device itself (if you're sharing through hardware) — you can protect the Internet activity on *all* the PCs on your network at one time.

✦ **Efficient:** Most folks I talk to are surprised that a shared Internet connection is so fast — even when multiple computers on the network are charging down the information superhighway at the same time.

A connection shared through a dedicated hardware device (like an Internet router) is always faster than a connection shared through software.

Speaking of convenience and efficiency, I should also mention that many hardware sharing devices also double as Ethernet *switches* (devices offering several wired Ethernet ports that are used to build a home or office Ethernet network). Hardware sharing devices allow you to build your entire home or office network around one central piece of hardware rather than use a separate switch and a PC running a software sharing program.

Sharing through Hardware

With a hardware device, all the PCs on your network can concentrate on their own work, eliminating the need to leave a PC running constantly as an "Internet server" as is the case if you choose to use Windows 8 Internet Connection Sharing. (After all, a PC that's capable of running Windows 8 at a decent clip is an expensive resource compared with an investment of $50–$100 (US) on a hardware sharing device.)

In this section, I familiarize you with the two different types of hardware sharing devices.

Wired sharing devices

For PC owners who either already have a traditional wired Ethernet network — or who are considering building one — a device like the combination switch-firewall-DHCP-server-sharing-thing you see in Figure 4-1 is the perfect solution to Internet connection sharing. (The *Dynamic Host*

Configuration Protocol, or *DHCP,* feature allows your hardware sharing device to automatically configure IP addresses on your network. If all that sounds like an alien language, visit Chapter 2 of this minibook, where I wax enthusiastic about DHCP.)

Perhaps I should be a little more specific in my description. (Not even Google returns many results if you search for *switch-firewall-DHCP server-sharing-thing.*) The illustrated device is actually a cable/DSL Internet router with a four-port switch.

Figure 4-1:
A candid shot of an Internet router.

For an idea of why hardware sharing is so popular, look at what you can buy — in one small, tidy box — online for a mere $50:

✦ **A built-in, four-port Ethernet 10/100 switch:** You can plug in four PCs, to start with, directly into the router for an instant Ethernet network. (For more information about network speeds, see Chapter 2 of this minibook.) You can also find routers with high-performance gigabit (10/100/1000) Ethernet ports for a slightly higher price.

✦ **A direct-connect port for your DSL or cable modem:** The port can also be used as a wide area network (WAN) connection to hook the sharing device to an existing external network.

✦ **A DHCP server:** It provides near-automatic network configuration for the PCs hooked into the device.

✦ **The hardware and software controls you need to block certain Internet traffic (both coming in and going out):** You can also lock out individual PCs from Internet access.

✦ **An easy-to-use, web-based configuration screen:** You can use it on any PC connected to the router. Figure 4-2 illustrates the web configuration screen from my router.

✦ **Built-in NAT functionality:** I dive into NAT in Chapter 5 of this minibook.

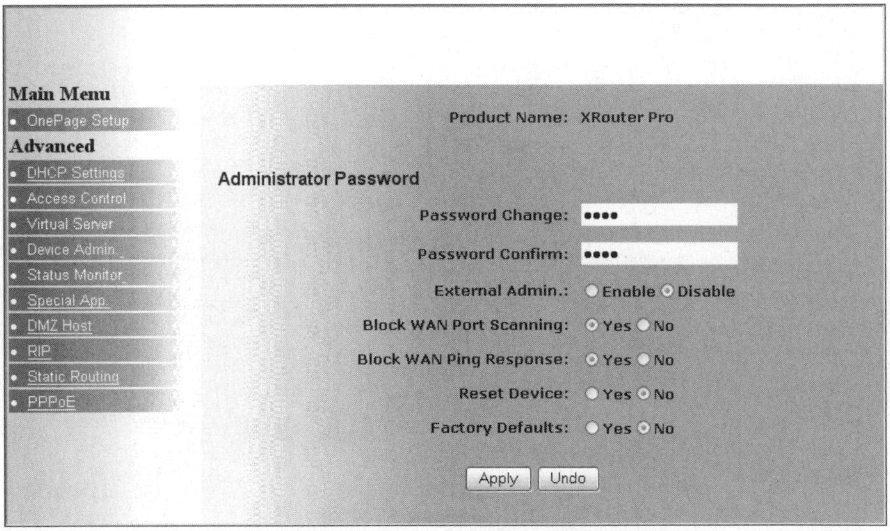

Figure 4-2:
Most
Internet
routers are
configured
through
your web
browser.

Pretty neat, eh? Remember that this device is used in tandem with your existing cable or DSL modem, which is typically included by your ISP as part of your Internet subscription (but you might be paying more because you're renting the modem).

I should also note that you can get a similar device with all these features *and* a built-in DSL or cable modem. Because you aren't charged a monthly rental fee for a modem, you can thumb your nose at your ISP and save money in the long run. (Please avoid mentioning my name when you gleefully return your modem to your ISP, or do any *visible* nose-thumbing in the direction of your ISP.)

Naturally, the setup procedure for each device on the market is different, but here's a sample of what's in store when you take your new Internet sharing router out of the box. (Don't plug your new toy's power supply into the wall yet.)

1. **If you're running a typical standalone network switch, you can either unplug the existing Ethernet cables from all existing computers and plug them into the new sharing device or connect the WAN port from the existing hub into one of the ports on the Internet sharing device.**

Ethernet

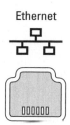

The device manual tells you how to take care of the latter method.

If you're setting up a new network, naturally, you just connect each Ethernet cable directly to the sharing device. See Figure 4-3.

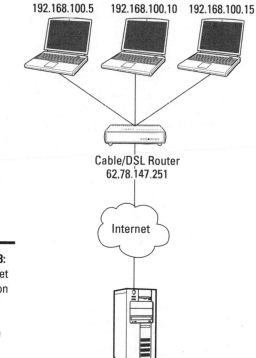

Figure 4-3:
An Internet connection shared using a hardware device.

2. **Plug the power supply from the sharing device into the AC socket.**

3. **Configure one of the PCs on your new network with the default network settings provided by the device manufacturer.**

4. **Run Internet Explorer on the PC you configured in Step 3 and use the web-based configuration utility to finish configuring the device.**

That's it! If you're running a typical home network or home office network, you'll likely keep the default settings for everything. For an idea of just what kind of power you can wield over your network as you share your Internet connection, take a gander at the sidebar "What the Sam Hill does *that* mean?" in Chapter 5 of this minibook. Luckily, you probably don't have to use any of those optional settings, but it's good to know that they're there.

Wireless sharing devices

Most folks think that sharing an Internet connection over a wireless network must be harder to set up than a traditional wired network — and that it's likely to be a tremendous security risk. I'm happy to tell you that both preconceptions are wrong. Wireless connection sharing with a hardware device is as simple to set up as the wired device that I discuss in the preceding section. And, with the settings I discuss in Chapter 5 of this minibook, you can make it very difficult (if not impossible) for someone to hack his way to your network or your Internet connection.

To see an example of a truly versatile all-in-one Internet sharing device, check out the device shown in Figure 4-4. Its antenna marks it as a wireless switch, but what you don't see is that it also sports four 10/100 Ethernet ports on the back for your old-fashioned wired network. Yep, you guessed it, this is just plain neat: It can accommodate multiple 802.11n wireless connections *and* four wired connections, all at the same time! (The somewhat spaghetti-fied world of wireless networking is covered in depth in Chapter 3 of this minibook.)

Figure 4-4: Is it wired? Is it wireless? This sharing device is both!

As you might expect, the cost on this puppy, about $125 online, is significantly higher than the wired-only device (see the preceding section). Another factor is the speed of the wireless connection; as you can read in Chapter 3 of this minibook, the older (and slower) 802.11g devices are rapidly disappearing from the market, so costs are dropping quickly on the faster 802.11n hardware. (And yes, if you opt for a wireless-only network, you can find a cheaper wireless sharing device that doesn't include any of those silly "antique" wired ports.) Wireless adapter cards (including the USB and PC Card varieties) are slightly more expensive than standard wired adapter cards, too.

As I mention in Chapter 5 of this minibook, don't forget to demand a wireless sharing device that offers Wi-Fi Protected Access (WPA2) private encryption. Use anything less and your wireless network will be much easier for outsiders to hack.

Sharing through Software in Windows 8

Time to be honest here; I think that using a hardware sharing device is *definitely* preferable to sharing a connection through software. For example, with a software solution

+ The Internet host PC on your network must always remain turned on if anyone wants to use the Internet.

+ You notice a significant slowdown on the host PC when several other PCs are using the Internet.

+ You can't use software sharing on a network that already has domain controllers, DNS servers, gateways, or DHCP servers.

+ You still need a switch or wireless base station.

If you decide to use the built-in Internet Connection Sharing (ICS) feature of Windows 8 — perhaps to avoid buying a hardware sharing device — first double-check to ensure that you already have everything in this list:

+ **A working Ethernet network:** Emphasis on "working" — don't try to share your connection if your network isn't already running like a well-oiled machine. Chapter 2 of this minibook will guide you through these fast-moving waters.

+ **A working broadband Internet connection to one of the PCs on your network:** Okay, you can use ICS with a dialup connection as well, but take my advice and *don't*. As I mentioned earlier in the chapter, everything works much faster with a DSL, cable, or satellite connection.

+ **An installed copy of Windows 8 on the host PC that's connected to the Internet:** This PC also needs two network cards installed — one

Book VIII
Chapter 4

Sharing Your
Internet Connection

that leads to the network switch and one that leads to the cable or DSL modem (as shown in Figure 4-5). Because many flavors of network cards exist (using many different connections, such as USB, PC Card, and the more traditional internal adapter card), follow the installation instructions provided by the card manufacturer to add both cards to your PC.

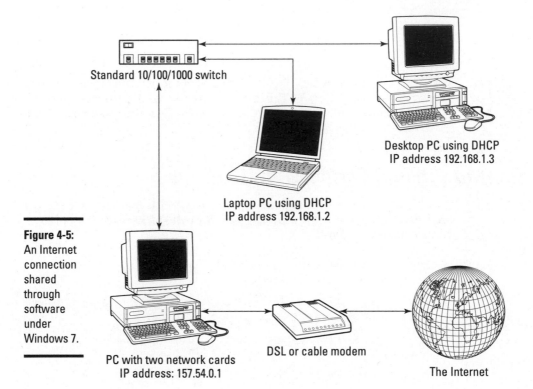

Figure 4-5:
An Internet
connection
shared
through
software
under
Windows 7.

Standard 10/100/1000 switch

Desktop PC using DHCP
IP address 192.168.1.3

Laptop PC using DHCP
IP address 192.168.1.2

PC with two network cards
IP address: 157.54.0.1

DSL or cable modem

The Internet

Everything shipshape? Good. Follow these steps to share that existing Internet connection on your host PC with the other computers on your network:

1. **Verify that you're connected to the Internet.**

I always open Internet Explorer and do the Google thing.

2. **Display the Charms bar, click Search and then click Settings. Type** Network **into the Search box.**

You should log in with an Administrator account, so that you'll have full rights to set things up — the account you used to install Windows 8 will be an Administrator account.)

3. **Click the Network and Sharing Center button in the Search results pane.**

4. **Click the Connections link for your Internet connection.**

   Typically, this reads *Ethernet*. Windows 8 displays the Status dialog box for your Internet connection.

5. **Click the Properties button.**

6. **Click the Sharing tab.**

   You won't see the Sharing tab unless you have at least two network connections (one to your DSL or cable modem, and one to your local network).

7. **Select the Allow Other Network Users to Connect through This Computer's Internet Connection check box.**

   I also recommend you disable the Allow Other Network Users to Control or Disable the Shared Internet Connection check box — this prevents someone on another of your network's PCs from accidentally disabling your shared Internet connection.

8. **Click OK to save your changes, and then click Close on the Status dialog box.**

   Windows 8 indicates that a connection is shared by adding a "couple of friends" badge under the connection icon.

**Book VIII
Chapter 4**

**Sharing Your
Internet Connection**

Chapter 5: Securing Your Home Network

In This Chapter

✔ **Keeping your wired network secure**

✔ **Ensuring that your wireless network is secure**

✔ **Working with shared folders**

✔ **Understanding NAT security**

✔ **Setting up virtual private networking (VPN) in Windows 8**

*P*robably the number-one question in my Outlook inbox these days is when readers ask me about home network security. "Am I opening my files to folks I don't know?" ranks right up there with "Am I sharing my Internet connection with the seedy teenager next door?" Frightening thoughts, indeed.

Regardless of whether you run a wired or wireless network — or some combination of both — I've got you covered in this chapter with a discussion of security tips and tricks you can use to help keep your network (and you) safe. Sure, a wired Ethernet network is easier to secure, but I have good news for the wireless network crowd, too. Read this chapter to see how to keep the private stuff private, even while sharing (using shared folders) the stuff you want to disseminate amongst others on your network.

And if you're always on the move, I also introduce you to the whiz-bang Windows 8 virtual private networking (VPN) feature, which enables you to reach your home network securely using any Internet connection!

Common Sense Tips for Wired Networks

Folks with wired home networks are often pretty doggone smug about their computer security because a connection to your network can occur only over a wired port or over the Internet. (In other words, you don't have to worry about broadcasting your address book across the street.)

What the Sam Hill does that mean?

When you're shopping for a wired or wireless Internet sharing device, you find that the side of the box mentions a number of nifty security features that seem to have been named by a very depressed engineer (who didn't speak common-folk English, either). Allow me to translate for you:

Static routing: This feature enables you to set up a preset network path between the device and an Internet host, which is likely to be an external network. Without static routing, you might not be able to use virtual private networking (VPN), which I discuss at the end of this chapter.

Dynamic routing: Basically, this concept is the reverse of static routing, which is a helpful feature for those who are continually yanking PCs, servers, and network hardware off the network and plugging stuff back in at other locations. With dynamic routing, the sharing device automatically compensates and adjusts for changes made to the *topology* (translation, *layout*) of your network.

Port forwarding: If you're running an e-mail, web, or File Transfer Protocol (FTP) server on your network, you can set the router to automatically divert any incoming traffic of that type — HyperText Transfer Protocol (HTTP) for the web server, for example — directly to the host PC.

I use this feature at my home office to provide my website, FTP server, and bulletin board system (BBS) to my visitors.

IP filtering: This feature allows you to block certain users or PCs from Internet access. It's also a helpful feature to have when you're using VPN.

WAN blocking: This term sounds like something that happens in a nuclear reactor, doesn't it? Luckily, this feature just prevents other PCs on the Internet from *pinging* (scanning) for your network, so it's a good idea to leave this one on. Another Mark's Maxim is in order: **It's generally a good thing to be invisible to other computers on the Internet.** ™ (More on this in Book III, Chapter 3.)

Demilitarized zone (DMZ) host: Finally, here's a feature that's designed just for us Internet gamers: You can set up your router with a special set of "holes" to "reveal" your PC to others on the Internet when you're connecting to an Internet game server (or if you're hosting your own server). Without a DMZ, your router's NAT firewall would likely block your PC from communicating with others (as I explain later in this chapter), and you wouldn't be able to join or create an Internet gaming battleground. Anyone for a fragfest in *Borderlands?*

First, the good news: If you followed my advice in earlier chapters about using the Windows 8 Firewall on each of your network PCs — or if you installed a third-party firewall application on each PC — you can be reasonably sure that your Internet connection is secure from The Bad Guys.

However, it's still possible to be a little *too* complacent about your wired network's security: Don't forget that the seedy teenager next door might end up dating your kid and spending time within the comfortable confines of your own home. Yep, it's Mark's Maxim time again:

> **Unless you can be absolutely certain that no one else has access to your wired network, it still pays to practice good network security policy!**™

With this Ultimate Truth in mind, here's a common sense checklist you can follow to help keep your wired network as secure as possible:

✦ **Use the armed guards supplied with Windows 8.** The moment you leave your PC unattended, you're opening the door for anyone else to step up and use it. For this reason, I recommend that you use a screen saver with the password feature enabled, and that you *always* assign a password to *every* account you create. Also, if security is an issue for your network, use the Windows 8 User Account Control (UAC) feature, which alerts you before running suspect applications or performing actions that could potentially harm your system. You can make this setting from the Windows 8 Charms bar: Click Search and then click Settings. Type **UAC** into the Search box. Click the Change User Account Control Settings button to display the window you see in Figure 5-1. Make sure that the Notify slider is set to either Always Notify (the first position) or the default (the second position). Click OK to save the change.

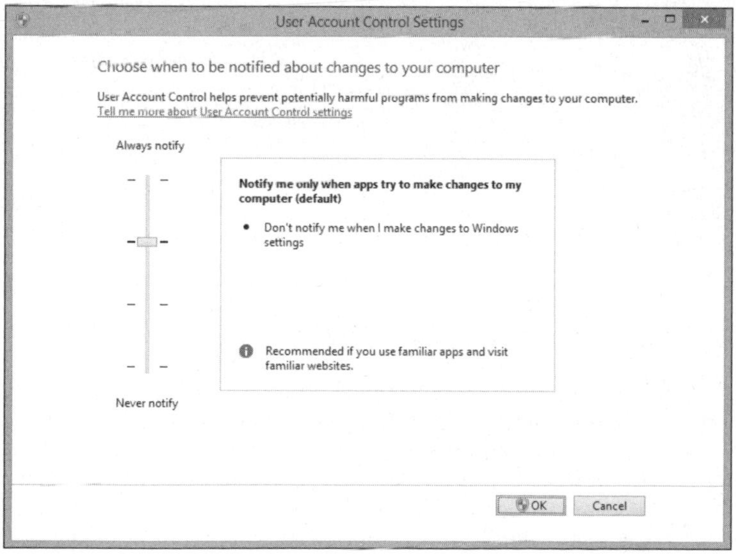

Figure 5-1:
Choosing
a User
Account
Control
setting
within
Windows 8.

![User Account Control Settings window]

User Account Control Settings

Choose when to be notified about changes to your computer

User Account Control helps prevent potentially harmful programs from making changes to your computer.
Tell me more about User Account Control settings

Always notify

— Notify me only when apps try to make changes to my computer (default)
  • Don't notify me when I make changes to Windows settings

Never notify

ⓘ Recommended if you use familiar apps and visit familiar websites.

OK   Cancel

✦ **Don't share passwords.** Do you regularly swap your credit card numbers with friends and relatives? I'm betting that you don't — and you should keep your login and screen saver passwords just as private.

✦ **Monitor your connections.** If you're using an Internet router or Internet sharing device, that device likely has a feature that enables you to see who's connected to your network (typically as part of the DHCP commands). Figure 5-2 illustrates my Internet router's DHCP connection table. Check your router's documentation to see how you can monitor who's connecting to it — and use this feature once a week or so, just to verify that the connections you see listed are the connections you *expected* to see. If you do encounter unwanted individuals who are using your wireless network, check your router's documentation to see whether it enables you to block them from connecting again.

✦ **Unplug unnecessary computers.** If a PC doesn't need a connection to your network, why keep it connected at all? Your wired network runs faster with fewer machines, and disconnecting that PC frees up a port on your switch or router for future use. (And, need I mention that another possible opening to your network has been closed?)

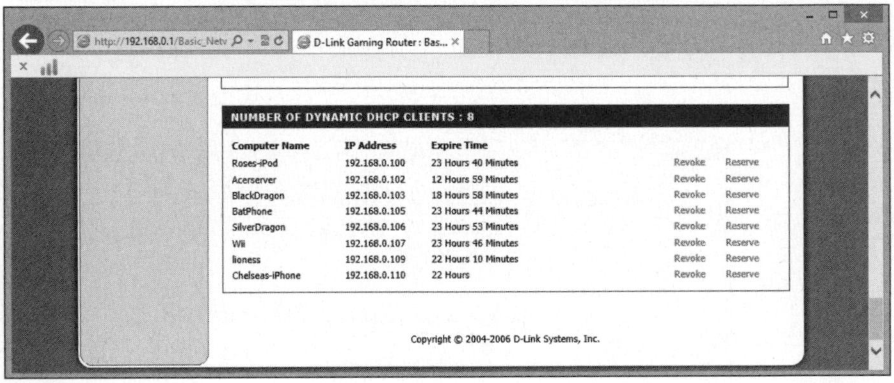

Figure 5-2:
Monitoring the machines on my wired Ethernet network.

Computer Name	IP Address	Expire Time		
Roses-iPod	192.168.0.100	23 Hours 40 Minutes	Revoke	Reserve
Acerserver	192.168.0.102	12 Hours 59 Minutes	Revoke	Reserve
BlackDragon	192.168.0.103	18 Hours 58 Minutes	Revoke	Reserve
BatPhone	192.168.0.105	23 Hours 44 Minutes	Revoke	Reserve
SilverDragon	192.168.0.106	23 Hours 53 Minutes	Revoke	Reserve
Wii	192.168.0.107	23 Hours 46 Minutes	Revoke	Reserve
lioness	192.168.0.109	22 Hours 10 Minutes	Revoke	Reserve
Chelseas-iPhone	192.168.0.110	22 Hours	Revoke	Reserve

NUMBER OF DYNAMIC DHCP CLIENTS : 8

Copyright © 2004-2006 D-Link Systems, Inc.

Ensuring Security on Your Wireless Network

If you're adding a wireless network to your home or office, security should be your first consideration before you send a single packet over the airwaves. First, if you're shopping for wireless hardware (as I discuss in Chapter 3 of this minibook), let me list the standards and features you should look for:

✦ **Do the WPA2.** WPA2 (blissfully short for *Wi-Fi Protected Access revision 2*) is a form of encryption that acts as your main defense against outside intrusion (as shown in Figure 5-3). Without the proper *key* (or, in human jargon, the proper *password*), a hacker is faced with a tough decoding job. The 256-bit WPA2 standard is the most common these days, and it does a creditable job of keeping your data secure. Choose hardware that supports the WPA2 standard whenever possible, and *make sure that WPA2 is enabled when you install the device.* (Note that devices older than three or four years may not support WPA2.)

Make your WPA2 key as long as allowed by your hardware, and also use the same common sense that you use when choosing your Internet passwords. Keys should be completely random. Don't use your middle name or your Social Security number, and remember to mix letters and numbers.

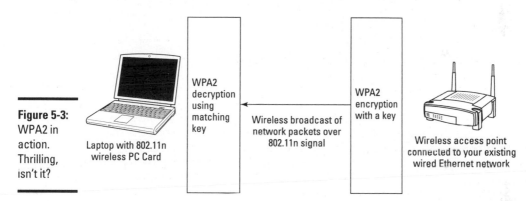

Figure 5-3:
WPA2 in action. Thrilling, isn't it?

Laptop with 802.11n wireless PC Card

WPA2 decryption using matching key

Wireless broadcast of network packets over 802.11n signal

WPA2 encryption with a key

Wireless access point connected to your existing wired Ethernet network

After you configure your wireless network, here are the security guidelines I recommend that you follow:

✦ **Use virtual private networking (VPN) for extra security.** As you can read in this chapter, VPN is a hard nut for an outsider to crack. When security is all-important, set up a VPN session.

✦ **Secure your SSID.** I know that statement sounds weird, but your *SSID* (service set identifier) is, essentially, the name for your wireless access point (WAP) or base station. Change your SSID immediately when you install your wireless base station or access point, making sure that you configured your system so that your SSID isn't broadcast to the outside world. (You have to configure your wireless connections manually; your WAP or base station doesn't show up automatically when your PC is in range.) Determining your SSID is the first step in hacking your wireless network. After you turn off the broadcast of your SSID, I guarantee that it's practically impossible for an outsider to guess that your SSID is *Bullwinkle007* (or something similar). Visit Chapter 3 of this minibook for all the details on WAPs and wireless base stations.

✦ **Change your access point or base station password.** Naturally, you also don't want anyone to be able to guess the password that secures your wireless access point or base station, so change that hardware password to something unique.

If anyone asks you to jump in his vehicle for a bit of "war driving," you'll understand why wireless security is so important. *War driving* occurs when hackers rig their cars with laptop PCs, equipped with a wireless network cards and cheap, omnidirectional antennas, and then drive around neighborhoods in their towns looking for unsecured wireless networks. When easy pickings are found, the hacker can use any broadband connection that's hooked up to that network (read that as "free Internet connection") or — much worse — haul away copies of the shared files and documents found on that network.

Using Shared Folders (the Right Way)

In Book II, Chapter 4, I mention the Public folder that resides in each of your Windows 8 Libraries — any file you store in the Public Documents, Public Music, Public Pictures, or Public Videos folders (or subfolders within) is immediately available to everyone else using your PC. You can always access your Public folders within each Library at the left side of an Explorer window; click the triangle next to the desired Library heading to expand it.

By default, the contents of your Windows 8 Libraries are private — no one else but you can access your files, and the files in each top-level Library aren't shared with other PCs across your network. On the other hand, the contents of the Public subfolder that appears within each Library *are* shared across your local network and among the user accounts on that lone PC.

Don't forget that you can also enable HomeGroup sharing for your Libraries at any time, allowing other PCs running Windows 7 or 8 in your HomeGroup to access files you specify inside your Libraries. If HomeGroup sharing isn't turned on, display the Charms bar, click Search, and then click Settings. Type **HomeGroup** into the Search box. Click the HomeGroup button in the Search results pane to display the HomeGroup settings. (If a HomeGroup is already set up on your network, you'll be prompted for the password.)

For multiple users sharing only one PC, Public folders are the bee's knees: They're already set up as soon as you install Windows 8. Likewise, you can share the contents of your Libraries across your network using the HomeGroup feature. But what if you need to share the contents of a folder *outside* the Windows 8 Libraries structure with others on your network? That's where *shared network folders* come in handy.

I show you how to create a shared network folder in Chapter 2 of this mini-book. I want to remind you, though, of these three important security guidelines that you should follow when using your Public Library folders, shared Libraries using HomeGroup, or the shared folders you create:

✦ **Never, never, *never* share an item unless it's necessary!** Remember that Windows 8 doesn't differentiate who gets to open which documents within your Public folders. The contents are available to everyone using your network. Perhaps that updated copy of your resume should be withheld from prying eyes. . . . And, while we're at it, I'd like to stress that you should *never* share one of your PC's hard drives across your network! (Microsoft warns you against such a gaping hole in your security as well, if you decide to try sharing a drive.) Why? Well, you're also sharing *everything* on that drive — *every last file in every last folder,* including the stuff you probably either don't know about or forgot was there. Share only what you need to share: 'Nuff said.

✦ **Assign the Read permission level.** When you share a folder, you set share permissions: that is, what rights you give the user. If you opt for the Owner permission level, that person can edit (or even delete) files. If you would rather keep these files pristine, go for the Read permission level; that way, other network users can open and print the documents in the folder but can't edit or delete them. (I cover these permission levels in Book II, Chapter 4.)

✦ **Use descriptive names for your shared folders.** It just makes good sense. I generally create only one shared folder for each PC on a network, and that folder name reflects the PC's network name (like Shared Folder – Den or Shared Folder – Rm 321), which helps you keep track of which shared resources are on which PC.

Knowing Why You Need NAT

Okay, you might have heard of NAT (Network Address Translation), and you think that it's probably important — but what does it *do?* Well, check out Figure 5-4. If your Internet sharing device (or your Internet sharing software) supports NAT, a number of different PCs — each with a different Internet Protocol (IP) address — are masked behind the single IP address that your ISP assigned to your cable or DSL modem. No one can tell which individual IP addresses are used behind your NAT device.

To hack a PC on your system, someone on the outside (meaning, elsewhere on the Internet) has to know the IP address of an individual computer on your system, and NAT prevents the intruder from learning just that. Instead, the only IP address that's visible is the modem or Internet-sharing device itself. Plus, a NAT blocks the most common weapon in the hacker arsenal: probing "port sniffers" that hunt for open, unprotected ports across the Internet.

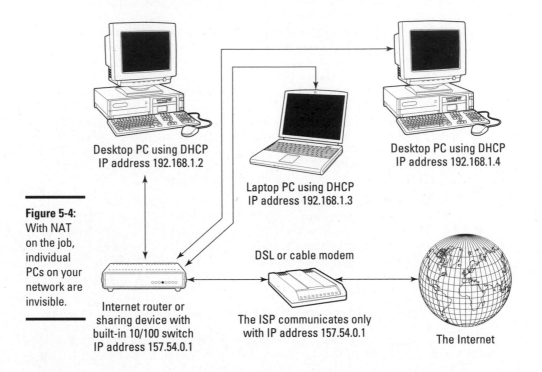

Figure 5-4: With NAT on the job, individual PCs on your network are invisible.

Desktop PC using DHCP
IP address 192.168.1.2

Laptop PC using DHCP
IP address 192.168.1.3

Desktop PC using DHCP
IP address 192.168.1.4

DSL or cable modem

Internet router or sharing device with built-in 10/100 switch
IP address 157.54.0.1

The ISP communicates only with IP address 157.54.0.1

The Internet

NAT isn't a complete firewall, but when your connection-sharing hardware or software uses NAT in conjunction with the Windows 8 Firewall, you effectively shut the door on Internet intruders! By the way, I discuss the built-in Windows 7 Firewall in Book III, Chapter 3.

Marveling at the Magic of Virtual Private Networking

Imagine if you could take your networking one step further. Rather than use wires or even a wireless network, what if you could create a secure network connection over the Internet into your private network? You could enjoy the benefits of using your private home network anywhere in the world — as long as an Internet connection was handy.

Such is the reality of virtual private networking — and the emphasis, of course, is on the words *private* and *secure*. (It's one thing to have access to your files from across the country, but giving that same access to an interested hacker is another thing entirely.) Your data is protected by encryption when it passes over the Internet; so for all intents and purposes, your connection is as well protected as a correctly configured wireless network.

VPN places you squarely back into the realm of client/server networking, where the VPN *client* is the PC that you're using remotely and the VPN *server* is the machine on your home network that you're connecting to.

In this section, I demonstrate how to set up your laptop PC (or a remote desktop) as a VPN client under Windows 8, with the following assumptions (based on how VPN is used most often in real-world situations):

✦ **You're using either**

   • *A broadband connection to the Internet*

      VPN over a dialup modem connection is the definition of the word *frustrating.* Don't.

   • *Another company's network Internet connection*

✦ **Your network administrator has provided you with the IP address of the VPN server (in an office environment) or you've configured a VPN server on a PC on your home network.**

✦ **You'll use your regular network username and password to log in.**

Follow these steps to create and use a VPN connection:

1. **Display the Charms bar, click Search, and then click Settings. Type VPN into the Search box. Click the Set Up a Virtual Private Network (VPN) Connection button in the Search results pane.**

   The Create a VPN Connection Wizard appears.

2. **Enter the following (as shown in Figure 5-5):**

   • The VPN server address, provided by your network administrator or displayed by your home network's host PC (such as 157.54.0.1), into the Internet Address text box

      This address can also be in the form of a host name in good ol' English (like **mlcbooks.com**).

Again, I'm a bit paranoid about enabling the Remember My Credentials check box because anyone using your (unattended) computer can simply log on as you. Weigh carefully the possible results of convenience.

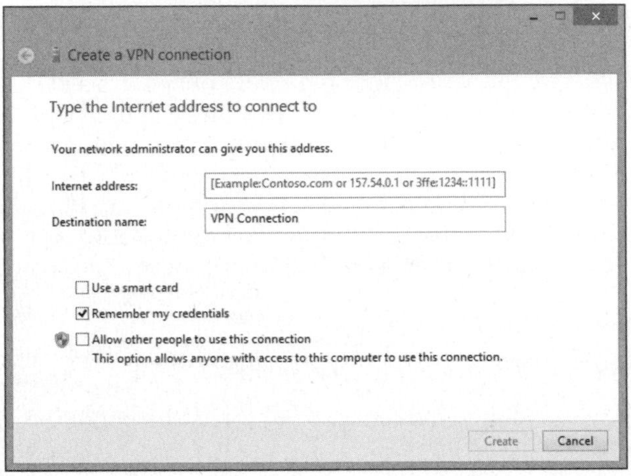

Figure 5-5:
Enter the IP address or host name for your VPN server.

• A *descriptive name* to help you keep track of the connection (such as **MLC Books VPN Client**) in the Destination Name text box

3. **(Optional) If you want to allow other user accounts on your PC to use this connection, select the Allow Other People to Use This Connection check box.**

As Windows 8 indicates with the "shield" security icon, allowing anyone with access to your PC to use a VPN connection might not be a good idea. Unless more than one user account on your computer has to have this VPN connection, I recommend that you leave this check box deselected and prudently keep your VPN connection to yourself!

4. **Click Create.**

Windows 8 creates the connection and displays it under the Networks heading in the Charms bar (as shown in Figure 5-6).

TIP

If you need to make changes to your VPN connection properties — for example, if you have to change the IP address of the VPN server on your network — open the Charms bar and click Settings, and then click Network to display the Networks list. Right-click your VPN connection and then choose View Connection Properties, which displays the VPN Connection Properties dialog box. From there, you can make any necessary changes.

When you're ready to use your VPN connection — and you're hooked up to the Internet during your travels — open the Charms bar and click Settings, and then click Network to display the Networks list. Click the VPN entry, and click Connect. Windows 8 prompts you for your username and password, as shown in Figure 5-7; type your username and password and then click the OK button to begin your VPN session, and you'll find that you can now access all the network resources that you're accustomed to on your host PC.

Figure 5-6:
Click
your VPN
connection
in the
Networks
list to start
the ball
rolling.

**Book VIII
Chapter 5**

Securing Your
Home Network

Figure 5-7:
Making
the VPN
connection.

Now tell me that technology ain't grand!

Book IX

Gaming

 Visit www.dummies.com/extras/pcsaio for more on top requirements for a gaming PC.

Contents at a Glance

Chapter 1: What's Different About a Gaming PC?

In This Chapter

✔ Understanding the gamer's primary needs

✔ Determining which version of Windows to use

✔ Discovering other internal performance upgrades

✔ Answering questions about overclocking

Hardcore PC gamers are demanding, impatient, and sometimes downright nitpicky. And those are often their *good* qualities. (I should know, I'm one myself.)

Even with our faults, however, you have to admit that we love immersing ourselves in The Game, whether it be the latest first-person slugfest, a multiplayer online role-playing game, or a thoughtful attempt to conquer any one of a thousand different worlds through stealth and strategy. If you'd like to join us, it's a great time to be a gamer!

Ah, but here's the catch: You've gotta have the right hardware to play with the big boys and girls at the highest resolutions and the fastest speeds. Gamers push their PCs to the limits because the most popular games typically demand it — if you've got a slower PC with stuttering graphics or a lousy Internet connection, you're already at a disadvantage.

In this chapter, I present the state of PC gaming hardware today, and what to look for when buying (or building) your own gaming monster machine!

But First, the Gamer Disclaimer

I know — catchy, right? More than any other chapter in this entire tome, the words that follow require a disclaimer. To wit: the gaming performance bar is raised practically *every month* with the introduction of all sorts of faster PC hardware (especially graphics cards). In the time it takes to publish and distribute a print book like this one, the CPU or graphics card that's the darling of the gaming community today will almost certainly be mediocre, old-school equipment! Such is the nature of power-hungry, cutting-edge PC games and the computer hardware required to play them at the highest possible quality levels.

Therefore, I won't make any specific (and soon-to-be-outdated) hardware recommendations in this chapter. Instead, I provide more general information in the form of tips and feature lists that you can use to shop around for the Latest and Greatest when you're ready to build or buy.

Introducing the Big Three

Where do you start when shopping or planning a rock-solid gaming machine? Sure, there's the flashy case with the lights — which really count as nothing but eye candy — and the hefty price tag, but the *real* brawn behind any high-performance PC depends on what I like to call the Big Three: your CPU, system memory, and graphics card. These are the foundations of good gaming hardware, and they're hidden in the innards of your computer.

I discuss all three of these PC components in general detail in Book VII, and the recommendations I make there still apply to a gaming PC — however, in this chapter, speed is everything (and prices are typically sky-high). Here, I concentrate on keeping your PC running fast enough to play the latest games. Let's dig in, shall we?

Your PC's processor

As you probably already know, your PC's CPU processes data according to the instructions provided by a program — in our case, a game or Windows itself — and it also sends commands and data to the various peripherals in your system. But why are games so demanding on your CPU? Consider the work involved in running a popular 3D first-person shooting game such as Crysis 3, where the processor in your gaming computer must handle all of these chores:

✦ **Artificial intelligence:** Your PC must react to your movements, calculate the appropriate strategy, and manipulate the computer players (which are becoming more and more sophisticated with every passing year).

✦ **Level control:** Your PC must calculate the appearance of both your character and your surroundings for your current position on the game level. Plus, your computer must process the results when your character interacts with traps, switches, doors, and their corresponding keys.

✦ **Calculations and events:** Your PC must calculate the path of your last missile launch, determine whether it hit its target, and alter the statistics of the target where appropriate.

✦ **Multiplayer support:** If you're participating in a multiplayer match or a multiplayer online world, your PC must send and receive data packets across the network (whether it's a local network or the Internet) from other computers and incorporate other players into your environment. In today's games, that may also include voice chatting between players as the fight continues!

Oh, and meanwhile your PC must still keep Windows running smoothly, as well as any other background tasks you're using. No wonder your CPU needs its own cooling system! Of course, your graphics card relieves your CPU from the lion's share of the low-level graphic calculations necessary for 3D gaming, but your CPU's performance still determines what types of games you can play. (In other words, even the fastest graphics card won't help you play a game with computing requirements that swamp your CPU.) Therefore, when you're building or buying a new gaming PC from scratch, the processor you select is a hugely important decision.

While shopping, consider a balance between the number of cores (in multicore processors like the AMD FX and Intel i7) and the processor's overall speed. I would definitely recommend at least a four-core processor, but there's typically not much need for additional cores after that in a gaming PC — instead, *concentrate on getting the highest processor speed you can afford* with four cores.

On-board cache memory is also important for the gamer's CPU because it's the fastest memory available on your PC. It acts as a temporary "waiting room" for data that your CPU is likely to need in the near future; some CPUs also use it to store data that has recently been accessed, so that it can be recalled again without reloading it from your hard drive or system RAM. The more cache you have, the better. It's also better to use *on-board* cache memory, which is actually built into the CPU itself; all current processors offer some amount of on-board cache.

Your PC's memory

Next up in our gamer's hardware Big Three list? It's our old friend RAM! Yep, I've already been harping on the importance of PC system memory throughout earlier chapters in this book, but a gaming PC with less than 8GB of RAM is doomed to slower performance with the latest titles.

And not just any RAM will do for a high-performance PC, either. Although most PC owners tend to think that "all memory is created equal," that's not the case with a gaming PC. At the time of this writing (and for at least the near future), your PC (or the motherboard you purchase, if you're assembling yourself) should use the fastest supported DDR3 memory your hardware can handle. Those memory modules should also be equipped with cooling fins or plates. (Yep, bunkie, you read that right. The memory a gamer demands can run so hot that — like your CPU — it needs additional cooling in order to avoid data errors!)

Now comes what folks my age still call the "64 thousand dollar question" — how much memory is necessary for a gaming PC? As I've already said, a minimum of 8GB is preferred, but as for a maximum, the sky (or, in this case, the motherboard) is the limit! As I discussed earlier in this book, the more memory you can afford to add to your motherboard, the faster everything runs (and that includes Windows and the other applications you run because most gamers use their hugely expensive toys for their other computing needs as well). Therefore, 16 to 32GB of system RAM is a zone I feel comfortable in recommending. (Personally, 64GB is out of the range of my wallet.)

Your PC's graphics card

The third element in any great gaming PC is the graphics card — in fact, most of my friends would revoke my membership in the hard-core gaming community if I didn't say graphics *cards* (in the plural) because most of the current crop of cards are designed to link together to provide even faster frame rates and detail.

And that, friends and neighbors, is what it's all about: Today's games provide 3D realism, Photoshop-quality visual effects, and a level of display complexity that would have been absolutely unthinkable a mere five years ago. (Of course, I was saying the same thing five years ago as well.) However, your PC must be able to deliver those details at an acceptable *frame rate* (that's the number of times the game can update the image you see, expressed as *frames per second* or *FPS*). If the frame rate is too low, the fluid motion you expect from the game slows to a jerky crawl. Today's PC games require at least 30 FPS (some can accommodate frame rates of over 100 FPS), and you can achieve that minimum 30 FPS in one of two ways:

✦ **Provide the performance.** If your PC's graphics hardware is up to the task, you can enjoy every detail and every 3D effect at the full settings, and at the full resolutions supported by today's high-definition monitors.

✦ **Turn stuff off.** If your graphics *aren't* fast enough for today's games, you'll have to disable details and 3D effects in order to reach that 30 FPS mark, significantly reducing the experience. You may also have to reduce the resolution of your system while you play. (In layman's terms, your game certainly won't look like it did on the back of the box.)

No need for speculation upon which option a hard-core gamer will choose.

Today's graphics cards carry their own on-board processors (called GPUs, short for *graphics processing units*), so don't be confused if I seem to be talking about more than one processor in this chapter. I am: the CPU, which resides on your motherboard, and the GPU, which resides on your motherboard (for integrated graphics hardware) or on a PCI adapter card (for a dedicated graphics card).

The truth about your built-in graphics hardware

Today's motherboards are equipped with built-in graphics hardware (although there should definitely be at least one dedicated graphics slot still available for you to use), and I'm often asked if a potential PC gamer can't save a little money and use the integrated graphics card rather than spend the money on an expensive PCI Express 3.0 card. The answer is a big "maybe" — everything hinges on the type of games you'd like to play. In general, integrated graphics hardware includes a cheaper GPU that's typically at least a generation old — if you're planning on playing older games or titles with less-demanding effects and lower resolutions (perhaps Civilization IV or something similar), your PC's integrated hardware should be able to deliver the goods.

However, a dedicated graphics card offers two advantages that will greatly enhance cutting-edge games: a whopping amount of on-board memory and a fan that will significantly reduce the heat generated by the card (especially if you've decided to overclock your graphics hardware). Without these extras, your integrated graphics hardware will almost certainly be unable to deliver higher frame rates within the most demanding games, and you'll be forced to skimp on detail, resolution, and effects.

Here's the recommendation that I give most often: You have nothing to lose if you try your built-in graphics hardware with the games you buy, so go ahead and put your PC through its paces with the integrated card. However, if you're disappointed with the results, start saving for that new PCI Express 3.0 x16 graphics card right now! (And don't forget, future requirements for new titles will only get more demanding, so your integrated hardware is eventually doomed to obsolescence anyway.)

With the latest features in mind (as of this writing), here's what to look for when shopping for high-end video cards from AMD and NVIDIA:

✦ **DirectX 11 support.** Games running on Windows Vista, 7, and 8 can use Microsoft's DirectX 11 graphics software to provide the most complex and detailed effects currently available on a PC. Any card you're considering should support DirectX 11.

✦ **A minimum of 1GB of on-board memory.** Most of the current crop of cards carry either 1 or 2GB of RAM on the card — this is dedicated graphics memory, so it's separate from your PC's system RAM.

✦ **A minimum of one on-board fan.** Again, adequate cooling is an absolute necessity for a high-performance gaming graphics card.

✦ **PCI Express 3.0 x16 connector.** Today's fastest graphics cards use a PCI Express 3.0 x16 slot on your motherboard. If you're unsure what type of card slots are available on your PC, check your user manual (or your motherboard's manual).

✦ **Support for linking cards.** Cards with NVIDIA processors can use SLI, while AMD cards offer CrossFireX — both technologies involve linking multiple cards together using cables. (Note that the cards must use the same brand of GPU, so choose the cards carefully and make sure that they are compatible — many gamers choose two of the same cards. Naturally, your motherboard also needs more than one dedicated graphics card slot.)

✦ **HDMI and DVI ports.** Cards with both DVI and HDMI ports can connect to a wide range of monitors and HD TVs.

Pay close attention to graphic benchmark results while shopping for a new PC, motherboard, or graphics card. Like most of the gaming community, I use 3DMark 11 benchmark software from Futuremark (www.3dmark.com) when comparing specific cards. Hardware review sites like Tom's Hardware (www.tomshardware.com) are a great resource when shopping, and it always helps to be able to benchmark your current graphics hardware as a starting point.

What Version of Windows Is Best for Gaming?

This is a question that crops up often in Internet gaming forums, and those discussions can get heated! Typically, the argument involves two camps, each of which offers a number of advantages they see as essential:

✦ **The latest and greatest:** Some gamers maintain that the latest version of Windows is always the best choice for a gaming PC because Microsoft typically adds support for the latest graphics cards, game controllers, and the like, as well as the latest version of DirectX. In the case of Windows 8, the operating system also boots and shuts down significantly faster.

✦ **The previous version of Windows:** Naturally, gamers can't hang on to a specific older version of Windows indefinitely — for example, a number of the latest games won't run on Windows XP — but many gamers insist that previous versions of Windows require less system RAM and provide better performance on a new gaming PC. They also point out that game patches and updates may not be available or adequately tested for older titles running on the latest version of Windows. (I've encountered this problem myself with games that were produced while Windows XP was current.)

At the time of this writing, this debate rests squarely between Windows 7 and Windows 8 because Windows Vista has been dropped from future DirectX support. Windows XP (although a dependable workhorse otherwise) shouldn't be considered at all for a gaming PC.

Which should you choose? The way I see it, personal preference is king — at the time of this writing, there are no games that demand Windows 8 as a requirement, so if you're comfortable running Windows 7, you should have a clear gaming horizon for some time to come.

Other Gaming Hardware that Pushes Performance

Now that you're familiar with the three most important components in any gaming PC, it's time to cover Mark's Additional Gaming Hardware — you're not quite done yet! Although these features may not be absolute require-ments for a well-rounded gaming PC, you shouldn't forget them while com-parison shopping, so add them to your list as well.

Don't forget that these components are all located *inside* your PC's case — I'll be discussing external gaming hardware in Chapter 2 of this minibook.

Fast hard drives

Gamers often get so wrapped up in the exotic that they forget about the mundane. For example, I've talked to dozens of fellow gamers who wax enthusiastic about their "incredibly-fast, state-of-the-art, high-end, unbe-lievably-expensive" graphics cards — and yet, when I ask what type of hard drive they're using in their PC, they can't even name the brand.

Sure, the graphics cards in a gaming PC are very important, but the speed of your hard drive subsystem is also important in determining your final score against Dr. Destructive and the Legion of Inter-dimensional Monstrosities. Plus, if you have a fast hard drive, that game (and Windows, and your other applications) will load much, *much* faster, which is probably just as beneficial for your gaming well-being, at least in the long run.

There are three storage features you should add to your shopping list while evaluating a gaming system (or a bare-bones hard drive, if you're building):

✦ **RPM:** The faster the rotation, the faster the data transfer — I recommend a minimum of 7,200 RPM, but I use a 10,000 RPM drive on my gaming PC, and there are a number of (quite expensive) 15,000 RPM drives on the market.

✦ **Cache:** Look for a drive with a minimum of 16MB of cache memory (the larger the cache, the more data your drive can accept while reading and writing data, and the faster your transfer rates).

✦ **Interface:** Today's fastest consumer drives run on SAS or SATA connections at 3.0 or 6.0Gb/second (the interface your PC can accept depends on what the motherboard supports, of course, but if you're shopping for components, this information can come in handy).

Today's gamers can also choose from SSD (*solid-state* drives) and *hybrid* drives (which offer solid-state storage and magnetic storage in the same drive). Typically, solid-state drives do not perform as well as magnetic hard drives while gaming, but hybrid drives (although expensive) are well-suited to a gaming PC.

External ports

Now consider the external connections you may need to make with your gaming PC: backup drives, media devices like digital cameras and camcorders, smartphones, and an ever-growing list of digital hangers-on that surround your system like an entourage around a movie star.

Although the fastest external connection available for PCs today is Intel's Thunderbolt port, there aren't yet many motherboards (or consumer systems) that support Thunderbolt (and the peripherals that are currently on the market are hideously expensive). In the next couple of years, however, I predict that Thunderbolt will become the gamer's connection of choice for external hard drives and multiple high-resolution monitors on one PC. If you can afford a gaming PC with Thunderbolt ports (or a motherboard that offers them), spending that money is an investment in the future.

At the time of this writing, the primary ports of choice are

✦ **USB 3.0:** Considerably faster than USB 2.0 ports, but still backwards-compatible (so you can use all those USB 2.0 gaming controllers, mice, and keyboards you already have).

✦ **eSATA:** eSATA ports are an excellent choice for an external backup drive, or an external drive array that includes multiple drives.

Sound hardware

Here's an item that you may very well be able to skip! Why? Luckily, today's motherboards typically include excellent integrated 3D-capable sound hardware, complete with support for 5.1 (six-channel) or 7.1 (eight-channel) surround sound. For example, my gaming PC's motherboard already included excellent built-in RealTek 7.1 sound hardware, complete with software mixer and all sorts of effects. I often use the card's 3D spatial audio with those games that support this feature.

If you do need to shop for a sound card, a 24-bit, 96KHz PCI sound card with 7.1 surround sound support should set you back no more than $40 or so.

Oh, and unlike the integrated graphics hardware found on a motherboard, you won't be overclocking your sound hardware! (More on overclocking in the next section.)

Heavy-duty cooling

I can't stress enough the importance of *powerful* cooling for your gaming PC — and that includes

✦ Multiple fans for the case itself

✦ A CPU-mounted fan

✦ A GPU-mounted fan on your graphics card

If you're buying an assembled gaming PC, make sure that the manufacturer has provided your case with a strong steady airflow from front to back (and perhaps even back to top, as with my Antec case, which features a saucer-sized fan on top of the case as well as two fans in front and two in back). If you're shopping for a bare case, airflow is a top priority, so ensure that the case you buy is made especially for gaming (and that it comes with the fans, or they're preinstalled for you).

You may have also heard bizarre tales of liquid-cooled gaming PCs — let me tell you that those aren't fairy tales, and that liquid-cooled gaming *does* indeed exist on Planet Earth! Liquid-cooled systems are generally favored by those gamers who are overclocking their PCs to exceptional levels because these cooling units can quickly dissipate far more heat than a standard fan/ heatsink combo. Today's liquid-cooling systems are far easier to install than those of three or four years ago, and the prices have dropped on these units dramatically as well. (For examples of liquid cooling units, visit www. corsair.com and check out the Hydro series of liquid CPU coolers.)

Should I Overclock My Processors?

Remember those custom hot rods and muscle cars of the 50s, 60s and 70s? Before the days of the sport utility vehicle, kids dreamed about adding huge superchargers and heavy transmissions to a sports car to make it a true hot rod. Sure, building a hot rod was more expensive than buying a typical car, but the raw power and speed of a souped-up Mustang, Camaro, or Javelin made it worthwhile. Unfortunately, most hot rods didn't last as long as a typical car, either — the high RPM and all that street racing took its toll on the car.

In a similar fashion, today's gamers often turn a typical CPU or GPU into a hot rod processor . . . but instead of adding a supercharger, they use a technique called *overclocking* to make a processor work harder and faster. Instead of adding high-performance parts, overclocking involves changing the bus speed and/or the clock multiplier on your motherboard or graphics hardware — although your CPU or GPU remains the same physically, it's running at a faster frequency (and therefore executing more instructions in the same time frame because a faster frequency means more instruction cycles per second).

Overclocking can be a complicated process, and it rarely provides a trouble-free boost the first time you try it. Although there are downsides to overclocking (which I list in a second), you'll find plenty of tutorials and articles on the web that will guide you through the process. You can locate these articles by simply searching for the word "overclocking" followed by your model of CPU or GPU on a search engine such as Google or Bing. Freeware and shareware overclocking software is also available for just about any processor.

Here's my honest opinion on overclocking . . . I personally don't recommend that you try it unless you know what you're doing, and your CPU or GPU is simply no longer fast enough to handle the games you want to play. (Overclocking is certainly cheaper than buying a new, faster PC!) Before you decide, here's a list of the important reasons why you should carefully consider the decision to overclock your CPU or GPU:

✦ **Your hardware must support overclocking.** Some CPU/motherboard and GPU/graphics card combinations are far more suitable for over-clocking than others — if your hardware doesn't support overclock-ing (and it's not something that's generally mentioned in a PC user's manual), there is a risk of damaging your hardware. If overclocking isn't mentioned in your motherboard (or PC) user manual, you may find over-clocking help on the Internet by searching for the model number of your motherboard or PC.

✦ **Overclocking usually voids a manufacturer's warranty.** If you do decide to overclock, you may be voiding the warranty from your PC's manufacturer. (This also applies to the manufacturer of your mother-board, CPU, and graphics card.)

✦ **Overclocking *will* shorten the life of your CPU/GPU.** Due to the effects of heat on the structure of today's chips, even processors running at their rated speed eventually degrade — this process takes many years, so it's not normally a concern. However, the extra heat produced by overclocking a processor automatically shortens its operational life. (Those who overclock are usually aware of this, but they argue that the rate of processor development will make any processor obsolete in three or four years anyway.)

Because of this ever-present danger from heat damage, smart PC owners who *do* overclock invariably invest in the best possible fans and cooling systems for their processors. Without such heavy-duty cooling, over-clocking a processor will quickly destroy it.

✦ **Overclocking can produce lockups and errors:** This makes sense — if you're pushing hardware beyond its design specifications, you're going to introduce problems if your overclocking configuration isn't exactly right. Overclocking usually involves a long process of tweaking your processor's frequency to achieve the most trouble-free operation — but even with the best settings, you're likely to experience occasional lock-ups. (An overclocking PC gamer accepts this as part of the deal.)

Chapter 2: Gaming Hardware That Helps You Win

In This Chapter

✔ Selecting the right controller

✔ Adding a gaming mouse or keyboard

✔ Using a gaming headset with VoIP

✔ Playing with glasses

The controllers that you use to play your favorite games might be the difference between a win and a loss — and that includes ordinary-looking mice, trackballs, and keyboards that hide features that can give you the edge!

However, there's more to gaming peripherals than just the hand-held tools of the trade: with the right gaming microphone and headphones, you can swap all sorts of jibes and laughter while playing your friends (or work together with your team to trounce the opposition). And why limit yourself to a mere two dimensions when you can use gaming glasses, which can immerse you in a 3D environment?

I'll be honest, I loved writing this chapter, and I only wish I could afford all the toys I mention. Prepare to enter the gamer's equipment closet!

Aren't All Controllers Created Equal?

Although I use *game controller* often in this minibook as a generic term (indicating any hand-held, desk-bound, or portable device that accepts player input), there are actually four basic types of controllers in use today — and I'd better define what they are before we go any further. Controllers are divided into

✦ **Traditional joysticks:** Although computer gaming on the Atari and Commodore started out with eight-position plastic joysticks (the four compass points and four angles), today's joysticks allow full 360-degree directional movement. Joysticks are almost exclusively used by flight simulators (both civilian and combat), so you may never need one unless your goal is to practice your pilot skills.

✦ **Gamepads:** These controllers are descended from the gamepads first introduced on the Nintendo and Sega home video game systems, and still popular on today's Xbox and Sony PlayStation systems. A typical gamepad has either one or two directional pads for movement and anywhere from two to eight buttons. Gamepads are often used in conjunction with a keyboard because most don't offer enough buttons to handle the baker's dozen of key commands in today's PC games.

✦ **Steering wheel/pedal combinations:** Racing fans will immediately fall in love with these controllers, which can even include a shifter. The typical steering wheel controller clamps to your desk or table, while the pedals are contained in a separate unit at your feet.

✦ **Mouse/trackball controllers:** These controllers are the most recent inventions in PC gaming technology, usually integrating a pointing device (either a mouse or a trackball) with a mini-keyboard or array of programmable buttons. Depending on the game, they may be used in conjunction with a keyboard, or they may have enough function buttons to be used alone.

Let's talk force-feedback and vibration

First, a definition: a *force-feedback controller* provides realistic tactile feedback each time the player's character in the game feels a jolt, bump, or impact. The best force-feedback joysticks and steering wheels can recreate the force of a missile hit, the resistance of your steering wheel as you speed around a corner at high speed, and the recoil of your railgun in a first-person shooting game. Gamepads use vibration for the same effect.

So why isn't force-feedback on my list of must-have controller features? For the simple reason that not everyone is a fan of force-feedback and vibration — they are definitely *not* necessary for good gameplay, and I've met many veteran players who find the feature distracting and scoff at the idea that a vibrating controller or a steering wheel that offers resistance is going to enhance anyone's enjoyment of a PC game. (The good news is that most controllers now allow you to switch off force-feedback if you wish.) I definitely recommend that you try a force-feedback controller before you buy.

No matter what type of controller you select, the features that every gamer desires on a controller are the same. Here's a short shopping list of features to look for when choosing a controller:

✦ **Programmable buttons:** This one's a no-brainer: Every gamer should invest in a controller with programmable buttons! Most games enable you to change the default keyboard assignments to other functions — essentially the same as programming the keyboard — but the same is usually not true for basic controllers without programmable buttons. With a programmable controller, you can assign virtually any possible keyboard or mouse function to your buttons (some high-end controllers can even run a simple "script" of sorts, which automatically performs multiple functions with a single press of a key). For example, you may assign a button for the 1 key, which swaps your weapon — or, with a macro, it can be a combination of the 1 key followed by the R key, which swaps the weapon and then reloads.

✦ **USB connection:** Today's controllers use your PC's USB port — if you're considering buying an antique joystick that uses a serial or gameport connection, make absolutely sure that your PC has the proper port to accommodate the controller, and make sure you can download a device driver for the controller that works with today's versions of Windows.

✦ **Wireless operation:** These controllers don't need a direct cable connection to your PC, which allows you to relax some distance away while gaming. Some wireless controllers include their own receiver unit, whereas others use Bluetooth technology — again, make sure your PC supports Bluetooth before you buy, or pick up a USB Bluetooth adapter.

✦ **A longer warranty:** Although you may not be one of those gamers who throws an innocent controller halfway across a room after losing a race, your controllers still take a heck of a beating . . . in fact, the typical gamepad endures more punishment than any other component on your PC. Because of this rough treatment, I highly recommend a controller that offers at least a two-year warranty, and the longer the better!

✦ **Support for lefties:** Are you a left-handed gamer? Suddenly, many of the high-end, ergonomic controllers are off-limits because they're especially made for the right hand. The best controllers on the market accept left or right-handed grips, from hands of all sizes, and the button design can be used by either "secondary" hand.

✦ **Auto-fire:** Although realism is important, you may also find yourself flying a Starfighter against the dreaded Space Gargoyles of Planet 99 — and that's when you'll appreciate the opportunity to fire your lasers as fast as possible! An auto-fire control will fire your weapons as fast as the game allows, and without interruption (sparing you a sore thumb).

As with other peripherals I mention in this book — like monitors, head-phones, and speakers — I highly recommend that you take time to play a few minutes of your favorite game in a computer store with the controller that you're considering, or buy from a store that accepts returns! *All* controllers look great in the box photographs, but it takes a few close calls in your favorite game to evaluate whether the layout, the buttons, and the *feel* of a controller are right for you.

Not Your Average Keyboard and Mouse

Next up on the gaming peripheral hit parade is the gaming keyboard and mouse/trackball combo that many ace players swear by. You may be wondering what could possibly be done to these two venerable input devices that would make them so attractive for gamers. Allow me to introduce you to a couple of good friends of mine, straight from my desk: the Logitech G19 gaming keyboard and the Logitech G700 Wireless Gaming Mouse (both from www.logitech.com). Did you notice that the mouse offers one of those prime features I mention earlier in the chapter already? (It's wireless.)

On the keyboard side, the G19 (which retails for $200) has four features that help illustrate the attraction of a gaming keyboard:

✦ **Customizable backlighting:** Like me, many gamers prefer a darkened room while playing, and you can choose the color and arrangement of backlighted keys to make them easy to spot.

✦ **12 programmable keys:** You can configure up to 3 macros (remember, macros are *strings* of keyboard commands, not just a single command) for each of these programmable keys. Each game you play can have its own 36 customized keys!

✦ **Windows keys disable:** Ever died because you pressed the Windows key on your keyboard by accident and found yourself staring at the Start screen? Not with the G19, which enables you to disable the Windows keys while playing.

✦ **LCD panel:** And the crowning touch? This keyboard has its own built-in LCD panel that's supported by many PC games, enabling you to display everything from the elapsed time you've spent playing to the number of kills and flags you've captured. *Sweet* indeed!

Besides the wireless connection, the G700 mouse (which retails for $100) differs from a typical PC mouse in three important ways:

✦ **A whopping 13 programmable controls:** The mix includes both buttons and the scroll wheel — this mouse looks (and feels) like something out of a science-fiction movie. Each button is carefully located so that a player can find it by touch (and doesn't have to look down, which can spell instant obliteration).

✦ **On-board memory:** If you're wondering how the G700 can keep track of all the macros and settings for up to five players (or five different games), it's because this mouse has its own memory.

✦ **High-speed optics:** A gaming mouse or trackball must provide the fastest and most precise response possible, so the tracking laser in this mouse can deliver up to 5,700 dpi (enabling you to cover the entire width of a high-definition monitor in a single swipe).

Oh, and don't sell these peripherals short — they're perfectly comfortable with Microsoft Word or Photoshop Elements as well as gaming, so you don't have to constantly swap your gaming gear when the real world intrudes.

Great Gamers Demand In-Game Chatter

Ah, dear reader, we've come a long way since Pong, the original home gaming system, and its series of beeps and tones! Today's PC gamer can take advantage of the 5.1 or 7.1 surround sound built-in to most motherboards, providing superb soundtracks and realistic sounds. (Not to mention the 3D spatial audio effects that can literally help you locate the direction of incoming fire or the location of your wingman.) You can use any good-quality PC speaker system, too — in my opinion, there's never been a need to shop for "gaming speakers" for your system.

But your motherboard's built-in sound hardware doesn't fit in the peripherals category, which is what this chapter's about — luckily, I can talk instead about one of the most appealing features of today's games, the capability to converse with other players in real time using *VoIP* (short for Voice over Internet Protocol). You may already be familiar with VoIP technology if you use an "Internet telephone" instead of a traditional landline.

Some of today's games have proprietary in-game VoIP support, so you don't have to run another program to chat. However, most gamers have already settled on one of two programs that enable you to chat while playing any game (or, if you like, without playing at all):

✦ **Ventrilo 3.0:** Ventrilo (commonly shortened to *Vent*) is free for non-business use, and you can freely download either the client (which everyone runs in order to talk) or the server (which provides the host that PCs running the client program can connect to) from the Flagship Industries website at www.ventrilo.com. Figure 2-1 illustrates the Ventrilo client in action.

✦ **TeamSpeak 3.0:** TeamSpeak is also free for non-profit use, and also works with a client/server system. You can download TeamSpeak client or server from TeamSpeak USA at www.teamspeakusa.com.

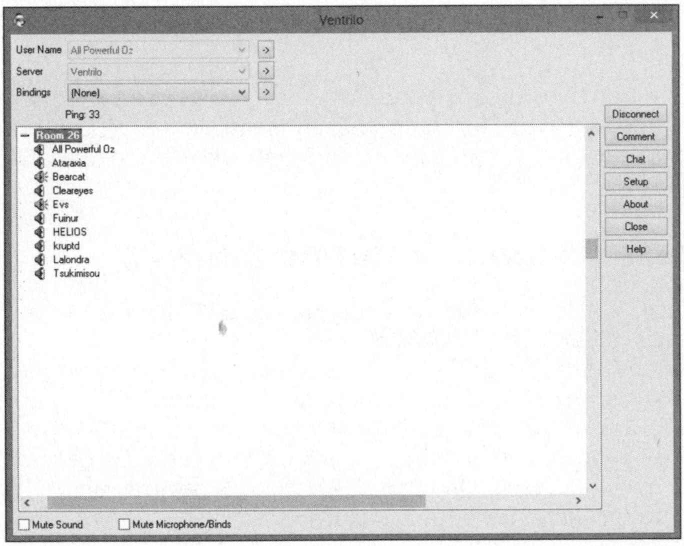

Figure 2-1:
Ventrilo is a popular VoIP client that enables players to converse in any game.

If you're itching to run a Ventrilo or TeamSpeak server on your gaming PC, I'd advise you to consider using an older PC on your home network as a dedicated VoIP server instead. Because of the processing time and resources needed to host a large chat room server, you're likely to see a significant drop in performance on your gaming PC.

To truly enjoy VoIP conversations while you're playing, you need to invest in a *gaming headset,* which enables you to keep both hands on your gaming controller and keyboard. These headsets incorporate both full headphones and a microphone, which is activated either by the press of a key or the sound of your voice.

Extreme gamers yearn for more

Some gamers aren't satisfied with ordinary visuals and audio — they look for peripherals that will add an extra level of realism, and price is often no object! For example, I've seen custom-built jet fighter "cockpits" that a player can sit in, complete with a canopy that closes and separate monitors for the instrument panel and view ahead. You'll spend thousands on such a setup, but for flight enthusiasts who crave realism, it's worth every penny. (I wonder if anyone's thought of building a tank interior yet?)

For something a little more in range with the typical hardcore gamer's budget, you can opt for an improvement on the gamepad vibration and controller feedback I mention earlier in the chapter: The Shell ShoXX system by Earthquake Sound is billed as a tactile transducer and amplifier, but you and I would think of it as vibration taken to a new level! With 300 watts of power, the Shell ShoXX includes a shaker unit that clamps to any gaming chair and provides vibrations synchronized with the low-level audio output of your game. (If you're as old as I am, think of the effect you felt when you watched the movie *Earthquake* in the theater as the entire seat shook along with the on-screen action.) The Shell ShoXX is available online for around $500.

Eye Candy for the Dedicated Gamer

Before we vacate the land of gaming peripherals, I should mention a recent arrival to gaming with close ties to the world of high-definition TVs: gaming glasses, which offer 1080p HD 3D play on your PC. You can also use these glasses to watch 3D Blu-Ray movies (if your system's graphics card, optical drive, and monitor support Blu-Ray) and view 3D photographs.

Although gaming glasses do indeed have a lot in common with the 3D glasses used with many of today's high-definition TVs, there's more to them than just simple blue and red lenses. For example, NVIDIA sells a pair of 3D glasses for gamers called the 3D Vision 2 that requires a 3D Vision-compatible monitor (or projector), an NVIDIA GeForce graphics card, and games and software especially written for 3D Vision 2. These glasses use a wireless infrared connection to your PC (the USB infrared receiver is included).

Naturally, because NVIDIA is a prime mover and shaker in the gaming community, 3D Vision 2 is already well-supported on the latest titles (currently, more than 600 games are compatible). The system sells for about $130 online.

As with 3D televisions that use glasses, it's a very good idea to try out 3D Vision locally (if possible) before you buy — some people experience severe eyestrain after a prolonged period of 3D viewing, and there are sometimes problems fitting 3D glasses over prescription glasses.

Chapter 3: Software for Gamers

In This Chapter

- ✔ Using Steam to buy and play games
- ✔ Comparing performance with a benchmark program
- ✔ Recording your gameplay
- ✔ Playing older games using emulators

*B*ack in the prehistoric age of computer gaming — the mid-80s to mid-90s, before the arrival of Windows 95 — PC owners coveted only the games themselves. Non-game software was typically centered on business, programming, or finance, and let's be honest: For gamers, productivity was boring.

The popularity of today's PC gaming, however, has produced a number of popular supporting software categories — programs that aren't games themselves, but enable players to measure (and gloat about) the performance of their systems, create movies from their games for a website or blog, and even play classic games written for antique computer systems.

And don't forget The Cloud. Yep, even gamers get a spot in the stratosphere: With Steam, you can buy, download, and archive your games online, rate them for other potential players, and compare scores and achievements. It's convenient and easy in the gaming cloud.

Welcome to the support software that no hard-core gamer can do without!

Gaming Through the Steam Cloud

If someone asks me what the biggest change in gaming has been over the last decade, there's only one answer to give: Steam. Before the arrival of Valve Corporation's Steam service, you kept your game discs on a shelf, and you laboriously installed and updated each one separately — but those days are gone for good! Steam is a free Internet service that puts your game software online, like the movies and music you've probably bought and downloaded from vendors like Apple's iTunes Store and Amazon's Cloud.

Steam requires an Internet connection, and I'll come right out and say you'll need a *broadband* Internet connection — without the speed of a DSL, cable, network, or satellite connection to the Internet, it will take forever to download your games. If you use a dialup modem connection, consider Steam off-limits.

Both PC and Mac gamers have wholeheartedly embraced the Steam system, and there are a number of important reasons why:

✦ **Buying games is a cinch.** Steam offers a wide range of different game genres, and after you've registered, buying a game is reduced to a few clicks of the mouse. Your games are automatically downloaded to your PC as soon as you buy them.

✦ **Steam organizes all your games in a single spot.** You can play any game that you've downloaded from a single list. Figure 3-1 illustrates an entry from my Steam library of games, complete with the latest news on the game and ratings from other players.

✦ **You can uninstall and reinstall games as necessary.** Steam keeps a permanent record of what you've bought, so if your hard drive is running low on space, you can uninstall as many Steam games as you like and reinstall them whenever you wish.

✦ **Steam provides automatic updates for your games.** No need to visit a dozen different websites like the old days to check for patches and updates — all Steam games are automatically updated for you.

✦ **Easily find others for multiplayer games.** Steam keeps track of your friends who play the same games, and you can invite a friend (or simply find an opponent) for a quick match.

✦ **Compare scores, achievements, and opinions with your gaming peers.** Steam offers discussion forums (where you can post and read messages) and leaderboards (where you can compare your highest scores in a game with others).

Getting started with Steam is easy: Visit `http://store.steampowered.com` and click on the Install Steam button at the top of the web page.

Figure 3-1:
Naturally,
my Steam
library
contains
Call of Duty
Black Ops II.

Comparing Hardware with Benchmarks

Benchmarks — when it comes to comparing graphics cards, the gaming
world seems to revolve directly around them. If you're not familiar with a
performance *benchmark,* it's a program (or suite of programs) that you run
on your PC to display the performance of a component, usually compared
against some form of proprietary scale in completely proprietary units of
measure. (Which confuses the issue even more because there are a large
number of benchmark programs out there.)

Many benchmarks are offered as freeware and shareware. Because this kind
of computer programming is practically a requirement to learning how to
address computer hardware in larger projects, most computer programming
students have written at least one benchmark program in the past. Some
benchmarks test the performance of your CPU, hard drives, and memory as
well as your graphics card.

The whole idea sounds very scientific, and a large majority of gamers rely almost entirely on benchmark performance figures when they buy new hardware. But are benchmark programs *completely* accurate? As a programmer and hardware tech, perhaps it's in my nature to be suspicious of the claims made by hardware manufacturers. Keep in mind that these programs can choose from a nearly unlimited combination of methods to test hardware (perhaps putting too much importance on one aspect of a graphics card, like memory handling, and not enough on texture mapping). Like statistics, take the results from a benchmark with a grain of salt.

Because your PC must "concentrate" on delivering the best possible graphics during a benchmark, it's important not to run any other programs in the background while the benchmark is running.

How do benchmarks work?

All benchmarks tend to use the same measures to arrive at their results — for example, a graphics benchmark program will likely measure the same arcane technical features as other benchmarks, including polygons created per second, frames per second, memory throughput, number of threads, and the GPU speed rating. (Don't worry, you won't be tested on the behind-the-scenes stuff.)

A graphics benchmark program runs a series of 3D scenes — which, by the way, are pretty doggone awesome viewing in their own right. (Figure 3-2 illustrates the advanced settings available for testing within Futuremark's 3DMark 11.) Each scene puts a specific type of effect through its paces, and the benchmark records the specifics on how well the card performed. At the end of the testing cycle, the final performance figure is calculated and displayed, ready to compare with other systems (as shown within PCMark 7 in Figure 3-3).

The real result you're looking for is the final performance figure — a card with a significantly higher benchmark figure should deliver better performance in your 3D games. As I mention earlier, most benchmarks report their findings in a totally proprietary result, so you need the same program's benchmark figures (run once using each device) to compare two or more different pieces of hardware.

Popular benchmark programs

When I need benchmark figures, they're usually delivered by one of these well-known and well-respected independent benchmark programs (rather than a proprietary benchmark from a hardware manufacturer). Downloading and installing any of them is time well spent, especially if you'd like to squeeze every last frame from your hardware:

✦ **3DMark 11 from Futuremark Corporation:** This is my high-intensity graphics benchmarking program of choice for PCs using DirectX 11 (which is installed by default within Windows 8, but is not supported by all graphics cards). 3DMark 11 focuses specifically on your CPU and graphics card performance in a gaming environment, so it tends to be the common denominator online when discussing 3D game performance. 3DMark 11 will set you back $20. Visit the company website at www.futuremark.com/ for more information. (The company also offers PCMark 7, which is a more comprehensive benchmark that tests your entire system.)

✦ **PerformanceTest 8 from PassMark Software:** This well-respected shareware (www.passmark.com, $26) offering dates all the way back to Windows 98. PerformanceTest 8 benchmarks your entire system — not just the graphics card — and the detailed results are probably the best in the business.

✦ **Sandra Lite 2013 from SiSoftware:** Sandra Lite is the freeware version of this classic shareware benchmark — the full Personal version costs $50 (www.sisoftware.co.uk). Sandra Lite benchmarks a number of PC features that the others don't, including virtual memory performance and advanced networking functions.

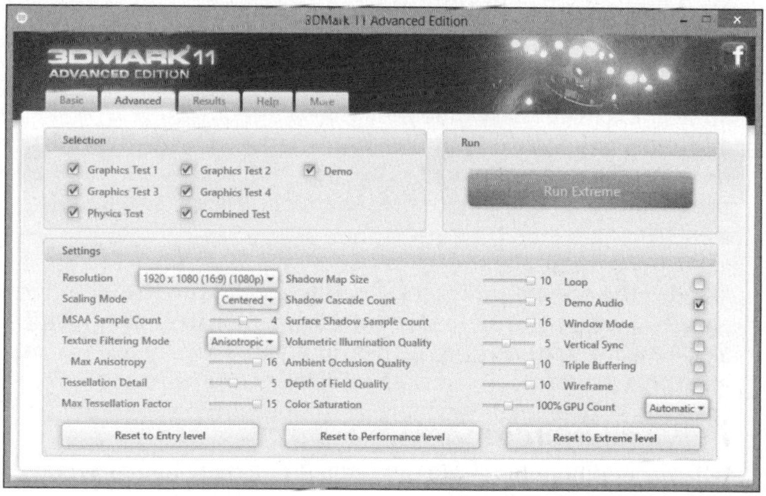

Figure 3-2:
3DMark 11
is a highly
configurable
PC graphics
benchmark
program.

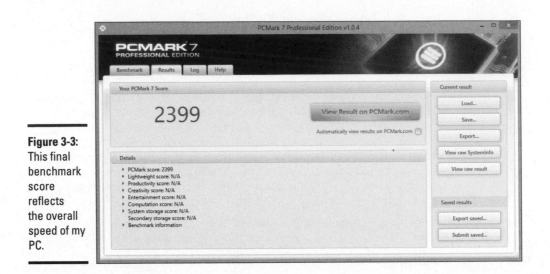

Figure 3-3:
This final benchmark score reflects the overall speed of my PC.

Recording Those Epic Battles

Ever wished that you could relive a particularly good match from one of your favorite games? Perhaps it was a good trouncing you gave your best friend within the latest 3D slugfest, or you wanted to share a particularly beautiful in-game landscape with others. Anyway, it's in the past, and you can't relive those moments again . . . but what if you could record the action from your favorite games?

Indeed you can, using today's crop of screen recording programs. These applications capture whatever's displayed on your screen as a video clip, and allow you to add your own narration (either in real-time, or after the fact). No special equipment is needed, although some screen recording programs do enable you to create a picture-in-picture display if you have a webcam connected to your PC.

Besides the opportunities for gloating and admiration that I mention earlier, gamers capture the action for tutorials and walk-through videos — check YouTube for your favorite games, and you'll see plenty of examples where an expert gamer demonstrates a tricky maneuver or complicated battle strategy, explaining how things are done with background narration.

Popular screen recording programs for games include

✦ **Fraps:** I know, a ridiculous name, but I've used this great utility a number of times (both for capturing in-game screenshots and gigabytes worth of video). Visit the application website at `www.fraps.com` to view sample clips and buy the software, which costs $37.

✦ **PlayClaw:** PlayClaw offers a unique voice overlay feature for TeamSpeak and Ventrilo (programs I discuss in Chapter 2 of this minibook), so you can listen in on the in-game conversations among players along with watching the action. The program can also capture full HD video. PlayClaw costs $38, and is available from `www.playclaw.com`.

✦ **ZD Soft Screen Recorder:** This $39 utility produces both AVI and WMV output and includes a timer that can automatically start and stop recording. Visit `www.zdsoft.com` for more information.

Playing Games for Other Systems

As a gamer, you're naturally interested in the latest releases — what's hot, what's coming up in the near future, and the games that are in development by your favorite companies. Like most other power gamers, I'll spend an entire evening looking over the titles on Steam, trying to figure out which one will actually live up to all the marketing hype that's splashed across the screen. After all, that money I'm spending on games doesn't grow on trees.

But what if I told you that some of my all-time favorite games were written as far back as 1981 — and for a totally different computer system? Actually, I've owned dozens of computers since the early '80s, each of which was "state-of-the-art" in its day; most used floppies because hard drives were so expensive, and one even loaded games from a cassette drive! Graphics were limited — in fact, many of my favorite classic games, like the original Zork series, Midway, and B1 Nuclear Bomber, did not have any graphics at all, and displayed only text — and sound was usually limited to an occasional beep or a quick melody. If you're old enough to remember classic games like Castle Wolfenstein on the Apple II, Star Raiders or M.U.L.E. on the Atari 400, or Jumpman Junior on the Commodore 64, you'll really enjoy reliving those hours you spent perfecting just the right moves in your favorite arcade game (and it won't cost you a single quarter)! Revisiting those adventure games and strategy games you used to play will feel like you're reunited with old friends.

So how do you relive those classic games without spending an arm and a leg on antique hardware? The answer is simple: Use your PC to "trick" those classic games into thinking that they're running on the original computer — the process is called *emulation,* and there are literally hundreds of emulators available these days, for just about any computer, video game console, or arcade machine that has ever been made. Many emulators use just the keyboard, but others can emulate joysticks, game paddles, and even trackballs.

Of course, most emulators also enable you to run applications originally written for the older computers too, so if you're interested in the history of the personal computer, you should grab every emulator you run across; besides games, you can try out programs like VisiCalc (the first spreadsheet program) and WordStar, the original word processor that started a revolution.

Game ROMs and binary files explained

You might be asking yourself, "How can I run a game that comes on a cartridge, or came on a floppy disk?" The answer to that question brings us to two of the requirements for most emulators:

✦ **Operating system ROMs:** ROM is one of the better-known acronyms among technotypes: It stands for *read-only memory*. All computers, arcade video games, and home video game consoles save some type of operating system data in a ROM chip, which enables you to turn off the machine without losing that data. Therefore, many emulators require the original ROM code used by the original computer in order to re-create the operating system; the ROM is typically downloaded from a site on the Internet as a file, and the emulator reads this file whenever it "boots." (Some emulators actually have the ROM incorporated into them, so they won't need that code as an additional file.)

✦ **Program binaries:** Naturally, most people don't have original games on their original media (usually either 5 ¼-inch disks or cartridges), and even if you did, there's no way you could use them with a modern computer. Therefore, a game must be converted into a *binary data file* before it can be loaded into an emulator — this also enables the game or application to be saved to your hard drive.

Where do binaries and ROMs come from? I'm happy to say that many computing old-timers want to ensure that future generations will be able to play these classic games and applications, and those who actually own the antique hardware and software run programs that create ROM and binary files for the rest of us. For example, I've converted cartridge games from my Atari 400 and 800 computers and created image files — because these antique computers are practically impossible to repair these days, emulation is the only certain method of preserving these games.

Are emulators legal?

Like any other original creation, all the computer and video games you've played — no matter when or on what machine — have been distributed under a copyright, and it's important to understand who has the rights to distribute the ROM and binary game code before you download and use an emulator. Of course, emulation is indeed legal, and emulators are generally released as either *freeware* (copyrighted programs that can be used free of charge by everyone) or *shareware* (copyrighted programs distributed by the author that you can purchase after you've tried them out). As long as the author gives you permission in the program's documentation, it's perfectly legal to distribute these emulator programs on a website or e-mail an emulator to a friend.

However, the legality of distributing either the operating system ROMs or the game binary files is less certain, and naturally many newcomers to the emulation scene are confused about the origin of these files. Without drawing legal boundaries, I can divide these data files into the following three categories:

✦ **The developer will not allow distribution.** Naturally, computer software developers and game console developers would certainly not approve of the distribution of the games that they're currently selling. The only legal way to emulate one of these games — for example, a PlayStation 3 or Wii console game — would be to legally own the game already, so you'll have to buy it before you can run the binary version of the game on the emulator — in fact, others even dispute that you have this right. (On the other hand, if you've already bought the console game, you probably have the genuine console — so why do you need an emulator?)

✦ **The developer is no longer in business.** Some computer and video game manufacturers have gone out of business in the intervening years — although the possibility of legal action greatly diminishes, that doesn't necessarily give you free reign to copy their ROM and game code.

✦ **The software has been rendered public domain or freeware.** When the demand for a certain computer has finally dropped to practically zero, many software developers decide to release their commercial software into the public domain or as freeware.

"So what rights do I *really* have to download ROM files or give them to my friends?" Unfortunately, there is no simple answer, and that's due to the "gray area" surrounding the emulation of both game consoles and computers that are still in production. The boundaries of legal ownership have not been set in stone (at least at the time of this writing). I'm not a lawyer, and I'm not qualified to tell you whether a specific ROM or binary file is safe to use or distribute — but I think it's a safe bet to assume that playing a binary file for a game currently on store shelves is certainly not legal, while playing a binary file for a game that has been released as freeware is perfectly okay. Most of the sites that distribute game files on the web look for binaries that fall into the second category, hoping that because the company is out of business, there's no danger in distributing the binary image — a dangerous assumption that is certainly not legally proven.

Also, ROM files are a prime target for distributing viruses and malicious spyware, so make sure that you thoroughly scan each ROM you download with your antivirus software, and visit such sites cautiously.

Top emulators for the PC

Now that you're familiar with emulation and its legality, I want to take you on a whirlwind tour around the world of emulators — I introduce you to some of the best-known emulators for the most popular antique computers, and also point you to where you can download them on the web. Remember, however, that you'll have to locate your own ROM images and program binary files yourself.

Each of the following emulation programs is freeware, so you won't spend a penny (or a quarter) on your classic gaming:

✦ **MAME (Multiple Arcade Machine Emulator):** MAME is it — the king of arcade machine emulators, and probably the best-known emulation project for any machine on the web. It's available for virtually every computer operating system available today, including DOS, Windows, Mac OS, and Linux. It runs literally thousands of games, which are ROM cartridge codes saved as binary files as of this writing. Best of all, to prove that you occasionally *can* get something for nothing, the complete source code for MAME is absolutely free, and it's constantly being updated by some of the best software developers on the Internet. MAME enables you to set "virtual" switches to configure different game features — for example, like the owner of the actual arcade game, you can change a setting to specify how many points you need for the game to award you a bonus ship. Other settings can include the game difficulty, the number of credits per coin, and different sets of sound effects. You don't need a joystick or trackball to play, but MAME will take advantage of these controllers if you have them. The emulator even saves your high scores for most of the games! For more information on MAME, visit the official website at `http://mamedev.org`.

✦ **Atari800:** Among the Atari emulation crowd, Atari800 has become the premiere emulator for the Atari 800/800XL/130XE, and it also emulates the Atari 5200 video game console. Atari800 is available for both the PC and Mac, and it emulates both Atari joystick and paddle controllers, as well as the Atari trackball and light gun. The emulator enables you to store Atari games and applications as binary images on your hard drive, and it can also handle cartridge and cassette images to boot. For the whole story on Atari800, visit the project's home page at `http://atari800.sourceforge.net`.

✦ **SDLTRS:** If you're a fan of the TRS-80 line of computers (as am I), you'll want to pick up this great emulator. SDLTRS supports the loading and saving of disk images, USB joysticks, dot-matrix printer emulation, and emulated cassette and hard drives. Visit the website at `http://sdltrs.sourceforge.net`.

✦ **AppleWin:** The freeware emulator AppleWin has an impressive list of features: It can emulate an Apple II+ or the enhanced Apple IIe (at several speeds, thanks to the custom CPU speed control), complete with twin disk drives, a joystick, and a serial card. AppleWin can handle all the IIe video modes, so it's perfect for games and graphics emulation. The program can also mimic both monochrome and color Apple monitors. Download AppleWin today at `http://applewin.berlios.de`.

Chapter 4: Playing Milestone PC Games

In This Chapter

✔ **Picking a milestone game**

✔ **Keeping tabs on upcoming releases**

✔ **Taking a peek at Mark's favorite milestone games**

*L*et's see: You've got your high-performance gaming PC running like a Swiss stopwatch, you've surrounded yourself with the right mix of gaming peripherals, and you've signed up with Steam. Now comes the most difficult decision of all: What the heck do you *play?*

Unless you're a millionaire or a game reviewer — or, in a cosmic stroke of luck, a professional game beta tester — you're simply going to have to pick and choose between the dozens of new PC game titles that appear each month. After I take care of family and work and my other obligations, there's little time left for serious gaming, so I have to be very careful to spend that time wisely. (I'll bet you're in the same boat.)

Hence this final chapter in this minibook — I outline the criteria I follow in selecting what I like to call *milestone* games, and where you can keep on top of the latest releases (and pick up some early reviews to boot). Finally, I introduce you to five of my past and current milestone games, as examples of the best in PC gaming in five major genres: first-person, turn-based, multi-player online, simulation, and puzzle games.

What Makes a Milestone Game?

Even if you're just getting started in PC gaming, you may already have an idea of what genre you'd like to play: flight or driving simulators, 3D first-person shooting games, real-time or turn-based strategy games, or pure arcade games with little or no plot (and no need for one). If you don't, however, I have some suggestions from my short list of milestone games. In my book — somewhat horrible pun unintended — there are a number of signs a game has reached milestone status:

✦ **It spawns a franchise.** Games like Civilization, Call of Duty, Halo, and Madden NFL have sequels for a reason. (Granted, some old-timers may cry over features and gameplay that have changed since the original game came out, but game developers don't usually stray far from a successful formula.)

✦ **It generates attention in popular culture.** Although most hard-core gamers I know would scoff at my labeling Angry Birds a milestone game, you have to admit that those silly pigs and birds have become cultural icons, just like Pac-Man and Sonic the Hedgehog . . . and such attention usually indicates an above-average game, no matter the genre.

✦ **It wins top gaming awards.** I always keep track of which games win the Spike Video Game Award for Game of the Year, as well as the Game of the Year for magazines like *PC Gamer* and *Computer Games Magazine.*

✦ **It's produced by a major game developer.** Blizzard Entertainment is a great example of this truism: Some developers reach for a level of polish, playability, and detail that ensures that just about any game they produce will turn into gold. I look to Electronic Arts and Activision for the same quality.

Of course, even a game that meets these criteria isn't an automatic best pick from your store shelf (or your Steam store), but it's far more likely that you'll get your money's worth with a milestone game (or its sequels).

Doing Your Gaming Homework

Naturally, the benchmarking and research you do before buying a new piece of hardware pays off — for example, you'll likely find the best graphics card for the least amount of money by comparing things like price, 3DMark benchmark figures, GPU speed, and the amount of memory on the card.

Although there's no such thing as a benchmark for comparing quality and playability for PC games, you can still do your research! Game companies tend to release all sorts of trailers, print advertisements, and even interviews on their upcoming titles, so it's easier to find out all about upcoming games than you might think. You can also search for reviews on current games to help you decide whether a specific title would interest you.

Where can you do your homework? Here's a list of the best places to learn more about today's PC games:

✦ **Gaming friends:** I tend to rely heavily on the opinion of my gaming friends when shopping for a new title — both the friends in my home-town and the friends I've met online in various groups. If a friend pans a game, that's typically all I need to know!

✦ **Gaming magazines:** Call me old-fashioned, but I still prefer a glossy game magazine to that same publisher's website or e-magazine. Whichever media you choose, gaming magazines like *PC Gamer* (www.pcgamer.com) and *Computer Games Magazine* (www.cgonline.com) are likely to be your primary news source for both upcoming titles and current hits. Publications like these are where those game developer advertising dollars get spent, and where reviewers are actually both unbiased and (somewhat) demanding.

✦ **Gaming fan sites:** If you need help or opinions on a specific game, use a search engine such as Google or Bing to search the web for fan sites dedicated to that title. (I must admit that I personally check these sites more to solve in-game problems than I do while deciding what to buy, simply because the folks that produce such fan sites are already hooked on the title! However, if you can't find the Glowing Golden Key and your patience has run out, the hints and tips on these sites can be invaluable.)

✦ **Developer sites:** Of course, don't forget to visit the developer's site for a game — you're likely to find screenshots, system requirements, and perhaps even a playable demo available for downloading.

The price of play

At this point in this gaming minibook, you've likely already ascertained a very important truism about PC gaming: It doesn't come cheap. After you've factored in the cost of building, buying, or upgrading a PC gaming machine, buying peripherals, and maintaining a broadband Internet connection, you've likely invested several hundred dollars . . . only to find out that you have to reach for your wallet or purse again for the $70 it takes to buy that latest mega-hit game you've just got to have.

There are, however, methods of playing for less. Consider these options:

Play for free. Steam offers a number of high-quality free-to-play games, like Gotham City Imposters (a favorite first-person team game that takes place in Batman's Gotham City). You can also find challenging word and puzzle games on Facebook and CNN.com.

Keep an eye out for game sales. Again, Steam comes in handy! You'll find that Steam often reduces prices for selected games on weekends.

Shop on eBay and other online stores. I buy a significant chunk of my new games on eBay, but be cautious: If a game has a serial number and it's been opened and used, you won't be able to successfully install that game on your PC! (The serial number will be rejected as having been used already.) Buy only brand-new, shrink-wrapped games from online stores.

Examples of Milestone Games

No chapter on milestone games would be complete without examples, right? In this section, I pick three game franchises from three different gaming genres that illustrate the points I make throughout this chapter. I can honestly make this unbiased statement: Each of these games has proven itself to be the best of the best, and every dollar you spend on any game in the series is money well spent.

First-person: The Call of Duty franchise

It's got campaign mode, it's got multiplayer, and — most importantly — Activision's Call of Duty Black Ops II has got the zombie enemies that every 3D first-person gaming fan craves! (In fact, I know players who've bought this latest game in the Call of Duty franchise specifically for the zombies.)

Besides the undead, Call of Duty has maintained a strong plotline throughout the entire franchise, with well-rounded NPCs (non-player characters), each with a full range of human personalities and frailties. The storyline has you fighting the enemy on the water, in the air, and on the ground, with stunning cinematics at every turn. (I love gliding toward an enemy base like a high-tech flying squirrel.)

As you can see in Figure 4-1, the level of detail is second-to-none in Black Ops II, and the action is perfectly paced. The Call of Duty franchise is known for its squad tactics — you rarely fight alone. Instead, your movement from place to place automatically pulls the rest of your squad with you, just as it would in real life.

As for weapons, there are literally dozens of accurately modeled rifles, handguns, and rockets for you to choose from, and you can specify your weapon load at the beginning of each mission. You also are given the opportunity to man rocket pods, Gatling guns, and the like from fixed emplacements.

Turn-based: The Civilization franchise

What gamer hasn't yearned to take over the world? In the Civilization franchise from Take-Two Interactive Software, you can meet the greatest leaders in human history — both warlike and peaceful — and match your ability to build a civilization against theirs.

I've often heard Civilization V compared to classic board games like Diplomacy and Risk, and there are certainly elements of a board game to this milestone franchise: Action is turn-based, and you can win a victory in all sorts of ways (through cultural means, by destroying other civilizations, and even a political victory by gaining control of the United Nations). Alliances can be made and broken at your whim, and the technology tree is logical, wonderfully detailed, and an integral part of the game. (For example, you won't be building that B-17 bomber before you discover both flight and combustion.)

Figure 4-1:
The action in Call of Duty Black Ops II is certainly realistic.

Civilization V offers another draw for gamers: The world is generated randomly for each game (although you can determine the size and even the general shape of the continents if you like), so discovery is a key factor. Will your band of settlers discover a river surrounded by gold you can mine, or will there be a barbarian encampment instead?

Multiplayer online: The World of Warcraft franchise

In the world of massive multiplayer online (or MMO), there is no competition for this game — Blizzard's World of Warcraft has outlasted all challengers, spawning expansion pack after expansion pack. (Each pack adds new areas to visit and new items.) If you've never tried World of Warcraft, you're missing out on the closest thing to a truly different world, and it will take months for you to see the highlights as you level your characters.

The world of Azeroth is a battleground between the Empire and the Horde, two groups made up of several different races (including humans). You can follow quests by yourself, join a guild of fellow players, or team up with others to accomplish the tougher quests. Player-versus-Player areas (PvP for short) enable you to battle against players from the opposing faction for special gear and weapons.

However, this is a multifaceted diamond of a game, and there's far more to World of Warcraft than simple combat. You'll find dozens of different occupations to fill your gaming hours: You can mine metals and craft weapons and armor, learn high-level alchemy and tailoring, or even cook and fish! Each occupation has its own achievements, and you can sell your finished items to the highest bidder in the auction house.

In Figure 4-2, my hunter and his lava dog companion are searching for enemies within a lush jungle environment — the many buttons arrayed below and to the side of the screen give you some idea of the complex combat and crafting commands offered to a high-end character.

Figure 4-2: My Tauren hunter and his lava dog, as seen by other players.

Simulation: The Tropico franchise

Tropico 4 holds a special spot in the world of simulation games — not only must you build a thriving city from a simple farm and a couple of paved streets, but you also must act as mayor across decades of strife, rebellion, and back-stabbing. And earthquakes. Lots of earthquakes, and tsunamis, and even a volcano or two!

In Campaign mode, you build the infrastructure of your cities in a wide range of challenging scenarios: some with extensive resources, some with practically no resources but a wealth of natural beauty. You can mine for iron and gold, grow all sorts of food crops, cut timber, fish, and develop all sorts of industries. (My favorite? Probably the cigar factory.) And of course, there's tourism, with everything from a simple beachfront motel to impressive high-rise condos and a floating cruise ship, with all the attractions to draw more visitors to your island paradise.

But is it a paradise for the natives? The challenges in Tropico are everywhere. You must provide for your people and keep them happy, or you'll be deposed by rebels in no time. If you don't keep relations with the U.S. and Russia well balanced, you could be invaded and your reign as dictator is over. Build a newspaper and TV station, and decide whether to broadcast propaganda or raise money through soap operas!

Each city comes with a series of goals you must complete — some through guile, some through brute force, and many through bribery and payoffs. Throughout this great game, you're treated to a wonderful soundtrack of island music, plenty of funny dialogue from your "somewhat less than competent" advisor Penultimo, and an ongoing litany of requests from characters like your town priest, your resident environmentalist, and your Communist party official.

Figure 4-3 illustrates the beginning of a city scenario. Each building can be individually managed, and your population can even be individually controlled if you like. It's the simulation lover's perfect game!

Puzzles: The Microsoft Classics franchise

Surprised? Don't be! No discussion of milestone PC games would be complete without the most successful (and most recognized) PC game in history: Microsoft's Windows Solitaire, which is now part of the Microsoft Solitaire Collection. Along with the other well-known games that have been bundled with Windows (such as Microsoft Minesweeper and Mahjong), Solitaire has accounted for more hours of simple gaming fun than any high-tech first-person game could ever hope to match.

Figure 4-3:
Tropico 4
addresses
the mayor
inside you.

In Windows 8, however, you'll find that the Windows Store offers new, improved versions of your favorite games, with enhanced graphics, visual themes, and more challenges. (Figure 4-4 illustrates a favorite of mine, Microsoft Mahjong, with an example of its stunning new tile designs and backgrounds.) Plus, many of the games in the Microsoft lineup are now part of Microsoft's online Xbox system, so you can compare scores with others, challenge your friends (for games with multiplayer support), and even win prizes. Everything is handled through your Windows 8 Microsoft account and your Internet connection.

The first versions of these games shipped as part of older versions of Windows (or were available free for the download) — the Windows 8 versions of these games, however, may require your wallet or purse. For example, many of the Microsoft titles in the Store are free, but others are for purchase only — so pay close attention to those prices as you shop. Other games may be free for downloading, but require you to pay for in-game purchases for new levels or enhanced features. You may also encounter video advertisements within some games when playing in Xbox monthly competitions.

Microsoft games automatically create a tile on the Start screen during installation, but you can also access your Microsoft games from the Games tile on your Startup screen (shown in Figure 4-5). From here, you can quickly check the leaderboards for your top games, learn about the latest PC game offerings with Xbox support, and see what your friends are playing.

Figure 4-4:
Microsoft
Mahjong is
the king of
Mahjong
solitaire
games.

Figure 4-5:
Click the
Games tile
on your
Windows 8
Start screen
to play and
socialize.

Index

B

C

F

G

S